MATH

Mc
Graw
Hill
Education

connectED.mcgraw-hill.com

STEM McGraw-Hill is committed to providing instructional materials in Science, Technology, Engineering, and Mathematics (STEM) that give all students a solid foundation, one that prepares them for college and careers in the 21st century.

Send all inquiries to:
McGraw-Hill Education
STEM Learning Solutions Center
8787 Orion Place
Columbus, OH 43240

ISBN: 978-0-07-665691-2
MHID: 0-07-665691-8

Printed in the United States of America.

5 6 7 8 9 RMN 16 15

CONTENTS IN BRIEF

Organized by Focal Areas

Your assignment's due tomorrow...

but your book is in your locker!

James Woodson/Digital Vision/Getty Images

NOW WHAT?

Even in crunch time, with ConnectED, we've got you covered!

With ConnectED, you have instant access to all of your study materials—anytime, anywhere. From homework materials to study guides—it's all in one place and just a click away. ConnectED even allows you to collaborate with your classmates and use mobile apps to make studying easy.

Resources built for you—available 24/7:

- Your eBook available wherever you are
- Personal Tutors and Self-Check Quizzes whenever you need them
- An Online Calendar with all of your due dates
- eFlashcard App to make studying easy
- A message center to stay in touch

Reimagine Learning

Go Online!

connectED.mcgraw-hill.com

Vocab

Learn about new vocabulary words.

Watch

Watch animations and videos.

Tutor

See and hear a teacher explain how to solve problems.

Tools

Explore concepts with virtual manipulatives.

Check

Check your progress.

eHelp

Get targeted homework help.

Worksheets

Access practice worksheets.

Chapter 1 Rational Numbers

Go to page 109 to learn about a 21st Century Career in **Fashion Design!**

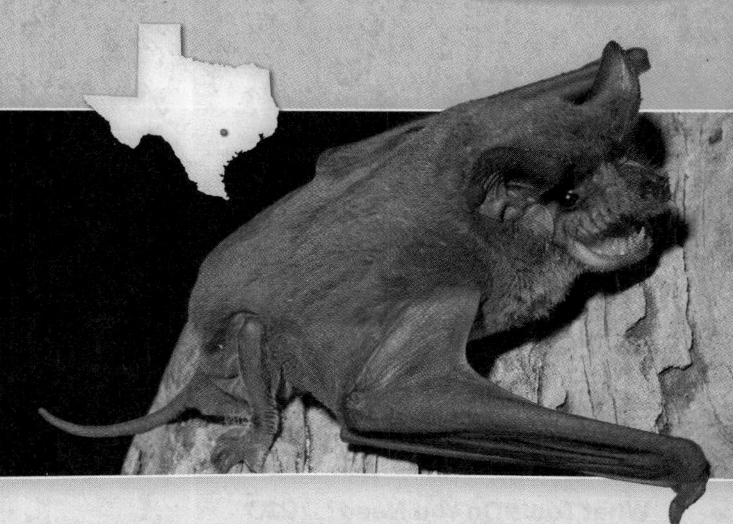

Chapter 2 Proportional Relationships

Go to page 203 to learn about a 21st Century Career in **Biomechanical Engineering!**

Chapter 3
Apply Proportionality to Percent

Go to page 293 to learn about a 21st Century Career in
Video Game Design!

Chapter 4
Apply Proportionality to Geometry

Go to page 353 to learn about a 21st Century Career in
Roller Coaster Design!

Chapter 5
Apply Proportionality to Probability

Go to page 427 to learn about a 21st Century Career in **Medicine!**

Chapter 6
Multiple Representations of Linear Relationships

Go to page 491 to learn about a 21st Century Career in **Animal Conservation!**

Chapter 7 Equations and Inequalities

Go to page 577 to learn about a 21st Century Career in **Veterinary Medicine!**

(t)Design Pics/Don Hammond, (b)Kenneth Garrett/National Geographic/Getty Images

Chapter 8 Develop Geometry with Algebra

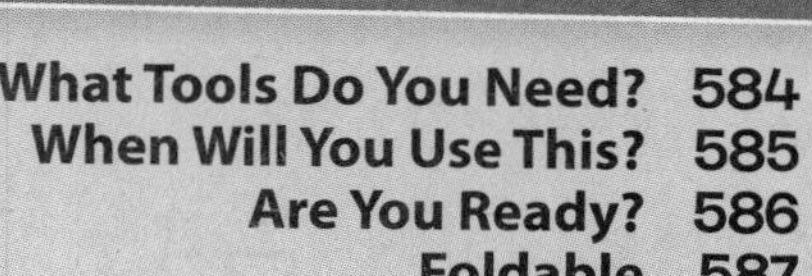

Go to page 693 to learn about a 21st Century Career in **Landscape Architecture!**

Chapter 9 Statistics and Sampling

Go to page 777 to learn about a 21st Century Career in **Market Research!**

Chapter 10 Personal Financial Literacy

Texas Essential Knowledge and Skills, Grade 7

Track Your TEKS Progress

The knowledge and skills that you will learn this year are listed on these pages. Throughout the year, your teacher will ask you to rate how confident you feel about your knowledge of each one. Don't worry if you have no clue **before** you learn about them. Your will rate your knowledge before and after you learn them. Your teacher will provide you with more instructions. Watch how your knowledge and skills grow as the year progresses!

☹ I have no clue. 😐 I've heard of it. ☺ I know it!

7.1 Mathematical Process Standards		Before ☹	Before 😐	Before ☺	After ☹	After 😐	After ☺
The student uses mathematical processes to acquire and demonstrate mathematical understanding. The student is expected to:							
7.1(A)	Apply mathematics to problems arising in everyday life, society, and the workplace;						
7.1(B)	Use a problem-solving model that incorporates analyzing given information, formulating a plan or strategy, determining a solution, justifying the solution, and evaluating the problem-solving process and the reasonableness of the solution;						
7.1(C)	Select tools, including real objects, manipulatives, paper and pencil, and technology as appropriate, and techniques, including mental math, estimation, and number sense as appropriate, to solve problems;						
7.1(D)	Communicate mathematical ideas, reasoning, and their implications using multiple representations, including symbols, diagrams, graphs, and language as appropriate;						
7.1(E)	Create and use representations to organize, record, and communicate mathematical ideas;						
7.1(F)	Analyze mathematical relationships to connect and communicate mathematical ideas; and						
7.1(G)	Display, explain, and justify mathematical ideas and arguments using precise mathematical language in written or oral communication.						

Before | After

7.2 Number and Operations

The student applies mathematical process standards to represent and use rational numbers in a variety of forms. The student is expected to:

Extend previous knowledge of sets and subsets using a visual representation to describe relationships between sets of rational numbers.

7.3 Number and Operations

The student applies mathematical process standards to add, subtract, multiply, and divide while solving problems and justifying solutions. The student is expected to:

7.3(A)	Add, subtract, multiply, and divide rational numbers fluently; and
7.3(B)	Apply and extend previous understandings of operations to solve problems using addition, subtraction, multiplication, and division of rational numbers;

7.4 Proportionality

The student applies mathematical process standards to represent and solve problems involving proportional relationships. The student is expected to:

7.4(A)	Represent constant rates of change in mathematical and real-world problems given pictorial, tabular, verbal, numeric, graphical, and algebraic representations, including $d = rt$;
7.4(B)	Calculate unit rates from rates in mathematical and real-world problems;
7.4(C)	Determine the constant of proportionality. $\left(k = \frac{y}{x}\right)$ within mathematical and real-world problems;
7.4(D)	Solve problems involving ratios, rates, and percents, including multi-step problems involving percent increase and percent decrease, and financial literacy problems; and
7.4(E)	Convert between measurement systems, including the use of proportions and the use of unit rates.

7.5 Proportionality	Before: 🙁	Before: 😐	Before: 🙂	After: 🙁	After: 😐	After: 🙂
The student applies mathematical process standards to use geometry to describe or solve problems involving proportional relationships. The student is expected to:						
7.5(A) Generalize the critical attributes of similarity, including ratios within and between similar shapes;						
7.5(B) Describe π as the ratio of the circumference of a circle to its diameter; and						
7.5(C) Solve mathematical and real-world problems involving similar shapes and scale drawings.						

7.6 Proportionality	Before: 🙁	Before: 😐	Before: 🙂	After: 🙁	After: 😐	After: 🙂
The student applies mathematical process standards to use probability and statistics to describe or solve problems involving proportional relationships. The student is expected to:						
7.6(A) Represent sample spaces for simple and compound events using lists and tree diagrams; and						
7.6(B) Select and use different simulations to represent simple and compound events with and without technology.						
7.6(C) Make predictions and determine solutions using experimental data for simple and compound events;						
7.6(D) Make predictions and determine solutions using theoretical probability for simple and compound events;						
7.6(E) Find the probabilities of a simple event and its complement and describe the relationship between the two;						
7.6(F) Use data from a random sample to make inferences about a population;						
7.6(G) Solve problems using data represented in bar graphs, dot plots, and circle graphs, including part-to-whole and part-to-part comparisons and equivalents;						
7.6(H) Solve problems using qualitative and quantitative predictions and comparisons from simple experiments; and						
7.6(I) Determine experimental and theoretical probabilities related to simple and compound events using data and sample spaces.						

7.7 Expressions, Equations, and Relationships	Before ☹	Before 😐	Before ☺	After ☹	After 😐	After ☺
The student applies mathematical process standards to represent linear relationships using multiple representations. The student is expected to:						
Represent linear relationships using verbal descriptions, tables, graphs, and equations that simplify to the form $y = mx + b$.						

7.8 Expressions, Equations, and Relationships	Before ☹	Before 😐	Before ☺	After ☹	After 😐	After ☺
The student applies mathematical process standards to develop geometric relationships with volume. The student is expected to:						
7.8(A) Model the relationship between the volume of a rectangular prism and a rectangular pyramid having both congruent bases and heights and connect that relationship to the formulas;						
7.8(B) Explain verbally and symbolically the relationship between the volume of a triangular prism and a triangular pyramid having both congruent bases and heights and connect that relationship to the formulas; and						
7.8(C) Use models to determine the approximate formulas for the circumference and area of a circle and connect the models to the actual formulas.						

7.9 Expressions, Equations, and Relationships	Before: ☹	Before: 😐	Before: ☺	After: ☹	After: 😐	After: ☺
The student applies mathematical process standards to solve geometric problems. The student is expected to:						
7.9(A) Solve problems involving the volume of rectangular prisms, triangular prisms, rectangular pyramids, and triangular pyramids;						
7.9(B) Determine the circumference and area of circles;						
7.9(C) Determine the area of composite figures containing combinations of rectangles, squares, parallelograms, trapezoids, triangles, semicircles, and quarter circles; and						
7.9(D) Solve problems involving the lateral and total surface area of a rectangular prism, rectangular pyramid, triangular prism, and triangular pyramid by determining the area of the shape's net.						

7.10 Expressions, Equations, and Relationships	Before: ☹	Before: 😐	Before: ☺	After: ☹	After: 😐	After: ☺
The student applies mathematical process standards to use one-variable equations and inequalities to represent situations. The student is expected to:						
7.10(A) Write one-variable, two-step equations and inequalities to represent constraints or conditions within problems;						
7.10(B) Represent solutions for one-variable, two-step equations and inequalities on number lines; and						
7.10(C) Write a corresponding real-world problem given a one-variable, two-step equation or inequality.						

7.11 Expressions, Equations, and Relationships		Before			After		
		☹	😐	☺	☹	😐	☺
The student applies mathematical process standards to solve one-variable equations and inequalities. The student is expected to:							
7.11(A)	Model and solve one-variable, two-step equations and inequalities;						
7.11(B)	Determine if the given value(s) make(s) one-variable, two-step equations and inequalities true; and						
7.11(C)	Write and solve equations using geometry concepts, including the sum of the angles in a triangle, and angle relationships.						

7.12 Measurement and Data		☹	😐	☺	☹	😐	☺
The student applies mathematical process standards to use statistical representations to analyze data. The student is expected to:							
7.12(A)	Compare two groups of numeric data using comparative dot plots or box plots by comparing their shapes, centers, and spreads;						
7.12(B)	Use data from a random sample to make inferences about a population; and						
7.12(C)	Compare two populations based on data in random samples from these populations, including informal comparative inferences about differences between the two populations.						

7.13 Personal Financial Literacy		Before ☹	Before 😐	Before ☺	After ☹	After 😐	After ☺
The student applies mathematical process standards to develop an economic way of thinking and problem solving useful in one's life as a knowledgeable consumer and investor. The student is expected to:							
7.13(A)	Calculate the sales tax for a given purchase and calculate income tax for earned wages;						
7.13(B)	Identify the components of a personal budget, including income, planned savings for college, retirement, and emergencies, taxes, and fixed and variable expenses, and calculate what percentage of each category comprises of the total budget;						
7.13(C)	Create and organize a financial assets and liabilities record and construct a net worth statement;						
7.13(D)	Use a family budget estimator to determine the minimum household budget and average hourly wage needed for a family to meet its basic needs in the student's city or another large city nearby;						
7.13(E)	Calculate and compare simple interest and compound interest earnings; and						
7.13(F)	Analyze and compare monetary incentives, including sales, rebates, and coupons.						

Chapter 6
Multiple Representations of Linear Relationships

Texas Essential Knowledge and Skills

Targeted TEKS

7.7 The student applies mathematical process standards to represent linear relationships using multiple representations. The student is expected to represent linear relationships using verbal descriptions, tables, graphs, and equations that simplify to the form $y = mx + b$.

Mathematical Processes

7.1, 7.1(A), 7.1(B), 7.1(C), 7.1(D), 7.1(E), 7.1(F), 7.1(G)

Essential Question

HOW can you express a linear relationship between two quantities in different ways?

Math in the Real World

Armadillos live in burrows. The nine-banded armadillo is found throughout much of Texas, absent from the Western Trans-Pecos. Because armadillos have sharp claws, they can dig at the rate of 0.2 inch per second. Complete the table to represent the distance dug by an armadillo.

Time (s)	Distance (in.)
1	
2	
3	
4	
5	

What Tools Do You Need?

Vocab
abc

Vocabulary

family of linear relationships
linear equation
linear relationship
slope
slope-intercept form
y-intercept

Reading Math

A word problem can be made easier to understand by rewriting it using fewer words. Work with a partner to complete the following steps.

Step 1 **Read the problem carefully to determine what information is needed to solve the problem.**
Camilo belongs to an online video club that charges a monthly fee of \$15, plus \$2.50 per video that he downloads to watch. Suppose Camilo can spend \$20 each month for his video club. How many videos can he download and watch?

Step 2 **Rewrite the problem to make it simpler. Keep all of the important words and numbers, but use fewer of them.**
The total monthly cost is \$15, plus \$2.50 times the number of videos downloaded. How many videos can he download and watch for \$20?

Step 3 **Simplify it again. Use a variable for the unknown.**
The cost of v videos at \$2.50 per download plus \$15 is \$20.

Work with a partner to rewrite each problem using the method above.

1. Irene is saving money to buy a new MP3 player that costs \$149. She has already saved \$96 and plans to save an additional \$7 each week. In how many weeks will she have enough money for the MP3 player?

2. Xavier wants to buy some books that are each on sale for \$12 plus a magazine that costs \$4. How many books and a magazine can he buy if he has \$45 to spend?

When Will You Use This?

Hiroshi, Caitlyn, and Dario in

Too Many Texts

Dario, why didn't you respond to my text last night?

Oh, sorry about that - I think I might have gone over my limit this month.

You know, you can check how many text messages you've sent online. Do you want to use my computer?

That's a great idea!

Oh, NO! What's THIS going to cost me?

Your plan:
1,000 text messages
= $10.00

Messages sent to date:
1,027

Uh-oh, sounds like you *did* go over the limit!

Hiroshi! Have you been paying attention to ANY of this?

Yes! I have the solution for him -- unlimited text messaging!

Your Turn! **You will solve this problem in the chapter.**

Are You Ready?

Quick Review

Review 6.9(A), 6.11 TEKS

Example 1

Name the ordered pair for point *A*.

Start at the origin. Move right along the *x*-axis until you reach 4. Then move down until you reach the *y*-coordinate, −3. Point *A* is located at (4, −3).

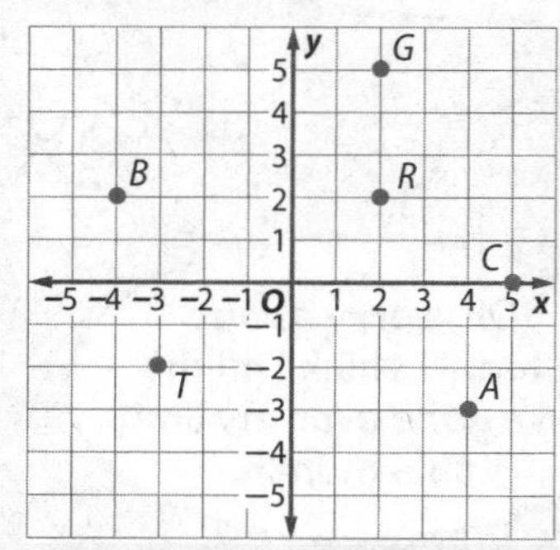

Example 2

Solve $3x = 36$. Check your solution.

$3x = 36$ Write the equation.

$\frac{3x}{3} = \frac{36}{3}$ Divide each side by 3.

$x = 12$ Simplify.

Check $3(12) = 36$ ✓

Quick Check

Coordinate Graphing **Name the ordered pair for each point.**

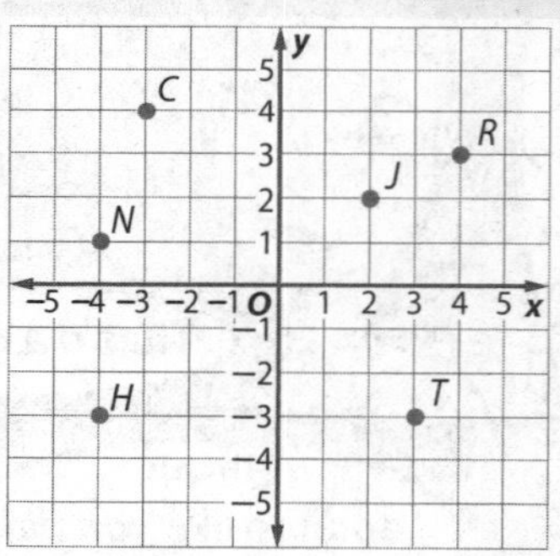

1. *C* ______
2. *H* ______
3. *J* ______
4. *N* ______
5. *R* ______
6. *T* ______

Solve Equations **Solve each equation. Check your solution.**

7. $x + 27 = 148$ ______
8. $k - 3.3 = 12.8$ ______
9. $13h = 32.5$ ______
10. $\frac{d}{4} = 19$ ______
11. The speed limit in a residential neighborhood is 35 miles per hour. This is one half the speed of a major interstate highway a few miles away. Write and solve a division equation to determine the speed limit of the interstate highway. ______

How Did You Do? **Which problems did you answer correctly in the Quick Check? Shade those exercise numbers below.**

① ② ③ ④ ⑤ ⑥ ⑦ ⑧ ⑨ ⑩ ⑪

Use the Foldable throughout this chapter to help you learn about linear relationships.

 cut on all dashed lines 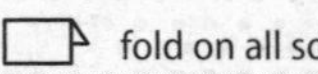 fold on all solid lines  tape to page 494

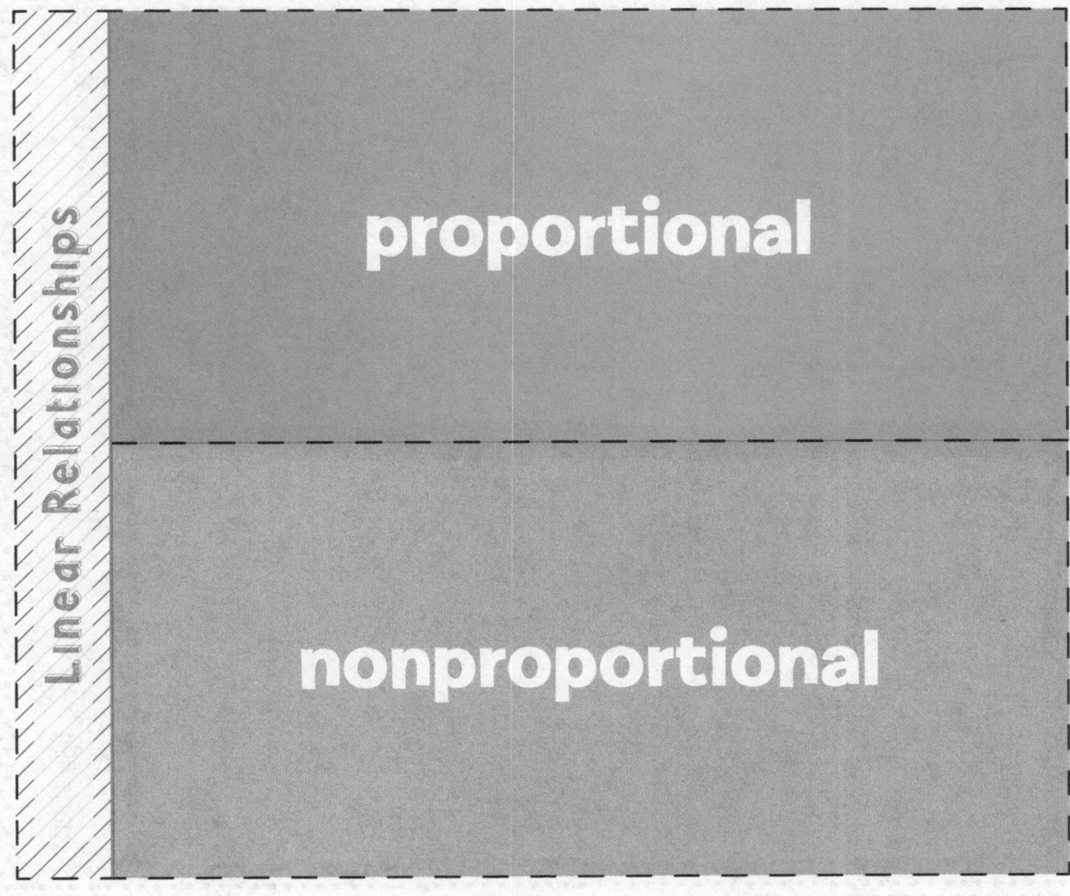

FOLDABLES® Use the Foldable throughout this chapter to help you learn about linear relationships.

 cut on all dashed lines 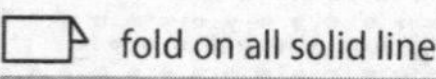 fold on all solid lines 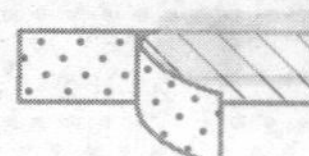 tape to page 494

Examples

Examples

page 494

Hands-On Lab 1-a

Linear Relationships

INQUIRY **HOW can I use multiple representations to display proportional linear relationships?**

Isaac will fence in a rectangular part of the backyard for his dog. The width is 3 yards. He wants to know how the amount of fencing he will need changes as he changes the length.

Texas Essential Knowledge and Skills

Targeted TEKS

7.7 The student applies mathematical process standards to represent linear relationships using multiple representations. The student is expected to represent linear relationships using verbal descriptions, tables, graphs, and equations that simplify to the form $y = mx + b$.

Mathematical Processes

7.1(C), 7.1(D), 7.1(E), 7.1(F), 7.1(G)

Hands-On Activity

Step 1 Use a separate piece of paper to draw several rectangles, each with a width of 3 units. Possible dimensions you can use for the lengths are 1 unit, 4 units, and 6 units.

Step 2 Complete the table to show how the perimeter of each rectangle changes as the length changes. Use a separate piece of paper, if needed, to draw more rectangles.

Length (units), x	Perimeter (units), y
1	
2	
3	
4	
5	
6	

1. **Analyze Relationships** Does the table display a constant rate of change? Explain.

____

____

____

Step 3 Graph the data in the table on the coordinate plane. Connect the points to see the pattern.

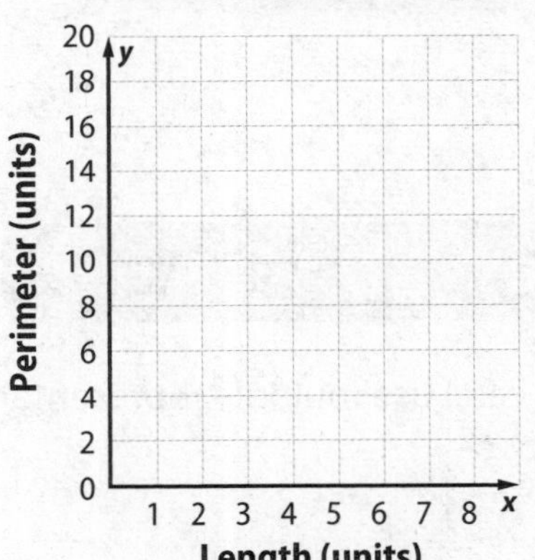

2. **Analyze Relationships** Does the graph display a constant ratio and a proportional relationship? Explain.

____

____

____

Investigate

Collaborate

Work with a partner to complete each table. Then graph the ordered pairs on a coordinate plane.

3.

Perimeter of Square	
Side Length (units), x	Perimeter (units), y
1	
3	
5	
7	

4.

Area of Square	
Side Length (units), x	Area (units^2), y
1	
3	
5	
7	

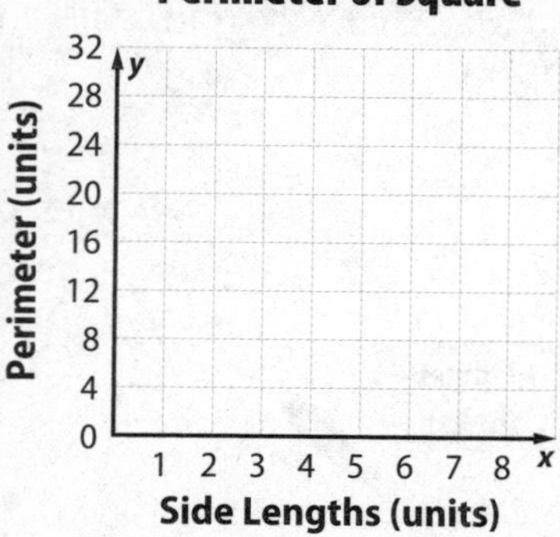

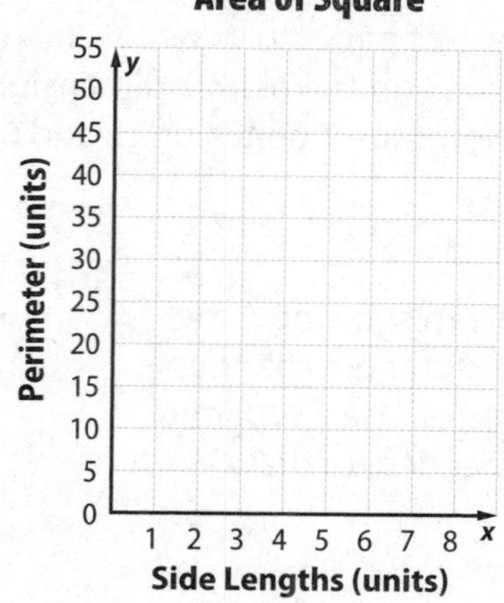

Analyze and Reflect

Collaborate

5. MP **Organize Ideas** A *proportional linear relationship* has a graph that is a straight line that passes through the origin. Compare the graphs above. Does either graph represent a proportional linear relationship? Explain.

Create

6. INQUIRY HOW can I use multiple representations to display proportional linear relationships?

Lesson 1

Identify Linear Relationships

Launch the Lesson: Real World

The table shows the approximate height and horizontal distance traveled by a football kicked at an angle of 30° with an initial velocity of 30 yards per second. Let's investigate which two quantities, time and height or time and length, have a constant rate of change.

Time (s)	Height (yd)	Length (yd)
0.0	0	0
0.5	6.2	13
1.0	9.7	26
1.5	10.5	39
2.0	8.7	52
2.5	4.2	65

1. Compare the rate of change for the height and length the football traveled each half-second.

2. Graph the ordered pairs (time, height) and (time, length) on a separate sheet of grid paper. Connect the points with a straight line or smooth curve. Then compare the graphs.

Which MP Mathematical Processes did you use? Shade the circle(s) that applies.

Ⓐ Apply Math to the Real World.
Ⓑ Use a Problem-Solving Model.
Ⓒ Select Tools and Techniques.
Ⓓ Use Multiple Representations.
Ⓔ Organize Ideas.
Ⓕ Analyze Relationships.
Ⓖ Justify Arguments.

Texas Essential Knowledge and Skills

Targeted TEKS

7.7 The student applies mathematical process standards to represent linear relationships using multiple representations. The student is expected to represent linear relationships using verbal descriptions, tables, graphs, and equations that simplify to the form $y = mx + b$.

Mathematical Processes

7.1(A), 7.1(B), 7.1(F)

Vocab

Vocabulary

linear relationship

Essential Question

HOW can you express a linear relationship between two quantities in different ways?

Work Zone

Identify Linear Relationships using Tables

A relationship between two quantities that have a constant rate of change and a straight-lined graph is called a **linear relationship**.

Examples

Determine whether the relationship in each table represents a linear relationship. Explain.

1.

x	y
2	50
4	35
6	20
8	5

+2, +2, +2 (x); −15, −15, −15 (y)

As *x* increases by 2, *y* decreases by 15 each time. The rate of change is constant, so this relationship is linear.

2.

x	y
1	1
4	16
7	49
10	100

+3, +3, +3 (x); +15, +33, +51 (y)

As *x* increases by 3, *y* increases by a greater amount each time. The rate of change is not constant, so this relationship is not linear.

Check Graph the points on a coordinate plane.

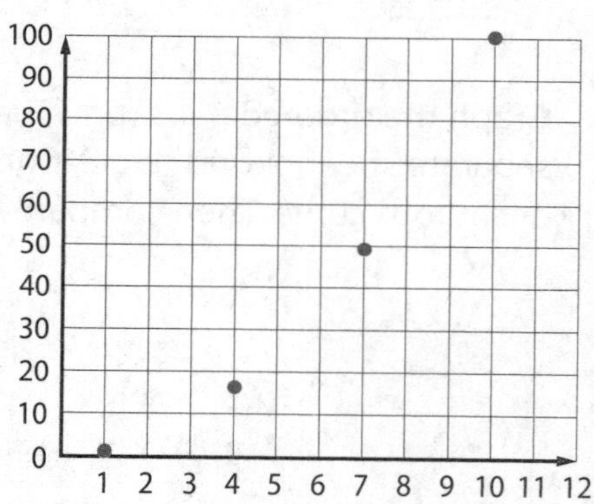

The points do not fall in a line. The relationship is not linear. ✓

Show your work.

Got It? Do these problems to find out.

Determine whether the relationship in each table represents a linear relationship. Explain.

a.

x	0	5	10	15
y	20	16	12	8

b.

x	0	2	4	6
y	0	2	8	18

a. ______

b. ______

Identify Linear Relationships using Graphs

You can use a graph to determine if a relationship between two quantities is a linear relationship.

Examples

Tutor

3. Use a graph to determine whether the relationship between a tiger cub's age, in weeks, and the minimum number of Calories it should eat is a linear relationship.

Age (weeks)	1	2	3	4	5
Minimum Calorie Intake	825	1,000	1,185	1,320	1,420

Graph the data on the coordinate plane to determine if the ordered pairs lie on a straight line.

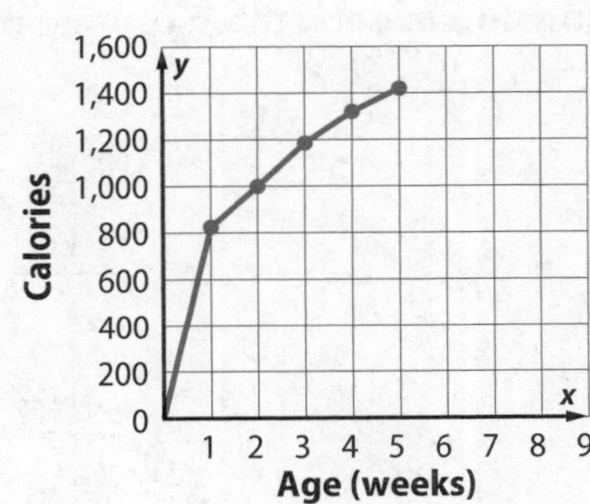

The relationship is not linear because the points (1, 825), (2, 1,000), (3, 1,185), (4, 1,320), and (5, 1,420) do not lie on a straight line. Therefore, this relationship is not linear.

4. A square has a side length of s inches. Use a graph to determine if the relationship between side length and area of the square a linear relationship.

Make a table to show the area of the square for side lengths of 1, 2, 3, 4, and 5 inches.

Side Length (in.)	1	2	3	4	5
Area (in^2)	1	4	9	16	25

Graph the relationship. The relationship is not linear because the points (1, 1), (2, 4), (3, 9), (4, 16), and (5, 25) do not lie on a straight line.

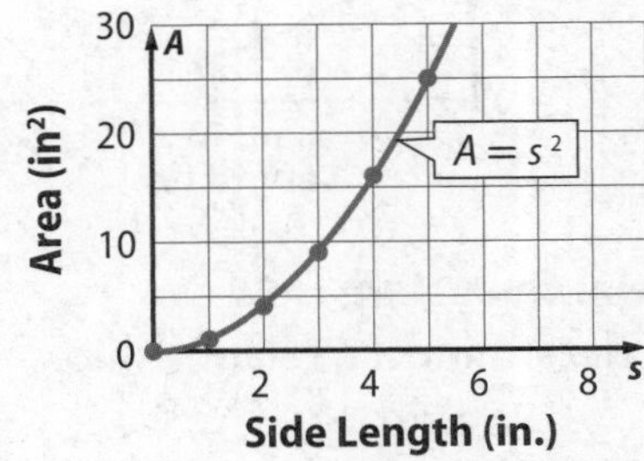

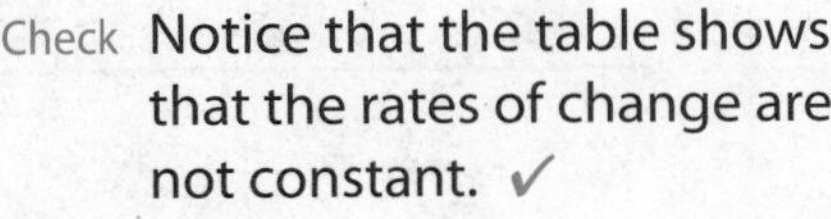

Check Notice that the table shows that the rates of change are not constant. ✓

Got It? Do this problem to find out.

c. Suri ordered running shirts for the cross country team online. Each shirt costs $15 plus $4 shipping for each item. Use a graph to determine if the relationship between total cost and the number of shirts sold a linear relationship. Explain.

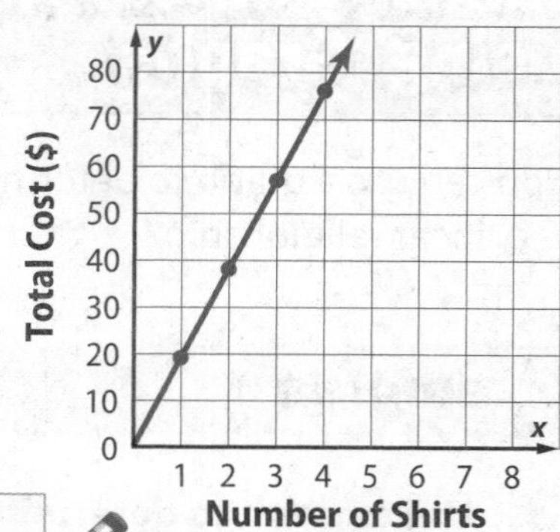

Number of Shirts	1	2	3	4
Total Cost ($)				

c. ______________

Guided Practice

Determine whether the relationship in each table represents a linear relationship. Explain. (Examples 1 and 2)

1.

x	0	1	2	3
y	1	3	6	10

2.

x	0	3	6	9
y	−3	9	21	33

3. The table shows the measures of the sides of several rectangles. Use a graph to determine if the relationship between the length and width of the rectangles is a linear relationship. Explain. (Examples 3 and 4)

Length (in.)	1	4	8	10
Width (in.)	64	16	8	6.4

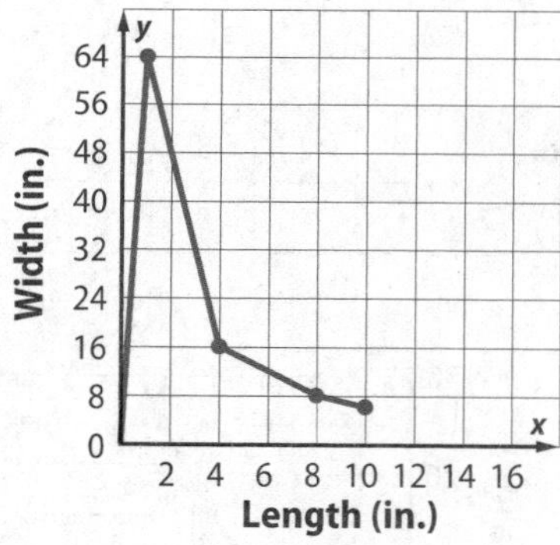

4. **Building on the Essential Question** How can you use a table or a graph to determine if a relationship is linear?

Rate Yourself!

How confident are you about linear relationships? Check the box that applies.

Find out online. Use the Self-Check Quiz.

Check

FOLDABLES Time to update your Foldable!

Name ______________________ My Homework ______________________

Independent Practice

7.7, 7.1(D) TEKS

Determine whether the relationship in each table represents a linear relationship. Explain. (Examples 1 and 2)

1.

x	−2	0	2	4
y	−1	0	1	2

2.

x	1	2	3	4
y	1	4	9	16

3.

x	5	10	15	20
y	13	28	43	58

4.

x	1	3	5	7
y	−2	−18	−50	−98

5. The Guzman family drove from Anderson, South Carolina, to Myrtle Beach, South Carolina. Use a graph to determine if the relationship between the distance traveled and time is a linear relationship. Explain. (Examples 3 and 4)

Time (h)	1	2	3	4
Distance (mi)	65	130	195	260

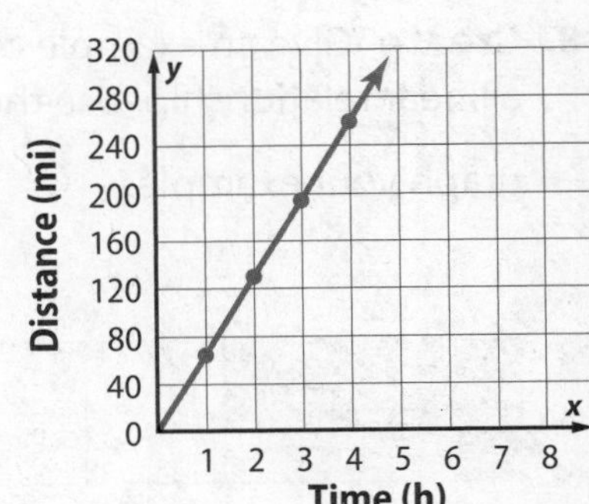

6. There are 3,600 seconds in one hour. The total seconds is a relationship of the hours. Complete the table and graph the ordered pairs to determine if the relationship between the hours and seconds is a linear relationship. Explain. (Examples 3 and 4)

Hours	1	2	3	4
Seconds	3,600			

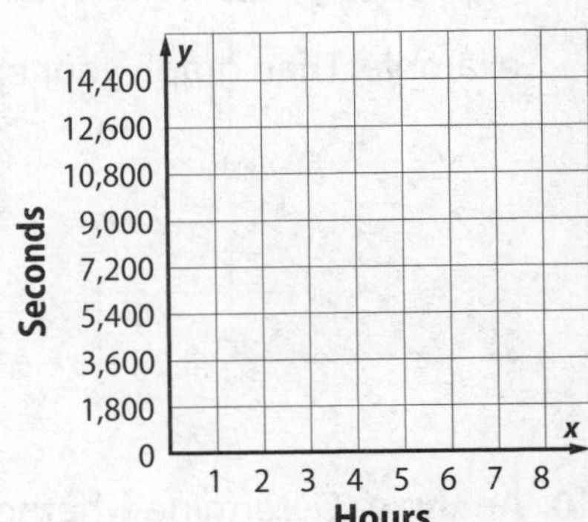

7. **Analyze Relationships** Complete the graphic organizer by determining if the graphs represent linear relationships.

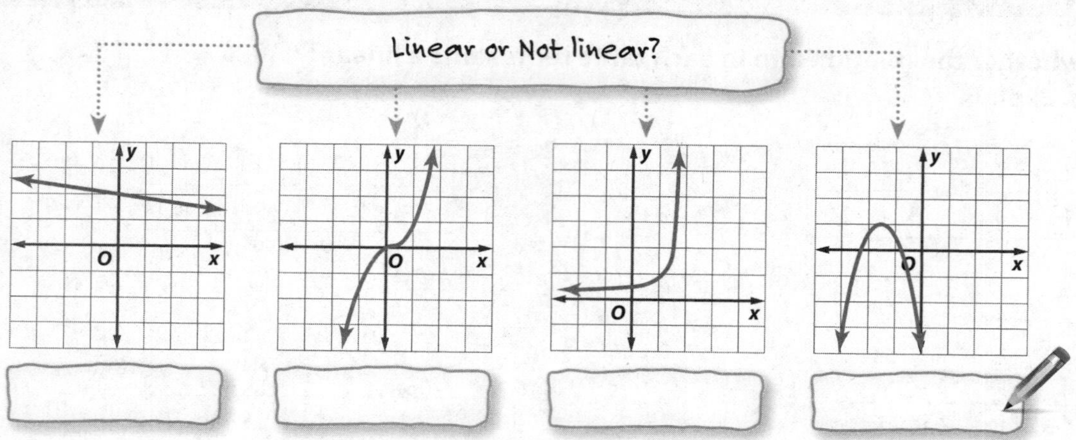

H.O.T. Problems Higher-Order Thinking

8. **Create** Give an example of a real-world situation that represents a linear relationship. Use the table to record your example. Then graph your example.

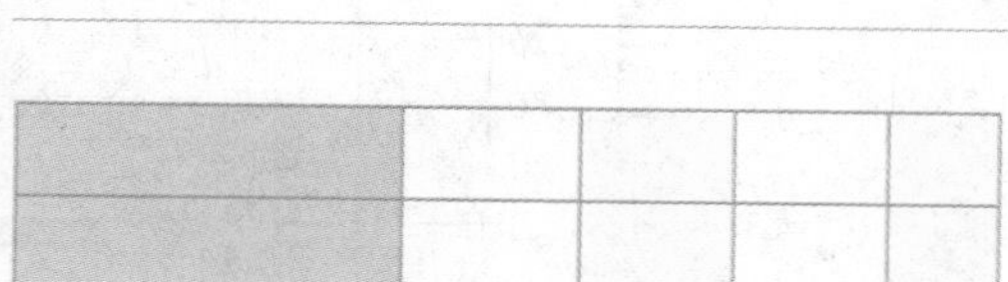

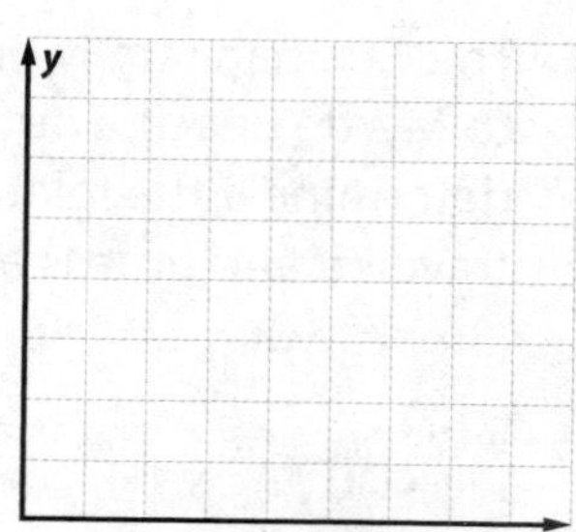

9. **Create** Give an example of a real-world situation that does not represent a linear relationship. Use the table to record your example. Then graph your example.

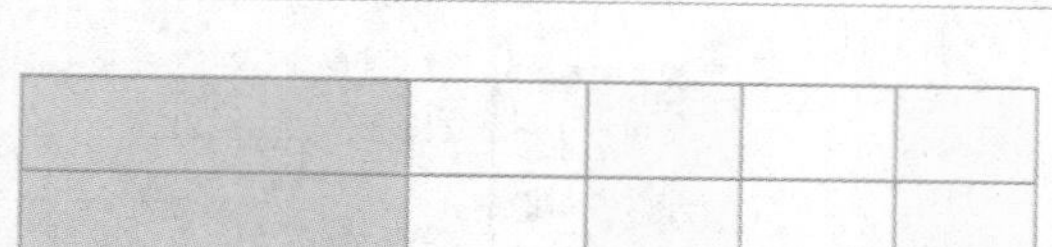

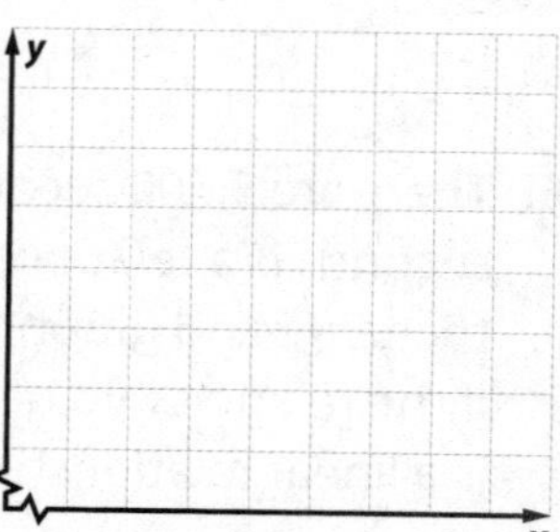

10. **Analyze** Determine whether the following statement is *always, sometimes,* or *never* true. Justify your reasoning.

A linear relationship that has a constant rate of change is a proportional relationship.

Name ______________________________

Multi-Step Problem Solving

11. Marco runs a tutoring business. The number of hours and the amount of money earned represents a linear relationship. Marco recorded his earnings for 4 days. He saves 35% of his earnings to pay income tax at the end of the year. How much does he save? EE P MP

Day	Total Money Earned ($)
Monday	125
Tuesday	75
Wednesday	150
Thursday	225

Ⓐ $172.50 Ⓒ $201.25

Ⓑ $192.50 Ⓓ $373.75

Use a problem-solving model to solve this problem.

1 Analyze

Read the problem. Circle the information you know. Underline what the problem is asking you to find.

2 Plan

What will you need to do to solve the problem? Write your plan in steps.

Step 1 Determine the ______________ in 4 days.

Step 2 Determine ______ of the total money he earned.

3 Solve

Use your plan to solve the problem. Show your steps.

Add the money he earned in 4 days.

$125 + 75 + 150 + 225 =$ ______

Determine 35% of the total money he earned.

$0.35 \times$ ______ $=$ ______

Marco should save ______.

So, the correct answer is ______. Fill in that answer choice.

Read to Succeed!

Since the relationship is linear, it must mean that Marco charges the same amount for the hours spent tutoring.

4 Justify and Evaluate

How do you know your solution is accurate?

____

____

____

EE = Expressions, Equations, and Relationships P = Proportionality MP = Mathematical Processes

More Multi-Step Problem Solving

Use a problem-solving model to solve each problem.

12. Rosa is training for a marathon. The amount of time and the number of miles ran represents a linear relationship. Rosa recorded her training for 3 days. The following week she ran 125% more miles. How many miles did she run the following week? EE P MP

Day	Distance (mi)
Monday	16
Wednesday	13
Friday	11

Ⓐ 10 miles

Ⓑ 40 miles

Ⓒ 50 miles

Ⓓ 50.5 miles

13. The table below represents a linear relationship. What is the sum of *a* and *b*? EE N P MP

x	y
2	−5
5	a
8	b
11	13

14. The graph shows the linear relationship between the amount of coffee purchased, in pounds, and the total cost, in dollars. How much more does it cost to buy 8 pounds of coffee than 4 pounds of coffee? EE N P MP

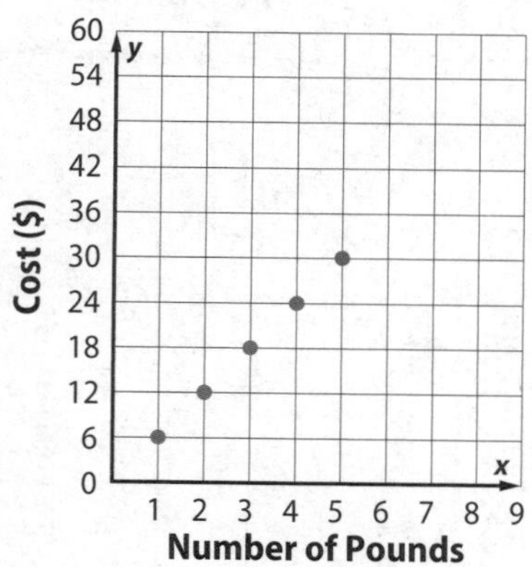

15. For a middle school fundraiser, 25% of the money raised by each grade level was donated to a local charity. The 6th grade raised a total of $200, the 7th grade raised a total of $148, and the 8th grade raised a total of $264. Determine whether the relationship between the amount raised and the amount donated to charity is a linear relationship. Justify your answer. EE P MP

EE = Expressions, Equations, and Relationships N = Number and Operations P = Proportionality MP = Mathematical Processes

Lesson 2

Equations of Linear Relationships

Launch the Lesson: Real World

Antonella's family is going on a trip to visit a museum. Each person must pay an admission fee of \$12. In addition, the museum charges a one-time fee of \$15 to cover the tour guide. Let's investigate the relationship of total cost to number of people.

1. Complete the table to determine the total cost of admission.
2. Graph the data in the table on the coordinate plane.
3. Does this situation represent a linear relationship? Explain.

Number of People, x	Total Cost (\$), y
0	
1	
2	
3	
4	
5	

4. Is this situation a proportional linear relationship? Explain.

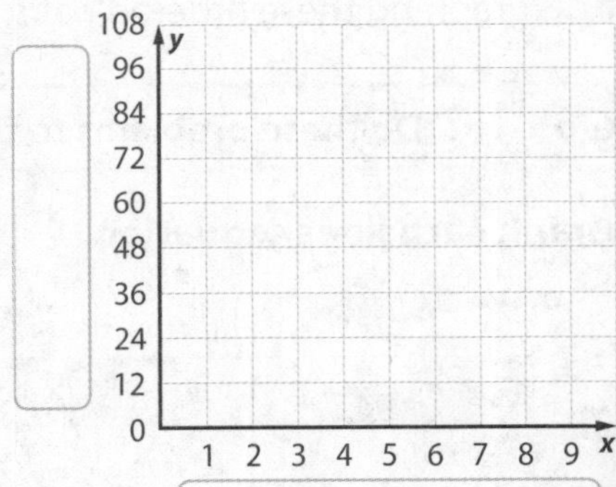

5. The equation that represents this situation is $y = 12x + 15$. Explain why the number 12 is multiplied by x.

Which MP Mathematical Processes did you use? Shade the circle(s) that applies.

Ⓐ Apply Math to the Real World.
Ⓑ Use a Problem-Solving Model.
Ⓒ Select Tools and Techniques.
Ⓓ Use Multiple Representations.
Ⓔ Organize Ideas.
Ⓕ Analyze Relationships.
Ⓖ Justify Arguments.

Texas Essential Knowledge and Skills

Targeted TEKS

7.7 The student applies mathematical process standards to represent linear relationships using multiple representations. The student is expected to represent linear relationships using verbal descriptions, tables, graphs, and equations that simplify to the form $y = mx + b$.

Mathematical Processes

7.1(A), 7.1(B), 7.1(D)

Vocabulary

linear equation

Essential Question

HOW can you express a linear relationship between two quantities in different ways?

Work Zone

Graph Linear Equations using Tables

An equation such as $y = 60x$ is called a linear equation. A **linear equation** is an equation whose graph is a line. You can graph a linear equation by making a table of ordered pairs.

Example

Tutor

1. Graph $y = 2x + 1$.

Select any four values for the independent variable x. We chose 2, 1, 0, and −1. Substitute these values for x to determine the dependent variable y.

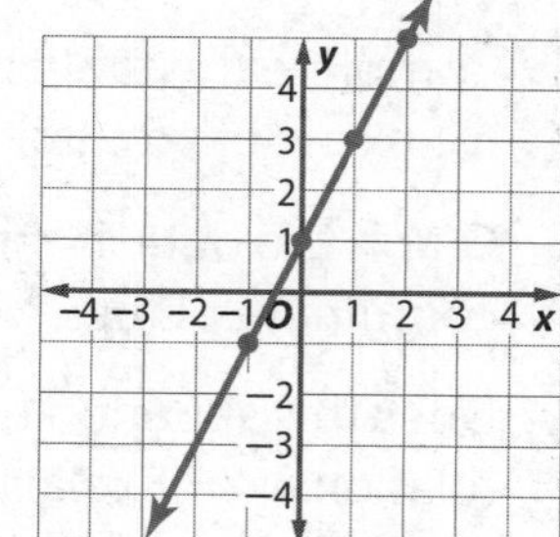

x	$2x + 1$	y	(x, y)
−1	$2(-1) + 1$	−1	(−1, −1)
0	$2(0) + 1$	1	(0, 1)
1	$2(1) + 1$	3	(1, 3)
2	$2(2) + 1$	5	(2, 5)

The ordered pairs (x, y) are (−1, −1), (0, 1), (1, 3), and (2, 5). By graphing these ordered pairs, you can create the graph of $y = 2x + 1$.

Defining Variables

The input value of a table is known as the independent variable and the output value is known as the dependent variable.

Got It? Do these problems to find out.

Graph each linear equation.

a. $y = x - 3$

x	$x - 3$	y	(x, y)

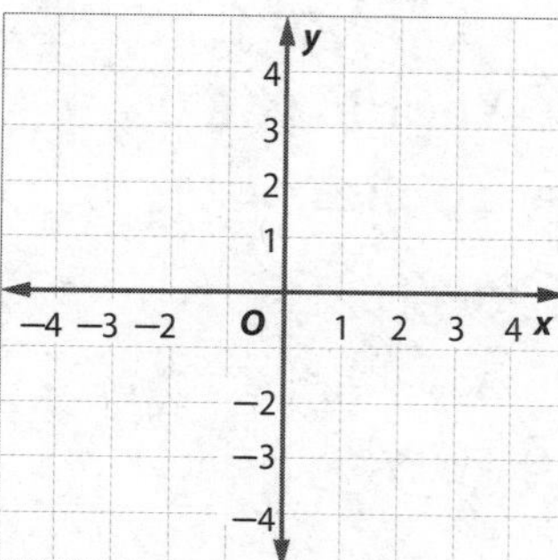

b. $y = -3x$

x	$-3x$	y	(x, y)

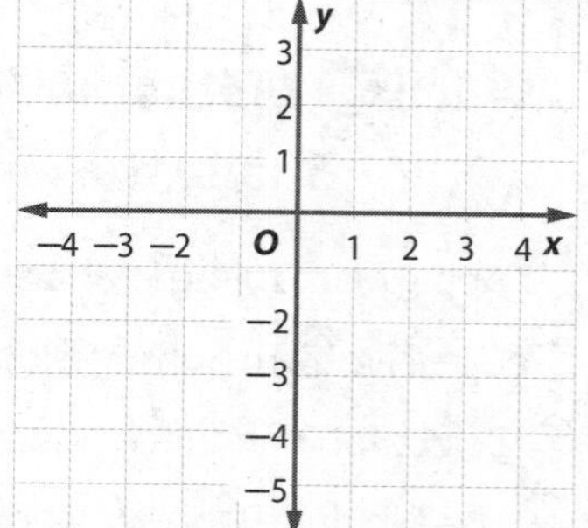

Graph Real-World Data

Real-world data can be modeled by a linear equation if there is a constant rate of change.

Multi-Step Example

Tutor

2. A outdoor adventure company charges $9 per hour for a mountain bike plus a $5 fee for a helmet. The equation $c = 9h + 5$ describes the total cost c for h hours to rent a bike. Represent this linear equation with a graph.

Step 1 Select any four values for h. Select only positive numbers because h represents time. Make a table.

h	$9h + 5$	c	(h, c)
1	$9(1) + 5$	14	(1, 14)
2	$9(2) + 5$	23	(2, 23)
3	$9(3) + 5$	32	(3, 32)
4	$9(4) + 5$	41	(4, 41)

Step 2 Graph the ordered pairs and draw a line connecting the points.

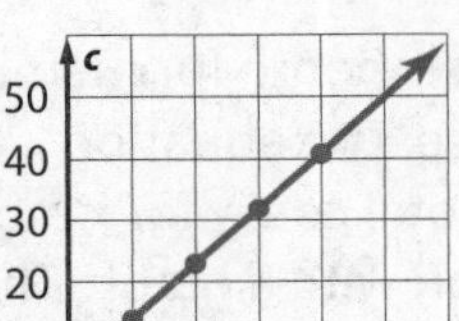

Show your work.

Got It? Do this problem to find out.

c. Malik's family decided to order premium cable that costs $34 per month. The company charges a one-time installation fee of $75. The equation $y = 34x + 75$ describes the total cost y for x months. Represent this linear equation with a graph.

x	$34x + 75$	y	(x, y)

c. ______

Example

3. A veterinarian charged a customer \$80 for an office visit. The veterinarian charges \$35 for office visits plus \$15 for vaccinations. The equation $80 = 15x + 35$ describes the total charge for x vaccinations. Use the equation and graph to determine how many vaccinations the customer's pet received.

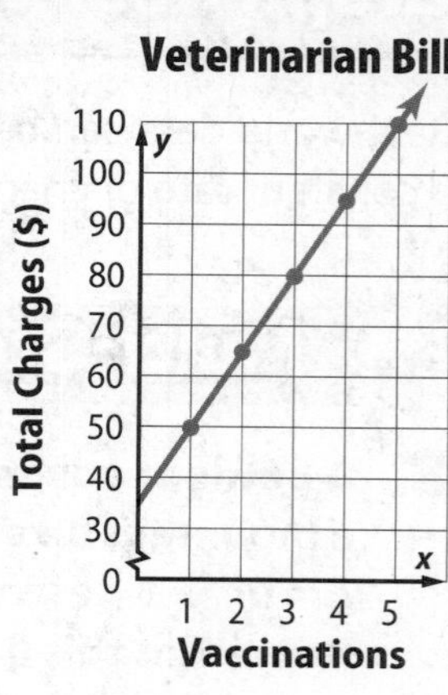

From the graph, it appears that when the total cost is \$80, there were 3 vaccinations administered.

Check Use the equation to check your answer. $15(3) + 35 = 80$ ✓

Guided Practice

1. Graph $y = 2x - 3$. (Example 1)

x				
y				

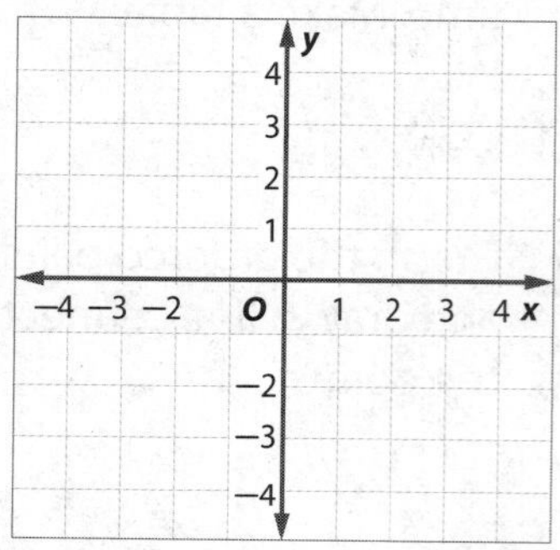

2. A health club charges \$20 per month for membership fees plus a \$45 enrollment fee. The equation $y = 20x + 45$ describes the total cost y for x months. Represent this linear equation with a graph. Then determine the number of months if the total charge is \$125. (Examples 2 and 3) ____________

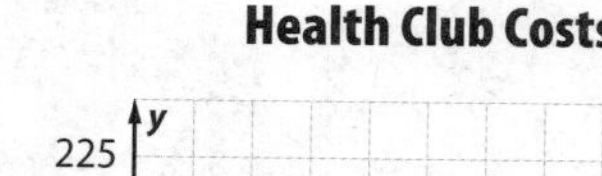

x	y

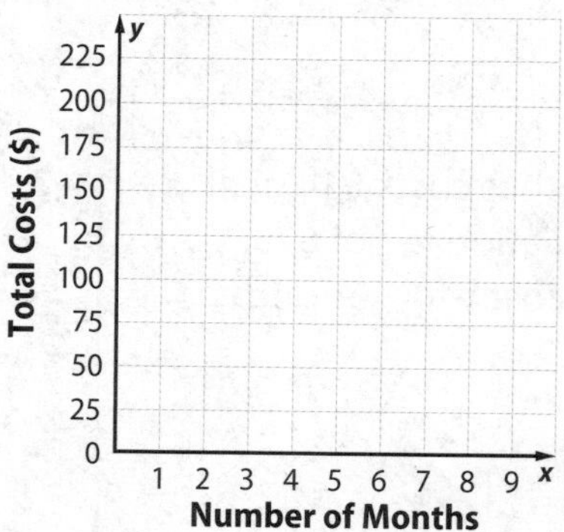

3. **Building on the Essential Question** How can linear relationships be represented?

____

____

Rate Yourself!

☐ I understand how to graph linear equations.

Great! You're ready to move on!

☐ I still have questions about graphing linear equations.

No problem! Go online to access a Personal Tutor.

Check

FOLDABLES Time to update your Foldable!

Independent Practice

7.7, 7.1(C), 7.1(D) TEKS

Graph each linear equation. (Example 1)

1. $y = x - 5$

x	y

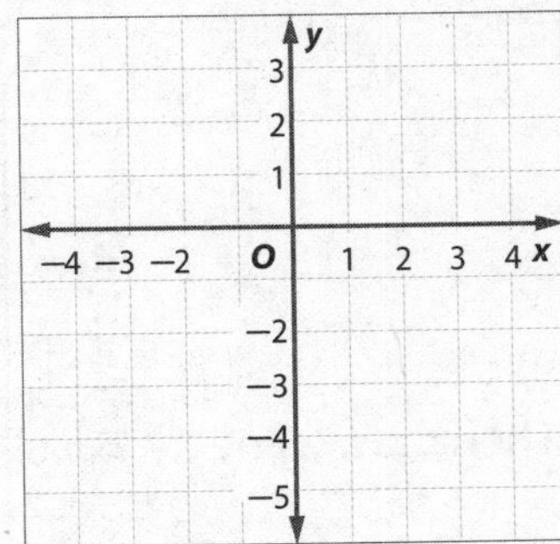

2. $y = 4x + 1$

x	y

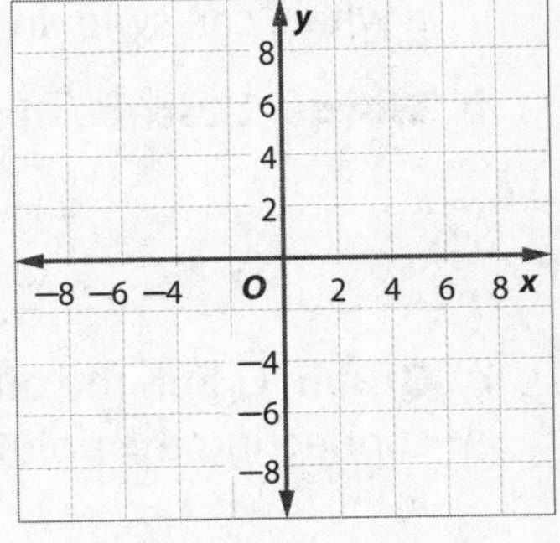

3. Financial Literacy Juliana wants to remodel her bathroom. Materials will cost her \$500 and the contractor charges \$40 per hour. The equation $y = 40x + 500$ represents the amount of money needed for x number of hours worked by the contractor. (Examples 2 and 3)

a. Represent this linear equation with a graph.

b. How much money would it cost if it took the contractor 12 hours to completely remodel her bathroom? ________

Remodeling

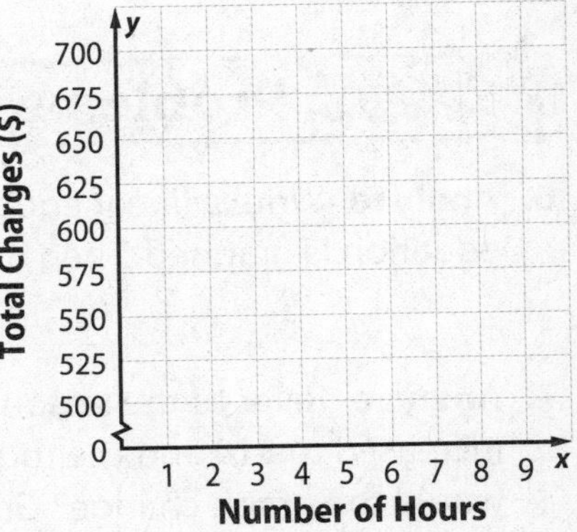

4. MP **Apply Math to the Real World** Refer to the graphic novel at the beginning of the chapter and the frame below. Let x represent the number of text messages over 1,000. The equation $y = 0.10x + 10$ gives the total cost y for x text messages of 1,000. What is the total cost for 1,027 text messages?

____

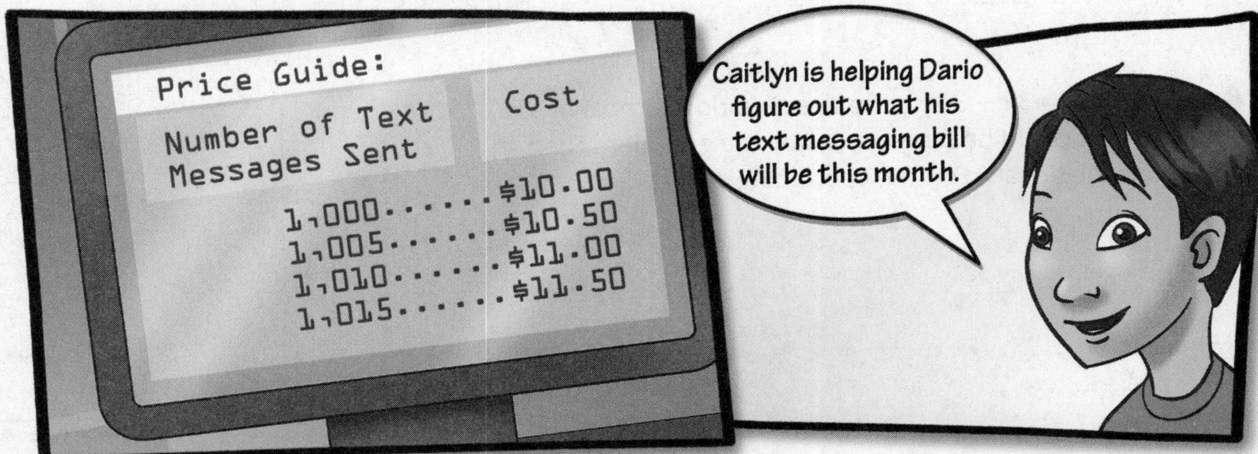

5. **MP Use Multiple Representations** A whale can swim half a mile per minute. The linear equation $y = 0.5x$ gives the distance y in miles that a whale can travel in x minutes.

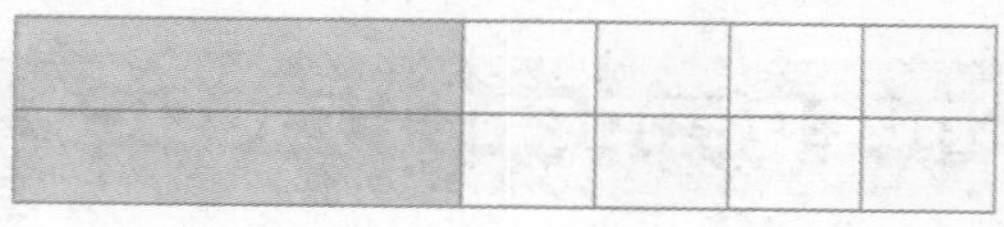

a. **Table** Make a table to determine the number of miles a whale can swim in 5, 10, 15, and 20 minutes.

b. **Words** Describe the rate of change.

c. **Graph** Graph the ordered pairs (time, distance). Then draw a line connecting the points.

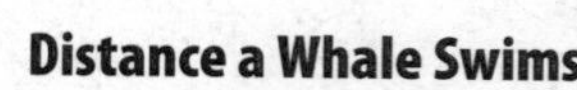

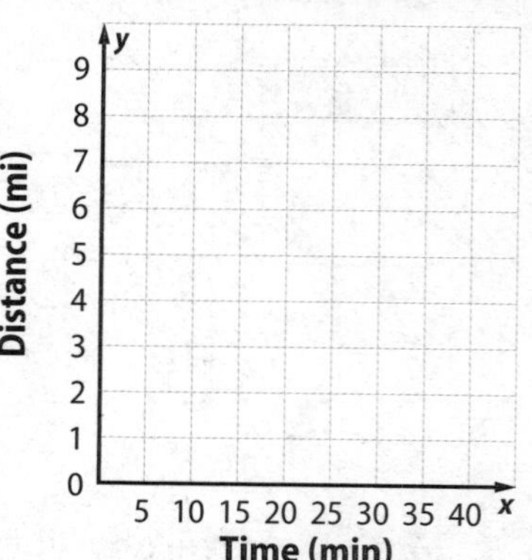

H.O.T. Problems Higher-Order Thinking

6. **Analyze** Write a linear equation that has (3, −2) as an ordered pair when the equation is graphed. Then determine another ordered pair.

7. **Analyze** Refer to the lesson opener. If the cost per person increased to \$14 and the tour guide fee stayed the same, how would the graph change? Graph the new relationship on the coordinate plane.

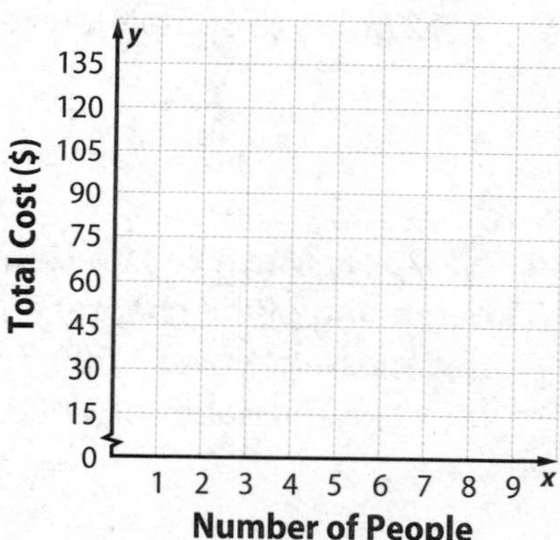

8. **Create** Refer to the lesson opener. Describe a situation regarding the cost per person and the tour guide fee that would result in a graph that passes through the point (0, 0).

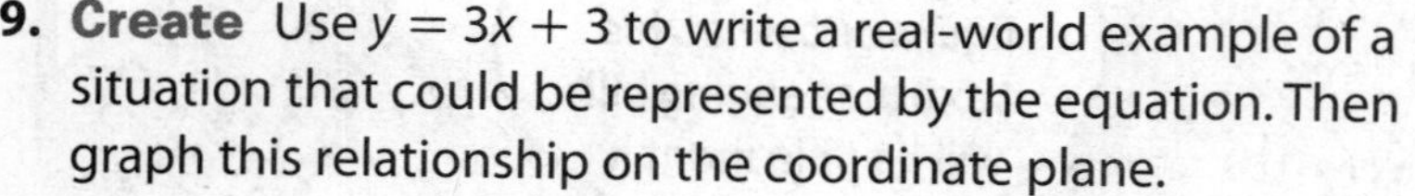

9. **Create** Use $y = 3x + 3$ to write a real-world example of a situation that could be represented by the equation. Then graph this relationship on the coordinate plane.

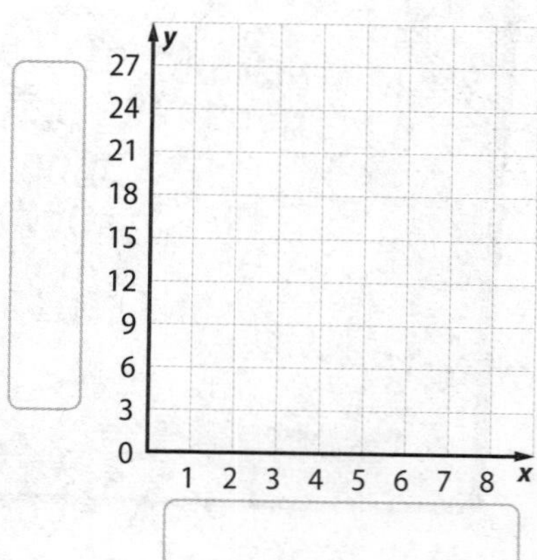

Name ______________________________

Multi-Step Problem Solving

10. A music subscription service charges an initial setup fee and also a monthly fee. The linear equation $y = 10x + 50$ gives the cost y in dollars for a monthly subscription x. How much less would a 6 month subscription be compared to a 1 year subscription? EE P MP

Ⓐ \$50 Ⓑ \$60 Ⓒ \$110 Ⓓ \$170

Use a problem-solving model to solve this problem.

1 Analyze

Read the problem. Circle the information you know.
Underline what the problem is asking you to find.

2 Plan

What will you need to do to solve the problem? Write your plan in steps.

Step 1 Determine the ____________ for each subscription.

Step 2 Subtract to determine how much less a ________ subscription costs.

3 Solve

Use your plan to solve the problem. Show your steps.

Use the equation to determine the total cost for each subscription.

$y = 10x + 50$ 6 month $y = 10x + 50$ 1 year

$y = 10(\_\_\_\_) + 50$ $y = 10(\_\_\_\_) + 50$

$y = \_\_\_\_$ $y = \_\_\_\_$

$\_\_\_\_ - \_\_\_\_ = \_\_\_\_$ Subtract.

A 6 month subscription is ______ less.

So, the correct answer is ____. Fill in that answer choice.

Read to Succeed!
The subscription is a monthly fee. Make sure you use months when you determine the cost for a 1 year subscription.

4 Justify and Evaluate

How do you know your solution is accurate?

____

____

____

EE = Expressions, Equations, and Relationships P = Proportionality MP = Mathematical Processes

More Multi-Step Problem Solving

Use a problem-solving model to solve each problem.

11. Jamie's car broke down and she has to take it to a mechanic. The part to fix the car costs \$450, plus the mechanic charges \$50 per hour for labor. The linear equation $y = 50x + 450$ gives the total cost y in dollars for x hours. Jamie has \$800 in her account. What is the maximum number of hours the mechanic can work on her car and still have enough money to pay her bill? EE N MP

Ⓐ 5 hours

Ⓑ 6 hours

Ⓒ 7 hours

Ⓓ 8 hours

12. Sarah is saving money. She already has \$30. To make more money, she babysits for \$12 per hour. How many hours will she have to babysit in order to save \$102? EE N MP

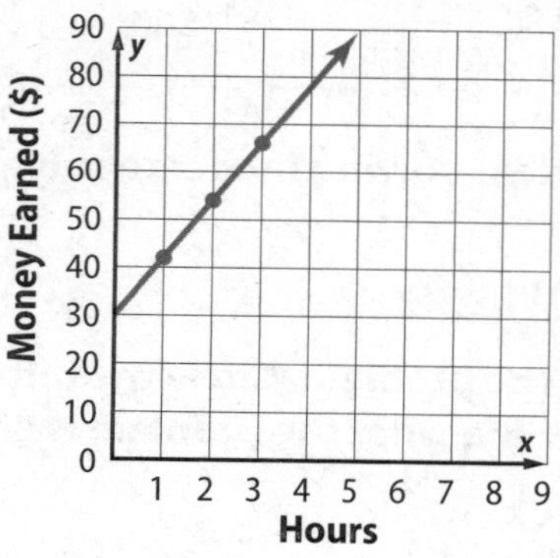

13. Robin bought 4 feet of string. She uses 10 inches to make each necklace and 6 inches to make each bracelet. If she makes 4 bracelets, how many necklaces can she make with the remaining string? EE N MP

14. Compare and contrast the graph of $y = x + 6$ and $y = \frac{1}{2}x + 6$. EE N MP

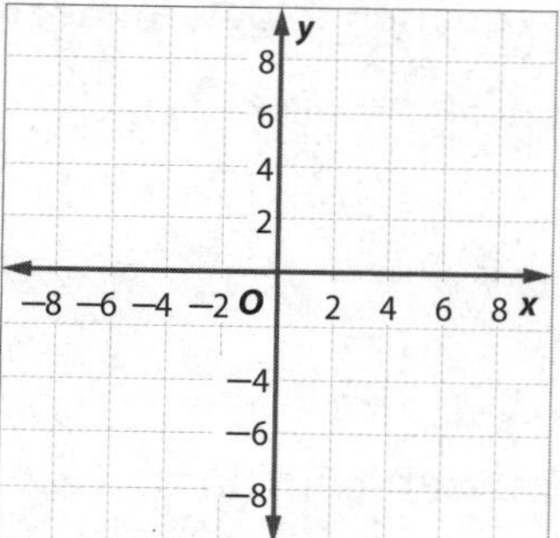

N = Number and Operations EE = Expressions, Equations, and Relationships MP = Mathematical Processes

Make a Table

Mathematical Process TEKS
7.1(B) Use a problem-solving model that incorporates analyzing given information, formulating a plan or strategy, determining a solution, justifying the solution, and evaluating the problem-solving process and the reasonableness of the solution.

Targeted TEKS 7.7

Dirt Bikes

Hoshi wants to purchase a membership to a dirt bike park. The cost of a membership is $10 per person plus a $5 group training fee. The equation $y = 10x + 5$ describes the total cost y for x people.

Determine if this situation represents a linear relationship. What is the total cost for 8 people?

Analyze

What are the facts?

The cost is $10 per person plus a $5 group training fee.

Plan

Choose a problem-solving strategy.

I will use the ________ strategy.

Solve

How can you apply the strategy?

Make a table. Then determine if the relationship is linear.

Number of People, x	Total Cost, y
1	
2	
3	
4	

+10, +10, +10

The rate of change is constant, so this represents a ________ relationship.

Use the equation to determine the cost for 8 people.

$y = 10x + 5$ $\quad$ $y = 10(8) + 5$ $\quad$ $y = \square$

So, the cost for 8 people is $\square$.

Justify and Evaluate

How do you know your solution is accurate?

____

____

Financial Literacy

Latoya is saving money to buy a saxophone. She already has \$75 and saves \$45 each month. The equation $y = 45x + 75$ describes the total amount saved y for x months.

Determine if this situation represents a linear relationship. Then determine how long it will take Latoya to save enough money to buy a saxophone that costs \$300.

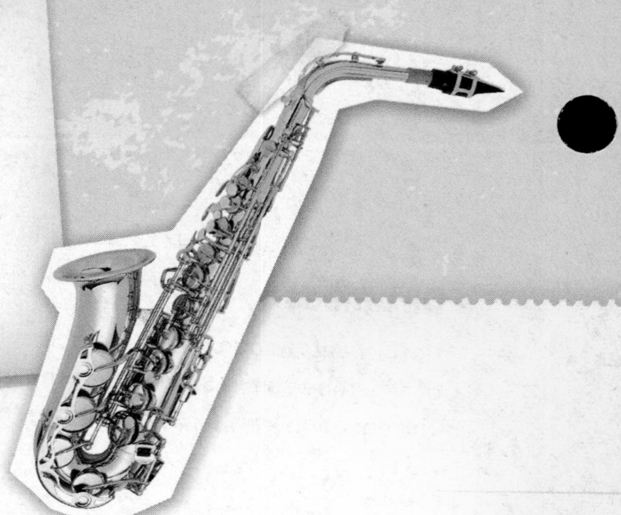

Analyze

Read the problem. Circle the information you know. Underline what the problem is asking you to find.

2 Plan

Choose a problem-solving strategy.

I will use the ______________________________ strategy.

3 Solve

How can you apply the strategy?

Justify and Evaluate

How do you know your solution is accurate?

____

____

C Squared Studios/Getty Images

Multi-Step Problem Solving

Work with a small group to solve the following problems. Show your work on a separate piece of paper.

1. Carnivals

For a carnival game, containers are arranged in a triangular display. The top row has 1 container. The second row has 2 containers. The third row has 3 containers. The pattern continues until the bottom row, which has 10 containers.

A contestant knocks down 29 containers on the first throw. How many containers remain?

2. Budget

Tamara earns $2,050 each month. She spends 65% of the amount she earns. The rest of the money is equally divided and deposited into two separate accounts.

How many months until Tamara has deposited more than $2,500 in one of her accounts?

3. Toothpicks

Write an expression to determine the number of toothpicks needed to make any figure. Then determine the number of toothpicks needed to make the 8th figure.

Figure 1 Figure 2 Figure 3

4. Diving

A diver descends to −15 feet after 1 minute, −30 feet after 2 minutes, and −45 feet after 3 minutes.

Determine if the relationship is linear. If the diver keeps descending at this rate, determine his position after 12 minutes.

TEKS Mid-Chapter Check

Vocabulary Check

1. What is a *linear relationship?* Give an example of a real-world example that is a linear relationship. TEKS 7.7, 7.1(D)

Key Concept Check

2. Complete the graphic organizer about linear relationships. Give three different ways that you can represent a linear relationship. TEKS 7.7, 7.1(E)

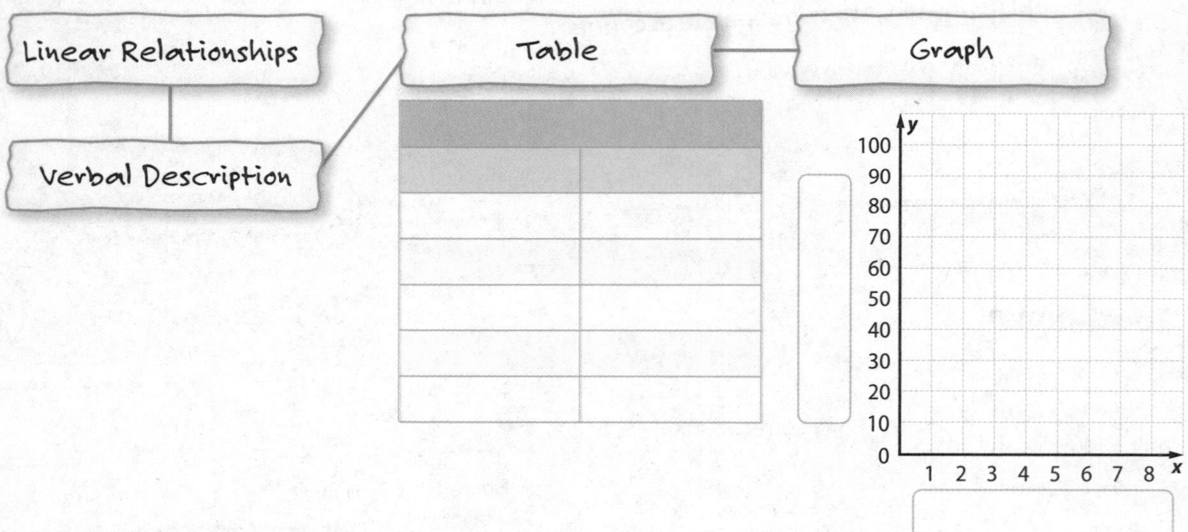

Multi-Step Problem Solving

3. Mr. Carter was comparing the cost to order running shoes for the track team online. Use the tables to compare the constant rate of change for each company. How much more for each pair of shoes will it cost Mr. Carter if he orders from Trail King?

Ⓐ \$3
Ⓑ \$6
Ⓒ \$12
Ⓓ \$24

Fast Feet	
Number of Shoes	Total Cost (\$)
2	86
4	172
6	258
8	344

Trail King	
Number of Shoes	Total Cost (\$)
2	92
4	184
6	276
8	368

EE = Expressions, Equations, and Relationships N = Number and Operations MP = Mathematical Processes

Lesson 3
Slope

Launch the Lesson: Real World

Hero Comics prints on recycled paper. The table shows the total number of pounds of recycled paper that has been used each day during the month. Let's investigate the properties of this relationship.

Day of Month	Total Recycled (lbs)
3	36
5	60
6	72
7	84
12	144

1. Graph the ordered pairs on the coordinate plane.

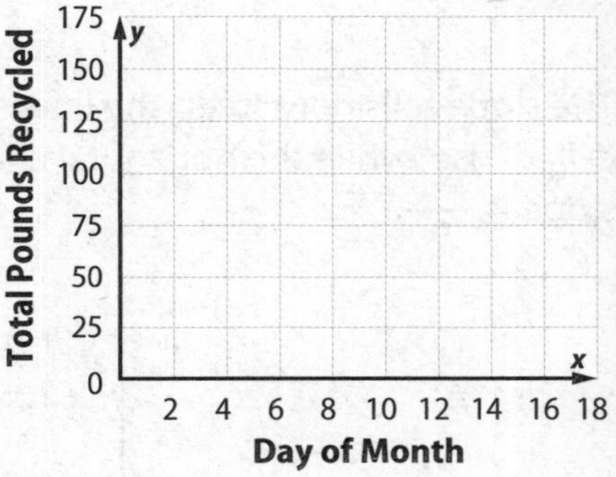

Total Pounds Recycled (y: 0, 25, 50, 75, 100, 125, 150, 175) vs. Day of Month (x: 2, 4, 6, 8, 10, 12, 14, 16, 18)

2. Explain why the graph is linear. ______________________

3. Use two points to determine the constant rate of change.

Point 1: ________ $\frac{\text{change in pounds}}{\text{change in days}}$ → $\frac{\square \text{ pounds}}{\square \text{ days}}$

Point 2: ________

The constant rate of change is $\frac{24}{2}$ or $\square$ pounds per day.

4. Choose a different pair of points and determine the constant rate of change. What do you notice? ______________________

Texas Essential Knowledge and Skills

Targeted TEKS

7.7 The student applies mathematical process standards to represent linear relationships using multiple representations. The student is expected to represent linear relationships using verbal descriptions, tables, graphs, and equations that simplify to the form $y = mx + b$.

Mathematical Processes

7.1(A), 7.1(B), 7.1(D), 7.1(E)

Vocab

Vocabulary

slope

Essential Question

HOW can you express a linear relationship between two quantities in different ways?

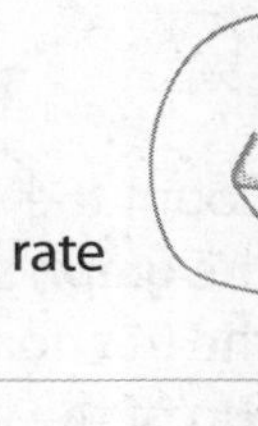

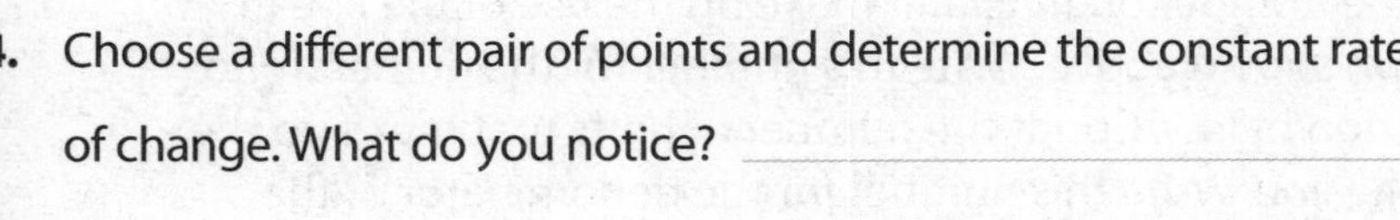

Which MP Mathematical Processes did you use? Shade the circle(s) that applies.

Ⓐ Apply Math to the Real World.
Ⓑ Use a Problem-Solving Model.
Ⓒ Select Tools and Techniques.
Ⓓ Use Multiple Representations.
Ⓔ Organize Ideas.
Ⓕ Analyze Relationships.
Ⓖ Justify Arguments.

Key Concept

Slope as Constant Rate of Change

Slope is the constant rate of change between any two points on a line.

$$\text{slope} = \frac{\text{change in } y}{\text{change in } x} \longrightarrow \begin{array}{l}\text{vertical change} \\ \text{horizontal change}\end{array}$$

$$= \frac{2}{1} \text{ or } 2$$

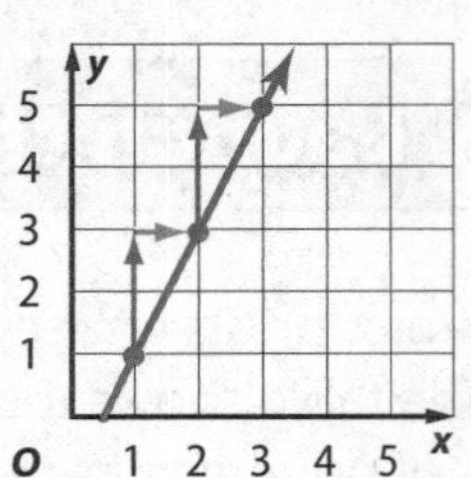

Work Zone

In a linear relationship, the vertical change (change in *y*-value) per unit of horizontal change (change in *x*-value) is always the same. This ratio is called the **slope** of the function. The constant rate of change, or unit rate, is the same as the slope of the related linear relationship.

The slope tells how steep the line is. The vertical change is sometimes called "rise" while the horizontal change is called "run." You can say that slope $= \frac{\text{rise}}{\text{run}}$.

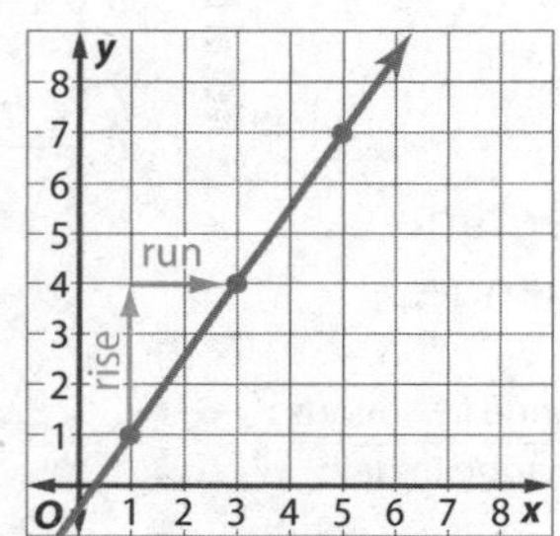

Count the number of units that make up the rise of the line in the graph shown above. Write this number for the numerator of the fraction below. Count the number of units that make up the run of the line. Write this number for the denominator of the fraction below.

$$\frac{\text{rise}}{\text{run}} = \frac{\square}{\square}$$

So, the slope of the line is $\frac{3}{2}$.

Example

1. The table below shows the relationship between the number of seconds y it takes to hear thunder after a lightning strike and the miles x you are from the lightning. Graph the data and determine the slope. Explain what the slope represents.

Miles (x)	0	1	2	3	4	5
Seconds (y)	0	5	10	15	20	25

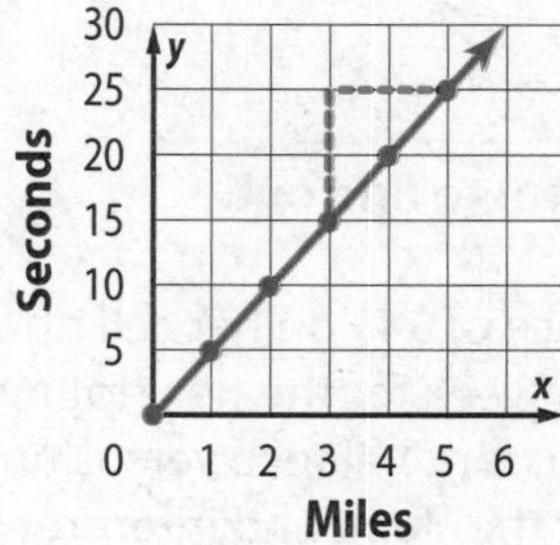

$$\text{slope} = \frac{\text{change in } y}{\text{change in } x}$$ Definition of slope

$$= \frac{25 - 15}{5 - 3}$$ Use (3, 15) and (5, 25).

$$= \frac{10}{2}$$ → seconds / → miles

$$= \frac{5}{1}$$ Simplify.

The slope, or constant rate of change is 5. So, for every 5 seconds between a lightning flash and the sound of thunder, there is 1 mile between you and the lightning strike.

Slope

In everyday language, slope means inclination or slant.

In math language, slope means the ratio of vertical change per unit of horizontal change; the steepness of a line.

Got It? Do this problem to find out.

a. Graph the data about plant height for a science fair project. Then determine the slope of the line. Explain what the slope represents in the work zone.

Week	Plant Height (cm)
1	1.5
2	3
3	4.5
4	6

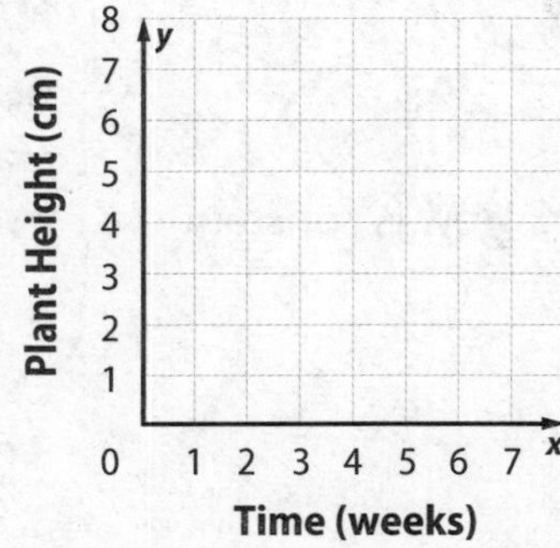

a. ______________

Example

2. Renaldo opened a savings account. Each week he deposits $300. Draw a graph of the account balance versus time. Determine the numerical value of the slope and interpret it in words.

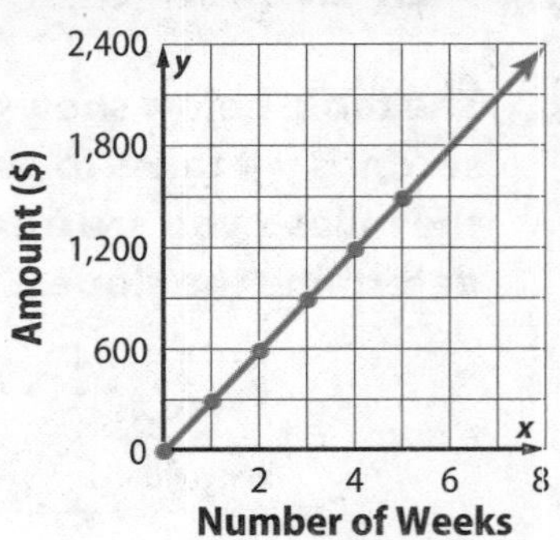

The slope of the line is the rate at which the account balance rises, or $\frac{\$300}{1 \text{ week}}$.

Show your work.

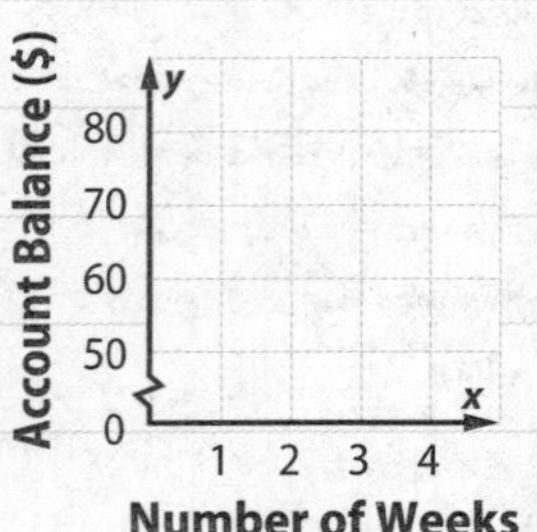

Got It? Do this problem to find out.

b. Jessica has a balance of $45 on her cell phone account. She adds $10 each week for the next four weeks. In the work zone, graph the account balance versus time. Determine the numerical value of the slope and interpret it in words.

b. ______________

Guided Practice

1. The table at the right shows the number of small packs of fruit snacks y per box x. Graph the data. Then determine the slope of the line. Explain what the slope represents. (Examples 1 and 2)

Boxes, x	3	5	7
Fruit Snacks, y	12	20	28

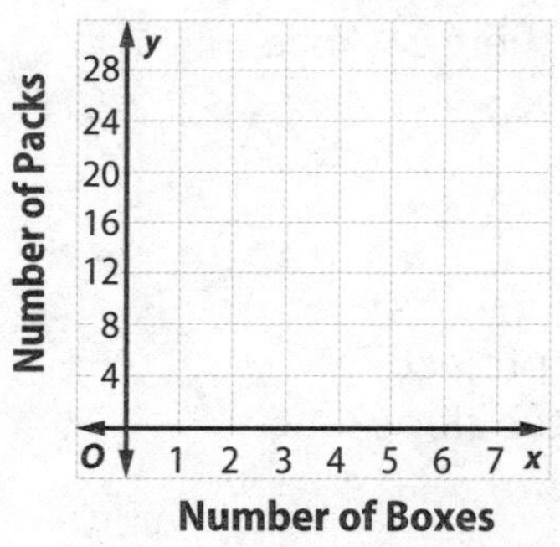

____

2. **Building on the Essential Question** How is constant rate of change related to slope? ______________________________

____

____

____

Rate Yourself!

How well do you understand slope? Circle the image that applies.

Clear

Somewhat Clear

Not So Clear

Find out online. Use the Self-Check Quiz.

Name ______ My Homework ______

Independent Practice

TEKS 7.7, 7.1(A), 7.1(D)

1. The table shows the number of pages Adriano read in x hours. Graph the data. Then determine the slope of the line. Explain what the slope represents. (Example 1)

Time (h)	1	2	3	4
Number of pages	50	100	150	200

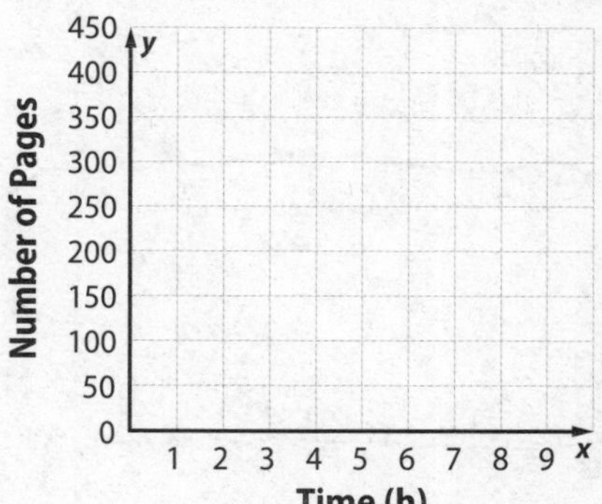

2. Graph the data. Determine the numerical value of the slope and interpret it in words. (Example 2)

Number of Yards	1	2	3
Number of Feet	3	6	9

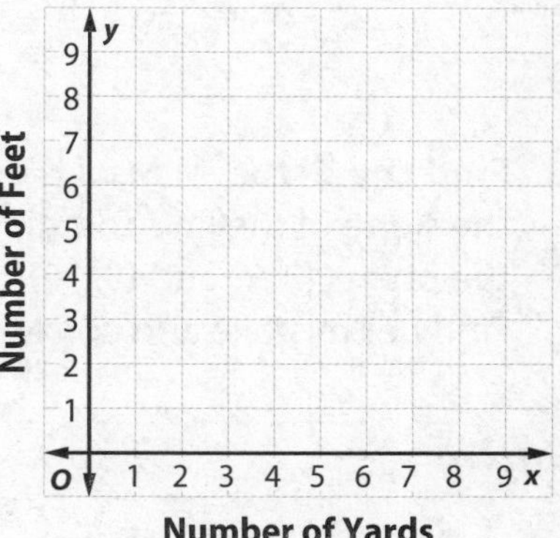

3. The graph shows the average speed of two cars on the highway.

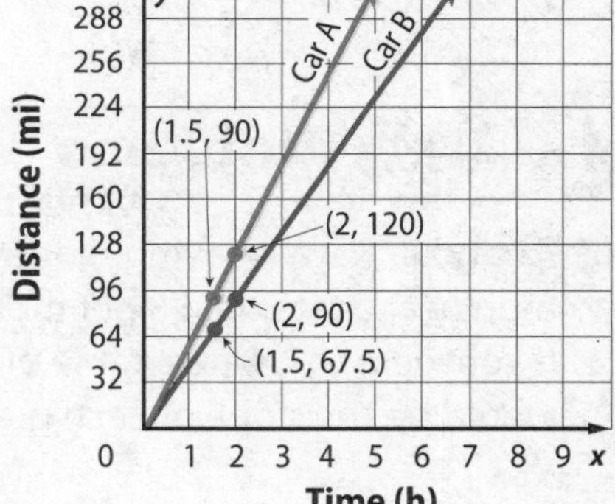

a. What does (2, 120) represent?

b. What does (1.5, 67.5) represent?

c. What does the ratio of the y-coordinate to the x-coordinate for each pair of points on the graph represent?

d. What does the slope of each line represent?

e. Which car is traveling faster? How can you tell from the graph?

4. **MP Use Multiple Representations** Complete the graphic organizer on slope.

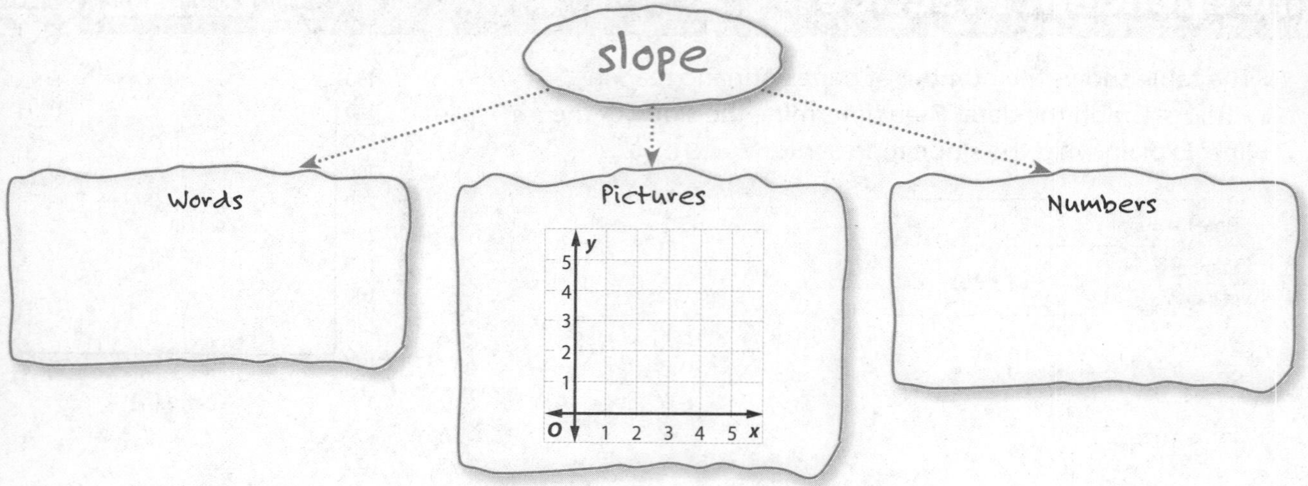

5. **Find the Error** Marisol is determining the slope of the line containing the points (3, 7) and (5, 10). Find her mistake and correct it.

H.O.T. Problems Higher-Order Thinking

6. **Analyze** Kaya is saving money at a rate of $30 per month. Edgardo is saving money at a rate of $35 per month. They both started saving at the same time. If you were to create a table of values and graph each relationship, what would be the slope of each graph?

7. **Analyze** Without graphing, determine whether $A(5, 1)$, $B(1, 0)$, and $C(-3, -3)$ lie on the same line. Explain.

8. **Create** Name two points on a line that has a slope of $\frac{3}{4}$.

Name ____________________

Multi-Step Problem Solving

9. The table represents the rates at Joe's Internet Café for last year. This year, his rates will be $1\frac{1}{4}$ times greater to help pay his increase of rent costs. How much more will a customer pay to use the Internet for 6 hours? EE P MP

Time (h) (x)	1	2	3	4
Cost ($) ($y$)	7	14	21	28

Ⓐ $1.75
Ⓑ $7.00
Ⓒ $10.50
Ⓓ $15.75

Use a problem-solving model to solve this problem.

1 Analyze

Read the problem. Circle the information you know.
Underline what the problem is asking you to find.

2 Plan

What will you need to do to solve the problem? Write your plan in steps.

Step 1 Determine the __________ for 6 hours of Internet usage.

Step 2 Multiply the cost by __________ and subtract the two costs.

Read to Succeed!
Interpret the slope in the table as the cost per hour for Internet usage. The slope shown in the table is $7 per hour.

3 Solve

Use your plan to solve the problem. Show your steps.

Determine the cost for 6 hours.

$7(6) = ____

Determine the increased cost for 6 hours. Then subtract.

$\_\_\_\_ \cdot \left(1\frac{1}{4}\right) = \_\_\_\_$

$\_\_\_\_ - \_\_\_\_ = \_\_\_\_$ Subtract.

The cost will be __________ greater.

So, the correct answer is ____. Fill in that answer choice.

4 Justify and Evaluate

How do you know your solution is accurate?

____

____

____

EE = Expressions, Equations, and Relationships P = Proportionality MP = Mathematical Processes

More Multi-Step Problem Solving

Use a problem-solving model to solve each problem.

10. The table represents the number of push-ups completed by Donald over the past 5 days. The next 5 days, he will increase the number of push-ups to be $2\frac{1}{2}$ times greater. How many more push-ups will he complete on day 5 after the increase compared to the number he completed on day 5 in the table below? EE N MP

Day	1	2	3	4	5
Push-Ups	10	20	30	40	50

Ⓐ 50 push-ups
Ⓑ 75 push-ups
Ⓒ 100 push-ups
Ⓓ 125 push-ups

11. Mr. Timken took his students on a hiking trip. He wants to avoid steep trails. On the steepest part of Evergreen Path, the path rises 12 feet over a horizontal distance of 60 feet. On Shady Glen Path, the path rises 18 feet over a horizontal distance of 45 feet. How much greater is the slope of the steeper path? Explain. EE N MP

12. The tables compare the number of bowling games and costs at two different bowling alleys. What is the difference in slopes? EE N MP

Number of Games	2	3	4
Cost ($)	9	10.50	12

Number of Games	2	3	5
Cost ($)	9	11	15

13. The slope of a line is −0.5. Two points on the line are (2, −1) and (6, *a*). What is the value of *a*? Use the graph to help you solve. EE N MP

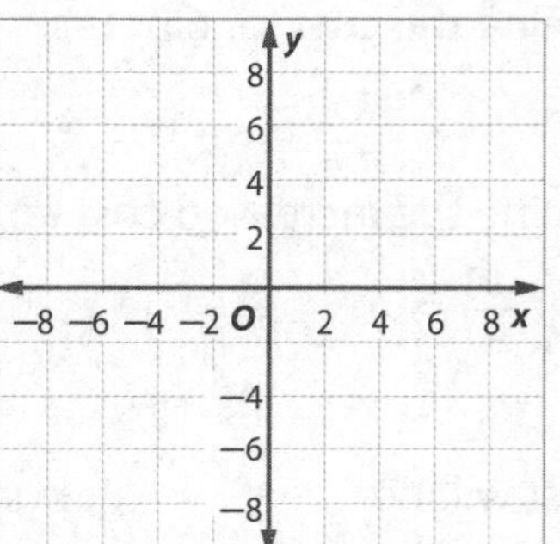

EE = Expressions, Equations, and Relationships N = Number and Operations MP = Mathematical Processes

Graphing Technology Lab 4-a

Nonproportional Linear Relationships

INQUIRY **HOW can I use multiple representations to analyze nonproportional linear relationships?**

Elisa is comparing two phone plans. If she goes with Plan A, she will need to buy the phone, which costs $175, and then pay a monthly fee of $80. With Plan B, she does not need to buy the phone, but the monthly fee is $110. How can she compare these two plans?

Texas Essential Knowledge and Skills TEKS

Targeted TEKS

7.7 The student applies mathematical process standards to represent linear relationships using multiple representations. The student is expected to represent linear relationships using verbal descriptions, tables, graphs, and equations that simplify to the form $y = mx + b$.

Mathematical Processes

7.1(C), 7.1(D), 7.1(E), 7.1(F), 7.1(G)

Hands-On Activity 1

Use a graphing calculator to graph equations for each plan. The linear equation that represents Plan A is $y = 175 + 80x$, where x represents the number of months and y represents the total cost in dollars. The linear equation that represents Plan B is $y = 110x$.

Step 1 Clear any equations from the Y = list by pressing [Y=] [CLEAR].

Step 2 Enter each equation. For Plan A, press 175 + 80 [X,T,θ,*n*] into Y_1. For Plan B, press 110 [X,T,θ,*n*] into Y_2.

Step 3 Press [WINDOW] to set an appropriate viewing window. Since x represents the number of months, select Xmin as 0, Xmax as 12 to display an entire year, and Xscl as 1. Since y represents the cost in dollars, set Ymin as 0, Ymax as 1,500 and Yscl as 100.

Step 4 Press [GRAPH]. Copy your calculator screen on the blank screen shown.

1. Are both graphs linear? For which plan is the graph nonproportional? Justify your response.

2. Compare the costs of the plans as the number of months increases.

Hands-On Activity 2

You can also use a graphing calculator to compare the two phone plans by looking at the tables that represent them.

Step 1 Press 2nd TABLE to view the tables of the two phone plans.

For how many months is Plan B less expensive than Plan A?

____

Step 2 Using the table, press the up or down arrows to determine the cost of each plan when the number of months is zero.

Plan A _______ Plan B: _______

Explain what each of these numbers means in the context of the phone plans.

____

____

Step 3 Press GRAPH. Then press TRACE. Press the up or down arrow to select each line. Then press the left arrow until you get to the point at which the graph crosses the y-axis. What do you notice?

____

____

Analyze and Reflect

3. **MP Organize Ideas** Compare the slope for each graph. What do you notice?

____

4. **MP Apply Math to the Real World** Compare the two phone plans. Write a few sentences describing how Elisa can use this information to make a decision on which phone plan to purchase.

____

____

____

____

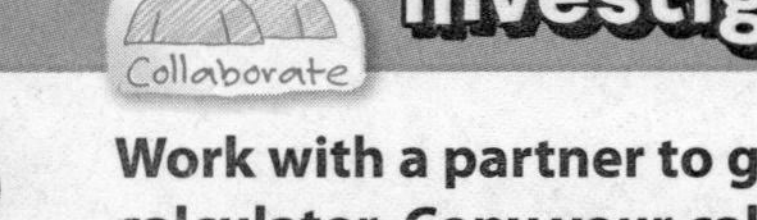

Work with a partner to graph each linear equation using a graphing calculator. Copy your calculator screens on the blank screens below. Press ZOOM 6 to select the standard viewing window.

5. $y = 2x$

6. $y = 0.5x + 3$

7. $y = -4 - 6x$

8. $y = -0.35x$

9. Which equations are linear? direct variations? Justify your response.

____

____

____

10. Complete the graphic organizer that shows which equations are proportional linear relationships and which equations are nonproportional linear relationships.

Analyze and Reflect

Refer to the equations and graphs in Activities 1–2 and in Exercises 3–8. Complete the table. The first one is done for you.

	Equation	Point at which crosses the y-axis	Proportional or Nonproportional?
	$y = 110x$	(0, 0)	proportional
11.	$y = 175 + 80x$		
12.	$y = 2x$		
13.	$y = 0.5x + 3$		
14.	$y = -4 - 6x$		
15.	$y = -0.35x$		

16. MP **Analyze Relationships** Study the equations that show nonproportional linear relationships. What do you notice about the y-coordinate of the point at which the graph crosses the y-axis?

Create

17. MP **Use Multiple Representations** Write an equation that represents a nonproportional linear relationship. Then graph the equation using the graphing calculator and copy your screen here.

18. INQUIRY HOW can I use multiple representations to analyze nonproportional linear relationships?

Lesson 4

Slope-Intercept Form

Launch the Lesson: Real World

Marissa wants to attend a space camp, which costs $125 per day. In addition, there is an application fee of $45, which is non-refundable even if Marissa does not attend the camp. How can you use multiple representations to illustrate the relationship between the number of days and the total cost?

1. Complete the table to show the total cost of space camp. Then graph the relationship on the coordinate plane.

Total Cost of Space Camp	
Number of Days, x	Total Cost ($), y
0	45

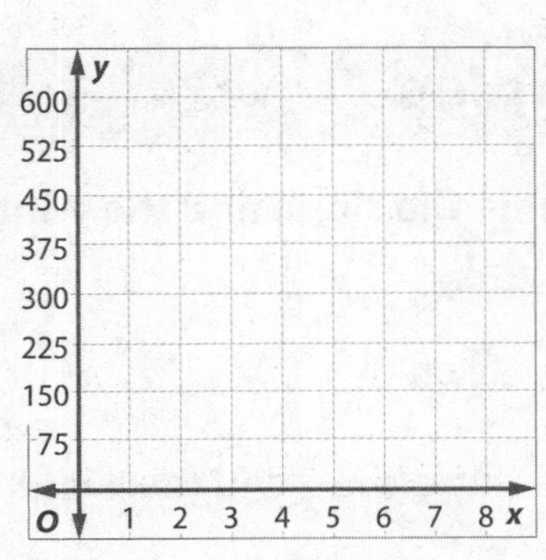

2. The **y-intercept** of a line is the y-coordinate of the point at which the line crosses the y-axis. What is the y-intercept of the line? ________

3. The equation that represents this situation is $y = 125x + 45$. How is the y-intercept represented in the equation?

____

____

Texas Essential Knowledge and Skills

Targeted TEKS

7.7 The student applies mathematical process standards to represent linear relationships using multiple representations. The student is expected to represent linear relationships using verbal descriptions, tables, graphs, and equations that simplify to the form $y = mx + b$.

Mathematical Processes

7.1(A), 7.1(B), 7.1(C), 7.1(D), 7.1(E)

Vocab

Vocabulary

slope-intercept form

y-intercept

Essential Question

HOW can you express a linear relationship between two quantities in different ways?

Which MP Mathematical Processes did you use? Shade the circle(s) that applies.

Ⓐ Apply Math to the Real World.
Ⓑ Use a Problem-Solving Model.
Ⓒ Select Tools and Techniques.
Ⓓ Use Multiple Representations.
Ⓔ Organize Ideas.
Ⓕ Analyze Relationships.
Ⓖ Justify Arguments.

Work Zone

Linear relationships can be written in the form $y = mx + b$. This is called the **slope-intercept form**. When an equation is written in this form, m represents the slope and b represents the y-intercept.

Key Concept Slope-Intercept Form

Words The slope-intercept form of an equation is $y = mx + b$, where m is the slope and b is the y-intercept.

Symbols $y = mx + b$

Example $y = 2x + 1$

slope (2), y-intercept (1)

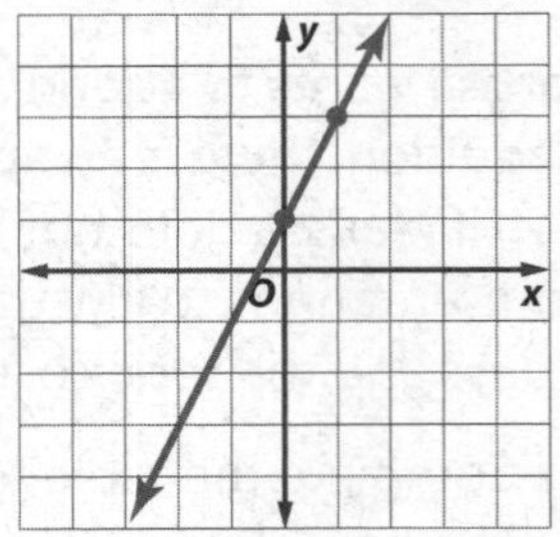

Tutor

Examples

Determine the slope and the y-intercept of each linear equation.

1. $y = -\frac{1}{2}x$

$y = -\frac{1}{2}x + 0$ Write the equation in the form $y = mx + b$.

The slope is $-\frac{1}{2}$ and the y-intercept is 0.

2. $y = 4x - 5$

$y = 4x + (-5)$ Write the equation in the form $y = mx + b$.

The slope is 4 and the y-intercept is -5.

Got It? Do these problems to find out.

Determine the slope and the y-intercept of each linear equation.

a. $y = 3x + 10$

b. $y = -\frac{2}{3}x$

c. $y = -5x - 4$

d. $y = \frac{1}{2}x + 21$

a. ________

b. ________

c. ________

d. ________

Graph Linear Equations

You can use the slope-intercept form of an equation to graph a line. First graph the y-intercept. Then use the slope to graph a second point on the line. Draw a line connecting these points.

Tutor

Multi-Step Example

3. Two leopard geckos were 3 inches long at birth. Gecko A grows at a rate of about $\frac{1}{3}$ inch per week and gecko B grows at a rate of about $\frac{1}{2}$ inch per week. The total length of gecko A y after x weeks can be represented by $y = \frac{1}{3}x + 3$ and the total length of gecko B y after x weeks can be represented by $y = \frac{1}{2}x + 3$.

a. Graph each equation.

Determine the slope and y-intercept for each equation.

Step 1 gecko A: slope $= \frac{1}{3}$ y-intercept $= 3$

gecko B: slope $= \frac{1}{2}$ y-intercept $= 3$

Step 2 Graph the y-intercept at (0, 3) for both equations.

Step 3 Write the slope as *rise* over *run*. Use it to locate a second point for each line.

$m = \frac{1}{3}$ ← change in y : up 1 unit / ← change in x : right 3 units

A second point on the line is at (3, 4).

$m = \frac{1}{2}$ ← change in y : up 1 unit / ← change in x : right 2 units

A second point on the line is at (2, 4).

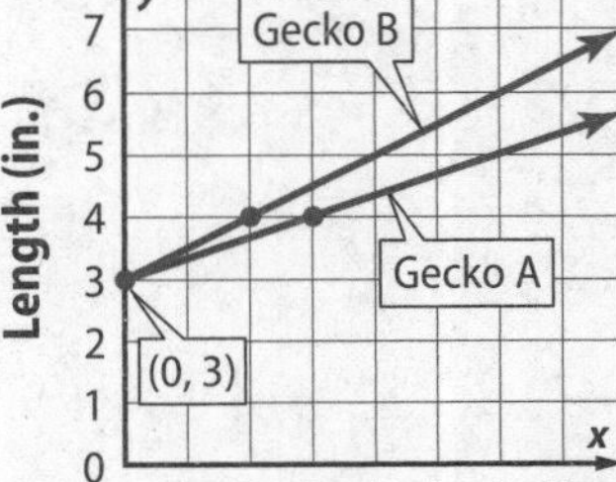

Step 4 Draw a line connecting the two points for each equation.

b. Compare the growth rate for each gecko.

The slope represents the growth rate in inches per week, which is the rate of change. The growth of gecko A is $\frac{1}{3}$ inch per week while gecko B is $\frac{1}{2}$ inch per week. Gecko B grows at a faster rate than gecko A.

Got It? Do this problem to find out.

e. Jack has written 30 pages of his novel. He plans to write 12 pages per week until he has completed his novel. Lauren has written 30 pages of her novel. She plans to write 15 pages per week until she has completed her novel. The total number of pages Jack has written y can be represented by $y = 12x + 30$, where x is the number of weeks. The total number of pages Lauren has written y can be represented by $y = 15x + 30$, where x is the number of weeks.

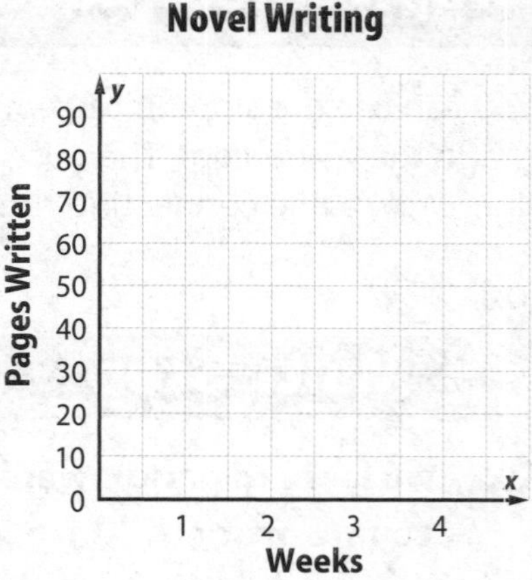

a. Graph each equation.

b. Compare the number of pages Jack and Lauren plan to write.

____

____

____

____

Guided Practice

Determine the slope and the *y*-intercept of each linear equation. (Examples 1 and 2)

1. $y = \frac{3}{4}x - 7$ ______________

2. $y = 4x$ ______________

3. $y = 6x + 3$ ______________

4. $y = 0.25x - 2.75$ ______________

5. **Building on the Essential Question** Describe how the slope-intercept form of an equation helps you graph the equation.

____

____

____

____

Independent Practice

7.7, 7.1(C) TEKS

Determine the slope and the *y*-intercept of each linear equation. (Examples 1 and 2)

1. $y = -\frac{5}{2}x - 2$ ______

2. $y = 6x$ ______

3. $y = \frac{3}{8}x + 7$ ______

4. $y = x - 4$ ______

5. $y = 8x - 5$ ______

6. $y = x$ ______

7. MP **Use Multiple Representations** In this problem, you will investigate graphs of equations. The Math Club is planning a trip to an amusement park. The table shows the bus prices to travel to each park and the admission price per student. (Example 3)

Park	Bus Fee ($)	Admission Price Per Student ($)
Wild Waves	200	16.50
Coaster Haven	250	14.50

a. Symbols Write an equation to represent the total cost *y* for *x* students at each park.

______

______

b. Graph Graph the two equations on the same coordinate plane. For how many students is the cost of both trips the same? Explain.

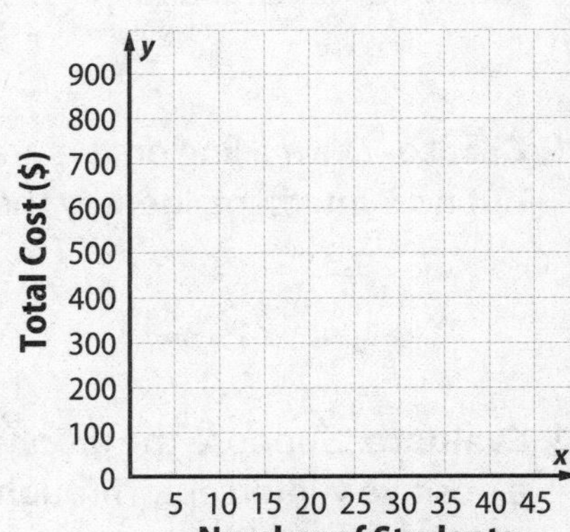

______

______

c. Numbers If 20 students decide to take the trip, which trip will cost less? If 28 students decide to take the trip, which trip will cost less? Justify your response.

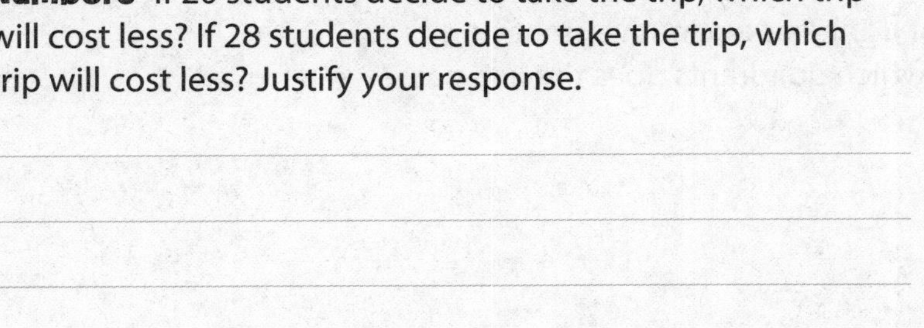

8. **Financial Literacy** Kelsey needs a new set of brakes. One auto mechanic quoted her a price of \$40 for parts plus \$50 per hour. Another mechanic gave her a quote of \$55 for parts and \$35 per hour. For the first quote, total cost y can be given by $y = 50x + 40$ for x hours. For the second quote, total cost y can be given by $y = 35x + 55$ for x hours.

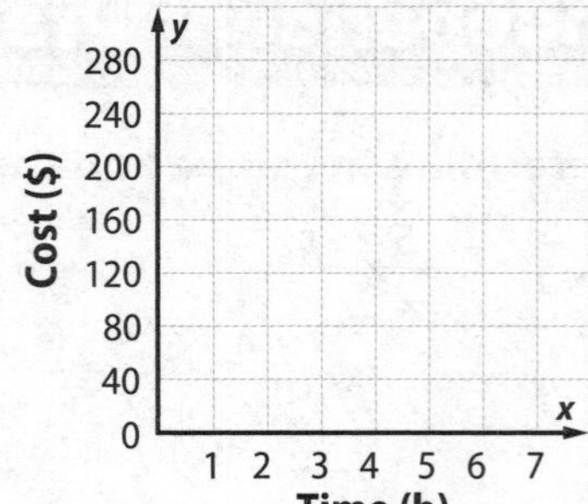

a. Graph each equation.

b. Compare the charges for each mechanic. Which mechanic should Kelsey go to? Explain.

9. **Find the Error** Theresa is determining the slope and y-intercept of $y = 3x - 4$. Find her mistake and correct it.

H.O.T. Problems Higher-Order Thinking

10. **Analyze** Describe what happens to the graph of $y = 3x + 4$ when the slope is changed to $\frac{1}{3}$.

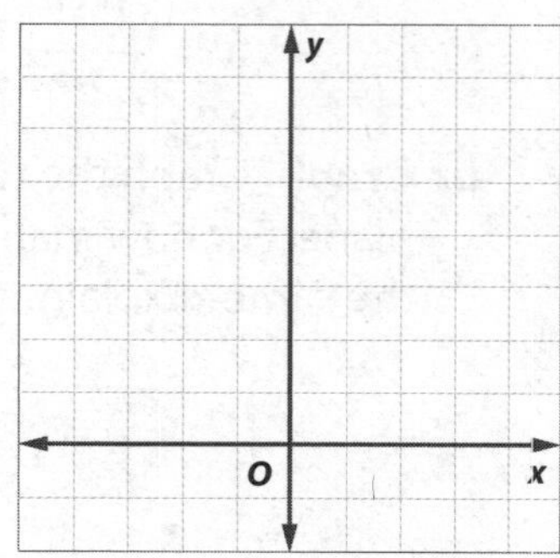

11. **Create** Draw a line on the graph at the right that has a y-intercept but no x-intercept. Identify the slope of the line.

12. **Evaluate** Suppose the graph of a line has a negative slope and a positive y-intercept. Through which quadrants does the line pass? Justify your reasoning.

Name ______________________________

Multi-Step Problem Solving

13. Bethany and Diego have decided to increase the size of their gardens each year. The table shows how many rows of corn they started with, and how many rows they plan to add each year. How many more rows will Bethany have after 4 years have passed compared to Diego? EE N MP

	Bethany	Diego
Starting Rows	16	6
Rows Added Each Year	4	6
Equation	$y = 4x + 16$	$y = 6x + 6$

Use a problem-solving model to solve this problem.

1 Analyze

Read the problem. Circle the information you know.
Underline what the problem is asking you to find.

2 Plan

What will you need to do to solve the problem? Write your plan in steps.

Step 1 Use each equation to determine the ______________ after 4 years.

Step 2 Compare the number of rows and __________ to determine the difference.

Read to Succeed! The y-intercept is the number of rows they started with and the slope represents the number of rows they add each year.

3 Solve

Use your plan to solve the problem. Show your steps.
Determine the number of rows after 4 years.

$y = 4x + 16$ $\quad$ $y = 6x + 6$

$y = 4(\_\_\_) + 16$ $\quad$ $y = 6(\_\_\_) + 6$

$y = \_\_\_$ $\quad$ $y = \_\_\_$

___ − ___ = ___ Subtract.

Bethany will have ____ more rows than Diego.
Complete the grid.

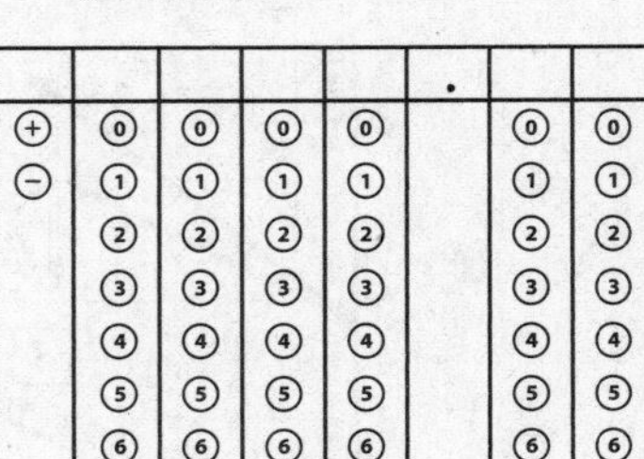

4 Justify and Evaluate

How do you know your solution is accurate?

____

____

____

EE = Expressions, Equations, and Relationships N = Number and Operations MP = Mathematical Processes

More Multi-Step Problem Solving

Use a problem-solving model to solve each problem.

14. Rajesh and Fala each bought a new car. The table shows the down payments each paid, and the amount of their monthly payments. After two years, how much more, in dollars, has Rajesh paid compared to Fala? EE N MP

	Rajesh	Fala
Down Payment ($)	1,900	3,000
Monthly Payment ($)	200	150
Equation	$y = 200x + 1{,}900$	$y = 150x + 3{,}000$

15. Zoe and Olivia are hiking on the same trail. In the equations below, the y-intercept represents how many miles up the trail they started, and the slope represents their hiking rate in miles per hour. If they meet after exactly 3 hours x, what is Olivia's rate m? EE N MP

Zoe	Olivia
$y = 1.5x + 3$	$y = mx + 1.5$

16. Sherwin paid $4.50 to sign up for an online music membership. He then paid $0.50 for each song he downloaded. Which line on the graph could represent Sherwin's music expense? EE N MP

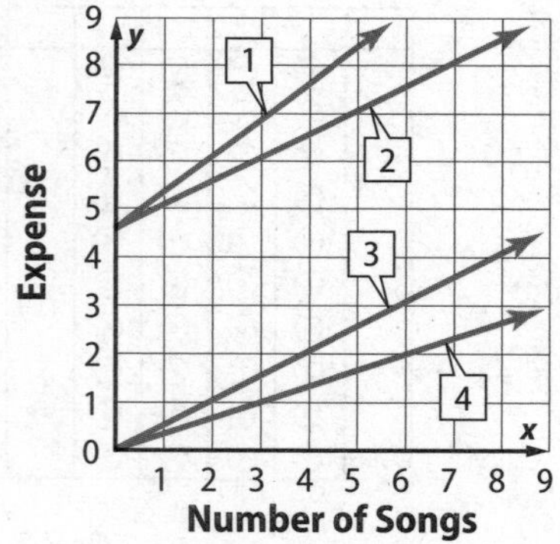

17. Write an equation in the form $y = mx + b$ based on the graph. Then, give the y-intercept, slope, and x-intercept. EE N MP

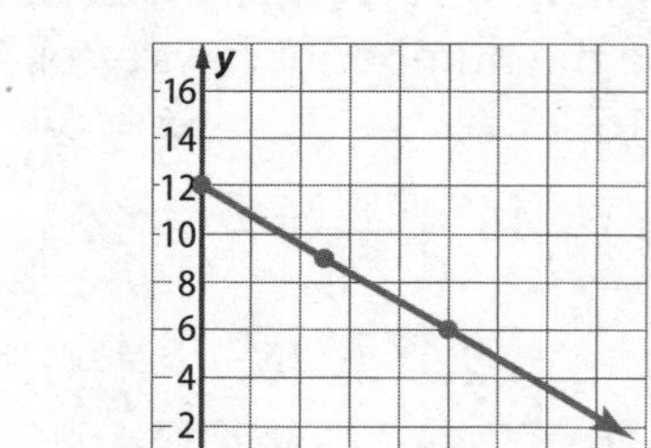

EE = Expressions, Equations, and Relationships N = Number and Operations MP = Mathematical Processes

Lesson 5

Write Equations from Tables and Graphs

Launch the Lesson: Real World

City Fitness offers a gym membership for \$35 per month with an initial activation fee of \$15. If Anthony paid a total of \$1,485, for how many months did he have a membership?

1. Work backward. Subtract the initial activation fee, 15.

$$\frac{1{,}485 - \square}{\square} = \square \text{ months}$$

Collaborate **Work with a partner to follow the steps below to see how to write a linear equation to represent this situation.**

2. Determine if this situation is a linear relationship. Explain.

____

3. Let x represent the number of months. Write an expression that represents the cost for x months, not including the activation fee. _______________

4. Write an expression that represents the cost for x months, including the activation fee. _______________

5. Let y represent the total cost. The slope-intercept form of a linear equation is $y = mx + b$. Write the linear equation in slope-intercept form that represents this situation. _______________

Texas Essential Knowledge and Skills

Targeted TEKS

7.7 The student applies mathematical process standards to represent linear relationships using multiple representations. The student is expected to represent linear relationships using verbal descriptions, tables, graphs, and equations that simplify to the form $y = mx + b$.

Mathematical Processes

7.1(A), 7.1(B), 7.1(D), 7.1(E)

Essential Question

HOW can you express a linear relationship between two quantities in different ways?

Which MP Mathematical Processes did you use? Shade the circle(s) that applies.

Ⓐ Apply Math to the Real World.
Ⓑ Use a Problem-Solving Model.
Ⓒ Select Tools and Techniques.
Ⓓ Use Multiple Representations.
Ⓔ Organize Ideas.
Ⓕ Analyze Relationships.
Ⓖ Justify Arguments.

Work Zone

Write a Linear Equation from a Table

You can write an equation from a table of values that represent a linear relationship. First, determine the constant rate of change, or slope. Then determine the y-intercept, or the value of y when $x = 0$. Write the equation in slope-intercept form, $y = mx + b$.

Tutor 

Examples

Write the equation of the line that is represented by each table.

1.

x	y
0	0
1	8
2	16
3	24

(+1 each row for x; +8 each row for y)

Step 1 Determine the rate of change. As x increases by 1, y increases by 8 each time. The rate of change is constant, so the slope is $\frac{8}{1}$, or 8.

Step 2 Determine the y-intercept. When $x = 0$, the value of y is 0. So, the y-intercept is 0.

The equation of the line, in slope-intercept form, is $y = 8x$.

2.

x	y
5	4
7	−2
9	−8
11	−14

(+2 each row for x; −6 each row for y)

Step 1 Determine the rate of change. As x increases by 2, y decreases by 6 each time. The rate of change is constant, so the slope is $\frac{-6}{2}$, or -3.

Step 2 Determine the y-intercept. Use the point (5, 4) to determine the value of y when $x = 0$.

$y = mx + b$ — slope-intercept form

$4 = -3(5) + b$ — $m = -3, x = 5, y = 4$

$4 = -15 + b$ — Multiply.

$19 = b$ — Add 15 to both sides.

So, the y-intercept is 19. The equation of the line, is $y = -3x + 19$.

Show your work.

a. ________

b. ________

Got It? **Do these problems to find out.**

Write the equation of the line that is represented by each table.

a.

x	0	4	8	12
y	13	29	45	61

b.

x	−2	0	2	4
y	6	0	−6	−12

Write a Linear Equation from a Graph

You can also write a linear equation from a graph. You can choose any two points to determine the slope.

Example

Tutor

3. Write an equation in slope-intercept form for the line.

The graph intersects the y-axis at 3. So $b = 3$.

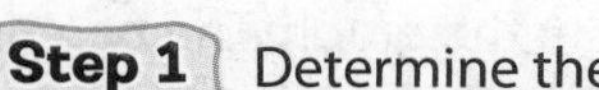

Step 1 Determine the slope.

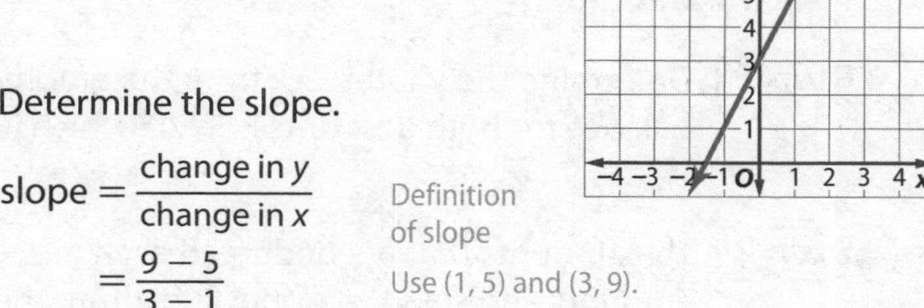

$$\text{slope} = \frac{\text{change in } y}{\text{change in } x}$$ Definition of slope

$$= \frac{9-5}{3-1}$$ Use (1, 5) and (3, 9).

$$= \frac{4}{2} \text{ or } 2$$ Simplify.

Step 2 Substitute the values into the slope-intercept equation.

$y = mx + b$

$y = 2x + 3$

The equation of the line, in slope-intercept form, is $y = 2x + 3$.

Got It? Do these problems to find out.

Write an equation in slope-intercept form for each line.

c.

d.

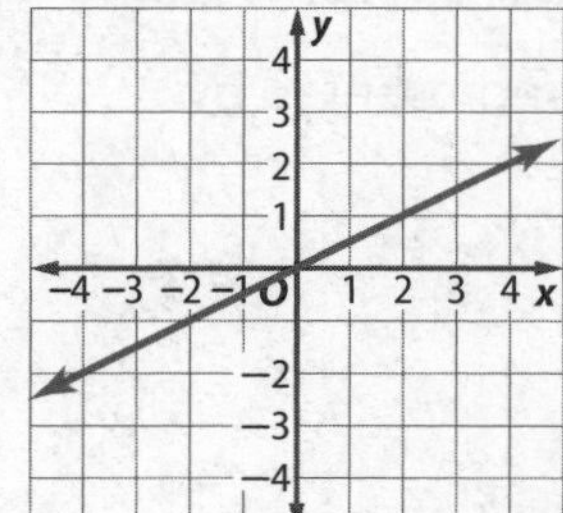

c. ____________

d. ____________

Multi-Step Example

4. Financial Literacy **Josefina and Dante both have $270 in their bank accounts. Each month, $30 is automatically deducted from Josefina's account to pay her cell phone bill. Dante has $45 automatically deducted from his account to pay his cell phone bill.**

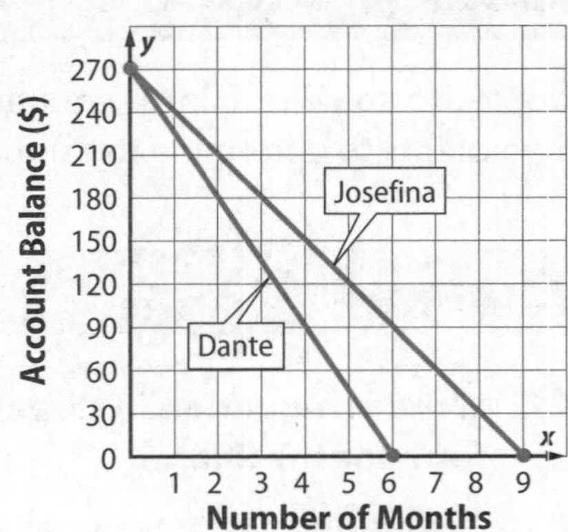

a. Write an equation for each situation.

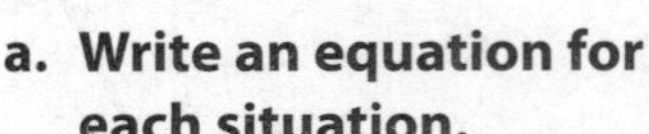

Step 1 Determine the y-intercept from the graph. The beginning balance for both accounts is $270, which is the y-intercept.

Step 2 The amounts that are deducted each month are negative amounts and so is the slope. Substitute the values into the slope-intercept equation.

Josefina	Dante
$y = mx + b$	$y = mx + b$
$y = -30x + 270$	$y = -45x + 270$

b. Compare each situation. If no deposits or additional withdrawals are made, who will have an account balance of $0 first?

Dante will have a balance of $0 after 6 months, which is 3 months before Josefina will have a balance of $0.

Guided Practice

1. Write the equation of the line that is represented by the table. (Examples 1 and 2)

x	0	−24	−48	−72
y	0	8	16	24

2. **Building on the Essential Question** How can you use a table or graph to write a linear equation?

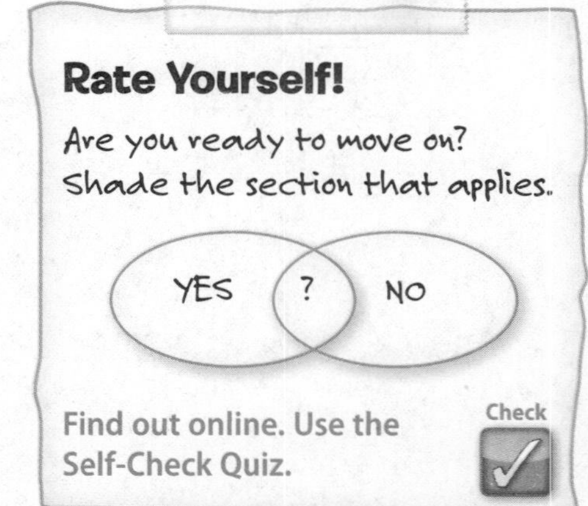

Independent Practice

7.7, 7.1(A), 7.1(D) TEKS

Write the equation of the line that is represented by each table. (Examples 1 and 2)

1.

x	−2	4	10	16
y	−4	8	20	32

2.

x	0	−2.5	−5	−7.5
y	3.25	9.5	15.75	22

Write an equation in slope-intercept form for each line. (Example 3)

3.

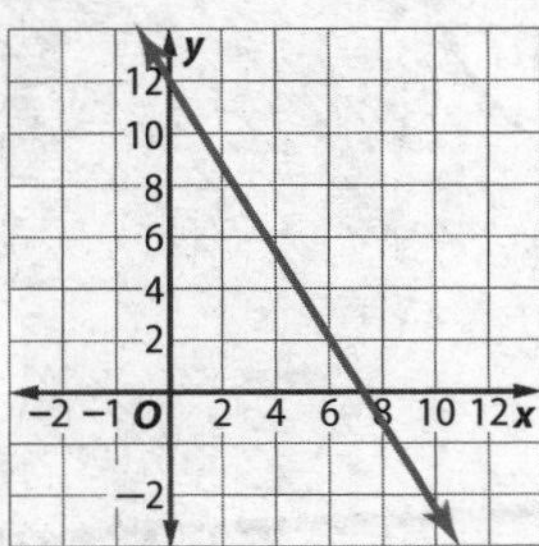

4.

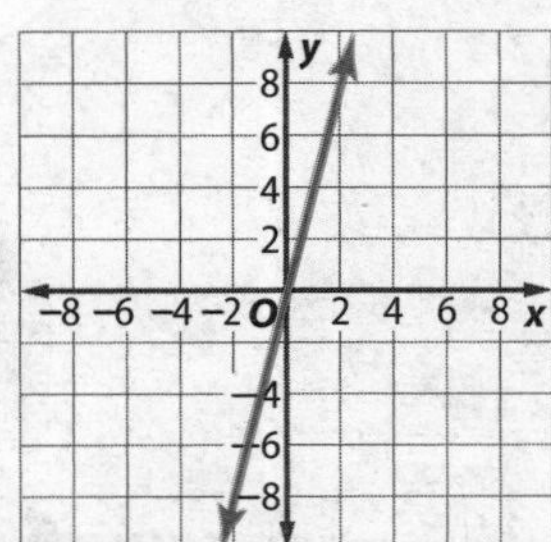

5. MP **Use Multiple Representations** Tomás has already hiked 35 feet to get to a trail. Tomás continues hiking at a rate of 3 feet per second. (Example 4)

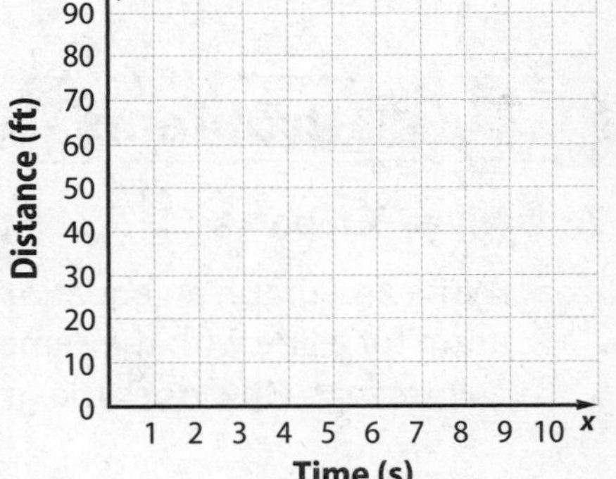

a. **Graph** Graph this relationship on the coordinate plane. What is the slope and y-intercept of the line?

b. **Symbols** Write an equation to represent the total distance hiked y for x seconds.

c. **Numbers** If Tomás hikes for 3 hours, what is the total distance he will travel? How many miles is this? Round to the nearest tenth.

d. **Words** Javier hiked 35 feet to get to the same trail Tomás used. Javier hikes at a rate of 4 feet per second. Compare and describe the meaning of the slope for each person.

6. **Apply Math to the Real World** Dario's cell phone company increased the charges for overage on text messages to \$0.15 per message sent over 1,000 messages. Write an equation to determine Dario's text messaging bill if he sends x number of text messages over 1,000. How much would it cost if he sent 1,038 text messages?

H.O.T. Problems Higher-Order Thinking

7. **Analyze** Graph $y = 2x + 3$ on the coordinate plane.

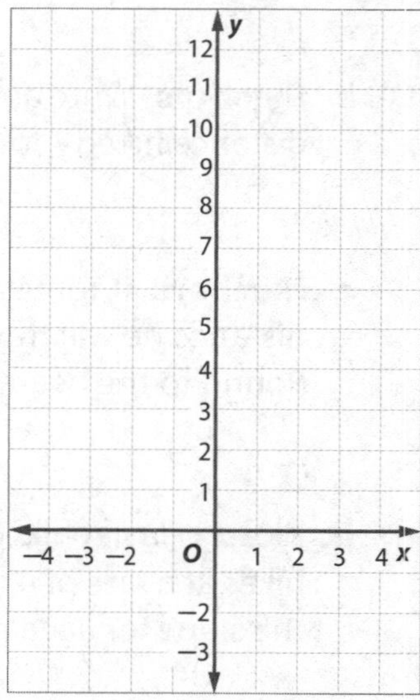

a. Write and graph an equation in slope-intercept form for a line with the same slope, but a different y-intercept. How does the graph change?

b. Write and graph an equation in slope-intercept form for a line with the same y-intercept, but a different slope. How does the graph change?

c. Write and graph equation in slope-intercept form for a line with the same y-intercept and a slope with the opposite numerical value. How does the graph change?

Name ___

Multi-Step Problem Solving

8. Sonia and Trey are tracking their reading progress. They read 2 pages of their assignment together as a class. The graph represents the number of pages they have read. How many more pages does Sonia read after 3 weeks compared to Trey? EE N MP

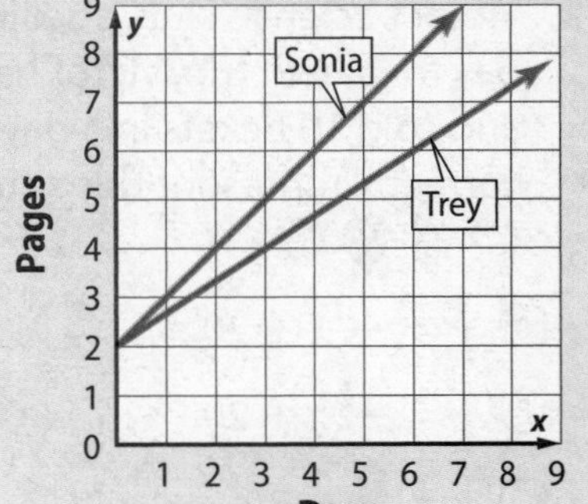

Ⓐ 1 page

Ⓑ $5\frac{1}{3}$ pages

Ⓒ $6\frac{2}{3}$ pages

Ⓓ 7 pages

Use a problem-solving model to solve this problem.

1 Analyze

Read the problem. Circle the information you know.
Underline what the problem is asking you to find.

2 Plan

What will you need to do to solve the problem? Write your plan in steps.

Step 1 Determine the ___ each student read in 21 days.

Step 2 ___ to determine the difference in the total pages read.

3 Solve

Use your plan to solve the problem. Show your steps.

Determine the number of pages read after 3 weeks or 21 days.

$y = \frac{2}{3}(\_\_\_) + 2$ $\qquad$ $y = \_\_\_ + 2$

$y = \_\_\_$ $\qquad$ $y = \_\_\_$

___ − ___ = ___ Subtract.

Sonia will read ___ more pages than Trey in 3 weeks.

So, the correct answer is ___. Fill in that answer choice.

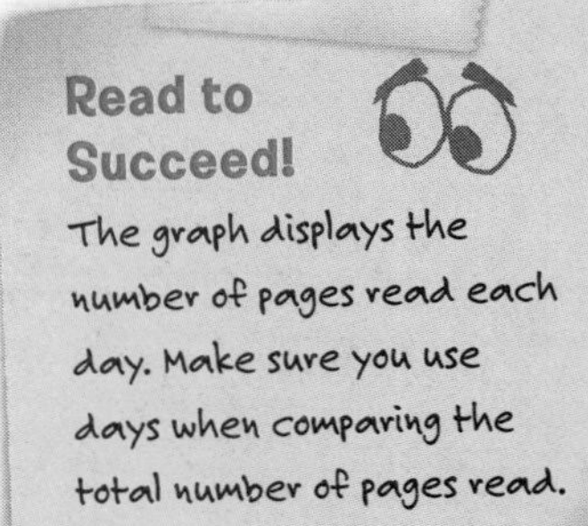

4 Justify and Evaluate

How do you know your solution is accurate?

___

___

___

EE = Expressions, Equations, and Relationships N = Number and Operations MP = Mathematical Processes

More Multi-Step Problem Solving

Use a problem-solving model to solve each problem.

9. Victor's science club is selling raffle tickets to pay for a field trip. Victor has 20 tickets to sell and sold 10 tickets in 4 days. Which equation correctly represent this situation?

Ⓐ $y = -\frac{2}{3}x + 20$

Ⓑ $y = -\frac{5}{2}x + 20$

Ⓒ $y = \frac{5}{2}x - 20$

Ⓓ $y = -\frac{5}{4}x + 8$

10. Coordinates for two lines are shown below. What is the slope of line B minus the slope of line A? Express your answer as a decimal. EE P N MP

Line A					
x	6.5	7.5	8.5	9.5	10.5
y	5	3	1	−1	−3

Line B					
x	10	4	−2	−8	−14
y	3	6	9	12	15

11. Ramona had money to spend during a visit with her grandparents. She recorded how much money she had left *y*, in dollars, after each day *x*. How much money did Ramona originally have to spend? EE N MP

x	*y*
2	34
4	28
6	22
10	10

12. Graph the following equations on the graph below: $y = -\frac{4}{3}x + 4$; $y = \frac{4}{3}x + 4$; $y = -\frac{4}{3}x - 4$; $y = \frac{4}{3}x - 4$. What shape did you make when you graphed all four equations on the same graph? EE N MP

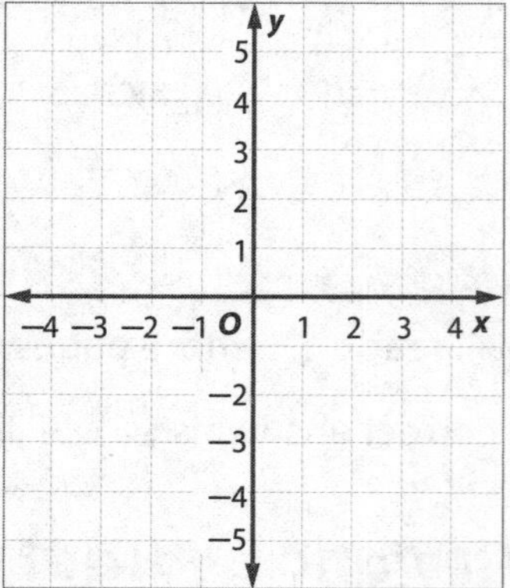

EE = Expressions, Equations, and Relationships   N = Number and Operations   P = Proportionality   MP = Mathematical Processes

Graphing Technology Lab 5-b

Family of Linear Relationships

INQUIRY **HOW can I analyze relationships to determine the effects of changing the slope or *y*-intercept of a linear equation on a graph?**

The taxi service Hugo uses charges \$6 plus an additional \$2 per mile x. The equation $y = 2x + 6$ represents the total cost y of a taxi ride.

A **family of linear relationships** is a set of relationships that is related in some way. The family of linear relationships has the parent relationship $y = x$.

A graphing calculator allows you to enter a relationship and manipulate the graph. This is useful for investigating families of linear relationships because you can easily compare characteristics such as slopes and y-intercepts.

Texas Essential Knowledge and Skills TEKS

Targeted TEKS

7.7 The student applies mathematical process standards to represent linear relationships using multiple representations. The student is expected to represent linear relationships using verbal descriptions, tables, graphs, and equations that simplify to the form $y = mx + b$.

Mathematical Processes

7.1(C), 7.1(D), 7.1(E), 7.1(F)

Hands-On Activity

Step 1 Graph $y = 2x + 6$ in the standard viewing window.

Clear any existing equations from the Y= list by pressing [Y=] [CLEAR].

Enter the equation and graph.

2 [X,T,θ,n] [+] 6 [GRAPH]

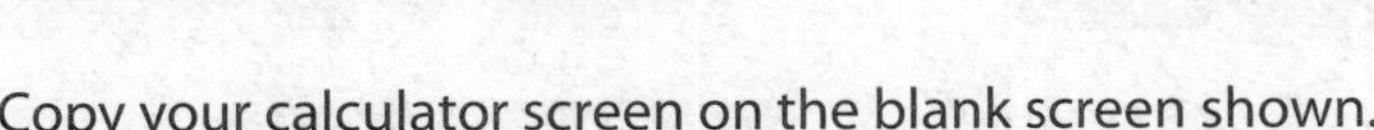

Copy your calculator screen on the blank screen shown.

Step 2 A different taxi service charges \$4 plus an additional \$2 per mile. Graph $y = 2x + 4$ and compare the two lines.

2 [X,T,θ,n] [+] 4 [GRAPH]

Step 3 A third taxi service charges \$6 plus an additional \$0.50 per mile. Graph $y = 0.5x + 6$ and compare all three lines.

0.5 [X,T,θ,n] [+] 6 [GRAPH]

Investigate

1. **MP Analyze Relationships** Compare and contrast the three graphs in the activity.

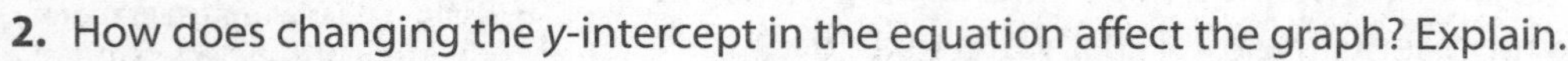

2. How does changing the y-intercept in the equation affect the graph? Explain.

3. How does changing the slope in the equation affect the graph? Explain.

Analyze and Reflect

4. Graph $y = \frac{1}{2}x + 2$, $y = 2x + 2$, and $y = 4x + 2$ in the standard viewing window. How does the steepness of the line change as the slope increases?

Create

5. **MP Use Multiple Representations** Three equations with a slope of 1 are graphed in the standard viewing window, shown at the right. Write an equation for each line.

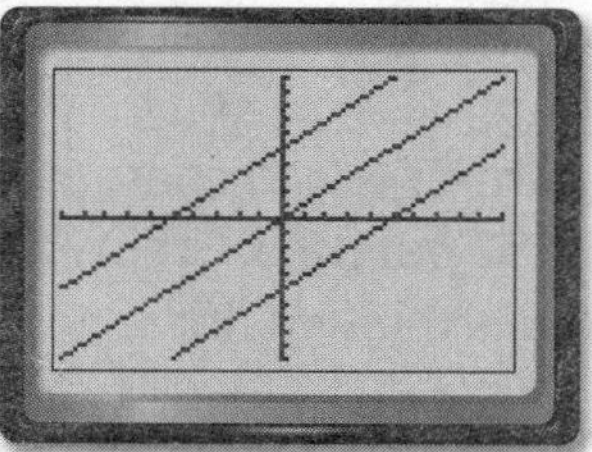

6. **INQUIRY** HOW can I analyze relationships to determine the effects of changing the slope or y-intercept of a linear equation on a graph?

21ST CENTURY CAREER

Shark Scientist

Are you fascinated by sharks, especially those that are found around the coasts of the United States? If so, you should consider a career as a shark scientist. Shark scientists use satellite-tracking devices, called tags, to study and track the movements of sharks. By analyzing the data transmitted by the tags, scientists are able to learn more about the biology and ecology of sharks. Their research is helpful in protecting shark populations around the world.

Mathematical Process
7.1(A) Apply mathematics to problems arising in everyday life, society, and the workplace.

Targeted TEKS 7.7

Is This the Career for You?

Are you interested in a career as a shark scientist? Take some of the following courses in high school.

- Algebra
- Calculus
- Physics
- Statistics

Explore college and careers at ccr.mcgraw-hill.com

Catch Me If You Can!

Use the information in the tables to solve each problem.

1. Determine whether the relationship in the tiger shark table represents a linear relationship. Explain your reasoning.

2. Is there a proportional linear relationship between time and distance for a white shark? Explain your reasoning.

3. Determine the slope of the line represented in the hammerhead shark table. What does the slope represent?

4. Write an equation to represent time x and distance y a hammerhead shark swims. How far will it swim in 12 hours?

5. If two sharks start swimming at the same location, how much further in distance will a white shark have traveled than a hammerhead shark after 8 hours?

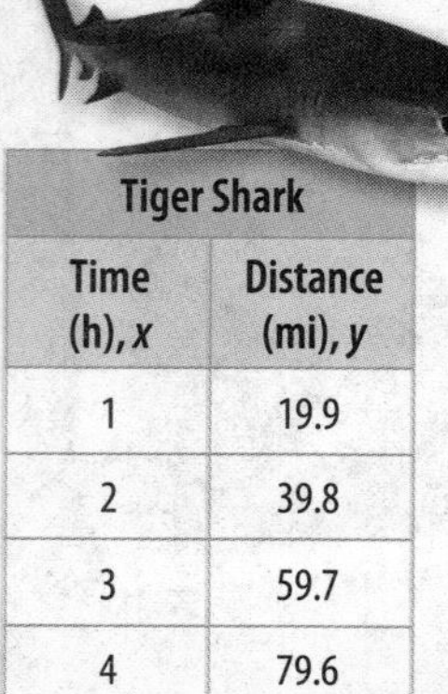

Tiger Shark

Time (h), x	Distance (mi), y
1	19.9
2	39.8
3	59.7
4	79.6

Hammerhead Shark

Time (h), x	Distance (mi), y
1	24.5
2	49
3	73.5
4	98

White Shark

Time (h), x	Distance (mi), y
1	24.9
2	49.8
3	74.7
4	99.6

TEKS Career Project

It's time to update your career portfolio! Prepare a brief oral presentation to present to your classmates describing the skills that would be necessary for a shark scientist to possess. Determine whether this type of career would be a good fit for you. As others are presenting, listen carefully to their presentations. At the end, ask any clarifying questions.

List several challenges associated with this career.

-
-
-
-
-

Chapter Review

Vocabulary Check

In the puzzle below, work with a partner to write a vocabulary term for each clue. Take turns reading each clue aloud, while the other student listens carefully. As students are determining the correct term, ask for and give help if needed.

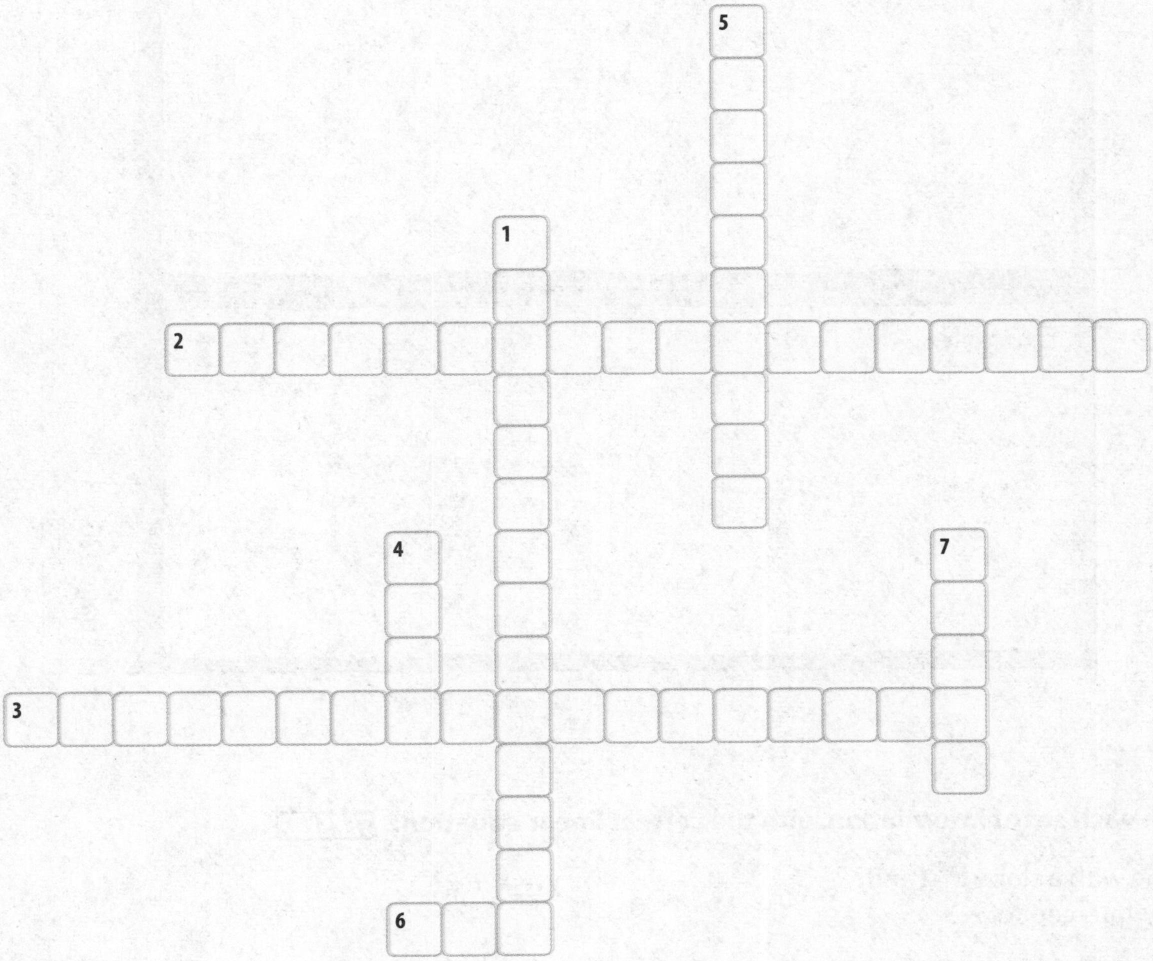

Across

2. linear relationships written in the form of $y = mx + b$
3. a relationship between two quantities that have a constant rate of change and a straight-lined graph
6. the horizontal change between the same two points

Down

1. an equation whose graph is a line
4. the vertical change between any two points
5. the y-coordinate of the point where the line crosses the y-axis
7. to describe the steepness of a straight line

Key Concept Check

Use Your FOLDABLES

Use your Foldable to help review the chapter. Share your Foldable with a partner and take turns summarizing what you learned in this chapter, while the other partner listens carefully. Ask for and give help of any concept if needed. TEKS 7.1(E)

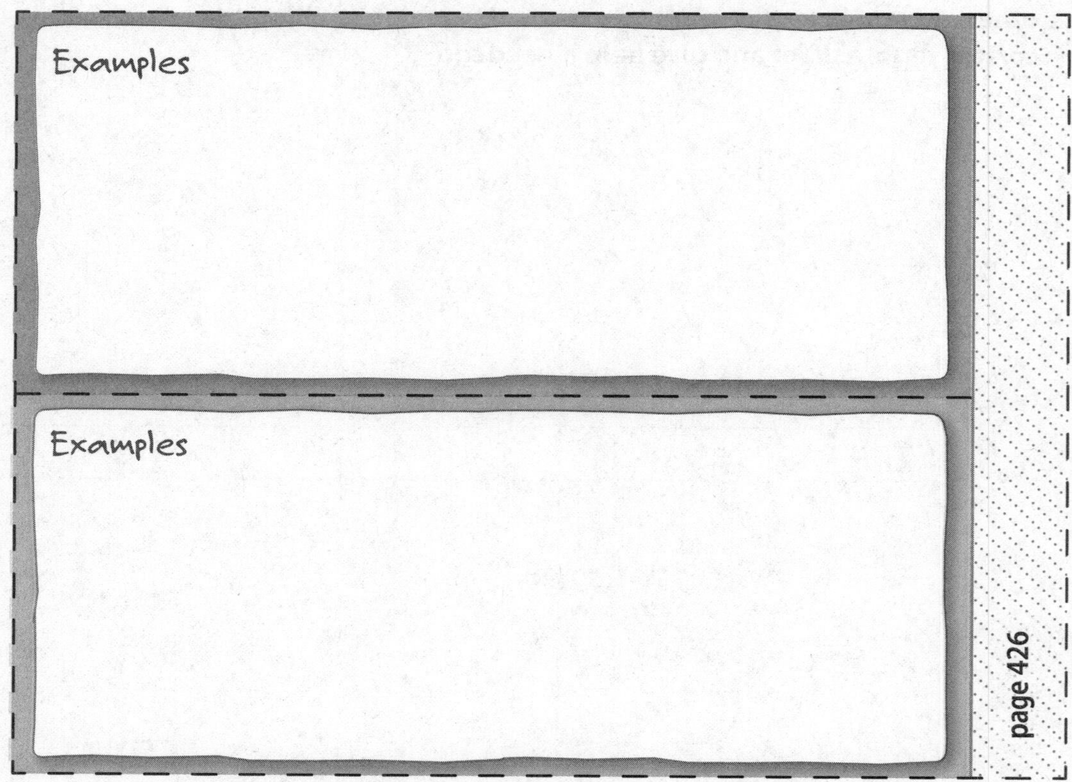

Got it?

Match each set of information with the correct linear equation. TEKS 7.7

1. line with a slope of 2 and a y-intercept of -3 — $y = x + 2$
2. line with a slope of 1 and a y-intercept of 2 — $y = -3x + 4$
3. line that passes through (3, 3) and the origin — $y = x$
4. line with a slope of 4 and a y-intercept of -3 — $y = 2x - 3$
5. line with a slope of -3 and a y-intercept of 4 — $y = 4x - 3$

Multi-Step Problem Solving

6. A farmer has two pumpkin patches that need to be harvested. Each day the farmer harvests 25 acres of each patch. The area of patch A is 400 acres and the area of patch B is 300 acres. For patch A, the total acreage harvested y can be given by $y = 400 - 25x$ for x days. For patch B, the total acreage harvested y can be given by $y = 300 - 25x$ for x days. Graph each equation and compare the acres harvested. How much longer will it take to harvest patch A? Justify your solution. EE N MP

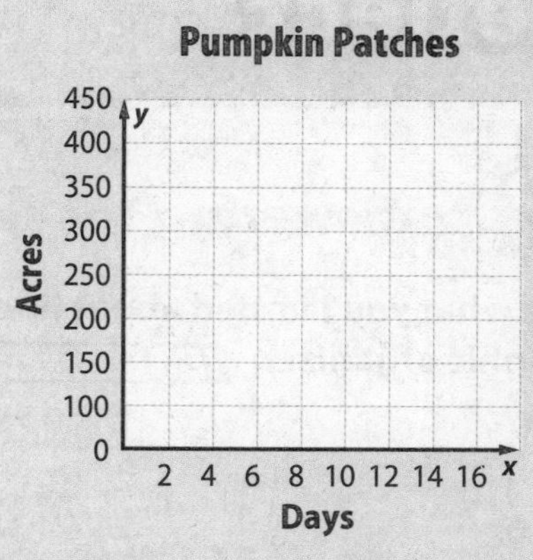

1 Analyze

2 Plan

3 Solve

4 Justify and Evaluate

Got it?

7. Jackson starts a lawn-mowing business. He pays \$56 for supplies and charges \$28 per lawn he mows. His profit y depends on the number of lawns he mows x can be given by $y = 28x - 56$. How many lawns must Jackson mow in order to have a profit of more than \$100? Explain. EE N MP

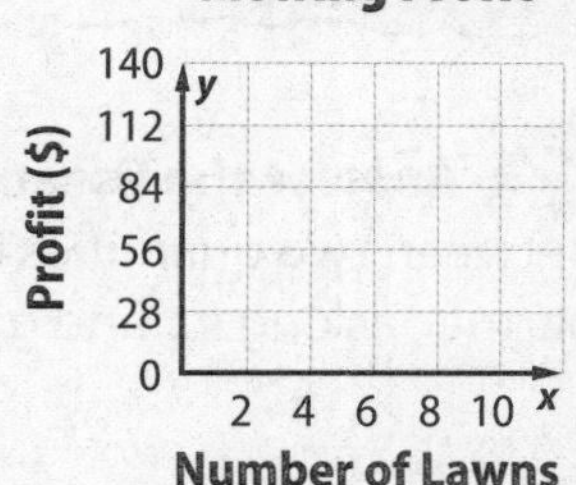

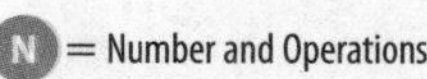
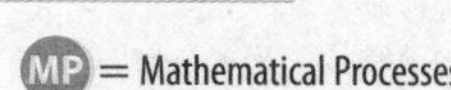

EE = Expressions, Equations, and Relationships N = Number and Operations MP = Mathematical Processes

Reflect

Answering the Essential Question

Use what you learned about linear relationships to complete the graphic organizer. TEKS 7.1(D), 7.1(F), 7.1(G)

Essential Question

HOW can you express a linear relationship between two quantities in different ways?

Use a Table

Example:

Use a Graph

Example:

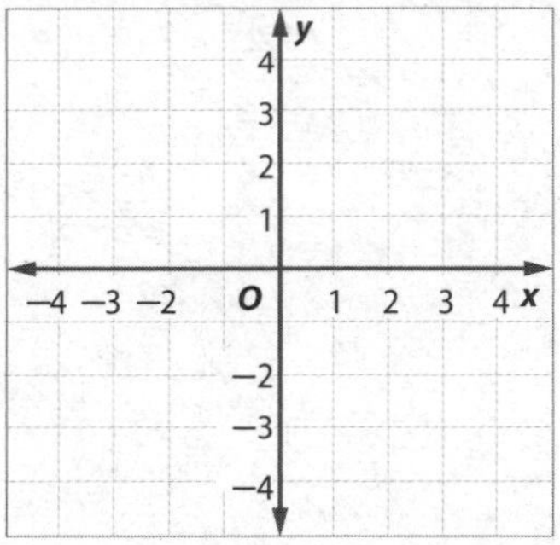

Graph Linear Equations

Example:

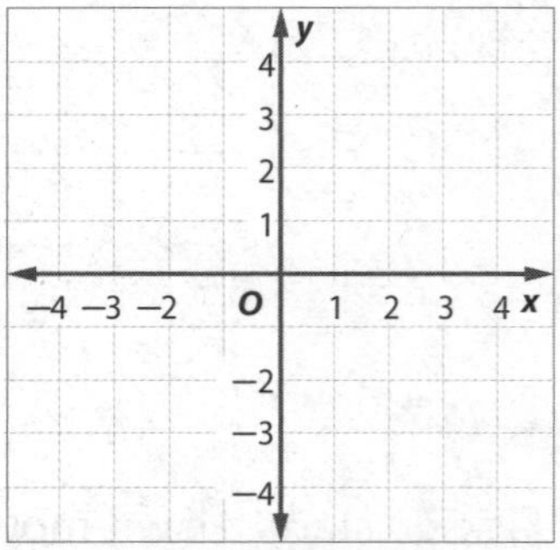

Answer the Essential Question. HOW can you express a linear relationship between two quantities in different ways? Verbally share your response with a partner, asking for and giving help if needed.

Chapter 7

Equations and Inequalities

Texas Essential Knowledge and Skills

Targeted TEKS

7.10 The student applies mathematical process standards to use one-variable equations and inequalities to represent situations. *Also addresses 7.11.*

Mathematical Processes

7.1, 7.1(A), 7.1(B), 7.1(C), 7.1(D), 7.1(E), 7.1(F), 7.1(G)

Essential Question

WHAT does it mean to say two quantities are equal?

Math in the Real World

King Ranch in Kingsville, Texas, is one of the largest ranches in the world. Its area is greater than the area of Rhode Island. The area of Rhode Island is 1,212 square miles. Circle the statement that represents the area a, in square miles, of King Ranch.

$a < 1,212$

$a > 1,212$

$a \leq 1,212$

Watch  Worksheets  Vocab    Tutor  Tools   Check 

What Tools Do You Need?

Vocab abc

Vocabulary

Addition Property of Equality
Addition Property of Inequality
coefficient
Division Property of Equality
Division Property of Inequality
equation
equivalent equation
inequality
Multiplication Property of Equality
Multiplication Property of Inequality
solution
Subtraction Property of Equality
Subtraction Property of Inequality
two-step equation
two-step inequality

Reading Math

Identify Key Information Have you ever tried to solve a word problem and didn't know here to start. Start by looking for key words in the text and images. Then write the important information in one sentence.

1. Highlight or circle key words in the following real-world problem.

   During a recent Super Bowl, millions of pounds of potato chips and tortilla chips were consumed. The number of pounds of potato chips consumed was 3.1 million pounds more than the number of pounds of tortilla chips. How many pounds of tortilla chips were consumed?

2. Write a sentence that summarizes the information provided. Include information from the text and the image. ______________________________

   ____

   ____

3. Work with a partner to share your answers to the exercises above, comparing and discussing any differences.

When Will You Use This?

Seth, Marisol, and Jamar in

Movie Night

Your Turn! **You will solve this problem in the chapter.**

Are You Ready?

Quick Review

Review 6.7(D), 6.10(B) TEKS

Example 1

Write the phrase as an algebraic expression.

Phrase: five dollars more than Jennifer earned

Variable: Let d represent the number of dollars Jennifer earned.

Expression: $d + 5$

Example 2

Is 3, 4, or 5 the solution of the equation $x + 8 = 12$?

Value of x	$x + 8 = 12$	Are both sides equal?
3	$3 + 8 \stackrel{?}{=} 12$ $11 \neq 12$	no
4	$4 + 8 \stackrel{?}{=} 12$ $12 = 12$	yes ✓
5	$5 + 8 \stackrel{?}{=} 12$ $13 \neq 12$	no

The solution is 4 since replacing x with 4 results in a true sentence.

Quick Check

Check

Words and Symbols **Write the phrase as an algebraic expression.**

1. 3 more runs than the Pirates scored

2. a number decreased by eight

3. ten dollars more than Grace has

One-Step Equations **Identify the solution of each equation from the list given.**

4. $8 + w = 17$; 7, 8, 9 ______

5. $d - 12 = 5$; 16, 17, 18 ______

6. $6 = 3y$; 2, 3, 4 ______

7. $7 \div c = 7$; 0, 1, 2 ______

8. $a + 8 = 23$; 13, 14, 15 ______

9. $10 = 45 - n$; 35, 36, 37 ______

How Did You Do?

Which problems did you answer correctly in the Quick Check? Shade those exercise numbers below.

① ② ③ ④ ⑤ ⑥ ⑦ ⑧ ⑨

FOLDABLES®

Use the Foldable throughout this chapter to help you learn about solving two-step equations.

cut on all dashed lines — fold on all solid lines — tape to page 580

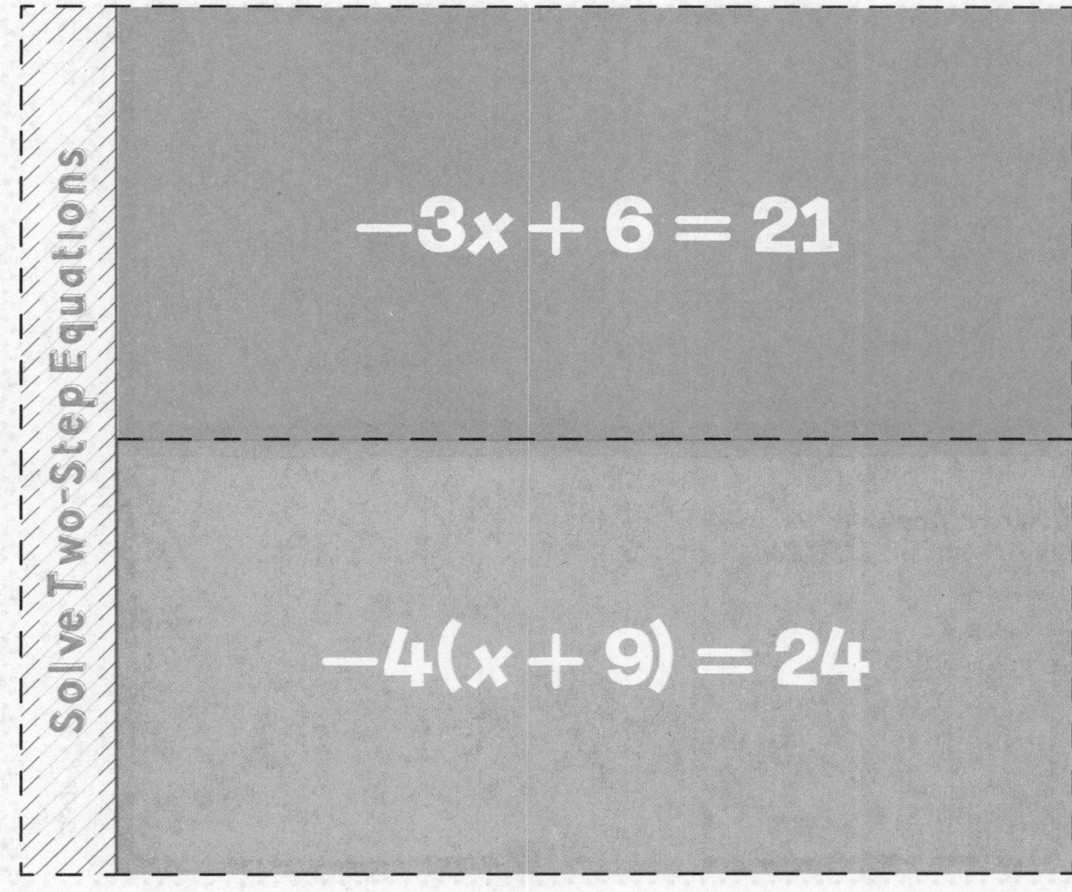

FOLDABLES®

Use this Foldable throughout this chapter to help you learn about solving two-step equations.

cut on all dashed lines

fold on all solid lines

tape to page 576

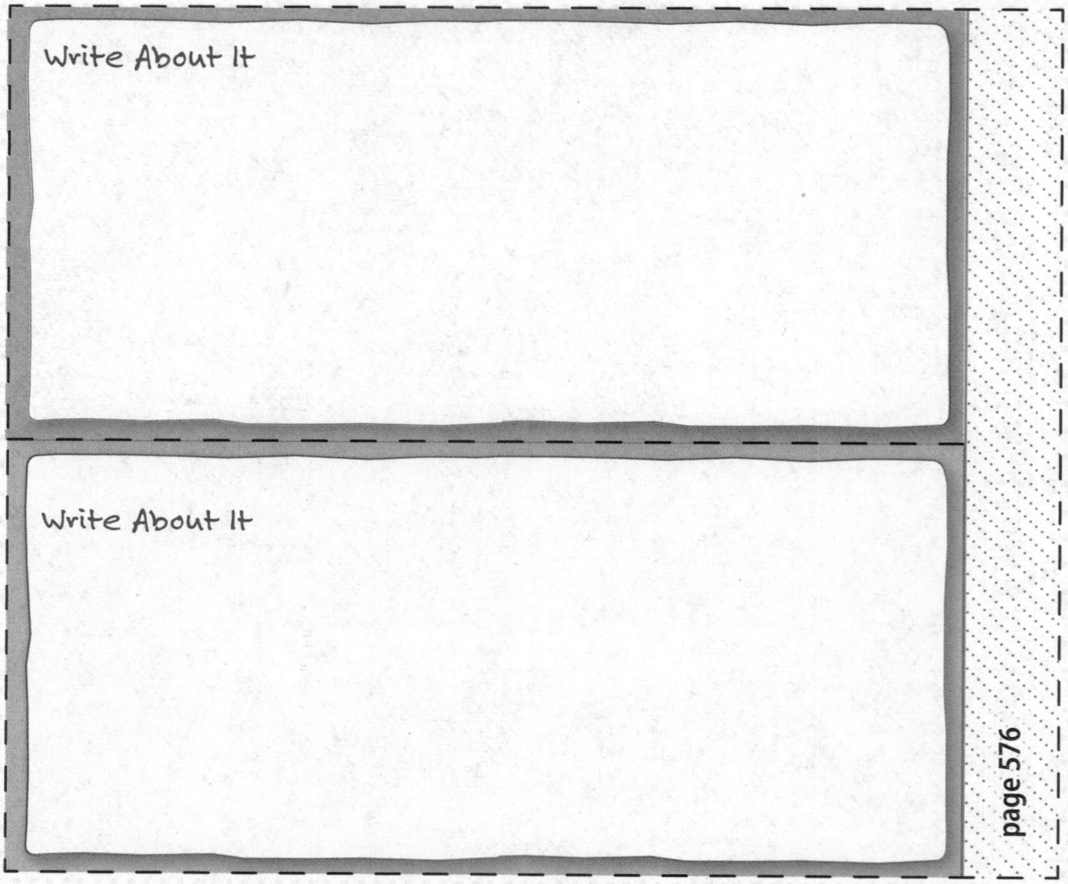

Write About It

Write About It

page 576

Lesson 1

Equations and Inequalities

Launch the Lesson: Vocabulary

Recall that an **equation** is a sentence stating that two quantities are equal. Equations often contain variables, or unknown values. Label the parts of the equation below with the terms *equation* and *variable*.

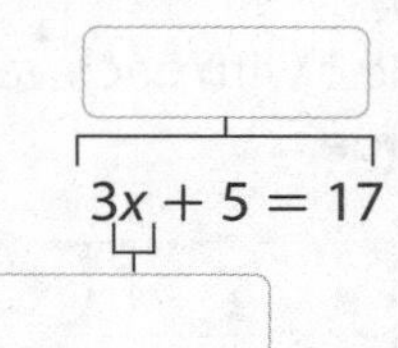

$3x + 5 = 17$

1. The value of a variable that makes an equation true is called the **solution** of the equation. Circle the equation that is true.

   $3(2) + 5 \stackrel{?}{=} 17$ $3(3) + 5 \stackrel{?}{=} 17$ $3(4) + 5 \stackrel{?}{=} 17$

2. Identify the solution to the equation $3x + 5 = 17$. ______
3. **Equivalent equations** have the same solution. Circle the equations that are equivalent to $3x + 5 = 17$.

   $x = 4$ $3x = 12$ $x + 1 = 6$

Real-World Link

Robyn had some video games, and then she bought 4 more games. Now she has 10 games. This scenario can be described using the equation $x + 4 = 10$.

4. What does x represent in the equation?

   ______

5. Circle the solution to the equation.

   4 5 6

Which MP Mathematical Processes did you use? Shade the circle(s) that applies.

Ⓐ Apply Math to the Real World.
Ⓑ Use a Problem-Solving Model.
Ⓒ Select Tools and Techniques.
Ⓓ Use Multiple Representations.
Ⓔ Organize Ideas.
Ⓕ Analyze Relationships.
Ⓖ Justify Arguments.

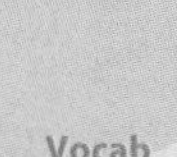

Texas Essential Knowledge and Skills

Targeted TEKS
7.11(B) Determine if the given value(s) make(s) one-variable, two-step equations and inequalities true.

Mathematical Processes
7.1(A), 7.1(B), 7.1(F)

Vocabulary
equation
solution
equivalent equation
inequality

Essential Question
WHAT does it mean to say two quantities are equal?

Work Zone

Determine Solutions of a Two-Step Equation

When you replace a variable with a value that results in a true sentence, that value is a solution for that equation.

Tutor

Examples

1. Determine if 4, 5, or 6 is the solution of the equation $2c + 5 = 17$.

Try each value. Replace the variable c with each value to determine which value makes the equation true.

value of c	4	5	6
$2c + 5 \stackrel{?}{=} 17$	$2(4) + 5 \stackrel{?}{=} 17$ $8 + 5 \stackrel{?}{=} 17$ $13 \neq 17$	$2(5) + 5 \stackrel{?}{=} 17$ $10 + 5 \stackrel{?}{=} 17$ $15 \neq 17$	$2(6) + 5 \stackrel{?}{=} 17$ $12 + 5 \stackrel{?}{=} 17$ $17 = 17$
True Sentence?	no	no	yes

Because $2(6) + 5 = 17$ is a true sentence, the solution of the equation, $2c + 5 = 17$ is 6.

2. Determine if 2.4, 2.7, or 3.6 is the solution of the equation $\frac{d}{3} - 1.4 = -0.5$.

Try each value. Replace the variable d with each value to determine which value makes the equation true.

value of d	2.4	2.7	3.6
$\frac{d}{3} - 1.4 \stackrel{?}{=} -0.5$	$\frac{2.4}{3} - 1.4 \stackrel{?}{=} -0.5$ $0.8 - 1.4 \stackrel{?}{=} -0.5$ $-0.6 \neq -0.5$	$\frac{2.7}{3} - 1.4 \stackrel{?}{=} -0.5$ $0.9 - 1.4 \stackrel{?}{=} -0.5$ $-0.5 = -0.5$	$\frac{3.6}{3} - 4 \stackrel{?}{=} -0.5$ $1.2 - 1.4 \stackrel{?}{=} -0.5$ $-0.2 \neq -0.5$
True Sentence?	no	yes	no

Because $\frac{2.7}{3} - 1.4 = -0.5$ is a true sentence, the solution of the equation, $\frac{d}{3} - 1.4 = -0.5$ is 2.7.

Got It? Do these problems to find out.

a. Determine if 2, 3, or 4 is the solution of the equation $6t - 7 = 11$.

b. Determine if 1.8, 2.6, or 2.8 is the solution of the equation $\frac{w}{2} + (-0.4) = 0.5$.

a. ________

b. ________

Determine Solutions of a Two-Step Inequality

An **inequality** is a mathematical sentence that compares quantities using $<$, $>$, $\leq$, or $\geq$. The table below gives some examples of the words you might use to describe different inequalities.

Words	• is less than • is fewer than	• is greater than • is more than	• is less than or equal to • is no more than	• is greater than or equal to • is no less than
Symbols	$<$	$>$	$\leq$	$\geq$

You can determine if given value(s) make(s) an inequality true by replacing the variable with the given value(s).

Tutor

Examples

3. **Determine if −4, −5, and/or −6 are solutions of $7 - 2x \leq 15$.**

value of c	−4	−5	−6
$7 - 2x \overset{?}{\leq} 15$	$7 - 2(-4) \overset{?}{\leq} 15$ $7 - (-8) \overset{?}{\leq} 15$ $15 \leq 15$	$7 - 2(-5) \overset{?}{\leq} 15$ $7 - (-10) \overset{?}{\leq} 15$ $17 \leq 15$	$7 - 2(-6) \overset{?}{\leq} 15$ $7 - (-12) \overset{?}{\leq} 15$ $19 \leq 15$
True statement?	yes; $15 = 15$	no; $17 > 15$	no; $19 > 15$

The only solution of the inequality is −4.

4. **Determine if 15, 24, and/or 27 are solutions of $5 - \frac{m}{3} < -2$.**

value of g	15	24	27
$5 - \frac{m}{3} \overset{?}{<} -2$	$5 - \frac{15}{3} \overset{?}{<} -2$ $5 - 5 \overset{?}{<} -2$ $0 < -2$	$5 - \frac{24}{3} \overset{?}{<} -2$ $5 - 8 \overset{?}{<} 5$ $-3 < -2$	$5 - \frac{27}{3} \overset{?}{<} -2$ $5 - 9 \overset{?}{<} -2$ $-4 < -2$
Are both sides equal?	no; $0 > -2$	yes; $-3 < -2$	yes; $-4 < -2$

The values 24 and 27 are both solutions of the inequality.

Got It? **Do these problems to find out.**

c. Determine if −24, −48, and/or −72 are solutions of $\frac{y}{12} + (-8) \leq -13$.

d. Determine if 2, 4, and/or 6 are solutions of $8b - 25 > 5$.

c. __________

d. __________

Example

5. Elías spends \$15.50 each week to buy lunch at school and a pack of gum. If a lunch at school costs \$3.50 and the pack of gum costs \$1.50, determine the solution to the equation $3.50x + 1.50 = 15.50$, where x represents the number of lunches he buys each week.

Use the *guess, check, and revise* strategy.

Try 2.	Try 3.	Try 4.
$3.50(2) + 1.50 \stackrel{?}{=} 15.50$ $7 + 1.50 \stackrel{?}{=} 15.50$ $8.50 \neq 15.50$	$3.50(3) + 1.50 \stackrel{?}{=} 15.50$ $10.50 + 1.50 \stackrel{?}{=} 15.50$ $12 \neq 15.50$	$3.50(4) + 1.50 \stackrel{?}{=} 15.50$ $14 + 1.50 \stackrel{?}{=} 15.50$ $15.50 = 15.50$

The equation $3.50(4) + 1.50 = 15.50$ is a true statement.

So, Elías buys 4 lunches each week.

Guided Practice

1. Determine if −10, −12, or −16 is the solution of $2t - 2 = -26$. (Examples 1 and 2) ______

2. Determine if 5.6, 5.2, or 4.8 is the solution of $\frac{m}{4} + (-0.8) = 0.5$. (Examples 1 and 2) ______

3. Determine if 15, 25, and/or 35 are solutions of $\frac{k}{5} - 12 \leq -8$. (Examples 3 and 4) ______

4. Jayla wants to buy some DVDs that each cost \$15, and a DVD player that costs \$45. She has \$105. Use the *guess, check,* and *revise* strategy to determine the solution to the equation $15d + 45 = 105$, where d represents the number of DVDs she can buy. (Example 5) ______

5. **Building on the Essential Question** How do you know whether a value is a solution to an equation or inequality? ______

Rate Yourself!

How confident are you about determining solutions to equations and in equalities? Check the box that applies.

Check

Find out online. Use the Self-Check Quiz.

Name ______________________ My Homework ______________________

Independent Practice

7.11(B), 7.1(F) TEKS

Determine the solution of each equation from the list given. (Examples 1 and 2)

1. $9m + 5 = -13; -2, -3, -4$ ________

2. $3t - 2 = -20; -4, -5, -6$ ________

3. $\frac{c}{-7} + 8 = 3; 14, 35, 49$ ________

4. $2.9 = -2b + 4.1; 0.5, 0.6, 0.7$ ________

Determine which number(s) are solutions of each inequality. (Examples 3 and 4)

5. $10 + \frac{a}{13} \geq 8; -13, -39, -65$ ________

6. $6x - 33 < -20; 1, 2, 3$

7. $-13.5 > -4z + 0.25; 2.5, 3.5, 4.5$ ________

8. $\frac{f}{-0.9} - 1.7 \leq -12; 7.2, 8.1, 9.9$ ________

MP Analyze Relationships For Exercises 9–11, solve using the *guess, check, and revise* strategy. (Example 5)

9. One season, the Tigers won 14 games and lost twice as many games as the Blue Jays. They played a total of 20 games. Use the equation $14 + 2g = 20$ to determine g, the number of games the Blue Jays lost.

____

10. Abril earned a total of $60 mowing lawns around her neighborhood. She charges $8 an hour and received $20 in tips. Use the equation $8h + 20 = 60$ to determine h, the number of hours she spent mowing lawns.

____

11. Connor wants to buy some books that each cost $7.95, and a MP3 player that costs $110.25. He has $150. Use the *guess, check,* and *revise* strategy to determine the solution to the equation $7.95b + 110.25 = 150$, where b represents the number of books he can buy.

____

12. Financial Literacy Mr. Kline works as a travel agent and earns a base pay of \$625 each week. He also receives 10% commission, or payment, of all his sales. In one week he earned \$925. Use the equation $625 + 0.1s = 925$ to determine s, the total amount in sales he had in one week. ____________

13. Which One Doesn't Belong? Circle the number that is *not* a solution to the inequality $2x + 3 \geq -1$.

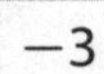

−3	−2	0	2

H.O.T. Problems Higher-Order Thinking

Analyze For Exercises 14 and 15, tell whether each statement is *true* or *false*. Then explain your reasoning.

14. In $3m + 13$, the variable m can have any value.

15. In $3m + 13 = 7$, the variable m can have any value and be a solution.

16. Create Give an example of a two-step equation that has a solution of 5.

17. Create Write an inequality for which −1, 0, and 2 are all solutions.

18. Analyze If $x = 1.5$, is the following inequality *true* or *false*? Explain.

$$\frac{x}{3} + 7.5 \geq 2.5 + 5x - 2$$

Name ___

Multi-Step Problem Solving

19. Levi is painting rectangular tabletops with a 16-square foot area. A bucket of paint will cover 1,000 square feet. The table shows orders waiting to be painted. Use the *guess, check, and revise* strategy and the equation $16t = 1{,}000$, where t represents the number of tables he can paint, to determine how many buckets he will need to paint all of the tables. EE N MP

Store	Tables Ordered
Fab Furniture	30
Tables R Tops	50
Deco Depot	90

Ⓐ 1 bucket Ⓑ 2 buckets Ⓒ 3 buckets Ⓓ 4 buckets

Use a problem-solving model to solve this problem.

1 Analyze

Read the problem. Circle the information you know.
Underline what the problem is asking you to find.

2 Plan

What will you need to do to solve the problem? Write your plan in steps.

Step 1 Use the equation to determine the ___ for the tables ordered.

Step 2 Divide the total area by the ___ each bucket of paint covers.

3 Solve

Use your plan to solve the problem. Show your steps.
Add the tables ordered. Then replace t in the equation with the sum.

$30 + 50 + 90 =$ ___
$16t = 1{,}000$

$16 \cdot$ ___ $=$ ___

___ $\div 1{,}000 =$ ___ Divide.

Levi will need ___ buckets of paint.

So, the correct answer is ___. Fill in that answer choice.

Read to Succeed!

Determine the total surface area Levi needs to paint first, before deciding how much paint he will need.

4 Justify and Evaluate

How do you know your solution is accurate?

___

___

___

___

EE = Expressions, Equations, and Relationships N = Number and Operations MP = Mathematical Processes

More Multi-Step Problem Solving

Use a problem-solving model to solve each problem.

20. Medha is paid \$300 to work as a nanny 20 hours each week. She is also paid \$20 per hour for each hour over 20 that she works. She wants her paycheck each week to be at least \$400. The table shows the hours she worked during the first four weeks. Which was the first week she met her goal? Use the inequality $300 + 20h \geq 400$, where h is the number of hours over 20 that she worked. EE N MP

Week	Hours Worked
1	20
2	24.5
3	27
4	29.5

Ⓐ week 1
Ⓑ week 2
Ⓒ week 3
Ⓓ week 4

21. At the book fair, Jasmeka bought a \$12 book and several pencils for \$1.50 each. She gave the cashier \$25 and received \$2.50 in change. Determine the amount that Jasmeka spent s. Then use the *guess, check, and revise* strategy to determine the solution to the equation $12 + 1.5p = s$, where p is the number of pencils she bought and s is the amount she spent. EE N MP

22. The dimensions of the triangle below will double to create a new triangle. Use the *guess, check, and revise* strategy to determine the solution to the equation $\frac{1}{2} \cdot 10 \cdot s = 17\frac{1}{2}$, where s is the side length of the triangle shown. Then use your solution to determine the area of the new triangle. EE N MP

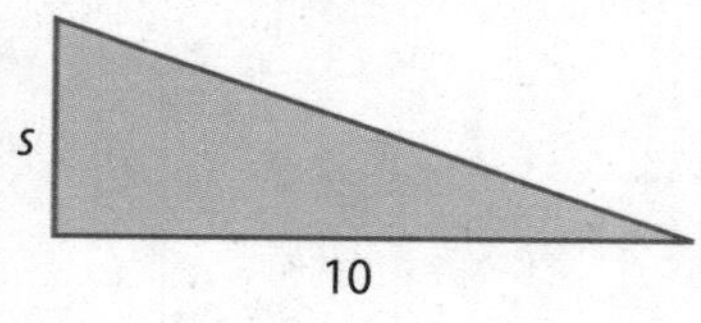

23. Cornelius bought \$50 worth of food at a store. He also bought some clothing. He pays 7% sales tax on clothing, but not food. He gives the cashier \$100 and receives change back. Use the inequality $50 + 1.07c < 100$, where c is the amount of money spent on clothing to determine the maximum amount he spent on clothes. Justify your answer. EE N MP

EE = Expressions, Equations, and Relationships N = Number and Operations MP = Mathematical Processes

Lesson 2

Solve One-Step Equations

Launch the Lesson: Vocabulary

The expression $3x$ means *3 times the value of x*. The numerical factor of a multiplication expression like $3x$ is called a **coefficient**. So, 3 is the coefficient of x.

The model below illustrates the multiplication equation $3x = 6$.

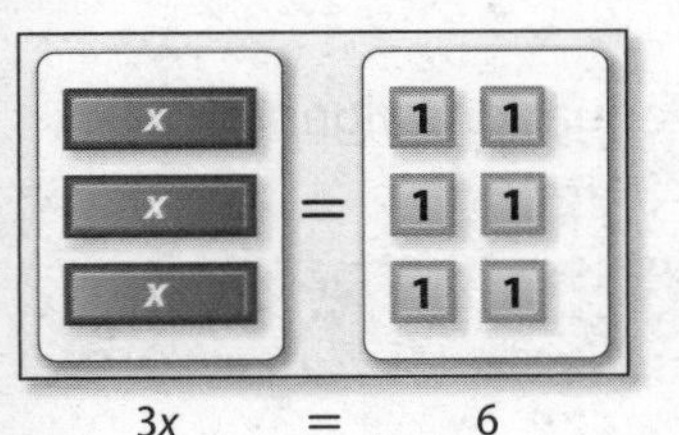

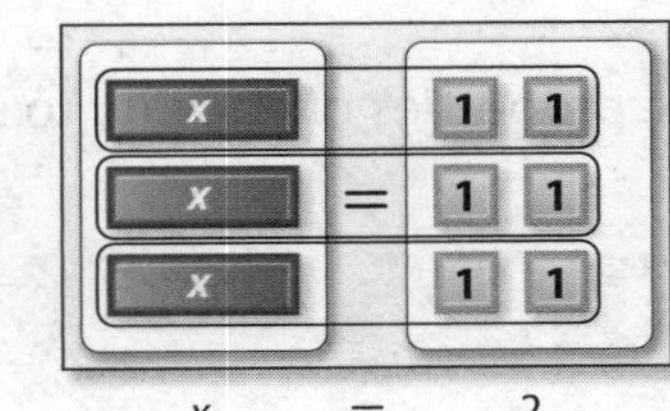

Since there are 3 *x*s each *x* is matched with 2.

The solution of $3x = 6$ is 2 because $3(2) = 6$.

Write an equation that represents each of the models below. Identify the coefficient in your equation. Then determine the solution.

1. 

Equation: ____________

Coefficient: ☐

Solution: ☐

2. 

Equation: ____________

Coefficient: ☐

Solution: ☐

Which MP Mathematical Processes did you use? Shade the circle(s) that applies.

Ⓐ Apply Math to the Real World.
Ⓑ Use a Problem-Solving Model.
Ⓒ Select Tools and Techniques.
Ⓓ Use Multiple Representations.
Ⓔ Organize Ideas.
Ⓕ Analyze Relationships.
Ⓖ Justify Arguments.

Texas Essential Knowledge and Skills

Targeted TEKS
Preparation for 7.10(A) Write one-variable, two-step equations and inequalities to represent constraints or conditions within problems.

Mathematical Processes
7.1(A), 7.1(B), 7.1(D), 7.1(F)

Vocab 

Vocabulary
coefficient
Subtraction Property of Equality
Addition Property of Equality
Division Property of Equality
Multiplication Property of Equality

Essential Question
WHAT does it mean to say two quantities are equal?

Key Concept

Properties of Equality

Words The **Subtraction Property of Equality** states that the two sides of an equation remain equal when you subtract the same number from each side.

Symbols If $a = b$, then $a - c = b - c$.

Words The **Addition Property of Equality** states that the two sides of an equation remain equal when you add the same number to each side.

Symbols If $a = b$, then $a + c = b + c$.

Work Zone

You can use the properties of equality to solve equations algebraically.

Examples

Solve each equation. Represent the solution on the number line. Check your solution.

1. $-5 = b + 8$

$$\begin{aligned} -5 &= b + 8 && \text{Write the equation.} \\ -8 &= \quad -8 && \text{Subtraction property of Equality} \\ -13 &= b && \text{Simplify.} \end{aligned}$$

So, the solution is −13.

Check $-13 + 8 = -5$ ✓

−15 −14 −13 −12 −11

2. $x - 3.2 = 2.1$

$$\begin{aligned} x - 3.2 &= \quad 2.1 && \text{Write the equation.} \\ +3.2 &\quad +3.2 && \text{Addition property of Equality} \\ x &= 5.3 \end{aligned}$$

The solution is 5.3.

Check $5.3 - 3.2 = 2.1$ ✓

5.1 5.2 5.3 5.4 5.5

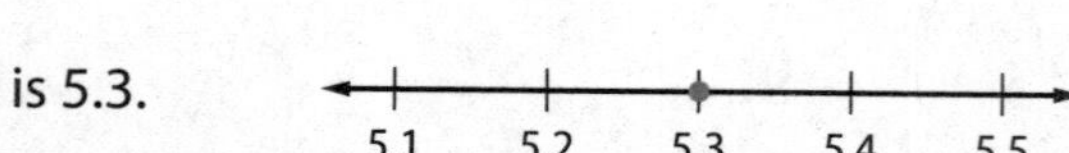

a. $x + 3.3 = 2.1$

b. $r - 4 = -6$

a. ________

b. ________

Properties of Equality

Key Concept

Words The **Division Property of Equality** states that two sides of an equation remain equal when you divide each side by the same nonzero number.

Symbols If $a = b$, and $c \neq 0$, then $\frac{a}{c} = \frac{b}{c}$.

Words The **Multiplication Property of Equality** states that two sides of an equation remain equal if you multiply each side by the same number.

Symbols If $a = b$, then $ac = bc$.

Use properties of equality to solve multiplication and division equations.

Examples

Tutor

Solve each equation. Represent the solution on the number line. Check your solution.

3. $-8y = 24$

$-8y = 24$ Write the equation.

$\frac{-8y}{-8} = \frac{24}{-8}$ Division Property of Equality

$y = -3$ Simplify.

So, the solution is −3.

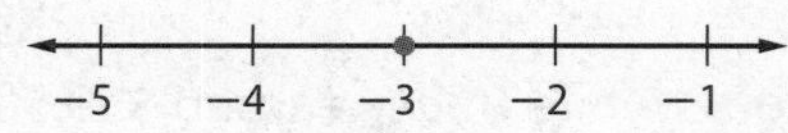

Check $-8(-3) = 24$ ✓

4. $\frac{a}{-4} = -9$

$\frac{a}{-4} = -9$ Write the equation.

$\frac{a}{-4}(-4) = -9(-4)$ Multiplication Property of Equality

$a = 36$ Simplify.

The solution is 36.

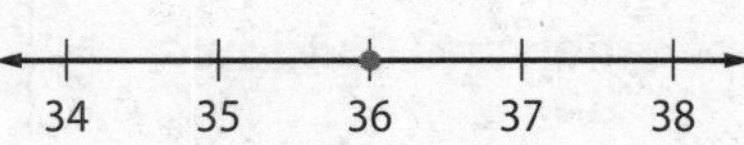

Check $36 \div -4 = -9$ ✓

Got It? Do these problems to find out.

c. $-6a = 36$

d. $-9d = -7.2$

c. ____________

d. ____________

Multi-Step Example

5. **Tina traveled 140 miles in 3.5 hours, while Loretta traveled 171 miles in 4.5 hours. Write and solve an equation to determine who traveled at a faster rate *r*.**

Step 1 Determine the rate each person traveled.

$\frac{140}{3.5} = r$ $\qquad$ $\frac{171}{4.5} = r$

$40 = r$ $\qquad$ $38 = r$

Step 2 Compare each rate. Tina traveled at a rate of 40 miles per hour and Loretta traveled at a rate of 38 miles per hour.

So, Tina traveled at a faster rate.

Distance Formula

The distance formula, distance = rate × time, can be written as $d = rt$, $r = \frac{d}{t}$, or $t = \frac{d}{r}$.

Guided Practice

Solve each equation. Represent the solution on the number line. Check your solution. (Examples 1–4)

1. $n + 6 = 4$ ______

2. $-7 = c - 6$ ______

3. $\frac{n}{-1.8} = -2.1$ ______

4. Antonia earned $45 for working 6 hours while Tracey earned $59.50 for working 7 hours. Write and solve an equation to determine who earned *e* more per hour. (Example 5)

5. **Building on the Essential Question** How is the process for solving one-step addition and subtraction equations like solving one-step multiplication and division equations?

Rate Yourself!

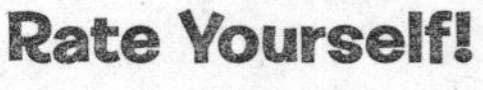

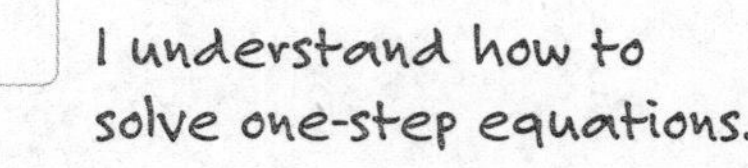

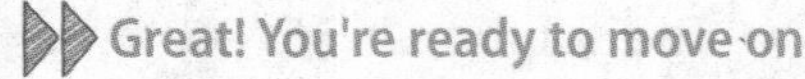

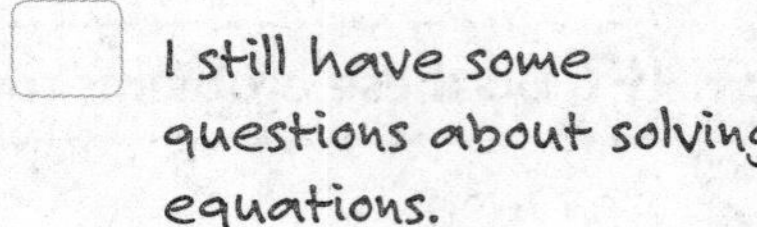

No problem! Go online to access a Personal Tutor.

Name ______ My Homework ______

Independent Practice

Preparation for 7.10(A), 7.1(D) TEKS

Solve each equation. Represent the solution on the number line. Check your solution. (Examples 1–4)

1. $-8 = \frac{c}{-10}$ ______

2. $-8 = p - 5$ ______

3. $-16 = -8v$ ______

4. $\frac{r}{2.4} = -2$ ______

5. $-7d = 56$ ______

6. $4.6 = x + 6.5$ ______

7. A race car can travel 615 miles in 3 hours. A small jet can travel 575 miles in 2.5 hours. Write and solve an equation to determine if the car or jet travels at a faster rate. (Example 5)

______

8. MP **Use Multiple Representations Refer to the table.**

Tallest Wooden Roller Coasters	Height (feet)	Drop (feet)	Speed (mph)
Colossos	h	159	68
T Express	184	151	65
El Toro	181	176	s
Voyage	163	d	67

a. **Symbols** The difference in speeds of El Toro and T Express is 5 miles per hour. If El Toro has the greater speed, write and solve a subtraction equation to determine its speed.

______

b. **Diagram** Voyage has a drop that is 22 feet less than El Toro. Draw a bar diagram below and write an equation to determine the height of Voyage.

______

c. **Words** Let h represent the height of the Colossos roller coaster. Explain why $h - 13 = 184$ and $h - 34 = 163$ are equivalent equations. Then explain the meaning of the solution.

______

______

9. **Find the Error** Aisha is determining $b + 5 = -8$. Find her mistake and correct it.

10. In a recent presidential election, Ohio had 20 electoral votes. This is 14 votes less than Texas had. How many electoral votes did Texas have? Write an equation and then solve.

 H.O.T. Problems Higher-Order Thinking

11. **Create** Write an addition equation and a subtraction equation that each have 10 as a solution.

12. **Evaluate** Suppose $x + y = 11$ and the value of x increases by 2. If their sum remains the same, what must happen to the value of y? Justify your response.

13. **Create** Describe a real-world situation in which you would use a division equation to solve a problem. Write an equation and then solve your problem.

14. **Analyze** *True* or *false*. To solve the equation $5x = 20$, you can use the Multiplication Property of Equality. Explain your reasoning.

15. **Analyze** Solve $3|x| = 12$. Explain your reasoning.

Name ______________________

Multi-Step Problem Solving

16. Devin recorded the percent humidity Monday through Saturday. The graph shows his measurements. On Sunday, he took the final measurement and calculated the average of all 7 days. The average humidity was 70%. How much greater was the humidity on Monday compared to Sunday? EE N MP

Ⓐ 11% Ⓑ 13% Ⓒ 14% Ⓓ 20%

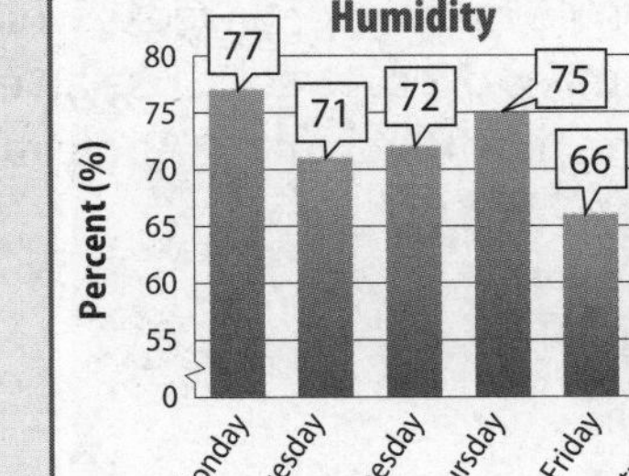

Use a problem-solving model to solve this problem.

1 Analyze

Read the problem. Circle the information you know. Underline what the problem is asking you to find.

2 Plan

What will you need to do to solve the problem? Write your plan in steps.

Step 1 Determine the ________ for Sunday.

Step 2 Subtract the humidity on ________ from ________.

3 Solve

Use your plan to solve the problem. Show your steps.

Write and solve an equation to determine the humidity on Sunday.

$$\frac{77 + 71 + 72 + 75 + 66 + 65 + x}{7} = 70 \qquad x = \_\_\_\_$$

77 − ____ = ____ Subtract.

The humidity on Monday was ______ greater than the humidity on Sunday.

So, the correct answer is ____. Fill in that answer choice.

Read to Succeed!

To determine the average humidity, add the humidity for each day, then divide by the total number of days.

4 Justify and Evaluate

How do you know your solution is accurate?

____

____

____

EE = Expressions, Equations, and Relationships N = Number and Operations MP = Mathematical Processes

More Multi-Step Problem Solving

Use a problem-solving model to solve each problem.

17. Angie ran 45 miles over 6 weeks while Hannah ran 59.5 miles over 7 weeks. Use an equation to determine how much more Angie ran per week. EE P N MP

Ⓐ 0.25 mile

Ⓑ 0.5 mile

Ⓒ 1.0 mile

Ⓓ 1.5 miles

18. The table shows how much Prisha read on Saturday and Sunday. If she read at the same rate on Sunday as she did on Saturday, what time did she start reading Sunday night? EE P N MP

Day	Start Time	End Time	Pages Read
Saturday	12:00 PM	12:30 PM	60
Sunday	?	8:40 PM	40

19. Josiah and Perry were painting their bedroom walls with a surface area of 196 square feet. Josiah can paint 16 square feet in 4 minutes, while Perry can paint 7 square feet in 2 minutes. After 10 minutes, how much more total area will Josiah and Perry have left to paint? EE P N MP

20. Zeshon drove 18 minutes to get to the highway. Once he got to the highway, he drove the same amount of time but covered two times the distance as he had before the highway. Compare the average rate he drove on the highway to the average rate he drove before the highway. Justify your solution.
EE   

EE = Expressions, Equations, and Relationships P = Proportionality 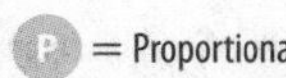 N = Number and Operations MP 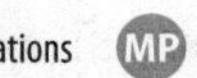 = Mathematical Processes

Hands-On Lab 3-a

Model and Solve Equations with Rational Coefficients

INQUIRY HOW can I use multiple representations to solve equations with rational coefficients?

Two thirds of Chen's homeroom class plan to participate in the school talent show. If 16 students from the class plan to participate, how many students are in the homeroom class?

What do you know? ______________________

____

What do you need to find? ______________________

____

Texas Essential Knowledge and Skills
TEKS

Targeted TEKS
Preparation for 7.10(A) Write one-variable, two-step equations and inequalities to represent constraints or conditions within problems.

Mathematical Processes
7.1(C), 7.1(D), 7.1(E), 7.1(F)

Hands-On Activity

You can represent the situation above with an equation.

Step 1 Draw a bar diagram that represents the total number of students in the class and how many plan to participate.

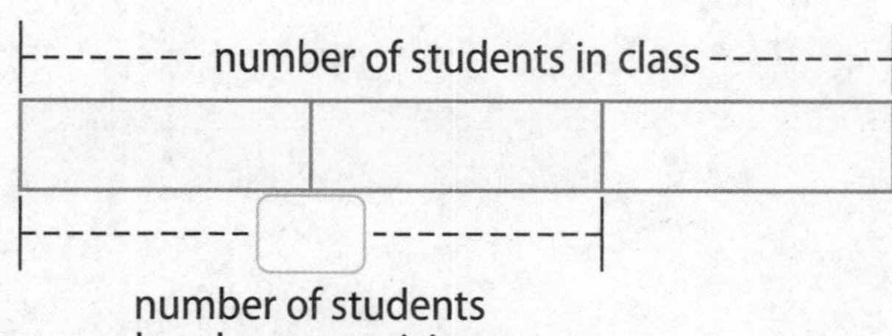

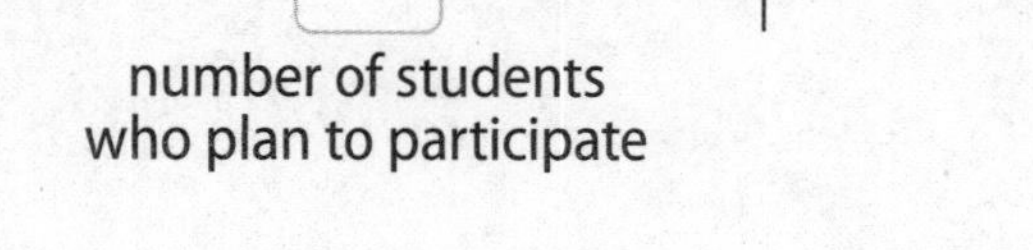

Step 2 Write an equation from the bar diagram. Let *c* represent the total number of students in the class. ______________________

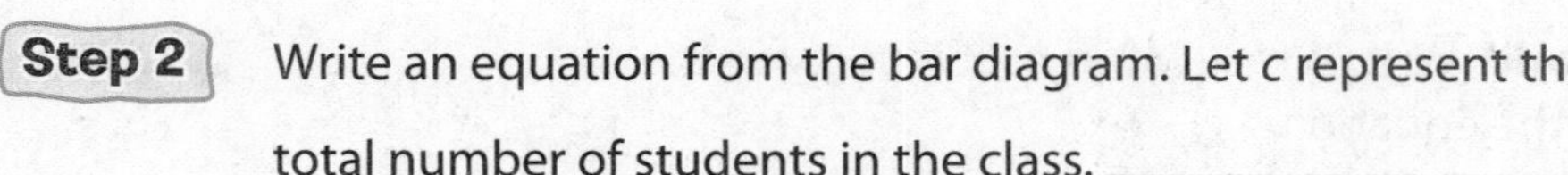

Step 3 Determine the number of students represented by the sections of the bar. Write that number in each section of the bar in Step 1.

Since each section represents 8 students, there are 8 × 3 or ☐ students in the class.

Check $\frac{2}{3} \times 24 = \frac{2}{3} \times \frac{24}{1}$

$= \frac{48}{3}$ or 16 ✓

Investigate

Work with a partner to solve the following problem.

1. Eliana is spending $\frac{3}{5}$ of her monthly allowance on a costume for the talent show. She plans to spend $24. Draw a bar diagram to represent the situation. Then write and solve an equation to determine the amount of Eliana's monthly allowance.

Equation: ________ Solution: ________

Analyze and Reflect

2. **MP Analyze Relationships** Suppose Eliana planned on spending $\frac{3}{4}$ of her monthly allowance on a costume. How would the diagram and equation be different?

Create

3. **MP Apply Math to the Real World** Write a real-world problem given the equation $\frac{2}{3}x = 12$. Then solve the equation.

4. **INQUIRY** HOW can I use multiple representations to solve equations with rational coefficients?

Lesson 3

Solve Equations with Rational Coefficients

Launch the Lesson: Real World

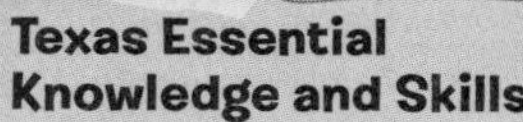

Texas Essential Knowledge and Skills

Targeted TEKS

Preparation for 7.10(A) Write one-variable, two-step equations and inequalities to represent constraints or conditions within problems.

Mathematical Processes

7.1(A), 7.1(B), 7.1(C), 7.1(E), 7.1(F)

Essential Question

WHAT does it mean to say two quantities are equal?

Three-fourths of the students in Aaliyah's class belong to a social network. There are 15 students in her class that belong to a social network. How many students are in Aaliyah's class?

1. Create a bar diagram and shade $\frac{3}{4}$, or 0.75, of it.

   Label 15 along the bottom to show the amount of the bar that represents 15 students.

2. Based on the diagram, circle the equations that can be used to determine *c*, the number of students in Aaliyah's class.

   $15c = \frac{3}{4}$ $\quad\quad$ $0.75c = 15$ $\quad\quad$ $\frac{3}{4}c = 15$

3. Based on what you know about solving equations, explain how you could solve the equations you circled in Exercise 2.

4. How many students are in Aaliyah's class?

Which MP Mathematical Processes did you use? Shade the circle(s) that applies.

Ⓐ Apply Math to the Real World.
Ⓑ Use a Problem-Solving Model.
Ⓒ Select Tools and Techniques.
Ⓓ Use Multiple Representations.
Ⓔ Organize Ideas.
Ⓕ Analyze Relationships.
Ⓖ Justify Arguments.

Work Zone

Decimal Coefficients

If the coefficient is a decimal, divide each side by the coefficient.

Tutor

Example

1. Solve $16 = 0.25n$. Check your solution.

$16 = 0.25n$	Write the equation.
$\frac{16}{0.25} = \frac{0.25n}{0.25}$	Division Property of Equality
$64 = n$	Simplify.
Check $16 = 0.25n$	Write the original equation.
$16 \stackrel{?}{=} 0.25 \cdot 64$	Replace n with 64.
$16 = 16$ ✓	This sentence is true.

The solution is 64.

Division with Decimals

$$0.25\overline{)16.00} = 64.$$
-150, 100, -100, 0

Got It? Do these problems to find out.

a. $6.4 = 0.8m$ **b.** $-2.8p = 4.2$ **c.** $-4.7k = -10.81$

a. ____________

b. ____________

c. ____________

Show your work.

Real World

Tutor

Example

2. Jaya's coach agreed to buy ice cream for all of the team members. Ice cream cones are \$2.40 each. Write and solve an equation to determine how many cones he can buy with \$30.

Let n represent the number of cones the coach can buy.

$2.4n = 30$	Write the equation; \$2.40 = 2.4.
$\frac{2.4n}{2.4} = \frac{30}{2.4}$	Division Property of Equality
$n = 12.5$	Simplify.

Since the number of ice cream cones must be a whole number, there is enough money for 12 ice cream cones.

Got It? Do this problem to find out.

d. Suppose the ice cream cones cost \$2.80 each. How many ice cream cones could the coach buy with \$42?

d. ____________

Fraction Coefficients

Recall that two numbers with a product of 1 are called multiplicative inverses, or reciprocals. If the coefficient in a multiplication equation is a fraction, multiply each side by the reciprocal of the coefficient.

Examples

Tutor

3. Solve $\frac{3}{4}x = \frac{12}{20}$.

$\frac{3}{4}x = \frac{12}{20}$ Write the equation.

$\left(\frac{4}{3}\right) \cdot \frac{3}{4}x = \left(\frac{4}{3}\right) \cdot \frac{12}{20}$ Multiply each side by the reciprocal of $\frac{3}{4}$, $\frac{4}{3}$.

$\frac{\cancel{4}^{1}}{\cancel{3}_{1}} \cdot \frac{\cancel{3}^{1}}{\cancel{4}_{1}}x = \frac{\cancel{4}^{1}}{\cancel{3}_{1}} \cdot \frac{\cancel{12}^{4}}{\cancel{20}_{5}}$ Divide by common factors.

$x = \frac{4}{5}$ Simplify. Check the solution.

4. Solve $-\frac{7}{9}d = 5$. Check your solution.

$-\frac{7}{9}d = 5$ Write the equation.

$\left(-\frac{9}{7}\right) \cdot \left(-\frac{7}{9}\right)d = \left(-\frac{9}{7}\right) \cdot 5$ Multiply each side by the reciprocal of $-\frac{7}{9}$, $-\frac{9}{7}$.

$\left(-\frac{9}{7}\right) \cdot \left(-\frac{7}{9}\right)d = \left(-\frac{9}{7}\right) \cdot \frac{5}{1}$ Write 5 as $\frac{5}{1}$.

$\left(-\frac{\cancel{9}^{1}}{\cancel{7}_{1}}\right) \cdot \left(-\frac{\cancel{7}^{1}}{\cancel{9}_{1}}\right)d = \left(-\frac{9}{7}\right) \cdot \frac{5}{1}$ Divide by common factors.

$d = -\frac{45}{7}$ or $-6\frac{3}{7}$ Simplify.

Check $-\frac{7}{9}d = 5$ Write the original equation.

$-\frac{7}{9}\left(-\frac{45}{7}\right) \stackrel{?}{=} 5$ Replace *d* with $-\frac{45}{7}$.

$\frac{315}{63} \stackrel{?}{=} 5$ Simplify.

$5 = 5$ ✓ This sentence is true.

Fractions as Coefficients

The expression $\frac{3}{4}x$ can be read as $\frac{3}{4}$ of x, $\frac{3}{4}$ multiplied by x, $3x$ divided by 4, or $\frac{x}{4}$ multiplied by 3.

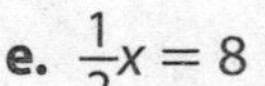

Do these problems to find out.

e. $\frac{1}{2}x = 8$

f. $-\frac{3}{4}x = 9$

g. $-\frac{7}{8}x = -\frac{21}{64}$

e. ____________

f. ____________

g. ____________

Example

5. Valerie needs $\frac{2}{3}$ yard of fabric to make each hat for the school play. Write and solve an equation to determine how many hats she can make with 6 yards of fabric.

Write and solve a multiplication equation. Let n represent the number of hats.

$$\frac{2}{3}n = 6$$ Write the equation.

$$\left(\frac{3}{2}\right) \cdot \frac{2}{3}n = \left(\frac{3}{2}\right) \cdot 6$$ Multiply each side by $\frac{3}{2}$.

$$n = 9$$ Simplify.

Valerie can make 9 hats.

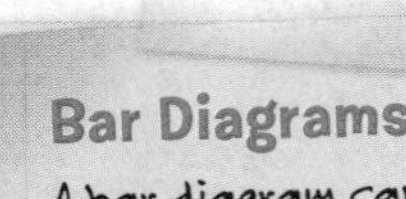

Bar Diagrams

A bar diagram can be used to represent this situation.

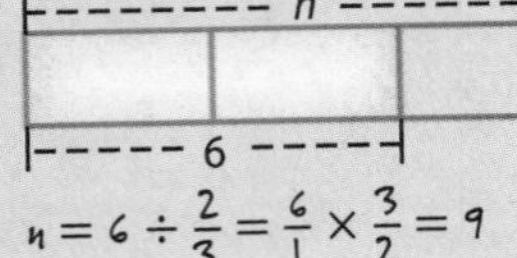

$n = 6 \div \frac{2}{3} = \frac{6}{1} \times \frac{3}{2} = 9$

Guided Practice

Solve each equation. Check your solution. (Examples 1, 3, and 4)

1. $1.6k = 3.2$ ______

2. $-2.5b = 20.5$ ______

3. $-\frac{1}{2} = -\frac{5}{18}h$ ______

Write and solve an equation. (Examples 2 and 5)

4. The average growth of human hair is 0.5 inch per month. Determine how long it takes a human to grow 3 inches of hair.

Equation: ______ Solution: ______

5. Three fourths of the fruit in a refrigerator are apples. There are 24 apples in the refrigerator. How many pieces of fruit are in the refrigerator?

Equation: ______ Solution: ______

6. **Building on the Essential Question** What is the process for solving a multiplication equation with a rational coefficient?

______

______

______

______

Rate Yourself!

Are you ready to move on? Shade the section that applies.

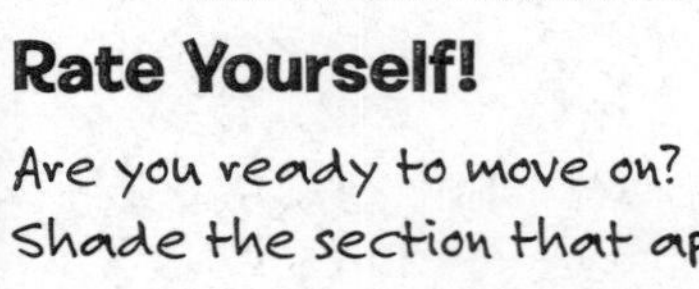

Find out online. Use the Self-Check Quiz.

Name ____________ My Homework ____________

Independent Practice

Preparation for 7.10(A), 7.1(G) TEKS

Solve each equation. Check your solution. (Examples 1, 3, and 4)

1. $1.2x = 6$ ______

2. $14.4 = -2.4b$ ______

3. $-3.6h = -10.8$ ______

Show your work.

4. $\frac{2}{5}t = \frac{12}{25}$ ______

5. $-3\frac{1}{3} = -\frac{1}{2}g$ ______

6. $-\frac{7}{9}m = \frac{11}{6}$ ______

7. **Financial Literacy** Dillon deposited $\frac{3}{4}$ of his paycheck into the bank. The deposit slip shows how much he deposited. Write and solve an equation to determine the amount of his paycheck. (Example 2)

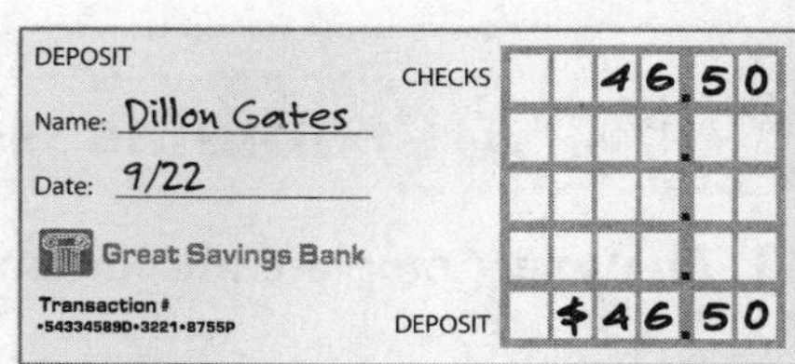

Equation: ______ Solution: ______

8. Twenty-four students brought their permission slips to attend the class field trip to the local art museum. If this represented eight tenths of the class, how many students are in the class? Use a bar diagram to solve arithmetically. Then use an equation to solve algebraically. (Example 5)

Equation: ______ Solution: ______

9. MP **Justify Arguments** Seventy-five percent, or 15, of the students in Emily's homeroom class are going on a field trip. Two thirds, or 12, of the students in Santiago's homeroom class are going on the field trip. Which class has more students? Justify your answer. ______

10. MP **Apply Math to the Real World** Refer to the graphic novel frame below. Write and solve an equation to determine how many movies they can show.

Equation: ______________ Solution: ______________

H.O.T. Problems Higher-Order Thinking

11. **Analyze** Complete the statement: If $8 = \frac{m}{4}$, then $m - 12 = $ ■. Explain.

12. **Evaluate** Identify the pair of numbers that does not belong with the other three. Explain.

$\frac{9}{6}, \frac{6}{9}$	$4, \frac{1}{4}$	$\frac{3}{5}, 5$	$\frac{2}{7}, \frac{7}{2}$

13. **Evaluate** The formula for the area of a trapezoid is $A = \frac{1}{2}h(b_1 + b_2)$, where b_1 and b_2 are both bases and h is the height. Determine the value of h in terms of A, b_1, and b_2. Justify your solution.

14. **Create** Write a real-world problem that can be represented by the equation $224 = 3.5r$. Then solve the problem and explain the solution.

Name ___

Multi-Step Problem Solving

15. The third quartile of the data set represented in the box plot at the right is the product of three-fourths and the median. The first quartile is the quotient of the median and four-sevenths. What is the interquartile range?
EE MD N MP

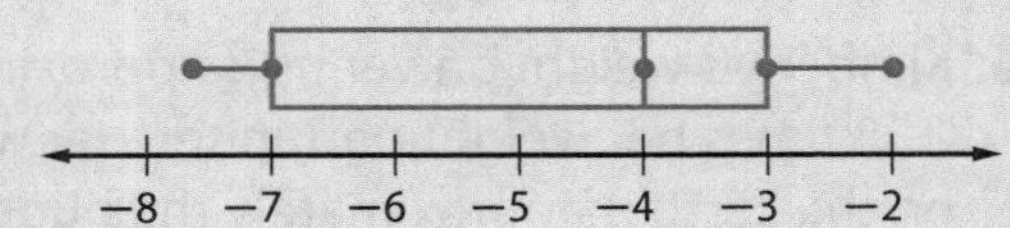

Use a problem-solving model to solve this problem.

1 Analyze

Read the problem. Circle the information you know.
Underline what the problem is asking you to find.

2 Plan

What will you need to do to solve the problem? Write your plan in steps.

Step 1 Use equations to determine the ___ and first quartile.

Step 2 Subtract the first quartile from the ___.

Read to Succeed!
Recall that the interquartile range is the distance between the first and third quartiles.

3 Solve

Use your plan to solve the problem. Show your steps.

Use equations to determine the median and first quartile.

$-3 = \frac{3}{4}m$ median = ___

$m \div \frac{4}{7} = q$ first quartile = ___

Determine the interquartile range.

___ − ___ = ___ Subtract.

The interquartile range is ___.

Complete the grid.

					.		
⊕	0	0	0	0		0	0
⊖	1	1	1	1		1	1
	2	2	2	2		2	2
	3	3	3	3		3	3
	4	4	4	4		4	4
	5	5	5	5		5	5
	6	6	6	6		6	6
	7	7	7	7		7	7
	8	8	8	8		8	8
	9	9	9	9		9	9

4 Justify and Evaluate

How do you know your solution is accurate?

___

___

___

EE = Expressions, Equations, and Relationships MD = Measurement and Data N = Number and Operations MP = Mathematical Processes

Use a problem-solving model to solve each problem.

16. Kimberly's weight on Venus is approximately 0.38 times her weight on Jupiter. Her weight on the Earth is approximately the quotient of her weight on Venus divided by 0.9. Her weight on the Earth is 100 pounds. What is her weight in pounds on Jupiter, rounded to the nearest whole number? EE N MP

17. A point on a number line moves to the right $\frac{1}{2}$ unit, to the left $5\frac{1}{2}$ units, and to the right 2 units, landing on the number line as shown. Where does the point start? Express your answer as a decimal. EE N P MP

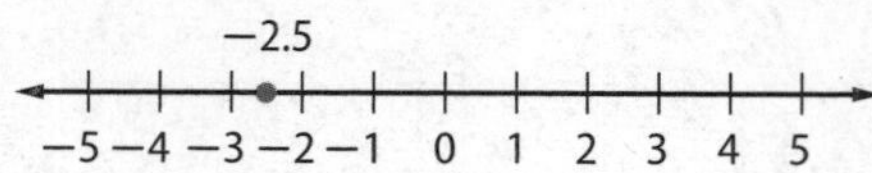

18. Tevon designates 40% of his income for spending. If he makes $10 per hour, how many hours per week does he have to work to have $100 to spend weekly? EE N P MP

19. The table below shows the withdrawals and deposits for a checking account. The ending balance is $51.20. Determine the starting balance. Explain. EE N FL MP

Transaction	Amount
Withdrawal	$30
Deposit	$10.20
Deposit	$45.50
Withdrawal	$60

EE = Expressions, Equations, and Relationships N = Number and Operations P = Proportionality FL = Personal Financial Literacy MP = Mathematical Processes

Hands-On Lab 4-a

Model and Solve Two-Step Equations

INQUIRY **HOW can I use multiple representations to help me solve a real-world problem?**

Texas Essential Knowledge and Skills TEKS

Targeted TEKS

7.11(A) Model and solve one-variable, two-step equations and inequalities. *Also addresses 7.10(A), 7.10(C).*

Mathematical Processes

7.1(C), 7.1(D), 7.1(E), 7.1(F), 7.1(G)

Latoya plays basketball and tennis. She has two basketballs and three tennis balls that weigh a total of 48 ounces. Each tennis ball weighs 2 ounces. What is the weight of a basketball?

Hands-On Activity 1

You can use models, such as a bar diagram, to represent the situation.

Step 1 Label the bar diagram below that represents the total weight.

48 oz

basketball		tennis	tennis	
?	?	2 oz	2 oz	____

Step 2 Write an equation that is modeled by the bar diagram. Let x represent the weight of a basketball.

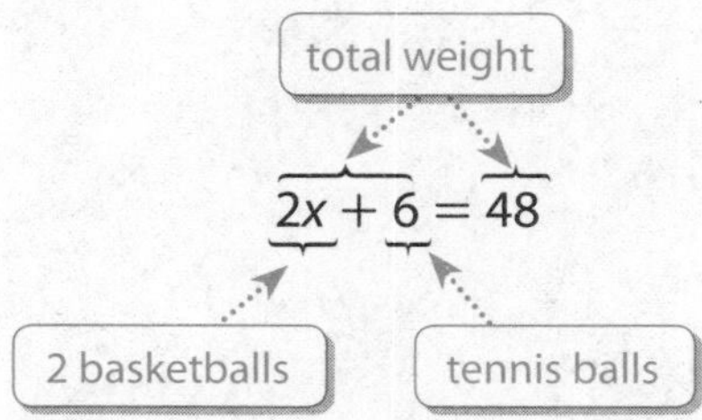

Step 3 Use the bar diagram to solve the equation. Subtract the weight of the tennis balls, ____ ounces, from the total weight, ____ ounces.

The two basketballs together weigh ____ − ____, or ____ ounces. Divide the weight by ____ to determine the weight of one basketball.

So, $x =$ ____. The weight of one basketball is ____ ÷ ____, or ____ ounces.

Check $2 \cdot$ ____ $+ 6 = 48$ ✓

The weight of one basketball is ____ ounces.

Hands-On Activity 2

You can use algebra tiles to model and solve the equation $4x - 2 = 10$.

Step 1 Model the equation.

$4x - 2 = 10$

Step 2 Add ☐ 1-tiles to each side of the mat to form zero pairs on the left side.

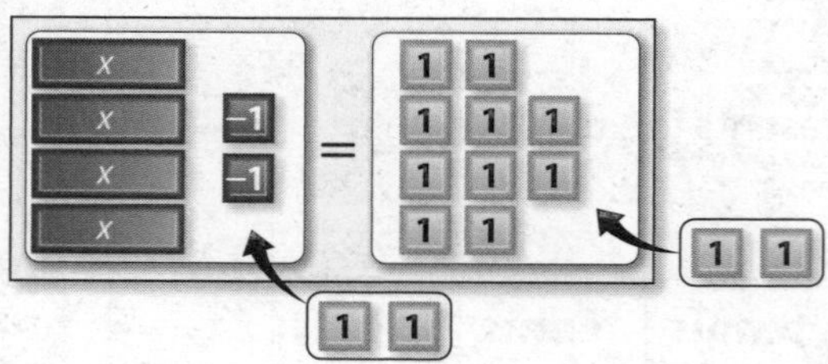

$4x - 2 + 2 = 10 + 2$

Step 3 Remove both zero pairs from the left side so that the variable is by itself.

$4x = 12$

Step 4 Divide the remaining tiles into ☐ equal groups.

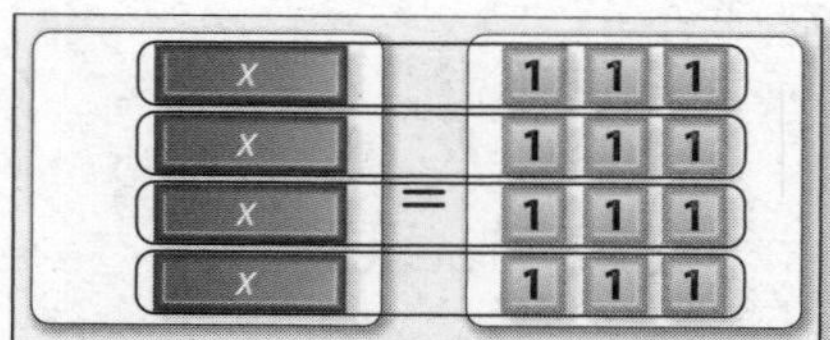

$\frac{4x}{4} = \frac{12}{4}$

So, $x =$ ☐.

Check $4 \cdot$ ☐ $- 2 = 10$ ✓

Investigate

Work with a partner to solve the following problem.

1. **Organize Ideas** Ryan is saving money to buy a skateboard that costs \$85. He has already saved \$40. He plans to save the same amount each week for three weeks. Draw a bar diagram. Then write an equation. How much should Ryan save each week?

Work with a partner to solve each equation. Use algebra tiles. Show your work using drawings.

2. $2x + 1 = 5$ $x =$ ______

3. $3x + 2 = 11$ $x =$ ______

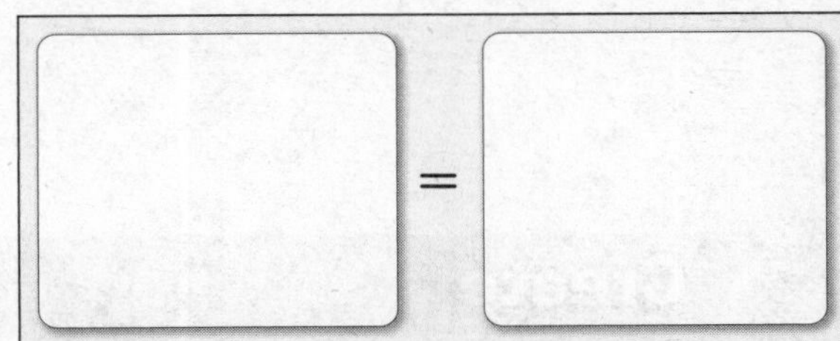

4. $4x + 3 = -5$ $x =$ ______

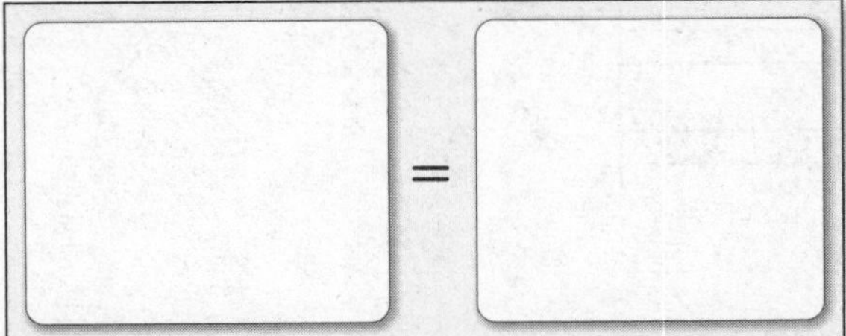

5. $2x - 1 = 7$ $x =$ ______

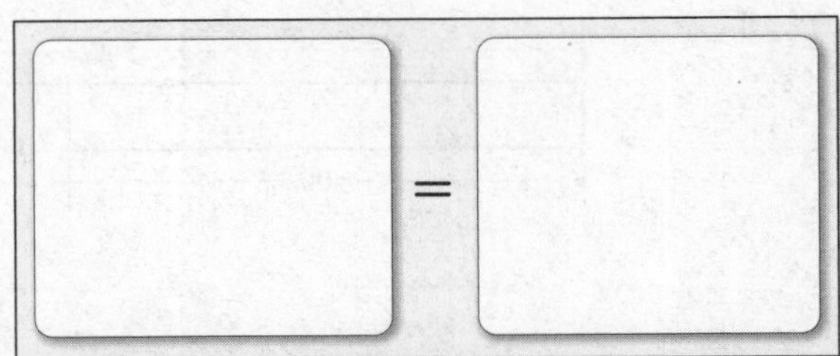

6. $5x - 2 = -7$ $x =$ ______

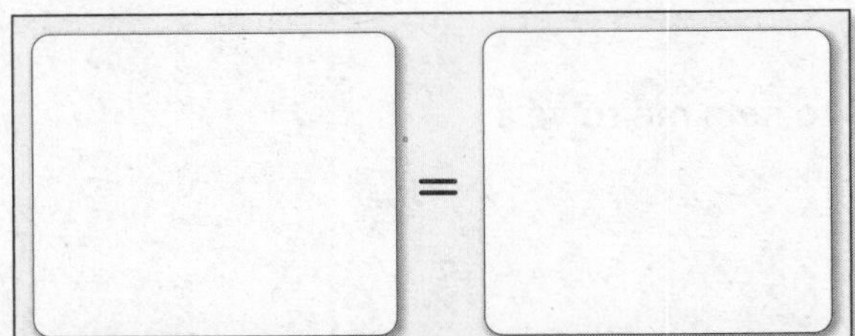

7. $3x - 4 = 5$ $x =$ ______

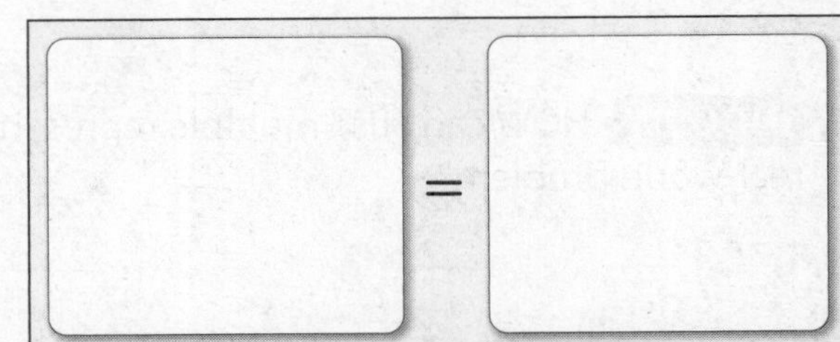

Analyze and Reflect

8. **MP Analyze Relationships** Work with a partner. Read the steps to model and solve an equation using algebra tiles. Then circle each correct equation.

Steps to Solve	Choices of Equation		
• Add three 1-tiles to each side of the mat. • Divide tiles into two equal groups.	$2x + 3 = 15$	$3x + 2 = 15$	$2x - 3 = 15$
• Add four 1-tiles to each side of the mat. • Divide tiles into three equal groups.	$3x - 4 = 11$	$3x + 4 = 11$	$4x - 3 = 11$
• Remove seven 1-tiles from each side of the mat. • Divide tiles into three equal groups.	$7x + 3 = 10$	$3x + 7 = 10$	$3x - 7 = 10$
• Add two −1-tiles to each side of the mat. • Remove two zero pairs from the left side of the mat. • Divide tiles into five equal groups.	$5x - 2 = -8$	$5x + 2 = -8$	$2x + 5 = -8$

9. **MP Justify Arguments** What did you observe while choosing the correct equations in the table above?

Create

10. **MP Apply Math to the Real World** Write a real-world problem and an equation that the bar diagram below could represent. Then solve your problem.

540

200 | ? | ?

11. **INQUIRY** HOW can I use multiple representations to help me solve a real-world problem?

Lesson 4

Solve and Write Two-Step Equations

Launch the Lesson: Real World

Watch

A company charges $2 for each balloon in an arrangement and a $3 delivery fee. You have $9 to spend. How many balloons you can purchase?

1. **Create** Draw a bar diagram to represent this situation.

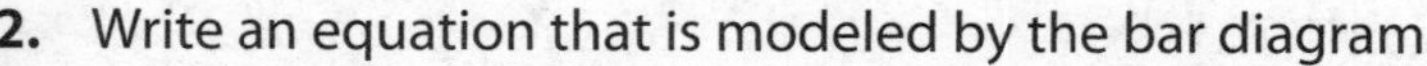

2. Write an equation that is modeled by the bar diagram.

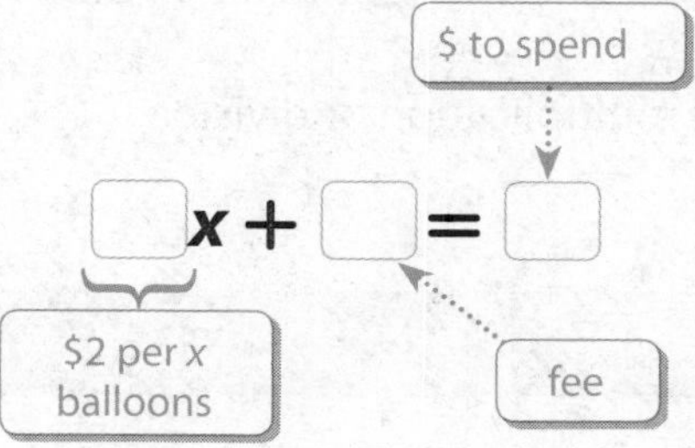

3. How can you use the bar diagram to determine the number of balloons you can purchase?

4. How would your equation and solution change if the delivery fee was only $1?

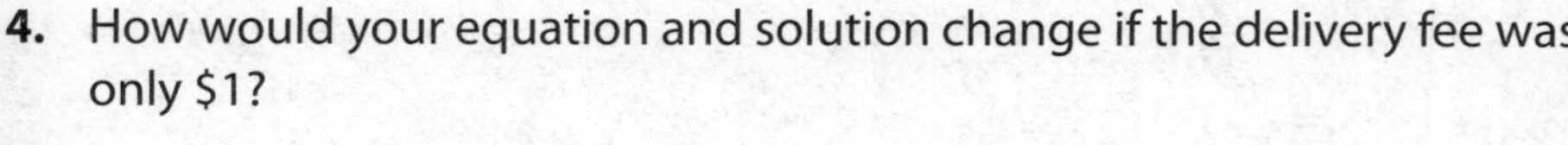

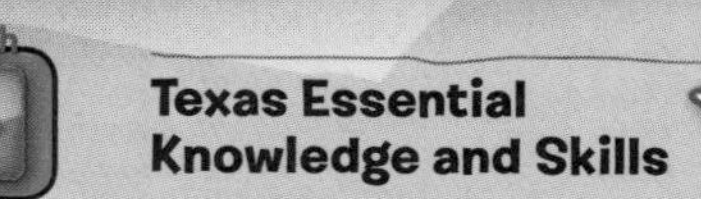

Texas Essential Knowledge and Skills

Targeted TEKS

7.11(A) Model and solve one-variable, two-step equations and inequalities. *Also addresses 7.10(A), 7.10(B), 7.10(C).*

Mathematical Processes

7.1(A), 7.1(B), 7.1(C), 7.1(D), 7.1(E)

Vocab

Vocabulary

two-step equation

Essential Question

WHAT does it mean to say two quantities are equal?

Which MP Mathematical Processes did you use? Shade the circle(s) that applies.

Ⓐ Apply Math to the Real World.
Ⓑ Use a Problem-Solving Model.
Ⓒ Select Tools and Techniques.
Ⓓ Use Multiple Representations.
Ⓔ Organize Ideas.
Ⓕ Analyze Relationships.
Ⓖ Justify Arguments.

Work Zone

Solve Two-Step Equations

Recall that the *order of operations* ensures that numerical expressions, such as $2 \cdot 5 + 3$, have only one value. To reverse the operations, undo them in reverse order.

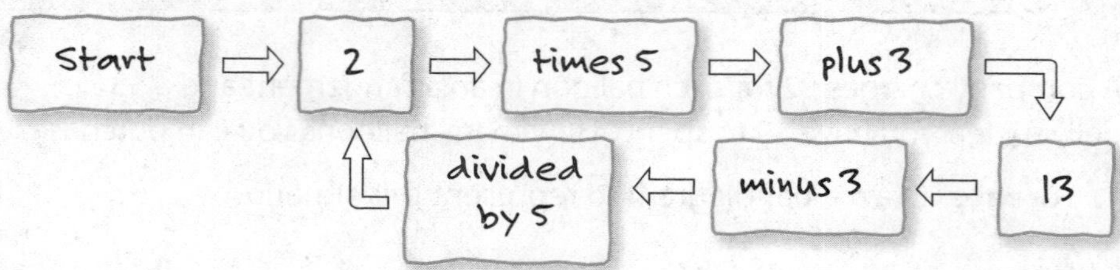

A **two-step equation**, such as $2x + 3 = 9$, has two different operations, multiplication and addition. To solve a two-step equation, undo the operations in reverse order of the order of operations.

This equation is written as $px + q = r$, where p, q, and r are rational numbers.

Step 1 Undo the addition or subtraction first.

Step 2 Undo the multiplication or division.

Examples

1. Solve $2x + 3 = 9$. Represent the solution on the number line. Check your solution.

$2x + 3 = 9$	Write the equation.
$-3 = -3$	Undo the addition first by subtracting 3 from each side.
$2x = 6$	
$\frac{2x}{2} = \frac{6}{2}$	Next, undo the multiplication by dividing each side by 2.
$x = 3$	Simplify.

The solution is 3.

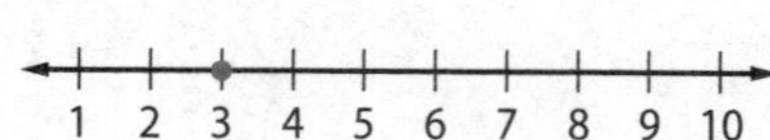

Check	$2x + 3 = 9$	Write the original equation.
	$2(3) + 3 \stackrel{?}{=} 9$	Replace x with 3.
	$9 = 9$ ✓	The sentence is true.

You can also use the number line to check your solution.

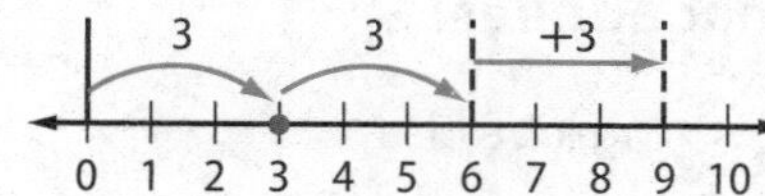

Starting at 0, 2 groups of 3 is equal to 6. Then add 3. The result is 9.

and Reflect

What are the two operations you would perform to solve $3x - 4 = 8$? Write your answer below.

2. Solve $-2y - 7 = 3$. Check your solution.

$-2y - 7 = 3$	Write the equation.
$\underline{\quad +7 = +7}$	Undo the subtraction first by adding 7 to each side.
$-2y = 10$	
$\frac{-2y}{-2} = \frac{10}{-2}$	Division Property of Equality
$y = -5$	Simplify.
The solution is -5.	Check the solution.

3. Solve $4 + \frac{1}{5}r = -1$. Check your solution.

$4 + \frac{1}{5}r = -1$	Write the equation.
$\underline{-4 \quad = -4}$	Undo the addition first by subtracting 4 from each side.
$\frac{1}{5}r = -5$	
$5 \cdot \frac{1}{5}r = 5 \cdot (-5)$	Multiplication Property of Equality
$r = -25$	Simplify.
The solution is -25.	Check the solution.

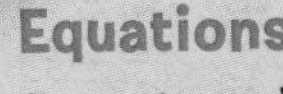

Equations
Remember, solutions of the new equation are also solutions of the original equation.

4. Write a real-world problem that can be represented by the equation $2x + 17 = 23$. Then solve the equation.

Bruno spent \$23 at the arcade. He purchased two drinks and spent \$17 on games. What was the cost of each drink?

$2x + 17 = 23$	Write the equation.
$\underline{-17 = -17}$	Undo addition first by subtracting 17 from each side.
$2x = 6$	
$\frac{2x}{2} = \frac{6}{2}$	Division Property of Equality
$x = 3$	Simplify.

The cost of each drink was \$3.

Got It? Do these problems to find out.

Solve each equation. Represent the solution on the number line. Check your solution.

a. $4x + 5 = 13$

b. $-5s + 8 = -2$

c. $-2 + \frac{2}{3}w = 10$

d. Write a real-world problem that can be represented by the equation $54 - 6d = 18$. Then solve the problem.

a. ________

b. ________

c. ________

d. ________

Example

5. Toya had her birthday party at the movies. It cost $27 for pizza and $8.50 per friend for the movie tickets. Write and solve an equation to determine the number of friends Toya had at her party if she spent $78.

Words	Cost of pizza	plus	Cost of 1 friend	times	number of friends	equals $78.
Variable	Let n represent the number of friends.					
Proportion	27	+	8.50	·	n	= 78

$27 + 8.50n = 78$ — Write the equation.

$-27 \quad = -27$ — Subtract 27 from each side.

$8.50n = 51$

$\frac{8.50n}{8.50} = \frac{51}{8.50}$ — Division Property of Equality

$n = 6$ — Simplify.

Toya had 6 friends at her party.

Solve Arithmetically

You can use a bar diagram to solve an equation arithmetically.

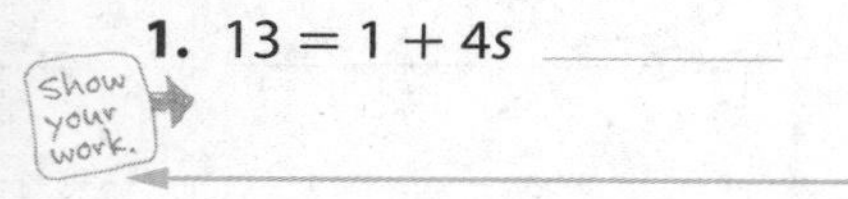

Subtract 27 from 78.
Then divide by 8.5.
$78 - 27 = 51; 51 \div 8.5 = 6$

Guided Practice

Solve each equation. Represent the solution on the number line. Check your solution. (Examples 1–3)

Show your work.

1. $13 = 1 + 4s$ ______

2. $-3y - 5 = 10$ ______

3. $-7 = 1 + \frac{2}{3}n$ ______

4. Syreeta wants to buy some CDs that each cost $14, and a DVD that costs $23. She has $65. Write and solve an equation to determine how many CDs she can buy. (Example 5)

   Equation: ______

   Solution: ______

5. **Building on the Essential Question** When solving an equation, explain why it is important to perform identical operations on each side of the equals sign.

Rate Yourself!

How well do you understand solving two-step equations? Circle the image that applies.

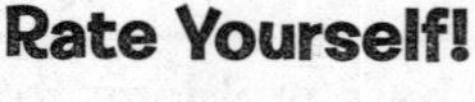

Clear | Somewhat Clear | Not So Clear

Find out online. Use the Self-Check Quiz.

FOLDABLES Time to update your Foldable!

Name ____________ My Homework ____________

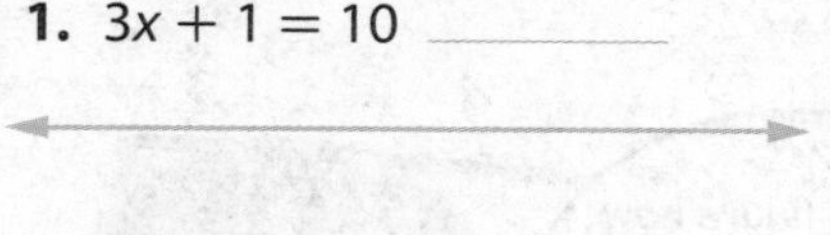

Independent Practice

7.10(A), 7.10(B), 7.10(C), 7.1(A) TEKS

Solve each equation. Represent the solution on the number line. Check your solution. (Examples 1–3)

1. $3x + 1 = 10$ ______

2. $-3 + 8n = -5$ ______

3. $4h - 6 = 22$ ______

Show your work.

4. $-8s + 1 = 33$ ______

5. $-4w - 4 = 8$ ______

6. $5 + \frac{1}{7}b = -2$ ______

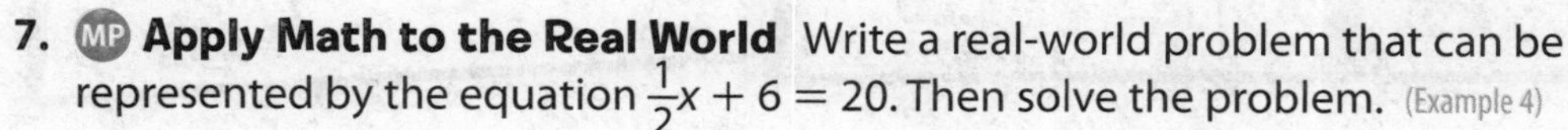

7. **Apply Math to the Real World** Write a real-world problem that can be represented by the equation $\frac{1}{2}x + 6 = 20$. Then solve the problem. (Example 4)

8. Cristiano is saving money to buy a bike that costs \$189. He has saved \$99 so far. He plans on saving \$10 each week. In how many weeks will he have enough money to buy the bike? Write and solve an equation to solve algebraically. (Example 5)

Solve each equation. Represent the solution on the number line. Check your solution.

9. $2r - 3.1 = 1.7$ ______

10. $4t + 3.5 = 12.5$ ______

11. $8m - 5.5 = 10.1$ ______

12. Temperature is usually measured on the Fahrenheit scale (°F) or the Celsius scale (°C). Use the formula $F = 1.8C + 32$ to convert from one scale to the other.

Alaska Record Low Temperatures (°F) by Month	
January	−80
April	−50
July	16
October	−48

a. Convert the temperature for Alaska's record low in July to Celsius. Round to the nearest degree.

b. Hawaii's record low temperature is −11°C. Determine the difference in degrees Fahrenheit between Hawaii's record low temperature and the record low temperature for Alaska in January.

13. MP **Apply Math to the Real World** Refer to the graphic novel frame below. Jamar figured that they will spend \$39 for popcorn. Each movie cost \$19. Write and solve an equation to determine how many movies they can purchase.

H.O.T. Problems Higher-Order Thinking

14. Analyze Refer to Exercise 12. Is there a temperature in the table at which the number of degrees Celsius is the same as the number of degrees Fahrenheit? If so, find it. If not, explain why not.

15. Create Suppose your school is selling magazine subscriptions. Each subscription costs \$20. The company pays the school half of the total sales in dollars. The school must also pay a one-time fee of \$18. Write and solve an equation to determine the fewest number of subscriptions that can be sold to earn a profit of \$200.

16. Create Write a real-world problem that can be represented by the equation $\frac{(12 + 14) \times h}{2} = 52$. Then solve the problem. (Example 4)

Name ____________________

Multi-Step Problem Solving

17. The graph shows the amount of money customers are charged to rent a moon bounce for an event. Write an equation to represent the total cost. Then use it to determine the cost for renting the moon bounce for 8.5 hours. EE N MP

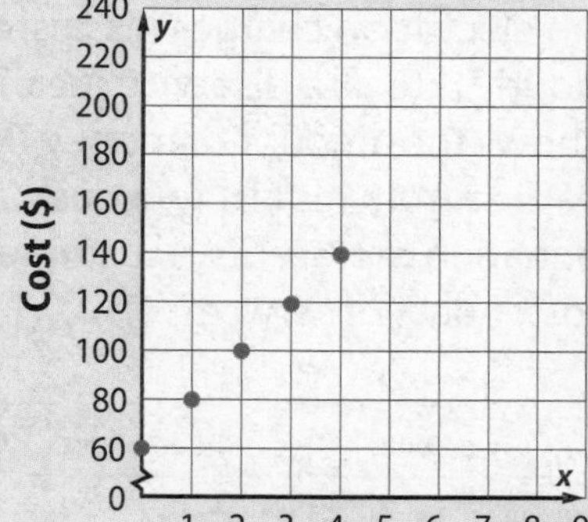

Ⓐ $200

Ⓑ $220

Ⓒ $230

Ⓓ $240

Use a problem-solving model to solve this problem.

1 Analyze

Read the problem. Circle the information you know.
Underline what the problem is asking you to find.

2 Plan

What will you need to do to solve the problem? Write your plan in steps.

Step 1 Determine the cost per ______ to rent the moon bounce.

Step 2 Determine the ______________ for 8.5 hours.

Read to Succeed! The cost for 0 hours is $60. This must mean there is a rental fee plus an hourly rate to rent the moon bounce.

3 Solve

Use your plan to solve the problem. Show your steps.

There is a ________ rental fee and the rate of change is _______.

$\_\_\_\_ h + 60 = t$ Let h represent hours and t represent total cost.

$\_\_\_\_ (8.5) + 60 = t$ Replace h with 8.5.

$\_\_\_\_\_\_ = t$

The cost for renting the moon bounce for 8.5 hours is _______.

The correct answer is _____. Fill in that answer choice.

4 Justify and Evaluate

How do you know your solution is accurate?

____

____

____

EE = Expressions, Equations, and Relationships N = Number and Operations MP = Mathematical Processes

More Multi-Step Problem Solving

Use a problem-solving model to solve each problem.

18. An electrician charges his customers an hourly rate plus a service fee of \$30. The table shows the amount of money the electrician earned from his last four customers. What equation represents a customer's charge, C, for x hours of service? EE P MP

Customer	Hours	Charge (\$)
Smith	3	94.50
Jones	2	73.00
Travers	6	159.00
Johnson	7	180.50

Ⓐ $C = 30x + 21.50$

Ⓑ $C = 21.50x + 30$

Ⓒ $C = 25.50x + 30$

Ⓓ $C = 30x + 25.50$

19. Valerie works at a local amusement park. She earns \$9.80 per hour. She is also paid \$7.00 for meals and \$3.00 for transportation each day. Last Friday, Valerie earned \$88.40. Write and solve an equation to determine how many hours Valerie worked on Friday. EE N MP

20. Write and solve an equation to determine the measures of the angles in the triangle below.

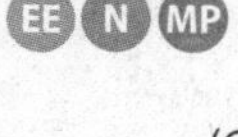

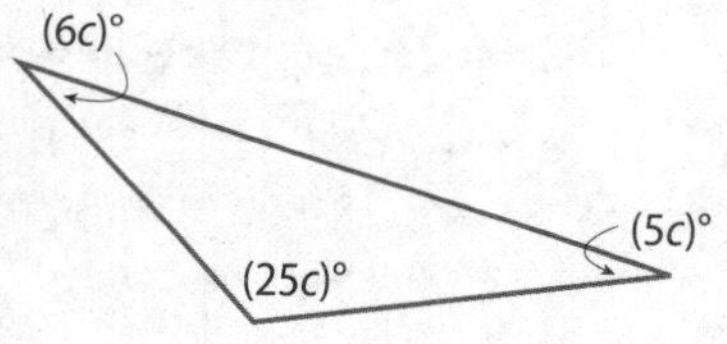

21. A seventh grade class is playing a game of *Guess My Rule*. As a student makes a guess, the teacher tells what number the rule gives back. Is it possible for a student to guess 10 with the teacher response being 3? Write a two-step equation that describes the rule to justify your answer. N EE MP

Student Guess (x)	Teacher Response (y)
2	−1
5	8
0	−7
6	11

EE = Expressions, Equations, and Relationships N = Number and Operations P = Proportionality MP = Mathematical Processes

Yard Work

Mike earned extra money by doing yard work for his neighbor. Then he spent \$5.50 at the convenience store and four times that amount at the bookstore. Now he has \$7.75 left.

How much money did Mike have before he went to the convenience store and the bookstore?

Mathematical Process
7.1(B) Use a problem-solving model that incorporates analyzing given information, formulating a plan or strategy, determining a solution, justifying the solution, and evaluating the problem-solving process and the reasonableness of the solution.

Targeted TEKS Preparation for 7.10(A)

Analyze *What are the facts?*

You know Mike has \$7.75 left. You need to determine the amount before his purchases.

Plan *Choose a problem-solving strategy.*

I will use the ________ strategy.

Solve *How can you apply the strategy?*

He has \$7.75 left.

Undo the four times \$5.50 spent at the bookstore.

Since \$5.50 × 4 is \$22, add \$7.75 and \$22.

\$7.75 + \$22.00 = \$ ☐

Undo the \$5.50 spent at the convenience store.

Add.

\$5.50 + ☐ = ☐

So, Mike's starting amount was ☐

Justify and Evaluate *How do you know your solution is accurate?*

____

____

____

Money

Marisa spent \$7.50 on a movie ticket. Then she spent \$4.50 on popcorn and one half of what was left on a drink. She had \$1.50 remaining.

How much did she have initially if she borrowed \$8 from her brother?

1 Analyze

Read the problem. Circle the information you know. Underline what the problem is asking you to find.

2 Plan

Choose a problem-solving strategy.

I will use the ______________ strategy.

3 Solve

How can you apply the strategy?

4 Justify and Evaluate

How do you know your solution is accurate?

____

____

____

____

Multi-Step Problem Solving

Work with a small group to solve the following problems. Show your work on a separate piece of paper.

1. Waterfalls

Angel Falls in Venezuela is 3,212 feet high. It is 29 yards higher than 2.5 times the architectural height of the Empire State Building.

Determine the architectural height, in feet, of the Empire State Building.

2. Number Theory

Travis works at Fantasy in Flight Factory. He checks all the kites before they are packaged. Travis discovered that for every 28 kites that passed inspection, there were 7 kites that did not pass: 4 kites did not have tails, and 3 kites had the wrong colors.

Of the 476 kites Travis examined, how many did not have tails and how many had the wrong colors?

3. Schedules

Timothy's morning schedule is shown.

At what time does Timothy wake up if he arrives at school at 7:35 A.M.?

Timothy's Schedules	
Activity	**Time**
Wake up	
Get ready for school — $\frac{3}{4}$ h	
Walk to School — $\frac{5}{12}$ h	7:35 A.M

4. Money

Antonio has saved $28 in cash to spend at the arcade.

If he has 5 bills, how many of each kind of bill does he have?

TEKS Mid-Chapter Check

Vocabulary Check

1. Define *equation*. Give an example of two equivalent equations.
TEKS 7.10(A), 7.1(D)

Key Concept Check

2. Complete the graphic organizer about equations below. TEKS 7.5(C), 7.1(E)

Show your work.

Equation example

Number line model

Write and solve your own real-world problem using $3x + 10 = 22$.

3. Cameron has 11 adult Fantail goldfish. This is 7 fewer Fantail goldfish than twice his friend Julia has. Write and solve an equation to determine the number of Fantail goldfish g that Julia has. (Lesson 1) TEKS 7.10(A), 7.1(D)

Equation: ________ Solution: ________

Multi-Step Problem Solving

4. The pentagon shown is a regular pentagon, so each side has the same length. The perimeter of the pentagon is 22.5 centimeters. What is the value of x? N EE MP

Ⓐ 4.2 cm Ⓒ 6.5 cm
Ⓑ 6 cm Ⓓ 7.2 cm

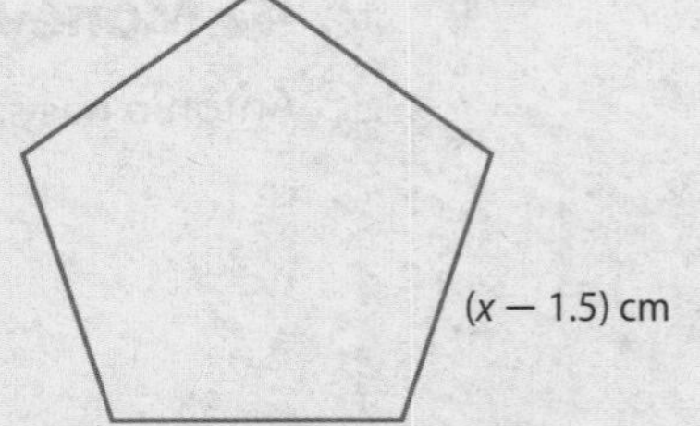

N = Number and Operations EE = Expressions, Equations, and Relationships MP = Mathematical Processes

Hands-On Lab 5-a

Model Two-Step Equations using the Distributive Property

INQUIRY How can I select tools to differentiate between equations written in $px + q = r$ and $p(x + q) = r$ forms?

Texas Essential Knowledge and Skills TEKS

Targeted TEKS
7.11(A) Model and solve one-variable, two-step equations and inequalities. *Also addresses 7.10(A), 7.10(C).*

Mathematical Processes
7.1(C), 7.1(D), 7.1(E), 7.1(F)

Mark has two summer jobs. He babysits and helps with the gardening. He works at each job three days a week and earns a total of $240. The table shows his earnings each day. How much does he earn each day babysitting?

Job	Daily Earnings ($)
Babysitting	x
Gardening	30

What do you know? ____________________

What do you need to determine? ____________________

Hands-On Activity 1

Step 1 Draw a bar diagram that represents the situation.

$\$x + \$30$	$\$x + \$30$	$\$x + \$30$
earnings each day	earnings each day	earnings each day

Step 2 Write an equation that is modeled by the bar diagram.

$3(\$x + \$30) =$ ☐

From the diagram, you can see that one third of Mark's total earnings is equal to $\$x + \$30$. So, $\$x + \$30 = \frac{\$240}{3}$ or ☐.

Mark earns ☐ − $30, or ☐ each day babysitting.

Vijay and his brother bought two hamburgers and two lemonades. The hamburgers cost $6 each. They spent a total of $16. How much did each lemonade cost?

Hands-On Activity 2

Use algebra tiles to model the situation described above.

Step 1 Model $2(x + 6) = 16$ using algebra tiles. Use ☐ groups of $(x + 6)$ tiles.

$2(x + 6) \quad = \quad 16$

Step 2 Divide the tiles into ☐ equal groups on each side of the mat.

Remove ☐ group from each side.

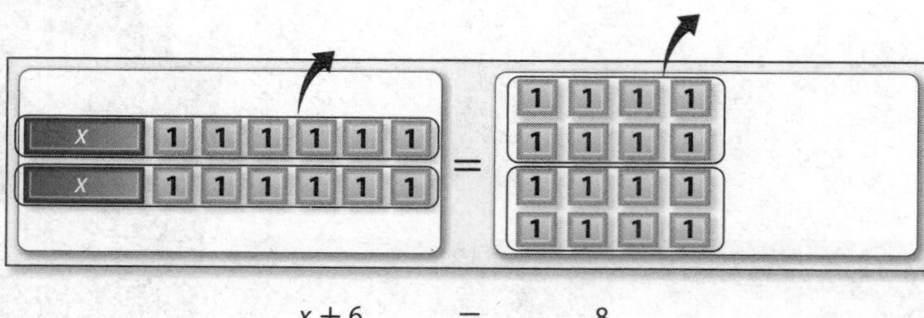

$x + 6 \quad = \quad 8$

Step 3 Remove the same number of 1-tiles from each side.

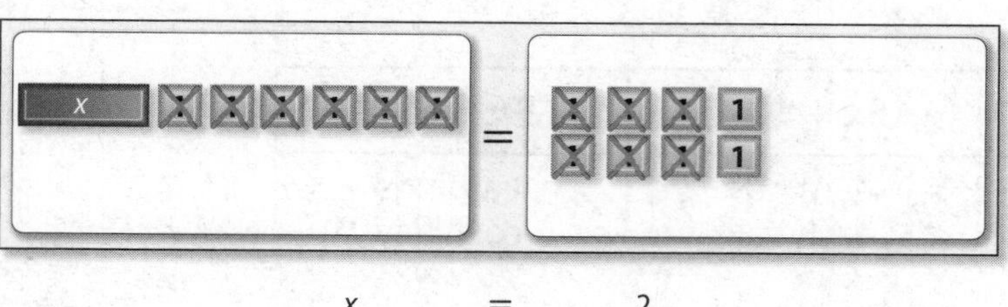

$x \quad = \quad 2$

So, $x =$ ☐. Each lemonade costs ☐.

Investigate

Work with a partner to model and solve each equation. Use a bar diagram for Exercises 1 and 2. Use algebra tiles for Exercises 3–6.

1. $3(x + 5) = 21$ $x =$ ______

2. $2(x - 3) = 10$ $x =$ ______

3. $4(x + 1) = 8$ $x =$ ______

4. $3(x + 2) = -12$ $x =$ ______

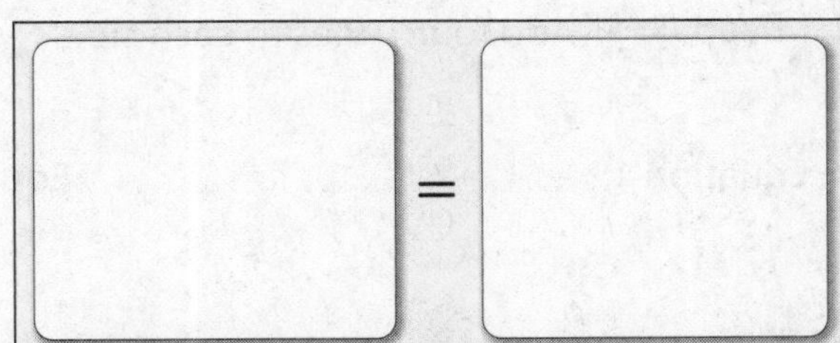

5. $2(x - 1) = 6$ $x =$ ______

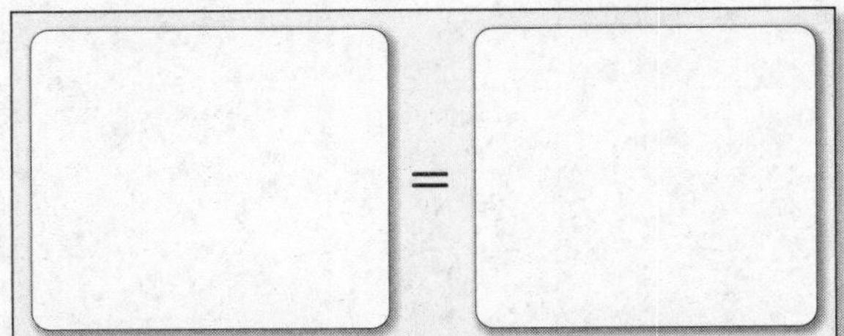

6. $3(x - 4) = -3$ $x =$ ______

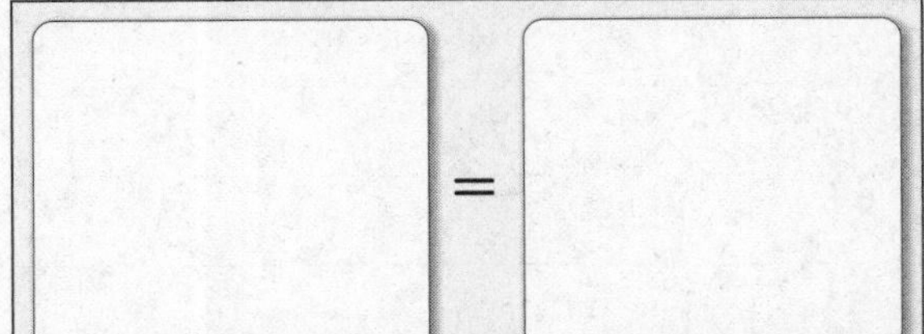

Analyze and Reflect

Work with a partner to write and solve an equation that represents each problem. Use a model if necessary.

7. Refer to Hands-On Activity 1. If Mark worked four days a week and made \$360, how much did he earn babysitting each day?

8. Refer to Hands-On Activity 2. If Vijay and his brother spent a total of \$15, how much did each lemonade cost?

9. MP **Analyze Relationships** After modeling an equation using algebra tiles, Angelina used the steps shown below to solve the equation. Write two different equations in $p(x + q) = r$ form that Angelina could have solved.

Step 1 Divide the tiles into three equal groups on both sides of the mat.

Step 2 Remove two groups from each side.

Step 3 Add four 1-tiles to each side.

Equation 1: ______________ Equation 2: ______________

Create

10. MP **Apply Math to the Real World** Write a real-world problem that can be represented by the equation $4(x + 15) = 140$. Then solve the problem.

11. INQUIRY HOW can I select tools to differentiate between equations written in $px + q = r$ and $p(x + q) = r$ forms?

Lesson 5

Solve Two-Step Equations using the Distributive Property

Launch the Lesson: Real World

Watch

Texas Essential Knowledge and Skills

Targeted TEKS

7.11(A) Model and solve one-variable, two-step equations and inequalities. *Also addresses 7.10(A), 7.10(B), 7.10(C).*

Mathematical Processes

7.1(A), 7.1(B), 7.1(C), 7.1(D), 7.1(E)

Essential Question

WHAT does it mean to say two quantities are equal?

A new exhibit about dinosaurs is being constructed. The exhibit is a rectangle that is 36 feet long. It has a perimeter of 114 feet. Write an equation that can be used to determine the width of the museum exhibit.

Step 1 Draw a diagram to help visualize the exhibit.

Label the length and width. Let w represent the width.

Step 2 Write an expression that represents the sum of the length and width of the exhibit. ________

Step 3 Write an expression that represents twice the sum of the length and width. ________

Step 4 Write an equation that represents the perimeter of the exhibit. ________

Which MP Mathematical Processes did you use? Shade the circle(s) that applies.

Ⓐ Apply Math to the Real World.
Ⓑ Use a Problem-Solving Model.
Ⓒ Select Tools and Techniques.
Ⓓ Use Multiple Representations.
Ⓔ Organize Ideas.
Ⓕ Analyze Relationships.
Ⓖ Justify Arguments.

Work Zone

Solve Two-Step Equations

An equation like $2(w + 36) = 114$ is in the form $p(x + q) = r$. It contains two factors, p and $(x + q)$, and is considered a two-step equation. Solve these equations using the properties of equality.

Examples

Tutor

1. Solve $3(x + 5) = 45$.

Method 1 **Solve using a model.**

Draw a bar diagram. From the diagram, you can see that $x + 5 = 45 \div 3$ or 15. So, $x = 15 - 5$ or 10.

Method 2 **Solve algebraically.**

$3(x + 5) = 45$	Write the equation.
$\frac{3(x + 5)}{3} = \frac{45}{3}$	Division Property of Equality
$x + 5 = 15$	Simplify.
$-5 = -5$	Subtraction Property of Equality
$x = 10$	Simplify. Check the solution.

Check Your Work

Remember to plug your solution back into the original equation to see if it makes a true statement.

2. Solve $5(n - 2) = -30$. Represent the solution on a number line.

$5(n - 2) = -30$	Write the equation.
$\frac{5(n - 2)}{5} = \frac{-30}{5}$	Division Property of Equality
$n - 2 = -6$	Simplify.
$+2 = +2$	Addition Property of Equality
$n = -4$	Simplify. Check the solution.

Use a number line to represent the solution to the equation.

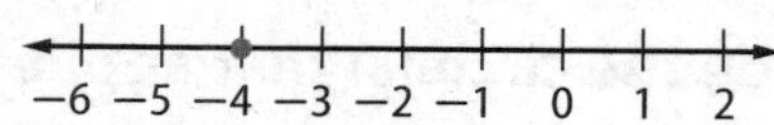

Show your work.

a. ________

b. ________

c. ________

Got It? Do these problems to find out.

a. $2(x + 4) = 20$ **b.** $3(b - 6) = 12$ **c.** $-7(6 + d) = 49$

Equations with Rational Coefficients

Sometimes the factor p, in $p(x + q)$, will be a fraction or decimal.

Examples

3. Solve $\frac{2}{3}(n + 6) = 10$. Check your solution.

$\frac{2}{3}(n + 6) = 10$	Write the equation.
$\frac{3}{2} \cdot \frac{2}{3}(n + 6) = \frac{3}{2} \cdot 10$	Multiplication Property of Equality
$(n + 6) = \frac{3}{\cancel{2}_1} \cdot \left(\frac{\cancel{10}^5}{1}\right)$	$\frac{2}{3} \cdot \frac{3}{2} = 1$; write 10 as $\frac{10}{1}$.
$n + 6 = 15$	Simplify.
$-6 = -6$	Subtraction Property of Equality
$n = 9$	Simplify.
Check $\frac{2}{3}(n + 6) = 10$	Write the original equation.
$\frac{2}{3}(9 + 6) \stackrel{?}{=} 10$	Replace n with 9. Is this sentence true?
$10 = 10$ ✓	The sentence is true.

4. Solve $0.2(c - 3) = -10$. Represent the solution on a number line. Check your solution.

$0.2(c - 3) = -10$	Write the equation.
$\frac{0.2(c - 3)}{0.2} = -\frac{10}{0.2}$	Division Property of Equality
$c - 3 = -50$	Simplify.
$+3 = +3$	Addition Property of Equality
$c = -47$	Simplify.

Use a number line to represent the solution to the equation.

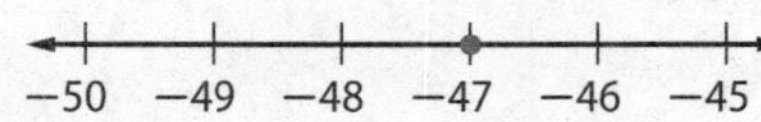

Check $0.2(c - 3) = -10$	Write the original equation.
$0.2(-47 - 3) \stackrel{?}{=} -10$	Replace c with -47. Is this sentence true?
$-10 = -10$ ✓	The sentence is true.

Reciprocals
The product of a number and its reciprocal is 1.

d. ____________

e. ____________

f. ____________

Got It? Do these problems to find out.

d. $\frac{1}{4}(d - 3) = -15$ **e.** $0.75(6 + d) = 12$ **f.** $(t + 3)\frac{5}{9} = 40$

Example

5. Jamal and two cousins received the same amount of money to go to a movie. Each boy spent \$15. Afterward, the boys had \$30 altogether. Write and solve an equation to determine the amount of money each boy received.

Let m represent the amount of money each boy received.

$3(m - 15) = 30$	Write the equation.
$\frac{3(m - 15)}{3} = \frac{30}{3}$	Division Property of Equality
$m - 15 = 10$	Simplify.
$+15 = +15$	Addition Property of Equality
$m = 25$	Simplify.

So, each boy received \$25.

STOP and Reflect

Solve the problem in Example 5 by using a bar diagram. How do the solutions compare? Write your answer below.

Guided Practice

Solve each equation. Represent the solution on the number line. Check your solution. (Examples 1–4)

1. $2(p + 7) = 18$

2. $(4 + g)(-11) = 121$

3. Mr. Singh had three sheets of stickers. He gave 20 stickers from each sheet to his students and has 12 total stickers left. Write and solve an equation to determine how many stickers were originally on each sheet. (Example 5)

Equation: ________

Solution: ________

4. **Building on the Essential Question** What is the difference between $px + q = r$ and $p(x + q) = r$?

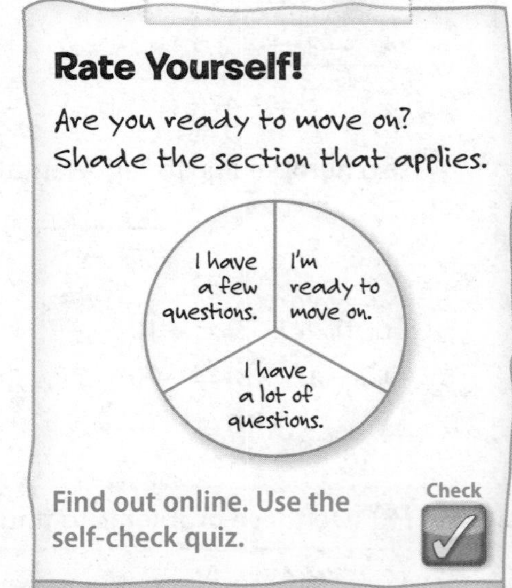

Name ______ My Homework ______

Independent Practice

7.10(A), 7.10(B), 7.1(D) TEKS

Solve each equation. Represent the solution on the number line. Check your solution. (Examples 1–4)

1. $8(s + 3) = 72$

2. $-7(z - 6) = -70$

3. $(t + 8)(-2) = 12$

4. $\frac{8}{11}(n - 10) = 64$

5. $-0.6(r + 0.2) = 1.8$

6. $\left(w - \frac{4}{9}\right)\left(-\frac{2}{3}\right) = -\frac{4}{5}$

7. The length of each side of an equilateral triangle is increased by 5 inches, so the perimeter is now 60 inches. Write and solve an equation to determine the original length of each side of the equilateral triangle. (Example 5)

Equation: ______ Solution: ______

8. MP **Use Multiple Representations** Miguel and three of his friends went to the movies. They originally had a total of $40. Each boy had the same amount of money and spent $7.50 on a ticket. How much money did each boy have left after buying his ticket?

a. Model Draw a bar diagram that represents the situation.

b. Algebra Write and solve an equation modeled by the diagram.

______

c. Words Explain how you solved your equation.

______

9. Mrs. Sorenstam bought one ruler, one compass, and one mechanical pencil at the prices shown in the table for each of her 12 students.

Item	Price ($)
compass	1.49
mechanical pencil	0.59
ruler	0.49

a. Suppose Mrs. Sorenstam had 36 cents left after buying the school supplies. Write an equation to determine the amount of money Mrs. Sorenstam initially had to spend on each student.

b. Describe a two-step process you could use to solve your equation. Then solve the equation.

10. **Find the Error** Marisol is solving the equation $6(x + 3) = 21$. Find her mistake and correct it.

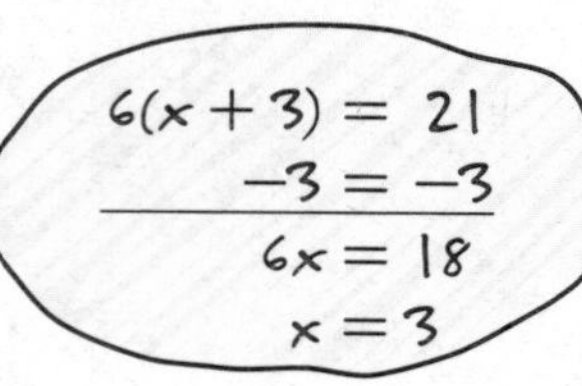

H.O.T. Problems Higher-Order Thinking

11. **Analyze** Solve $p(x + q) = r$ for x.

12. **Create** Use the bar diagram to solve the following problems.

12		
x−8	**x−8**	**x−8**

a. **Algebra** Use the bar diagram to write an equation.

b. **Words** Write a real-world problem that can be represented by the bar diagram.

13. **Analyze** Suppose for some value of k the solution of the equation $3.1(x - k) = 0$ is $x = 7$. What must be true about k? Justify your conclusion.

Name ______________________________

Multi-Step Problem Solving

14. Pierre uses two rectangular pieces of paper as bookmarks. The width of the larger bookmark is equal to the length of the smaller bookmark. The length of the larger bookmark is equal to half the perimeter of the smaller bookmark which is 14 centimeters. What is the perimeter of the larger bookmark? EE N MP

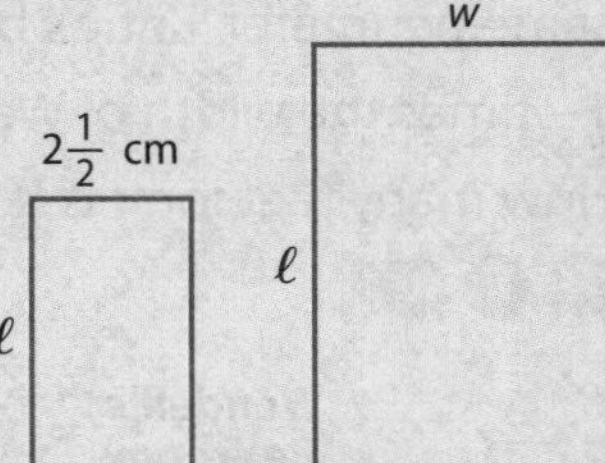

Ⓐ 32 cm
Ⓑ 30 cm
Ⓒ 26 cm
Ⓓ 23 cm

Use a problem-solving model to solve this problem.

1 Analyze

Read the problem. Circle the information you know.
Underline what the problem is asking you to find.

2 Plan

What will you need to do to solve the problem? Write your plan in steps.

Step 1 Use the perimeter to determine the ______ of the smaller bookmark.

Step 2 Determine the ______________ of the larger bookmark.

3 Solve

Use your plan to solve the problem. Show your steps.

Determine the length of the smaller bookmark.

$14 = 2\left(2\frac{1}{2}\right) + 2(\ell)$ $\ell =$ ________

Determine the perimeter of the larger bookmark. The length is 7 centimeters, half of 14 centimeters.

$P = 2($____$) + 2(7)$ $P =$ ________

The perimeter of the larger bookmark is _____ centimeters.

So, the correct answer is _____. Fill in that answer choice.

Read to Succeed!
Use the width of the smaller bookmark to solve the equation for the larger bookmark to determine the perimeter.

4 Justify and Evaluate

How do you know your solution is accurate?

____

____

____

EE = Expressions, Equations, and Relationships N = Number and Operations MP = Mathematical Processes

More Multi-Step Problem Solving

Use a problem-solving model to solve each problem.

15. Wendell and Katie have bedrooms with the same perimeter. Katie's bedroom has a width $1\frac{1}{3}$ times the width of Wendell's bedroom. How many feet long is Katie's bedroom?

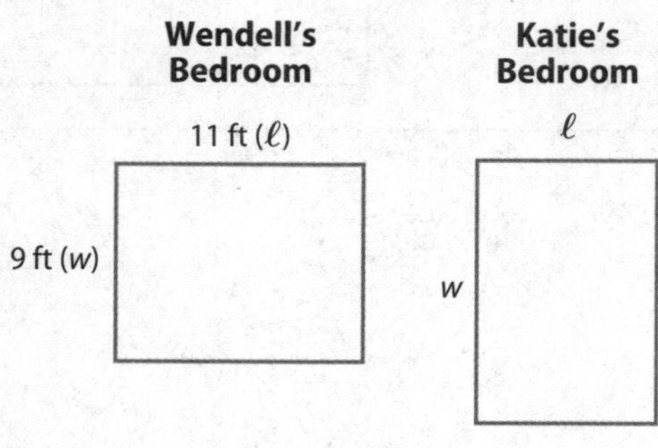

Ⓐ 8 ft
Ⓑ 10 ft
Ⓒ 12 ft
Ⓓ 14 ft

16. Diego and two friends are going skating and will choose between two skating rinks. Skate-O-Rama charges \$5 admission plus a skate rental fee, which comes to \$20.25 for Diego and his friends. Ice Stars charges one dollar less for admission but twice the skate rental fee. If all three friends plan to rent skates, how much more will they spend, in dollars, at Ice Stars than at Skate-O-Rama? EE N MP

17. Ella solved the equation $0.5(3 + x) = 2.5$ and then the equation $0.25(4 + y) = x$. If the value of x is the same for both equations, what is the value of y? EE N MP

18. Write and solve a real-world problem based on the equation $5(1\frac{3}{8} + x) = 8\frac{3}{4}$. EE N MP

EE = Expressions, Equations, and Relationships N = Number and Operations MP = Mathematical Processes

Lesson 6

Solve One-Step Inequalities

Launch the Lesson: Real World

Watch

An astronaut in a space suit weighs about 300 pounds on Earth, but only 50 pounds on the Moon. Is the weight of one astronaut greater on the Moon or on Earth?

weight on Earth   weight on Moon
300 lb $>$ 50 lb

1. If the astronaut and space suit each weighed half as much, would the inequality still be true?

$$\frac{300}{2} > \frac{50}{2}$$ Divide each side by 2.

$\square > \square$

Is the inequality still true? Circle yes or no.

Yes   No

2. Is the weight of one astronaut greater on Pluto or Earth? Would the weight of 5 astronauts be greater on Pluto or on Earth? Explain by using an inequality.

Location	Weight of Astronaut (lb)
Earth	300
Moon	50
Pluto	67
Jupiter	796

3. Is the weight of one astronaut greater on Jupiter or on Earth? Would the weight of 5 astronauts be greater on Jupiter or on Earth? Explain by using an inequality.

Which MP Mathematical Processes did you use? Shade the circle(s) that applies.

Ⓐ Apply Math to the Real World.
Ⓑ Use a Problem-Solving Model.
Ⓒ Select Tools and Techniques.
Ⓓ Use Multiple Representations.
Ⓔ Organize Ideas.
Ⓕ Analyze Relationships.
Ⓖ Justify Arguments.

Texas Essential Knowledge and Skills

Targeted TEKS
Preparation for 7.10(A) Write one-variable, two-step equations and inequalities to represent constraints or conditions within problems.

Mathematical Processes
7.1(A), 7.1(B), 7.1(E), 7.1(F)

Vocab

Vocabulary
Subtraction Property of Inequality
Addition Property of Inequality
Division Property of Inequality
Multiplication Property of Inequality

Essential Question
WHAT does it mean to say two quantities are equal?

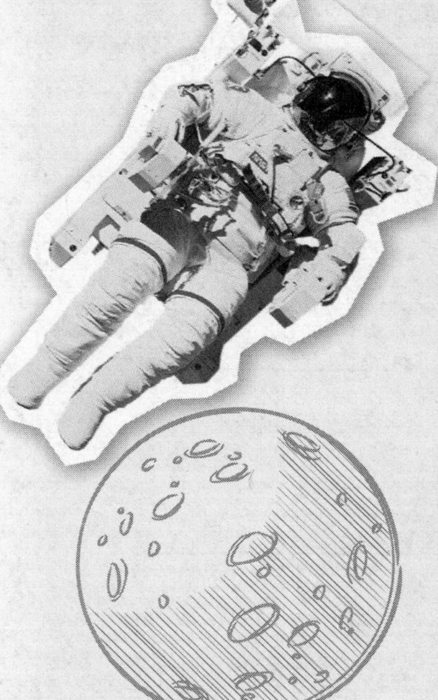

Key Concept

Solve Addition and Subtraction Inequalities

Work Zone

Words You can solve inequalities by using the **Addition Property of Inequalities** and the **Subtraction Property of Inequalities.** When you add or subtract the same number from each side of an inequality, the inequality remains true.

Examples

$$\begin{array}{rr} 2 < & 4 \\ +3 & +3 \\ \hline 5 < & 7 \end{array} \qquad \begin{array}{rr} 6 > & 3 \\ -4 & -4 \\ \hline 2 > & -1 \end{array}$$

Examples

Tutor

Solve each inequality. Represent the solution set on the number line provided.

1. $a + \frac{1}{2} < 2$

$a + \frac{1}{2} < 2$ Write the inequality

$-\frac{1}{2} \quad -\frac{1}{2}$ Subtract $\frac{1}{2}$ from each side.

$a < 1\frac{1}{2}$ Simplify.

The solution is $a < 1\frac{1}{2}$. Check your solution.

Represent the solution.

Place an open dot at $1\frac{1}{2}$. Draw a line and an arrow to the left.

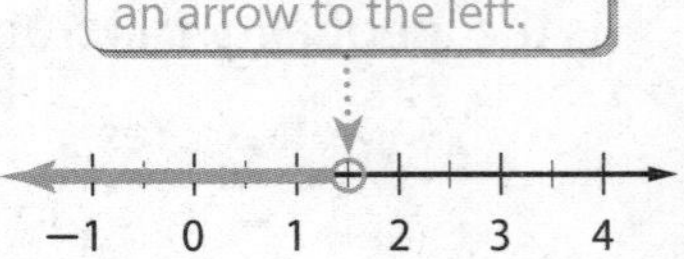

2. $-6 \geq n - 5$

$-6 \geq n - 5$ Write the inequality.

$+5 \quad +5$ Add 5 to each side.

$-1 \geq n$ Simplify.

The solution is $-1 \geq n$ or $n \leq -1$.

Represent the solution.

Place a closed dot at −1. Draw a line and arrow to the left.

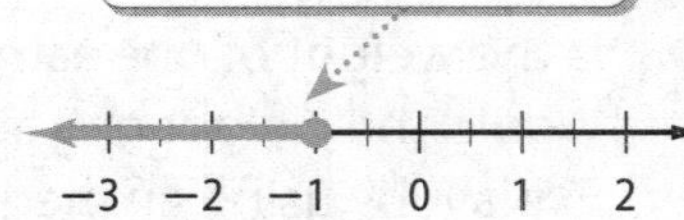

Open and Closed Dots

When graphing inequalities, an open dot is used when the value should not be included in the solution, as with > and < inequalities. A closed dot indicates the value is included in the solution, as with ≤ and ≥ inequalities.

Show your work.

Got It? Do these problems to find out.

a. $h + 4 > 4$

b. $x - 6 \leq 4$

a. ______

b. ______

Solve Multiplication and Division Inequalities

Key Concept

Words The **Multiplication Property of Inequality** and the **Division Property of Inequality** state that an inequality remains true when you multiply or divide each side of an inequality by a positive number. It also states that when you multiply or divide by a negative number, the inequality symbol must be reversed for the inequality to remain true.

Examples

$7 > 1$	$-4 < 16$	
$2(7) > 2(1)$	$\frac{-4}{-4} > \frac{16}{-4}$	Reverse the symbols.
$14 > 2$	$1 > -4$	

Examples

Tutor

Solve each inequality. Represent the solution set on the number line provided.

3. $-2g < 10$

$-2g < 10$ Write the inequality.

$\frac{-2g}{-2} > \frac{10}{-2}$ Divide each side by −2 and reverse the symbol.

$g > -5$ Simplify.

−7 −6 −5 −4 −3

4. $\frac{x}{3} \geq -4$

$\frac{x}{3} \geq -4$ Write the inequality.

$3\left(\frac{x}{3}\right) \geq 3(-4)$ Multiply each side by 3.

$x \geq -12$ Simplify.

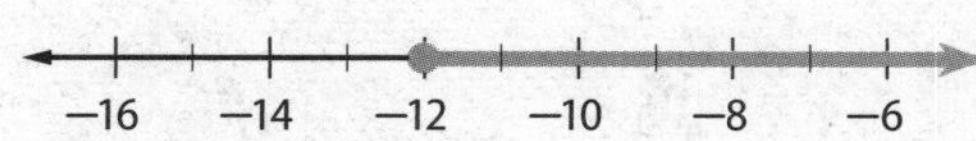

Negative in Inequalities

In Example 4, you do not reverse the inequality symbol even though the inequality contains a negative number. The number by which you are multiplying is positive, so the inequality symbol remains the same.

Got It? Do these problems to find out.

c. $\frac{k}{-2} < 9$

d. $5b \leq -5$

c. ____________

d. ____________

Example

5. Ling earns $8 per hour working at the zoo. Write and solve an inequality that can be used to determine how many hours she must work to earn at least $120. Interpret the solution.

Words	Amount earned per hour	times	number of hours	is at least	amount earned each week.
Variable	Let x represent the number of hours.				
Inequality	8	$\cdot$	x	$\geq$	120

$8x \geq 120$ Write the inequality.

$\frac{8x}{8} \geq \frac{120}{8}$ Divide each side by 8.

$x \geq 15$ Simplify.

So, Ling must work at least 15 hours.

Guided Practice

Solve each inequality. Represent the solution set on a number line. (Examples 1–4)

1. $6 + h \geq 12$ ______

2. $\frac{t}{-4} < -11$ ______

3. At a baseball game you can get a single hot dog for $2. You have $10 to spend. Write and solve an inequality to determine the number of hot dogs you can buy. Interpret the solution. (Example 5)

4. **Building on the Essential Question** Explain when you should not reverse the inequality symbol when solving an inequality.

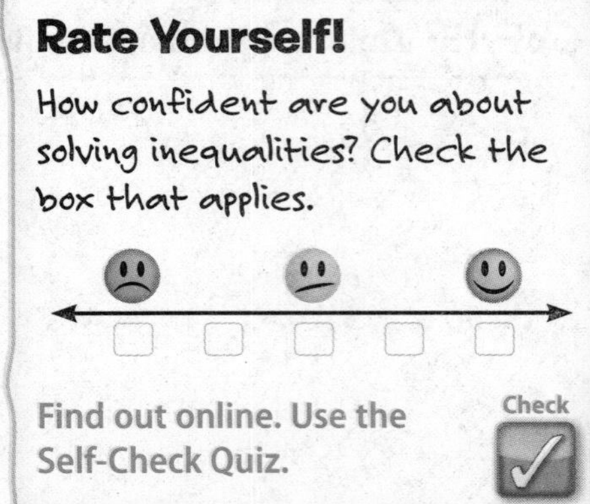

Name ______________________ My Homework ______________________

Independent Practice

Preparation for 7.10(A), 7.1(E) TEKS

Solve each inequality. Represent the solution set on a number line. (Examples 1–4)

1. $m + 5 \geq -1$ ________

2. $-11 > t + 7$ ________

3. $-4x \leq -36$ ________

4. $20 < 5t$ ________

5. $\frac{s}{6} < 16$ ________

6. $\frac{x}{-4} \geq 8$ ________

7. The high school soccer team can have no more than 26 players. Write and solve an inequality to determine how many more players can make the team if the coach has already chosen 17 players. Then interpret the solution. (Example 5)

Inequality: ________ Solution: ________

Interpretation: ________________________

8. At a softball game you can get a bratwurst for \$4.50. You have \$18 to spend. Write and solve an inequality to determine the number of bratwursts you can buy. Then interpret the solution. (Example 5)

Inequality: ________ Solution: ________

Interpretation: ________________________

9. MP **Apply Math to the Real World** Write a real-world problem that can be represented by the inequality $4x > 100$. Then solve the problem and interpret the solution.

10. MP **Analyze Relationships** Cross out the inequality that does not belong in the organizer shown at the right. Then explain your reasoning.

$-2x > 12$	$-2 < x + 4$
$\frac{x}{2} < -3$	$-7 > x - 1$

Write an inequality for each sentence. Then solve the inequality.

11. Sixteen is less than eight times a number.

Inequality: ____________ Solution: ____________

12. The product of a number and five is at the most 30.

Inequality: ____________ Solution: ____________

H.O.T. Problems Higher-Order Thinking

13. Analyze Compare and contrast the solution(s) of $a - 3 = 15$ and $a - 3 \geq 15$.

14. Create Write two different inequalities that have the solution $y > 6$. One inequality should be solved using multiplication properties, and the other should be solved using division properties.

15. Analyze Solve $x + b > c$ for x.

16. Create Write a real-world problem involving an addition inequality for the solution set represented at the right. Then solve the problem and interpret the solution.

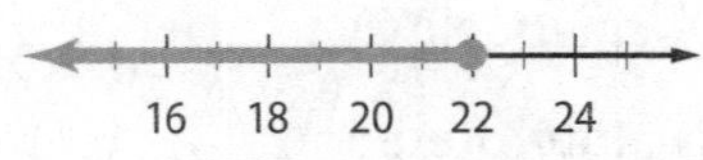

17. Create The inequalities $3x > 2$ and $9x > 6$ are equivalent inequalities. Write another inequality that is equivalent to $3x > 2$ and $9x > 6$.

Name ___

Multi-Step Problem Solving

18. To get the grade she wants in her English class, Elspeth needs an average of 85% from her quiz scores. Each quiz is worth 20 points. The scores of her first four quizzes are shown in the table. There will be one more quiz. What is the minimum score she can receive to earn at least an 85% grade? EE N MP

Quiz	Score
1	18
2	16
3	19
4	14

Ⓐ at least 15 points
Ⓑ at least 16 points
Ⓒ at least 17 points
Ⓓ at least 18 points

Use a problem-solving model to solve this problem.

1 Analyze

Read the problem. Circle the information you know.
Underline what the problem is asking you to find.

2 Plan

What will you need to do to solve the problem? Write your plan in steps.

Step 1 Determine the ___ she earned on the first four quizzes.

Step 2 Write an inequality to determine what she must score on the ___.

Read to Succeed!
To determine her score as a percent, add the score she earns divided by the total points possible. Then express the decimal as a percent.

3 Solve

Use your plan to solve the problem. Show your steps.

$18 + 16 + 19 + 14 =$ ___ Add the scores for quizzes 1–4.

Write and solve an inequality, where x is the score she needs to earn.

$\frac{67 + x}{100} \geq 0.85$ $x \geq$ ___

Elspeth needs to earn at least ___ points on her fifth quiz.

So, the correct answer is ___. Fill in that answer choice.

4 Justify and Evaluate

How do you know your solution is accurate?

___

___

___

EE = Expressions, Equations, and Relationships N = Number and Operations MP = Mathematical Processes

More Multi-Step Problem Solving

Use a problem-solving model to solve each problem.

19. Phong and Janice are collecting action cards for a strategy game. They want to collect more than 30 new action cards. Action cards come in packs of 5. What is the least number of packs of action cards they will need to buy to have at least 30 new action cards?

Ⓐ at least 6

Ⓑ at least 5

Ⓒ at least 4

Ⓓ at least 3

20. Jihan plans to spend no more than $50 at the grocery store and $25 at the hardware store. His shopping lists include milk that costs $3.50 and cereal that costs $2.95 at the grocery store, and duct tape that costs $3.95 and a hammer that costs $4.75 at the hardware store. What is the difference between the maximum amounts, in dollars, he has left to spend at the two stores? EE N MP

21. Edward is painting the rectangle, which has a rectangular hole in the middle. The rectangular hole in the center is less than 40% of the area of the larger rectangle. What is the greatest possible length of the rectangular hole? EE N P MP

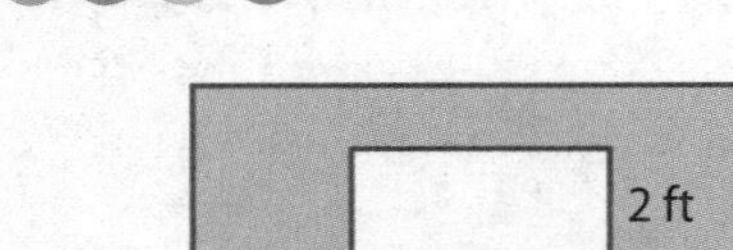

22. Write and solve a real-world problem involving the addition inequality below. Then, graph it on a number line. EE N MP

$5 + x \leq 12$

EE = Expressions, Equations, and Relationships N = Number and Operations P = Proportionality MP = Mathematical Processes

Hands-On Lab 7-a

Model and Solve Two-Step Inequalities

INQUIRY **HOW can I select tools to model and solve two-step inequalities?**

Texas Essential Knowledge and Skills

Targeted TEKS

7.11(A) Model and solve one-variable, two-step equations and inequalities. *Also addresses 7.10(A), 7.10(C).*

Mathematical Processes

7.1(C), 7.1(D), 7.1(E), 7.1(F), 7.1(G)

Natalia can spend no more than \$7 to buy some school supplies. A notebook costs \$3, and each pen costs \$2. If she wants to buy one notebook, how many pens can she buy?

Hands-On Activity 1

The real-world situation described above can be represented by the inequality $2x + 3 \leq 7$. Let x represent the number of pens Natalia can buy.

$$\underline{2x} + \underline{3} \leq \underline{7}$$

Each pen costs \$2.

The notebook costs \$3.

The maximum money she can spend is \$7.

You can use a balance to model and solve the inequality $2x + 3 \leq 7$.

Step 1 On one side of a balance, place two paper bags and ☐ cubes to represent $2x + 3$.

Step 2 On the other side of a balance, place ☐ cubes to represent 7.

Add one cube to each bag one at a time. Then complete the table.

Number of Pens, x	Cost, $\$2x + \$3$	Less than or equal to \$7?
1		
2		
3		
4		

So, Natalia can buy up to ☐ pens.

Hands-On Activity 2

An airline charges for checked luggage that weighs more than 50 pounds. Mia's suitcase currently weighs 36 pounds and she still needs to pack two pairs of shoes. Determine the maximum amount each pair of shoes can weigh so Mia will not be charged a fee.

Step 1 In the bar diagram, write the maximum weight Mia's luggage can be without a fee. Label the weight of Mia's luggage without her shoes.

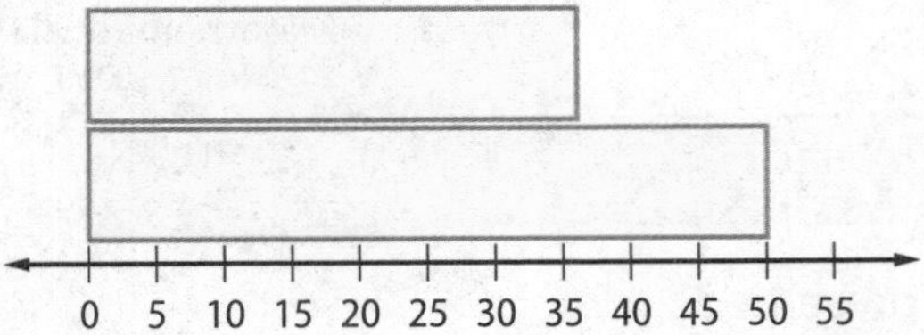

Step 2 In the bar diagram, write a $2x$ beside the bar that represents the weight of Mia's luggage.

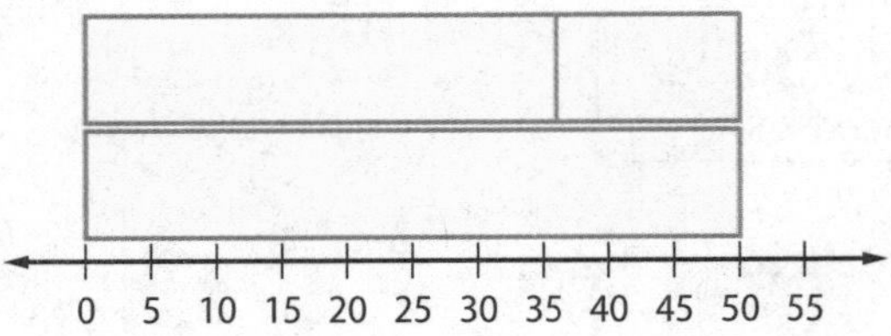

Fill in the boxes below with a description using the bar diagram above.

$$36 + 2x \leq 50$$

The weight of Mia's suitcase plus the weight of her shoes must be less than or equal to the maximum luggage weight.

What inequality symbol represents less than or equal to? ☐

This can be written as $36 + 2x \leq 50$.

Using the bar diagram, both pairs of Mia's shoes cannot weigh more than $50 - 36$, or ☐ pounds.

So, each pair cannot weigh more than $14 \div 2$, or ☐ pounds.

Investigate

Work with a partner to solve the following problems.

Analyze Relationships For Exercises 1–3, assume the paper bags are weightless. Write the inequality represented by each balance. Then write the different possible numbers of cubes in each paper bag if the sides of each balance remain unlevel.

1.

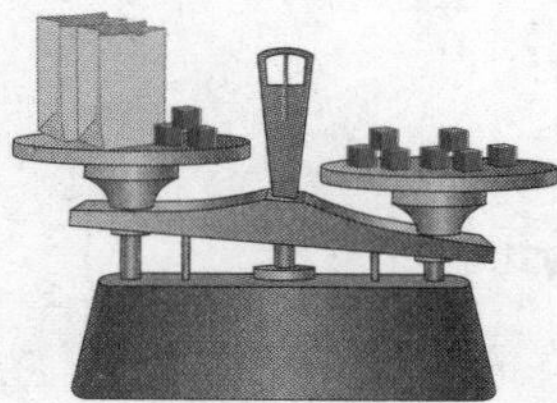

Inequality: ______

Number of Cubes: ______

2.

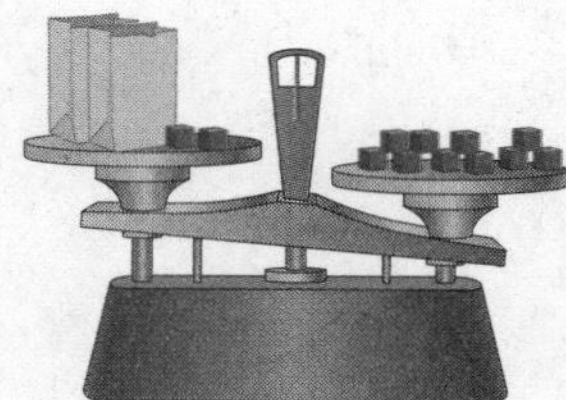

Inequality: ______

Number of Cubes: ______

3.

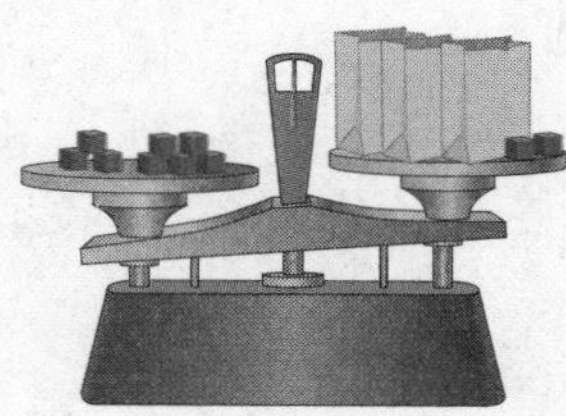

Inequality: ______

Number of Cubes: ______

4. **Analyze Relationships** At an amusement park, roller coaster riders are required to be at least 48 inches tall. Last year, Myron was 42 inches tall. He has been growing at a rate of 2 inches each year. Complete the bar diagram to determine the number of years x before Myron will be able to ride the roller coaster. Then write an inequality to represent the situation.

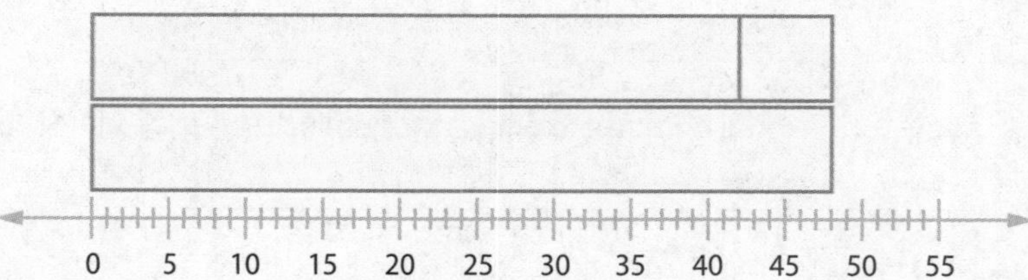

Inequality: ______

So, it will take Myron at least ____ years in order to be tall enough to ride the roller coaster.

Analyze and Reflect

Work with a partner to circle the correct inequality for each situation.

5. Kai has \$4.95 left on a music download gift card. She has a download costing \$1.98 in her online shopping cart. How many more songs x can she download if each song costs \$0.99?

$0.99x + 1.98 \geq 4.95$ $\quad$ $0.99x + 1.98 \leq 4.95$

6. The Walter family budgets a maximum amount of \$124 for a camping trip. Mr. Walter already spent \$40. How many people x can go canoeing if the cost is \$21 per person?

$21x + 40 \geq 124$ $\quad$ $21x + 40 \leq 124$

$40x + 21 \leq 124$ $\quad$ $21x + 40 > 124$

7. A car sales associate receives a monthly salary of \$1,700 plus \$140 for every car they sell. How many cars must they sell monthly to earn at least \$4,500?

$4{,}500 - 140x \geq 1{,}700$ $\quad$ $1{,}700 + 140x \leq 4{,}500$

$1{,}700 - 140x \geq 4{,}500$ $\quad$ $1{,}700 + 140x \geq 4{,}500$

8. A community needs to raise at least \$5,000 for a new park. They have raised \$1,250 so far and are selling flowers for \$20 each. How many flowers x do they need to sell to raise at least \$5,000?

$1{,}250 + 20x < 5{,}000$ $\quad$ $1{,}250 + 20x \leq 5{,}000$

$1{,}250 + 20x \geq 5{,}000$ $\quad$ $1{,}250x + 20 \geq 5{,}000$

Create

9. MP **Apply Math to the Real World** Write a real-world problem that could be represented by $10x + 20 \geq 50$.

10. INQUIRY HOW can I select tools to model and solve two-step inequalities?

Lesson 7

Solve and Write Two-Step Inequalities

Launch the Lesson: Real World

Kaitlyn is placing an ad in the local newspaper for a pottery class. The cost of placing an ad is shown in the table. Kaitlyn has $50. Is this enough to place an ad with 5 lines?

Service	Cost ($)
10-day ad with 3 lines	38.00
each additional line	9.00

1. Complete the equation to determine the total cost c of an ad with 4 or more lines. Use *x* as the variable.

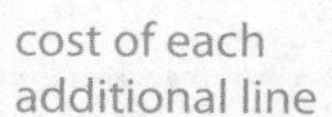

cost of a 10-day add with only 3 lines | cost of each additional line | total cost

 +  x = 

2. How much will it cost to place the ad if it is 5 lines long?

____

3. Does Kaitlyn have enough money to place the ad? Circle yes or no.

yes   no

If the answer is no, how much more money will Kaitlyn need?

Explain. ______________________________

____

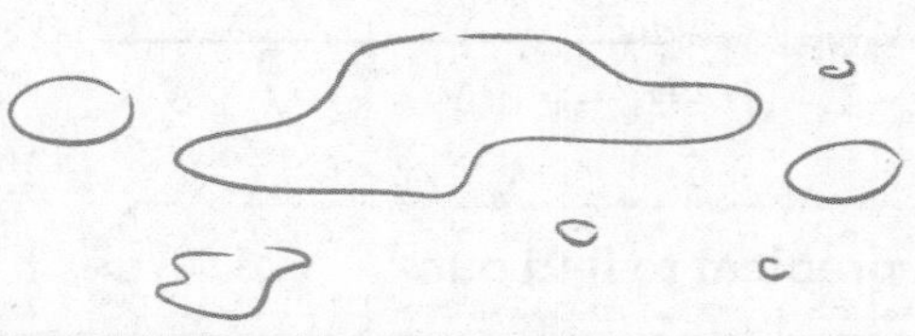

Which MP Mathematical Processes did you use? Shade the circle(s) that applies.

Ⓐ Apply Math to the Real World.
Ⓑ Use a Problem-Solving Model.
Ⓒ Select Tools and Techniques.
Ⓓ Use Multiple Representations.
Ⓔ Organize Ideas.
Ⓕ Analyze Relationships.
Ⓖ Justify Arguments.

Texas Essential Knowledge and Skills

Targeted TEKS

7.11(A) Model and solve one-variable, two-step equations and inequalities. *Also addresses 7.10(A), 7.10(B), 7.10(C).*

Mathematical Processes

7.1(A), 7.1(B), 7.1(C), 7.1(D), 7.1(E)

Vocabulary

two-step inequality

Essential Question

WHAT does it mean to say two quantities are equal?

Work Zone

Solve a Two-Step Inequality

A **two-step inequality** is an inequality that contains two operations. To solve a two-step inequality, use inverse operations to undo each operation in reverse order of the order of operations.

Tutor

Examples

1. Solve $3x + 4 \geq 16$. Graph the solution set on a number line.

$3x + 4 \geq 16$	Write the inequality.
$\quad -4 \quad -4$	Subtract 4 from each side
$3x \geq 12$	Simplify.
$\frac{3x}{3} \geq \frac{12}{3}$	Divide each side by 3.
$x \geq 4$	Simplify.

Graph the solution set.

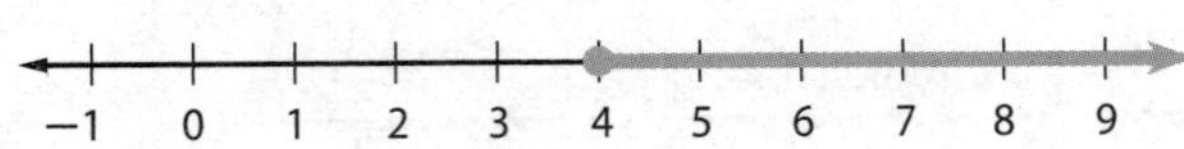

Draw a closed dot at 4 with an arrow to the right.

2. Solve $7 - 2x > 11$. Graph the solution set on a number line.

$7 - 2x > 11$	Write the inequality.
$-7 \quad\quad -7$	Subtract 7 from each side.
$-2x > 4$	Simplify.
$\frac{-2x}{-2} < \frac{4}{-2}$	Divide each side by −2. Reverse inequality symbol.
$x < -2$	Simplify. Check your solution.

Graph the solution set.

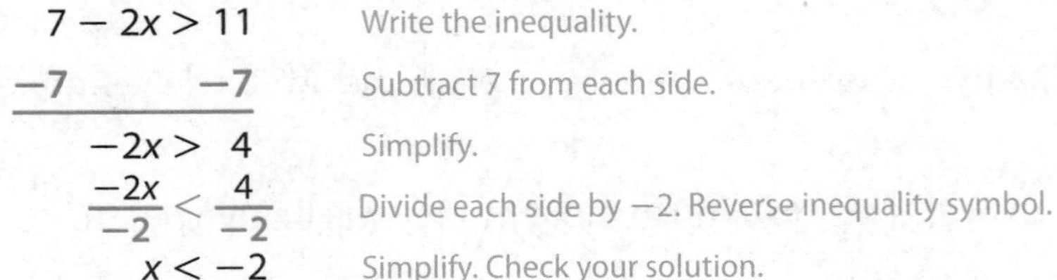

Solving Inequalities
Remember that if multiplying or dividing by a negative number when solving inequalities, reverse the direction of the inequality symbol.

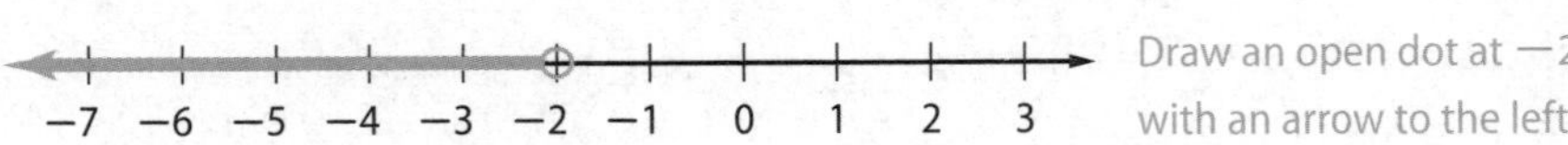

Draw an open dot at −2 with an arrow to the left.

Got It? Do this problem to find out.

Solve each inequality. Graph the solution set on the number line.

a. $2x + 8 > 24$

b. $4x - 13 \leq 7$

a. ____________

b. ____________

Tutor

Examples

3. Solve $\frac{x}{2} - 5 < -8$. Graph the solution set on a number line.

$\frac{x}{2} - 5 < -8$ Write the inequality.

$+5 \quad +5$ Add 5 to each side.

$\frac{x}{2} < -3$ Simplify.

$\frac{x}{2}(2) < -3(2)$ Multiply each side by 2.

$x < -6$ Simplify. Check your solution.

Graph the solution set.

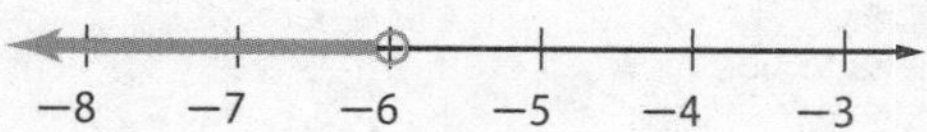

Draw an open dot at −6 with an arrow to the left.

4. Write and solve a real-world problem that can be represented by the inequality $0.25x + 20 \leq 30$.

Addison can spend up to $30 each month for her cell phone. The cell phone company charges $20 for her plan and $0.25 for each text message. How many text messages can Addison send without going over $30?

$0.25x + 20 \leq 30$ Write the inequality.

$-20 \leq -20$ Subtract 20 from each side.

$0.25x \leq 10$ Simplify.

$\frac{0.25x}{0.25} \leq \frac{10}{0.25}$ Divide each side by 0.25.

$x \leq 40$ Simplify.

Addison can send up to 40 text messages.

c. 

d. 

e. 

Got It? Do these problems to find out.

Solve each inequality. Graph the solution set on the number line.

c. $\frac{x}{2} + 9 \geq 5$

d. $8 - \frac{x}{3} \leq 7$

e. Write and solve a real-world problem that can be represented by the inequality $21 + 7.25h \geq 50$.

Example

5. Halfway through the bowling league season, Stewart has 34 strikes. He averages 2 strikes per game. Write and solve an inequality to determine how many more games it will take for Stewart to have at least 61 strikes, the league record. Interpret the solution.

The number of strikes plus two strikes per game is at least 61. Let g represent the number of games he needs to bowl.

$34 + 2g \geq 61$	Write the inequality.
$-34 \quad -34$	Subtract 34 from each side.
$2g \geq 27$	Simplify.
$\frac{2g}{2} \geq \frac{27}{2}$	Divide each side by 2.
$g \geq 13.5$	Simplify.

Stewart should have at least 61 strikes after 14 more games.

Guided Practice

Solve each inequality. Graph the solution set on a number line. (Examples 1–4)

1. $5x - 7 \geq 43 =$ ______

2. $11 \leq 7 + \frac{x}{5}$ ______

3. Financial Literacy A rental car company charges \$45 plus \$0.20 per mile to rent a car. Mr. Lawrence does not want to spend more than \$100 for his rental car. Write and solve an inequality to determine how many miles he can drive and not spend more than \$100. Interpret the solution. (Example 5)

4. Building on the Essential Question Compare $2x + 8 > 18$ and $2x + 8 \leq 18$.

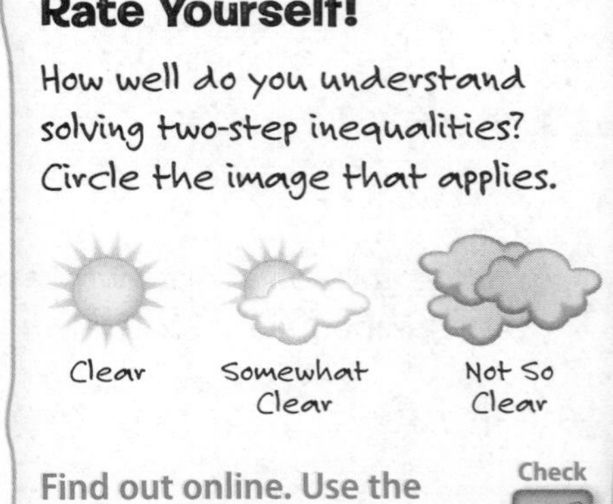

Find out online. Use the Self-Check Quiz.

Name ______________________ My Homework ______________________

Independent Practice

7.10(B), 7.11(A), 7.1(A), 7.1(E)

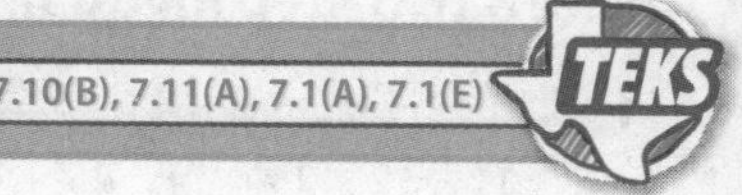

Solve each inequality. Graph the solution set on a number line. (Examples 1–4)

1. $6x + 14 \geq 20$ ________

2. $4x - 13 < 11$ ________

3. $-20 > -2x + 4$ ________

4. $\frac{x}{13} + 3 \geq 4$ ________

5. Tyler needs at least \$205 for a new video game system. He has already saved \$30. He earns \$7 an hour at his job. Write and solve an inequality to determine how many hours he will need to work to buy the system. Interpret the solution. (Example 5)

   Inequality: ________ Solution: ________

   Interpretation: ________

6. Write and solve a real-world problem that can be represented by the inequality $45 + 3p \leq 75$.

Organize Ideas Write and solve an inequality for each sentence.

7. Three times a number increased by four is less than −62.

8. The quotient of a number and −5 increased by one is at most 7.

9. The quotient of a number and 3 minus two is at least −12.

10. The product of −2 and a number minus six is greater than −18.

Write a two-step inequality that could be represented by each number line.

11. 11 12 13 14 15 16

12. 4 5 6 7 8 9

13. 93 94 95 96 97 98

14. 48 49 50 51 52 53

H.O.T. Problems Higher-Order Thinking

15. Create Write a real-world example that could be solved by using the inequality $4x + 8 \geq 32$. Then solve the inequality.

16. Evaluate In five games, you score 16, 12, 15, 13, and 17 points. Write and solve an inequality to determine how many points must you score in the sixth game to have an average of at least 15 points.

17. Analyze Solve $-x + 6 > -(2x + 4)$. Then graph the solution set on the number line.

Solution: ______

18. Create Write and solve a real-world problem that can be represented by the inequality $4(x - 2.8) \leq 45$.

Name ______________________________

Multi-Step Problem Solving

19. Benjamin cannot exceed 10 hours of watching television in a week. He plans to watch a $2\frac{1}{2}$ hour movie on Friday night and not watch any television on Saturday. He writes an inequality to determine how much time he can spend watching television on the other days of the week, if he watches the same amount each day. Which number line represents the solution set of the inequality? EE N MP

Ⓐ 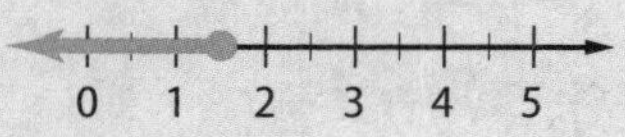

Ⓒ 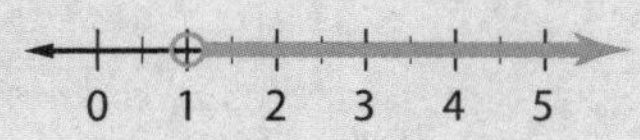

Ⓑ 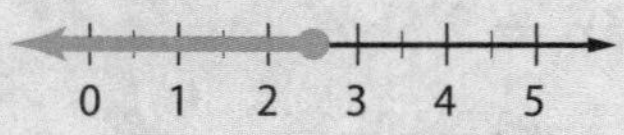

Ⓓ 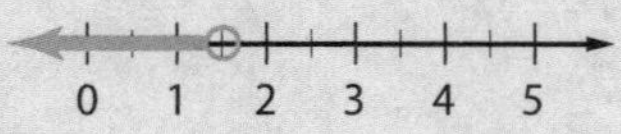

Use a problem-solving model to solve this problem.

1 Analyze

Read the problem. Circle the information you know.
Underline what the problem is asking you to find.

2 Plan

What will you need to do to solve the problem? Write your plan in steps.

Step 1 Write an __________ to represent the situation.

Step 2 Solve the inequality and compare __________.

3 Solve

Use your plan to solve the problem. Show your steps.

Write an inequality to represent the situation where x is the amount of time he can watch television on the other five days in the week.

$2\frac{1}{2} + 5x \leq 10$ $x \leq$ __________

The graph that represents the solution set for the inequality is ____.

The correct answer is ____. Fill in that answer choice.

Read to Succeed!
Determine the appropriate inequality symbol to use. He cannot exceed 10 hours, which means he can watch less than or equal to 10 hours of television.

4 Justify and Evaluate

How do you know your solution is accurate?

____

____

____

EE = Expressions, Equations, and Relationships N = Number and Operations MP = Mathematical Processes

More Multi-Step Problem Solving

Use a problem-solving model to solve each problem.

20. Peta has studied $2\frac{1}{2}$ hours for a test and plans to continue studying at the rate of $\frac{3}{4}$ hour per day. She writes an inequality to determine how many more days she needs to study to meet her goal of at least 7 hours total. Which number line represents the solution set of the inequality? EE N MP

Ⓐ 0 1 2 3 4 5 6 7 8

Ⓑ 0 1 2 3 4 5 6 7 8

Ⓒ 0 1 2 3 4 5 6 7 8

Ⓓ 0 1 2 3 4 5 6 7 8

21. Jala wrote and correctly solved the two inequalities shown below and then compared their solution sets. What whole number is a solution in both inequalities? EE N MP

Jala's Inequalities

$\frac{1}{2}a + 5 \leq 6\frac{1}{2}$

$3b - 2 > 4$

22. Reggie solved the inequality $1.2x + 4 < 10$. Faith solved the inequality $5x - 3 > 14$. What is the difference in the value of x in Reggie's and Faith's solutions? EE N MP

23. Stephanie is solving $-11 < 3x - 3.5$ and $3x - 3.5 \leq 14.5$. Help her solve each inequality and graph the solution sets. Then write the complete whole-number solution set. EE N MP

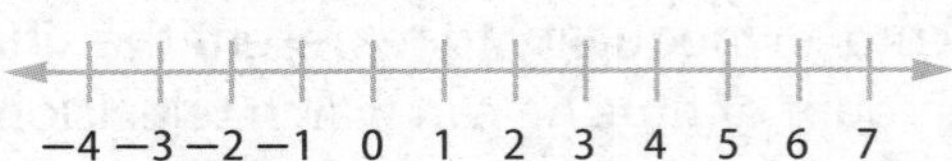

EE = Expressions, Equations, and Relationships N = Number and Operations MP = Mathematical Processes

21ST CENTURY CAREER

Veterinary Technician

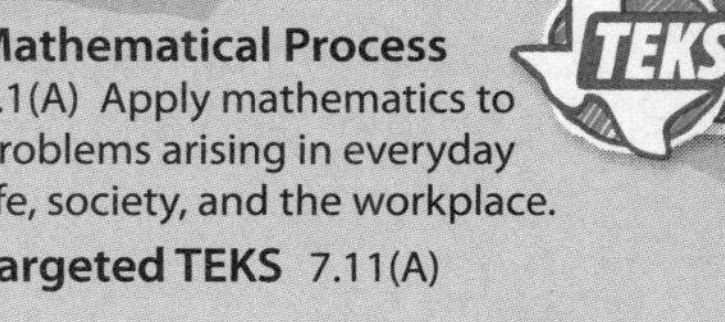

Mathematical Process
7.1(A) Apply mathematics to problems arising in everyday life, society, and the workplace.

Targeted TEKS 7.11(A)

If you love being around animals, enjoy working with your hands, and are good at analyzing problems, a challenging career in veterinary medicine might be a perfect fit for you. Veterinary technicians help veterinarians by helping to diagnose and treat medical conditions. They may work in private clinics, animal hospitals, zoos, aquariums, or wildlife rehabilitation centers.

Is This the Career for You?

Are you interested in a career as a veterinary technician? Take some of the following courses in high school.

- Algebra
- Animal Science
- Biology
- Chemistry
- Veterinary Assisting

Explore college and careers at ccr.mcgraw-hill.com

Vet Techs Don't Monkey Around

For each problem, use the information in the tables to write an equation. Then solve the equation.

1. The minimum tail length of an emperor tamarin is 1.6 inches greater than that of a golden lion tamarin. What is the minimum tail length of a golden lion tamarin?

____

2. The minimum body length of a golden lion tamarin is 5.3 inches less than the maximum body length. What is the maximum body length? _______________

3. Tamarins live an average of 15 years. This is 1 year more than half the years that one tamarin in captivity lived. How long did the tamarin in captivity live? _______________

4. The maximum weight of a golden lion tamarin is about 0.4 ounce less than 2 times the maximum weight of an emperor tamarin. What is the maximum weight of an emperor tamarin? Round to the nearest tenth.

____

5. For an emperor tamarin, the maximum total length, including the body and tail, is 27 inches. What is the maximum body length of an emperor tamarin?

____

Golden Lion Tamarin Monkeys		
Measure	**Minimum**	**Maximum**
Body length	7.9 in.	ℓ
Tail length	t	15.7 in.
Weight	12.7 oz	28 oz

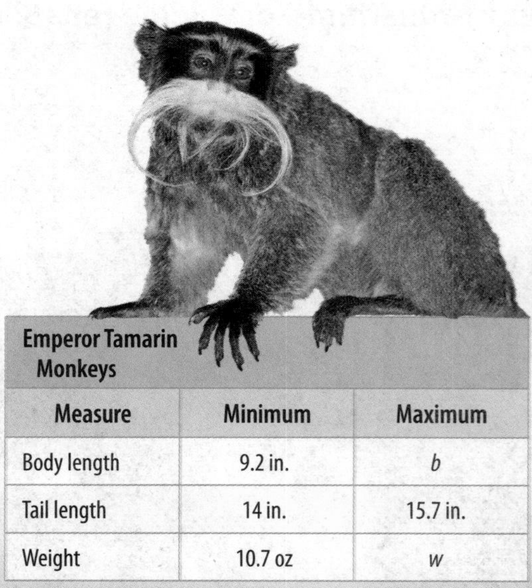

Emperor Tamarin Monkeys		
Measure	**Minimum**	**Maximum**
Body length	9.2 in.	b
Tail length	14 in.	15.7 in.
Weight	10.7 oz	w

Career Project

It's time to update your career portfolio! Go to the Occupational Outlook Handbook online and research a career as a veterinary technician. Prepare a brief oral presentation to present to your classmates of the work environment, education and training requirements, and job outlook. At the end, ask any clarifying questions.

____

____

____

Do you think you would enjoy a career as a veterinary technician? Why or why not?

____

____

____

____

____

Chapter Review TEKS

Vocabulary Check

Work with a partner to unscramble each of the clue words. Take turns saying each word aloud while the other student listens carefully. Then give the definition of each word in your own words. Ask for and give help if needed for each word.

TOW-SETP

☐☐☐ – ☐☐☐☐ (7 under box 1)

PYORERPT

☐☐☐☐☐☐☐☐ (8 under box 8)

DODTIINA

☐☐☐☐☐☐☐☐ (4 under box 1)

NIIOSDIV

☐☐☐☐☐☐☐☐ (6 under box 4)

AILEYQUITN

☐☐☐☐☐☐☐☐☐☐ (2 under box 4)

BISTAUTORNC

☐☐☐☐☐☐☐☐☐☐☐ (3 under box 2)

NUATIEQO

☐☐☐☐☐☐☐☐ (1 under box 1)

TIULINTICPOLMA

☐☐☐☐☐☐☐☐☐☐☐☐☐☐ (5 under box 7)

Use the numbered letters to find another vocabulary term from this chapter.

☐☐☐☐☐☐☐☐

1 2 3 4 5 6 7 8

Key Concept Check

Use Your FOLDABLES

Use your Foldable to help review the chapter. Share your Foldable with a partner and take turns summarizing what you learned in this chapter, while the other partner listens carefully. Ask for and give help of any concept if needed. TEKS 7.1(E)

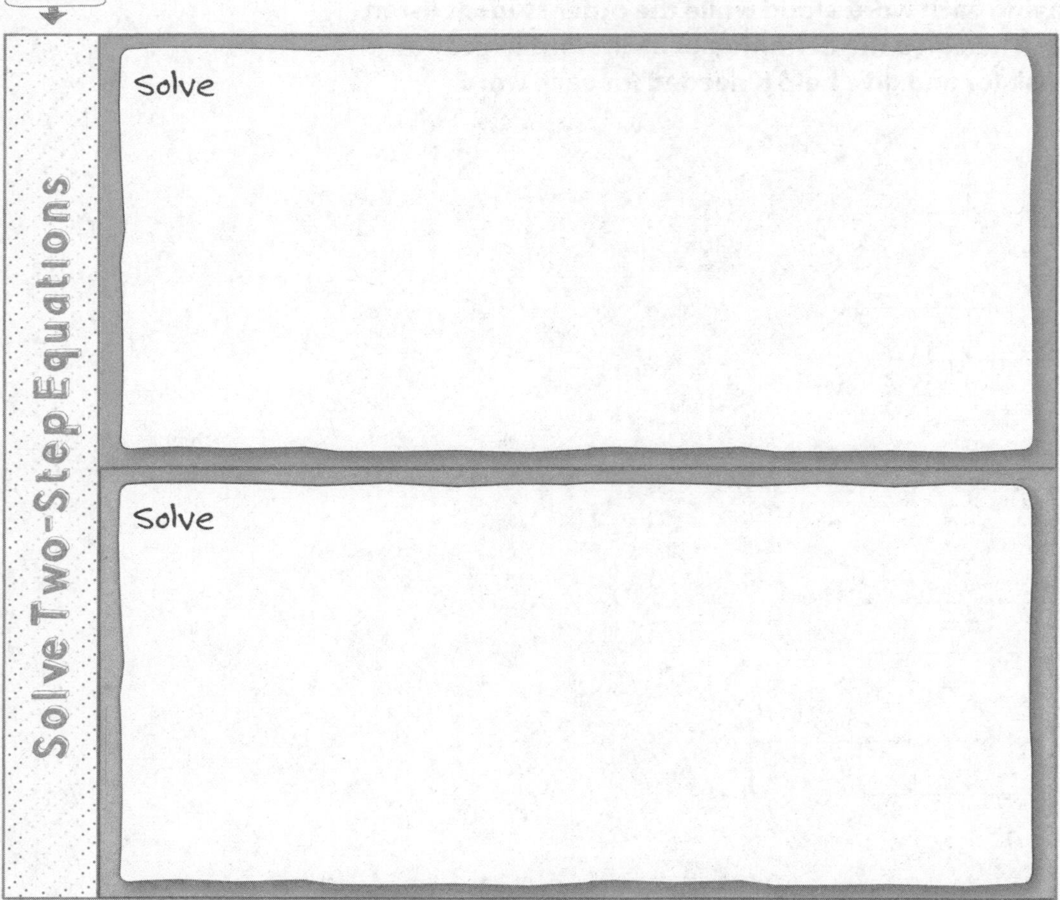

Got it?

Match each phrase with the correct term. TEKS 7.1(D)

1. The value of a variable that makes an equation true
2. The numerical factor in a multiplication expression
3. Equations that have the same solution
4. A sentence stating that two quantities are equal

a. equivalent equations

b. equation

c. Addition Property of Equality

d. coefficient

e. formula

f. solution

Multi-Step Problem Solving

Use a problem-solving model to solve the problem.

5. The tread depth on the Lopez's new car is $\frac{11}{32}$ inch. It is recommended that you replace your tires when the tread depth reaches $\frac{1}{8}$ inch. Suppose the wear on the Lopez's tires each year is $\frac{3}{64}$ inch. How soon will the Lopez family need to replace their tires? Justify your solution. EE N MP

1 Analyze

2 Plan

3 Solve

4 Justify and Evaluate

Got it?

6. The width of the game board shown is x inches. The length of the game board is $6\frac{1}{4}$ inches longer than the width of the game board. What is the area of the game board? Justify your solution. EE N MP

$P = 66\frac{1}{2}$ in.

EE = Expressions, Equations, and Relationships 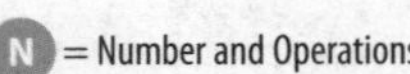 N = Number and Operations 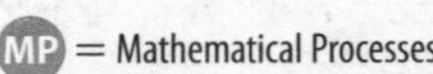 MP = Mathematical Processes

Reflect

Answering the Essential Question

Use what you learned about equations and inequalities to complete the graphic organizer. TEKS 7.1(D), 7.1(F), 7.1(G)

When do you use an equals sign?

Essential Question

WHAT does it mean to say two quantities are equal?

When do you use an inequality symbol?

Answer the Essential Question. WHAT does it mean to say two quantities are equal? Verbally share your response with a partner, asking for and giving help if needed.

Chapter 8

Develop Geometry with Algebra

Texas Essential Knowledge and Skills

Targeted TEKS

7.8 The student applies mathematical process standards to develop geometric relationships with volume. *Also addresses 7.9.*

Mathematical Processes

7.1, 7.1(A), 7.1(B), 7.1(C), 7.1(D), 7.1(E), 7.1(F), 7.1(G)

Essential Question

HOW do measurements help you describe real-world objects?

Math in the Real World

Soccer The Plano Labor Day Invitational held in Plano, Texas, is a soccer tournament that is played on a rectangular field. The dimensions of the regulation size field are 100 yards long and 60 yards wide.

What is the area of the soccer field shown?

$A =$ ______ square yards

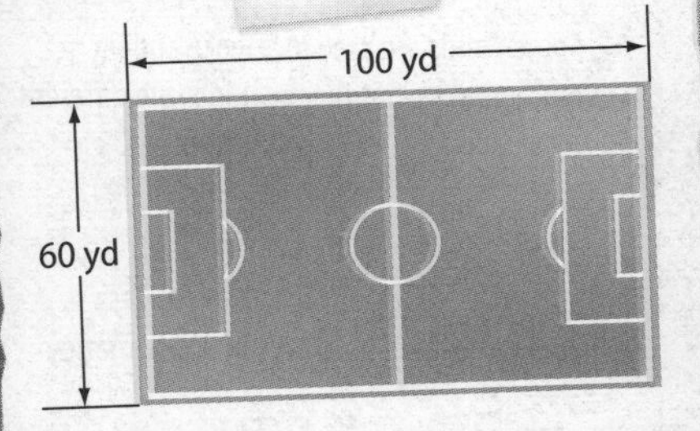

Go Online! www.connectED.mcgraw-hill.com

Watch  Worksheets  Vocab  Tutor  Tools  Check 

What Tools Do You Need?

Vocab abc

Vocabulary

acute angle
acute triangle
adjacent angles
complementary angles
composite figure
congruent
congruent segments
equilateral triangle
isosceles triangle
lateral face
lateral surface area
net
obtuse angle
obtuse triangle
prism
pyramid
quarter circle
right angle
right triangle
scalene triangle
semicircle
slant height
straight angle
supplementary angles
surface area
triangle
vertex
vertical angles
volume

Reading Math

The Language of Mathematics Many of the words you use in math and science are also used in everyday language, such as the leg of a person and the leg of a right triangle.

Usage	Example
Some words are used in science and in mathematics, but the meanings are different.	$x + 4 = -2$ $x = -6$ solution (125, 100, 75, 50)
Some words are used only in mathematics.	hypotenuse

Verbally explain to a classmate how the everyday meaning of *face* is different than its mathematical meaning.

Everyday meaning: ______________________________

____

Mathematical meaning: ______________________________

____

When Will You Use This?

Caitlyn, Dario, and Hannah in

The Dunk Tank

Your Turn! **You will solve this problem in the chapter.**

Are You Ready?

Quick Review

Example 1

Determine the area of the rectangle.

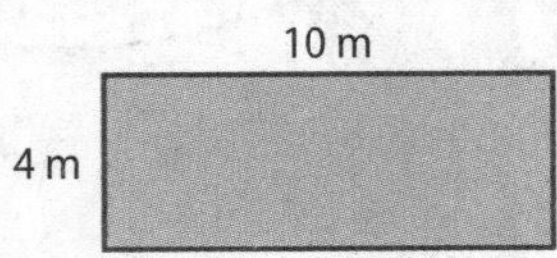

$A = \ell w$ Area of a rectangle

$A = (10)(4)$ Replace ℓ with 10 and w with 4.

$A = 40$ Simplify.

The area of the rectangle is 40 square meters.

Example 2

Determine the area of the triangle.

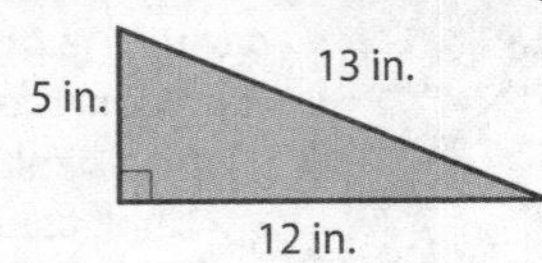

$A = \frac{1}{2}bh$ Area of a triangle

$A = \frac{1}{2}(12)(5)$ Replace b with 12 and h with 5.

$A = \frac{1}{2}(60)$ Multiply.

$A = 30$ Simplify.

The area of the triangle is 30 square inches.

Quick Check

Area **Determine the area of each figure.**

1. 14 m, 3 m

Show your work.

$A =$ ______

2.

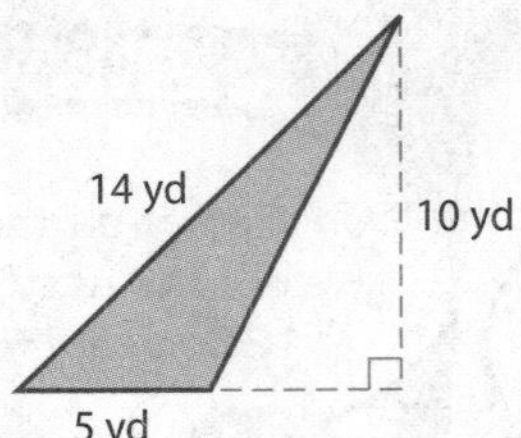

$A =$ ______

3.

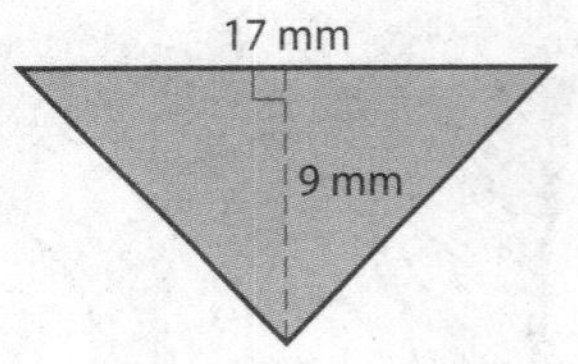

$A =$ ______

4. Anita's yard is in the shape of a triangle. It has a height of 35 feet and a base of 50 feet. What is the area of the yard?

______

How Did You Do?

Which problems did you answer correctly in the Quick Check? Shade those exercise numbers below.

① ② ③ ④

FOLDABLES®

Use the Foldable throughout this chapter to help you learn about volume and surface area.

cut on all dashed lines

fold on all solid lines

tape to page 696

Volume

prism	prism
pyramid	pyramid

Surface Area

FOLDABLES®

Use the Foldable throughout this chapter to help you learn about volume and surface area.

cut on all dashed lines — fold on all solid lines — tape to page 694

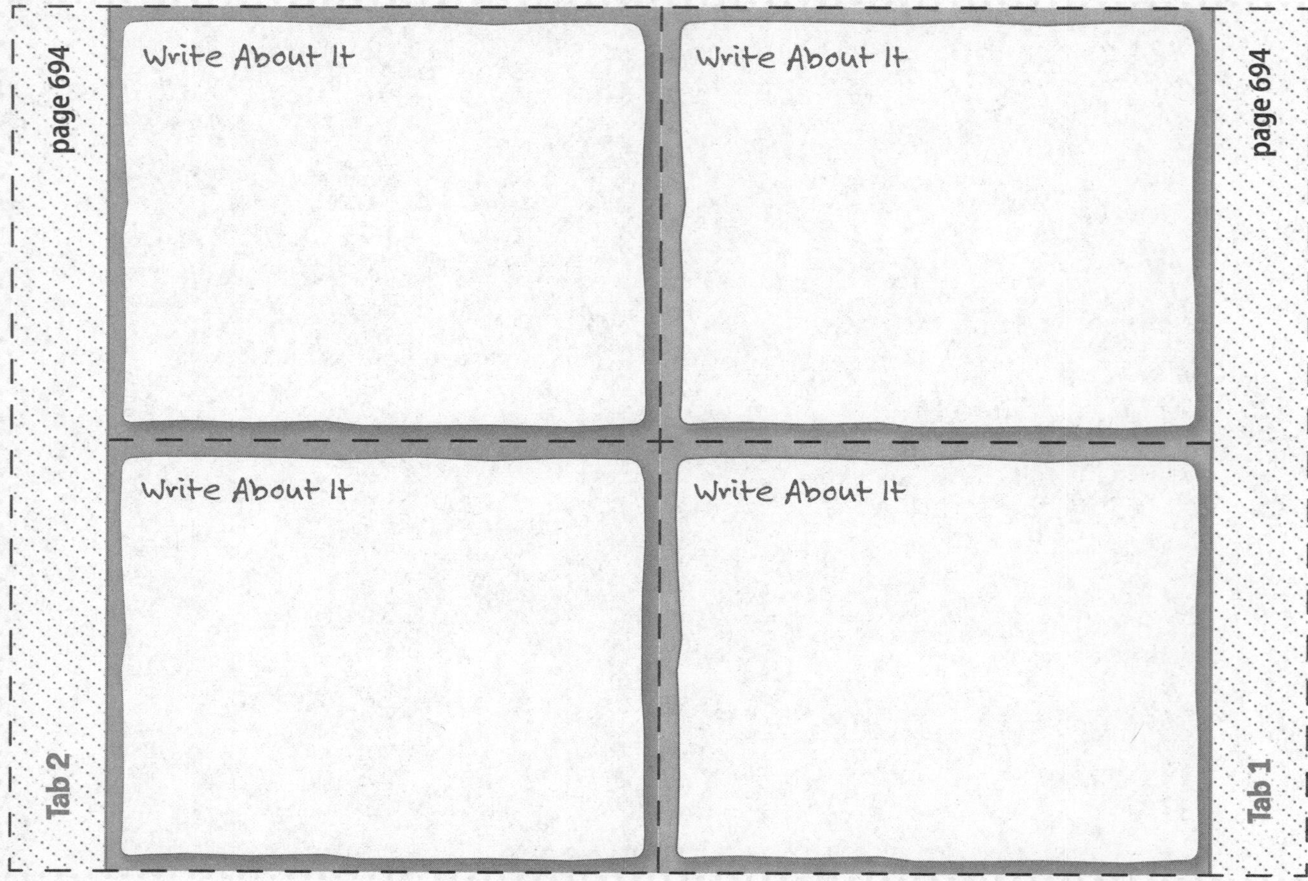

Lesson 1

Angle Relationships

Launch the Lesson: Vocabulary

An angle is formed by two rays that share a common endpoint. The **vertex** is the point where the two rays meet.

Complete the table by drawing the hands of a clock to represent each angle.

Type of Angle			
Right	Acute	Obtuse	Straight
exactly 90°	less than 90°	greater than 90°	exactly 180°

Texas Essential Knowledge and Skills

Targeted TEKS

7.11(C) Write and solve equations using geometry concepts, including the sum of the angles in a triangle, and angle relationships.

Mathematical Processes

7.1(A), 7.1(B), 7.1(E), 7.1(F)

Vocabulary

vertex
right angle
acute angle
obtuse angle
straight angle
vertical angles
congruent
adjacent angles

Math Symbols

∠
≅

Essential Question

HOW do measurements help you describe real-world objects?

Real-World Link

The angle formed by a bike ramp is shown at the right.

1. What type of angle is formed?

2. Estimate the measure of the angle.

Which MP Mathematical Processes did you use? Shade the circle(s) that applies.

Ⓐ Apply Math to the Real World.
Ⓑ Use a Problem-Solving Model.
Ⓒ Select Tools and Techniques.
Ⓓ Use Multiple Representations.
Ⓔ Organize Ideas.
Ⓕ Analyze Relationships.
Ⓖ Justify Arguments.

Key Concept

Name and Identify Angles

Work Zone

Words	Models	Symbols
Two angles are **vertical** if they are opposite angles formed by the intersection of two lines. Vertical angles are **congruent** or have the same measure.	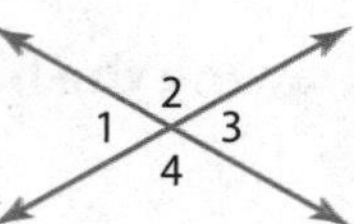 $\angle 1$ and $\angle 3$, $\angle 2$ and $\angle 4$	$\angle 1 \cong \angle 3$ $\angle 2 \cong \angle 4$
Two angles are **adjacent** if they share a common vertex, a common side, and do not overlap.	(model: intersecting lines with angles 1, 2, 3, 4)	Adjacent angle pairs are $\angle 1$ and $\angle 2$, $\angle 2$ and $\angle 3$, $\angle 3$ and $\angle 4$, and $\angle 4$ and $\angle 1$.

You can name an angle by its vertex and by its points.

Tutor

Example

Symbols
The symbol for angle is $\angle$.
The symbol $\cong$ means is congruent to.

1. Name the angle shown at the right. Then classify it as *acute*, *right*, *obtuse*, or *straight*.

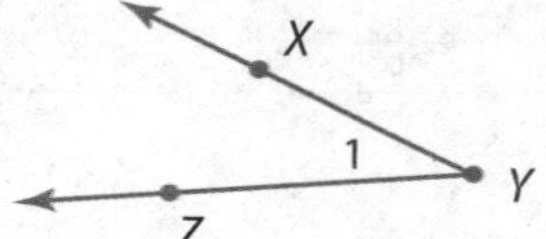

- Use the vertex as the middle letter and a point from each side, $\angle XYZ$ or $\angle ZYX$.
- Use the vertex only, $\angle Y$.
- Use a number, $\angle 1$.

Since the angle is less than 90°, it is an acute angle.

Show your work.

Got It? Do these problems to find out.

Name each angle in four ways. Then classify each angle as *acute*, *right*, *obtuse*, or *straight*.

a. 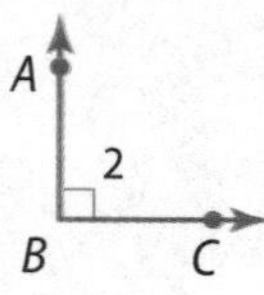

b. 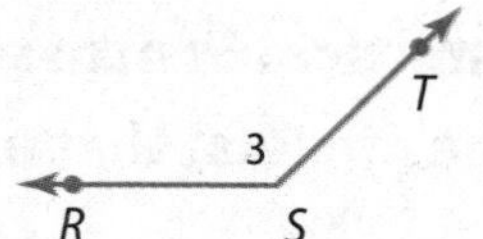

c. 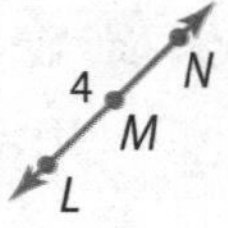

a. ______

b. ______

c. ______

Example

2. Identify a pair of vertical angles and adjacent angles in the diagram at the right. Justify your response.

Since ∠2 and ∠4 are opposite angles formed by the intersection of two lines, they are vertical angles.

Since ∠1 and ∠2 share a common side and vertex, and they do not overlap, they are adjacent angles.

Got It? Do this problem to find out.

d. Refer to the diagram in Example 2. Identify different pairs of vertical and adjacent angles. Justify your response.

d. ______

Determine a Missing Measure

Use what you learned about vertical and adjacent angles to determine the value of a missing measure. To do so, write and solve an equation.

Example

3. Write and solve an equation to determine the value of x in the figure.

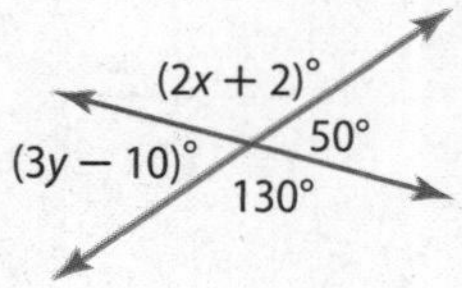

(Figure: angles labeled $(2x + 2)°$, $50°$, $(3y - 10)°$, $130°$)

The angle labeled $(2x + 2)°$ and the angle labeled 130° are vertical angles.

Since vertical angles are congruent, $(2x + 2)°$ equals 130°.

$2x + 2 = 130$	Write the equation.
$-2 = -2$	Subtract 2 from each side.
$\frac{2x}{2} = \frac{128}{2}$	Divide each side by 2.
$x = 64$	

So, the value of x is 64.

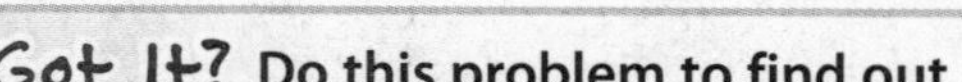

e. Write and solve an equation to determine the value of y in the figure in Example 3.

e. ______

Example

4. Write and solve an equation to determine the value of *x* show in the sidewalk.

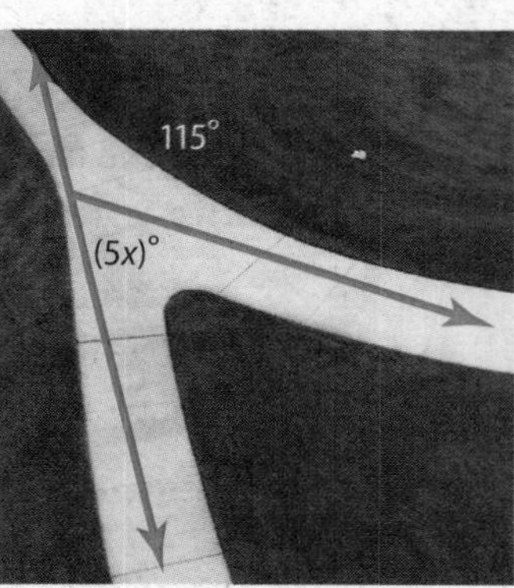

The angle labeled 115° and the angle labeled $5x$ are adjacent. Together they form a straight angle or 180°.

$115 + 5x = 180$	Write the equation.
$-115 \quad = -115$	Subtract 115 from each side.
$\frac{5x}{5} = \frac{65}{5}$	Divide each side by 5.
$x = 13$	

So, the value of x is 13.

Guided Practice

1. Name the angle below in four ways. Then classify it as *acute, right, obtuse,* or *straight*. (Example 1)

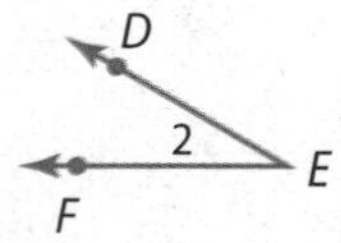

2. Write and solve an equation to determine the value of x in the figure. (Examples 3–4)

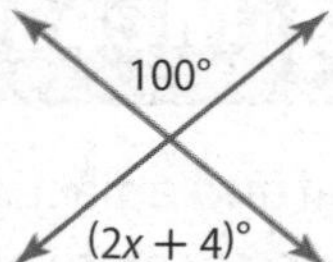

3. Identify a pair of vertical angles and adjacent angles on the railroad crossing sign. Justify your response. (Example 2)

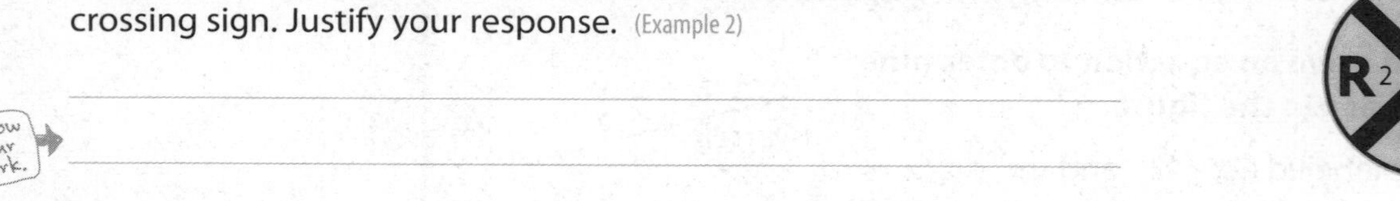

4. **Building on the Essential Question** Describe the differences between vertical and adjacent angles.

Rate Yourself!

How confident are you about classifying angles? Check the box that applies.

Find out online. Use the Self-Check Quiz.

Name ______________________ My Homework ______________________

Independent Practice

7.11(C), 7.1(C) TEKS

Name each angle in four ways. Then classify the angle as *acute, right, obtuse,* or *straight.* (Example 1)

1.

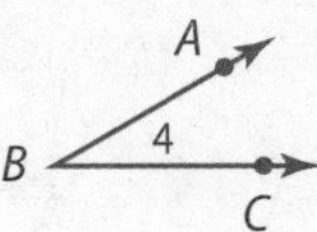

Show your work.

2.

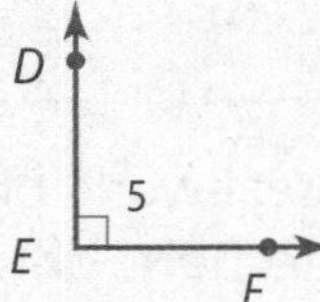

3.

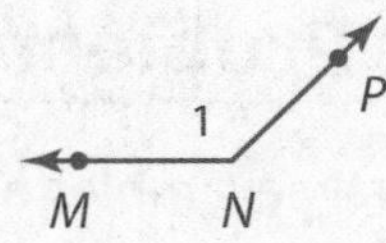

MP **Analyze Relationships** **Refer to the diagram at the right. Identify each angle pair as *adjacent, vertical,* or *neither.*** (Example 2)

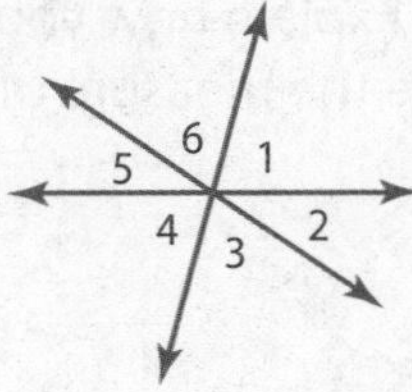

4. ∠2 and ∠5 ______

5. ∠4 and ∠6 ______

6. ∠3 and ∠4 ______

7. ∠5 and ∠6 ______

8. ∠1 and ∠3 ______

9. ∠1 and ∠4 ______

10. Write and solve an equation to determine the value of *x* in the figure at the right. (Examples 3 and 4)

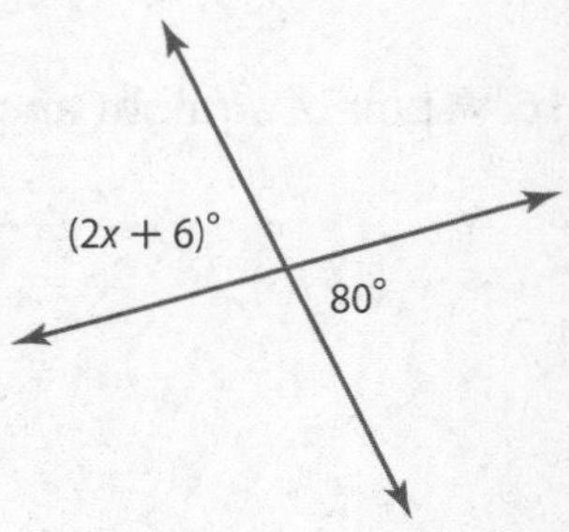

11. Write and solve an equation to determine the value of *x* in the figure at the right. (Examples 3 and 4)

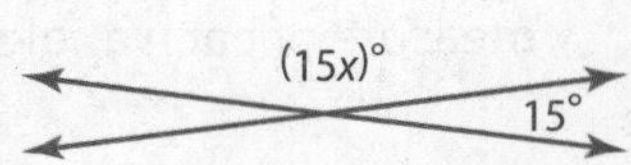

12. Angles *ABC* and *DBE* are adjacent angles. Together they form a straight angle. If the measure of $\angle ABC$ is $(4x)°$, and the measure of $\angle ABD$ is $(14x)°$, what is the value of *x*? Write and solve an equation. ______

H.O.T. Problems Higher-Order Thinking

13. **Create** Draw examples of angles that represent real-world objects. Be sure to include at least three of the following angles: acute, right, obtuse, straight, vertical, and adjacent. Verify by measuring the angles.

______

14. **Analyze** Explain how you can use a protractor to measure the angle shown. Determine the measure of the angle.

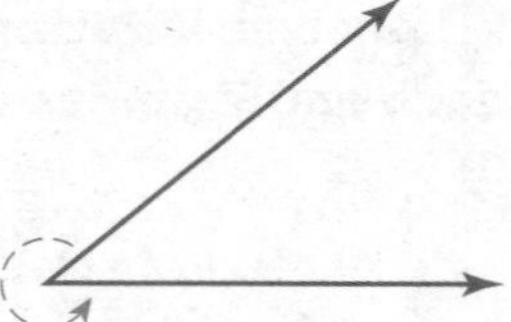

______

______

Evaluate Determine whether each statement is *true* or *false*. If the statement is true, provide a diagram to support it. If the statement is false, explain why.

15. A pair of obtuse angles can also be vertical angles.

______

16. A pair of straight angles can also be adjacent angles.

______

17. **Analyze** Lines ℓ and *k* shown at the right are parallel and are intersected by line *j*. Explain how you can write and solve equations to determine the measure of each angle.

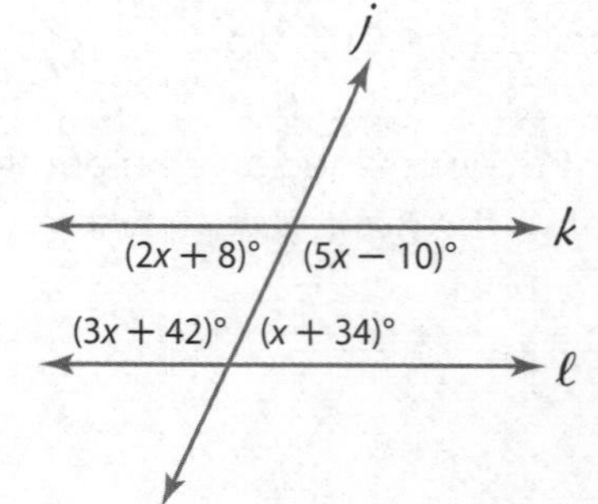

______

______

______

Name ______________________________

Multi-Step Problem Solving

18. The value of the variable in the circle is also equal to the radius of the circle. What is the circumference of the circle? Use 3.14 for π. EE N MP

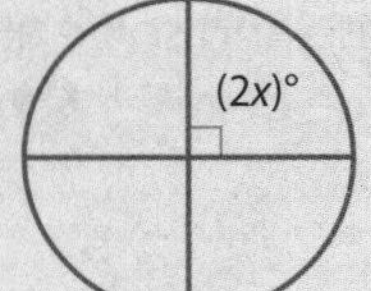

Ⓐ 141.3

Ⓑ 282.6

Ⓒ 565.2

Ⓓ 847.8

Use a problem-solving model to solve this problem.

1 Analyze

Read the problem. Circle the information you know.
Underline what the problem is asking you to find.

2 Plan

What will you need to do to solve the problem? Write your plan in steps.

Step 1 Determine the value of ____ by solving an equation.

Step 2 Determine the ______________ of the circle.

3 Solve

Use your plan to solve the problem. Show your steps.

Write and solve an equation.

$2x = 90$ $\frac{2x}{2} = \frac{90}{2}$ $x =$ ______

$C = 2\pi r$ $C = 2(3.14)($____$)$ $C =$ ______

The circumference of the circle is ____________ units.

So, the correct answer is ____. Fill in that answer choice.

Read to Succeed!
The angle symbol in the circle represents a right angle. All right angles measure 90°. Use this to solve the equation.

4 Justify and Evaluate

How do you know your solution is accurate?

____

____

____

EE = Expressions, Equations, and Relationships 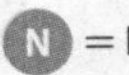 N = Number and Operations MP = Mathematical Processes

More Multi-Step Problem Solving

Use a problem-solving model to solve each problem.

19. Write and solve an equation to determine the value of x. EE N MP

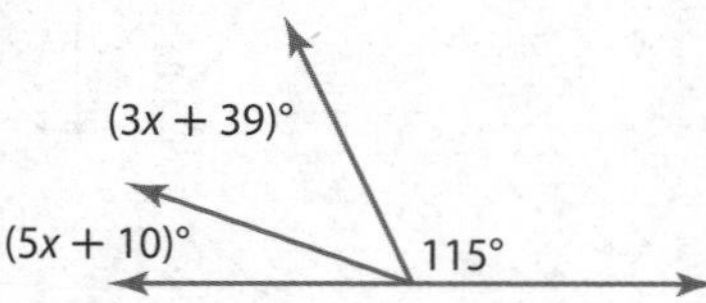

Ⓐ 2

Ⓑ 7

Ⓒ 21

Ⓓ 34

20. The time shown on a clock is 6:00 P.M. The seconds hand is at 11 seconds. The angles formed between the seconds hand and the hour and minute hands are adjacent angles. At what time will those adjacent angles be equal? EE N MP

21. A class of students was asked for their favorite color. The circle graph shows the results. The sum of the vertical angles for yellow and red in the circle graph is 40° and represents $\frac{1}{9}$ of the students. There are 360° in a circle and 18 students in the class. How many students chose yellow? EE N P MP

Favorite Color

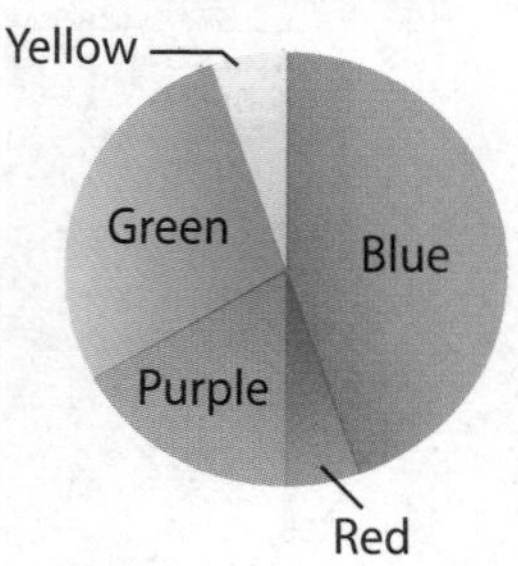

22. An obtuse angle is divided into a right angle and $\angle A$. If the measures of the angles are whole numbers, what are the possible measures of $\angle A$? EE N MP

N = Number and Operations P = Proportionality EE = Expressions, Equations, and Relationships MP = Mathematical Processes

Lesson 2

Complementary and Supplementary Angles

Launch the Lesson: Real World

Watch

Engineers use angles to construct bridges. The Golden Gate Bridge is created by combining angles as shown. How are these angles related?

1. What types of angles make up the two angles marked in the drawing of the bridge? ____________

2. What is the sum of the measures of the two angles marked in the drawing of the bridge? ____________

3. In the space below, draw a figure that contains two angles with measures that have a sum of 90°.

Texas Essential Knowledge and Skills

Targeted TEKS

7.11(C) Write and solve equations using geometry concepts, including the sum of the angles in a triangle, and angle relationships.

Mathematical Processes

7.1(A), 7.1(B), 7.1(E), 7.1(G)

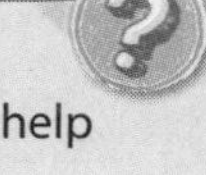

Vocab

Vocabulary

complementary angles

supplementary angles

Math symbols

$m\angle 1$

Essential Question

HOW do measurements help you describe real-world objects?

Which MP Mathematical Processes did you use? Shade the circle(s) that applies.

Ⓐ Apply Math to the Real World.

Ⓑ Use a Problem-Solving Model.

Ⓒ Select Tools and Techniques.

Ⓓ Use Multiple Representations.

Ⓔ Organize Ideas.

Ⓕ Analyze Relationships.

Ⓖ Justify Arguments.

Key Concept

Pairs of Angles

Words	Models	Symbols
Two angles are **complementary** if the sum of their measures is 90°.		$m\angle 1 + m\angle 2 = 90°$
Two angles are **supplementary** if the sum of their measures is 180°.		$m\angle 3 + m\angle 4 = 180°$

Work Zone

A special relationship exists between two angles with a sum of 90°. A special relationship also exists between two angles with a sum of 180°. The symbol $m\angle 1$ means *the measure of angle 1*.

Tutor

Examples

Identify each pair of angles as *complementary, supplementary,* or *neither*.

1.

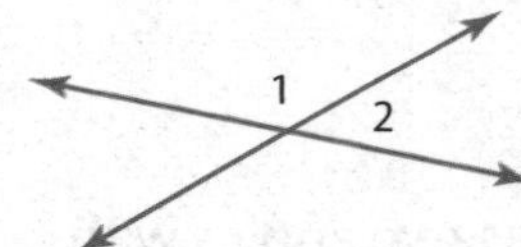

$\angle 1$ and $\angle 2$ form a straight angle. So, the angles are supplementary.

2.

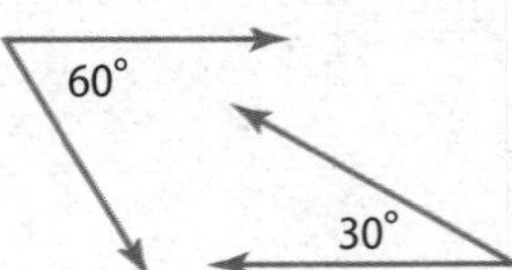

$60° + 30° = 90°$ The angles are complementary.

Adjacent

As shown in Example 2, angles do not need to be adjacent to be complementary or supplementary angles.

Show your work.

Got It? Do these problems to find out.

a.

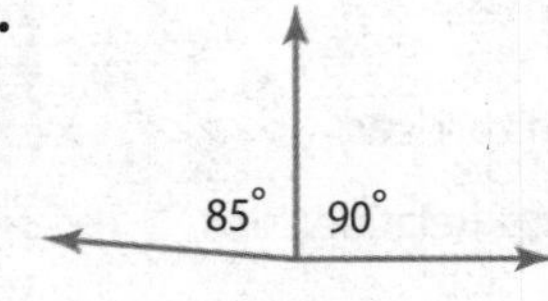

b.

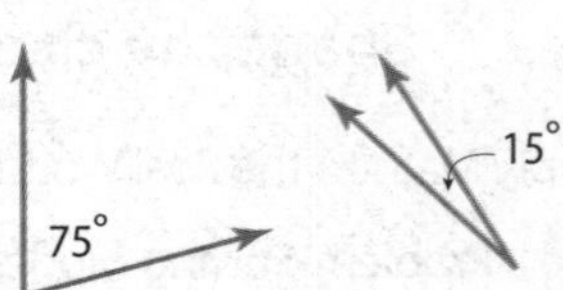

a. ______________

b. ______________

Determine a Missing Measure

You can use angle relationships to write and solve equations in order to determine missing measures.

Examples

3. Write and solve an equation to determine the value of x.

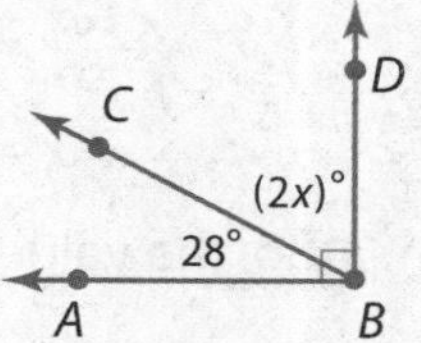

Since the two angles form a right angle, they are complementary.

Words	The sum of the measures of $\angle ABC$ and $\angle CBD$	is	90°.
Variable	Let $2x$ represent the measure of $\angle CBD$.		
Equation	$28 + 2x$	$=$	90

$$\begin{aligned} 28 + 2x &= 90 && \text{Write the equation.} \\ -28 &= -28 && \text{Subtract 28 from each side.} \\ \frac{2x}{2} &= \frac{62}{2} && \text{Divide each side by 2.} \\ x &= 31 \end{aligned}$$

So, the value of x is 31.

4. The angles shown are supplementary. Write and solve an equation to determine the value of x.

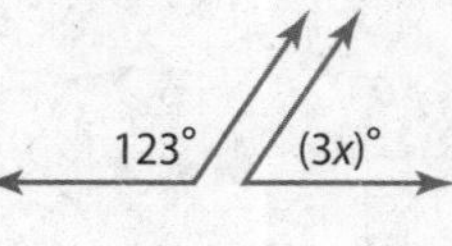

$$\begin{aligned} 123 + 3x &= 180 && \text{Write the equation.} \\ -123 &= -123 && \text{Subtract 123 from each side.} \\ \frac{3x}{3} &= \frac{57}{3} && \text{Divide each side by 3.} \\ x &= 19 \end{aligned}$$

So, the value of x is 19.

and Reflect

Circle true or false.
The sum of two angles that are supplementary is 180°.

True False

Got It? Do this problem to find out.

c. Write and solve an equation to determine the value of x.

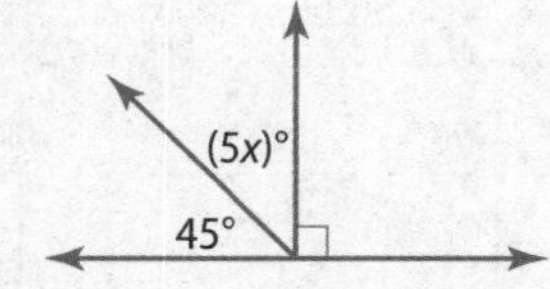
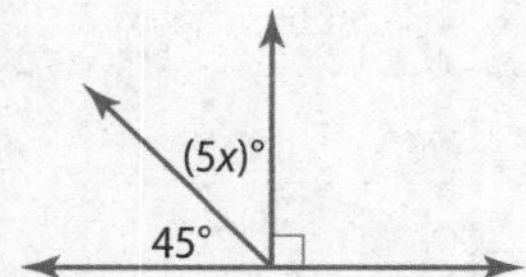

c. ____________

Example

Tutor

5. The picture shows a support brace for a gate. Write and solve an equation to determine the value of *x*.

The angle labeled 80° and the angle labeled 10*x* are supplementary angles.

$80 + 10x = 180$ — Write the equation.

$-80 \quad = -80$ — Subtract 80 from each side.

$\frac{10x}{10} = \frac{100}{10}$ — Divide each side by 10.

$x = 10$

So, the value of *x* is 10.

Got It? Do this problem to find out.

d. ______

d. The opening of the scissors forms an angle. Write and solve an equation to determine the value of *x*.

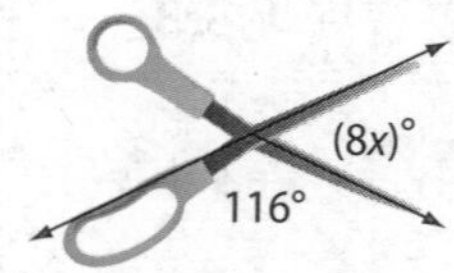

Guided Practice

Identify each pair of angles as *complementary, supplementary,* or *neither*. (Examples 1 and 2)

1.

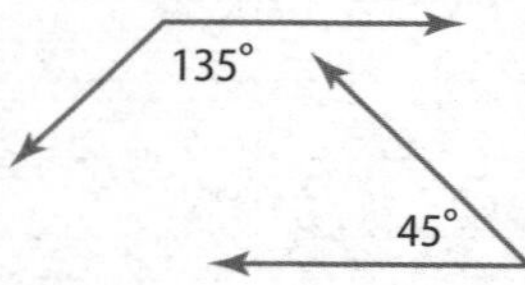

______

2.

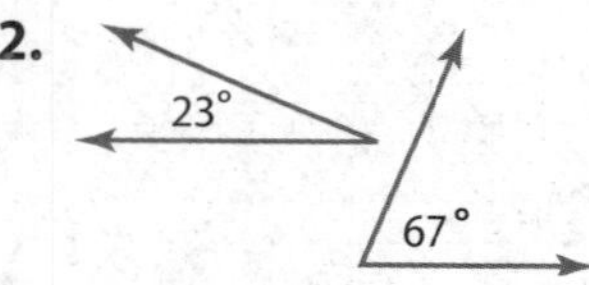

______

3. Write and solve an equation to determine the value of *x*. (Examples 3–5)

______

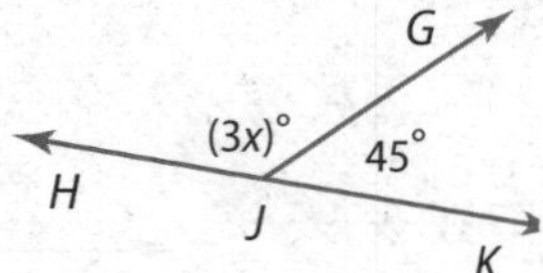

4. **Building on the Essential Question** How are vertical, adjacent, complementary, and supplementary angles related? ______

Rate Yourself!

Are you ready to move on? Shade the section that applies.

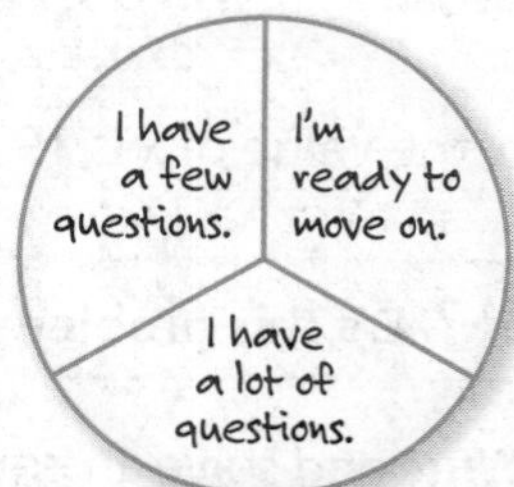

Find out online. Use the Self-Check Quiz.

Check

Name ______________________ My Homework ______________________

Independent Practice

7.11(C), 7.1(E), 7.1(G) TEKS

Identify each pair of angles as *complementary, supplementary,* or *neither*.
(Examples 1 and 2)

Show your work.

1.

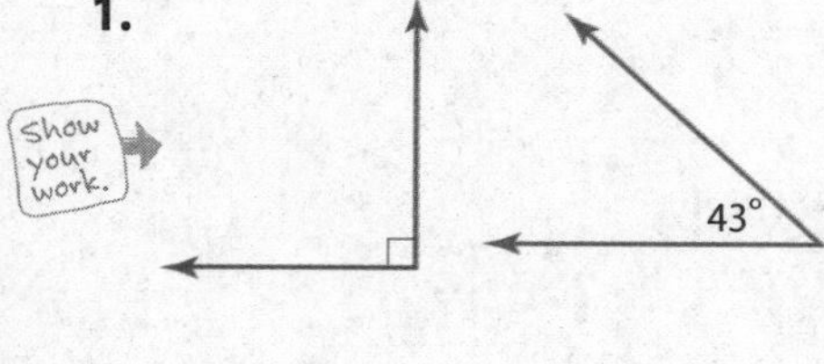

____

2.

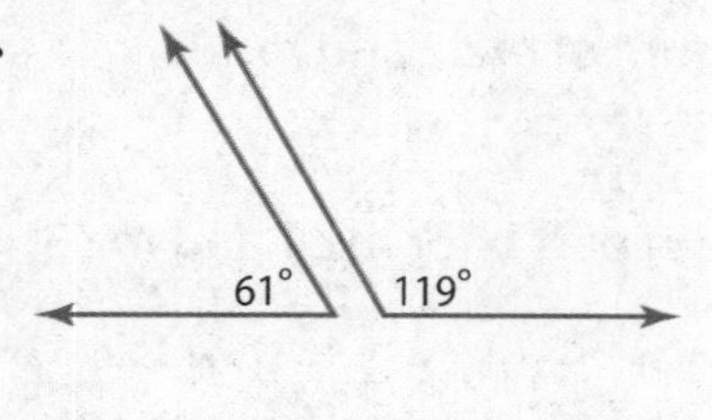

____

3.

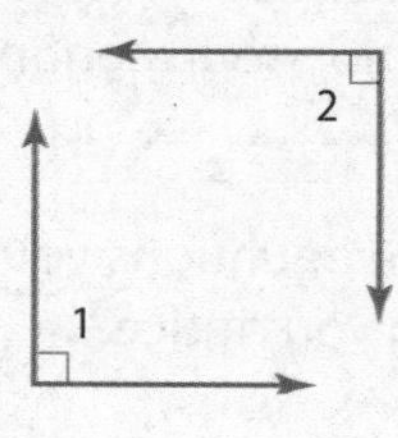

____

Write and solve an equation to determine the measure of *x* in each figure.
(Examples 3 and 4)

4.

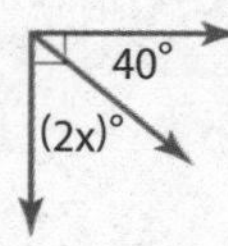

____

5.

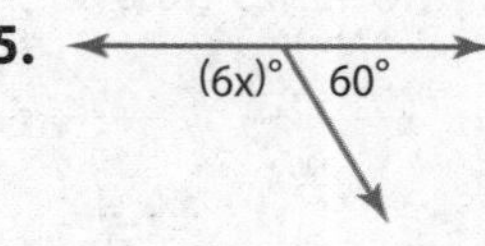

6. ∠A and ∠B are complementary angles. The measure of ∠B is $(4x)°$, and the measure of ∠A is 50°. Write and solve an equation to determine the value of x. (Example 5)

____

7. A skateboard ramp forms a 42° angle as shown. Write and solve an equation to determine the value of x. (Example 5)

____

Use the figure at the right to name the following.

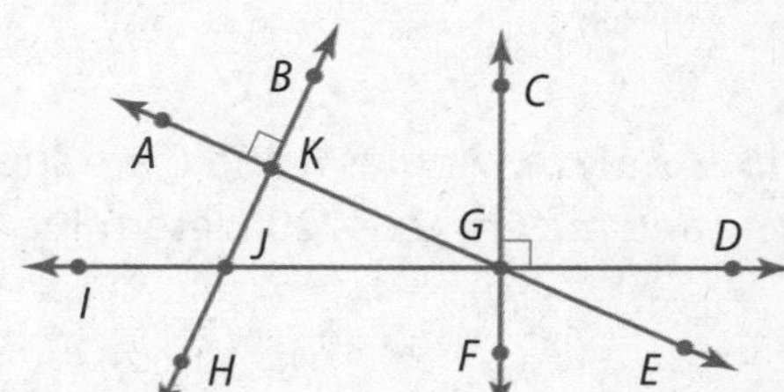

8. a pair of supplementary angles

____

9. a pair of complementary angles

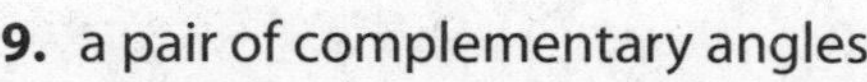

10. a pair of vertical angles

____

11. Use the figure at the right.

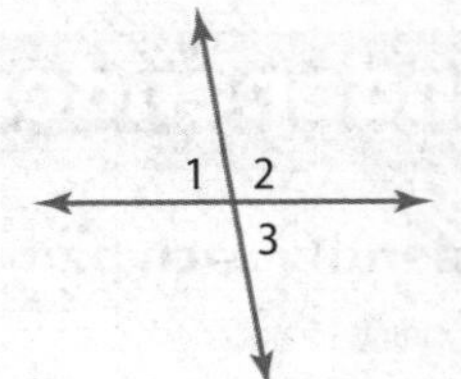

a. Are $\angle 1$ and $\angle 2$ vertical angles, adjacent angles, or neither? $\angle 2$ and $\angle 3$? $\angle 1$ and $\angle 3$?

b. Write an equation representing the sum of $m\angle 1$ and $m\angle 2$. Then write an equation representing the sum of $m\angle 2$ and $m\angle 3$.

c. Solve the equations you wrote in part **b** for $m\angle 1$ and $m\angle 3$, respectively. What do you notice?

d. MP **Justify Arguments** Use your answer from part **c** to make a conjecture as to the relationship between vertical angles.

 H.O.T. Problems Higher-Order Thinking

12. Evaluate When a basketball hits a hard, level surface, it bounces off at the same angle at which it hits. Use the figure to determine the angle at which the ball hit the floor.

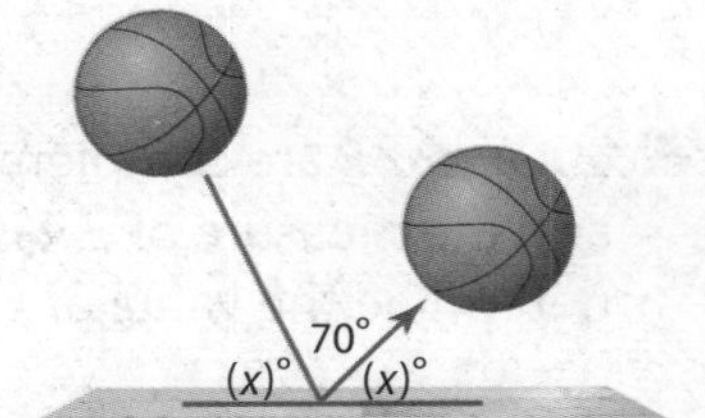

13. Evaluate Angles E and F are complementary. If $m\angle E = x - 10$ and $m\angle F = x + 2$, determine the measure of each angle.

14. Create Draw a pair of complementary adjacent angles. Label the measures of the angles.

15. Analyze Angles B and C are supplementary. If $m\angle B = 2x - 40$ and $m\angle C = 2x + 20$, determine the measure of each angle.

16. Analyze Explain the statement below.

If two angles are right angles, they must be supplementary.

Name ______

Multi-Step Problem Solving

17. The angle shown represents a building support joist. Engineers determined that the measure of angle x needs to be about 7% less to be more supportive. What is the measure of the new angle rounded to the nearest tenth? EE N MP

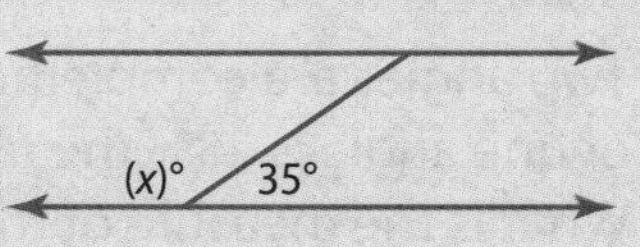

Ⓐ 134.9°
Ⓑ 145°
Ⓒ 155.2°
Ⓓ 165.9°

Use a problem-solving model to solve this problem.

1 Analyze

Read the problem. Circle the information you know.
Underline what the problem is asking you to find.

2 Plan

What will you need to do to solve the problem? Write your plan in steps.

Step 1 Determine the value of ___ by solving an equation.

Step 2 Determine ___ of the measure of angle x.

3 Solve

Use your plan to solve the problem. Show your steps.

Write and solve an equation.

$35 + x = 180$ $x =$ ______

Determine 7% of the measure of angle x.

______ $\times 0.07 =$ ______

______ $-$ ______ $=$ ______

The measure of the new angle is ______ degrees.

So, the correct answer is ___. Fill in that answer choice.

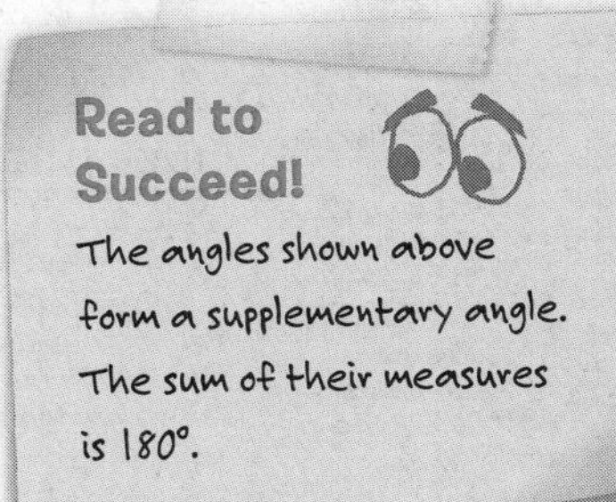

4 Justify and Evaluate

How do you know your solution is accurate?

______

______

______

 = Expressions, Equations, and Relationships N = Number and Operations MP = Mathematical Processes

More Multi-Step Problem Solving

Use a problem-solving model to solve each problem.

18. Two angles are complementary. The measure of one angle is 25% the measure of the other. What is the measure of the smaller angle?

Ⓐ 4.5°

Ⓑ 18°

Ⓒ 36°

Ⓓ 72°

19. The time on a clock is 10:00 A.M. The second hand creates a supplementary angle to the angle formed by the hour and minute hands on a clock. What time, in seconds, does the second hand point to? EE N MP

20. What is the measure, in degrees, of the angle x that is complementary to the angle with a measure $(160y)°$? EE N MP

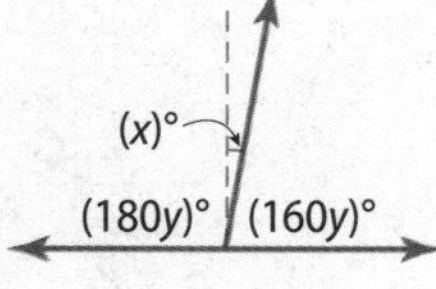

21. Two lines intersect to form vertical angles that are supplementary. What do you know about the measures of the four angles formed by the lines? EE N MP

EE = Expressions, Equations, and Relationships N = Number and Operations P = Proportionality MP = Mathematical Processes

Geometry Software Lab 3-a

Angles in Triangles

INQUIRY HOW can I select tools to explore angles in triangles?

Texas Essential Knowledge and Skills

Targeted TEKS

7.11(C) Write and solve equations using geometry concepts, including the sum of the angles in a triangle, and angle relationships.

Mathematical Processes

7.1(C), 7.1(D), 7.1(E), 7.1(F)

The Spirit Club is selling triangular-shaped pennants for Homecoming. Teresa is making a poster to advertise the pennants. She wants to use a computer program to draw a model of the pennant.

Hands-On Activity 1

Tools

You can use dynamic geometry software such as The Geometer's Sketchpad® to draw triangles given three angle measures. In this investigation, you will draw a triangle with angle measures of 30°, 60°, and 90°.

Step 1 First, click on **Edit**. Go to **Preferences**. Change the angle precision from *hundredths* to *units*. Next, use the **Straightedge (segment)** tool. Click and drag three times to create a triangle like the one shown.

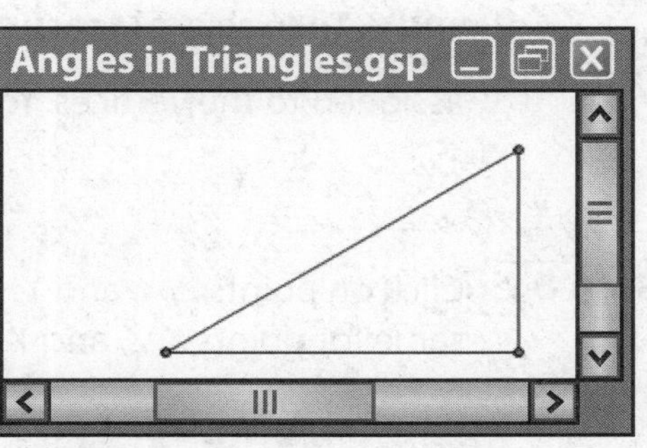

Step 2 Using the **Selection Arrow**, click on each of the vertex points *A*, *B*, and *C*. Then select **Measure** and **Angle**. Labels will automatically be assigned to the vertices. You found that the measure of $\angle ABC$ is ______.

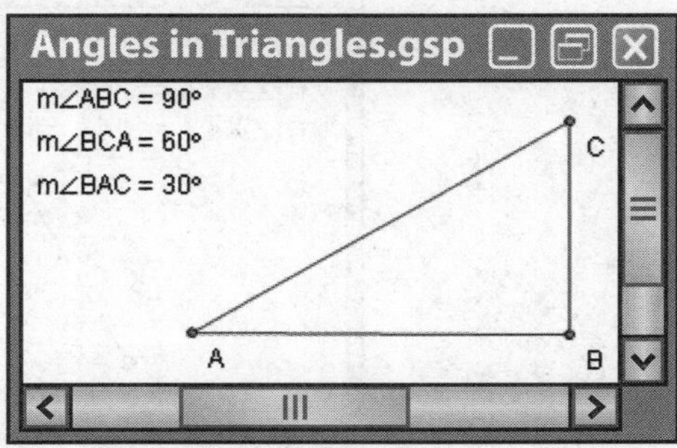

Step 3 Click on points *B*, *C*, and *A*. Click **Measure** and **Angle** again. Repeat for points *B*, *A*, and *C*. The angle measures should be displayed on your screen.

Step 4 If the angles do not measure 30°, 60°, and 90°, use the **Selection Arrow** to move the vertices. Click and drag one or more points so that the angles move.

1. What is the sum of the angle measures in the triangle? ______

Hands-On Activity 2

You can also use The Geometer's Sketchpad® to measure the angles of any triangle created.

Step 1 Construct a triangle using the **Straightedge (segment)** tool. Click and drag three times to create a triangle.

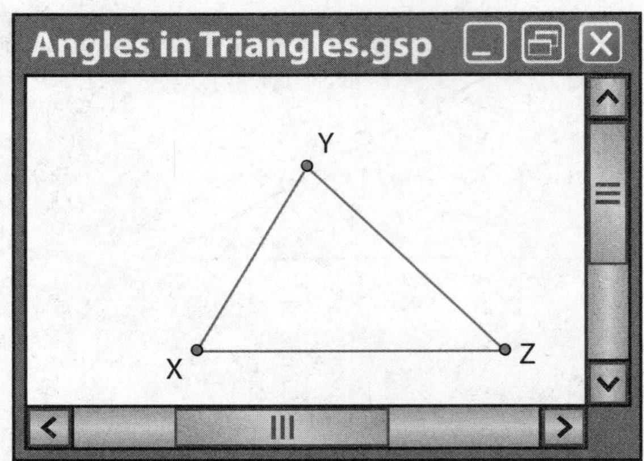

Step 2 Using the **Selection Arrow**, click on each of the vertex points *X*, *Y*, and *Z*. Then select **Measure**, and **Angle**. Labels will automatically be assigned to the vertices. You found that the measure of $\angle XYZ$ is ☐.

Step 3 Click on points *Z*, *X*, and *Y*. Click **Measure**, and **Angle** again. Do the same for points *X*, *Z*, and *Y*. The angle measures should display.

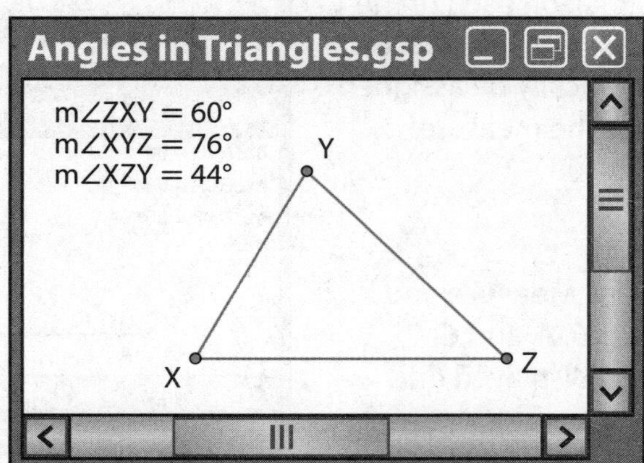

Step 4 Add the measure of the angles of the triangle you created.

☐ + ☐ + ☐ = ☐

Investigate

Select Tools and Techniques Work with a partner to construct each triangle. Once you have constructed a triangle, draw the text and image that appears on your display.

2. $\angle ABC = 90°$

$\angle BCA = 70°$

$\angle BAC = 20°$

Show your work.

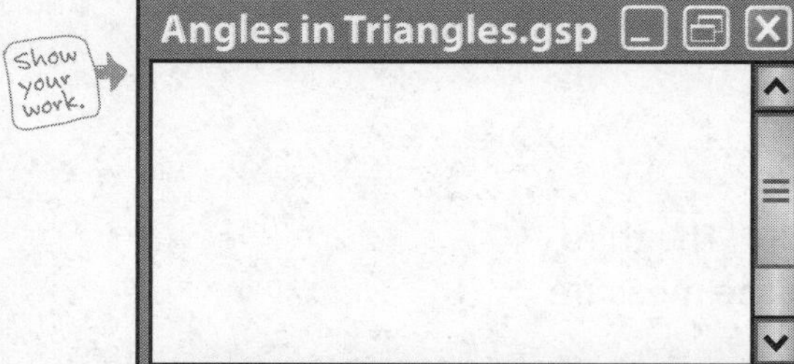

3. $\angle ABC = 90°$

$\angle BCA = 45°$

$\angle BAC = 45°$

Select Tools and Techniques Work with a partner to construct two different triangles. Once you have constructed each triangle, draw the triangle and list the angle measures of the triangle.

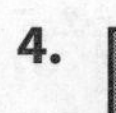

4.

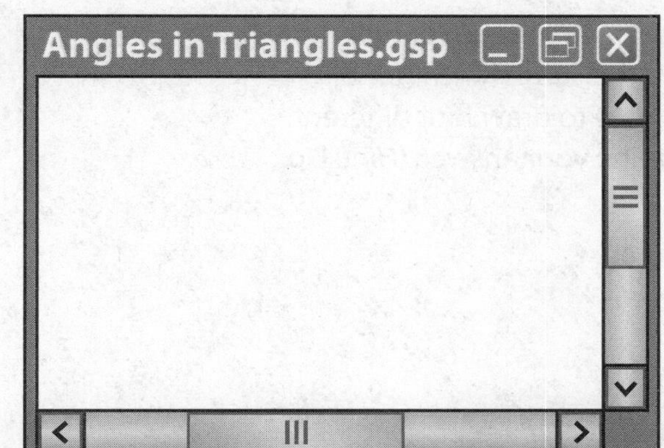

5.

6. Determine the sum of the angle measures of each triangle in Exercises 2–5. What do you notice?

____

7. **Organize Ideas** Make a conjecture about the sum of measures of the angles on any triangle.

____

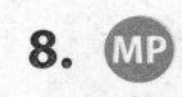

8. **Justify Arguments** Explain the steps you would take to create a triangle if you were given the measures of all three angles.

____

____

____

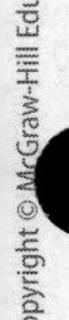

Analyze and Reflect

Work with a partner to answer each of the following questions.

9. Is it possible to use dynamic geometry software to draw a triangle with angles of 50°, 65°, and 70°? Explain.

10. MP **Analyze Relationships** A triangle has angles of 37° and 53°. The third angle is unknown. Based on your findings, write and solve an equation to determine the measure of the third angle. ______

11. MP **Analyze Relationships** A triangle has angles of 58° and 79°. The third angle is unknown. Write and solve an equation to determine the measure of the third angle. ______

Create

12. MP **Analyze Relationships** You know the rule to determine the sum of the interior angles of a triangle. Does a similar rule exist for the sum of the interior angles of a quadrilateral? Use dynamic geometry software to draw four different quadrilaterals and complete the table below to determine your answer. (*Hint*: Do not draw more than one square or rectangle.)

	$m\angle 1$	$m\angle 2$	$m\angle 3$	$m\angle 4$	Sum of Angles
Quadrilateral 1					
Quadrilateral 2					
Quadrilateral 3					
Quadrilateral 4					

13. INQUIRY HOW can I select tools to explore angles in triangles?

Lesson 3

Sum of Angles in Triangles

Launch the Lesson: Real World

Julia practices jumping on a ski ramp. The front of the ramp is a triangle like the one shown below. Determine the measure of the unknown angle.

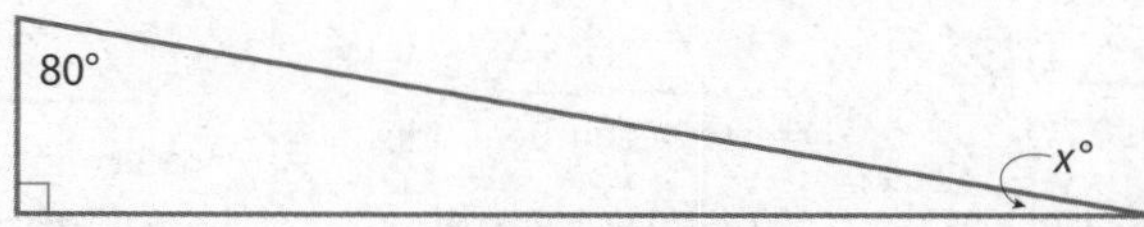

1. Draw an X through the type of angle that is not shown in the triangle.

right acute obtuse

2. Measure the unknown angle. Describe the relationship between the 80° angle and the unknown angle. __________

3. Draw a triangle with one obtuse angle.

4. Is it possible to draw a triangle with two obtuse angles? Explain.

Texas Essential Knowledge and Skills

Targeted TEKS

7.11(C) Write and solve equations using geometry concepts, including the sum of the angles in a triangle, and angle relationships.

Mathematical Processes

7.1(A), 7.1(B), 7.1(E), 7.1(G)

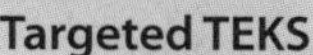

Vocabulary

acute triangle
right triangle
obtuse triangle
scalene triangle
isosceles triangle
equilateral triangle
triangle
congruent segments

Math symbols

△

Essential Question

HOW do measurements help you describe real-world objects?

Which MP **Mathematical Processes** did you use? Shade the circle(s) that applies.

Ⓐ Apply Math to the Real World.
Ⓑ Use a Problem-Solving Model.
Ⓒ Select Tools and Techniques.
Ⓓ Use Multiple Representations.
Ⓔ Organize Ideas.
Ⓕ Analyze Relationships.
Ⓖ Justify Arguments.

Key Concept

Classify Triangles

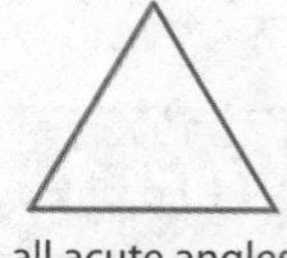

all acute angles

acute triangle

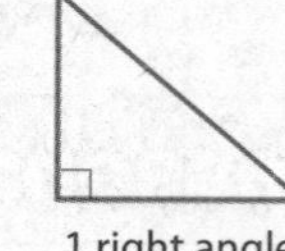

1 right angle

right triangle

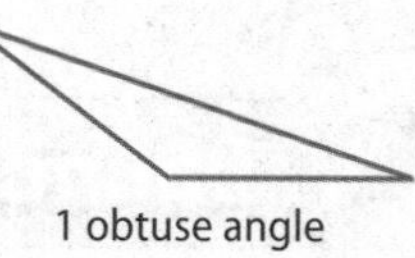

1 obtuse angle

obtuse triangle

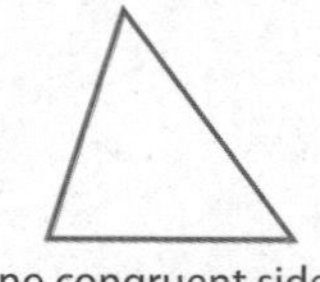

no congruent sides

scalene triangle

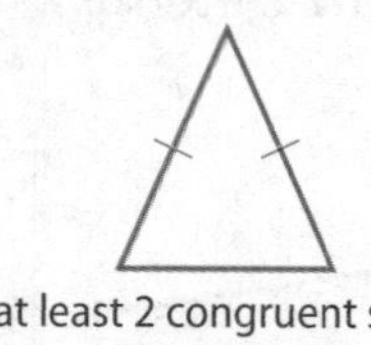

at least 2 congruent sides

isosceles triangle

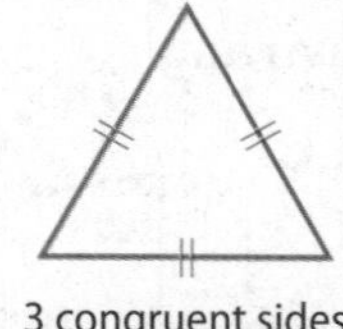

3 congruent sides

equilateral triangle

Work Zone

Congruent Segments

The tick marks on the sides of the triangle indicate that those sides are congruent.

A **triangle** is a figure with three sides and three angles. The symbol for triangle is △.

Every triangle has at least two acute angles. One way you can classify a triangle is by using the third angle. Another way to classify triangles is by their sides. Sides with the same length are **congruent segments**.

Example

Tutor

1. **Draw a triangle with one obtuse angle and no congruent sides. Then classify the triangle.**

Show your work.

Draw an obtuse angle. The two segments of the angle should have different lengths.

Connect the two segments to form a triangle.

The triangle is an obtuse scalene triangle.

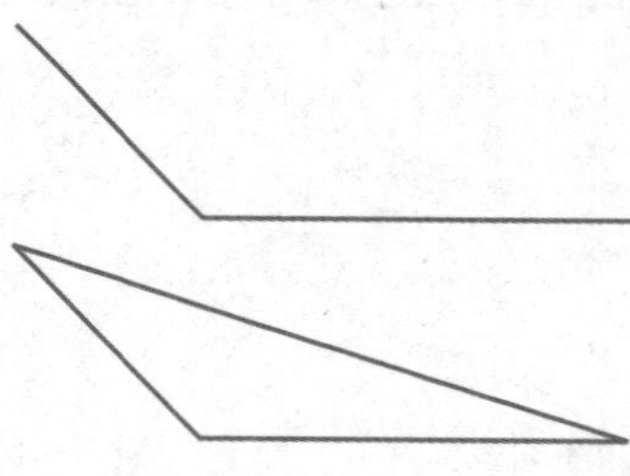

Got It? **Do this problem to find out.**

Draw a triangle that satisfies the set of conditions below. Then classify the triangle.

a. a triangle with one right angle and two congruent sides

a. __________

Example

2. Classify the triangle on the building by its angles and by its sides.

The triangle has one obtuse angle and two congruent sides. It is an obtuse isosceles triangle.

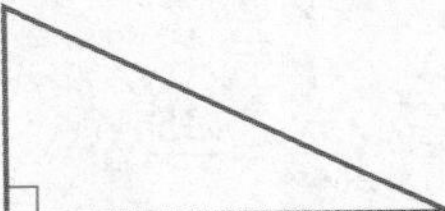

STOP and Reflect

How would you classify a triangle with a right angle and two congruent sides?

Got It? Do this problem to find out.

b. Classify the triangle shown by its angles and by its sides.

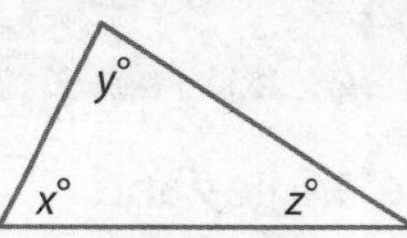

b. ______

Angles of a Triangle

Key Concept

Words	The sum of the measures of the angles of a triangle is 180°.	**Model**
Algebra	$x + y + z = 180$	

You can write and solve an equation to determine the missing angle measure of a triangle.

Example

Tutor

3. Write and solve an equation to determine the value of *x*.

The sum of the angle measures in a triangle is 180°.

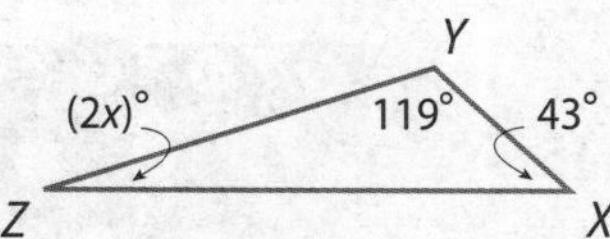

$2x + 43 + 119 = 180$	Write the equation.
$2x + 162 = 180$	Simplify.
$-162 = -162$	Subtract 162 from each side.
$2x = 18$	Divide each side by 2.
$\frac{2x}{2} = \frac{18}{2}$	Simplify.
$x = 9$	

So, the value of *x* equals 9.

Got It? Do this problem to find out.

c. In $\triangle ABC$, the $m\angle A = 25°$, $m\angle B = 107°$ and $m\angle C = (3x)°$. Write and solve an equation to determine the value of *x*.

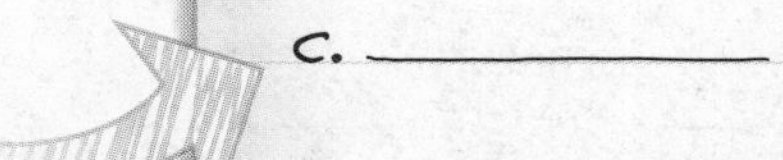

c. ______

Example

Tutor

4. The Alabama state flag is shown. Write and solve an equation to determine the value of x in the triangle.

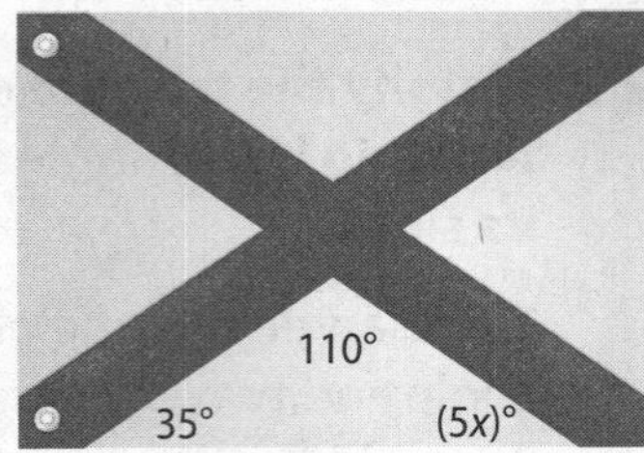

To find the missing measure, write and solve an equation.

$5x + 110 + 35 = 180$	The sum of the measures is 180.
$5x + 145 = 180$	Simplify.
$-145 = -145$	Subtract 145 from each side.
$5x = 35$	Simplify.
$\frac{5x}{5} = \frac{35}{5}$	Divide each side by 5.
$x = 7$	Simplify.

The value of x is 7.

Guided Practice

1. Draw a triangle with three acute angles and two congruent sides. Classify the triangle. (Examples 1 and 2) ______

2. Write and solve an equation to determine the value of x if $m\angle T = (8x)°$ in $\triangle RST$ and the $m\angle R = 37°$ and $m\angle S = 55°$. (Example 3)

______

3. A triangle is used in the game of pool to rack the pool balls. Write and solve an equation to determine the missing measure of the triangle. (Example 4)

______

4. **Building on the Essential Question** How can algebraic reasoning help you develop and represent geometry concepts? ______

______

______

______

Rate Yourself!

Are you ready to move on? Shade the section that applies.

YES ? NO

Find out online. Use the Self-Check Quiz.

Check

Name ______ My Homework ______

Independent Practice

7.11(C), 7.1(E) TEKS

Draw a triangle that satisfies each set of conditions. Then classify the triangle. (Example 1)

1. a triangle with three acute angles and three congruent sides ______

2. a triangle with one right angle and no congruent sides ______

Classify the marked triangle by its angles and by its sides. (Example 2)

3.

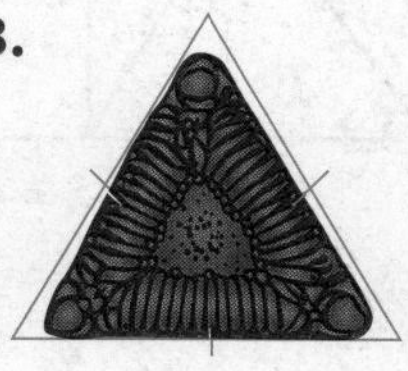

______

4.

______

5.

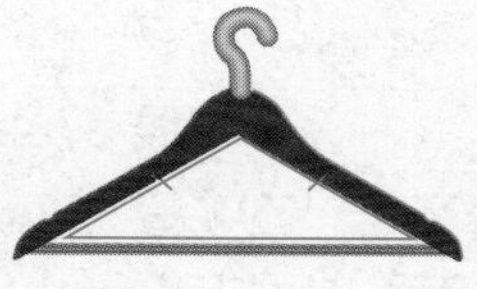

______

Write and solve an equation to determine the value of *x*. (Examples 3 and 4)

6.

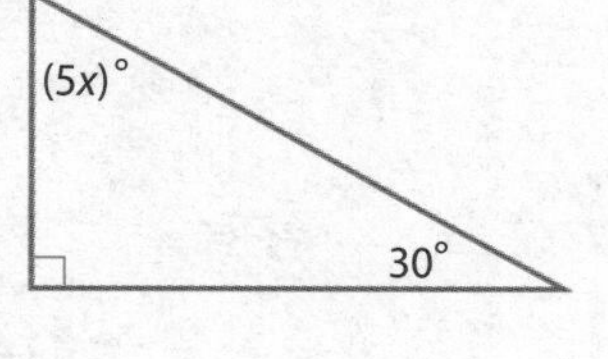

______

7.

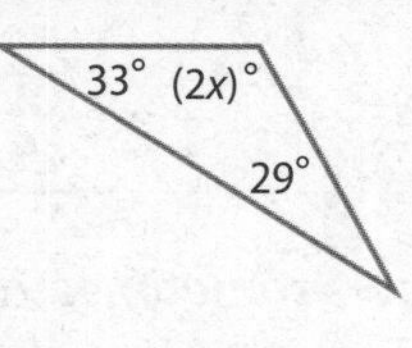

______

8.

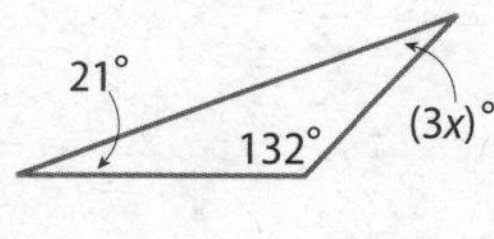

______

Write and solve an equation to determine the measures of the angles in each triangle.

9.

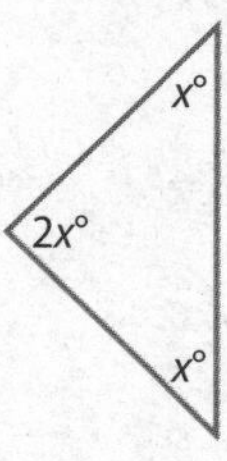

______

10.

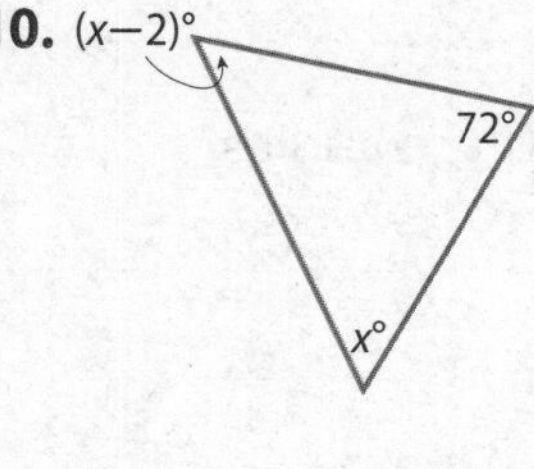

______

11.

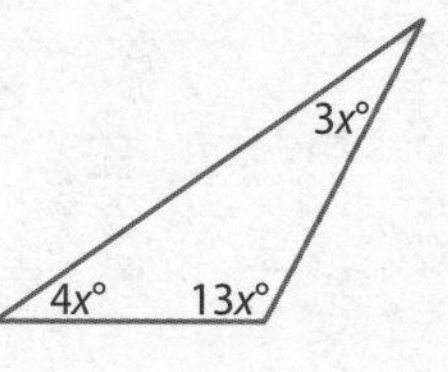

______

12. Write and solve an equation to determine the value of x of a right triangle if one of the angles measures $(2.5x)°$ and the other angle measures $(3.5x)°$.

______

13. A Triangle is formed by two parallel lines and two other intersecting lines. Write and solve equations to determine $m\angle A$.

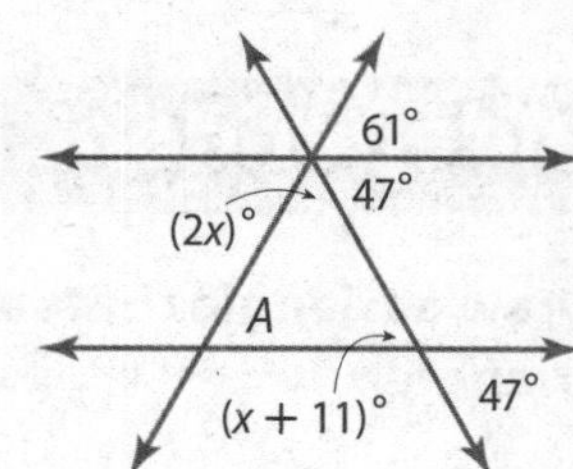

MP Analyze Relationships The measures of the sides of a triangle are given. Classify each triangle by its sides.

14. $5x$, $8x$, $11x$ ________

15. $4b$, $4b$, $4b$ ________

16. $1.7x$, $3.6x$, $1.7x$ ________

H.O.T. Problems Higher-Order Thinking

17. Analyze Apply what you know about triangles to write and solve equations to determine the missing angle measures in the figure.

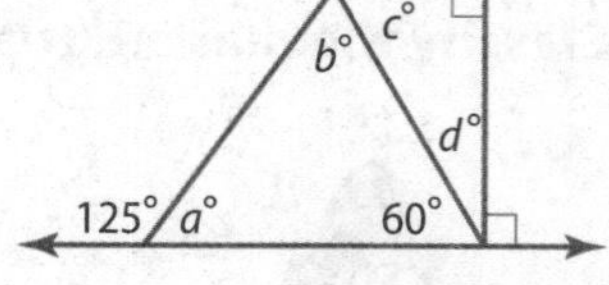

18. Create Draw an acute scalene triangle. Describe the angles and sides of the triangle.

19. Evaluate Determine whether each statement is *sometimes*, *always*, or *never* true. Justify your answer.

a. It is possible for a triangle to have two right angles.

b. It is possible for a triangle to have two obtuse angles.

c. Every triangle has at least 2 acute angles.

Name ______________________________

Multi-Step Problem Solving

20. Amie drew an acute triangle as shown. Her teacher instructed her to use this triangle to create a new right triangle by moving point *C* to the right. What is the area of the right triangle? EE N MP

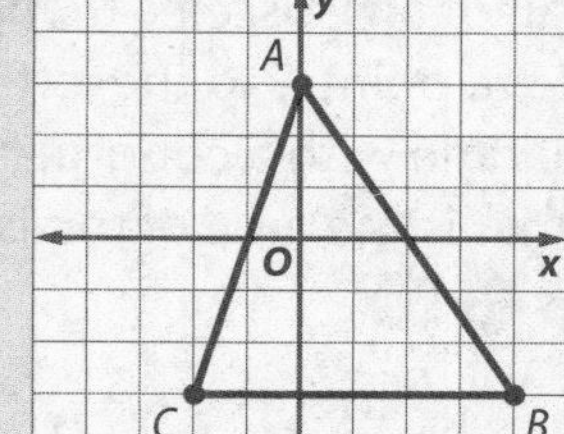

Ⓐ 10 square units
Ⓑ 12 square units
Ⓒ 18 square units
Ⓓ 24 square units

Use a problem-solving model to solve this problem.

1 Analyze

Read the problem. Circle the information you know.
Underline what the problem is asking you to find.

2 Plan

What will you need to do to solve the problem? Write your plan in steps.

Step 1 Determine the ____________ of point *C* after moving to the right.

Step 2 Determine the ________ of the right triangle.

3 Solve

Use your plan to solve the problem. Show your steps.

If you move point *C* to the right ___ units, it will form a right triangle.

The ordered pair for point *C* is ________.

Use the base and height of the right triangle to determine the area.

$A = \frac{1}{2}bh$ $A = \frac{1}{2} \times$ ___ $\times$ ___ $A =$ _____

The area of the right triangle is _____ square units.

So, the correct answer is ____. Fill in that answer choice.

Read to Succeed!
In order for her triangle to be a right triangle, the measure of ∠C needs to equal 90°. Move point C to the right until the angle measures 90°.

4 Justify and Evaluate

How do you know your solution is accurate?

____

____

____

EE = Expressions, Equations, and Relationships N = Number and Operations MP = Mathematical Processes

More Multi-Step Problem Solving

Use a problem-solving model to solve each problem.

21. Half of an isosceles triangle is shown below. Move point C to the left to create an isosceles triangle with a congruent base and height. What is the area of the isosceles triangle?

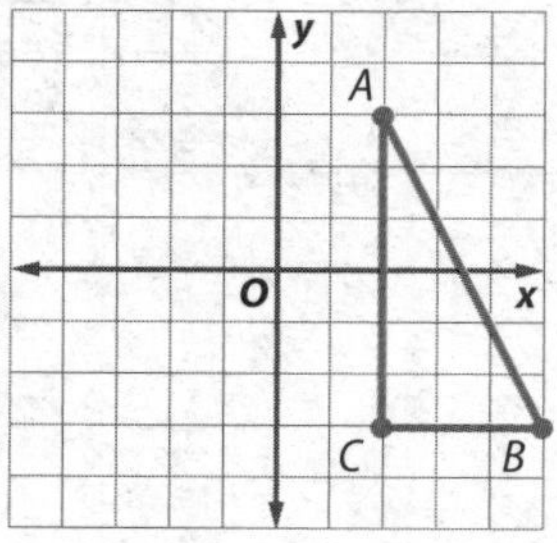

Ⓐ 9 square units

Ⓑ 12 square units

Ⓒ 15 square units

Ⓓ 18 square units

22. What is the value of x in the triangle shown?

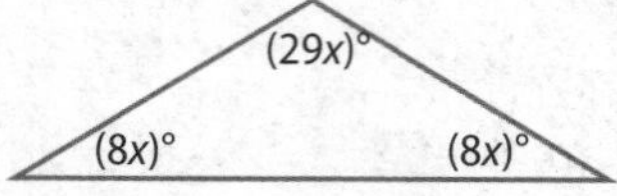

23. What is the measure of the smallest angle in the largest triangle in the picture? EE N MP

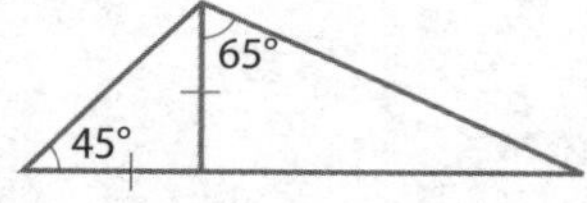

24. What is the measure of $\angle A$?

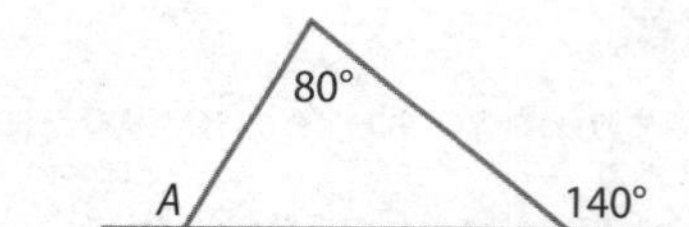

EE = Expressions, Equations, and Relationships N = Number and Operations MP = Mathematical Processes

Hands-On Lab 4-a

Model Area of Circles

INQUIRY **HOW can I select tools to connect models to the formula for the area of a circle?**

Mrs. Allende wants to create a family message center on a wall in her house. There are 4 family members, including Mrs. Allende. She decides to paint 1 circle for each family member using magnetic paint. Each circle will have a 12-inch radius. How do you find the area of a circle?

Texas Essential Knowledge and Skills TEKS

Targeted TEKS
7.8(C) Use models to determine the approximate formulas for the circumference and area of a circle and connect the models to the actual formulas.
Also addresses 7.9(B).

Mathematical Processes
7.1(C), 7.1(D), 7.1(E), 7.1(F)

Hands-On Activity

Let's connect models to a formula for determining the area of a circle.

Step 1 Fold a paper plate in half four times to divide it into 16 equal sections.

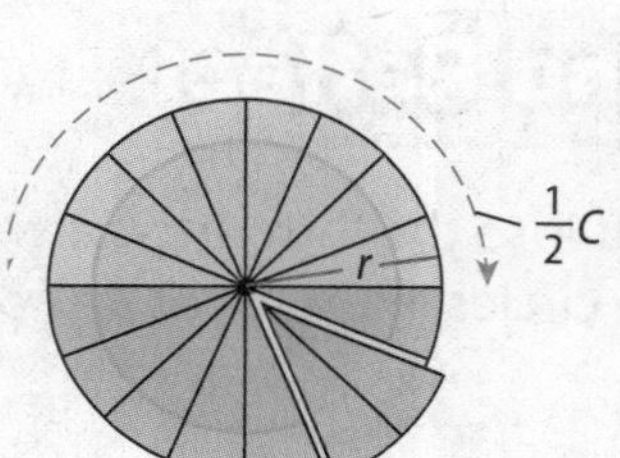

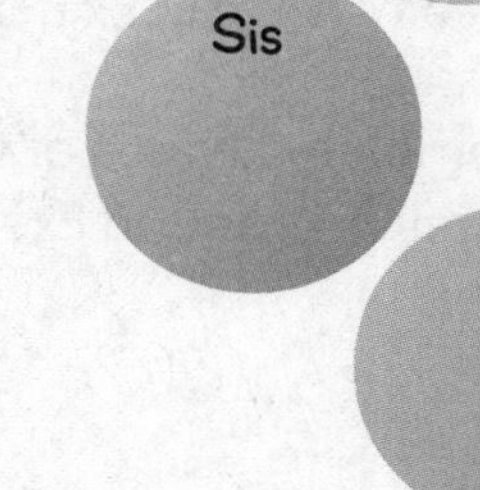

Step 2 Label the radius r as shown. Let C represent the circumference of the circle.

Step 3 Cut out each section. Reassemble the sections to form a parallelogram-shaped figure.

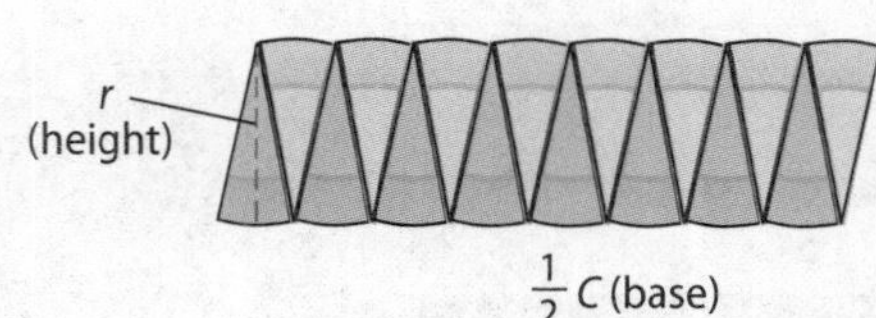

1. What expressions represent the measurements of the base and the height of the parallelogram?

Base: ______________ Height: ______________

2. **MP Organize Ideas** Substitute these values into the formula for the area of a parallelogram, $A = b \times h$. Write the new formula. ______________

3. **Connect Models to Rules** Replace C with the expression for the circumference of a circle, $2\pi r$. Simplify the equation and describe what it represents.

____

Investigate

Work with a partner. Use the circle to draw and label a parallelogram that would result from cutting and reassembling the circle. Use 3.14 for π.

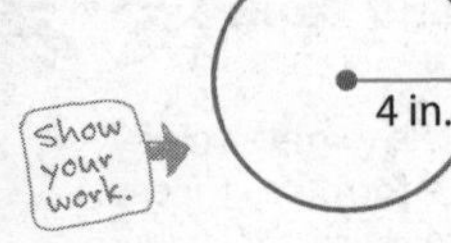

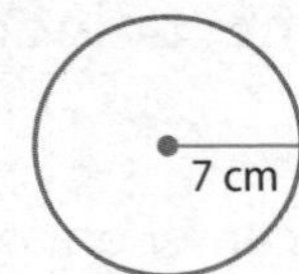

4. Base: ______ Height: ______

Area of Parallelogram: ______

5. Base: ______ Height: ______

Area of Parallelogram: ______

Analyze and Reflect

6. MP **Analyze Relationships** Use the formula you wrote in Exercise 3 to determine the area of the circles in Exercises 4 and 5 above. Use 3.14 for π.

Area of circle in Exercise 4: ______

Area of circle in Exercise 5: ______

7. Compare the area of the circles you found in Exercise 6 to the area of the parallelograms in Exercises 4 and 5. What do you notice? Explain.

Create

8. MP **Apply Math to the Real World** Find a real-world example of a circle. Measure the radius of the circle. Draw a resulting parallelogram from reassembling the circle on a piece of paper. Then calculate the circle's area.

9. INQUIRY HOW can I select tools to connect models to the formula for the area of a circle?

Lesson 4

Area of Circles

Launch the Lesson: Real World

Adrianne bought an 8-foot leash for her dog. How much running room will her dog have with the leash fully extended?

1. Should she calculate the circumference or area? Explain. ______

2. The circle above was cut and reassembled to form the parallelogram shown. Label the parallelogram with the appropriate measures.

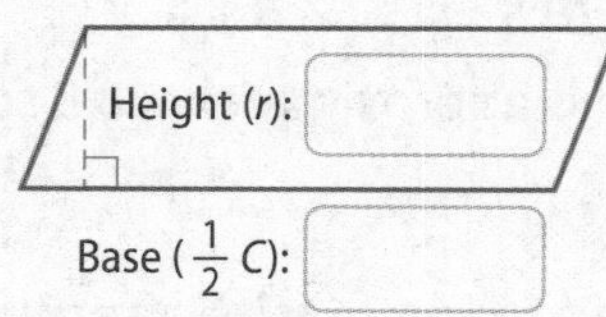

3. Determine the area of running room the dog has with the leash fully extended. Use 3.14 for π. ______

4. **Connect Models to Rules** Write a formula that you can use to determine the area of a circle.

5. Describe a real-world situation that would involve the area of circles.

Texas Essential Knowledge and Skills

Targeted TEKS
7.9(B) Determine the circumference and area of circles. *Also addresses 7.8(C).*

Mathematical Processes
7.1(A), 7.1(B), 7.1(E), 7.1(G)

Vocabulary
semicircle
quarter circle

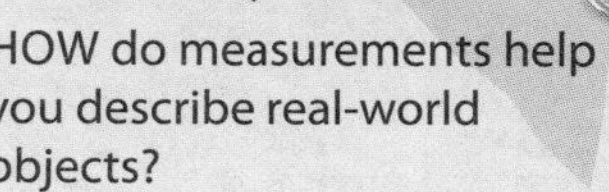

Essential Question
HOW do measurements help you describe real-world objects?

Which MP Mathematical Processes did you use? Shade the circle(s) that applies.

Ⓐ Apply Math to the Real World.
Ⓑ Use a Problem-Solving Model.
Ⓒ Select Tools and Techniques.
Ⓓ Use Multiple Representations.
Ⓔ Organize Ideas.
Ⓕ Analyze Relationships.
Ⓖ Justify Arguments.

Key Concept

Determine the Area of a Circle

Words The area A of a circle equals the product of π and the square of its radius r.

Symbols $A = \pi r^2$

Model

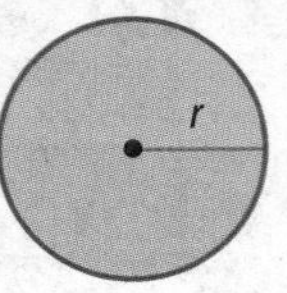

Work Zone

Tutor

Examples

1. Determine the area of the circle. Use 3.14 for π.

5 in.

Estimate $3 \times 5 \times 5 = 75$

$A = \pi r^2$	Area of a circle
$A \approx 3.14 \cdot 5^2$	Replace r with 5.
$A \approx 3.14 \cdot 25$	$5^2 = 5 \cdot 5 = 25$
$A \approx 78.5$	Multiply.

Check for Reasonableness $78.5 \approx 75$ ✓

The area of the circle is approximately 78.5 square inches.

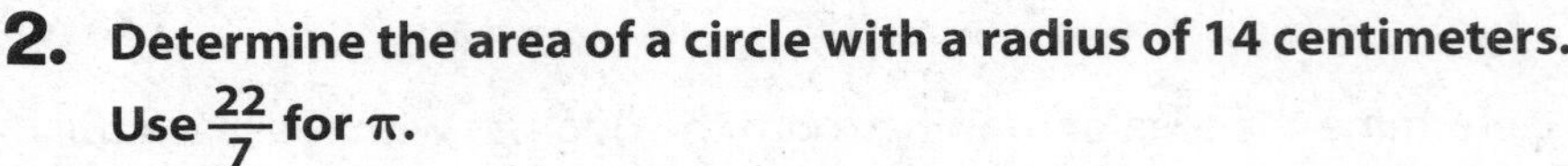

2. Determine the area of a circle with a radius of 14 centimeters. Use $\frac{22}{7}$ for π.

Estimate $3 \times 14 \times 14 = 588$

$A = \pi r^2$	Area of a circle
$A \approx \frac{22}{7} \cdot 14^2$	Replace π with $\frac{22}{7}$ and r with 14.
$A \approx \frac{22}{7} \cdot 196$	$14^2 = 14 \cdot 14 = 196$
$A \approx \frac{22}{\cancel{7}_1} \cdot \cancel{196}^{28}$	Divide by the GCF, 7.
$A \approx 616$	Multiply.

Check for Reasonableness $616 \approx 588$ ✓

The area of the circle is approximately 616 square centimeters.

and Reflect

Cross out the formula that is not used for determining the area of a circle.

$A = \pi r^2$ $A = 3.14r^2$

$A = \frac{22}{7}r^2$ $A = \frac{1}{2}bh$

Got It? Do this problem to find out.

a. Determine the area of a circle with a radius of 3.2 centimeters. Use 3.14 for π. Round to the nearest tenth.

b. Determine the area of a circle with a diameter of 30 feet. Use 3.14 for π. Round to the nearest tenth.

a. ____________

b. ____________

Area of Semicircles and Quarter Circles

A **semicircle** is half of a circle. The formula for the area of a semicircle is $A = \frac{1}{2}\pi r^2$. A **quarter circle** is one-fourth of a circle. The formula for the area of a quarter circle is $A = \frac{1}{4}\pi r^2$.

Calculating with π
When evaluating expressions involving π, using the π key on a calculator will result in a different approximation.

Examples

Tutor

3. Determine the area of the semicircle. Use 3.14 for π. Round to the nearest tenth.

18 mm

$A = \frac{1}{2}\pi r^2$ Area of a semicircle

$A \approx \frac{1}{2}\pi 9^2$ Replace *r* with 9.

$A \approx 0.5(3.14)(9^2)$ Multiply. Use 3.14 for π.

$A \approx 127.2$ Simplify.

The area of the semicircle is approximately 127.2 square millimeters.

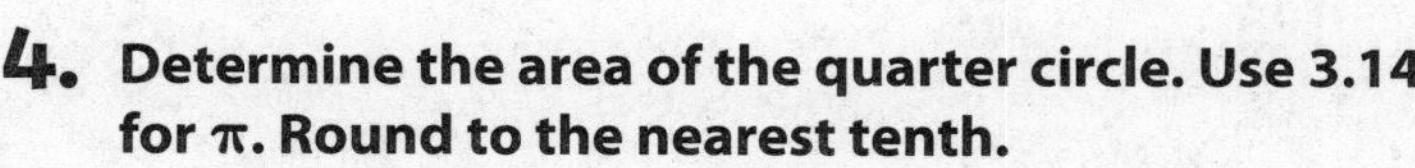

4. Determine the area of the quarter circle. Use 3.14 for π. Round to the nearest tenth.

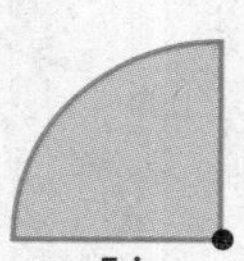

$A = \frac{1}{4}\pi r^2$ Area of a quarter circle

$A \approx \frac{1}{4}\pi 5^2$ Replace *r* with 5.

$A \approx 0.25(3.14)5^2$ Multiply. Use 3.14 for π.

$A \approx 19.6$ Simplify.

The area of the quarter circle is approximately 19.6 square inches.

Got It? Do these problems to find out.

Determine the approximate area of each semicircle or quarter circle. Use 3.14 for π. Round to the nearest tenth.

c.

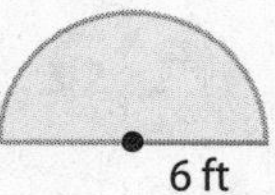

d.

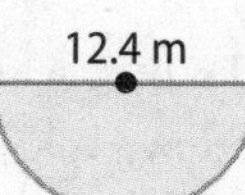

e.

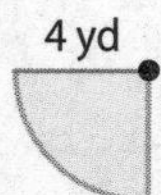

c. ______________

d. ______________

e. ______________

Example

Tutor

5. On a basketball court, there is a semicircle above the free-throw line that has a radius of 6 feet. Determine the area of the semicircle. Use 3.14 for π. Round to the nearest tenth.

$A = \frac{1}{2}\pi r^2$	Area of a semicircle
$A \approx 0.5(3.14)(6^2)$	Replace π with 3.14 and r with 6.
$A \approx 0.5(3.14)(36)$	$6^2 = 6 \cdot 6 = 36$
$A \approx 56.5$	Multiply.

So, the area of the semicircle is approximately 56.5 square feet.

Guided Practice

Determine the area of each circle. Use 3.14 or $\frac{22}{7}$ for π. Round to the nearest tenth. (Examples 1 and 2)

1.

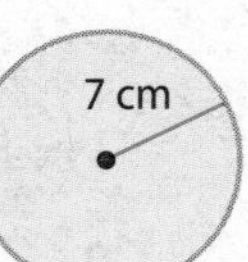

2.

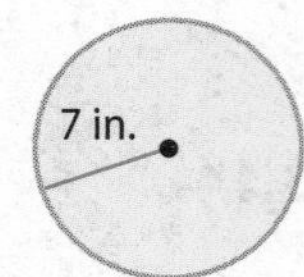

3. diameter = 16 m

4. Rondell draws the semicircle shown at the right. What is the area of the semicircle? Use 3.14 for π. (Examples 3 and 5)

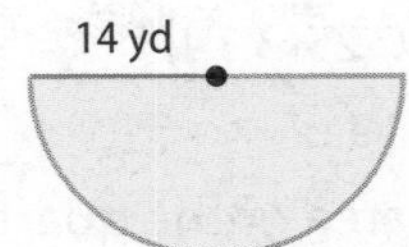

5. Refer to Exercise 4. Rondell decides to cut his semicircle in half to make a quarter circle. What is the area of the quarter circle? Use 3.14 for π. Round to the nearest tenth. (Example 4)

6. **Building on the Essential Question** How can you connect models to the formula for the area of a circle?

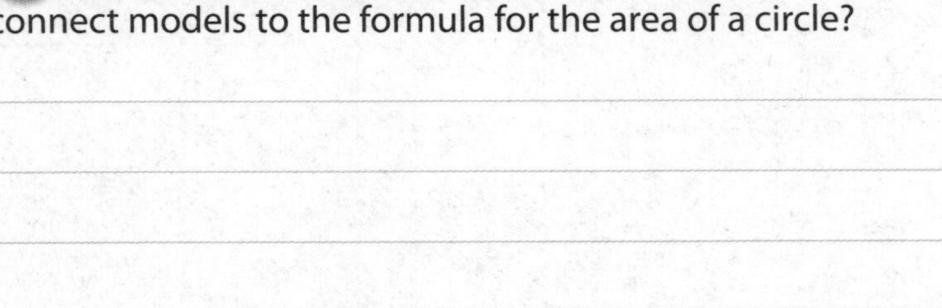

Rate Yourself!

Are you ready to move on? Shade the section that applies.

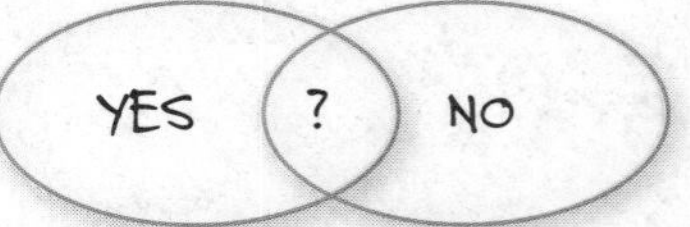

Find out online. Use the Self-Check Quiz.

Name ______________________ My Homework ______________________

Independent Practice

7.9(B), 7.8(C), 7.1(A) TEKS

Determine the area of each circle. Use 3.14 or $\frac{22}{7}$ for π. Round to the nearest tenth. (Examples 1 and 2)

1. 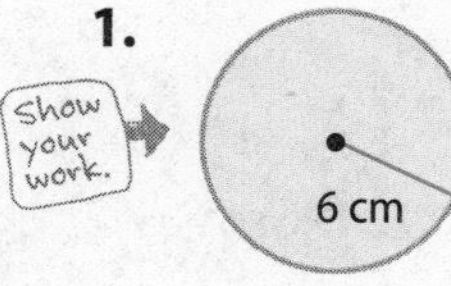

2. 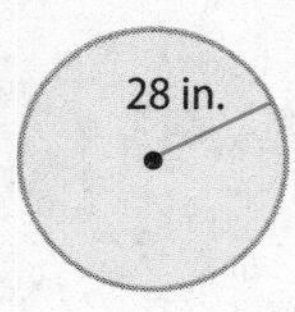

3. 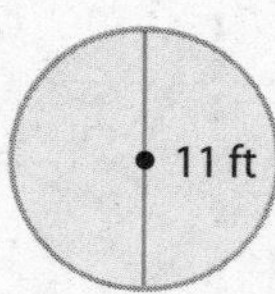

4. diameter = 10.5 in.

5. radius = 6.3 mm

6. radius = $3\frac{1}{4}$ yd

7. Mrs. Corwin has a contractor install a new quarter circle window in her house like shown at the right. What is the area of the window? Use 3.14 for π. Round to the nearest tenth. (Example 4)

8. A rotating sprinkler that sprays water at a radius of 11 feet is used to water a lawn. Determine the area of the lawn that is watered. Use 3.14 for π. Round to the nearest tenth. (Examples 1 and 2)

Determine the area of each semicircle or quarter circle. Use 3.14 for π. Round to the nearest tenth. (Examples 3 and 4)

9. 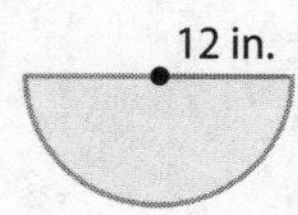

10. 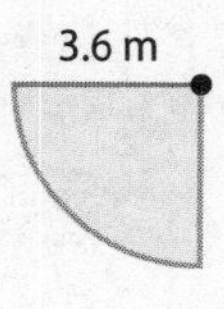

11. 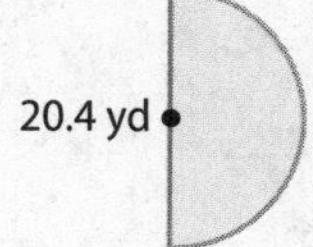

12. The tunnel opening shown is a semicircle. Determine the area, to the nearest tenth, of the opening of the tunnel enclosed by the semicircle. Use 3.14 for π. (Example 5)

13. MP **Justify Arguments** Harry's Pizzeria is having a sale on medium and large pizzas. Medium pizzas are 10 inches in diameter and cost $7.99. Large pizzas are 14 inches in diameter and cost $14.99. Which size pizza is the better deal? Explain. (*Hint*: Determine the cost per square inch of each pizza.)

H.O.T. Problems Higher-Order Thinking

14. **Create** Write a real-world problem that involves determining the area of two circles. Then solve your problem.

15. **Analyze** If the length of the radius of a circle is doubled, how does that affect the circumference and area? Explain.

Analyze Determine the area of the shaded region in each figure. Round to the nearest tenth.

16

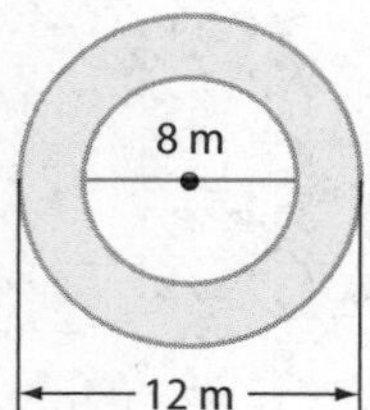

17.

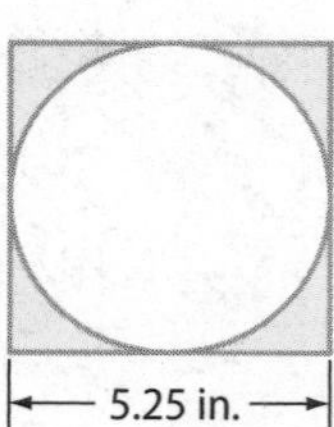

18.

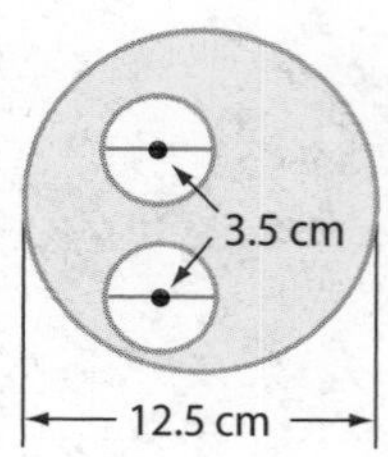

19. **Create** Draw and label a quarter circle that has an area between 100 square meters and 120 square meters. Label the length of the radius and state the area of the circle to the nearest tenth.

Name ____________________

Multi-Step Problem Solving

20. Julian and Ava are raking the leaves around a tree in their backyard. The tree is 2 feet in diameter and is surrounded by a circle of leaves that is 24 feet in diameter. What is the area in square feet of the ground covered by leaves? Use 3.14 for π. EE N MP

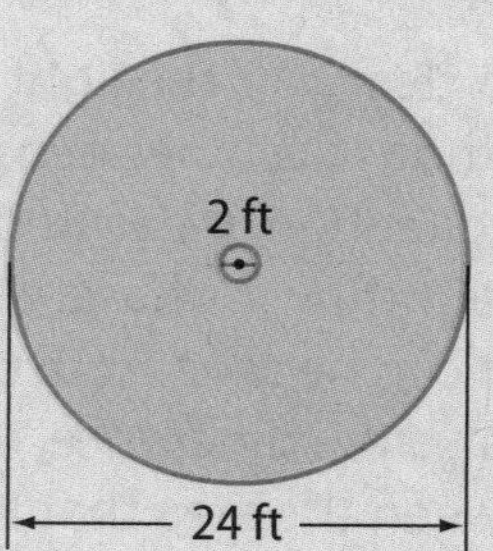

Use a problem-solving model to solve this problem.

1 Analyze

Read the problem. Circle the information you know.
Underline what the problem is asking you to find.

2 Plan

What will you need to do to solve the problem? Write your plan in steps.

Step 1 Determine the ________ of both circles.

Step 2 Subtract the area of the ____________________ from the area of the ____________.

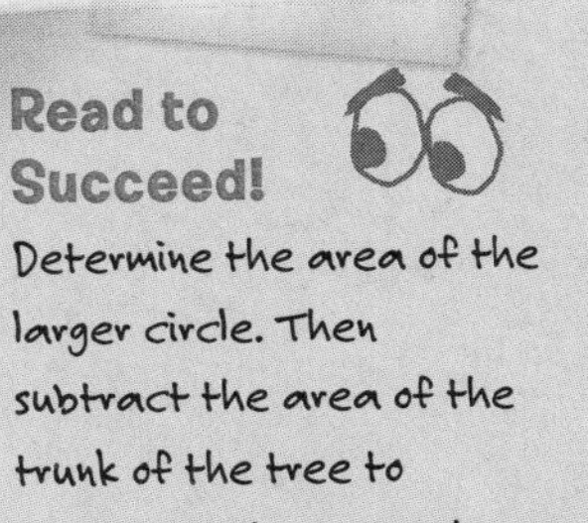

3 Solve

Use your plan to solve the problem. Show your steps.

Write and solve equations to determine the median and lower quartile.

$A = \pi r^2$ $\quad$ $A = \pi(1^2)$ $\quad$ $A =$ ________

$A = \pi r^2$ $\quad$ $A = \pi(12^2)$ $\quad$ $A =$ ________

________ − ________ = ________ Subtract.

The area of the ground covered by leaves is ________ square feet.

Complete the grid.

					.		
⊕	0	0	0	0		0	0
⊖	1	1	1	1		1	1
	2	2	2	2		2	2
	3	3	3	3		3	3
	4	4	4	4		4	4
	5	5	5	5		5	5
	6	6	6	6		6	6
	7	7	7	7		7	7
	8	8	8	8		8	8
	9	9	9	9		9	9

4 Justify and Evaluate

How do you know your solution is accurate?

____

____

____

EE = Expressions, Equations, and Relationships N = Number and Operations MP = Mathematical Processes

More Multi-Step Problem Solving

Use a problem-solving model to solve each problem.

21. On a clear day, the light from a certain lighthouse can be seen from 10 miles away in any direction, measured from the center of the lighthouse's base. On a cloudy day, the light can be seen from only half the distance. What is the difference, in square miles, between the area that the light is visible on a clear day and on a cloudy day? Use 3.14 for π. EE N MP

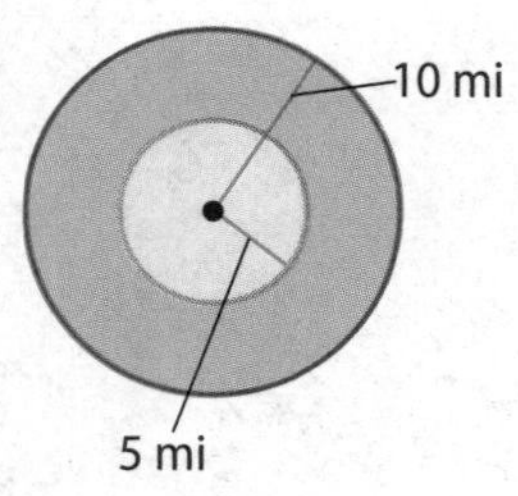

22. Two semicircles are drawn in a rectangle as shown.

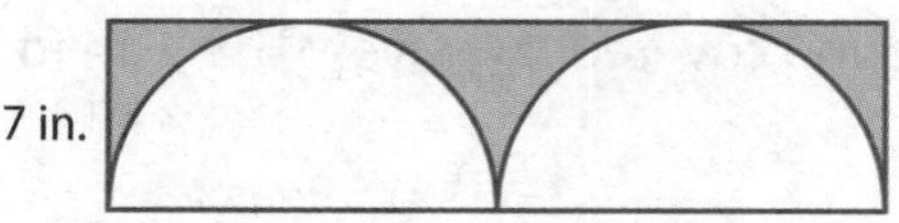

Determine the area of the shaded region in the figure shown. Use $\frac{22}{7}$ for π. EE N MP

23. Carter has 88 feet of fencing to enclose a dog pen in his yard. He is trying to decide whether to make the pen circular or square. Assuming he uses all of the fencing, what is the difference between the area of the circular pen and the square pen? Use $\frac{22}{7}$ for π.

24. Brian is performing in a play at the community theater. The theater is round with seating area around a circular stage as shown below. One quarter of the seating area is taken up by the orchestra and the rest is for audience seating. What is the area of the audience seating? Use 3.14 for π. Explain your method. EE N MP

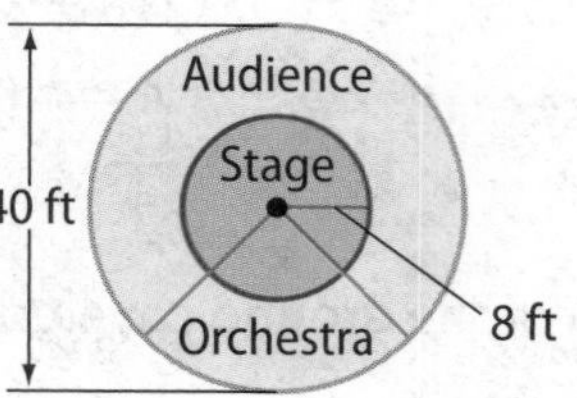

EE = Expressions, Equations, and Relationships N = Number and Operations MP = Mathematical Processes

Lesson 5

Area of Composite Figures

Launch the Lesson: Real World

An image of a stained glass window is shown below.

1. Identify two of the shapes that make up the window.

____

____

2. How could you find the area of the entire window except for the shapes you identified in Exercise 1?

____

____

____

3. Draw a figure that is made up of a triangle and a rectangle on the grid below. Then determine the area of your figure by counting square units.

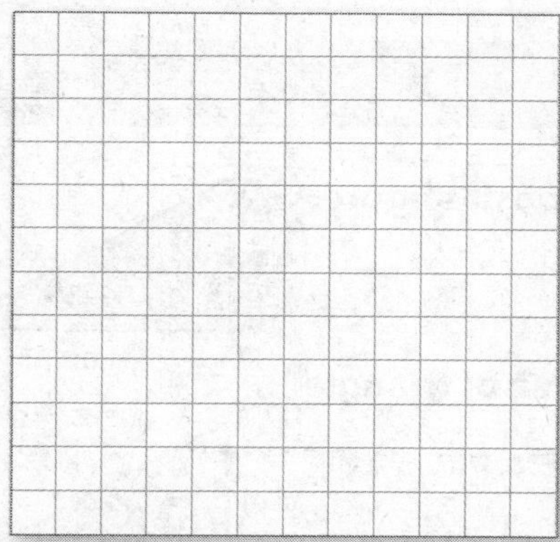

Area: __________ square units

Which MP Mathematical Processes did you use? Shade the circle(s) that applies.

Ⓐ Apply Math to the Real World.
Ⓑ Use a Problem-Solving Model.
Ⓒ Select Tools and Techniques.
Ⓓ Use Multiple Representations.
Ⓔ Organize Ideas.
Ⓕ Analyze Relationships.
Ⓖ Justify Arguments.

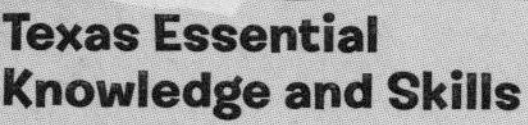

Texas Essential Knowledge and Skills

Targeted TEKS

7.9(C) Determine the area of composite figures containing combinations of rectangles, squares, parallelograms, trapezoids, triangles, semicircles, and quarter circles.

Mathematical Processes

7.1(A), 7.1(B), 7.1(E), 7.1(F)

Vocab

Vocabulary

composite figure

Essential Question

HOW do measurements help you describe real-world objects?

Work Zone

Determine Area of a Composite Figure

A **composite figure** is made up of two or more shapes.

To determine the area of a composite figure, decompose the figure into shapes with areas you know. Then determine the sum of these areas.

Shape	Words	Formula
Parallelogram	The area *A* of a parallelogram is the product of any base *b* and its height *h*.	$A = bh$
Triangle	The area *A* of a triangle is half the product of any base *b* and its height *h*.	$A = \frac{1}{2}bh$
Trapezoid	The area *A* of a trapezoid is half the product of the height *h* and the sum of the bases, b_1 and b_2.	$A = \frac{1}{2}h(b_1 + b_2)$
Circle	The area *A* of a circle is equal to π times the square of the radius *r*.	$A = \pi r^2$

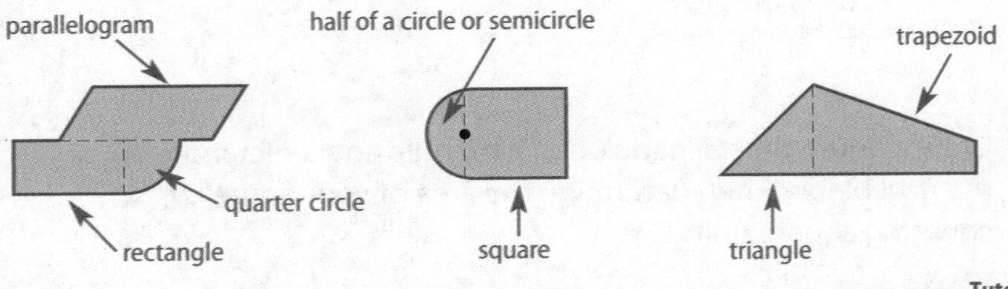

Example

1. Determine the area of the composite figure.

The figure can be separated into a semicircle and a triangle.

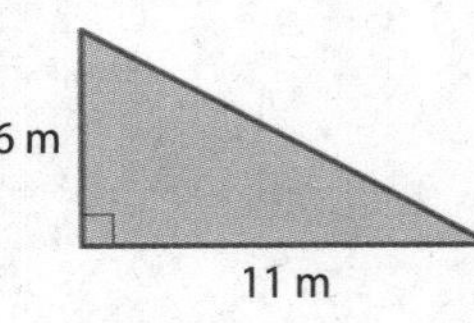

Area of semicircle

$A = \frac{1}{2}\pi r^2$

$A \approx \frac{1}{2} \cdot 3.14 \cdot 3^2$

$A \approx 14.1$

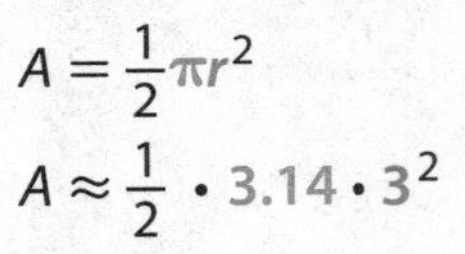

Area of triangle

$A = \frac{1}{2}bh$

$A = \frac{1}{2} \cdot 11 \cdot 6$

$A = 33$

The area of the figure is about 14.1 + 33 or 47.1 square meters.

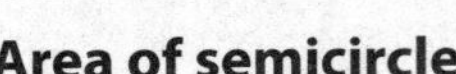

Show your work.

Got It? Do this problem to find out.

a. Determine the area of the figure. Round to the nearest tenth if necessary.

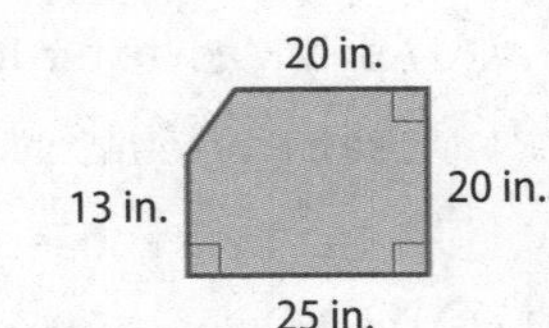

a. ____________

Example

2. **Daniel is constructing a deck like the one shown. How many square feet of decking with Daniel need?**

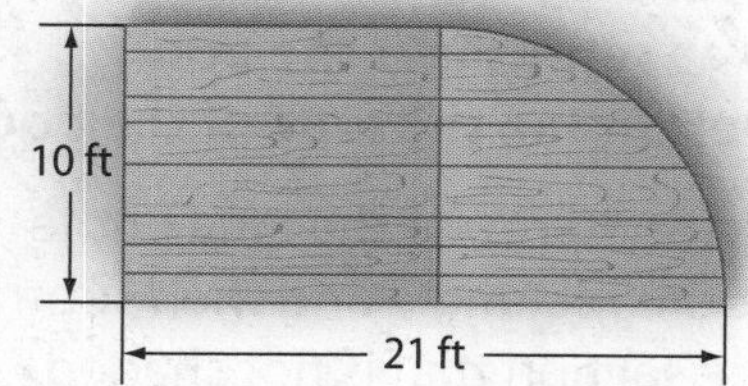

Area of rectangle

$A = bh$

$A = 11 \cdot 10$

$A = 110$

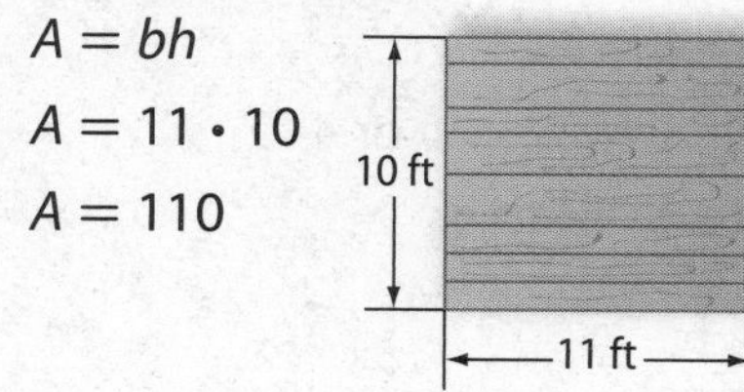

Area of quarter circle

$A = \frac{1}{4}\pi r^2$

$A \approx \frac{1}{4}\pi 10^2$

$A \approx 0.25(3.14)10^2$

$A \approx 78.5$

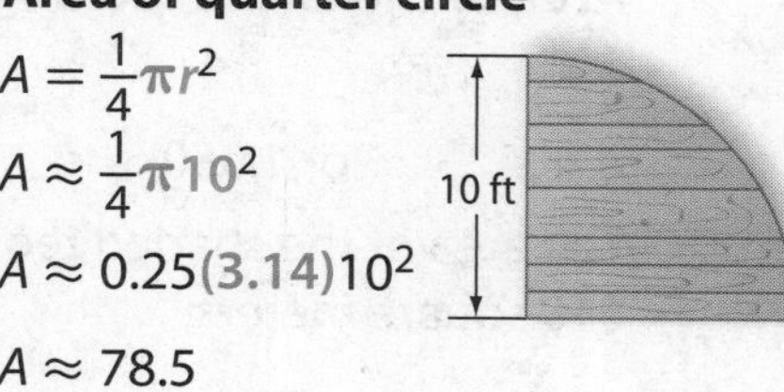

So, 110 + 78.5 or about 188.5 square feet of decking will be needed.

Got It? **Do this problem to find out.**

b. Pedro's father is building a shed. How many square feet of wood are needed to build the back of the shed shown at the right?

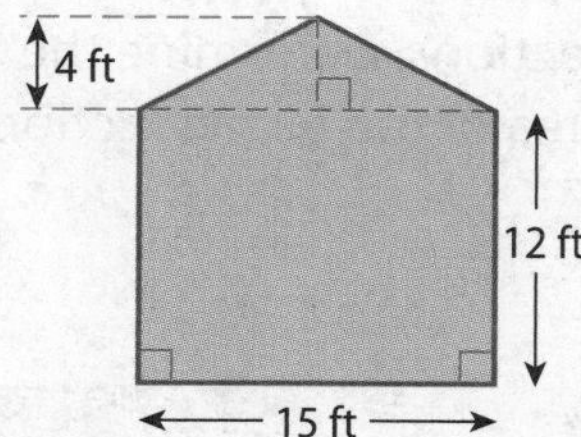

Show your work.

b. ____________

Determine Area of a Shaded Region

Use the areas you know to determine the area of a shaded region.

Multi-Step Examples

3. **Determine the area of the shaded region.**

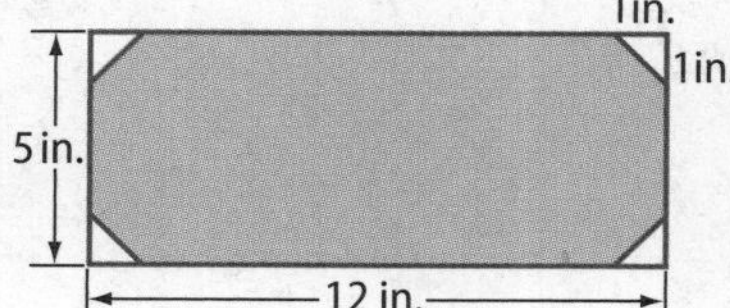

First determine the area of the rectangle and then subtract the area of the four triangles.

Area of rectangle

$A = \ell w$

$A = 12 \cdot 5$ $\quad \ell = 12, w = 5$

$A = 60$ Simplify.

Area of triangles

$A = 4 \cdot \left(\frac{1}{2}bh\right)$

$A = 4 \cdot \frac{1}{2} \cdot 1 \cdot 1$ $\quad b = 1, h = 1$

$A = 2$ Simplify.

The area of the shaded region is 60 − 2 or 58 square inches.

Congruent Triangles

Congruent triangles have corresponding sides and angles that are congruent.

4. The blueprint for a hotel swimming area is represented by the figure shown. The shaded area represents the pool. Determine the area of the pool.

20 m
25 m
22 m
42 m

First determine the area of the entire rectangle and then subtract the section that is not shaded.

Area of the entire rectangle

$A = \ell w$

$A = 42 \cdot 25$ or 1,050

Area not shaded

$A = \ell w$

$A = 22 \cdot 20$ or 440

The area of the shaded region is 1,050 − 440 or 610 square meters.

Got It? Do this problem to find out.

c. A diagram for a park is shown. The shaded area represents the picnic sections. Determine the area of the picnic sections.

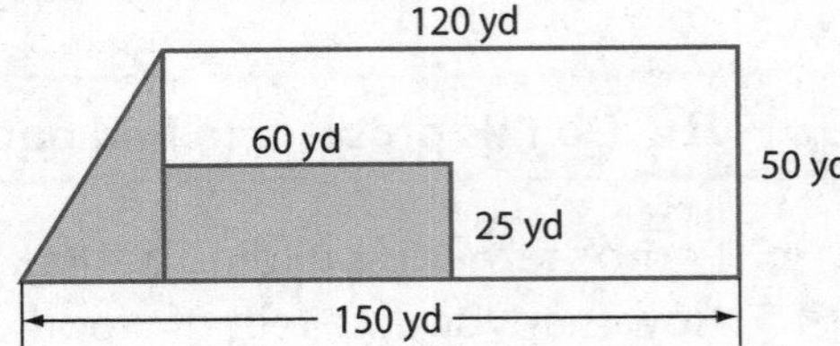

c. ______

Guided Practice

1. Mike installed the window shown. How many square feet is the window? Use 3.14 for π. Round to the nearest tenth.

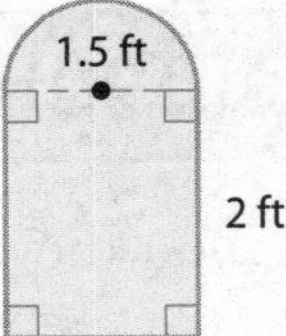

Show your work. (Examples 1 and 2) ______

2. A triangle is cut from a rectangle. Determine the area of the shaded region.

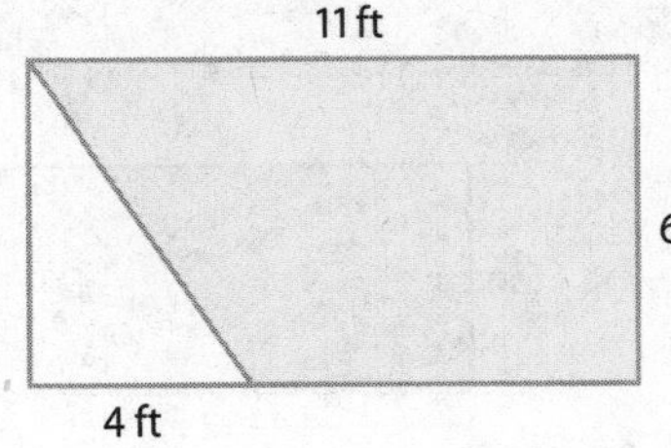

(Examples 3 and 4) ______

3. **Building on the Essential Question** Is your answer to Exercise 1 an exact or approximate answer? Explain.

______

Rate Yourself!

How confident are you about determining the area of composite figures? Check the box that applies.

☐ ☐ ☐ ☐ ☐

Check

Find out online. Use the Self-Check Quiz.

Name ______________________ My Homework ______________________

Independent Practice

7.9(C), 7.1(E) TEKS

Determine the area of each composite figure. Round to the nearest tenth if necessary. (Example 1)

1. ____________

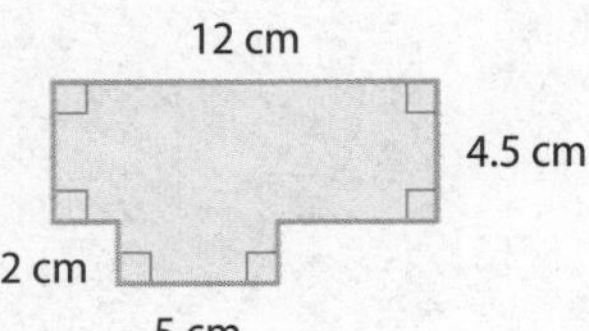

Show your work.

2. ____________

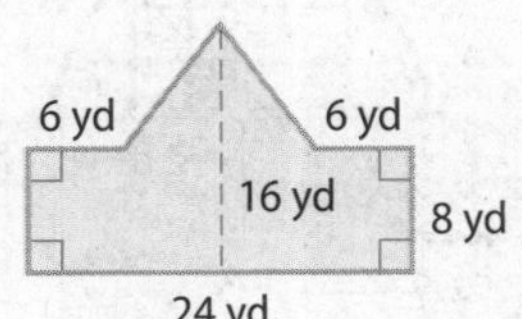

3. ____________

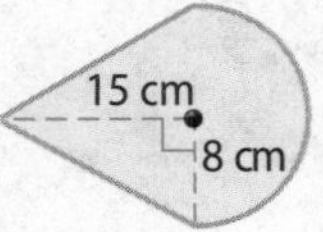

4. ____________

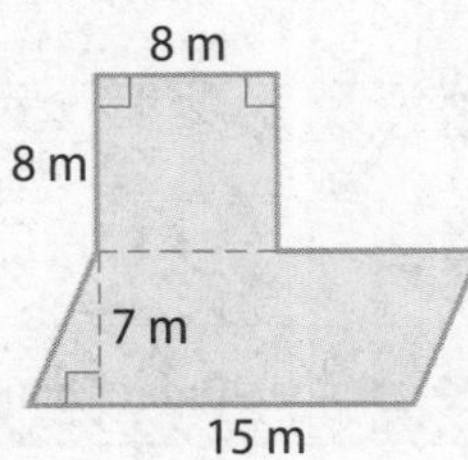

5. ____________

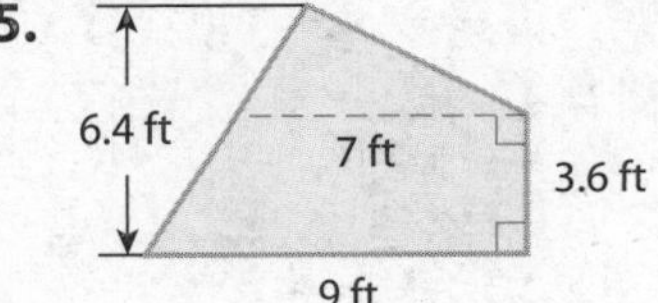

6. ____________

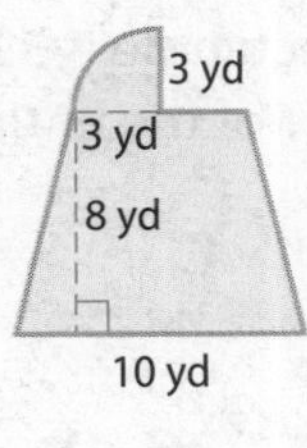

Determine the area of the shaded region. Round to the nearest tenth if necessary. (Examples 3 and 4)

7.

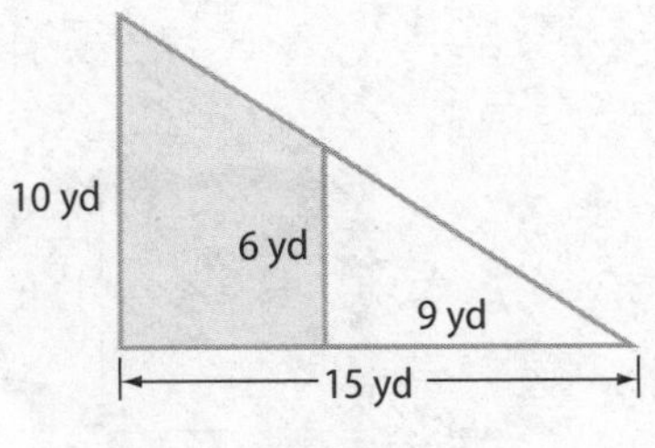

____

8.

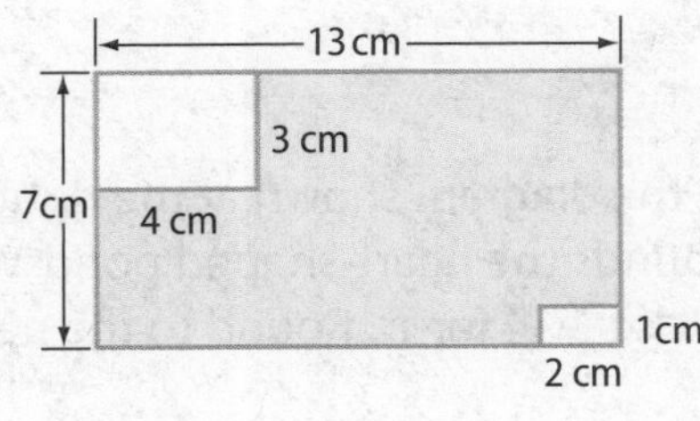

____

9. MP **Use a Problem-Solving Model** Zoe's mom is carpeting her bedroom and needs to know the amount of floor space. How many square feet of carpeting are needed for the room? If she is also installing baseboards on the bottom of all the walls,

how many feet of baseboards are needed? ____________

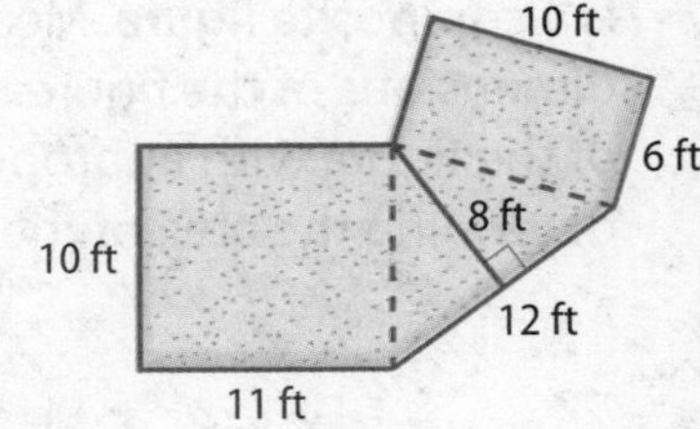

10. Violeta's parents just installed a new front window like shown below. Approximately how many square feet of glass were used to construct the window? Use 3.14 for π. Round to the nearest tenth. ______

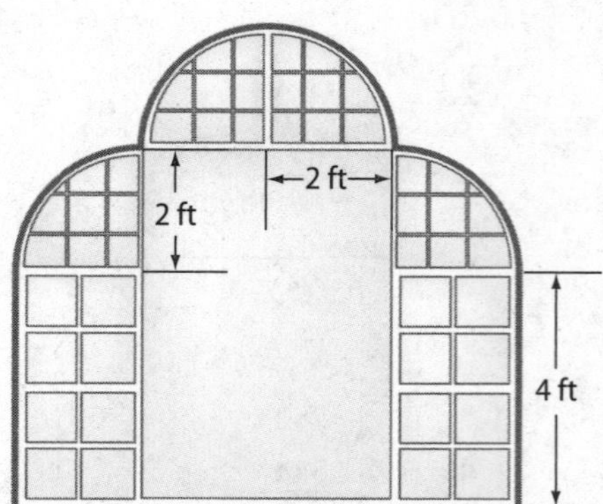

H.O.T. Problems Higher-Order Thinking

11. Analyze The composite figure shown is made from a rectangle and a quarter circle. The area of the rectangle is 32 square feet. Determine the approximate area and perimeter of the entire figure. Use 3.14 for π. Round to the nearest tenth.

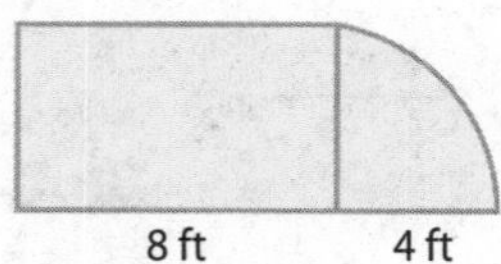

______

12. Analyze The side length of the square in the figure at the right is x units. Write expressions that represent the perimeter and area of the figure.

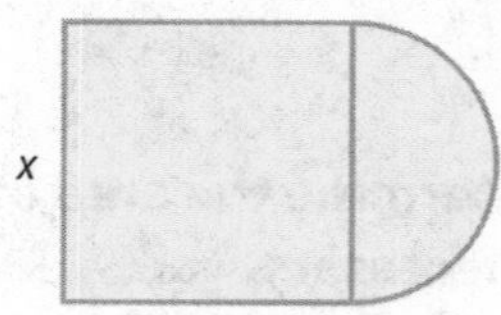

______

13. Analyze In the diagram shown at the right, a 2-foot-wide flower border surrounds the heart-shaped pond. What is the area of the border? Use 3.14 for π. Round to the nearest tenth.

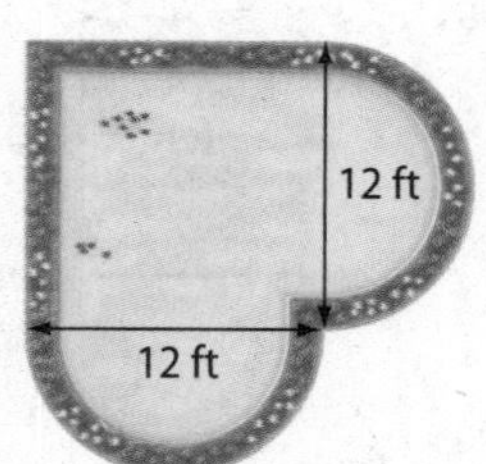

______

14. Create Find a real-world object that is a composite figure. Measure the dimensions of the figure. Draw a model of the figure with appropriate labels. Then determine the area of the composite figure.

______

Name ______________________________

Multi-Step Problem Solving

15. Erin is putting wallpaper on her bedroom wall shown at the right. Determine the area of wallpaper needed for the wall shown. EE N MP

Ⓐ 63 square feet

Ⓑ 75 square feet

Ⓒ 84 square feet

Ⓓ 96 square feet

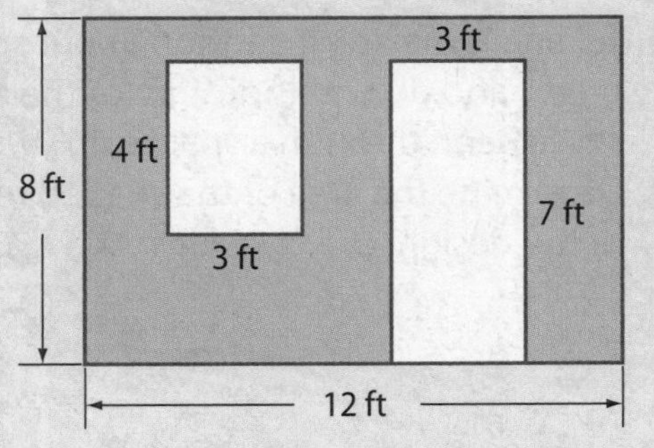

Use a problem-solving model to solve this problem.

1 Analyze

Read the problem. Circle the information you know.
Underline what the problem is asking you to find.

2 Plan

What will you need to do to solve the problem? Write your plan in steps.

Step 1 Determine the ______ of the entire larger rectangle.

Step 2 Subtract ______ of the two smaller rectangles.

Read to Succeed!
Erin will not put wallpaper over the window or doorway. You will need to subtract those areas from the area of the wall.

3 Solve

Use your plan to solve the problem. Show your steps.

The area of the entire wall is 12 × 8 or _____ square feet.

The area of the window is 4 × 3 or _____ square feet.

The area of the door is 3 × 7 or _____ square feet.

Subtract the window and door area from the wall area.

_____ − _____ − _____ = _____

The area of the wall that will need wallpaper is _____ square feet.

So, the correct answer is _____. Fill in that answer choice.

4 Justify and Evaluate

How do you know your solution is accurate?

____

____

____

EE = Expressions, Equations, and Relationships N = Number and Operations MP = Mathematical Processes

More Multi-Step Problem Solving

Use a problem-solving model to solve each problem.

16. Juliana is making a cartoon about space travel, and drew this design for the Moon and sky as seen through a spaceship's window. Determine the area of the shaded region of her design. Use 3.14 for π. EE N MP

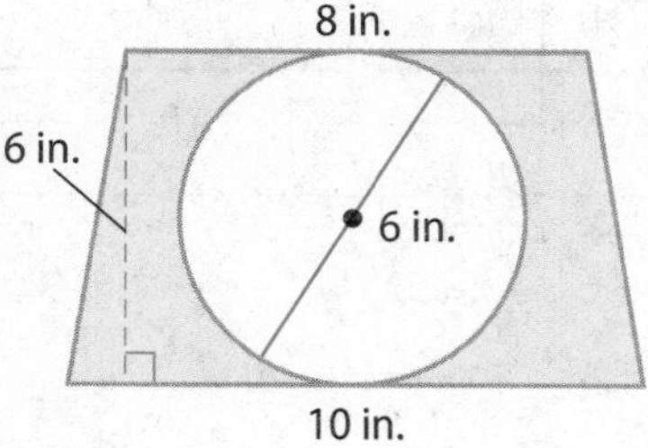

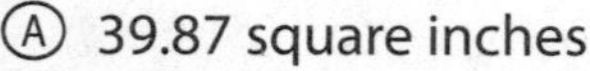

Ⓐ 39.87 square inches

Ⓑ 31.74 square inches

Ⓒ 28.26 square inches

Ⓓ 25.74 square inches

17. The figure shows the dimensions of a home plate for baseball, rounded to the nearest half-inch. If the plate is cut from a two-foot square piece of plastic, what is the area of the unused plastic? EE N MP

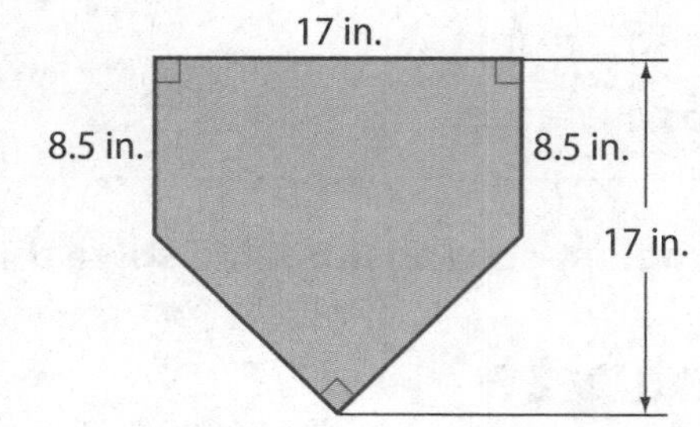

18. Felipe's backyard has a two-foot walkway with outside dimensions of 64 feet long and 36 feet wide. He wants to seed a lawn inside the area enclosed by the walkway. There is a pool, with dimensions shown, at one end of the yard. What is the total area in square feet of the lawn Felipe will plant? Use 3.14 for π. EE N MP

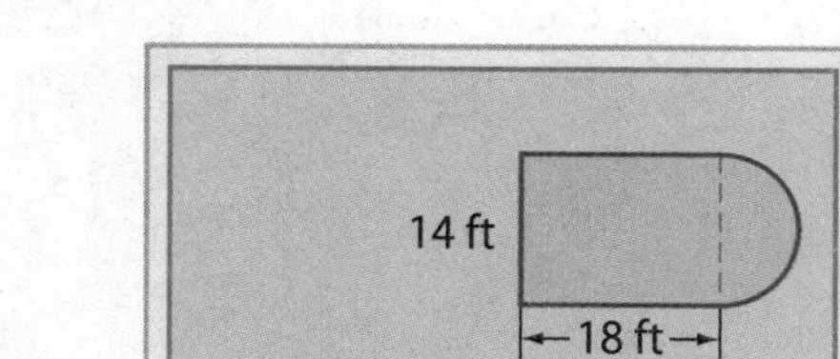

19. The floor plan shows Carmen's studio apartment. She is installing new carpeting, which will cover the entire area except a triangular entertainment center, a closet, and a 10-foot wall with kitchen appliances as shown in the sketch. How many square feet of carpet will Carmen need? Show your calculations. EE N MP

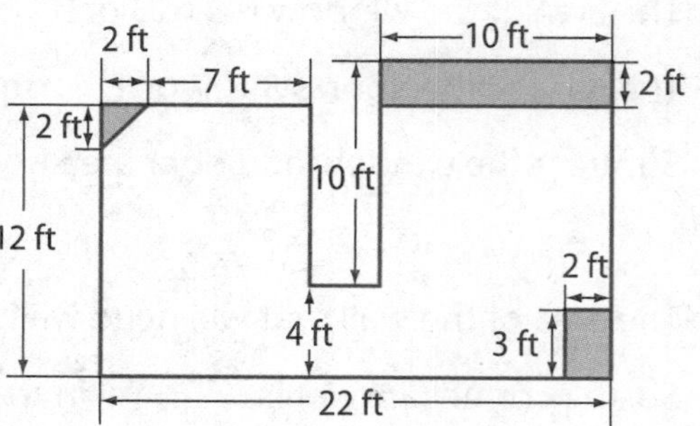

EE = Expressions, Equations, and Relationships N = Number and Operations MP = Mathematical Processes

Solve a Simpler Problem

Playgrounds

Liam is helping to mulch the play area at the community center. The diagram shows the dimensions of the play area.

If a bag of mulch covers 24 square feet, about how many bags of mulch do they need? Round to the nearest tenth if necessary.

Mathematical Process
7.1(B) Use a problem-solving model that incorporates analyzing given information, formulating a plan or strategy, determining a solution, justifying the solution, and evaluating the problem-solving process and the reasonableness of the solution.

Targeted TEKS 7.9(C)

Analyze *What are the facts?*

You know the shape and dimensions of the play area and how much area each bag covers, 24 square feet.

Plan *Choose a problem-solving strategy.*

I will use the ______________ strategy.

Solve *How can you apply the strategy?*

Area of Rectangle 1	**Area of Rectangle 2**	**Area of Semicircle**
$A = \ell w$	$A = \ell w$	$A = \frac{1}{2}\pi r^2$
$A = 5 \cdot 10$	$A = 8 \cdot 7$	$A \approx 0.5\,(3.14)3.5^2$
$A =$ ☐	$A =$ ☐	$A \approx$ ☐

The total area is ☐ + ☐ + ☐ or about ☐ square feet.

Divide the total area by the area each bag covers.

$125.2 \div 24 =$ ☐

So, Liam will need at least ☐ bags of mulch to cover the playground.

Justify and Evaluate *How do you know your solution is accurate?*

____

____

____

Paint

Dora is painting a wall in her house.

If a quart of paint covers about 100 square feet, how many quarts of paint should Dora buy?

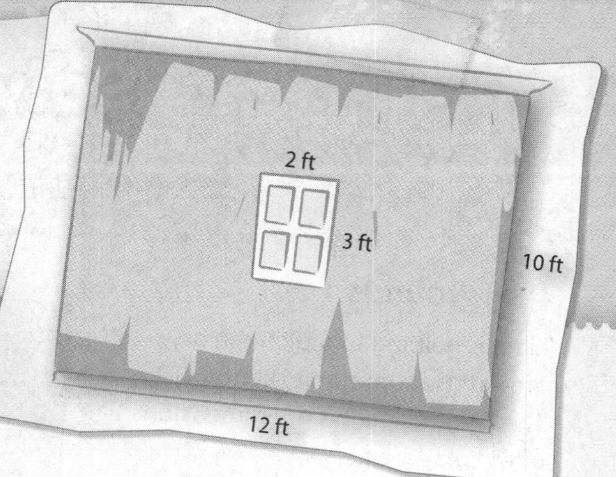

Analyze

Read the problem. Circle the information you know.
Underline what the problem is asking you to find.

Plan

Choose a problem-solving strategy.

I will use the ______________________________ strategy.

Solve

How can you apply the strategy?

Justify and Evaluate

How do you know your solution is accurate?

Multi-Step Problem Solving

Work with a small group to solve the following problems. Show your work on a separate piece of paper.

1. Woodworking

Two workers can make two chairs in two days.

How many chairs can 8 workers working at the same rate make in 20 days?

2. Tips

Ebony wants to leave an 18% tip for a $19.82 restaurant bill. The tax is 6.25%, which is added to the bill before the tip.

How much money does Ebony spend at the restaurant? Explain.

3. Continents

The land area of Earth is 57,505,708 square miles.

Approximately how much larger is the land area of Asia than North America? Explain.

Continent	Percent of Earth's Land
Asia	30
Africa	20.2
North America	16.5

4. Fountains

Mr. Flores has a circular fountain with a radius of 5 feet. He plans of installing a brick path around the fountain.

If each brick covers 2 square feet, how many bricks will he need to buy?

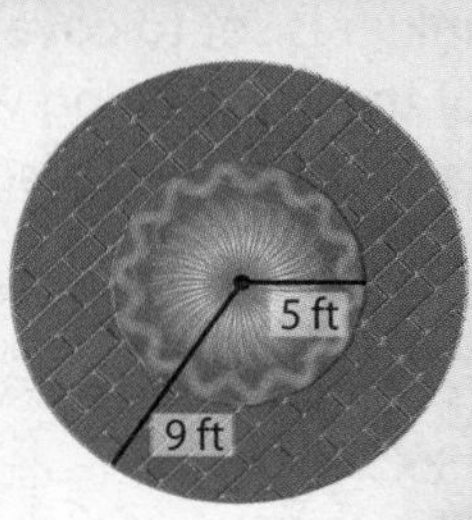

TEKS Mid-Chapter Check

Vocabulary Check

1. MP **Organize Ideas** Define *complementary angles.* Give an example of two angles that would be complementary. TEKS 7.1(D)

Key Concept Check

2. Label the triangles below with the terms *acute, right, obtuse, scalene, isosceles*, and *equilateral*. Then find a real-world object that is a triangle. Explain how you would classify the triangle you found. TEKS 7.11(C), 7.1(E)

Multi-Step Problem Solving

3. A sprinkler is set to cover the area shown. Determine the area of the grass being watered if the sprinkler reaches a distance of 10 feet. Use 3.14 for π. EE N MP

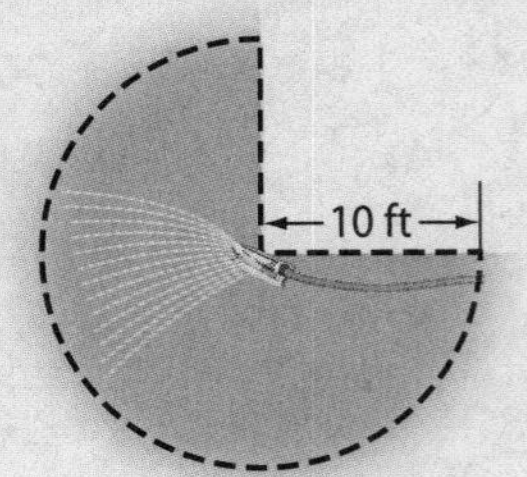

Ⓐ 47.1 ft^2

Ⓑ 157.1 ft^2

Ⓒ 235.5 ft^2

Ⓓ 314 ft^2

EE = Expressions, Equations, and Relationships N = Number and Operations MP = Mathematical Processes

Lesson 6

Volume of Prisms

Launch the Lesson: Vocabulary

A **prism** is a three-dimensional figure with at least two parallel, congruent faces called bases that are polygons. The bases of a *rectangular prism* are rectangles, and the bases of a *triangular prism* are triangles.

Write *rectangular prism* or *triangular prism* on the line below each figure.

1. 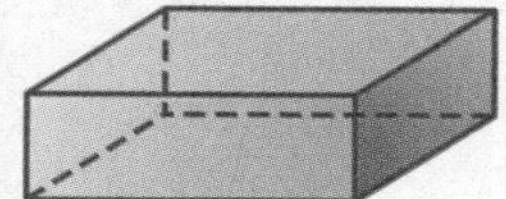

____

2. 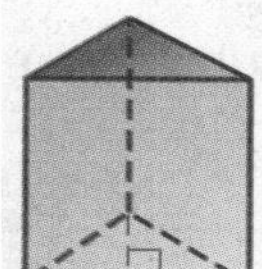

____

Texas Essential Knowledge and Skills

Targeted TEKS

7.9(A) Solve problems involving the volume of rectangular prisms, triangular prisms, rectangular pyramids, and triangular pyramids.

Mathematical Processes

7.1(A), 7.1(B), 7.1(E)

Vocab

Vocabulary

prism

volume

Essential Question

HOW do measurements help you describe real-world objects?

Real-World Link

3. Suppose you observed the camping tent shown from directly above. What geometric figure would you see?

____

4. What formula would you use to determine the area of this figure?

____

5. The length of the tent is 8 feet and the width is 4 feet, use your formula to determine the area.

____

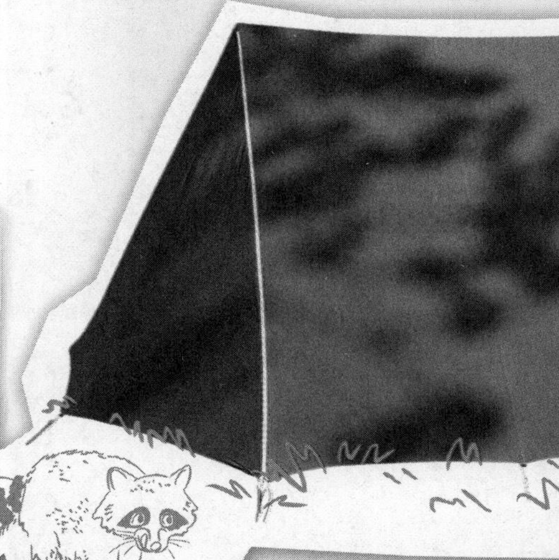

Which MP **Mathematical Processes** did you use? Shade the circle(s) that applies.

Ⓐ Apply Math to the Real World.
Ⓑ Use a Problem-Solving Model.
Ⓒ Select Tools and Techniques.
Ⓓ Use Multiple Representations.
Ⓔ Organize Ideas.
Ⓕ Analyze Relationships.
Ⓖ Justify Arguments.

Key Concept

Volume of a Rectangular Prism

Words The volume V of a rectangular prism is the product of the area of the rectangular base B and the height h. Because the base is a rectangle, the volume V is also the product of the length ℓ, the width w, and the height h.

Model

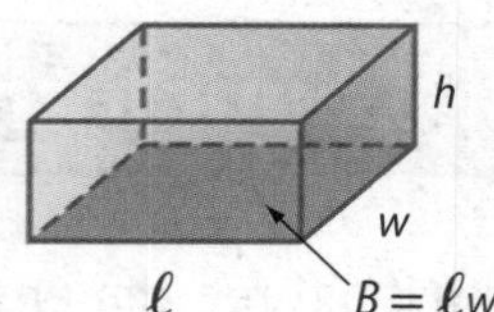

Symbols $V = Bh$ or $V = \ell wh$

Work Zone

The **volume** of a three-dimensional figure is the measure of space it occupies. It is measured in cubic units such as cubic centimeters (cm^3) or cubic inches (in^3).

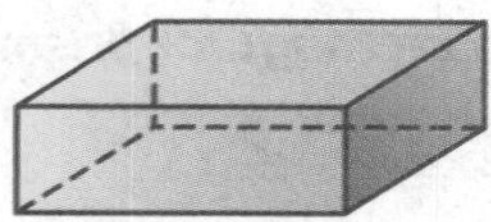

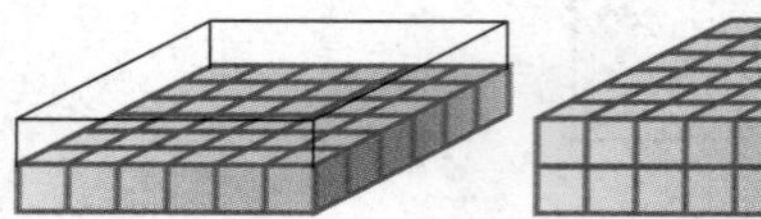

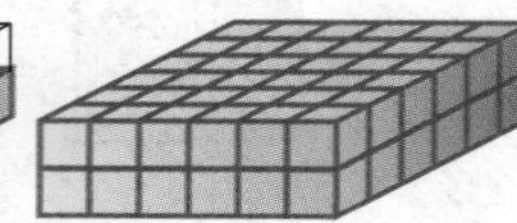

$V = Bh$	Volume formula
$V = (6 \cdot 6) \cdot 2$	$B = \ell w, h = 2$
$V = 36 \cdot 2$, or 72	Multiply.

It takes 2 layers of 36 cubes to fill the box. So, the volume of the box is 72 cubic centimeters.

Decomposing Figures

Think of the volume of the prism as consisting of three congruent slices. Each slice contains the base area, 20 square centimeters, and a height of 1 centimeter.

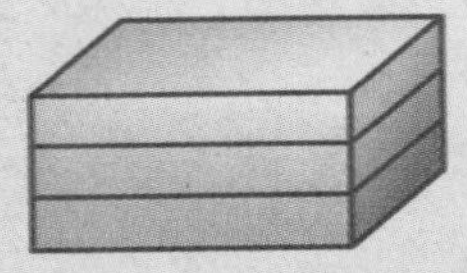

Example

Tutor

1. Determine the volume of the rectangular prism.

$V = \ell wh$	Volume of a prism
$V = 8 \cdot 6 \cdot 4$	$\ell = 8$, $w = 6$, and $h = 4$
$V = 192$	Multiply.

The volume is 192 cubic centimeters or 192 cm^3.

4 cm

6 cm

8 cm

Got It? **Do this problem to find out.**

Show your work.

a. Determine the volume of the rectangular prism shown below.

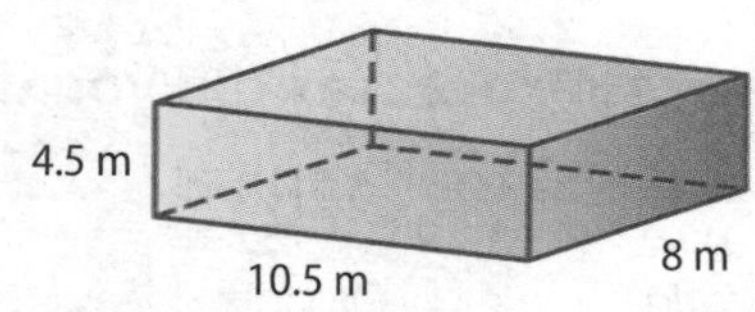

a. ____________

Volume of a Triangular Prism

Key Concept

Words The volume V of a triangular prism is the area of the triangular base B times the height h.

Symbols $V = Bh$, where B is the area of the triangular base.

Model

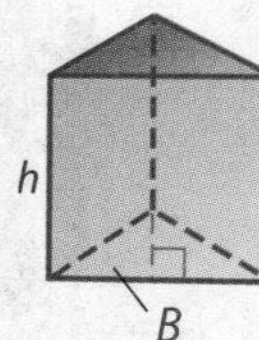

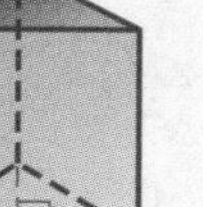

Height

Do not confuse the height of the triangular base with the height of the prism.

The diagram below shows that the volume of a triangular prism is also the product of the area of the triangular base B and the height h of the prism.

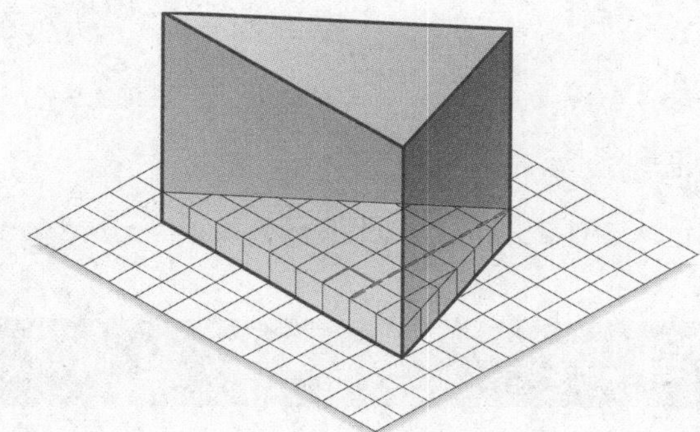

Example

Tutor

2. Determine the volume of the triangular prism shown.

The area of the triangle is $\frac{1}{2} \cdot 5 \cdot 7$, so replace B with $\frac{1}{2} \cdot 5 \cdot 7$.

5 ft, 10 ft, 7 ft

$V = Bh$	Volume of a prism
$V = \left(\frac{1}{2} \cdot 5 \cdot 7\right)h$	Replace B with $\frac{1}{2} \cdot 5 \cdot 7$.
$V = \left(\frac{1}{2} \cdot 5 \cdot 7\right)10$	The height of the prism is 10.
$V = 175$	Multiply.

The volume is 175 cubic feet or 175 ft^3.

Before determining the volume of a prism, identify the base. In Example 2, the base is a triangle, so you replace B with $\frac{1}{2}bh$.

Got It? Do this problem to find out.

b. Determine the volume of the triangular prism.

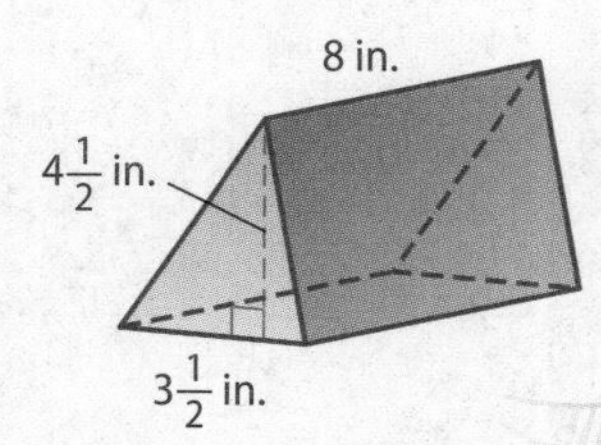

b. ______

Multi-Step Example

3. **Which lunch box holds more food?**

Determine the volume of each lunch box. Then compare.

Lunch Box A

$V = \ell wh$

$V = 7.5 \cdot 3.75 \cdot 10$

$V = 281.25 \text{ in}^3$

Lunch Box B

$V = \ell wh$

$V = 8 \cdot 3.75 \cdot 9.5$

$V = 285 \text{ in}^3$

Since $285 \text{ in}^3 > 281.25 \text{ in}^3$, Lunch Box B holds more food.

Guided Practice

Determine the volume of each rectangular or triangular prism. Round to the nearest tenth if necessary. (Examples 1–2)

1.

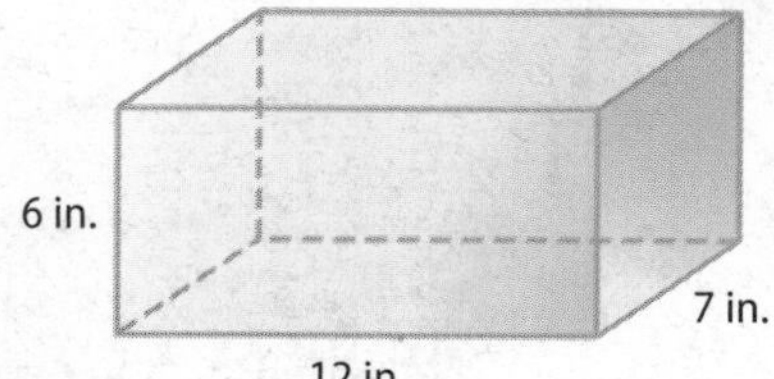

Show your work.

2.

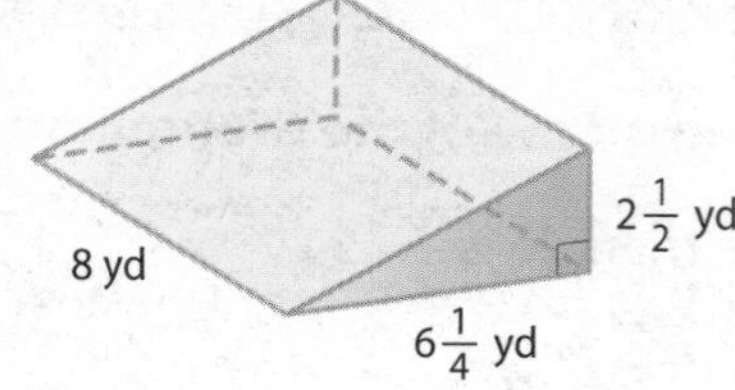

3. One cabinet measures 3 feet by 2.5 feet by 5 feet. A second measures 4 feet by 3.5 feet by 4.5 feet. Which volume is greater? Explain. (Example 3)

4. **Building on the Essential Question** Compare and contrast determining the volume of a rectangular prism and a triangular prism.

Rate Yourself!

How confident are you about determining volume for prisms? Check the box that applies.

Find out online. Use the Self-Check Quiz.

FOLDABLES Time to update your Foldable!

Name ______________________ My Homework ______________________

Independent Practice

7.9(A), 7.1(A) TEKS

Determine the volume of each rectangular or triangular prism. Round to the nearest tenth if necessary. (Examples 1–2)

1. 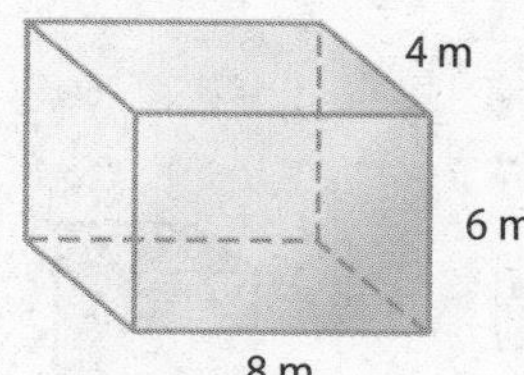

2. 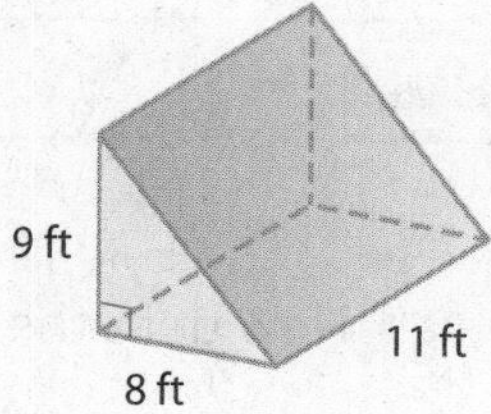

3. 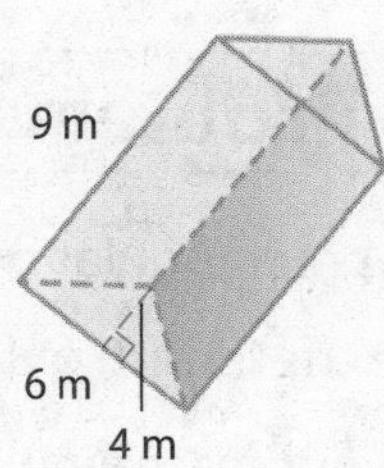

Show your work.

4. Which package has a greater volume? Justify your answer. (Example 3)

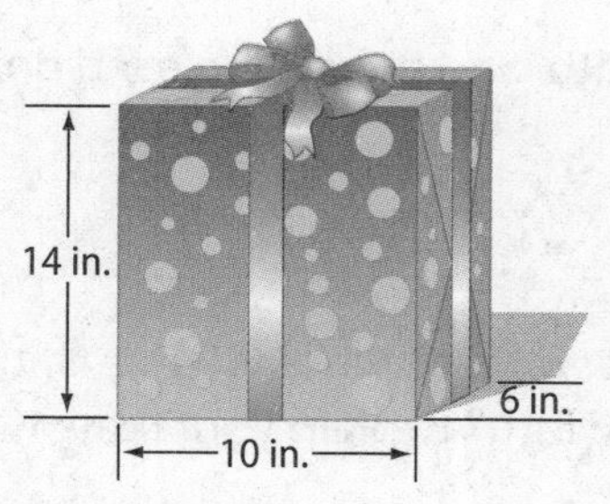

Package A

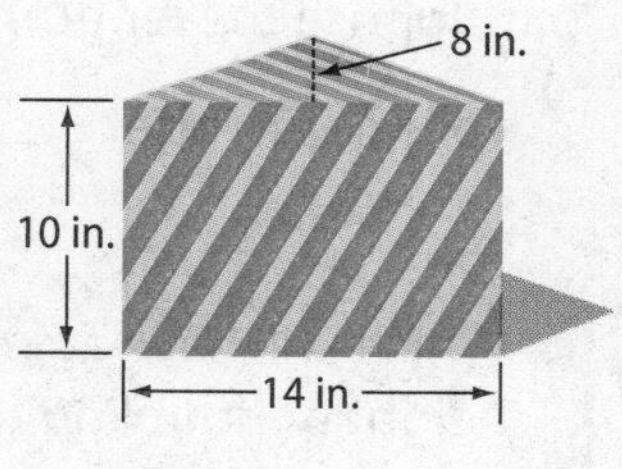

Package B

5. MP **Apply Math to the Real World** Refer to the graphic novel frame below. The table shows possible dimensions for the dunk tank.

Length(ft)	Width(ft)	Height(ft)
2	12	4
4	4	8
4	7	6
8	5	4
10	4	3

a. Determine the volume of each given dunk tank.

b. Which dimensions are reasonable for a dunk tank? Explain.

6. The diagram shows the dimensions of an office. It costs about $0.11 per year to air condition one cubic foot of space. On average, how much does it cost to air condition the office for one month? ______

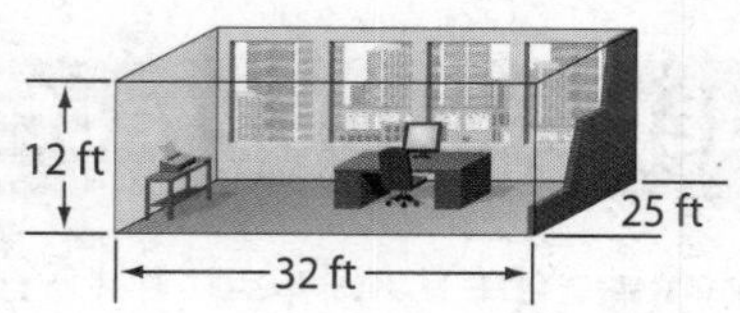

H.O.T. Problems Higher-Order Thinking

7. Evaluate A rectangular prism is shown.

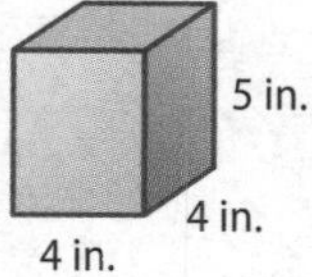

a. Suppose the length of the prism is doubled. How does the volume change? Explain your reasoning. ______

b. Suppose the length, width, and height are each doubled. How does the volume change? ______

c. Which will have a greater effect on the volume of the prism: doubling the height or doubling the width? Explain your reasoning.

8. Analyze The prism shown has a base that is a trapezoid. Determine the volume of the prism. ______

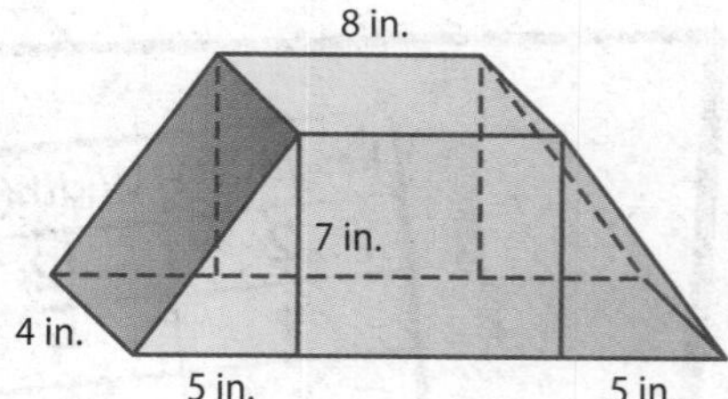

9. Create Find the volume of a real-world object that is in the shape of a rectangular or triangular prism using appropriate units. Draw a model of the prism including the dimensions.

10. Analyze Compare the formula $V = Bh$ for a rectangular prism to a triangular prism. Explain the difference between the two.

Name ______________________

Multi-Step Problem Solving

11. A drink cooler is in the shape of a rectangular prism. How many liters of lemonade will it hold if half of the volume is taken up by ice? (*Hint*: 1 L = 1,000 cm^3) EE N MP

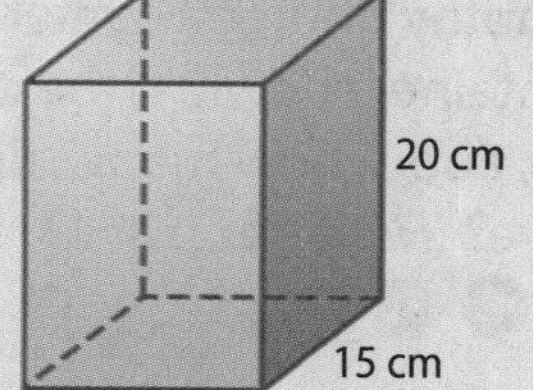

Ⓐ 1.65 L

Ⓑ 2.25 L

Ⓒ 4.5 L

Ⓓ 9 L

Use a problem-solving model to solve this problem.

1 Analyze

Read the problem. Circle the information you know.
Underline what the problem is asking you to find.

2 Plan

What will you need to do to solve the problem? Write your plan in steps.

Step 1 Determine the ________ of the rectangular prism.

Step 2 Determine half of the volume, then ________ to liters.

3 Solve

Use your plan to solve the problem. Show your steps.

Read to Succeed!

To convert cubic centimeters to liters, you will need to divide the volume in cubic centimeters by 1,000.

The volume of the cooler is 15 × 15 × 20 or ________ cubic centimeters.

Half of the volume is ________ ÷ 2, or ________ cubic centimeters.

Convert cubic centimeters to liters.

________ ÷ 1,000 = ________

The cooler will hold ______ liters of lemonade.

So, the correct answer is _____. Fill in that answer choice.

4 Justify and Evaluate

How do you know your solution is accurate?

____

____

____

More Multi-Step Problem Solving

Use a problem-solving model to solve each problem.

12. Timothy poured vegetable broth into the container shown. If the container is now 75% full, about how many cups of broth did he have? (*Hint*: 1 cup $\approx$ 14.4 cubic inches)

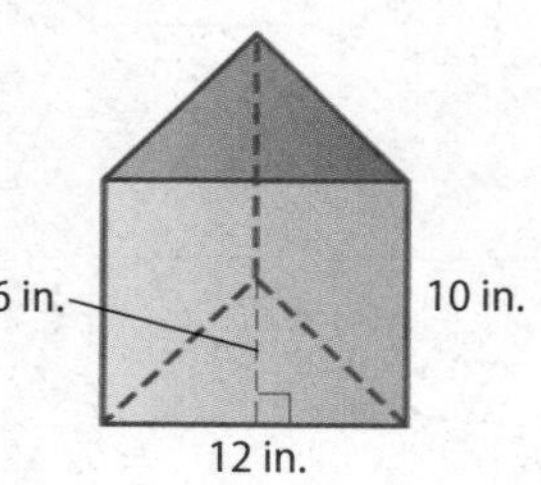

Ⓐ 12.5 cups

Ⓑ 15.25 cups

Ⓒ 18.75 cups

Ⓓ 25 cups

13. Thema has a raised garden bed in her backyard that is a rectangular prism with dimensions 6 feet by 3 feet by $\frac{2}{3}$ feet. How many bags of soil should Thema buy to fill the bed if each bag holds 960 cubic inches of soil?

14. The base of a triangular prism has dimensions with a base of 3 meters and a height of 2.5 meters. If the volume of the triangular prism is 5.625 cubic meters, what is the height of the triangular prism?

15. Compare the volume of the two triangular prisms shown. What do you notice? Explain.

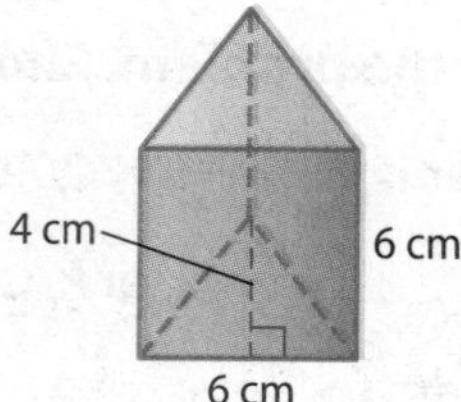

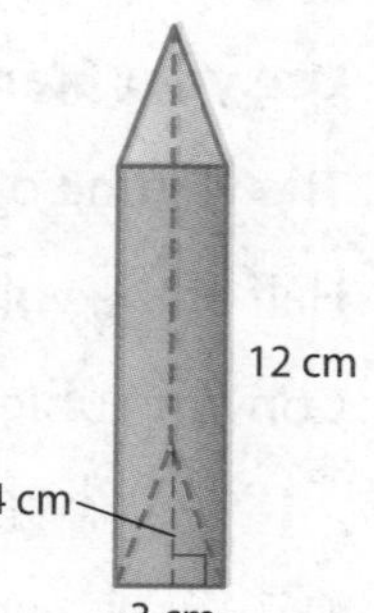

EE = Expressions, Equations, and Relationships N = Number and Operations MP = Mathematical Processes

Hands-On Lab 7-a

Volume Relationships of Prisms and Pyramids

INQUIRY HOW can I select tools to model the relationship between the volume of a prism and a pyramid having both congruent bases and heights?

Texas Essential Knowledge and Skills

TEKS

Targeted TEKS

7.8(A) Model the relationship between the volume of a rectangular prism and a rectangular pyramid having both congruent bases and heights and connect that relationship to the formulas. *Also addresses 7.8(B), 7.9(A).*

Mathematical Processes

7.1(C), 7.1(D), 7.1(E), 7.1(F), 7.1(G)

A movie theater offers two different containers of popcorn: a square prism and a square pyramid. Both containers are 4 inches tall and have congruent base areas of 16 square inches. Determine the container that holds more popcorn.

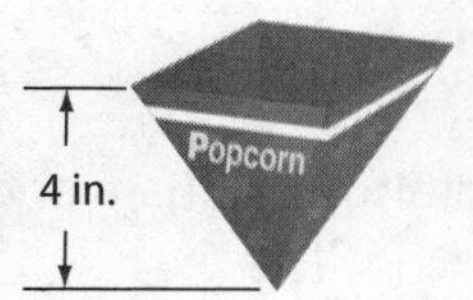

Hands-On Activity 1

A **pyramid** is a three-dimensional figure with one base that is a polygon.
A **net** is a two-dimensional pattern of three-dimensional figure.

Let's connect models to the formulas for the volume of the prism and the pyramid.

Step 1 Draw the nets of the popcorn containers shown below onto card stock. Cut out and tape each net to form its shape. The prism and pyramid will be open. The pyramid is composed of ☐ congruent isosceles triangles with bases of 4 inches and heights of $4\frac{1}{2}$ inches.

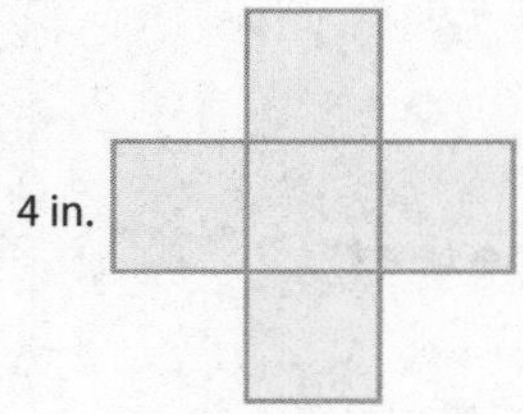

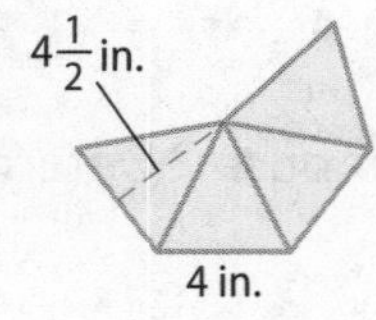

Step 2 Fill the pyramid with rice. Pour the rice from the pyramid into the prism and repeat until the prism is full. Slide a ruler across the top to level the amount.

It took ☐ pyramids of rice to fill the prism.

So, the square ________ container holds ________ times as much popcorn than the square ________ container.

Select Tools and Techniques **Work with a partner to repeat Activity 1 with a rectangular prism and a rectangular pyramid. Use the nets below.**

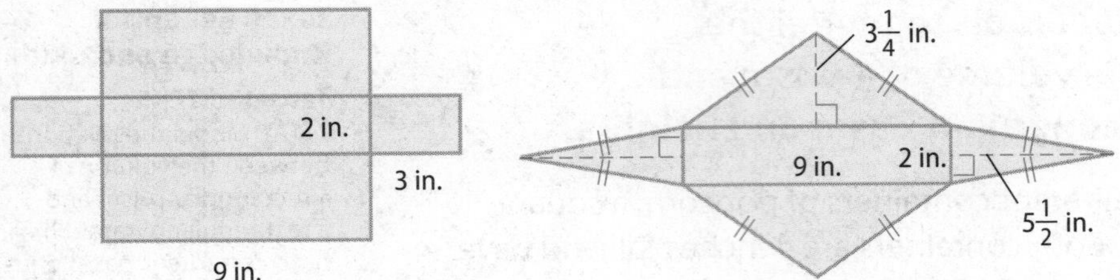

1. How many pyramids of rice did it take to fill the prism?

2. What is true about the bases of your rectangular prism and rectangular pyramid? the heights?

3. Refer to Activity 1. What is true about the bases of the square prism and square pyramid? the heights?

Analyze and Reflect

Collaborate

4. **Analyze Relationships** Explain verbally the relationship between the volume of a rectangular prism and a rectangular pyramid having both congruent bases and heights. ______

5. What is the formula for the volume of a rectangular prism? Determine the volume of the rectangular prism above Exercise 1.

6. **Connect Models to Rules** Connect the relationship you found in Exercise 4 to the formula for the volume of a rectangular prism. Then write a formula that can be used to determine the volume of a rectangular pyramid, having both congruent bases and heights. ______

7. Determine the volume of the rectangular pyramid above Exercise 1.

Hands-On Activity 2

You can also use nets to model the relationship between a triangular prism and a triangular pyramid having both congruent bases and heights. You can connect this relationship to the formulas.

Step 1 Draw the nets of the triangular prism and triangular pyramid shown below onto card stock. Cut out and tape each net to form its shape. The prism and pyramid will be open. The pyramid is composed of ☐ congruent equilateral triangles with bases of 4 inches and heights of $4\frac{1}{2}$ inches.

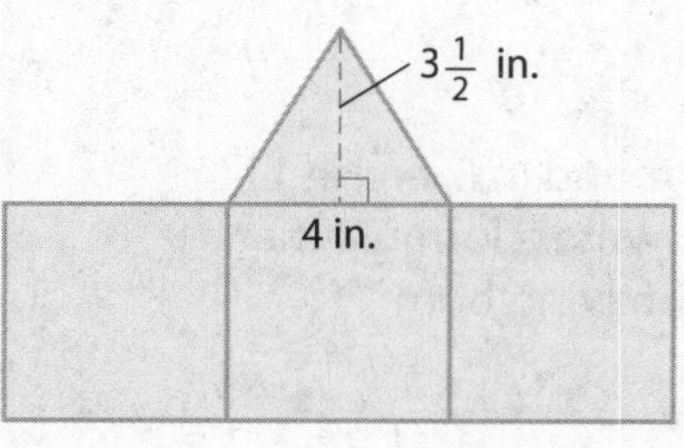

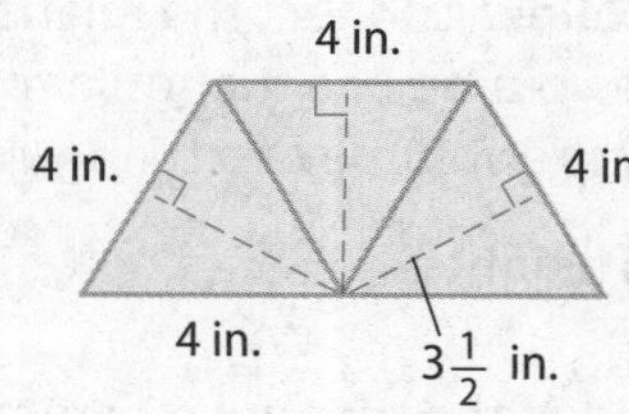

Step 2 Fill the pyramid with rice. Pour the rice from the pyramid into the prism and repeat until the prism is full. Slide a ruler across the top to level the amount.

It took ☐ pyramids of rice to fill the prism.

So, the triangular ________ holds ________ times as much rice than the triangular ________. Since the formula for the volume of a triangular prism is $V = Bh$, then the formula for the volume of a triangular pyramid is $V = \frac{\square}{\square}Bh$.

8. How many pyramids of rice did it take to fill the prism?

____

9. What is true about the bases of your triangular prism and triangular pyramid? the heights?

____

10. What fraction of the volume of the triangular prism is the volume of the triangular pyramid?

____

Analyze and Reflect

11. MP **Analyze Relationships** Explain verbally the relationship between the volume of a triangular prism and a triangular pyramid having both congruent bases and heights. ______

12. What is the formula for the volume of a triangular prism? Determine the volume of the triangular prism in Activity 2.

13. **Connect Models to Rules** Connect the relationship you found in Exercise 11 to the formula for the volume of a triangular prism. Then write a formula that explains symbolically the volume of a triangular pyramid, having both congruent bases and heights. ______

14. Determine the volume of the triangular pyramid in Activity 2.

Create

15. MP **Analyze Relationships** Draw a net of a rectangular pyramid that has a congruent base and height to the net of the rectangular prism shown. Then determine the volume of the pyramid. (*Hint*: The height of the pyramid is 4 feet.)

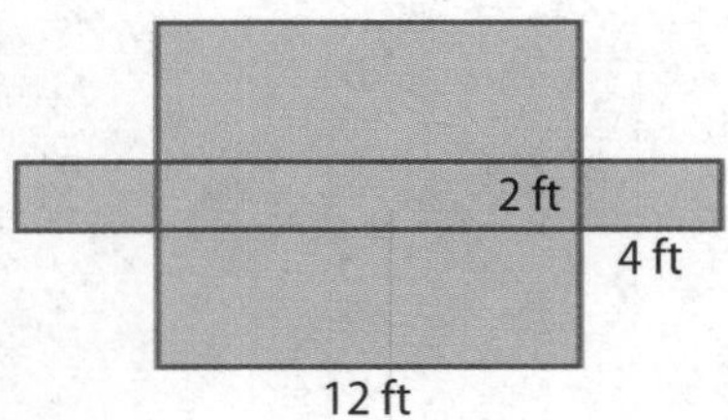

16. INQUIRY HOW can I select tools to model the relationship between the volume of a prism and a pyramid having both congruent bases and heights?

Lesson 7

Volume of Pyramids

Launch the Lesson: Real World

Dion is helping his mother build a sand sculpture at the beach in the shape of a rectangular pyramid. The pyramid has a base with a length and width of 12 inches each and a height of 14 inches. How can we model the relationship between the volume of the pyramid and a rectangular prism with congruent bases and heights?

1. Label the dimensions on the pyramid. Then draw and label a rectangular prism next to it with a congruent base and height.

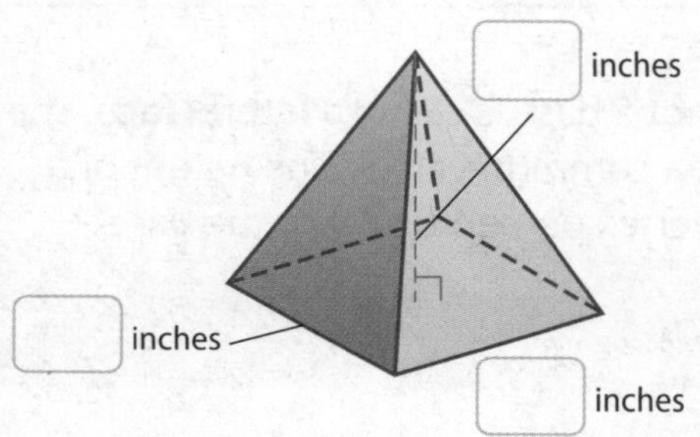

2. Explain verbally the relationship between the volume of the rectangular pyramid and the volume of the rectangular prism. ______________________

____

3. **Connect Models to Rules** Write two formulas that symbolically explain this relationship.

Volume of Rectangular Prism: ____________

Volume of Rectangular Pyramid: ____________

Which MP Mathematical Processes did you use? Shade the circle(s) that applies.

Ⓐ Apply Math to the Real World.
Ⓑ Use a Problem-Solving Model.
Ⓒ Select Tools and Techniques.
Ⓓ Use Multiple Representations.
Ⓔ Organize Ideas.
Ⓕ Analyze Relationships.
Ⓖ Justify Arguments.

Texas Essential Knowledge and Skills

Targeted TEKS

7.9(A) Solve problems involving the volume of rectangular prisms, triangular prisms, rectangular pyramids, and triangular pyramids. *Also addresses 7.8(A), 7.8(B).*

Mathematical Processes

7.1(A), 7.1(B), 7.1(D), 7.1(E)

Vocab

Vocabulary

lateral face

Essential Question

HOW do measurements help you describe real-world objects?

Key Concept

Volume of a Pyramid and Prism

Work Zone

Explain Verbally

The volume V of a pyramid is one third the volume of a prism with a congruent base B and height h.

Explain Symbolically

Volume of a Prism: $V = Bh$

Volume of a Pyramid, with congruent base and height: $V = \frac{1}{3}Bh$

Models

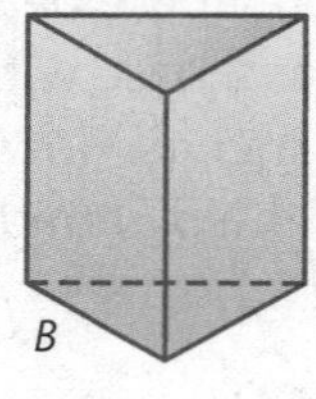

$V = Bh$

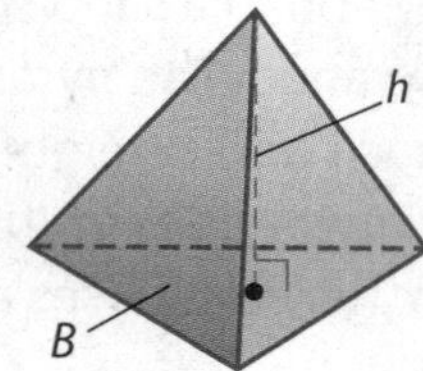

$V = \frac{1}{3}Bh$

In a polyhedron, any face that is not a base is called a **lateral face**. The lateral faces of a pyramid meet at a common vertex. The height of a pyramid is the distance from the vertex perpendicular to the base.

Tutor

Examples

1. Determine the volume of the rectangular pyramid. Round to the nearest tenth.

$V = \frac{1}{3}Bh$ — Volume of a pyramid

$V = \frac{1}{3}(3.2 \cdot 1.4)2.8$ — $B = 3.2 \cdot 1.4, h = 2.8$

$V \approx 4.2$ — Simplify.

The volume is about 4.2 cubic inches.

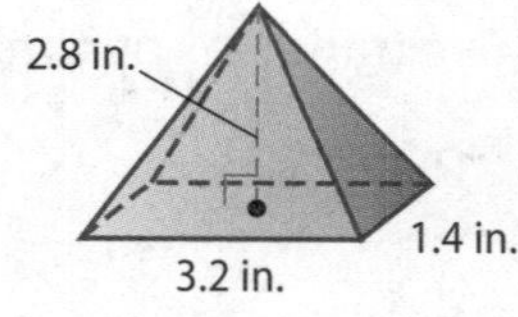

2. Determine the volume of the triangular pyramid. Round to the nearest tenth.

$V = \frac{1}{3}Bh$ — Volume of a pyramid

$V = \frac{1}{3}\left(\frac{1}{2} \cdot 8.1 \cdot 6.4\right)11$ — $B = \frac{1}{2} \cdot 8.1 \cdot 6.4, h = 11$

$V = 95.04$ — Simplify.

The volume is about 95.0 cubic meters.

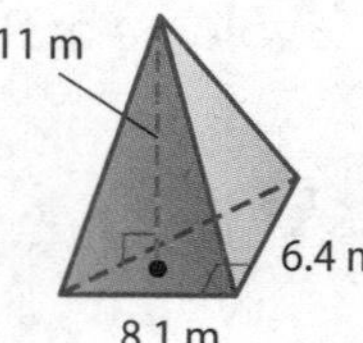

Got It? Do this problem to find out.

a. Determine the volume of a pyramid that has a height of 9 centimeters and a rectangular base with a length of 7 centimeters and a width of 3 centimeters.

a. ________

Determine the Height of a Pyramid

You can also use the formula for the volume of a pyramid to determine a missing height.

Examples

3. The rectangular pyramid shown has a volume of 90 cubic inches. Determine the height of the pyramid.

$V = \frac{1}{3}Bh$	Volume of a pyramid
$90 = \frac{1}{3}(9 \cdot 5)h$	$V = 90, B = 9 \cdot 5$
$90 = 15h$	Multiply.
$\frac{90}{15} = \frac{15h}{15}$	Divide by 15.
$6 = h$	Simplify.

5 in.
9 in.
h

The height of the pyramid is 6 inches.

4. A triangular pyramid has a volume of 44 cubic meters. It has an 8-meter base and a 3-meter height. Determine the height of the pyramid.

$V = \frac{1}{3}Bh$	Volume of a pyramid
$44 = \frac{1}{3}\left(\frac{1}{2} \cdot 8 \cdot 3\right)h$	$V = 44, B = \frac{1}{2} \cdot 8 \cdot 3$
$44 = 4h$	Multiply.
$\frac{44}{4} = \frac{4h}{4}$	Divide by 4.
$11 = h$	Simplify.

3 m
8 m
h

The height of the pyramid is 11 meters.

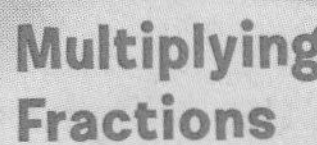

Multiplying Fractions

To determine $\frac{1}{3} \cdot \frac{1}{2} \cdot 8 \cdot 3$, multiply $\frac{1}{3} \cdot \frac{1}{2}$ and $8 \cdot 3$ to get $\frac{1}{6}$ and 24, then determine $\frac{1}{6}$ of 24.

Got It? Do these problems to find out.

b. A triangular pyramid has a volume of 840 cubic inches. The triangular base has a base length of 20 inches and a height of 21 inches. Determine the height of the pyramid.

c. A rectangular pyramid has a volume of 525 cubic feet. It has a base of 25 feet by 18 feet. Determine the height of the pyramid.

b. ________

c. ________

Example

5. Kamilah is making a model of the Food Guide Pyramid for a class project. Determine the volume of the square pyramid.

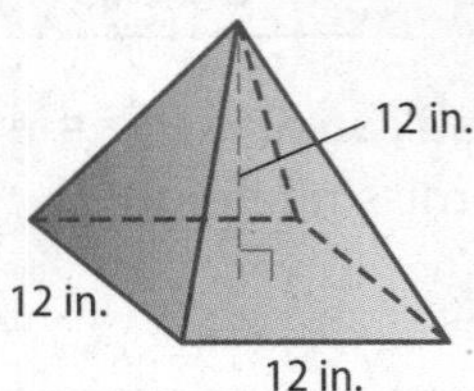

$V = \frac{1}{3}Bh$ Volume of a pyramid

$V = \frac{1}{3}(12 \cdot 12)12$ $B = 12 \cdot 12, h = 12$

$V = 576$ Multiply.

The volume is 576 cubic inches.

Guided Practice

Determine the volume of each rectangular pyramid. Round to the nearest tenth if necessary. (Examples 1 and 2)

1. ____________

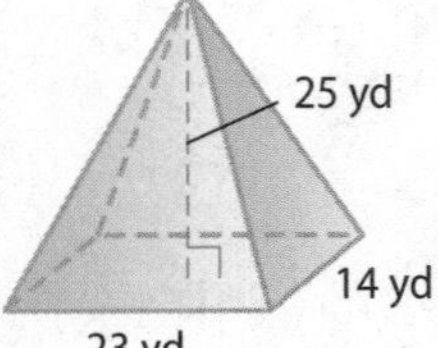

2. ____________

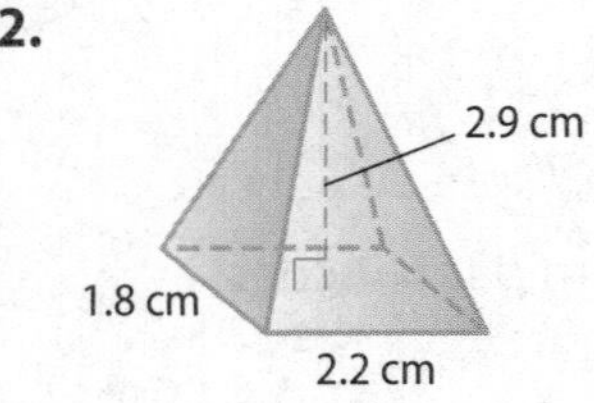

Determine the height of each square or triangular pyramid. (Examples 3 and 4)

3. square pyramid: volume 1,024 cm^3; base edge 16 cm ____________

4. triangular pyramid: volume 48 in^3; base edge 9 in.; base height 4 in. ____________

5. The Transamerica Pyramid is a skyscraper in San Francisco. The rectangular base has a length of 175 feet and a width of 120 feet. The height is 853 feet. Determine the volume of the building. (Example 5) ____________

6. **Building on the Essential Question** Your friend forgot the formula for the volume of a pyramid. Explain how to use the relationship between prisms and pyramids with congruent bases and heights to determine the volume of a pyramid.

____

____

____

____

Rate Yourself!

How well do you understand volume of pyramids? Circle the image that applies.

Find out online. Use the Self-Check Quiz.

FOLDABLES Time to update your Foldable!

Name ______________________ My Homework ______________________

Independent Practice

7.9(A), 7.1(B) TEKS

Determine the volume of each rectangular or triangular pyramid. Round to the nearest tenth if necessary. (Examples 1 and 2)

1. 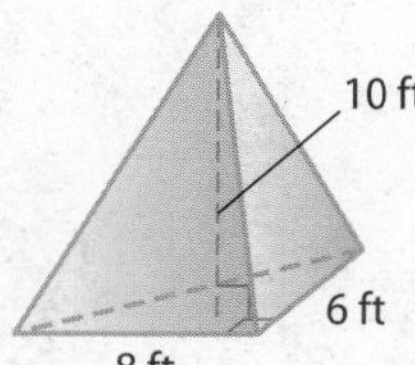

______

2. 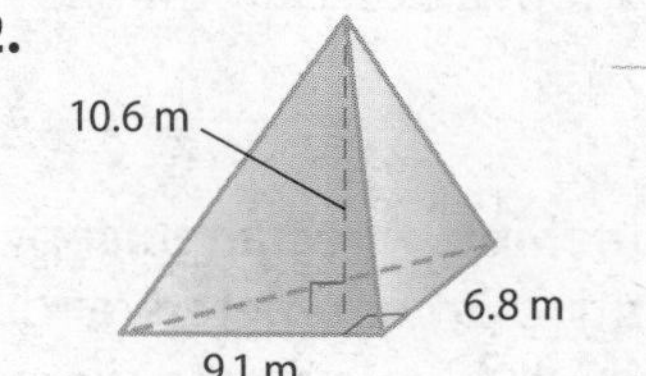

______

3. 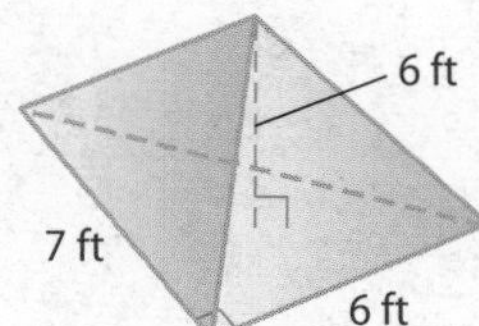

______

4. 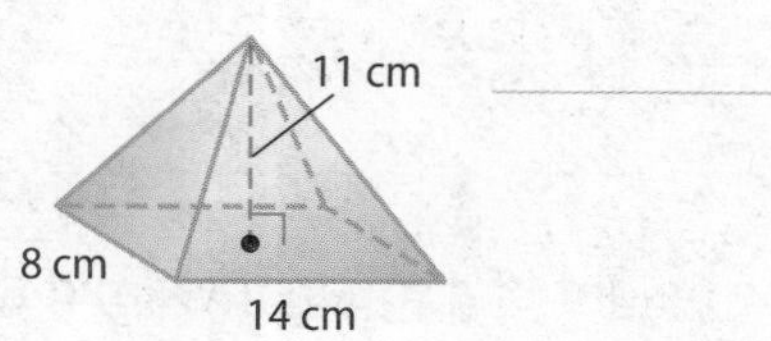

______

Determine the height of each rectangular or triangular pyramid. (Examples 3 and 4)

5. rectangular pyramid: volume 448 in^3; base edge 12 in.; base length 8 in.

______

6. triangular pyramid: volume 270 cm^3; base edge 15 cm; height of base 4 cm

______

7. **MP Use Multiple Representations** Consider the pyramids shown.

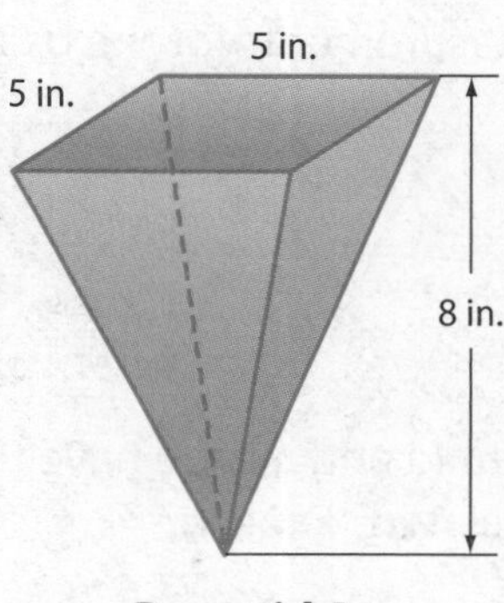

Pyramid A

5 in. 8 in. 5 in. 5 in. 4.3 in.

Pyramid B

a. **Models** Draw a model of a rectangular prism with a congruent base and a congruent height as Pyramid A. Then draw a model of a triangular prism with a congruent base and height as Pyramid B.

b. **Numbers** Determine the volume of each pyramid and prism. ______

______

______

Prism A

Prism B

c. **Words** Explain verbally the relationship between the volume of a pyramid and the volume of a prism with congruent bases and heights. ______

______

______

d. **Symbols** Write two formulas to symbolically explain this relationship.

______

8. A glass pyramid has a height of 4 inches. Its rectangular base has a length of 3 inches and a width of 2.5 inches. Determine the volume of glass used to create the pyramid. (Example 5) ______

9. The Pyramid Arena in Memphis, Tennessee, is a square pyramid that is 321 feet tall. The base has 600-foot sides. Determine the volume. (Example 5)

______

10. MP **Analyze Relationships** A rectangular pyramid has a length of 14 centimeters, a width of 9 centimeters, and a height of 10 centimeters. Explain the effect on the volume if each dimension were doubled.

______

______

11. Determine the height of a square pyramid that has a volume of $25\frac{3}{5}$ meters and a base with 4 meter sides. ______

H.O.T. Problems Higher-Order Thinking

12. **Evaluate** A rectangular pyramid has a volume of 160 cubic feet. Determine two possible sets of measurements for the base area and height.

______

______

______

13. **Analyze** A square pyramid and a cube have the same bases and volumes. How are their heights related? Explain.

______

______

14. **Analyze** The two figures shown have congruent bases. How does the volume of the two square pyramids in Figure B compare to the volume of the square pyramid in Figure A?

______

______

Figure A

Figure B

15. **Evaluate** *True* or *false*? The volume of a rectangular-based pyramid and a triangular-based pyramid with congruent heights and congruent base areas are equal. Explain. ______

Name ____

Multi-Step Problem Solving

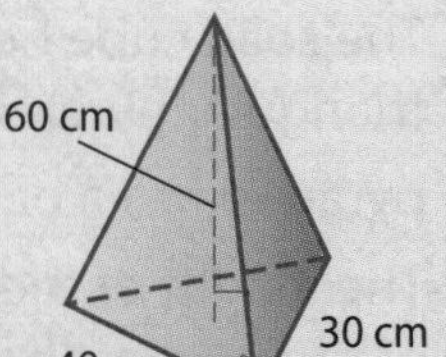

16. Yukiko has 10,000 cubic centimeters of sand. She pours it into the pyramid shown. What fraction of the pyramid can she fill with sand? EE N MP

Ⓐ $\frac{1}{2}$
Ⓑ $\frac{5}{9}$
Ⓒ $\frac{3}{4}$
Ⓓ $\frac{5}{6}$

Use a problem-solving model to solve this problem.

1 Analyze

Read the problem. Circle the information you know.
Underline what the problem is asking you to find.

2 Plan

What will you need to do to solve the problem? Write your plan in steps.

Step 1 Determine the ________ of the triangular pyramid.

Step 2 Determine the ________ of the pyramid that is filled.

Read to Succeed!
The pyramid shown is a triangular pyramid. Use the formula for a triangle when determining the base *B*.

3 Solve

Use your plan to solve the problem. Show your steps.

Determine the volume.

$V = \frac{1}{3}Bh$ $V = \frac{1}{3}\left(\frac{1}{2} \cdot 40 \cdot 30\right) \cdot 60$ $V =$ ________ cm^3

Write the volume of sand Yukiko has over the volume of the pyramid.

$\frac{\_\_\_\_}{\_\_\_\_}$ or $\frac{\_\_\_\_}{\_\_\_\_}$

The pyramid will be ____ full.

So, the correct answer is ____. Fill in that answer choice.

4 Justify and Evaluate

How do you know your solution is accurate?

____

____

____

EE = Expressions, Equations, and Relationships N = Number and Operations MP = Mathematical Processes

More Multi-Step Problem Solving

Use a problem-solving model to solve each problem.

17. The solid cube below fits inside a hollow triangular pyramid. The triangular base of the pyramid has a base of $7\frac{1}{2}$ and a height of 4. The height of the pyramid is 5. What percent of the pyramid's volume is filled by the cube? Round your answer to the nearest thousandth, if necessary. EE N P MP

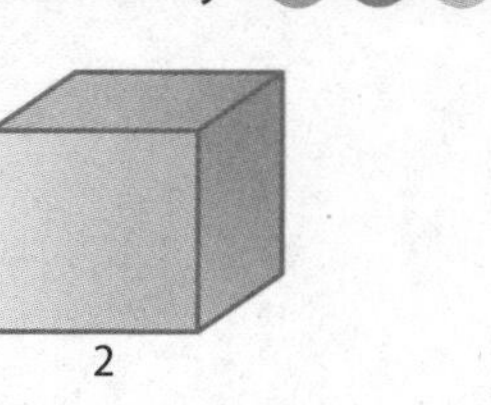

Ⓐ 5%
Ⓑ 16.7%
Ⓒ 25%
Ⓓ 32%

18. A square pyramid trophy is being shipped in a rectangular prism shaped package. The square pyramid has a base edge of 6 inches and height of 8 inches. What is the minimum volume that the package must be in order for the trophy to fit inside? EE N MP

19. The rectangular pyramid block shown was cut in half. What is the volume of each half of the pyramid block? EE N MP

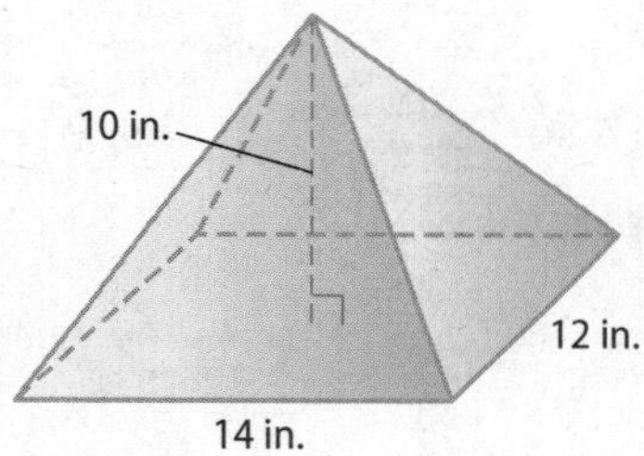

20. A triangular pyramid is placed on top of a triangular prism with a congruent base. If the volumes are equal, and the height of the prism is 1 unit, what is the total height of the both figures? Explain. EE N MP

EE = Expressions, Equations, and Relationships 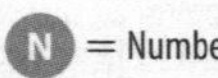 N = Number and Operations P = Proportionality MP = Mathematical Processes

Hands-On Lab 8-a

Nets of Rectangular Prisms

INQUIRY HOW can I select tools and techniques to model surface area?

Texas Essential Knowledge and Skills

Targeted TEKS

7.9(D) Solve problems involving the lateral and total surface area of a rectangular prism, rectangular pyramid, triangular prism, and triangular pyramid by determining the area of the shape's net.

Mathematical Processes

7.1(C), 7.1(D), 7.1(E), 7.1(F)

If you want to know the amount of cereal that can fit in the box, you would determine the volume. But if you want to know how much cardboard is needed to make the box, you would find the *surface area*.

Hands-On Activity 1

One way to determine the surface area is to use a *net*. Nets are two-dimensional patterns of three-dimensional figures. When you construct a net, you are decomposing the three-dimensional figure into separate shapes.

Step 1 Use a cereal box in the shape of a rectangular prism. Measure and record the length, width, and height of the box on the lines below.

Length: ____________

Width: ____________

Height: ____________

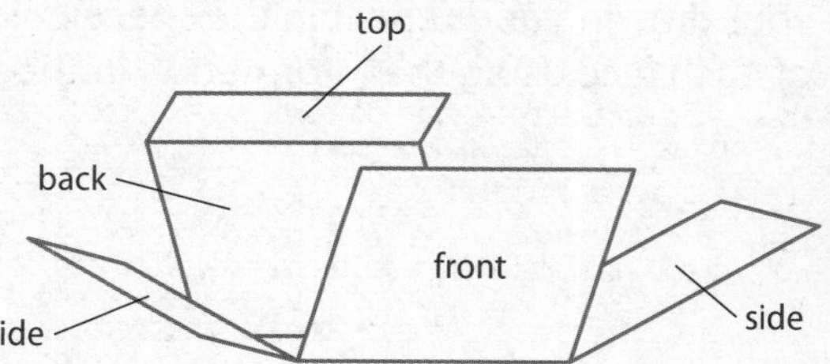

Step 2 Using a marker, label the top, bottom, front, back and side faces of the box.

Step 3 Using scissors, carefully cut along three edges of the top face and then cut down each vertical edge.

Step 4 Measure and record the area of each face, using the dimensions of the box shown in the table.

Face	Length	Width	Area of Face
Front			
Back			
Side 1			
Side 2			
Top			
Bottom			

Step 5 Add the areas of each face to determine the surface area of the box.

☐ + ☐ + ☐ + ☐ + ☐ + ☐ = ☐

So, the surface area of the box is ☐ square inches.

Hands-On Activity 2

Orthogonal drawings consist of separate views of an object taken from different angles. You can make a net from orthogonal drawings.

Step 1 Determine the dimensions of each side of a rectangular prism from the orthogonal drawing.

Orthogonal Drawing		
View	**Drawing**	**Dimensions**
Front and Back		×
Sides		×
Top and Bottom		×

Step 2 Use grid paper to draw a net from the orthogonal drawing. Trace and cut out your drawing and tape it in the space below. Check the dimensions of each face using the information in the table.

Step 3 Fold the net into a three-dimensional figure. Draw the resulting figure in the space provided.

So, the figure is a ______________________.

It has a surface area of [ ] square units.

Investigate

MP Select Tools and Techniques Work with a partner. Use a net to determine the surface area of each prism. Draw a net of each prism on the provided grid.

1. ________ mm^2

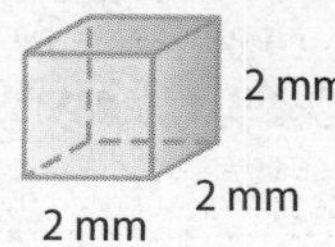

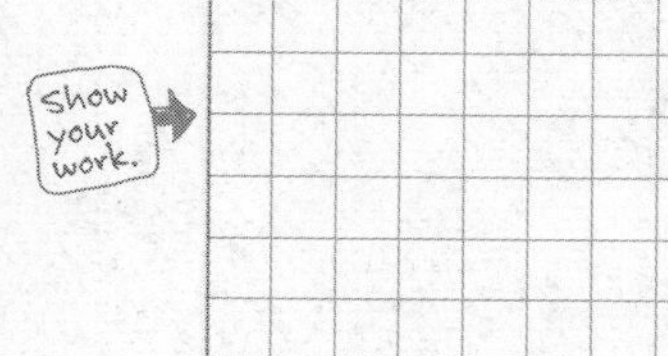

2. ________ in^2

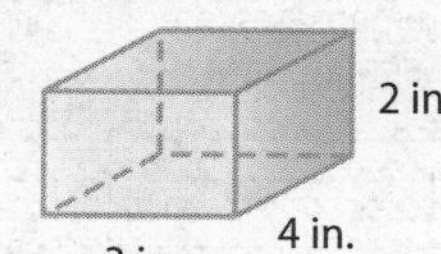

3. ________ ft^2

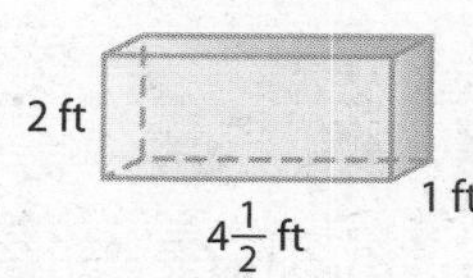

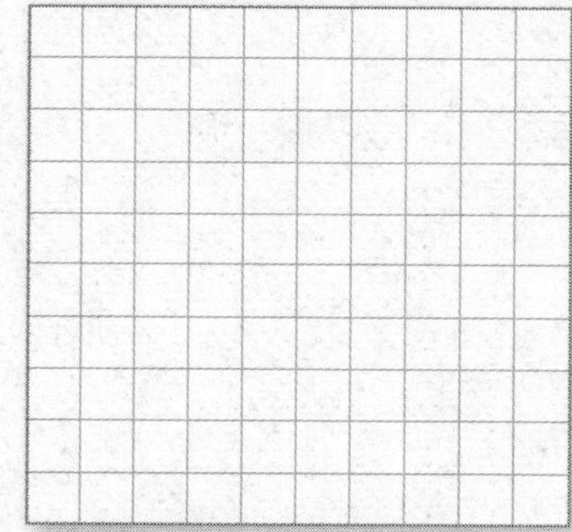

4. ________

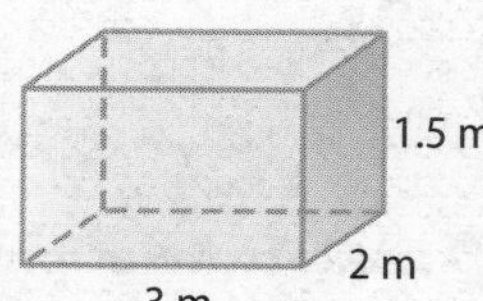

Draw a net on the grid from the orthogonal drawing. Then determine the surface area of the prism.

5. ________ square units

Orthogonal Drawing	
View	**Drawing**
Front and Back	
Sides	
Top and Bottom	

Work with a partner to complete the table. The first one is done for you.

	Dimensions of Rectangular Prism	Area of Top (units^2)	Area of Bottom (units^2)	Area of Side 1 (units^2)	Area of Side 2 (units^2)	Area of Front (units^2)	Area of Back (units^2)	Surface Area (units^2)
	1 × 2 × 3	2	2	6	6	3	3	22
6.	2 × 2 × 3							
7.	3 × 3 × 3							
8.	3 × 2 × 8							
9.	6 × 6 × 6							

10. Compare the surface area for Exercise 7 to the surface area for Exercise 9. How does doubling each dimension affect the surface area?

11. MP **Analyze Relationships** Write a formula to determine the surface area of a rectangular prism. Use your formula to determine the surface area of the prism in Investigation 2. ______

Create

12. MP **Apply Math to the Real World** Write a real-world problem that involves the surface area of rectangular prisms. Provide the dimensions and the surface area.

13. Will the surface area of a cube ever have the same numerical value as the volume of the cube?

14. **INQUIRY** HOW can I select tools and techniques to model surface area?

Lesson 8

Surface Area of Rectangular Prisms

Launch the Lesson: Vocabulary

Define Surface	Define Area
What is surface area?	**Example:**

Texas Essential Knowledge and Skills

Targeted TEKS

7.9(D) Solve problems involving the lateral and total surface area of a rectangular prism, rectangular pyramid, triangular prism, and triangular pyramid by determining the area of the shape's net.

Mathematical Processes

7.1(A), 7.1(B), 7.1(E)

Vocabulary

surface area

lateral surface area

Essential Question

HOW do measurements help you describe real-world objects?

Real-World Investigation

Roberta is wrapping a gift for her sister's quinceañera. She places it in a box with the measurements shown below.

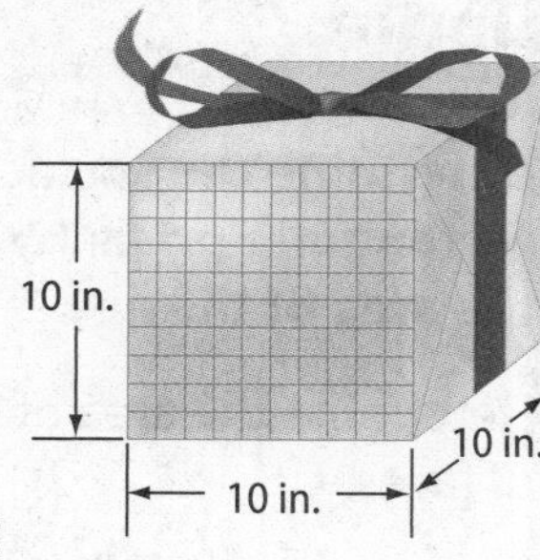

1. What is the area of one face of the box?

____

2. How many faces does the box have? ☐

3. What operations would you use to determine the surface area of the box? _______________

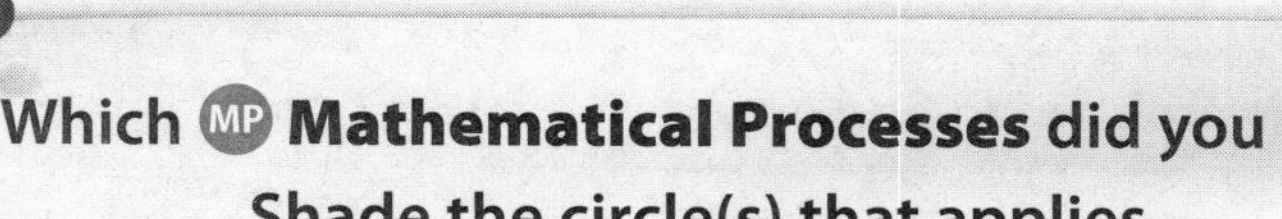

Which MP **Mathematical Processes** did you use? Shade the circle(s) that applies.

Ⓐ Apply Math to the Real World.

Ⓑ Use a Problem-Solving Model.

Ⓒ Select Tools and Techniques.

Ⓓ Use Multiple Representations.

Ⓔ Organize Ideas.

Ⓕ Analyze Relationships.

Ⓖ Justify Arguments.

Work Zone

Key Concept — Surface Area of a Rectangular Prism

Words The surface area of a rectangular prism with length ℓ, width w, and height h is the sum of the areas of the faces.

Model

h w ℓ

The **surface area** of a prism is the sum of the areas of its faces. You can determine the surface area by determining the area of the prism's net.

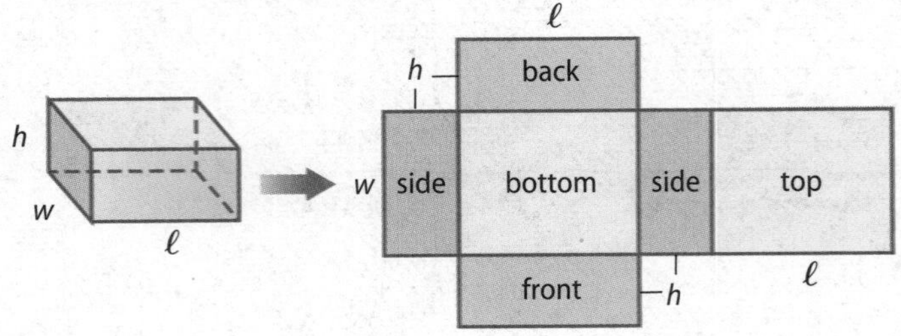

Notice that the rectangles for the front and back are congruent. The top and bottom are congruent and both sides are congruent.

You can determine the area of one rectangle, then double it to determine the total area for the two congruent shapes.

Example

1. Determine the surface area of the rectangular prism by determining the area of the net.

8 m
48 m²
6 m
6 m
6 m
8 m
7 m
42 m²
56 m²
42 m²
56 m²
48 m²
6 m

Determine the area of each pair of faces.

front and back: $2(8 \cdot 6) = 2(48)$

top and bottom: $2(7 \cdot 8) = 2(56)$

sides: $2(7 \cdot 6) = 2(42)$

$48 + 48 + 56 + 56 + 42 + 42 = 292$ Add the area of each face.

So, the surface area is 292 square meters.

Nets

The net shows that a rectangular prism has six faces. The faces can be grouped as three pairs of congruent sides. The colors indicate which faces are congruent.

Got It? Do this problem to find out.

a. Determine the surface area of the rectangular prism by determining the area of the net.

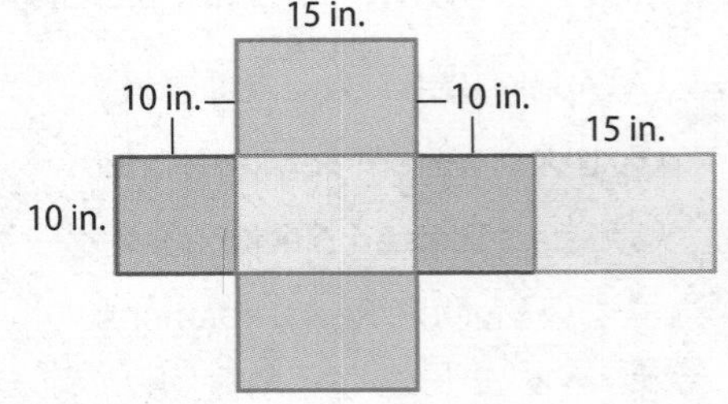

Show your work.

a. ____________

Determine Lateral Surface Area

You can use a net to determine the lateral surface area of a rectangular prism. The **lateral surface area** is the sum of the areas of all its lateral faces. The lateral faces do not include the top or bottom faces.

Multi-Step Example

2. Iker is painting his bedroom that measures 12 feet long, 10 feet wide, and 7 feet high. He has 1 gallon of paint that covers about 350 square feet of surface. Does he have enough to paint the lateral surface area of his room with two coats of paint? Justify your answer.

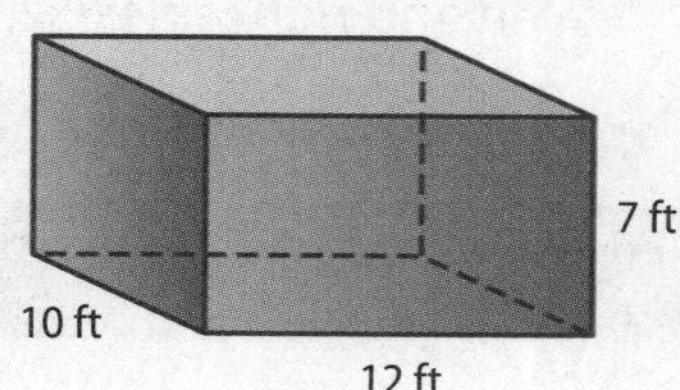

Step 1 Determine the lateral surface area.
front and back: 2(12)(7) or 168
left and right sides: 2(10)(7) or 140
Add to determine the lateral surface area. The lateral surface area is 168 + 140 or 308 square feet.

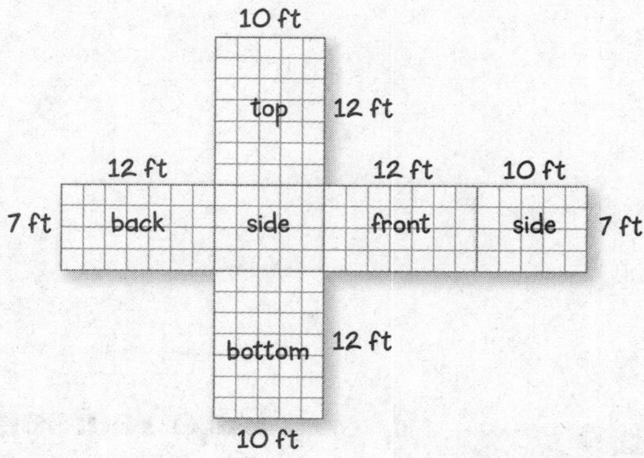

Step 2 Determine the total number of square feet he will paint.
308 + 308 or 616 square feet

Step 3 Divide the total area by the number of square feet the paint will cover. $616 \div 350 = 1.76$

So, Iker will need at least 2 gallons of paint.

Got It? Do this problem to find out.

b. Desmona is building a doll house that measures 24 inches long, 18 inches wide, and 15 inches high. She has 10 square feet of material. Does she have enough material to build the walls or lateral surface area of her doll house? Justify your answer.

b. __________

Example

3. STEM A geode is being sent as a gift. It is packed in a box that measures 7 inches long, 3 inches wide, and 16 inches tall. What is the surface area of the box?

Determine the area of the prism's net. There are 6 faces.
Determine the area of each pair of faces.
front and back: 2(7)(16) or 224
top and bottom: 2(3)(7) or 42
left and right sides: 2(3)(16) or 96

The surface area is 224 + 42 + 96 or 362 square inches.

Guided Practice

Determine the lateral area and the surface area of each rectangular prism by determining the area of the shape's net. (Examples 1–3)

1. ______

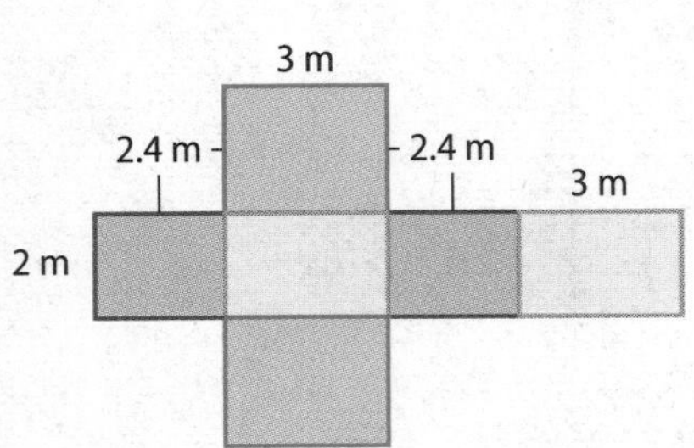

Show your work.

2. ______

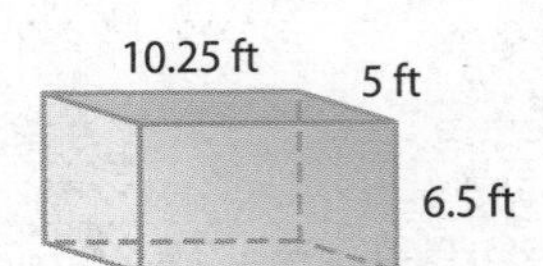

3. ______

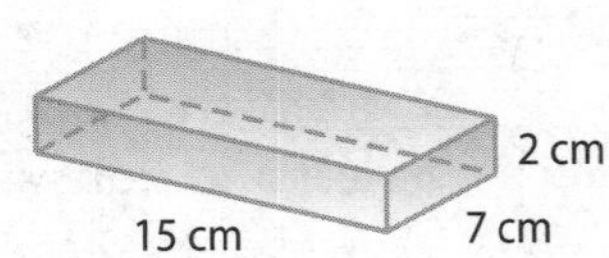

4. Tomás keeps his diecast car in a glass display case as shown. What is the surface area of the glass, including the bottom? (Example 3)

______

5. Building on the Essential Question What is the relationship between area and surface area?

______

Name ______________________ My Homework ______________________

Independent Practice

7.9(D), 7.1(A), 7.1(G) TEKS

Determine the lateral area and the surface area of each rectangular prism by determining the area of the shape's net. (Example 1)

1. ______________________

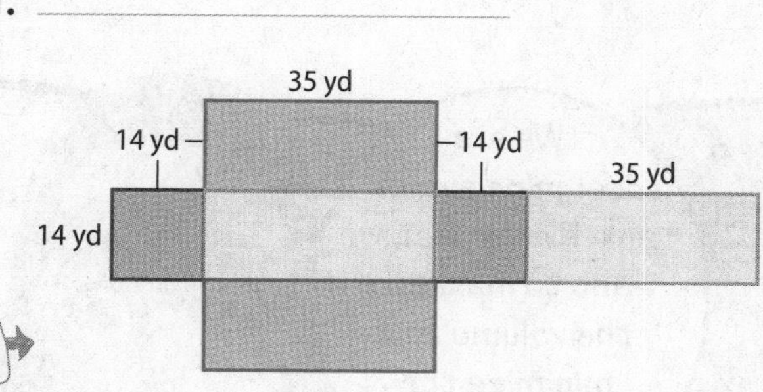

Show your work.

2. ______________________

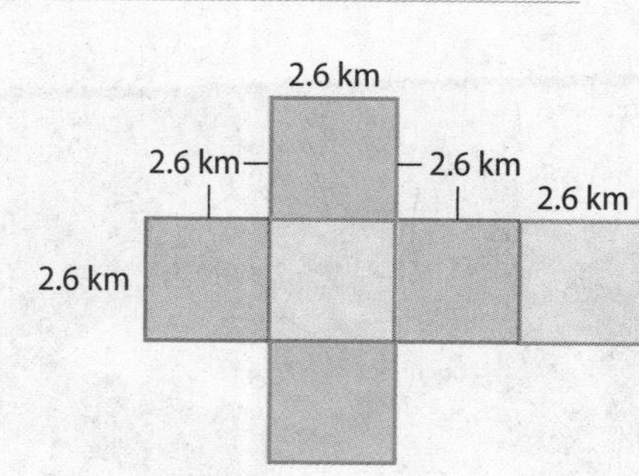

3. ______________________

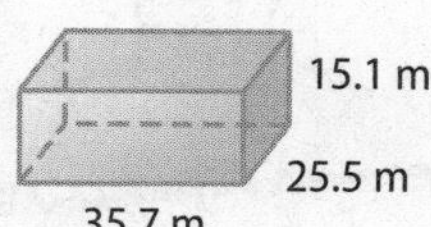

4. ______________________

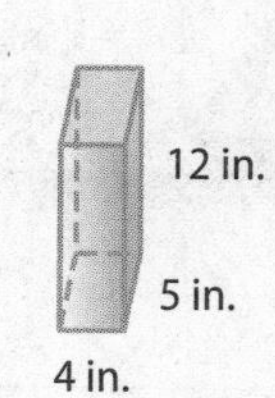

5. A game box for video games is shaped like a rectangular prism. What is the surface area of the game box? (Example 3)

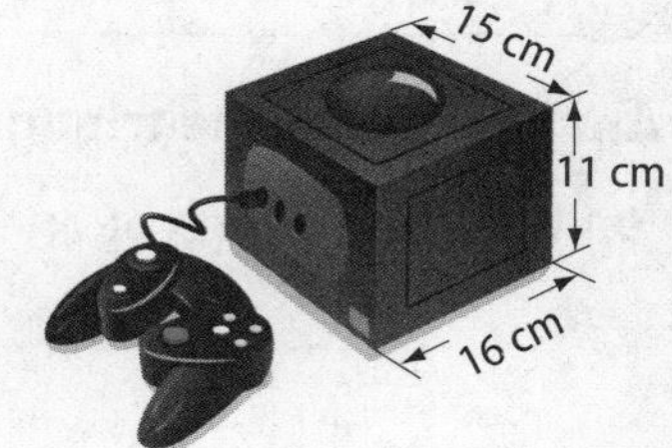

____

6. **MP Justify Arguments** Martina estimates that the lateral surface area of a rectangular prism with a length of 13.2 feet, a width of 6 feet, and a height of 8 feet is about 304 square feet. Is her estimate reasonable? Explain your reasoning.

____

____

7. **MP Justify Arguments** Determine the surface area of each shipping package. Which package has the greater surface area? Does the same package have a greater volume? Explain your reasoning to a classmate.

Package A

Package B

____

____

8. Apply Math to the Real World Refer to the graphic novel in Lesson 6 and the one below. What whole number dimensions would allow the students to maximize the volume while keeping the surface area at most 160 square feet? Draw a net if necessary. Explain.

 H.O.T. Problems Higher-Order Thinking

Analyze All of the triangular faces of the figure are congruent.

9. What is the area of one of the triangular faces? the square face?

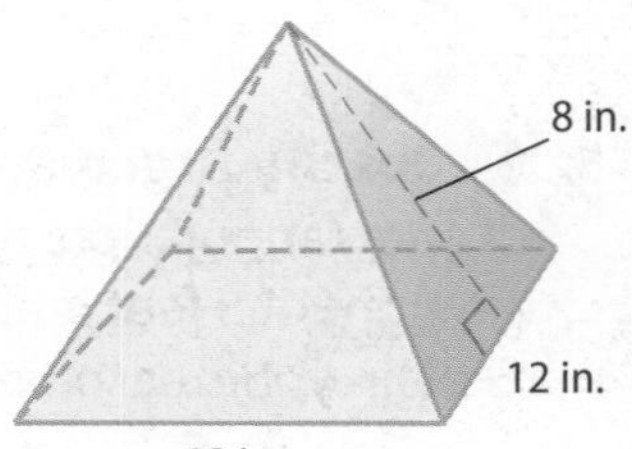

10. Use what you know about determining the surface area of a rectangular prism to determine the surface area of the square pyramid.

11. **Create** Draw two prisms on a separate sheet of paper. Draw one with a greater volume and the other with a greater surface area. Use real-world units. Then give a description of your prisms.

12. **Analyze** Explain the difference between surface area and lateral surface area.

Name ______________________________

Multi-Step Problem Solving

13. Determine the surface area for each package. How much greater is the surface area of package B? EE N MP

Ⓐ 10 square inches

Ⓑ 12 square inches

Ⓒ 20 square inches

Ⓓ 24 square inches

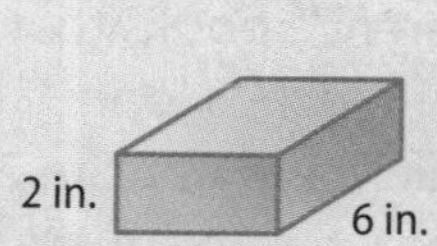

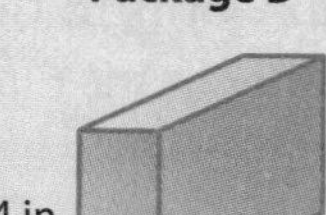

Use a problem-solving model to solve this problem.

1 Analyze

Read the problem. Circle the information you know. Underline what the problem is asking you to find.

2 Plan

What will you need to do to solve the problem? Write your plan in steps.

Step 1 Determine the ______________ for each prism.

Step 2 __________ the surface areas.

Read to Succeed!

You may need to draw a net of each prism to help you visualize the area of each face.

3 Solve

Use your plan to solve the problem. Show your steps.

Package A surface area:

front and back: $2(2 \cdot 4) =$ ____

top and bottom: $2(6 \cdot 4) =$ ____

sides: $2(2 \cdot 6) =$ ____

____ + ____ + ____ = ____ Add.

Package B surface area:

front and back: $2(2 \cdot 4) =$ ____

top and bottom: $2(2 \cdot 7) =$ ____

sides: $2(7 \cdot 4) =$ ____

____ + ____ + ____ = ____ Add.

____ − ____ = ____ square inches greater Subtract.

So, the correct answer is ____. Fill in that answer choice.

4 Justify and Evaluate

How do you know your solution is accurate?

____

____

____

EE = Expressions, Equations, and Relationships N = Number and Operations MP = Mathematical Processes

Multi-Step Problem Solving

Use a problem-solving model to solve each problem.

14. Talin wants to build a storage box that will exactly fit his 6 reference books that are each 8 inches wide and 11 inches long. If half of his books are 1 inch thick, and half are 2 inches thick, how much material, in square feet, will he need to make the storage box? Round your answer to the nearest thousandth. EE N P MP

Ⓐ 3.597 square feet

Ⓑ 3.65 square feet

Ⓒ 4.735 square feet

Ⓓ 5.375 square feet

15. The coordinate grid shows the base of a rectangular prism. If the prism has a surface area of 170 units, what is its height, in units?

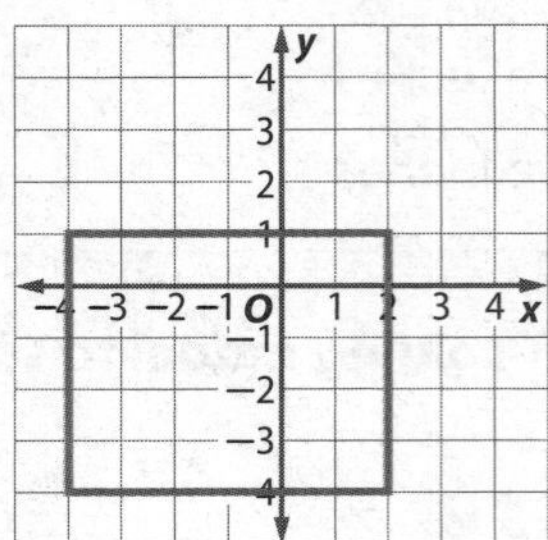

16. Each side length of a unit cube measure 2 units and increases by 50% every minute. What is the ratio of the surface area after 3 minutes to the original surface area? Write your answer as a decimal rounded to the nearest tenth. EE N P MP

17. A chemical company wants to reduce the cost of their shipping containers. The measurements of the containers are shown. They pay for the containers by the amount of material required to make them. If they want to ship the greatest volume of chemicals at the lowest cost, which container should they use? Justify your answer. EE N P MP

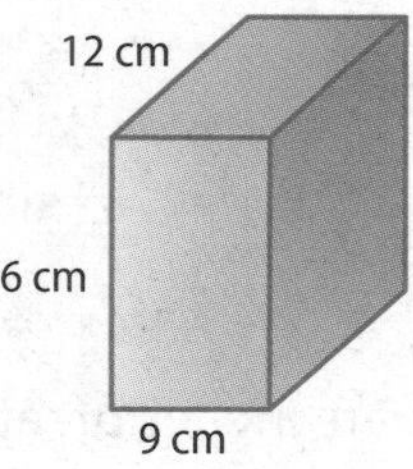

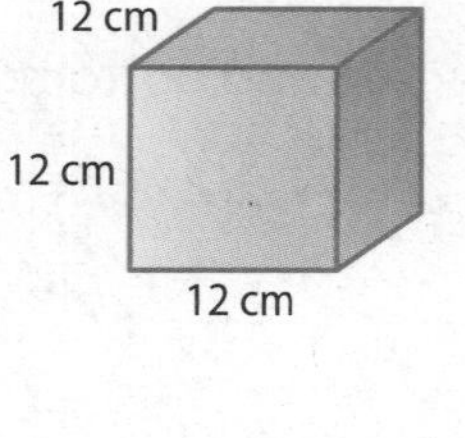

EE = Expressions, Equations, and Relationships N = Number and Operations P = Proportionality MD = Measurement and Data MP = Mathematical Processes

Hands-On Lab 9-a

Nets of Triangular Prisms

INQUIRY **HOW can I select tools and techniques to model the surface area of a triangular prism?**

A computer hardware company packages batteries and cords in boxes shaped like triangular prisms. You can use nets and drawings to determine the surface area of the box.

Texas Essential Knowledge and Skills TEKS

Targeted TEKS

7.9(D) Solve problems involving the lateral and total surface area of a rectangular prism, rectangular pyramid, triangular prism, and triangular pyramid by determining the area of the shape's net.

Mathematical Processes

7.1(C), 7.1(D), 7.1(E), 7.1(F)

Hands-On Activity

Step 1 Use grid paper to draw a net using the dimensions of each face of the triangular prism.

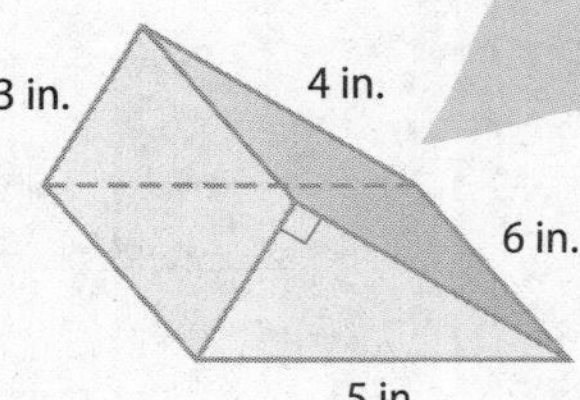

The triangular prism is made up of ☐ triangles and ☐ rectangles.

What is true about the triangles?

______

Compare the dimensions of the rectangles. What do you notice?

______

______

Explain one way to determine the total surface area of a triangular prism.

______

______

Step 2 Add the area of each face to determine the surface area of the figure. Remember, there are two bases.

☐ + ☐ + ☐ + ☐ + ☐ = ☐

So, the surface area is ☐ square units.

Investigate

Collaborate

MP Select Tools and Techniques Work with a partner. Use nets to determine the surface area of each prism. Draw a net of each prism on the provided grid paper.

1. __________ m²

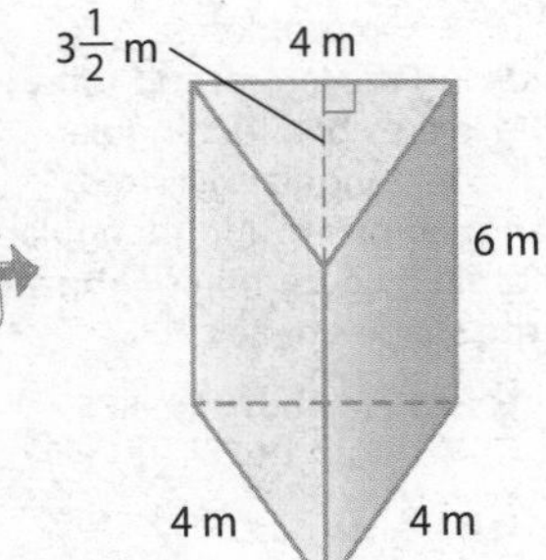

2. __________ cm²

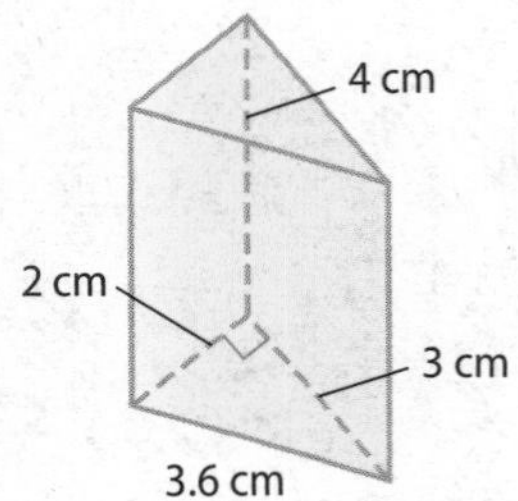

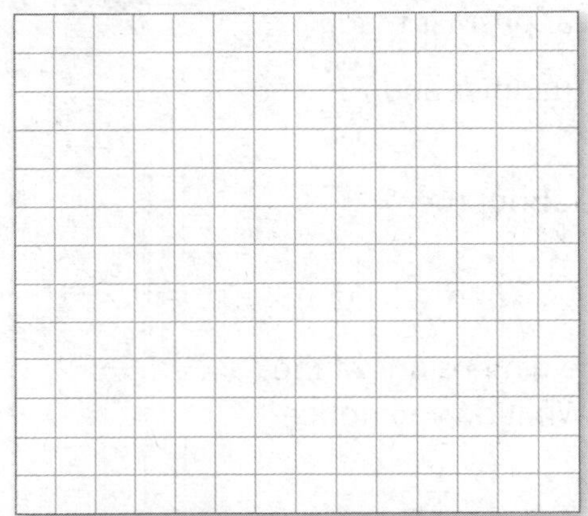

Create

On Your Own

3. **MP Analyze Relationships** Explain how to determine the surface area of a triangular prism, using only the dimensions of the figure. Use the dimensions in Exercise 2 to explain your answer.

____

____

4. **INQUIRY** HOW can I select tools and techniques to model the surface area of a triangular prism?

____

____

____

Lesson 9

Surface Area of Triangular Prisms

Launch the Lesson: Real World

Raj and his dad are building a ramp to move his dirt bike onto a trailer. What shapes are used to build the ramp?

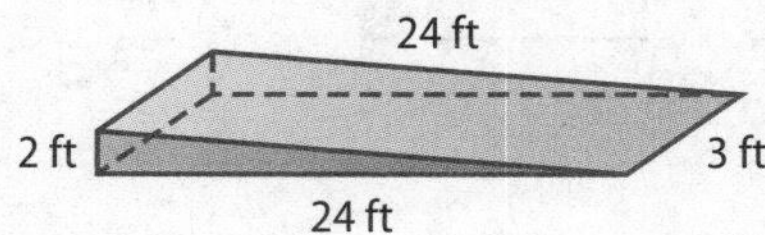

Fill in the table by drawing the sides of the ramp and identifying the shape of each face.

	Face	Draw the Face	Shape of the Face
1.	Front		
2.	Back		
3.	Top		
4.	Bottom		
5.	Side		

Which MP Mathematical Processes did you use?
Shade the circle(s) that applies.

Ⓐ Apply Math to the Real World.
Ⓑ Use a Problem-Solving Model.
Ⓒ Select Tools and Techniques.
Ⓓ Use Multiple Representations.
Ⓔ Organize Ideas.
Ⓕ Analyze Relationships.
Ⓖ Justify Arguments.

Texas Essential Knowledge and Skills

Targeted TEKS
7.9(D) Solve problems involving the lateral and total surface area of a rectangular prism, rectangular pyramid, triangular prism, and triangular pyramid by determining the area of the shape's net.

Mathematical Processes
7.1(A), 7.1(B), 7.1(D), 7.1(E)

Essential Question
HOW do measurements help you describe real-world objects?

Key Concept

Surface Area of a Triangular Prism

Words

The surface area of a triangular prism is the sum of the areas of the two triangular bases and the three rectangular faces.

Model

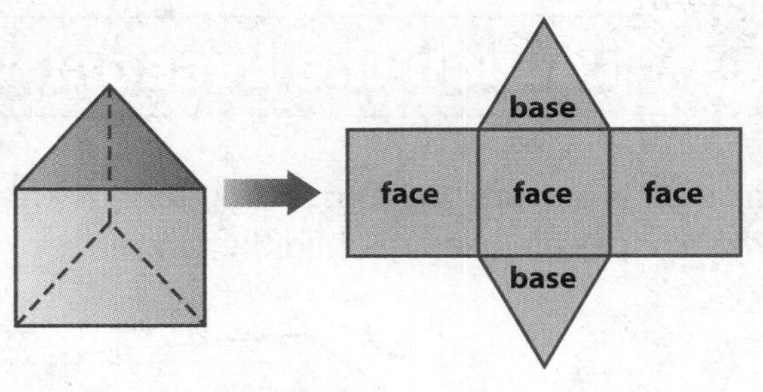

Work Zone

A triangular prism is a prism that has triangular bases. When the bases are equilateral triangles, the areas of the three rectangular faces are equal. You can determine the surface area of a triangular prism by determining the area of the shape's net.

Tutor

Example

1. Determine the surface area of the triangular prism by determining the area of the shape's net.

To determine the surface area of the triangular prism, determine the area of each face and add.

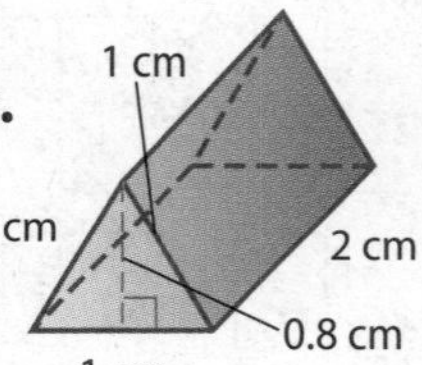

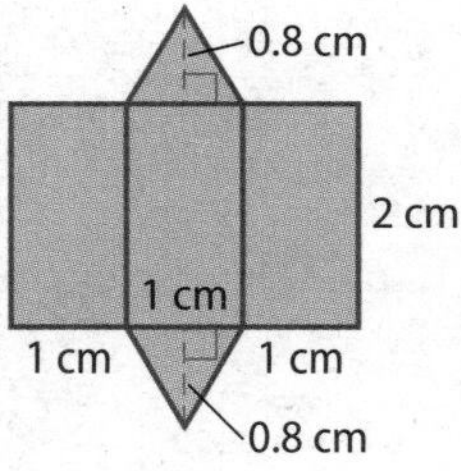

area of each triangular base: $\frac{1}{2}(1)(0.8) = 0.4$

area of each rectangular face: $1(2) = 2$

Add to determine the surface area.

$0.4 + 0.4 + 2 + 2 + 2 = 6.8$ square centimeters

Got It? Do this problem to find out.

a. Determine the surface area of the triangular prism by determining the area of the shape's net.

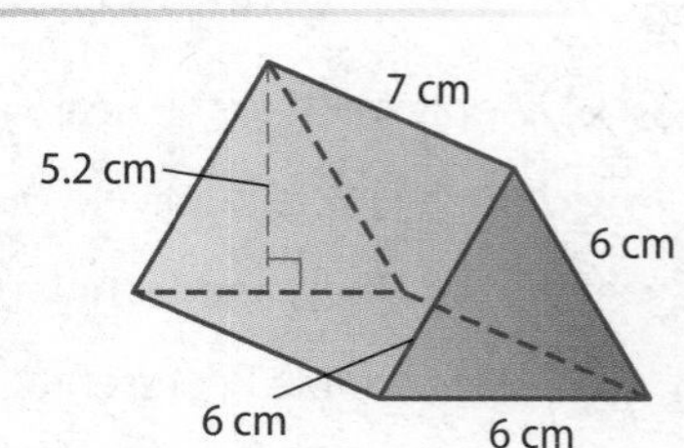

a. ____________

Determine Lateral Surface Area

You can use a net to determine the lateral surface area of a triangular prism. Recall that the lateral surface area is the sum of the areas of all its lateral faces.

Multi-Step Example

Tutor

2. Lucia is covering a box with fabric. It is a triangular prism with the measurements as shown at the right. Determine the amount of fabric she needs to cover the lateral surface area. How much will it cost her if the fabric costs $2.50 per square yard?

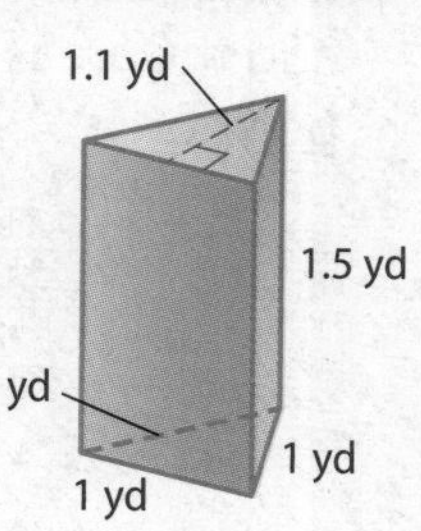

Step 1 Determine the lateral surface area.
All of the lateral faces are congruent rectangles.
lateral faces: 3(1.5)(1) or 4.5

The lateral surface area is 4.5 square yards.

Step 2 Multiply the lateral surface area by the cost per square yard to determine the total cost of the fabric.
$4.5 \times 2.50 = 11.25$

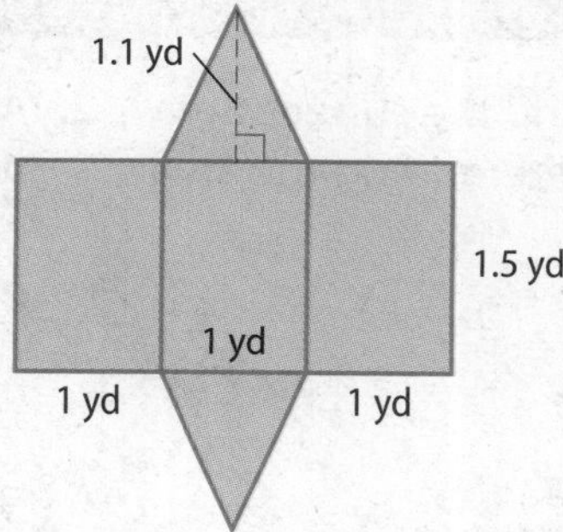

So, it will cost Lucia $11.25 to buy fabric to cover her box.

Got It? Do this problem to find out

b. Gary is painting a decorative box. It is a triangular prism with the measurements as shown at the right. He bought 1 pint of paint that covers about 25 square feet of surface. Does he have enough to paint the lateral surface area of his box with three coats of paint? Justify your answer.

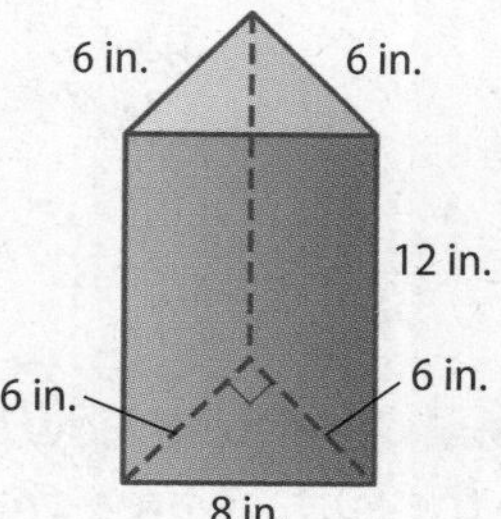

b. ____________

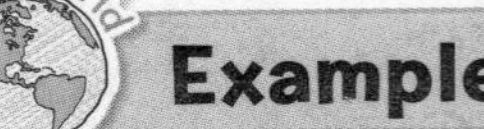

Example

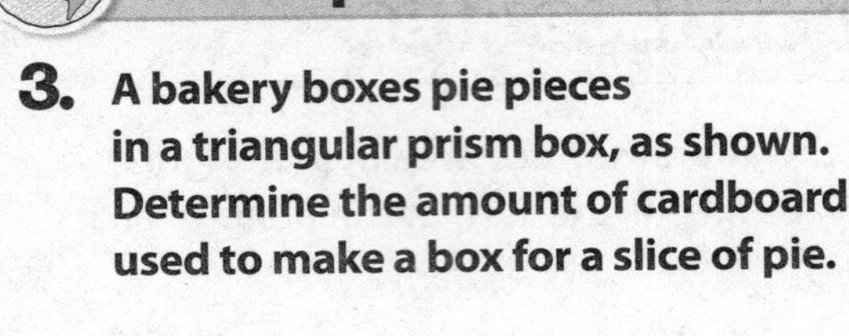

3. A bakery boxes pie pieces in a triangular prism box, as shown. Determine the amount of cardboard used to make a box for a slice of pie.

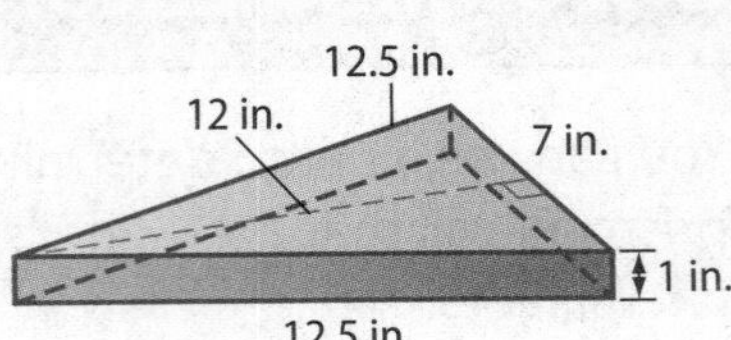

Sketch and label the bases and faces of the triangular prism. Then add the areas of the polygons.

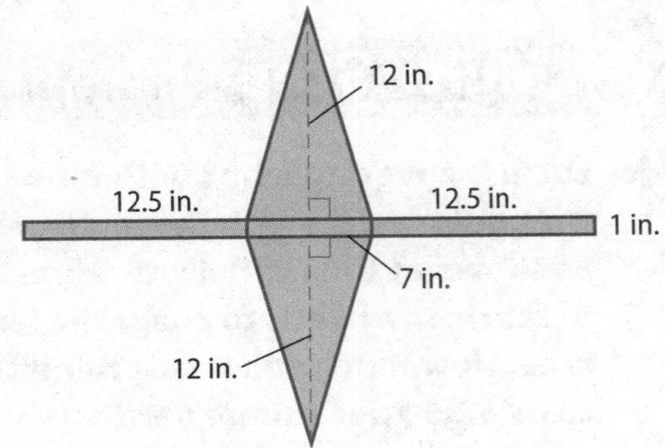

$$\text{Surface area} = 2\left(\frac{1}{2} \cdot 7 \cdot 12\right) + 2(1 \cdot 12.5) + (1 \cdot 7)$$
$$= 84 + 25 + 7 \text{ or } 116$$

So, 116 square inches of cardboard are needed to make a box.

Guided Practice

1. Determine the lateral area and the surface area of the triangular prism by determining the area of the shape's net. (Examples 1–2) ______

Show your work.

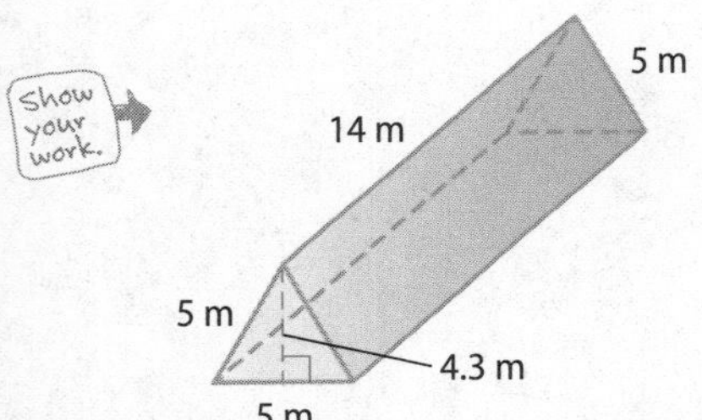

2. A skateboarding ramp is in the shape of a triangular prism. If the entire ramp is to be painted, what is the surface area to be painted by determining the area of the shape's net? (Example 3) ______

50 in.
14 in.
36 in.
48 in.

3. **Building on the Essential Question** How is the area of a rectangle related to the surface area of a triangular prism? ______

______

______

______

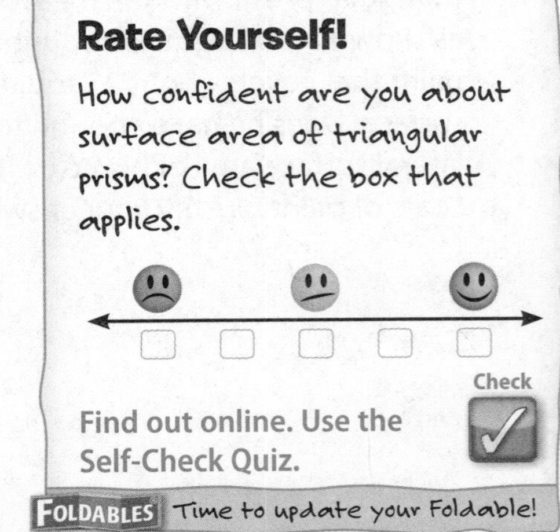

Name ______________________ My Homework ______________________

Independent Practice

7.9(D), 7.1(A) TEKS

Determine the lateral area and the surface area of each triangular prism by determining the area of the shape's net. (Examples 1–2)

1. ____________

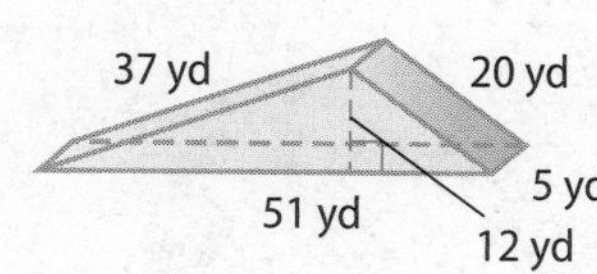

2. ____________

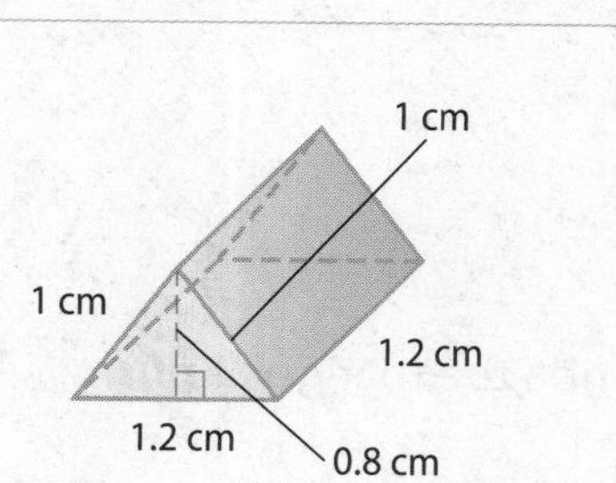

3. ____________

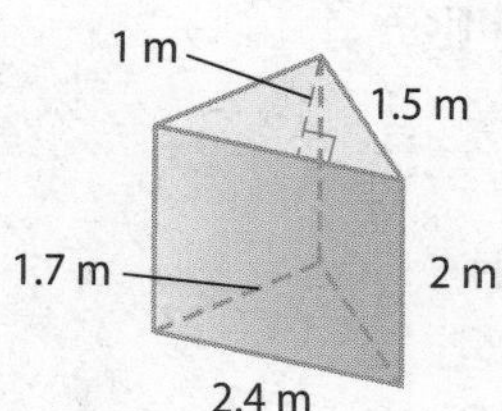

4. ____________

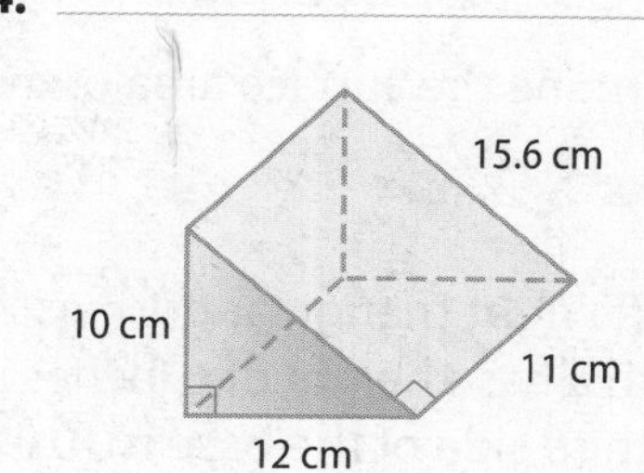

5. A tent is in the shape of a triangular prism. About how much canvas, including the floor, is used to make the tent? Draw a net if necessary. (Example 3)

____

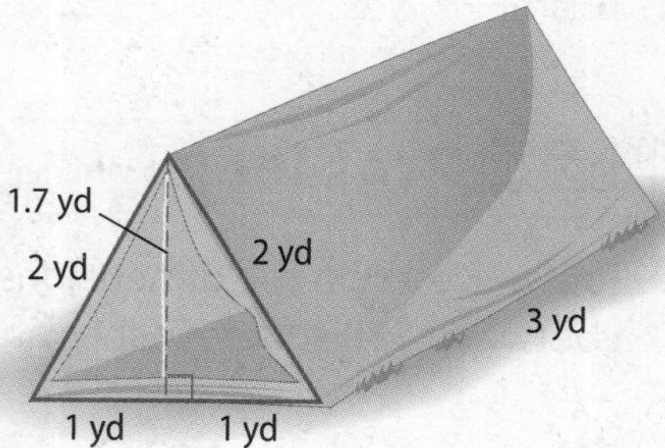

6. A decorative gift box is in the shape of a triangular prism as shown. What is the lateral surface area of the box? Draw a net if necessary. (Example 2) ____________

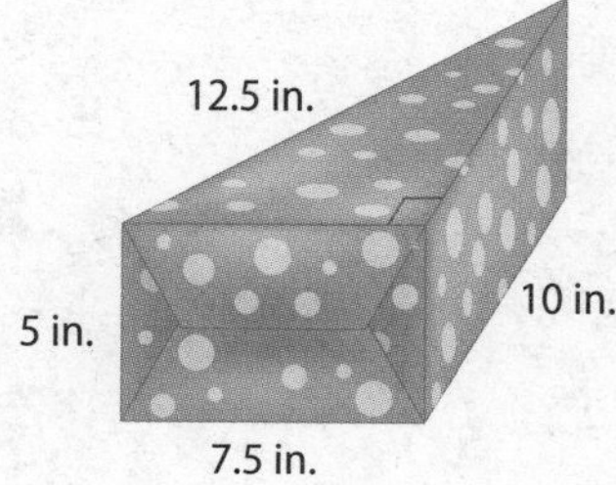

7. A mailer for posters is a triangular prism as shown. Determine the lateral surface area of the mailer. Draw a net if necessary. (Example 2) ____________

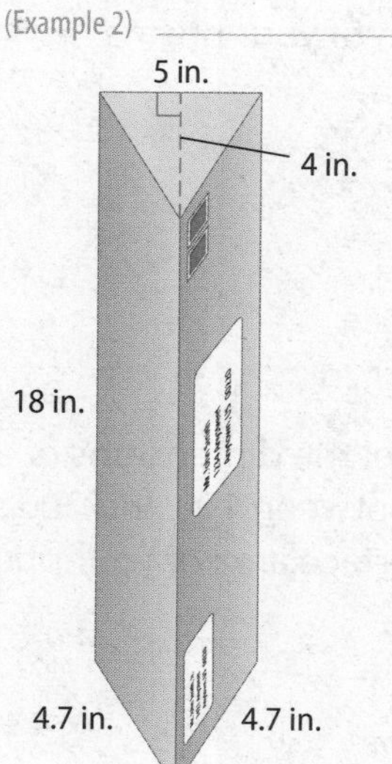

8. MP **Use Multiple Representations** The figure shows the dimensions of a triangular prism.

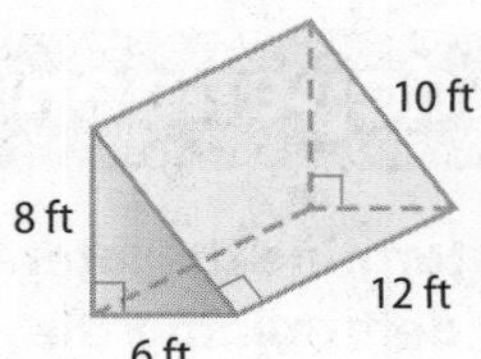

a. **Models** Draw a model of the faces and bases of the triangular prism.

b. **Words** Describe the triangular prism. ______________________________

____

____

c. **Numbers** Determine the surface area of the triangular prism using addition.

____

9. The surface area of a right triangular prism is 228 square inches. The base is a right triangle with a base height of 6 inches and a base length of 8 inches. The length of the third side of the base is 10 inches. Determine the height of the prism. ______________________________

H.O.T. Problems Higher-Order Thinking

10. **Evaluate** Describe the dimensions of a triangular prism that has a surface area between 550 square inches and 700 square inches.

____

____

11. **Create** Draw and label two triangular prisms on a separate sheet of paper. Draw one with a greater volume and the other with a greater surface area. Then give a description of your prisms.

____

____

____

____

12. **Create** Draw and label the dimensions of a triangular prism with a lateral surface area between 100 and 200 square meters. Then determine the total surface area of your prism.

____

Name ______________________________

Multi-Step Problem Solving

13. Two tunnels at a children's gym are shown at the right. How much greater, in square feet, is the lateral surface area of the larger tunnel than the smaller tunnel? EE N MP

Ⓐ 100.4 square feet

Ⓑ 110.2 square feet

Ⓒ 112.4 square feet

Ⓓ 307.6 square feet

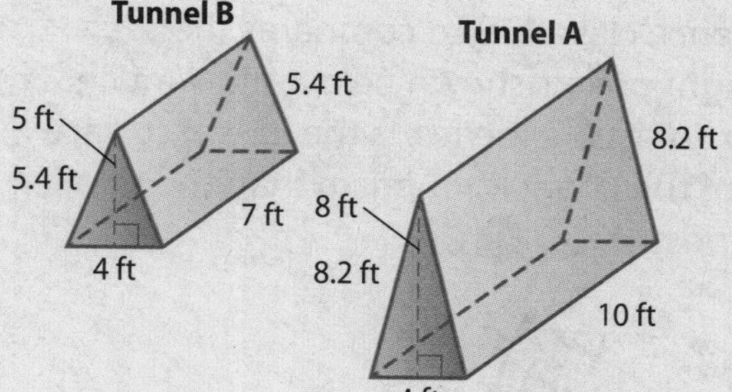

Use a problem-solving model to solve this problem.

1 Analyze

Read the problem. Circle the information you know. Underline what the problem is asking you to find.

2 Plan

What will you need to do to solve the problem? Write your plan in steps.

Step 1 Determine the ______________ for each triangular prism.

Step 2 ________ the lateral surface areas.

3 Solve

Use your plan to solve the problem. Show your steps.

Tunnel A lateral surface area:

base: $4 \cdot 10 =$ ____

sides: $2(8.2 \cdot 10) =$ ____

____ + ____ = ____ Add.

____ − ____ = ____ square feet Subtract.

Tunnel B lateral surface area:

base: $4 \cdot 7 =$ ____

sides: $2(5.4 \cdot 7) =$ ____

____ + ____ = ____ Add.

So, the correct answer is ___. Fill in that answer choice.

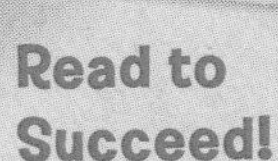

Read to Succeed!

You may need to draw a net of each prism to help you visualize the area of each face.

4 Justify and Evaluate

____

____

____

EE = Expressions, Equations, and Relationships N = Number and Operations MP = Mathematical Processes

More Multi-Step Problem Solving

Use a problem-solving model to solve each problem.

14. In science class, Marco compares the two light prisms shown below. How much larger, in square inches, is the lateral surface area of the larger light prism than the smaller light prism? EE N MP

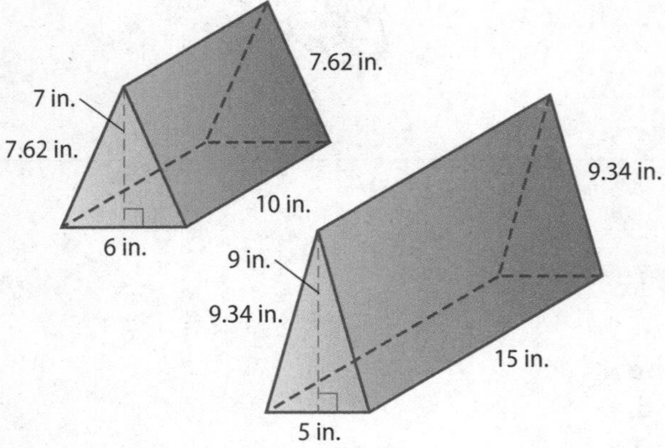

Ⓐ 142.8 square feet

Ⓑ 145.8 square feet

Ⓒ 212.4 square feet

Ⓓ 567.6 square feet

15. The net below represents a portion of a mural on a park sidewalk. If the dimensions are doubled, how many times greater is the surface area of the similar net, in square yards? EE N MP

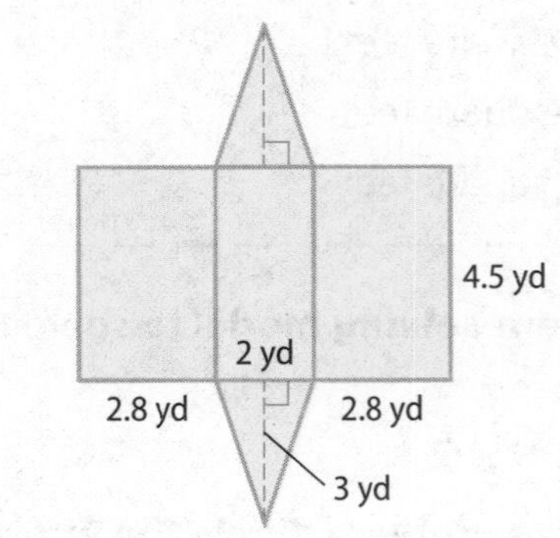

16. Gloria purchased a wedge pillow as shown below. She wants to make a pillow case for it. She has 500 square inches of fabric. How many more square inches of fabric does she need for the pillow case? EE N MP

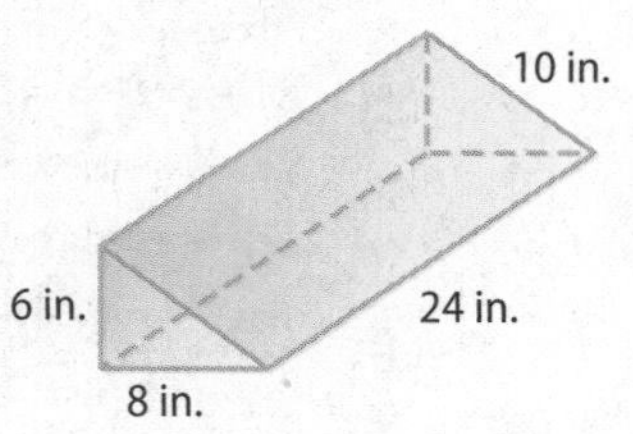

17. The rectangular prism shown is cut in half diagonally to create the triangular prism. Is the surface area of the right triangular prism equal to one-half the surface area of the rectangular prism? Explain. EE N MP

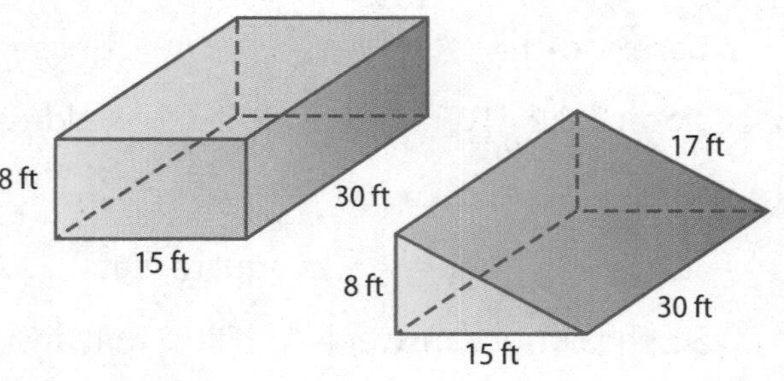

EE = Expressions, Equations, and Relationships N = Number and Operations MP = Mathematical Processes

Hands-On Lab 9-b

Relate Surface Area and Volume

INQUIRY HOW can I analyze relationships to connect the shape of a rectangular prism to its volume and surface area?

You can arrange blocks in many ways. How can you arrange 8 blocks to create the least possible surface area?

What do you know? ______________________________

____

What do you need to find? ______________________________

____

Texas Essential Knowledge and Skills TEKS

Targeted TEKS
7.9(D) Solve problems involving the lateral and total surface area of a rectangular prism, rectangular pyramid, triangular prism, and triangular pyramid by determining the area of the shape's net. *Also addresses 7.9(A).*

Mathematical Processes
7.1(C), 7.1(D), 7.1(E), 7.1(G)

Hands-On Activity 1

Tools

Step 1 Create a rectangular prism using 8 centimeter cubes. Record the dimensions in the table below. Determine and record the volume and surface area of the prism.

Rectangular Prism	Length (cm)	Width (cm)	Height (cm)	Volume (cm^3)	Surface Area (cm^2)
1	2	2			
2					
3					

Step 2 Repeat Step 1 for as many different rectangular prisms as you can create with 8 cubes.

Does the volume change when the prism changes? Explain.

____

____

The rectangular prism measuring ☐ × ☐ × ☐ has the least surface area.

Hands-On Activity 2

Suppose you make structures in the shape of the ones shown below. What is the volume of each structure? Which structure has the lesser surface area? Draw a net if necessary.

Figure 1

Figure 2

Step 1 Use centimeter cubes to create the rectangular prism shown in Figure 1. Write its dimensions, volume, and surface area in the table below.

Rectangular Prism	Length (cm)	Width (cm)	Height (cm)	Volume (cm^3)	Surface Area (cm^2)
Figure 1	3				
Figure 2					

Step 2 Use centimeter cubes to create the rectangular prism shown in Figure 2. Write its dimensions, volume, and surface area in the table.

Step 3 Compare the volume and surface areas of Figure 1 and Figure 2.

What do you notice about the volume of Figure 1 and Figure 2?

____

The surface area of Figure 1 is ☐ square centimeters.

The surface area of Figure 2 is ☐ square centimeters.

Compare the surface areas using an inequality.

☐ square centimeters < ☐ square centimeters

So, Figure ☐ has the lesser surface area.

Work with a partner. Compare the two figures that have the same volume. Then determine which figure has a greater surface area. Draw a net if necessary.

1.

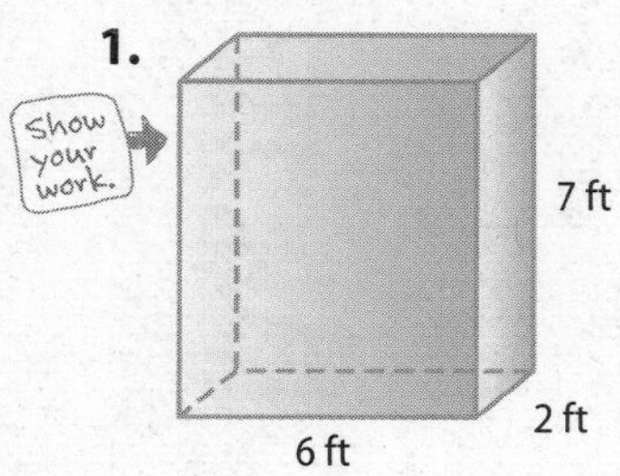

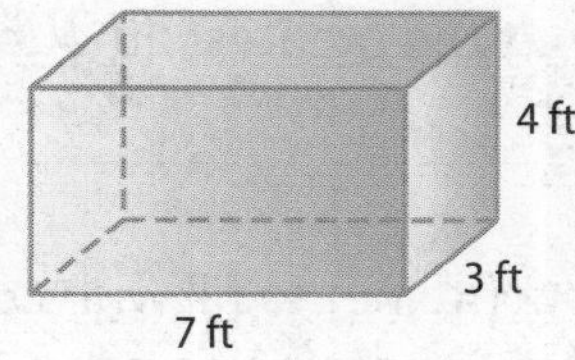

Figure 1 Surface Area: ______

Figure 2 Surface Area: ______

2.

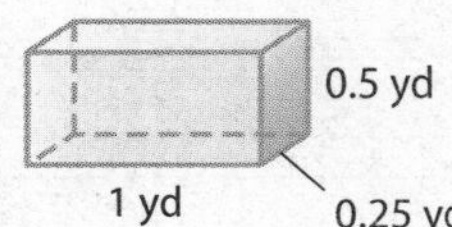

Figure 1 Surface Area: ______

Figure 2 Surface Area: ______

3.

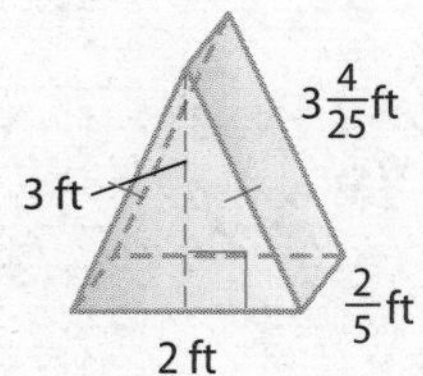

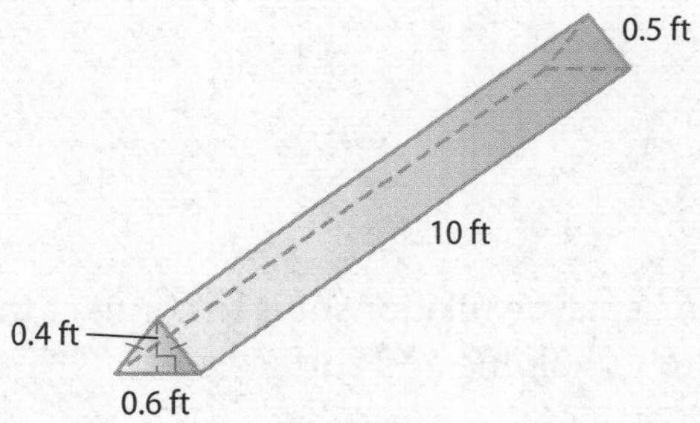

Figure 1 Surface Area: ______

Figure 2 Surface Area: ______

Analyze and Reflect

Work with a partner to solve the following problems. Draw a net if necessary.

4. Monique sews together pieces of fabric to make rectangular gift boxes. She only uses whole numbers. What are the dimensions of a box with a volume of 50 cubic inches that has the greatest amount of surface area?

5. Thomas is creating a decorative container to fill with colored sand. He uses only whole numbers. The top of the container is open. What are the dimensions of the rectangular prism that holds 100 cubic inches with the least amount of surface area?

6. MP **Justify Arguments** Zack needs to melt a stick of butter that measures 5 inches by 1 inch by 1 inch. He is going to put the butter in a pan on top of the stove. Explain why cutting the butter into smaller pieces will help the butter melt faster.

Create

7. MP **Select Tools and Techniques** Draw a sketch of a triangular prism with a volume of 120 cubic units and a surface area of 184 square units.

8. INQUIRY HOW can I analyze relationships to connect the shape of a rectangular prism to its volume and surface area?

Lesson 10

Surface Area of Pyramids

Launch the Lesson: Vocabulary

Texas Essential Knowledge and Skills

Targeted TEKS

7.9(D) Solve problems involving the lateral and total surface area of a rectangular prism, rectangular pyramid, triangular prism, and triangular pyramid by determining the area of the shape's net.

Mathematical Processes

7.1(A), 7.1(B), 7.1(E), 7.1(F)

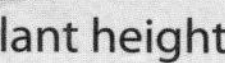

Vocabulary

slant height

Essential Question

HOW do measurements help you describe real-world objects?

Ancient Egyptians built pyramids, such as the one shown in the photo below. A right square pyramid has a square base and four isosceles triangles that make up the lateral faces. The lateral surface area is the sum of the areas of all its lateral faces. The height of each lateral face is called **slant height**.

1. Fill in the blanks on the diagram below with the terms *slant height* and *lateral face*.

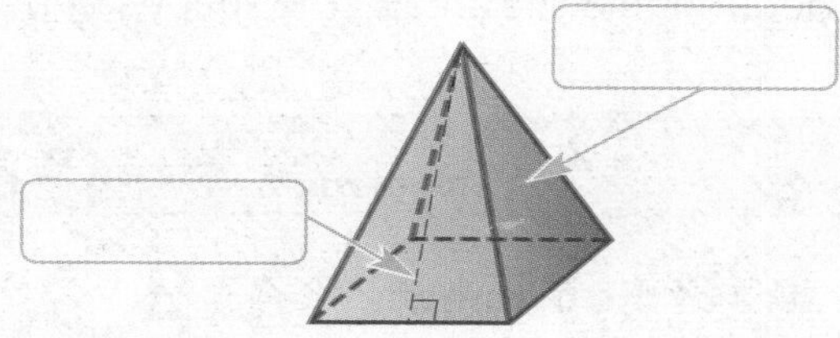

2. Draw a net of a square pyramid.

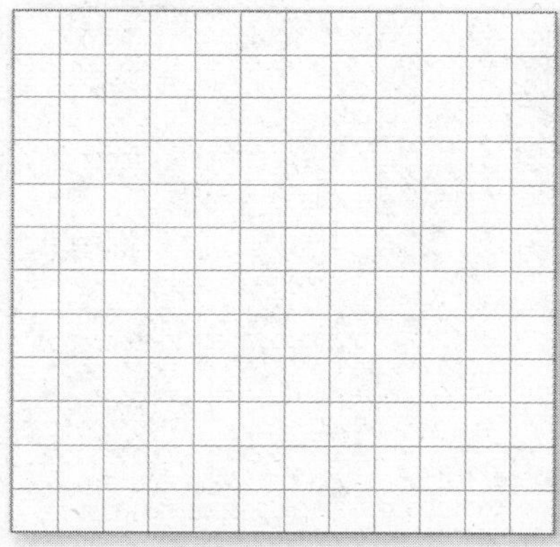

Which MP Mathematical Processes did you use? Shade the circle(s) that applies.

Ⓐ Apply Math to the Real World.
Ⓑ Use a Problem-Solving Model.
Ⓒ Select Tools and Techniques.
Ⓓ Use Multiple Representations.
Ⓔ Organize Ideas.
Ⓕ Analyze Relationships.
Ⓖ Justify Arguments.

Key Concept

Surface Area of a Pyramid

Work Zone

Words The surface area of a pyramid is the sum of the area of the base and the areas of the lateral faces.

Model vertex, lateral face, slant height, base → lateral face, base, slant height

Some pyramids have square or rectangular bases. You can determine the surface area of a pyramid by determining the area of the shape's net.

Tutor 

Example

1. Determine the surface area of the pyramid.

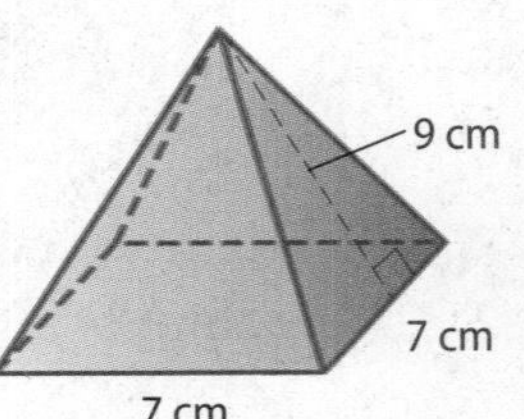

Determine the area of the pyramid's net.

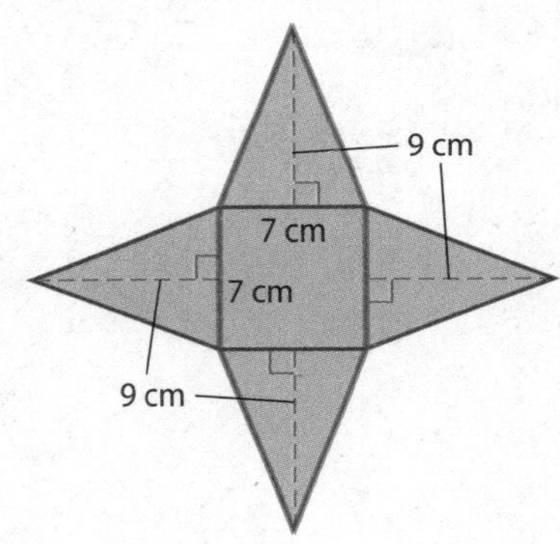

area of base: $7(7) = 49$

area of each triangular side: $\frac{1}{2}(7)(9) = 31.5$

Add to determine the surface area.

$49 + 31.5 + 31.5 + 31.5 + 31.5 = 175$ square centimeters

Got It? **Do these problems to find out.**

a. ____________

b. ____________

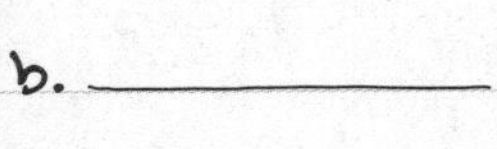

a.

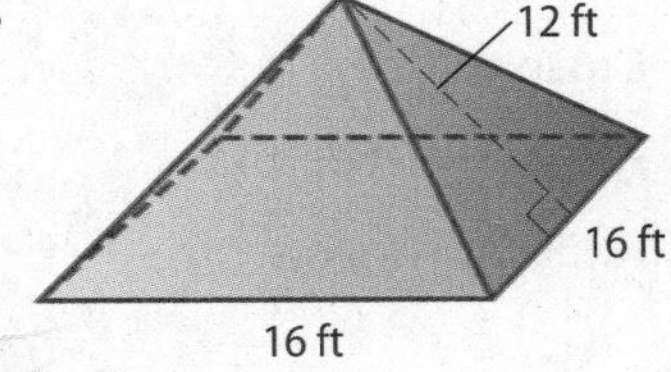

b.

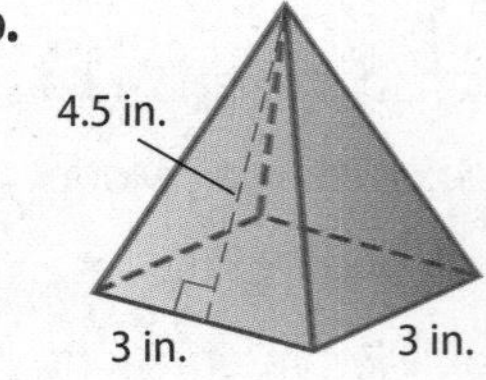

Lateral and Total Surface Area of Pyramids with Triangular Bases

A triangular pyramid has one triangular base, and three triangular faces. If the base is an equilateral triangle, all three lateral faces are congruent. If the sides of the base triangle are different lengths, the areas of the lateral faces will also vary.

Example

Tutor

2. Determine the lateral surface area and total surface area of the pyramid.

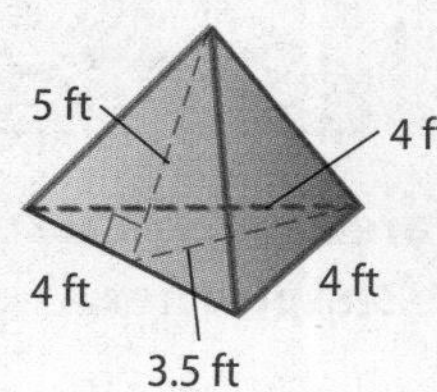

Determine the area of each face and add. The triangular base is an equilateral triangle because all three sides are 4 feet long.

base **lateral faces**

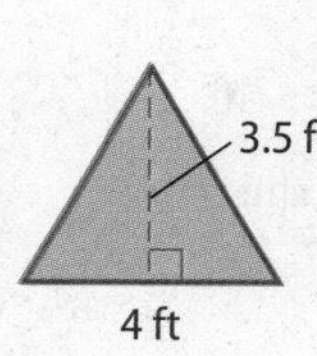

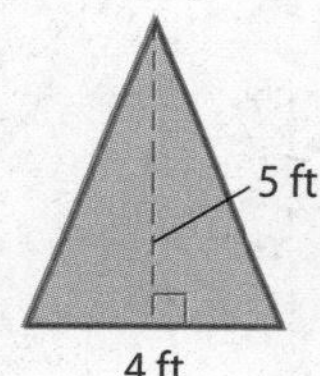

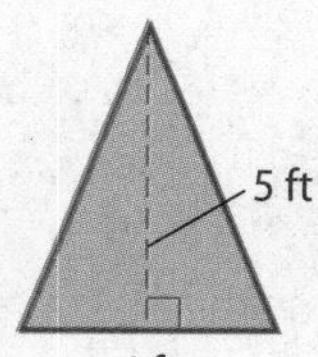

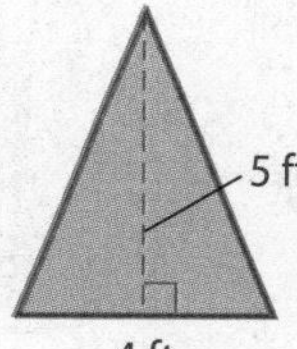

Determine the area of each lateral face.

area of each lateral face: $\frac{1}{2}(4)(5) = 10$

The lateral surface area is $3 \cdot 10$ or 30 square feet.

Determine the total surface area.

area of base: $\frac{1}{2}(4)(3.5) = 7$

Add the surface area of the base to the lateral surface area.

$7 + 30 = 37$ square feet

Got It? Do these problems to find out.

Show your work.

c.

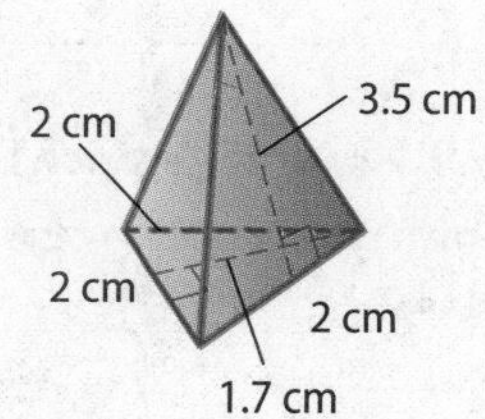

d.

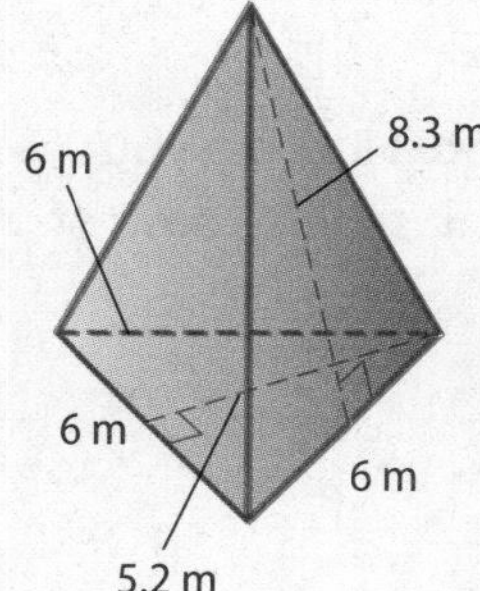

c. ________

d. ________

Example

3. A pyramid puzzle has all sides that are equilateral triangles. Each triangle has side lengths of 8 centimeters. The slant height is 6.9 centimeters. Determine the surface area of the puzzle.

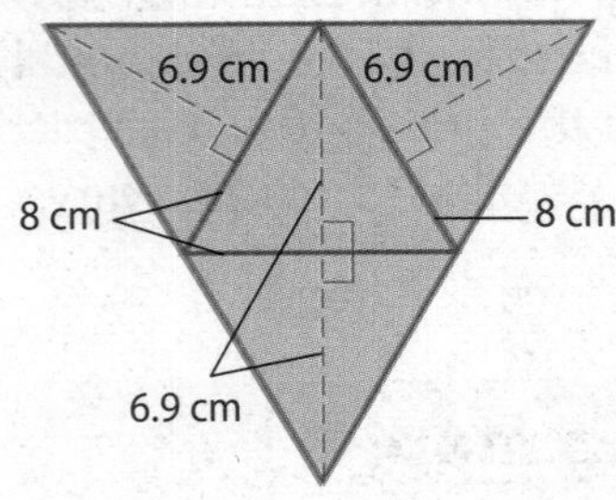

Create a net and then use it to determine the surface area of the pyramid.

Each face has an area of $\frac{1}{2}(8)(6.9)$ or 27.6 square centimeters. So, the surface area of the puzzle is $4 \cdot 27.6$ or 110.4 square centimeters.

Guided Practice

Determine the lateral surface area and total surface area of each pyramid by determining the area of the shape's net. (Examples 1–2)

1. ______

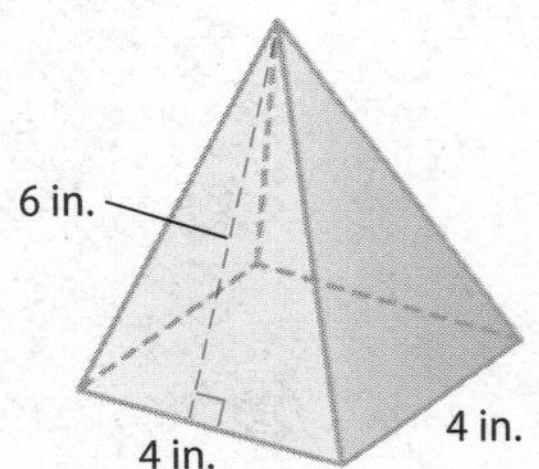

2. ______

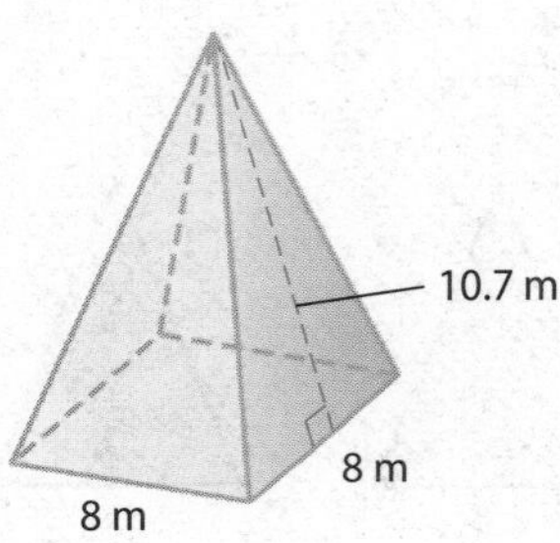

3. ______

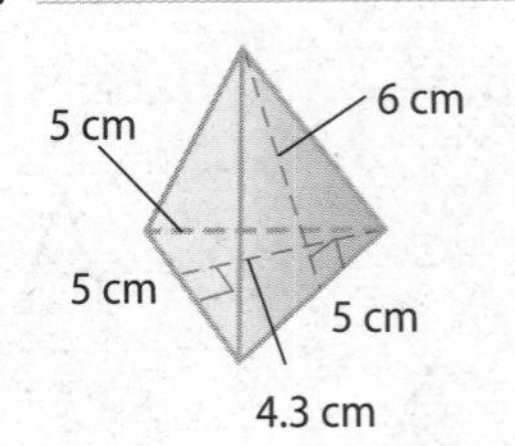

Show your work.

4. Pyramid-shaped gift boxes have square bases that measure 5 inches on each side. The slant height is 6.5 inches. How much cardboard is used to make each box? (Example 3)

5. **Building on the Essential Question** How do you use the area of a triangle to determine the surface area of a triangular pyramid?

Rate Yourself!

☐ I understand surface area of pyramids.

Great! You're ready to move on!

☐ I still have questions about surface area of pyramids.

No problem! Go online to access a Personal Tutor.

FOLDABLES Time to update your Foldable!

Name ______________________ My Homework ______________________

Independent Practice

7.9(D), 7.1(A), 7.1(F) TEKS

Determine the lateral surface area and total surface area of each pyramid by determining the area of the shape's net. (Examples 1–2)

1. ______________

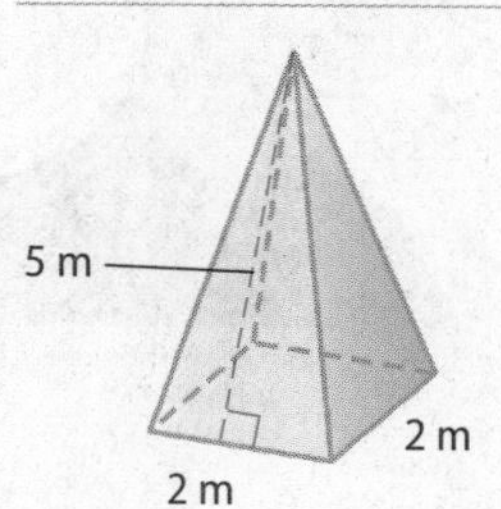

2. ______________

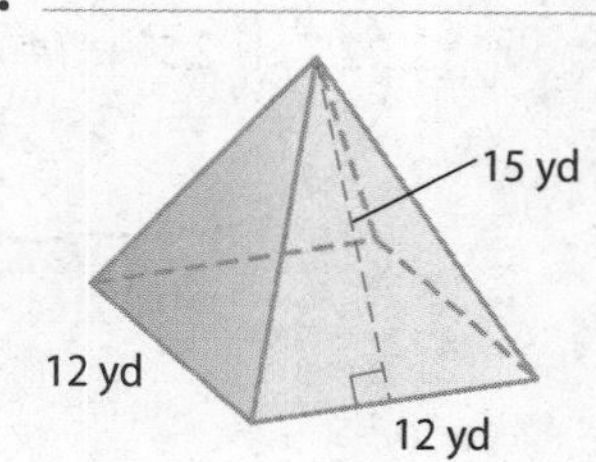

3. ______________

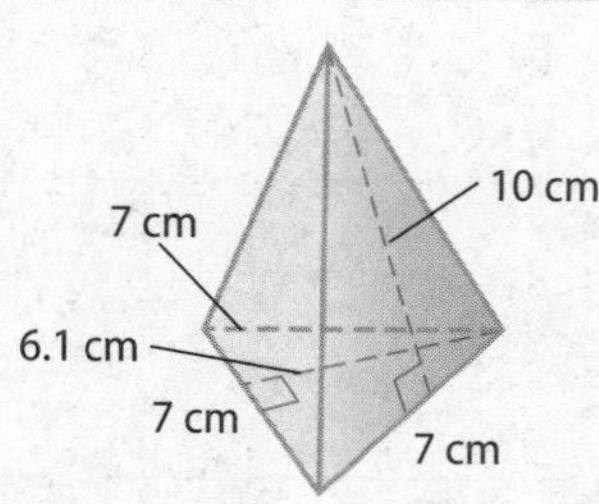

4. ______________

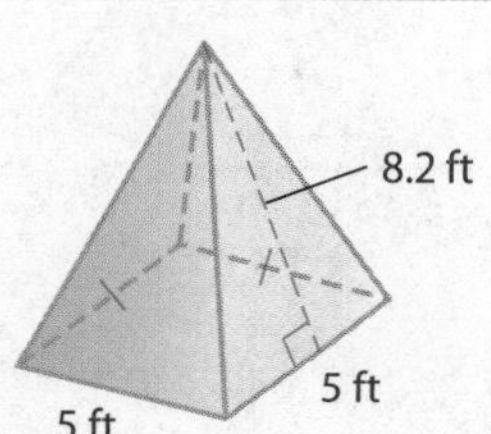

5. ______________

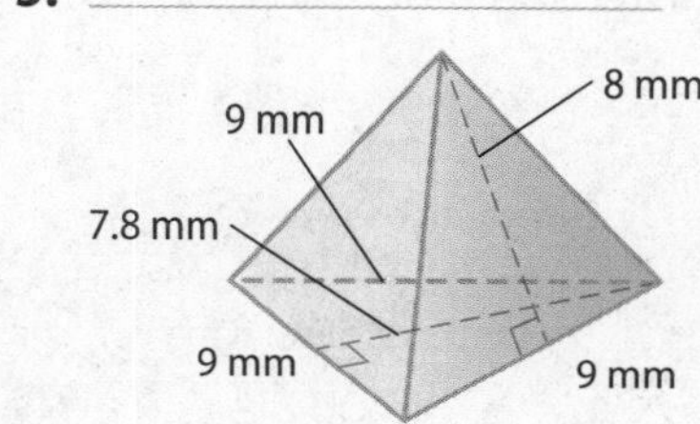

6. ______________

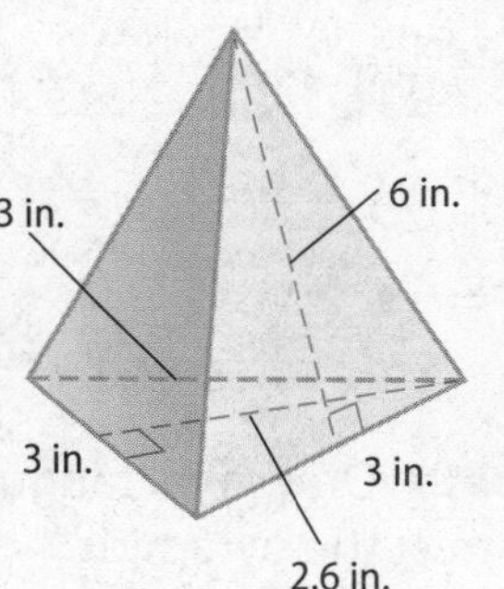

7. An acting award is a square pyramid with a base that measures 6 inches on each side. The slant height is 8 inches. What is the surface area of the award? (Example 3)

____

8. MP **Analyze Relationships** Refer to the figures listed in the table. Determine the number of faces the figure has of each two-dimensional shape. Explain.

Figure	Rectangular Faces	Triangular Faces
Rectangular Prism		
Triangular Prism		
Square Pyramid		
Triangular Pyramid		

____

____

____

9. **Find the Error** Raul is determining the surface area of the pyramid shown. Find his mistake and correct it.

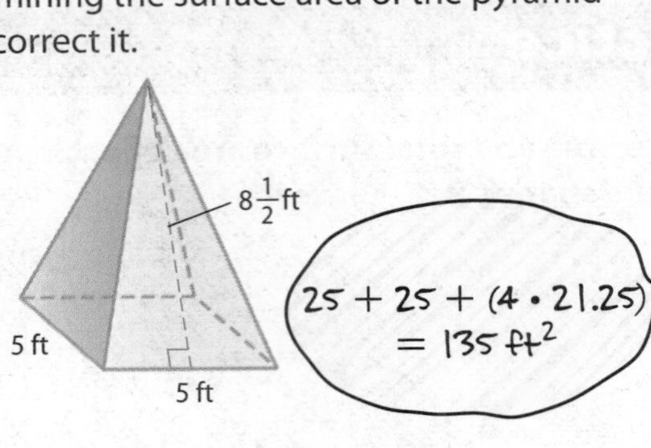

H.O.T. Problems Higher-Order Thinking

10. **Analyze** The *lateral surface area L.A.* of a pyramid is the area of its lateral faces. Use the square pyramid at the right to complete each step to determine the lateral surface area of any pyramid.

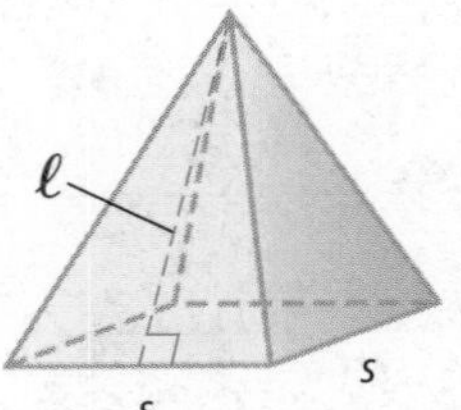

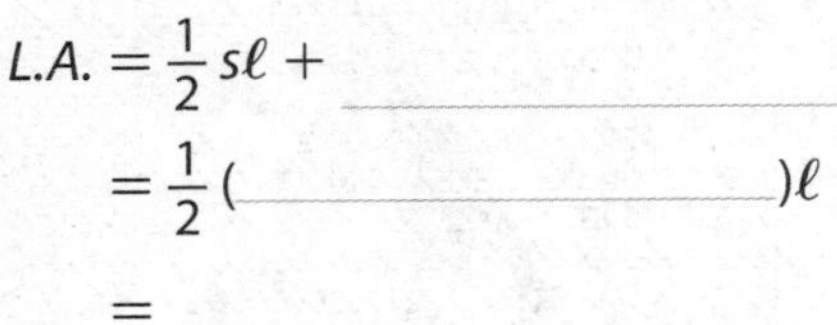

$L.A. = \frac{1}{2}s\ell +$ ______ Lateral surface area

$= \frac{1}{2}($ ______ $)\ell$ Distributive Property

$=$ ______ Perimeter of base: $P = s + s + s + s$

11. **Create** Draw a rectangular pyramid and a square pyramid. Compare and contrast the pyramids.

Rectangular Pyramid **Square Pyramid**

12. **Analyze** What is the difference between the slant height and the height of a pyramid? Explain.

Name ____________________

Multi-Step Problem Solving

13. The table shows the dimensions of three different square pyramids. What is difference between the greatest and least surface area, in square inches? EE N MP

Pyramid	Base Edge (in.)	Slant Height (in.)
A	2	5
B	5	12
C	3.5	9

Ⓐ 51.25 square inches
Ⓑ 69.75 square inches
Ⓒ 96 square inches
Ⓓ 121 square inches

Use a problem-solving model to solve this problem.

1 Analyze

Read the problem. Circle the information you know.
Underline what the problem is asking you to find.

2 Plan

What will you need to do to solve the problem? Write your plan in steps.

Step 1 Determine the __________ for each square pyramid.

Step 2 __________ the least from the greatest surface areas.

3 Solve

Use your plan to solve the problem. Show your steps.

Determine the area of each base and lateral face:

A: (2)(2) = ___ B: (5)(5) = ___ C: (3.5)(3.5) = ___

A: $\frac{1}{2}$(2)(5) = ___ B: $\frac{1}{2}$(5)(12) = ___ C: $\frac{1}{2}$(3.5)(9) = ___

A: ___ + ___ + ___ + ___ + ___ = ___ Add.

B: ___ + ___ + ___ + ___ + ___ = ___ Add.

C: ___ + ___ + ___ + ___ = ___ Add.

___ − ___ = ___ square inches Subtract.

So, the correct answer is ___. Fill in that answer choice.

Read to Succeed!
A square pyramid has four triangular sides. Determine the area of one side, then add the area four times to determine the lateral surface area.

4 Justify and Evaluate

How do you know your solution is accurate?

____

____

____

EE = Expressions, Equations, and Relationships N = Number and Operations MP = Mathematical Processes

More Multi-Step Problem Solving

Use a problem-solving model to solve each problem.

14. The table shows the dimensions of three different square pyramids. What is difference between the greatest and least surface area, in square inches? EE N MP

Pyramid	Base Edge (cm)	Slant Height (cm)
1	5	8.5
2	8	5
3	6	10

Ⓐ 12 square inches

Ⓑ 34 square inches

Ⓒ 46 square inches

Ⓓ 55 square inches

15. The net of Alana's crystal square pyramid is shown below. She wants to wrap the pyramid in three layers of tissue paper so she can put it in storage. What is the area, in square centimeters, of tissue paper will she need? EE N MP

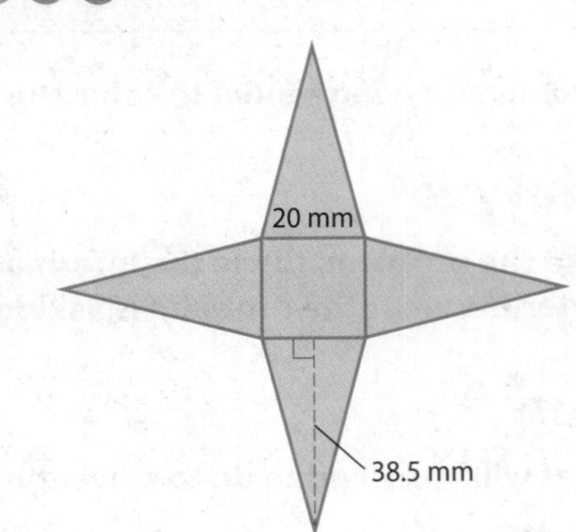

16. The pyramid below represents a sign at the entryway to a state park. The sign is going to be covered using advertisements on a large canvas. The bottom of the sign does not need to be covered since it is on the ground. There will only be advertisements on two lateral faces of the pyramid. Determine the lateral surface area, in square feet, to cover the two sides of the sign. EE N MP

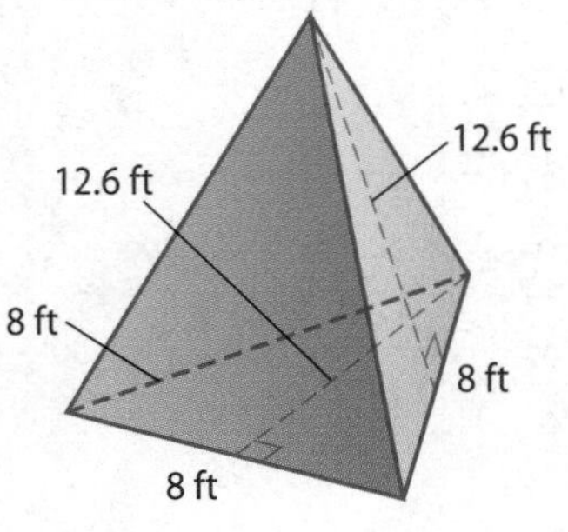

17. The square pyramids below are congruent. What is the surface area of the composite figure? Explain. EE N MP

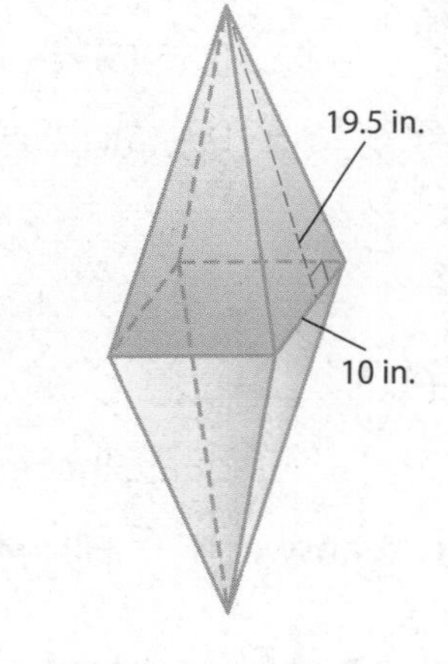

EE = Expressions, Equations, and Relationships N = Number and Operations MP = Mathematical Processes

21ST CENTURY CAREER

Mathematical Process
7.1(A) Apply mathematics to problems arising in everyday life, society, and the workplace.
Targeted TEKS 7.9(B)

Landscape Architect

Do you have an artistic side, and do you enjoy being outdoors? If so, a career in landscape design might be a perfect fit for you. Landscape architects design outside areas such as yards, parks, playgrounds, campuses, shopping centers, and golf courses. Their designed areas are not only meant to be beautiful, but also functional and compatible with the natural environment. A landscape architect must be proficient in mathematics, science, and the use of computer-aided design.

Is This the Career for You?

Are you interested in a career as a landscape architect? Take some of the following courses in high school.

- Algebra
- Architectural Design
- Botany
- Drafting/Illustrative Design Technology
- Geometry

Explore college and careers at ccr.mcgraw-hill.com

Planting in Circles

For each problem, use the information in the designs.

1. In Design 2, what is the radius of the larger grassy area? ______

2. The small circular fountain in Design 1 is surrounded by a stone wall. Determine the circumference of the wall. Use $\frac{22}{7}$ for π.

______

3. Determine the circumference of the smaller grassy area in Design 2. Use 3.14 for π.

______

4. In Design 2, how much greater is the lawn area in the larger circle than in the smaller circle? Use 3.14 for π. ______

5. In Design 2, the smaller circle is surrounded by a path 1 meter wide. What is the circumference of the outside edge of the path? Use the π key on a calculator and round to the nearest tenth.

______

6. In Design 1, the area of the large circular patio is about 201.1 square feet. What is the radius of the patio? Round to the nearest foot. ______

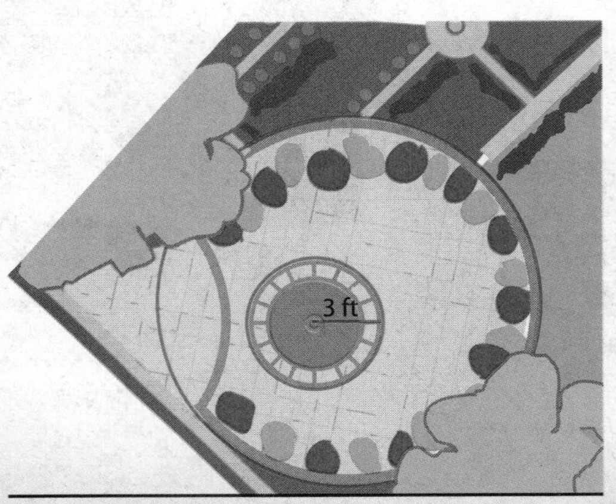

Design 1

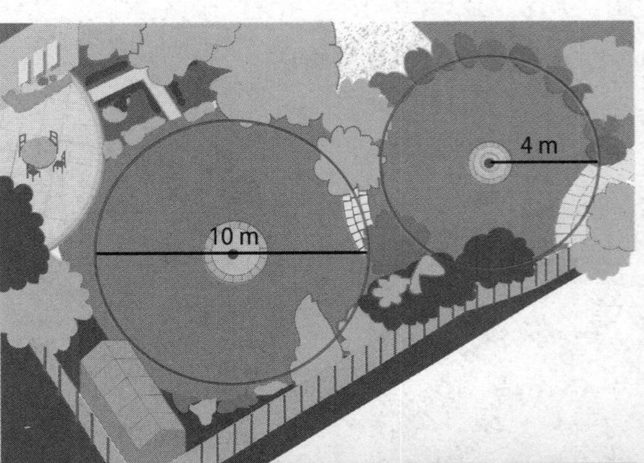

Design 2

TEKS Career Project

It's time to update your career portfolio! Download free landscaping software from the Internet and use it to create your own landscape design. Include a list of all the plants and materials used in your design. Also, provide an estimate of the total cost of the landscaping project. Then prepare a brief oral presentation to present to your classmates. As others are presenting, listen carefully. Ask clarifying questions as needed.

______

______

______

What is something you really want to do in the next ten years?

- ______
- ______
- ______
- ______
- ______

Chapter Review

Vocabulary Check

Work with a partner to complete the crossword puzzle using the vocabulary list at the beginning of the chapter. Take turns reading each sentence aloud while the other student listens carefully.

Across

1. segments with the same length
4. half of a circle
5. a three-dimensional figure with two parallel, congruent bases that are polygons
6. the measure of the space a three-dimensional figure occupies
7. opposite angles that are formed by the intersection of two lines
8. an angle less than 90 degrees

Down

2. a triangle with an angle greater than 180 degrees
3. two angles with a sum of 90 degrees
4. two angles with a sum of 180 degrees
6. where two rays meet to form an angle

Key Concept Check

Use Your FOLDABLES®

Use your Foldable to help review the chapter. Share your Foldable with a partner and take turns summarizing what you learned in this chapter, while the other partner listens carefully. Ask for and give help of any concept if needed. TEKS 7.1(E)

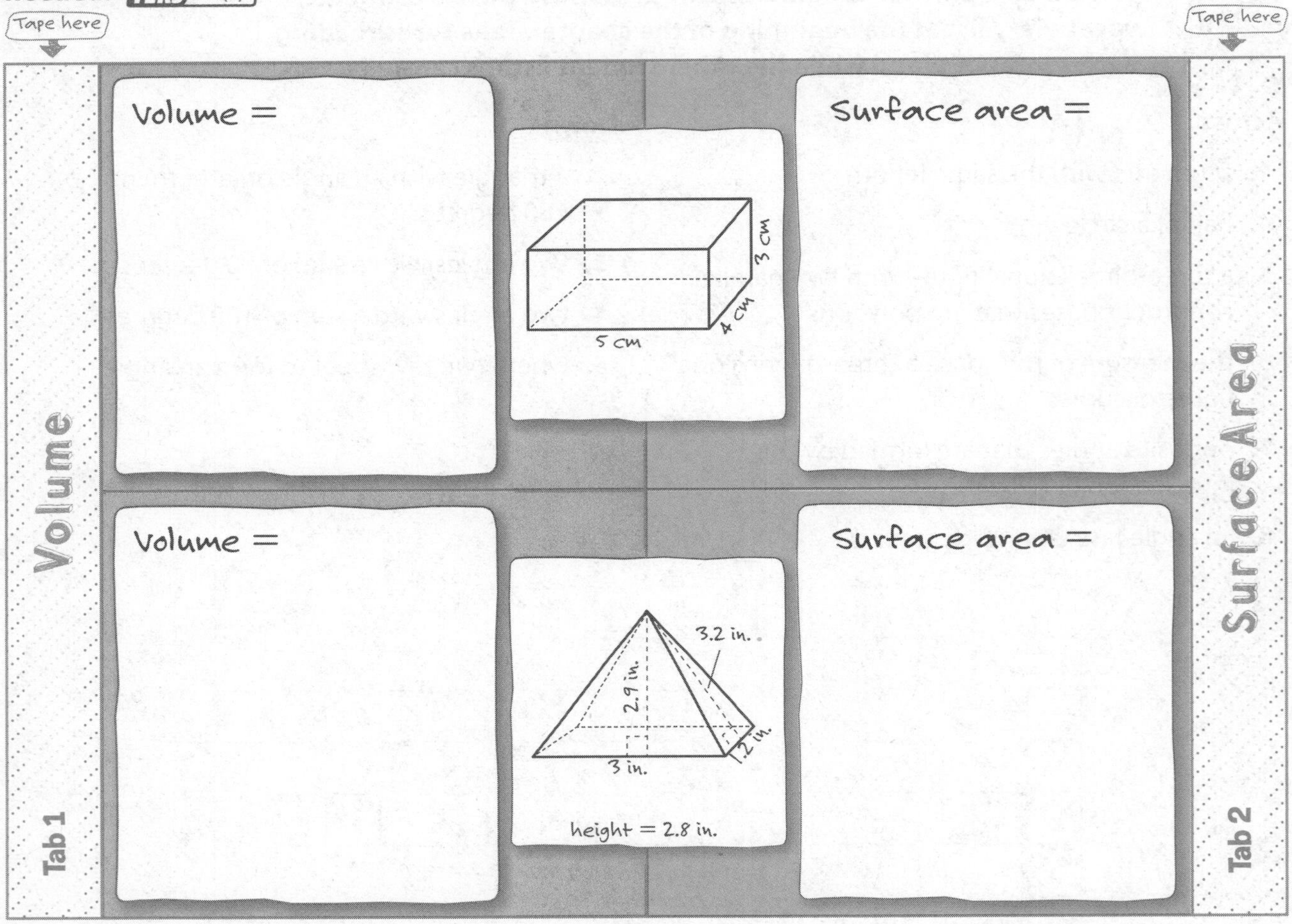

Tape here

Tape here

Volume

Tab 1

Volume =

5 cm

4 cm

3 cm

Surface area =

Volume =

3.2 in.

2.9 in.

2 in.

3 in.

height = 2.8 in.

Surface area =

Surface Area

Tab 2

Got it?

Circle the correct term or number to complete each sentence. TEKS 7.1(D)

1. The diameter of a circle is (twice, three times) its radius.
2. The area of a circle equals the product of pi and the square of its (radius, diameter).
3. The volume of a rectangular prism can be found by multiplying the area of the base times the (length, height).
4. To determine the surface area of a triangular prism, draw a net to determine the area of each face and calculate the (sum, product) of all the faces.

Multi-Step Problem Solving

5. The scale drawing at the right represents a circle fountain. The circumference of circular fountain drawing is 78.5 centimeters. The actual circumference of the fountain is 9.42 meters. What is the area of the actual fountain? Justify your solution. EE P MP

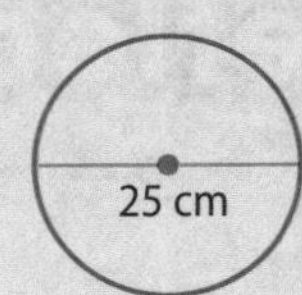

1 Analyze

2 Plan

3 Solve

4 Justify and Evaluate

Got it?

6. A children's rectangular pool has a length of $3\frac{1}{2}$ feet, a width of 5 feet, and a height of 1 foot. If the pool will be filled at a rate of $2\frac{1}{2}$ cubic feet per minute, how many minutes will it take until the pool is completed filled? Justify your solution. EE P MP

EE = Expressions, Equations, and Relationships  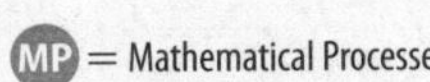
P = Proportionality
MP = Mathematical Processes

Reflect

Answering the Essential Question

Use what you learned about measuring figures to complete the graphic organizer. TEKS 7.1(D), 7.1(F), 7.1(G)

Angles

Area

Essential Question

HOW do measurements help you describe real-world objects?

Volume

Surface Area

Answer the Essential Question. HOW do measurements help you describe real-world objects? Verbally share your response with a partner, asking for and giving help if needed.

Chapter 9
Statistics and Sampling

Texas Essential Knowledge and Skills

Targeted TEKS

7.12 The student applies mathematical process standards to use statistical representations to analyze data. *Also addresses 7.6.*

Mathematical Processes

7.1, 7.1(A), 7.1(B), 7.1(C), 7.1(D), 7.1(E), 7.1(F), 7.1(G)

Essential Question

HOW do you know which type of graph to use when displaying data?

Math in the Real World

Corpus Christi covers 452.2 square miles. The table shows the area covered by land and by water for Corpus Christi.

On the circle graph, write the percent, rounded to the nearest percent, of the land area and the water area for Corpus Christi.

Corpus Christi	Area (sq. mi)
Land	124.3
Water	327.9
Total	452.2

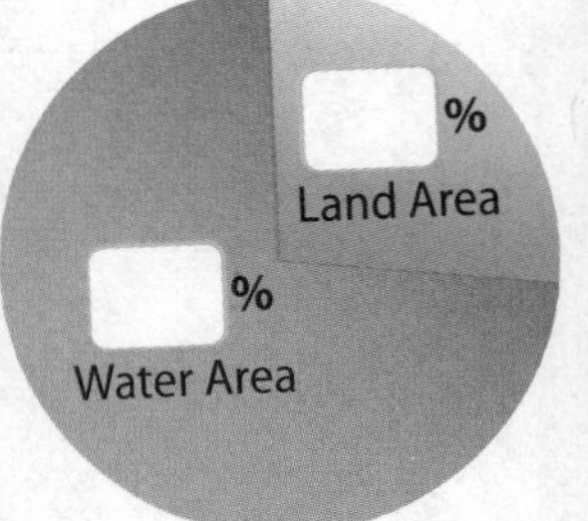

Go Online!
www.connectED.mcgraw-hill.com

What Tools Do You Need?

Vocab

Vocabulary

bar graph
biased sample
circle graph
convenience sample
dot plot
double box plot
double dot plot
population
sample
simple random sample
statistics
survey
systematic random sample
unbiased sample
voluntary response sample

Writing Math

Describe Data When you *describe* something, you represent it in words.

The table shows the prices for takeout orders at Lombardo's Restaurant.

Takeout	Price ($)
Main Dish	8.00
Side Dish	2.50
Dessert	4.00

With a partner, use the table to complete the following statements.

1. The price of a dessert is ______________________.

2. The price of a main dish is twice the price of ______________________.

3. A ______________________ is the least expensive item.

Write two other statements that describe the data. Then work with a partner to compare your answers, discussing any differences.

4. ______________________

5. ______________________

When Will You Use This?

Blake, Hannah, and Jamar in

Record Highs

For our report we decided to compare record temperatures for 2 of the hottest places in the U.S.

Let's find the U.S. city that is closest to the equator.

I'm sure it must be some place in Texas. I'll look it up.

Wow! The southern most point in the U.S. is actually Key West, FL!

I'll get the weather data.

Key West! Ok, great. Let's compare that with another place that gets lots of sun.

Well, my cousin lives in Phoenix, Arizona. He always tells me how hot it gets there.

Phoenix, Arizona! Coming right up!

Ok, I got a set of monthly record highs for both places.

What's the best way to compare the data?

Key West FL		Phoenix, AZ	
Jan:	86°	Jan:	88°
Feb:	85°	Feb:	92°
Mar:	88°	Mar:	100°
Apr:	90°	Apr:	105°
May:	91°	May:	114°
Jun:	94°	Jun:	122°
Jul:	95°	Jul:	121°
Aug:	95°	Aug:	116°
Sep:	94°	Sep:	116°
Oct:	93°	Oct:	107°
Nov:	89°	Nov:	96°
Dec:	88°	Dec:	87°

Boy, I sure wish I was in either place right now.

Your Turn! **You will solve this problem in the chapter.**

Are You Ready?

Quick Review

Review 5.9(C) TEKS

Example 1

Which players average more than 10 points per game?

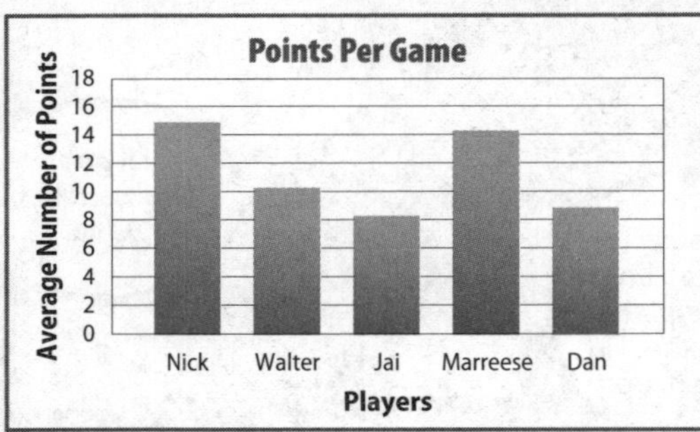

Nick, Walter, and Marreese averaged more than 10 points per game.

Example 2

Use the circle graph. Suppose 300 people were surveyed. How many people have two accounts?

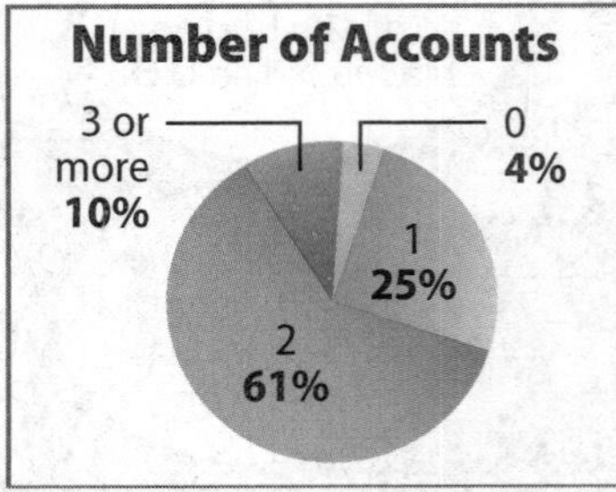

Determine 61% of 300.

$61\% \text{ of } 300 = 61\% \times 300$

$= 0.61 \times 300 \text{ or } 183$

So, 183 people have two accounts.

Quick Check

Check

Graphs **The bar graph at the right shows the number of items each student obtained during a scavenger hunt.**

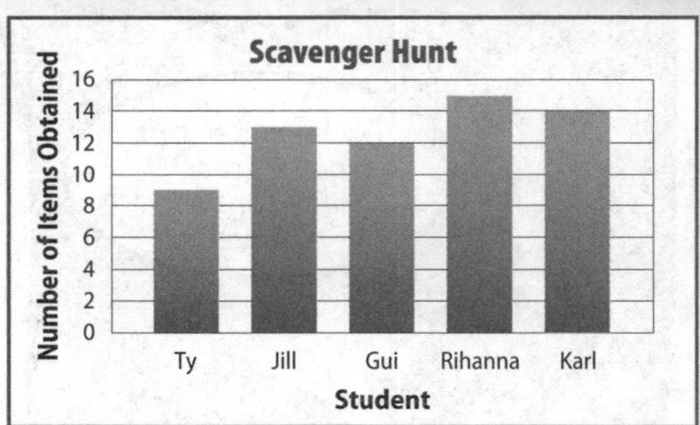

1. Who obtained the most items?

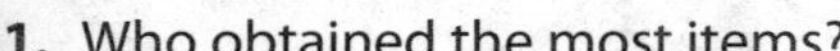

2. Who obtained the least items?

3. Refer to the circle graph in Example 2. Suppose 300 people were surveyed. How many people have 1 account?

How Did You Do?

Which problems did you answer correctly in the Quick Check? Shade those exercise numbers below.

FOLDABLES®

Use the Foldable throughout to help you learn about samples.

cut on all dashed lines

fold on all solid lines

tape to page 780

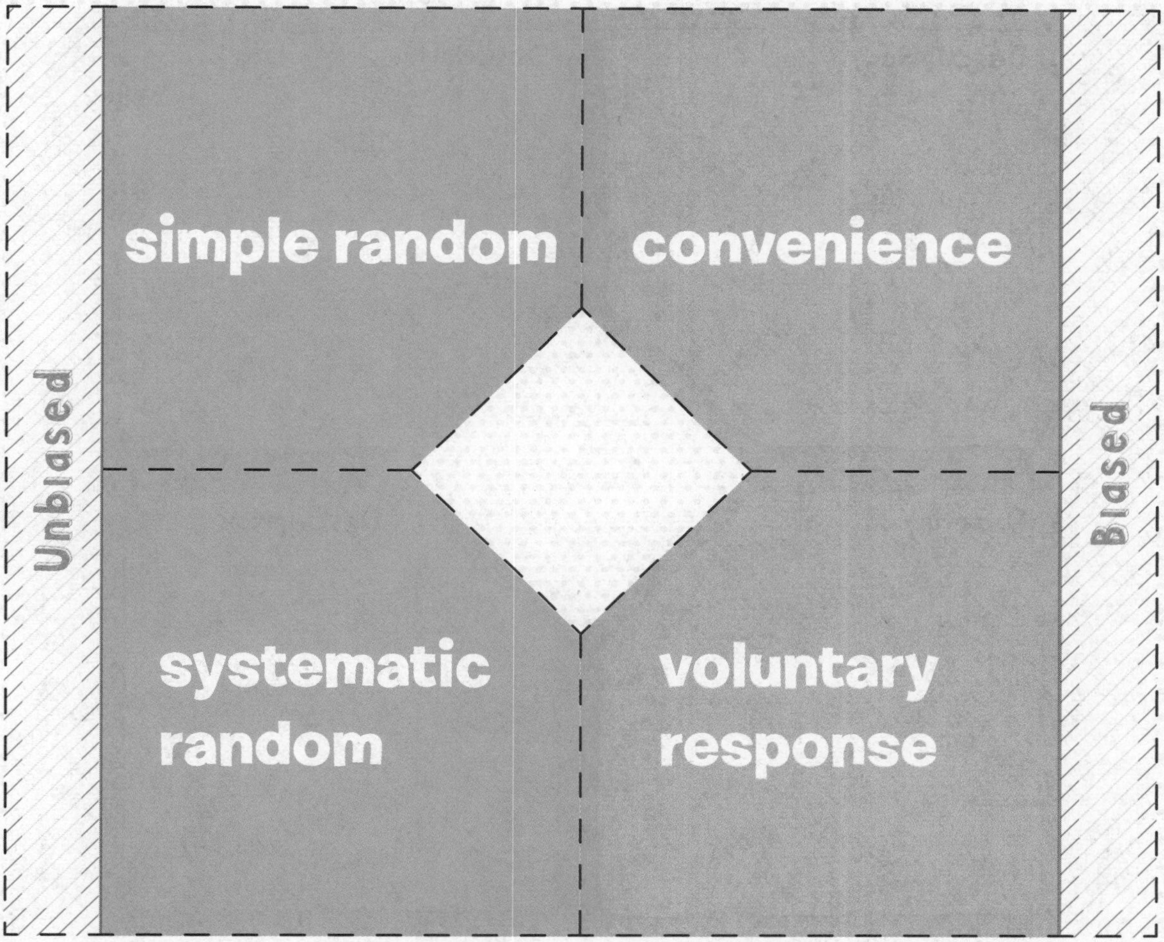

Unbiased

simple random

convenience

systematic random

voluntary response

Biased

Use the Foldable throughout to help you learn about samples.

cut on all dashed lines

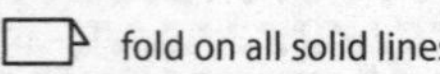
fold on all solid lines

tape to page 780

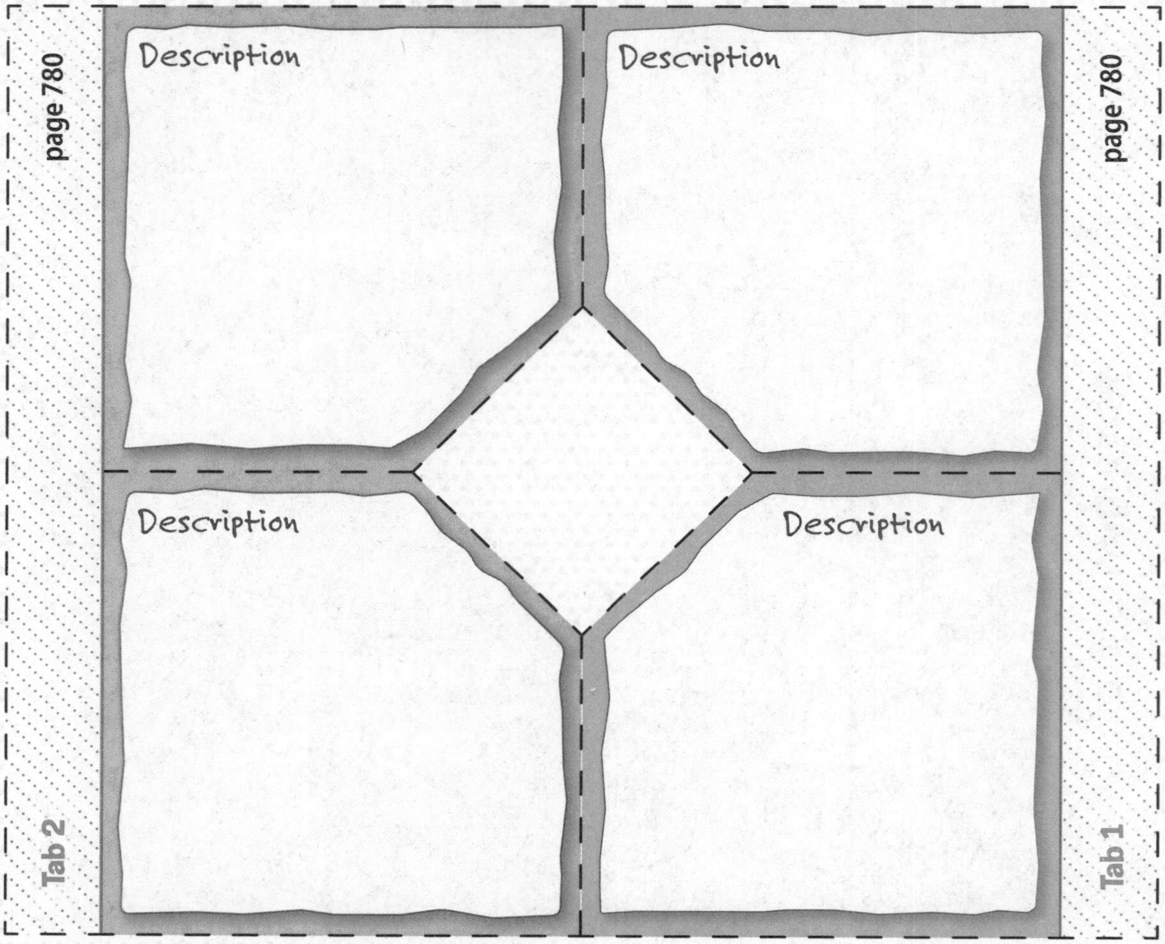

page 780

Description

Description

page 780

Description

Description

Tab 2

Tab 1

Lesson 1

Bar Graphs and Dot Plots

Launch the Lesson: Real World

The students in Mr. Morgan's class were asked how many sibling they have. The table shows the results of the survey. Use the data to construct a bar graph.

1. Fill in the frequency column on the frequency table below.

Siblings		
Number	**Tally**	**Frequency**
0	IIII	
1	~~IIII~~ III	
2	~~IIII~~ II	
3	III	
4	I	

2. Construct a bar graph.

3. What fraction of the students have 1 sibling? ________

4. What fraction of the students have 2 or more siblings? ________

Which MP Mathematical Processes did you use? Shade the circle(s) that applies.

Ⓐ Apply Math to the Real World.
Ⓑ Use a Problem-Solving Model.
Ⓒ Select Tools and Techniques.
Ⓓ Use Multiple Representations.
Ⓔ Organize Ideas.
Ⓕ Analyze Relationships.
Ⓖ Justify Arguments.

Texas Essential Knowledge and Skills

Targeted TEKS
7.6(G) Solve problems using data represented in bar graphs, dot plots, and circle graphs, including part-to-whole and part-to-part comparisons and equivalents.

Mathematical Processes
7.1(A), 7.1(B), 7.1(D), 7.1(F)

Vocab

Vocabulary
bar graph
dot plot

Essential Question
HOW do you know which type of graph to use when displaying data?

Work Zone

Part-to-Whole Comparisons and Equivalents

One type of graph that shows the number of items in a specific category is called a **bar graph**. Another type of graph that shows the frequency of data with a number line is called a **dot plot**. You can use a bar graph or dot plot to make part-to-whole comparisons and equivalents.

Multi-Step Example

Tutor

1. Use the bar graph to compare the total number of students surveyed to the ones who chose volleyball.

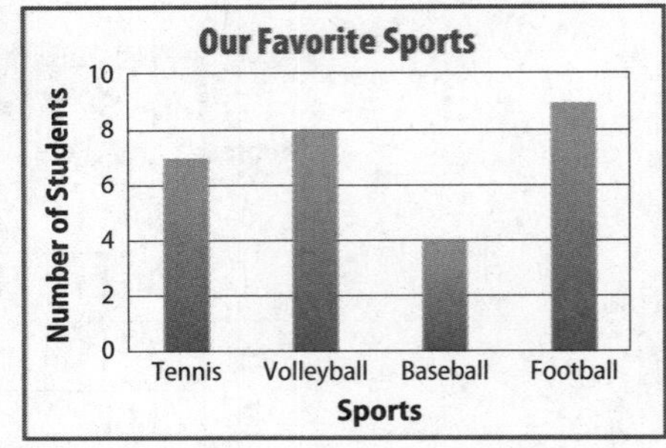

Step 1 Determine the total number of students surveyed.
$7 + 8 + 4 + 9 = 28$

Step 2 Divide the total number of students by the number of students who chose volleyball.
$28 \div 8 = 3.5$

So, 3.5 times as many students were surveyed than chose volleyball.

Example

Tutor

2. The dot plot shows the number of televisions that families own. What fraction of the total families own 2 televisions? Express in simplest form.

Number of Televisions

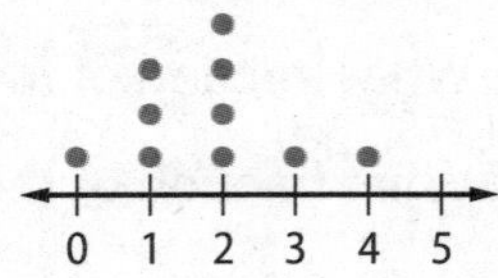

There are 4 families who own 2 televisions. A total of 10 families were surveyed.

$\frac{4}{10} = \frac{2}{5}$ Write 4 out of 10 as an equivalent fraction in simplest form.

So, $\frac{2}{5}$ of the families own 2 televisions.

Show your work.

Got It? **Do this problem to find out.**

a. ________

a. Refer to the dot plot in Example 2. Compare the number of families surveyed to those who own 2 televisions.

Part-to-Part Comparisons and Equivalents

You can use bar graphs and dot plots to make part-to-part comparisons and equivalents.

Example

Tutor

3. The bar graph shows grades that students received on a test. Write a ratio that compares the number of students who received a B on their test to the number of students who received a C on their test. Express this ratio as a fraction, decimal, and a percent. Then interpret the ratio's meaning.

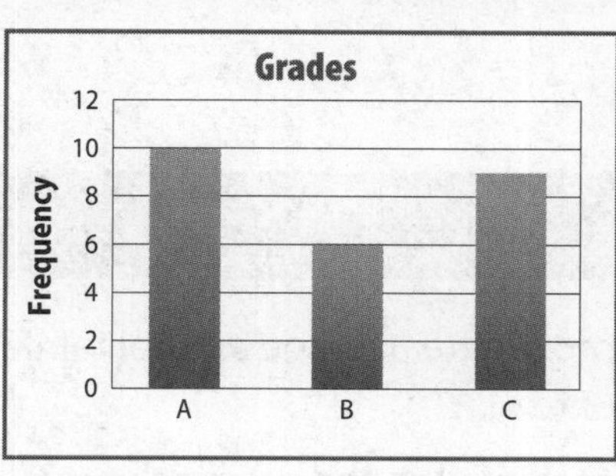

$6:9 = \frac{6}{9}$ or $\frac{2}{3}$ Write a ratio and fraction comparing these quantities.

As a decimal, the ratio is equivalent to $0.\overline{6}$. As a percent, the ratio is equivalent to $66.\overline{6}\%$.

For every six students who received a B, nine students received a C.

Multi-Step Example

Tutor

4. The dot plot shows the number of times per week that students visit the library. How many more students visit four or more times per week than students that visit less than two times per week?

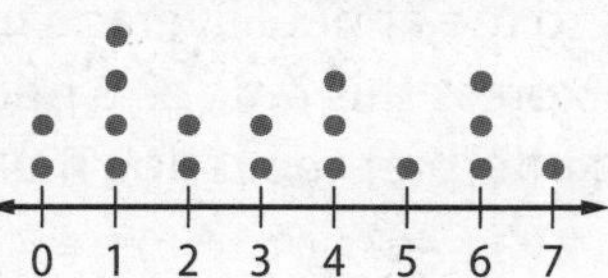

Step 1 Determine the number of students that visit the library four or more times per week. There are $3 + 1 + 3 + 1$, or 8 students who visit the library four or more times per week.

Step 2 Determine the number of students that visits the library less than two times per week. There are $4 + 2$, or 6 students who visit the library less than two times per week.

So, $8 - 6$, or 2 more students visit the library four or more times per week than those who visit less than two times per week.

b. ____________ Show your work.

c. ____________

Got It? Do these problems to find out.

b. Refer to the bar graph in Example 3. How many more students received an A or B than those who received a C?

c. Refer to the dot plot in Example 4. Write a ratio that compares the number of students who visit the library 2 times per week to the number of students who visit the library 1 time per week. Express this ratio as a fraction, decimal, and a percent. Then interpret the ratio's meaning.

Guided Practice

1. The bar graph shows the approximate average annual rainfall for different cities in Texas. (Examples 1–4)

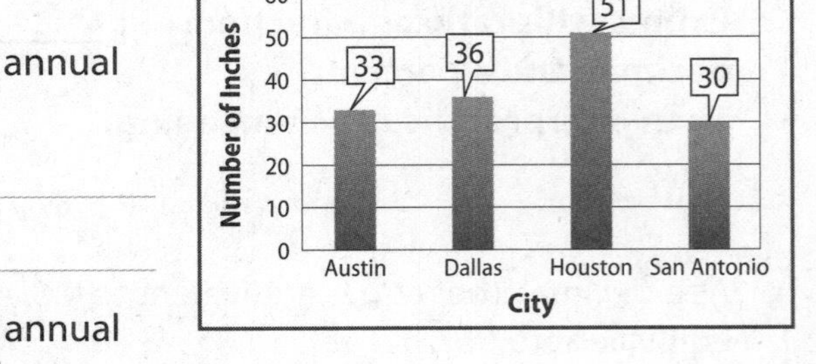

a. Compare the total inches of rainfall to the average annual rainfall in San Antonio?

b. Compare the total inches of rainfall to the average annual rainfall in Austin and Dallas combined? Round to the nearest tenth.

c. Write a ratio that compares the average annual inches of rainfall San Antonio receives to the annual average inches of rainfall that Dallas receives. Express this ratio as a fraction, decimal, and a percent. Then interpret the ratio's meaning.

2. **Building on the Essential Question** How can I use a bar graph or dot plot to make comparisons and equivalents?

Rate Yourself!

☐ I understand how to make comparisons and equivalents from data.

Great! You're ready to move on!

☐ I still have questions about making comparisons and equivalents from data.

No problem! Go online to access a Personal Tutor. Check

Name ______________________ My Homework ______________________

Independent Practice

1. The dot plot shows the number of movies students watched at the movie theater in a month. (Examples 1–4)

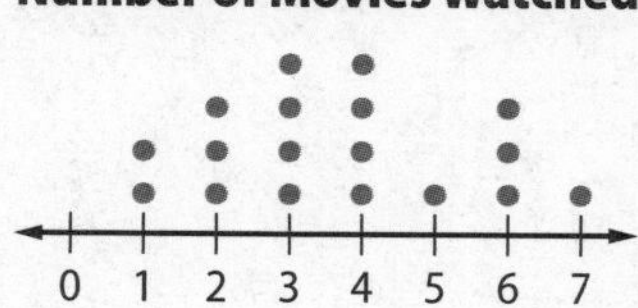

a. Compare the total number of students that went to the movie theater four or more times to the number of students that went less than three times?

____

____

b. What fraction of the students that went to the movie theater went to 4 movies? Express in simplest form.

____

c. Compare the total number of students that were surveyed to those who went to watch 2 or less movies at the theater?

____

____

2. The bar graph shows the approximate number of visitors at a state park. (Examples 1–4)

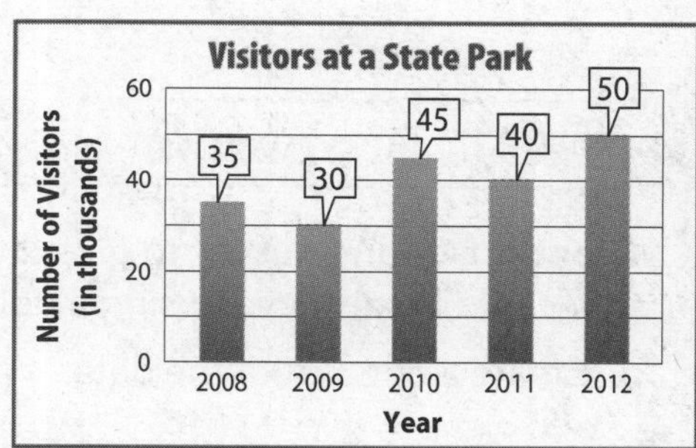

a. What fraction of the total number of visitors visited in 2012? Express in simplest form.

____

b. What fraction of the total number of visitors visited in 2008 and 2009 combined? Express in simplest form.

____

c. How many more visitors were there in 2011 and 2012 than in 2009 and 2010?

____

d. Write a ratio that compares the number of visitors at a state park in 2009 to the number of visitors at a state park in 2012. Express this ratio as a fraction, decimal, and a percent. Then interpret the ratio's meaning.

____

____

____

3. **MP Use Multiple Representations** The table shows the results of a survey of students' favorite food.

Number	Tally
Pizza	30
Spaghetti	13
Hamburgers	8
Chicken	12
Lasagna	17
Steak	20

a. **Graph** Create a bar graph for the data in the table.

b. **Numbers** What fraction of the total number of students prefer pizza?

Express in simplest form. ____________

c. **Words** Write a ratio that compares the number of students who prefer steak to the number of students who prefer spaghetti and lasagna combined. Express this ratio as a fraction, decimal, and a percent. Then interpret the ratio's meaning.

____

____

H.O.T. Problems Higher-Order Thinking

4. **Create** Design a survey to give to your classmates that could be displayed using a dot plot.

a. Create a dot plot of the data.

b. Write and solve a problem that could be used to make a part-to-whole comparison based on your data.

____

____

____

5. **Analyze** Compare and contrast using bar graphs and dot plots to make comparisons and equivalents.

____

____

____

Name ______________________________

Multi-Step Problem Solving

6. The dot plot shows the number of vacations that students have taken to South Padre Island, Texas. How many more total vacations were taken compared to the number of students that have vacationed there 3 or more times? P N MD MP

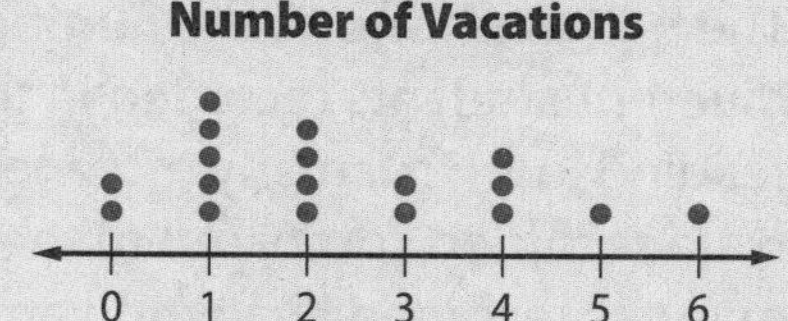

Ⓐ 10 vacations

Ⓑ 11 vacations

Ⓒ 12 vacations

Ⓓ 13 vacations

Use a problem-solving model to solve this problem.

1 Analyze

Read the problem. Circle the information you know.
Underline what the problem is asking you to find.

2 Plan

What will you need to do to solve the problem? Write your plan in steps.

Step 1 Determine the ________ number of vacations.

Step 2 Subtract the number of vacations that are ________.

Read to Succeed!
Read the question carefully. It asks you to compare to 3 or more using the dot plot. That means you need to include the 2 dots above 3.

3 Solve

Use your plan to solve the problem. Show your steps.

Determine the total number of vacations.

There were ______ students that have taken a vacation to South Padre Island.

There were ______ students that have taken 3 or more vacations.

______ − ______ = ______ vacations Subtract.

So, the correct answer is ______. Fill in that answer choice.

4 Justify and Evaluate

How do you know your solution is accurate?

____

____

____

P = Proportionality 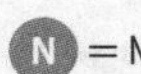 N = Number and Operations 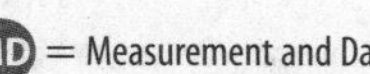 MD = Measurement and Data 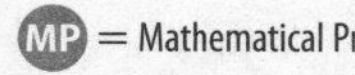 MP = Mathematical Processes

More Multi-Step Problem Solving

Use a problem-solving model to solve each problem.

7. The bar graph shows the number of minutes different students recorded in their daily reading log. How many more total minutes were recorded compared to the number of minutes recorded by Vernon and Shelli? P N MD MP

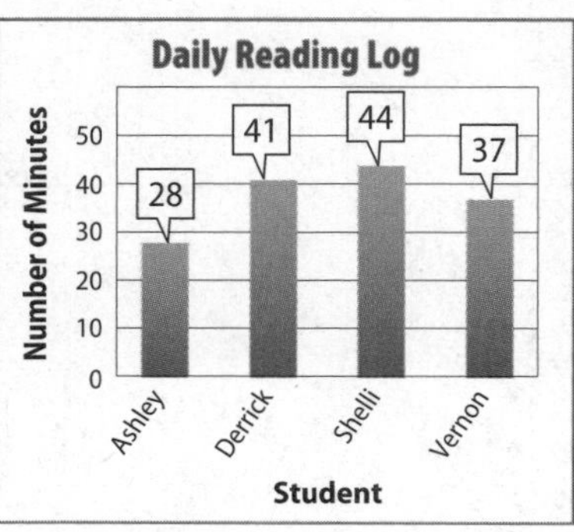

8. The dot plot shows the approximate number of hours students watched television in a week. What fraction more of the students watched television more than 4 hours during the week compared to those who watched less than 4 hours? Express in simplest form.

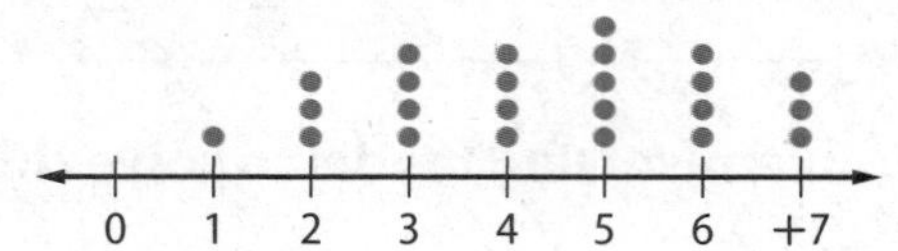

9. The bar graph shows the approximate population of Texas over the past four U.S. Census reports. Write a ratio that compares the population in 2000 to the population in 2010. Express this ratio as a fraction, decimal, and a percent. Then interpret the ratio's meaning. P N MD MP

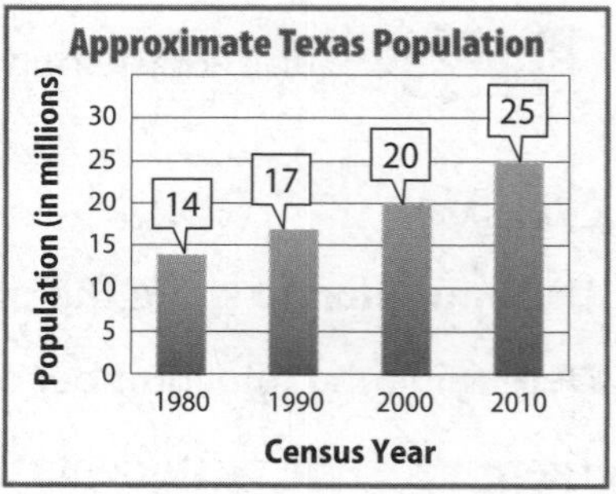

P = Proportionality N = Number and Operations MD = Measurement and Data MP = Mathematical Processes

Hands-On Lab 2-a

Connect Bar Graphs to Circle Graphs

INQUIRY **HOW can I select tools and techniques to connect bar graphs to circle graphs?**

You can create a *circle graph* from a bar graph to compare data.

Texas Essential Knowledge and Skills TEKS

Targeted TEKS

7.6(G) Solve problems using data represented in bar graphs, dot plots, and circle graphs, including part-to-whole and part-to-part comparisons and equivalents.

Mathematical Processes

7.1(C), 7.1(D), 7.1(E), 7.1(F), 7.1(G)

Hands-On Activity

Tools

The table at the right shows the results of a survey about which sports students prefer to watch. Display the data in a bar graph.

Sport	Number of
Baseball	6
Basketball	7
Football	9
Other	3

Step 1 Using different colors of construction paper, measure and cut out a bar to represent each category. The height of each bar, in centimeters, should be the same as the number of students. Label each bar.

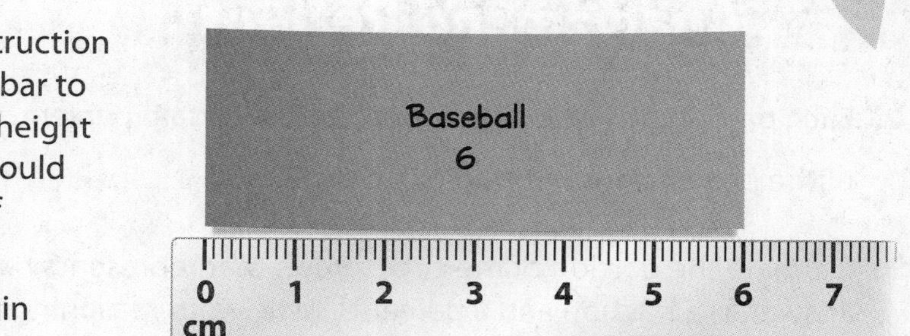

Step 2 On a large piece of paper, begin constructing your bar graph. Remember to include all the necessary labels for the bar graph.

Step 3 Use different color markers to trace the outline of each bar. Draw the bar diagram you created in the space below.

1. What is the sum of all of the categories? ______________

Step 4 Remove the pieces of construction paper used in the bar graph. Tape the ends together to form one bar. Do not overlap the bar. Then tape the two ends of the bar together to form a circle. Do not overlap the bar.

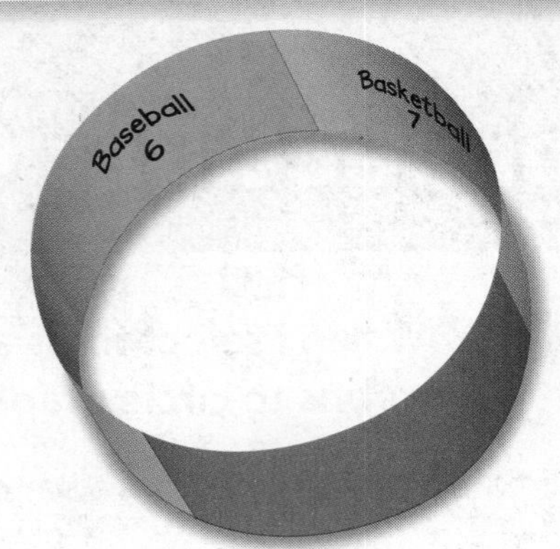

Step 5 Use a marker to outline the circle on a piece of paper. Carefully mark a point where each section meets on the outline. Remove the circle and place a point in the center of your drawing. Draw a line from the center point to each point on the circle. Label each section and include a title. Draw the circle graph you created at the right.

Analyze and Reflect

2. Each part of the circle graph represents a certain percent. What is the sum of the percents for the whole circle graph? ______

3. Estimate the portion of the circle graph that represents baseball. Express your answer as a fraction and a percent. Justify your reasoning.

______

______

Create

4. MP **Select Tools and Techniques** The table shows the number of people who prefer cars that are different colors. Construct a bar graph and a circle graph of the data on a separate sheet of paper. Which graph allows you to compare the part of people who prefer a red car compared to the total number of people surveyed? Justify your reasoning.

Car Color	Number of People
Red	4
Silver	7
Black	10
Navy	3

5. **INQUIRY** HOW can I select tools and techniques to connect bar graphs to circle graphs? ______

______

______

Lesson 2
Circle Graphs

Launch the Lesson: Real World

The students at Pine Ridge Middle School were asked to identify their favorite class. The table shows the results of the survey. How can we compare these percents?

Favorite Class	
Class	**Percent (%)**
Math	25
Science	23
Language Arts	27
Social Studies	14
Other	11

1. Without knowing how many students participated in the survey, how can you determine which subjects were chosen by about the same number of students?

2. How can you compare the number of students who chose language arts to social studies without knowing how many students participated in the survey?

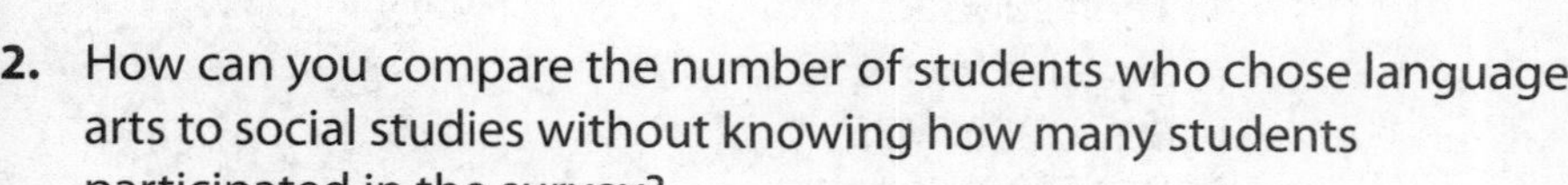

3. Complete the circle graph using the data from the table above.

Favorite Class

25%
Math

Texas Essential Knowledge and Skills

Targeted TEKS

7.6(G) Solve problems using data represented in bar graphs, dot plots, and circle graphs, including part-to-whole and part-to-part comparisons and equivalents.

Mathematical Processes

7.1(A), 7.1(B), 7.1(D), 7.1(F)

Vocabulary

circle graph

Essential Question

HOW do you know which type of graph to use when displaying data?

Which MP Mathematical Processes did you use? Shade the circle(s) that applies.

Ⓐ Apply Math to the Real World.
Ⓑ Use a Problem-Solving Model.
Ⓒ Select Tools and Techniques.
Ⓓ Use Multiple Representations.
Ⓔ Organize Ideas.
Ⓕ Analyze Relationships.
Ⓖ Justify Arguments.

Work Zone

Part-to-Whole Comparisons and Equivalents

A graph that displays data as parts of a whole is called a **circle graph**. In a circle graph, the percents add up to 100 since the entire circle represents the whole. You can solve problems, using data represented in a circle graph, including part-to-whole comparisons and equivalents.

Multi-Step Examples

The graph shows the percent of favorite single topping pizzas.

Favorite Pizza Toppings

1. A total of 250 students were surveyed. How many more total students were surveyed than prefer pepperoni?

Method 1 Determine 30% of 250. Then subtract that amount from 250.
$0.3 \times 250 = 75$
$250 - 75 = 175$

Method 2 Subtract 30% from 100%. 100% − 30%
Then determine 70% of 250.
$0.7 \times 250 = 175$

So, there were 175 more students surveyed than prefer pepperoni.

2. A total of 250 students were surveyed. What fraction of the total number of students prefer mushrooms as their favorite topping?

Method 1 Determine 20% of 250. Express in simplest form.
$0.2 \times 250 = 50 \quad \rightarrow \quad \frac{50}{250} = \frac{1}{5}$

Method 2 Express 20% of 100% as a fraction in simplest form.
$\frac{20}{100} = \frac{1}{5}$

So, $\frac{1}{5}$ of the total students surveyed prefer mushrooms.

Got It? Do this problem to find out.

a. Refer to the circle graph above. A total of 300 students were surveyed. What fraction of the total number of students prefer cheese as their favorite topping?

a. ________

Part-to-Part Comparisons and Equivalents

Use a circle graph to make part-to-part comparisons and equivalents.

Multi-Step Examples

The circle graph shows the percent of automobiles registered in parts of the United States in a recent year.

3. **A total of 79 million automobiles were registered in these states. How many more automobiles were registered in Texas than in Florida?**

Registered Automobiles

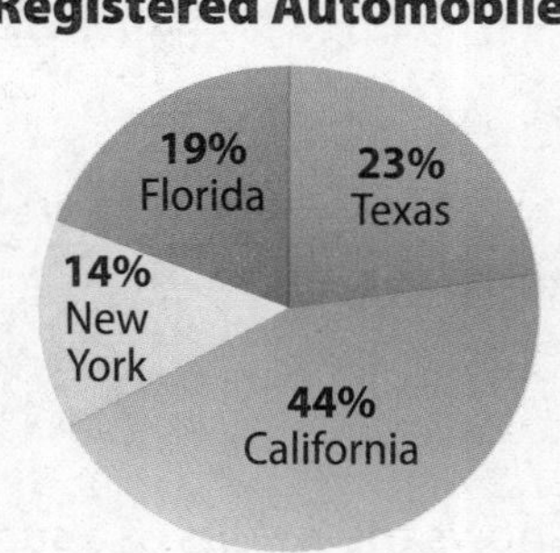

Method 1 Determine 23% of 79. Then subtract 19% of 79.

$0.23 \times 79 = 18.17$

$0.19 \times 79 = 15.01$

$18.17 - 15.01 = 3.16$

Method 2 Subtract 19% from 23%. $23\% - 19\% = 4\%$
Then determine 4% of 79. $0.04 \times 79 = 3.16$

There were 3.16 million more automobiles in Texas than Florida.

4. **A total of 79 million automobiles were registered in these states. Write a ratio that compares the part of automobiles that were registered in New York to the part of automobiles registered in California. Express this ratio as a fraction, decimal, and a percent. Then interpret the ratio's meaning.**

Step 1 The ratio is 14 : 44. As a fraction, this is $\frac{14}{44}$ or $\frac{7}{22}$.

As a decimal, this is $0.3\overline{18}$. As a percent, this is $31.\overline{81}\%$.

Step 2 For every 7 of automobiles registered in New York, there are 22 of automobiles registered in California.

Got It? **Do this problem to find out.**

b. A total of 79 million automobiles were registered in these states. How many more automobiles were registered in Florida than New York?

b. ________________

Guided Practice

1. The circle graph at the right shows the results of a middle school survey about favorite states to visit on vacation. (Examples 1–4)

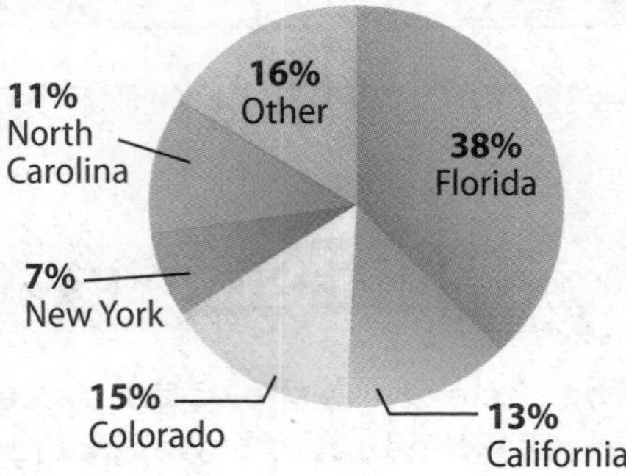

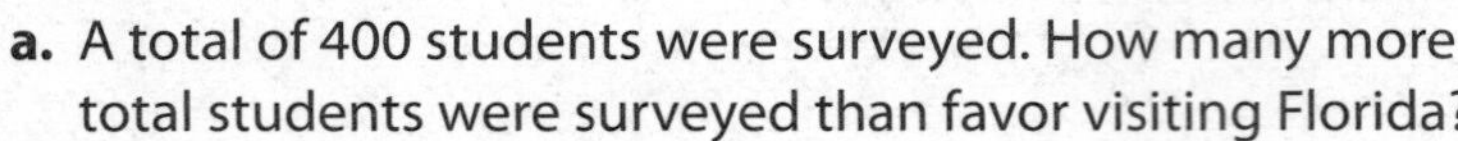

a. A total of 400 students were surveyed. How many more total students were surveyed than favor visiting Florida?

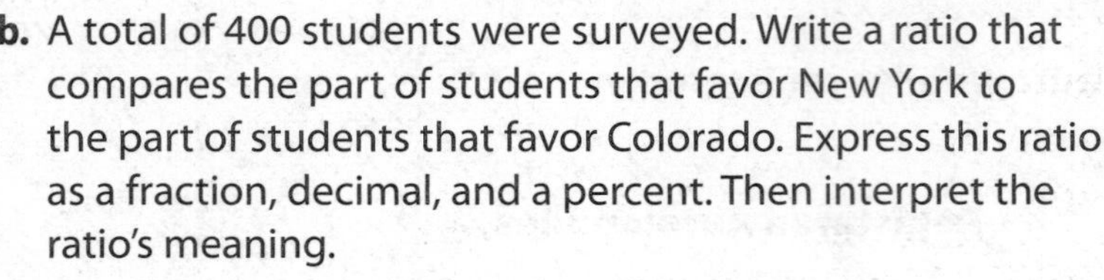

b. A total of 400 students were surveyed. Write a ratio that compares the part of students that favor New York to the part of students that favor Colorado. Express this ratio as a fraction, decimal, and a percent. Then interpret the ratio's meaning.

2. The circle graph at the right shows the results of a survey about the number of televisions per household. (Examples 1–4)

Number of Televisions in a Household

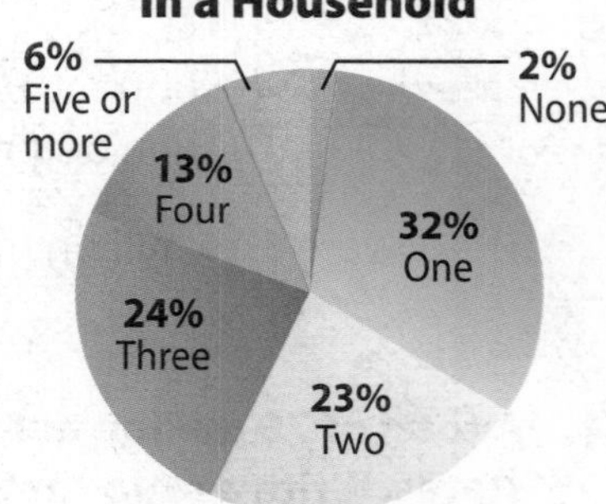

a. A total of 250 households were surveyed. How many more households have one television than three televisions?

b. A total of 250 households were surveyed. What fraction of the total number of households have three televisions?

c. A total of 250 households were surveyed. How many more households have two or more televisions than less two televisions?

3. **Building on the Essential Question** How is using a circle graph useful to analyze and compare data?

Rate Yourself!

Are you ready to move on?
Shade the section that applies.

I have a few questions. | I'm ready to move on. | I have a lot of questions.

Find out online. Use the Self-Check Quiz.

Check

Name ______________________ My Homework ______________________

Independent Practice

7.6(G), 7.1(A), 7.1(F) TEKS

1. The circle graph at the right shows the results of a survey about favorite pets. (Examples 1–3)

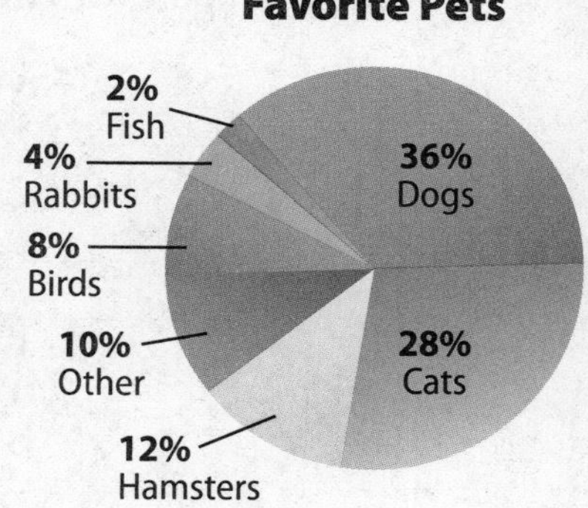

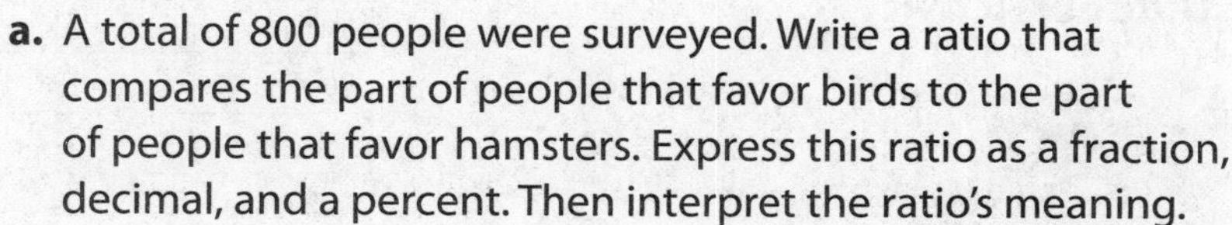

a. A total of 800 people were surveyed. Write a ratio that compares the part of people that favor birds to the part of people that favor hamsters. Express this ratio as a fraction, decimal, and a percent. Then interpret the ratio's meaning.

____

____

____

b. A total of 800 people were surveyed. How many more total people were surveyed than favor cats?

____

c. A total of 800 people were surveyed. How many more people favor dogs than favor fish and rabbits combined?

____

2. The circle graph at the right shows what is in U.S. landfills. (Examples 4 and 5)

What is in U.S. Landfills?

8% Metal; 24% Plastic; 11% Food and Yard Waste; 6% Rubber and Leather; 21% Other Trash; 30% Paper

a. The U.S. landfills contain a total of 200 million tons of trash. What fraction of the total tons of trash is metal?

____

b. The U.S. landfills contain a total of 200 million tons of trash. How many more million tons of trash is from paper than rubber and leather?

____

3. MP **Analyze Relationships** The circle graph at the right shows the favorite book types of students.

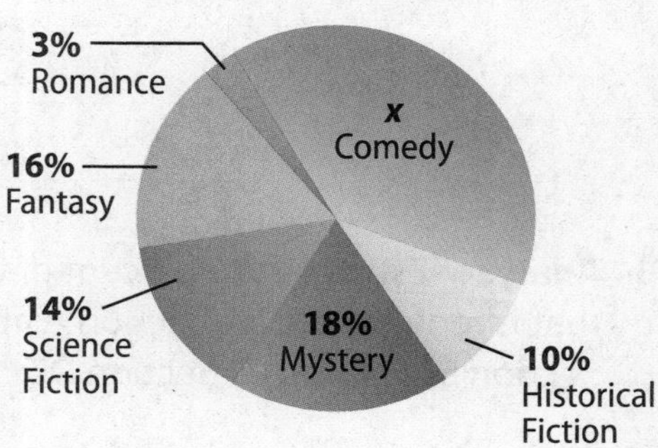

a. Determine the missing value in the circle graph. What fraction of the total number of students surveyed is comedy?

____

b. A total of 300 students were surveyed. How many more total students were surveyed than favor mystery books?

____

4. **MP Use Multiple Representations** The table at the right shows the results of a survey of students' favorite outdoor activity.

Favorite Outdoor Activity	
Activity	Number of Students
Walking	20
Hiking	18
Skiing	31
Running	9
Rollerblading	12
Swimming	29

a. **Graph** Complete the circle graph for the data in the table by labeling each part with the correct activity and percent.

Favorite Outdoor Activity

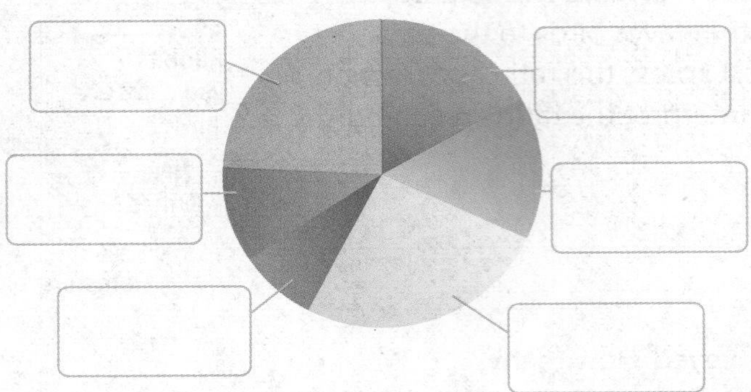

b. **Numbers** There were 119 students surveyed. About how many more students favor walking than rollerblading? ______

c. **Words** Compare each part of the graph. What parts combine to make up 50% of the entire circle graph? Explain.

______

______

H.O.T. Problems Higher-Order Thinking

5. **Create** Design a survey to give to your classmates.

a. Create a circle graph of the data.

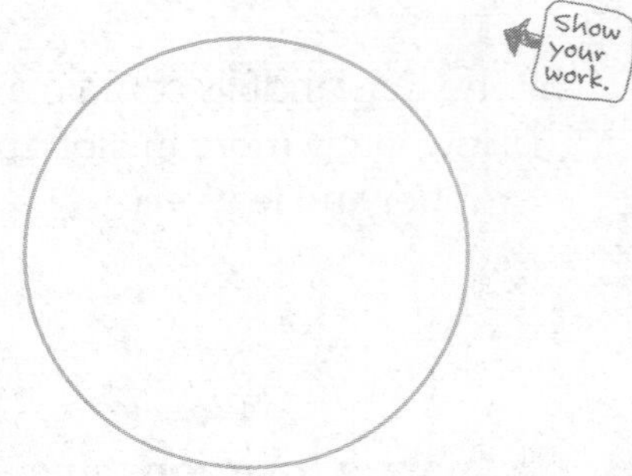

b. Write and solve two questions based on your data.

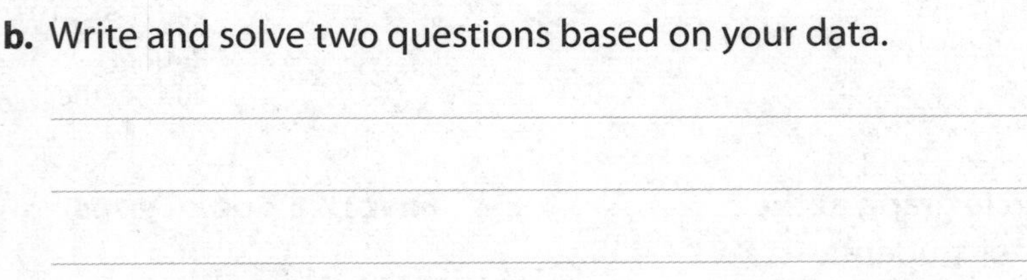

6. **Analyze** Estimate the percent of the circle graph at the right that is represented by Section A and B combined? Section A? Section B? Section C? Section D?

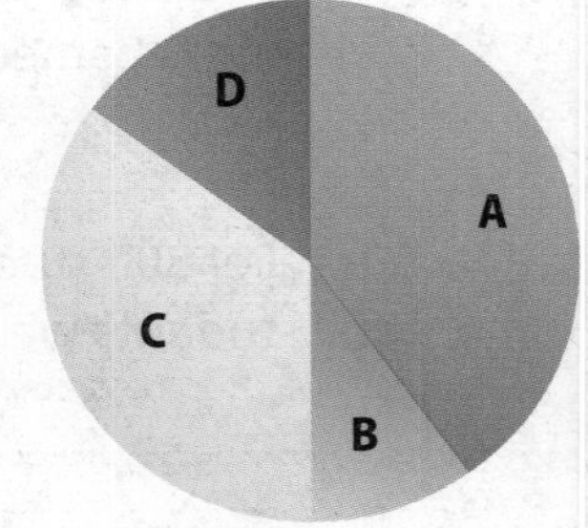

______

______

Name ____________________

Multi-Step Problem Solving

7. Adrian's class surveyed 150 students to determine their favorite ice cream flavors. The results are shown in the circle graph at the right. How many more students favored vanilla than mint chocolate chip? P N MD MP

Use a problem-solving model to solve this problem.

1 Analyze

Read the problem. Circle the information you know.
Underline what the problem is asking you to find.

2 Plan

What will you need to do to solve the problem?
Write your plan in steps.

Step 1 Determine ______ of 150 and ______ of 150.

Step 2 Then subtract the ______________.

3 Solve

Use your plan to solve the problem. Show your steps.

Determine 24% of 150. Determine 18% of 150.

$0.24 \times 150 =$ ____ $0.18 \times 150 =$ ____

____ − ____ = ____ Subtract.

There are ____ more students who favor vanilla than mint chocolate chip. Complete the grid.

					.		
⊕	0	0	0	0		0	0
⊖	1	1	1	1		1	1
	2	2	2	2		2	2
	3	3	3	3		3	3
	4	4	4	4		4	4
	5	5	5	5		5	5
	6	6	6	6		6	6
	7	7	7	7		7	7
	8	8	8	8		8	8
	9	9	9	9		9	9

4 Justify and Evaluate

How do you know your solution is accurate?

____

____

____

P = Proportionality N = Number and Operations MD = Measurement and Data MP = Mathematical Processes

More Multi-Step Problem Solving

Use a problem-solving model to solve each problem.

8. All the seventh graders in Carla's school voted on where to go for their class trip. There are a total of 350 students in the seventh grade. How many fewer students voted for the two least popular choices than for the two most popular choices? 

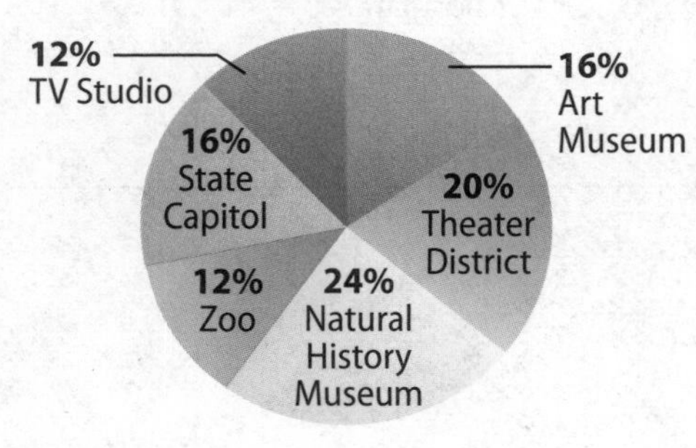

9. Billy spent $500 on his dog last year, and he made a circle graph to show how he spent the money. This year, he spent $100 less on the veterinarian but the same amount on every other category. This year, what percent of dog expenses was spent on the veterinarian?

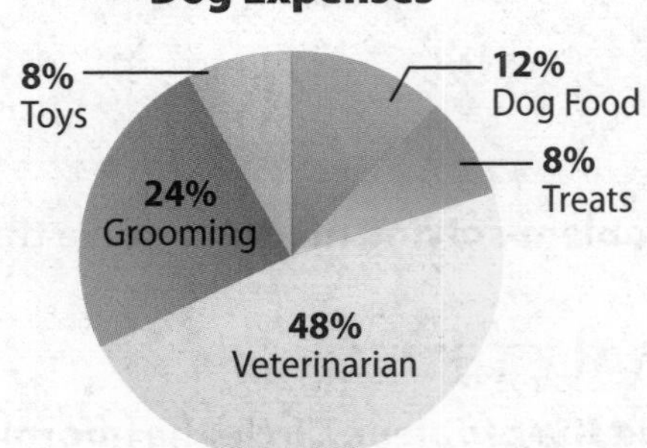

10. Kya and Nicholas each kept a list of trees that their class saw during a nature project. To show their results, Kya made a circle graph and Nicholas made a table. If Kya's circle graph represents 27 beech trees, how many more total trees are represented on her graph than on Nicholas's table? P N MD MP

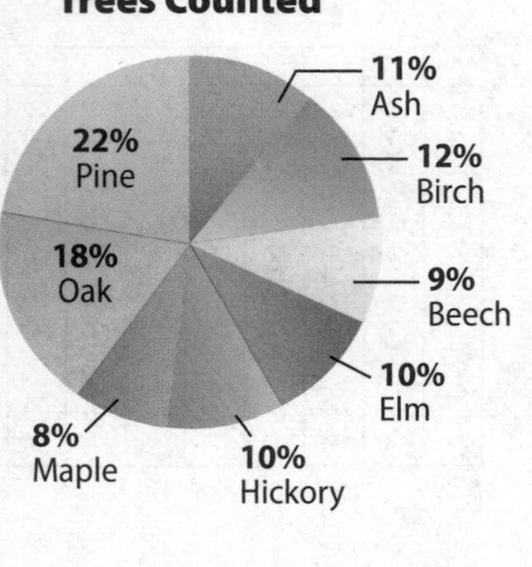

Trees Counted

Tree	Number
Ash	33
Birch	29
Beech	27
Elm	30
Hickory	30
Maple	20
Oak	52
Pine	22

11. Look at the divisions on the circle graph. Assign approximate percents to each section. Then, write a real-world problem about the graph. P N MD MP

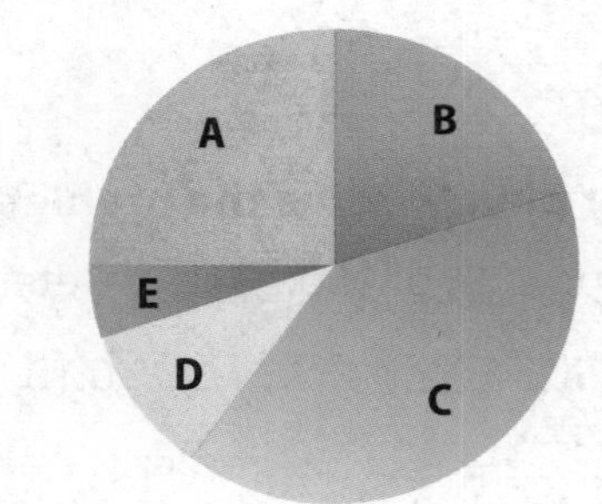

P = Proportionality N = Number and Operations MD = Measurement and Data MP = Mathematical Processes

Lesson 3

Make Predictions about a Population

Launch the Lesson: Vocabulary

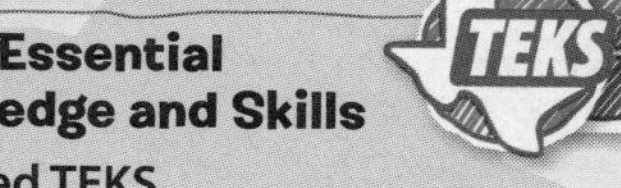

Texas Essential Knowledge and Skills

Targeted TEKS
7.6(F) Use data from a random sample to make inferences about a population. *Also addresses 7.6(G), 7.12(B).*

Mathematical Processes
7.1(A), 7.1(B), 7.1(E)

Vocabulary
statistics
survey
population
sample

Essential Question
HOW do you know which type of graph to use when displaying data?

Statistics deal with collecting, organizing, and interpreting data. A **survey** is a method of collecting information. The group being studied is the **population**. Sometimes the population is very large. To save time and money, part of the group, called a **sample**, is surveyed.

For each survey topic, determine which set represents the population and which represents a sample of the population. Write *population* or *sample*.

	Survey Topic	Set A	Set B
1.	dress code changes	the students in a middle school ______	the seventh graders in the middle school ______
2.	favorite flavors of ice cream	the customers at an ice cream shop in the town ______	the residents of a town ______

Real-World Investigation

Logan wants to survey students in his school about their favorite and least favorite ice cream flavors. Describe a possible sample Logan could survey instead of surveying the entire school.

____

____

Which MP Mathematical Processes did you use? Shade the circle(s) that applies.

Ⓐ Apply Math to the Real World.
Ⓑ Use a Problem-Solving Model.
Ⓒ Select Tools and Techniques.
Ⓓ Use Multiple Representations.
Ⓔ Organize Ideas.
Ⓕ Analyze Relationships.
Ⓖ Justify Arguments.

Work Zone

Make Predictions Using Ratios

You can use the results of a survey or past actions to predict the actions of a larger group. Since the ratios of the responses of a good sample are often the same as the ratios of the responses of the population.

Examples

The students in Mr. Blackwell's class brought photos from their summer break. The bar graph shows how many students brought each type of photo.

1. What is the probability that a student brought a photo taken at a theme park?

$$P(\text{theme park}) = \frac{\text{number of theme park photos}}{\text{number of students with a photo}} = \frac{11}{28}$$

So, the probability of a theme park photo is $\frac{11}{28}$.

2. There are 560 students at the school where Mr. Blackwell teaches. Predict how many students would bring in a photo taken at a theme park.

Let s represent the number of theme park photos.

$\frac{11}{28} = \frac{s}{560}$ Write equivalent ratios.

$\frac{11}{28} = \frac{s}{560}$ (×20 top and bottom) Since $28 \times 20 = 560$, multiply 11 by 20 to determine s.

$\frac{11}{28} = \frac{220}{560}$ $s = 220$

Of the 560 students, you can expect about 220 to bring a photo from a theme park.

Got It? Do these problems to find out.

A survey found that 6 out of every 10 students have a blog.

a. What is the probability that a student at the school has a blog?

b. Suppose there are about 250 students at the school. About how many have a blog?

a. ________

b. ________

Make Predictions Using Equations

You can also use the percent equation to make predictions.

Examples

3. A survey found that 85% of people use emoticons on their instant messengers. Predict how many of the 2,450 students at Washington Middle School use emoticons.

Words	What number of students is 85% of 2,450 students?
Variable	Let n represent the number of students.
Equation	$n = 0.85 \cdot 2{,}450$

$n = 0.85 \cdot 2{,}450$ Write the percent equation.

$n = 2{,}082.5$ Multiply.

About 2,083 of the students use emoticons.

What proportion could you use to solve Example 3? Write your answer below.

4. The circle graph shows the results of a survey in which students were asked whether they have a television in their bedroom. Predict how many more students would not have a television in their bedroom than those who do have a television out of 1,725 students.

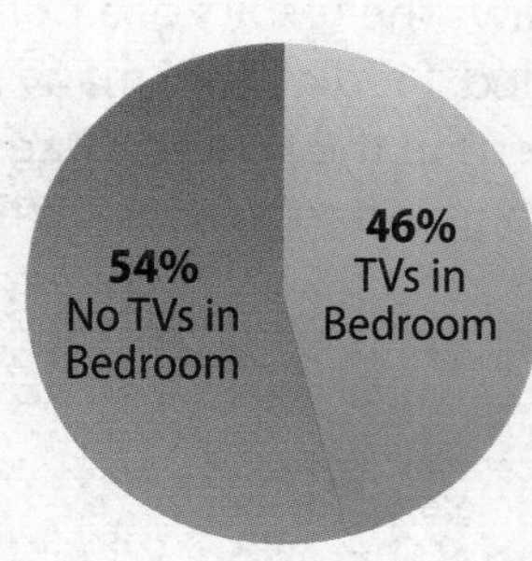

You can use the percent equation and the survey results to predict what part p of the 1,725 students have no TV in their bedroom.

Part of whole that do not have TV	Part of whole that have TV
$p = 0.54 \cdot 1{,}725$ or 931.5	$p = 0.46 \cdot 1{,}725$ or 793.5

Make a part-to-part comparison. About $931.5 - 793.5$ or 138 more do not have a television in their bedroom than those who do.

Got It? Do this problem to find out.

c. Refer to Example 4. Predict how many less students have a television in their bedroom compared to those who do not have a television out of 1,370 students.

c. __________

Guided Practice

The bar graph shows the results of a survey of Hamilton Middle School seventh graders. Use the bar graph to determine the following probabilities. (Examples 1 and 2)

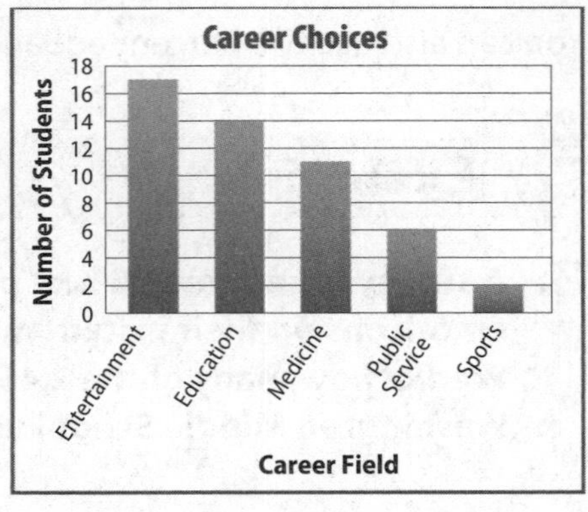

1. the probability of choosing a career in public service

2. the probability of choosing a career in education

3. the probability of choosing a career in sports

4. Predict how many students out of 400 will enter the education field.

5. Predict how many students out of 500 will enter the medical field.

6. Use the circle graph that shows the results of a poll to which 60,000 teens responded. Predict how many more of the approximately 28 million teens in the United States would buy a music CD compared to going to a movie if they were given $20. (Examples 3 and 4)

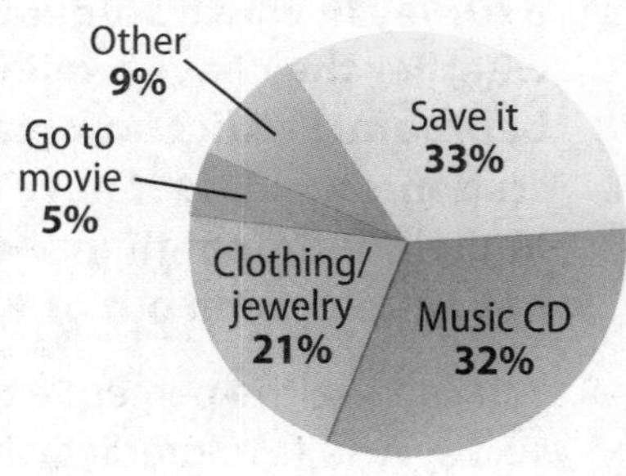

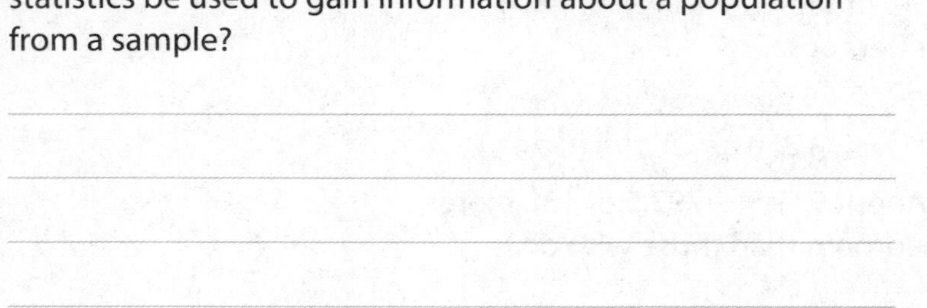

7. **Building on the Essential Question** When can statistics be used to gain information about a population from a sample?

Rate Yourself!

How confident are you about making predictions? Check the box that applies.

Find out online. Use the Self-Check Quiz.

Name ______________________ My Homework ______________________

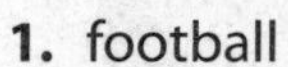

Independent Practice

7.6(F), 7.6(G), 7.1(A), 7.1(E) TEKS

The bar graph shows the results of a survey of 150 students. Use the bar graph to determine the probability of a student participating in each sport. (Example 1)

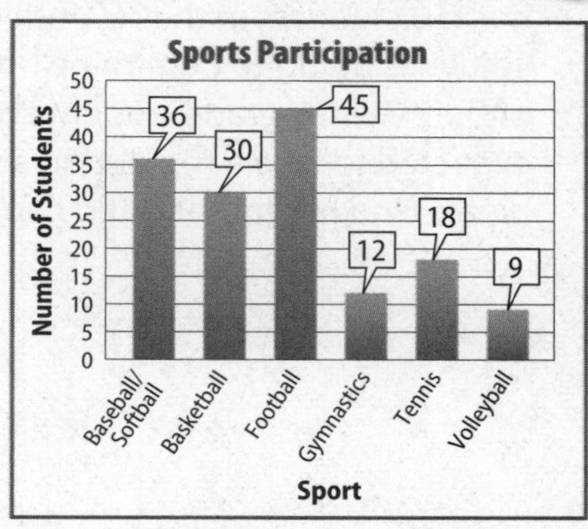

1. football

____

2. tennis

____

3. gymnastics

____

4. volleyball

____

5. Three out of every 10 students ages 6–14 have a magazine subscription. Suppose there are 30 students in Annabelle's class. About how many will have a magazine subscription? (Example 2)

____

6. Use the graph that shows the percent of cat owners who train their cats in each category. (Examples 3 and 4)

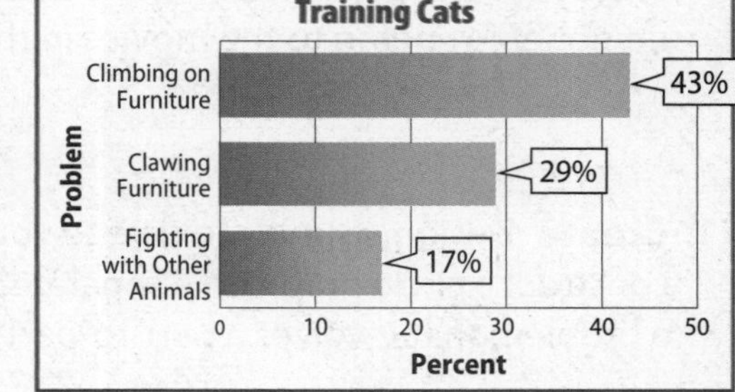

   a. Out of 255 cat owners, predict how many more owners trained their cat not to climb on furniture than clawing furniture.

   ____

   b. Out of 316 cat owners, predict how many more cat owners trained their cat not to claw on furniture than fighting with other animals.

   ____

7. MP **Organize Ideas** The school librarian recorded the types of books students checked out on a typical day. Suppose there are 605 students enrolled at the school. Predict the number of students that prefer humor books. Compare this to the number of students at the school who prefer nonfiction.

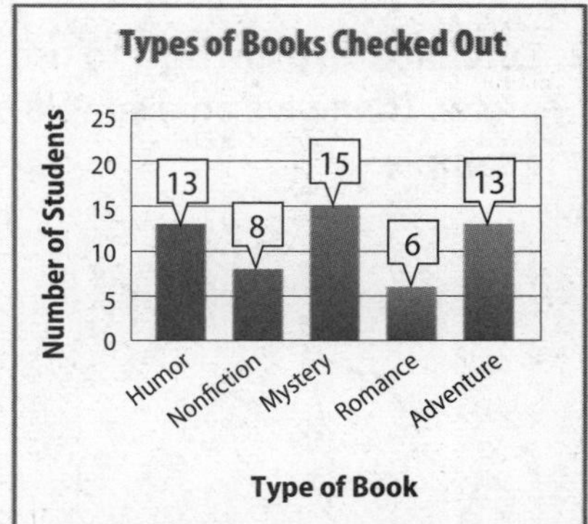

____

____

____

8. **Find the Error** A survey of a seventh-grade class showed that 4 out of every 10 students are taking a trip during spring break. There are 150 students in the seventh grade. Caitlyn is trying to determine how many of the seventh-grade students can be expected to take a trip during spring break. Find her mistake and correct it.

H.O.T. Problems Higher-Order Thinking

9. **Evaluate** One letter tile is drawn from the bag and replaced 300 times. Predict how many times a consonant will not be picked.

10. **Evaluate** A survey found that 80% of teens enjoy going to the movies in their free time. Out of 5,200 teens, predict how many said that they do not enjoy going to the movies in their free time.

11. **Create** Design a survey to give to your classmates. Use your results to construct a circle graph on a separate sheet of paper. Then write and solve a problem that involves a part-to-part comparison using the circle graph.

12. **Evaluate** Explain how to use a sample to predict what a group of people prefer. Then give an example of a situation in which it makes sense to use a sample.

Name ______________________________

Multi-Step Problem Solving

13. The table shows the results of a survey of students in Janette's class about their favorite pencil-and-paper puzzles. If there are 360 students in Janette's grade, predict how many more favor word searches compared to word scrambles. 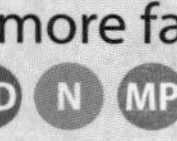 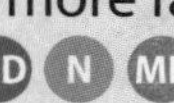

Ⓐ 36   Ⓒ 144
Ⓑ 72   Ⓓ 216

Kind of Puzzle	Students
Crossword	6
Sudoku	8
Word Search	14
Word Scramble	7

Use a problem-solving model to solve this problem.

1 Analyze

Read the problem. Circle the information you know.
Underline what the problem is asking you to find.

2 Plan

What will you need to do to solve the problem? Write your plan in steps.

Step 1 Determine how many more students favor ______________ compared to ______________ written as a fraction.

Step 2 Determine the ______________ out of 360 students.

3 Solve

Use your plan to solve the problem. Show your steps.

There were 35 students surveyed. Write the number of students that prefer each puzzle over 35. Then subtract.

$\frac{14}{35} - \frac{7}{35} =$ ________ or ________ Subtract.

________ $\times\ 360 =$ ________ Multiply.

There would be ________ students more that favor word searches.

So, the correct answer is ________. Fill in that answer choice.

Read to Succeed!
You can also express the difference as a decimal before multiplying. One-fifth is equal to 0.2 or 20%.

4 Justify and Evaluate

How do you know your solution is accurate?

____

____

____

 P = Proportionality 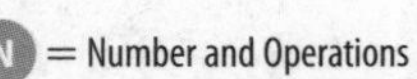 MD = Measurement and Data N = Number and Operations MP = Mathematical Processes

More Multi-Step Problem Solving

Use a problem-solving model to solve each problem.

14. The table shows the results of a student survey at a shopping mall in which they asked people what store they were visiting first. During the survey, the students observed 30 shoppers entering the mall. If 390 people were surveyed, predict how many more would have said they were visiting the electronics store or clothing store compared to the bookstore. P MD N MP

Store	Shoppers
Bookstore	8
Electronics	11
Clothing	7
Sporting Goods	4

Ⓐ 234

Ⓑ 195

Ⓒ 130

Ⓓ 104

15. Jack surveyed two classes in his school to determine how many students had savings accounts. The circle graphs show his results. If there are 250 total seventh-graders and 220 eighth-graders in Jack's school, predict the difference in the number of students who have savings accounts between the two grades. P MD N MP

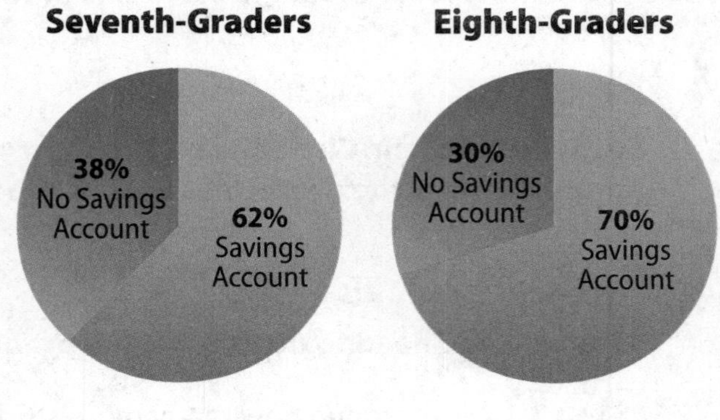

16. Kristen at the Yummy Lunch restaurant kept track of how many people ordered different dishes in one day. She used the results to predict how many orders the restaurant would receive during the following week. If 750 people visited Yummy Lunch that week, predict how many more people ordered salad than soup. P MD N MP

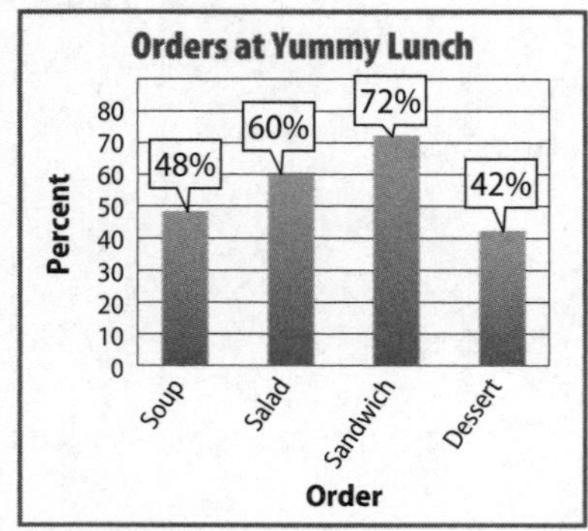

17. The graph shows the results of a survey of families in the town of Jefferson about their household's newspaper subscriptions. If there are a total of 4,300 households in Jefferson, predict how many more families subscribe to State Telegram or Jefferson Gazette compared to County Journal or The City Sentinel.

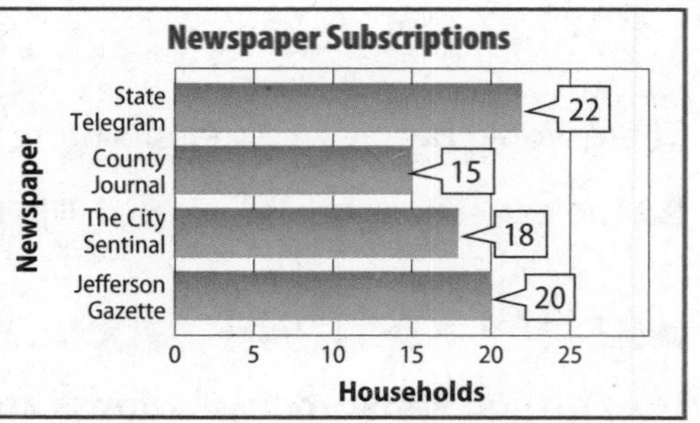

P = Proportionality MD = Measurement and Data N = Number and Operations MP = Mathematical Processes

Lesson 4

Unbiased and Biased Samples

Launch the Lesson: Real World

A T.V. programming manager wants to conduct a survey to determine which reality television show is the favorite of viewers in a certain viewing area. He is considering the three samples shown. Draw an X through the two samples that would not fairly represent all of the people in the viewing area.

Sample 1
100 people that are trying out for a reality show

Sample 2
100 students at your middle school

Sample 3
Every 100th person at a shopping mall

1. Explain why the two samples that you crossed out do *not* fairly represent all of the people in the viewing area? Explain.

____

____

____

____

Texas Essential Knowledge and Skills

Targeted TEKS

7.6(F) Use data from a random sample to make inferences about a population. *Also addresses 7.12(B).*

Mathematical Processes

7.1(A), 7.1(B), 7.1(C)

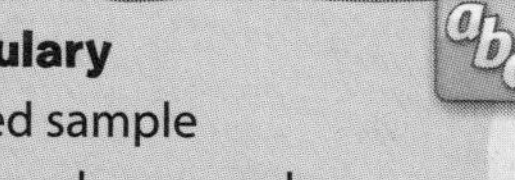

Vocabulary

unbiased sample
simple random sample
systematic random sample
biased sample
convenience sample
voluntary response sample

Essential Question

HOW do you know which type of graph to use when displaying data?

Which MP Mathematical Processes did you use?
Shade the circle(s) that applies.

Ⓐ Apply Math to the Real World.
Ⓑ Use a Problem-Solving Model.
Ⓒ Select Tools and Techniques.
Ⓓ Use Multiple Representations.
Ⓔ Organize Ideas.
Ⓕ Analyze Relationships.
Ⓖ Justify Arguments.

Work Zone

Biased and Unbiased Samples

To get valid results, a sample must be chosen very carefully. An **unbiased sample** is selected so that it accurately represents the entire population. Two ways to pick an unbiased sample are listed below.

Unbiased Samples		
Type	**Description**	**Example**
Simple Random Sample	Each item or person in the population is as likely to be chosen as any other.	Each student's name is written on a piece of paper. The names are placed in a bowl, and names are picked without looking.
Systematic Random Sample	The items or people are selected according to a specific time or item interval.	Every 20th person is chosen from an alphabetical list of all students attending a school.

In a **biased sample**, one or more parts of the population are favored over others. Two ways to pick a biased sample are listed below.

Everyday Use
Bias is a tendency or prejudice

Math Use
Bias is an error introduced by selecting or encouraging a specific outcome

Biased Samples		
Type	**Description**	**Example**
Convenience Sample	A convenience sample consists of members of a population that are easily accessed.	To represent all the students attending a school, the principal surveys the students in one math class.
Voluntary Response Sample	A voluntary response sample involves only those who want to participate in the sampling.	Students at a school who wish to express their opinions complete an online survey.

Tutor

Examples

Determine whether the conclusion is valid. Justify your answer.

1. A random sample of students at a middle school shows that 10 students prefer listening to rock, 15 students prefer listening to hip hop, and 25 students prefer no music while they exercise. It can be concluded that half the students prefer no music while they exercise.

This is a simple random sample. So, the sample is unbiased and the conclusion is valid.

Determine whether each conclusion is valid. Justify your answer.

2. **Every tenth person who walks into a department store is surveyed to determine his or her music preference. Out of 150 customers, 70 stated that they prefer rock music. The manager concludes that about half of all customers prefer rock music.**

Since the population is every tenth customer of a department store, the sample is an unbiased, systematic random sample. The conclusion is valid.

3. **The customers of a music store are surveyed to determine their favorite leisure time activity. The results are shown in the graph. The store manager concludes that most people prefer to listen to music in their leisure time.**

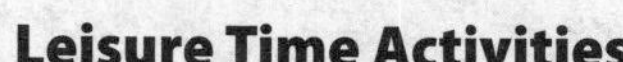

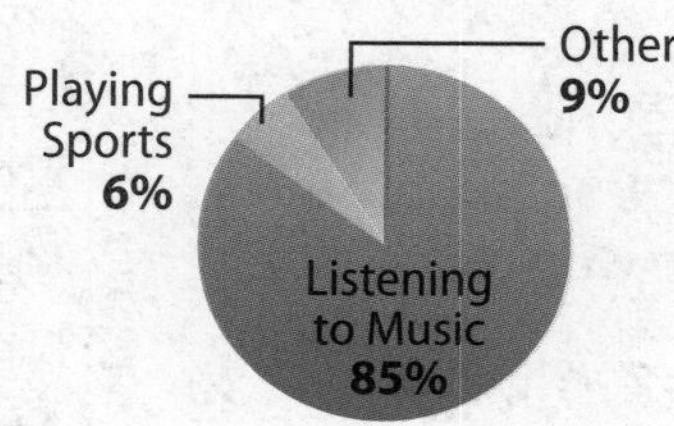

The customers of a music store probably like to listen to music in their leisure time. The sample is a biased, convenience sample since all of the people surveyed are in one specific location. The conclusion is not valid.

Got It? **Do this problem to find out.**

a. A radio station asks its listeners to indicate their preference for one of two candidates in an upcoming election. Seventy-two percent of the listeners who responded preferred candidate A, so the radio station announced that candidate A would win the election. Is the conclusion valid? Justify your answer.

Show your work.

a. ______________

Make Inferences About a Population

A valid sampling method uses unbiased samples. If a sampling method is valid, you can use data from the random sample to make *inferences*, or conclusions, about the population.

Example

4. A store sells 3 types of pants: jeans, capris, and cargos. The store workers survey 50 customers at random about their favorite type of pants. The survey responses are indicated at the right. If 450 pairs of pants are ordered, how many should be jeans?

Type	Number
Jeans	25
Capris	15
Cargos	10

First, determine whether the sample method is valid. The sample is a simple random sample since customers were randomly selected. Thus, the sample method is valid.

$\frac{25}{50}$ or 50% of the customers prefer jeans. So, determine 50% of 450.

$0.5 \times 450 = 225$, so about 225 pairs of jeans should be ordered.

Guided Practice

1. Zach is trying to decide which of three golf courses is the best. He randomly surveyed people at a sports store and recorded the results in the table. Is the sample method valid? If so, suppose Zach surveyed 150 more people. How many people would be expected to vote for Rolling Meadows? (Example 4)

Course	Number
Whispering Trail	10
Tall Pines	8
Rolling Meadows	7

2. To find how much money the average American family spends to cool their home, 100 Alaskan families are surveyed at random. Of the families, 85 said that they spend less than $75 per month on cooling. The researcher concluded that the average American family spends less than $75 on cooling per month. Is the conclusion valid? Explain. (Examples 1–3)

3. **Building on the Essential Question** How can you use data from a random sample to make inferences about a population?

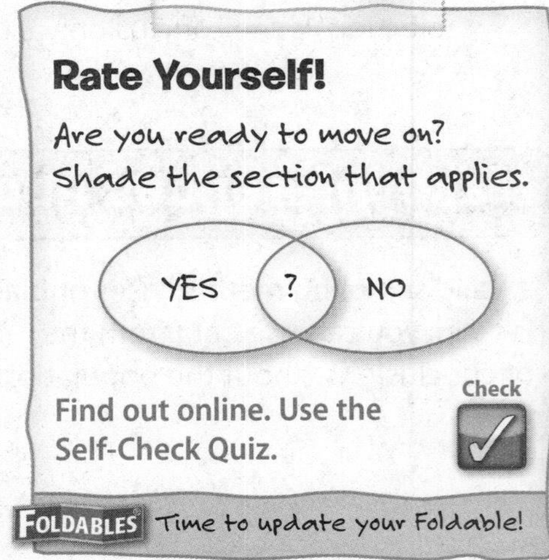

Name ______________________ My Homework ______________________

Independent Practice

7.6(F), 7.12(B), 7.1(A), 7.1(C) TEKS

Determine whether each conclusion is valid. Justify your answer. (Examples 1–3)

1. To evaluate the quality of their product, a manufacturer of cell phones checks every 50th phone off the assembly line. Out of 200 phones tested, 4 are defective. The manager concludes that about 2% of the cell phones produced will be defective.

____

____

2. To determine whether the students will attend an arts festival at the school, Oliver surveys his friends in the art club. All of Oliver's friends plan to attend. So, Oliver assumes that all the students at his school will also attend.

____

____

3. A random sample of people at a mall shows that 22 prefer to take a family trip by car, 18 prefer to travel by plane, and 4 prefer to travel by bus. Is the sample method valid? If so, make an inference to determine how many people out of 500 would you expect to say they prefer to travel by plane. (Example 4)

Preferred Ways to Travel

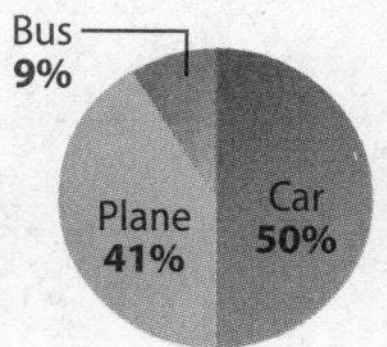

____

____

4. MP **Select Tools and Techniques** Use the organizer to determine whether the conclusion is valid.

Step 1: Read the situation. → Marcus wants to predict the next student council president. He polls every fourth person from each grade level as they exit the cafeteria. In his poll, 65% chose Sophia. So, Marcus predicts Sophia will win the election.

Step 2: Determine the type of sample taken. 

Step 3: Determine if the conclusion is valid. → 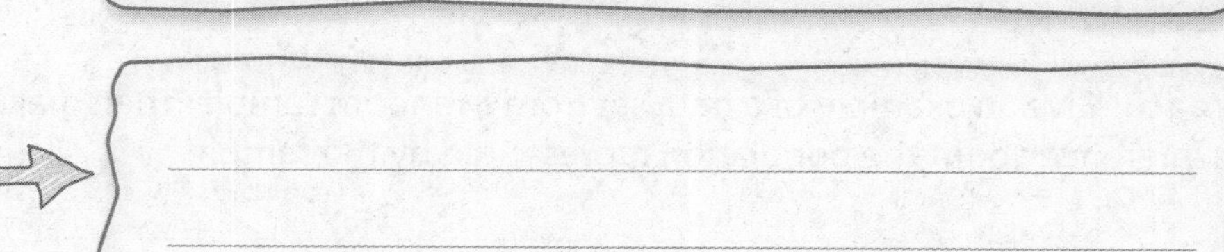

5. **Find the Error** Marisol wants to determine how many students plan to attend the girls' varsity basketball game. Find her mistake and correct it.

I will survey students at the boys' varsity basketball game.

 H.O.T. Problems Higher-Order Thinking

6. **Evaluate** How could the wording of a question or the tone of voice of the interviewer affect a survey? Provide an example.

Analyze Determine whether each statement is *sometimes*, *always*, or *never* true. Explain your reasoning to a classmate.

7. A biased sample is valid.

8. A simple random sample is valid.

9. A voluntary response sample is valid.

10. **Create** Give an example of a data set from a random sample. Then make an inference about the population represented by the sample.

Name ________________________________

Multi-Step Problem Solving

11. A furniture store sells wood, metal, and wicker chairs. The store workers survey 80 customers at random about their favorite type of chair. The table shows the results of this survey. If 200 chairs are ordered, about how many more should be wood than metal?

P MD N MP

Chair Type	Number
Wood	45
Metal	27
Wicker	8

Ⓐ 18 Ⓒ 68

Ⓑ 45 Ⓓ 113

Use a problem-solving model to solve this problem.

1 Analyze

Read the problem. Circle the information you know.
Underline what the problem is asking you to find.

2 Plan

What will you need to do to solve the problem? Write your plan in steps.

Step 1 Determine how many more people favor ________ compared to ________ written as a fraction.

Step 2 Determine the ________ out of 200 chairs.

3 Solve

Use your plan to solve the problem. Show your steps.

There were 80 people surveyed. Write the number of people that prefer each chair type over 80. Then subtract.

$\frac{45}{80} - \frac{27}{80} =$ ____ or ____ Subtract.

____ $\times$ 200 = ____ Multiply.

The store would expect about ____ more wood chair orders than metal.

So, the correct answer is ____. Fill in that answer choice.

Read to Succeed!
You can also express the difference as a decimal before multiplying. It can be expressed as 0.225 or 22.5%.

4 Justify and Evaluate

How do you know your solution is accurate?

____

____

____

P = Proportionality MD = Measurement and Data N = Number and Operations MP = Mathematical Processes

More Multi-Step Problem Solving

Use a problem-solving model to solve each problem.

12. A toy store sells three different versions of a popular game as a board game, electronic, or a travel-size version. The store workers survey 120 customers at random about their favorite version of the game. The table shows the results of this survey. If 420 games are ordered, about how many more should be electronic than travel-size? P MD N MP

Game Type	Number
Board	42
Electronic	50
Travel-Size	28

Ⓐ 273

Ⓑ 175

Ⓒ 98

Ⓓ 77

13. A sporting goods store sells three different versions of athletic shoes. The store workers surveyed 200 customers at random. The results are shown in the table. The store ordered 500 shoes. Out of the shoes they ordered, 220 were cross trainers. Based on the survey, make an inference about how cross trainers they will still need. P MD N MP

Shoe Type	Number in Survey
Cross Trainer	100
High Top	24
Tennis Shoes	76

14. Two pharmacies on opposite sides of town each surveyed a random sample of customers in their store about what type of cold medicine they prefer. If store A and store B each order 150 units of cold medicine, make an inference to determine how many more should be in the pill form for store A compared to store B. P MD N MP

Medicine Form	Store A	Store B
Pill	33	38
Syrup	10	15
Spray	2	4

15. A jewelry store wanted to survey customers to determine if they preferred silver, gold, or platinum chain. The store surveyed 67 customers who made a purchase and 23 customers who did not make a purchase. Explain why neither of the data collection methods is valid, and what would be a better way to collect the data. P MD MP

P = Proportionality MD = Measurement and Data N = Number and Operations MP = Mathematical Processes

Hands-On Lab 4-b

Multiple Samples of Data

INQUIRY **HOW can I organize ideas to analyze multiple samples of data before making predictions?**

Texas Essential Knowledge and Skills

Targeted TEKS
7.6(F) Use data from a random sample to make inferences about a population. *Also addresses 7.12(B).*

Mathematical Processes
7.1(C), 7.1(D), 7.1(E), 7.1(G)

A hostess at a restaurant randomly hands out crayons to young children. There are three different color crayons: green (G), red (R), and blue (B). The hostess gives out the green crayon 40% of the time, the red crayon 40% of the time, and the blue crayon 20% of the time.

Hands-On Activity 1

When you draw a conclusion about a population from a sample of data, you are making *inferences* about that population. Sometimes, making inferences about a population from only one sample is not as accurate as using multiple samples of data.

Use a spinner to simulate the situation above.

Step 1 Create a spinner with five equal sections. Label two sections G. Label another two sections R and label one section B.

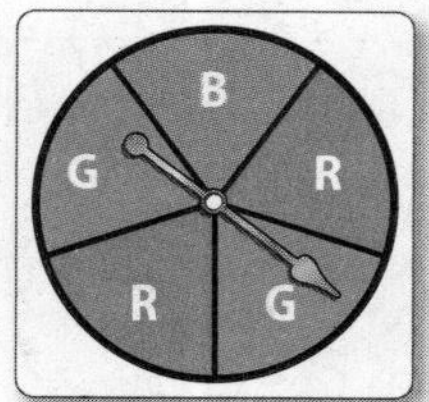

Step 2 Each spin of the spinner represents a young child receiving a crayon. Spin the spinner 20 times. Record the number of times each color of crayon was received in the column labeled Sample 1 in the table below. Repeat two more times. Record the results in the columns labeled Sample 2 and Sample 3 in the table.

Color	Sample 1 Frequency	Sample 2 Frequency	Sample 3 Frequency
Green			
Red			
Blue			

1. Compare the results of the 3 samples. Do you notice any differences?

The most commonly used keyboard is the QWERTY keyboard. However, there is another type of keyboard called the Dvorak keyboard that is based on letter frequency. Complete the Activity below about letter frequencies.

Hands-On Activity 2

The table below contains fifteen randomly selected words from the English language dictionary.

Sample 1		
airport	juggle	sewer
blueberry	lemon	standard
costume	mileage	thread
doorstop	percentage	vacuum
instrument	print	whale

Step 1 Determine the frequency of each letter. Record the frequencies in the Sample 1 rows of the tables below.

Letter	a	b	c	d	e	f	g	h	i	j	k	l	m
Sample 1 Frequency													
Sample 2 Frequency													
Sample 3 Frequency													

Letter	n	o	p	q	r	s	t	u	v	w	x	y	z
Sample 1 Frequency													
Sample 2 Frequency													
Sample 3 Frequency													

Step 2 Randomly select another 15 words from a dictionary. Record the frequency of the letters in the rows labeled Sample 2 in the tables above.

Step 3 Repeat Step 2. Record the frequency of the letters in the rows labeled Sample 3.

Work with a partner to collect multiple samples based on the following situation.

Janet and Masao are making centerpieces for their school's fall dance. They randomly select a ribbon to use in each centerpiece. There are four different colors of ribbon to choose from: brown (B), green (G), orange (O), and yellow (Y).

2. MP **Apply Math to the Real World** Design a method to simulate how many times each ribbon will be selected. Describe your simulation.

Show your work.

3. Use the method you described in Exercise 1 to simulate the ribbon selection 20 times. Record the frequency of each color selection in the Sample 1 Frequency column of the table below.

Color	Sample 1 Frequency	Sample 2 Frequency	Sample 3 Frequency
Brown			
Green			
Orange			
Yellow			

4. Repeat the process described in Exercise 2 two more times. Record the frequencies of each color selection in the Sample 2 and Sample 3 columns.

5. Make an inference to determine which color was selected the most often in each sample.

6. The *relative frequency* of a color being selected is the ratio of the number of times the color was selected to the total number of selections. Find the relative frequency of an orange ribbon being selected for each sample.

Sample 1: ______ Sample 2: ______ Sample 3: ______

7. Masao predicts that 5 out of 10 centerpieces will have an orange ribbon. How far off is Masao's prediction? Explain.

Analyze and Reflect

Work with a partner to answer the following questions. Refer to Activity 2.

8. What is the relative frequency for the letter *e* for each sample? Round to the nearest hundredth.

Sample 1: ____________ Sample 2: ________ Sample 3: ____________

9. What is the mean relative frequency of the letter *e* for the three samples? the median relative frequency? Round to the nearest tenth if necessary.

mean relative frequency: _______ median relative frequency: _______

10. MP **Select Tools and Techniques** Research on the Internet to determine the actual relative frequency of the letter *e* for words in the English language. How do your sample results compare to the actual relative frequency?

11. MP **Organize Ideas** Write a few sentences describing the inferences you can make about the frequency of letters in the words in the English language using your three samples.

On Your Own

Create

12. MP **Organize Ideas** Research on the Internet to determine the relative frequency of other letters in words in the English language. Write how your sample results compare to the actual frequencies. Note any differences.

13. INQUIRY HOW can I organize ideas to analyze multiple samples of data before making predictions?

Use a Graph

Fish

Tess is making a display of the length of various fish at the pet store. She uses the information in the table to make a dot plot.

Length of Fish (in.)									
2	2	3	1	5	3	2	2	2	2
1	3	4	2	1	4	5	4	3	1

How many fish have a length that is 3 inches or longer?

Mathematical Process
7.1(B) Use a problem-solving model that incorporates analyzing given information, formulating a plan or strategy, determining a solution, justifying the solution, and evaluating the problem-solving process and the reasonableness of the solution.
Targeted TEKS 7.6(G)

Analyze *What are the facts?*

You know the length of various fish that are shown in the table.

Plan *Choose a problem-solving strategy.*

I will use the ______ strategy.

Solve *How can you apply the strategy?*

Using the dot plot, count the number of fish for each length that is 3 inches or greater.

Length of Fish (in.)

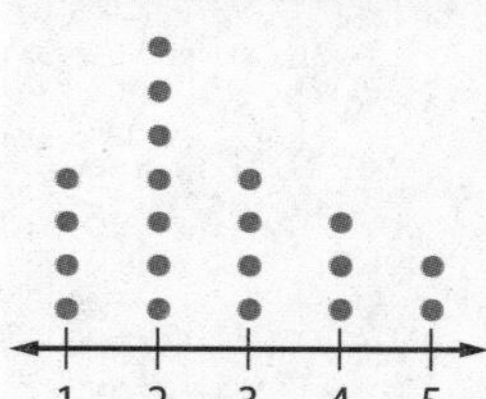

3 inches: ____

4 inches: ____

5 inches: ____

There are ____ fish that are 3 inches or longer.

Justify and Evaluate *How do you know your solution is accurate?*

____

____

____

____

Sleep

The bar graph shows the average number of hours students sleep each night.

If 225 students were surveyed, what percent more of students sleep 8 hours compared to those who sleep 6 hours?

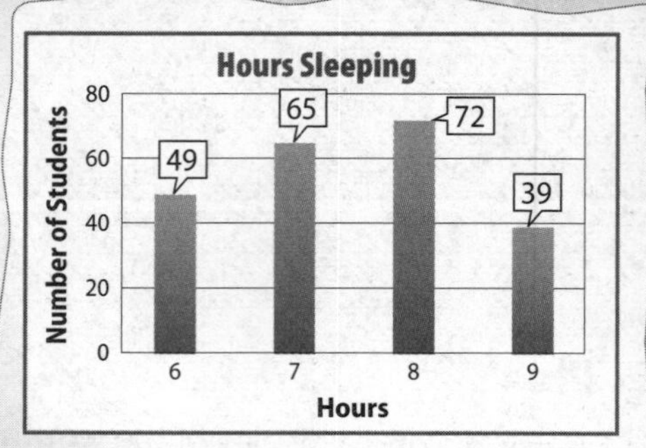

1 Analyze

Read the problem. Circle the information you know. Underline what the problem is asking you to find.

2 Plan

Choose a problem-solving strategy.

I will use the ____________ strategy.

3 Solve

How can you apply the strategy?

Justify and Evaluate

How do you know your solution is accurate?

____

____

____

Multi-Step Problem Solving

Work with a small group to solve the following problems. Show your work on a separate piece of paper.

1. Postage

The table shows the postage stamp rate from 1999 to 2009.

Make a graph of the data. Predict the year the postage rate will reach $0.52.

Postage Stamp Rates	
Year	**Cost ($)**
1999	0.33
2001	0.34
2002	0.37
2006	0.39
2007	0.41
2008	0.42
2009	0.44

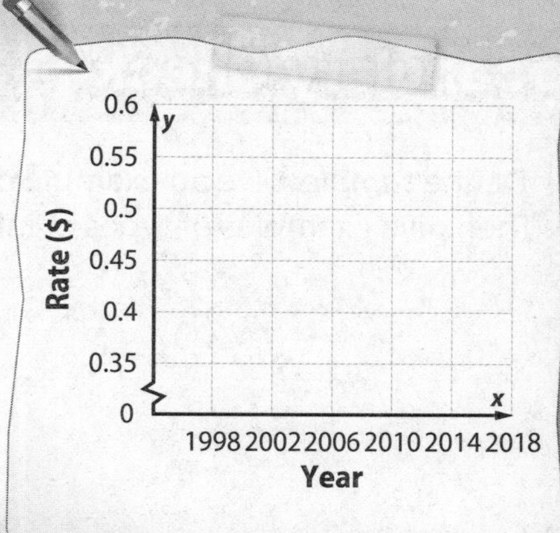

2. Trains

The lengths of various train rides are 4, 1, 2, 3, 6, 2, 3, 2, 5, 8, and 4 hours.

Draw a box plot for the data set. What percent of the train rides are longer than 3 hours?

3. Advertising

A local newspaper charges $15.30 for every three lines of a classified ad plus a 7% sales tax.

What is the cost of a 7-line ad? Round to the nearest hundredth.

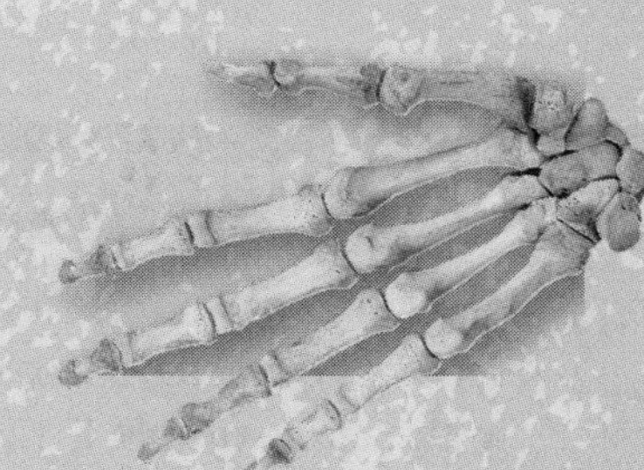

4. Anatomy

Each human hand has 27 bones. There are 6 more bones in the fingers than in the wrist. There are 3 fewer bones in the palm than in the wrist.

How many bones are in each part of the hand?

TEKS Mid-Chapter Check

Vocabulary Check

Vocab

1. Define *sample*. Give an example of a sample of the students in a middle school. Then give examples of types of inferences can be made from that sample? TEKS 7.12(B), 7.1(D)

Key Concept Check

2. Use the graphic organizer to write a real-world example of a biased sample and an unbiased sample. TEKS 7.6(F), 7.1(E)

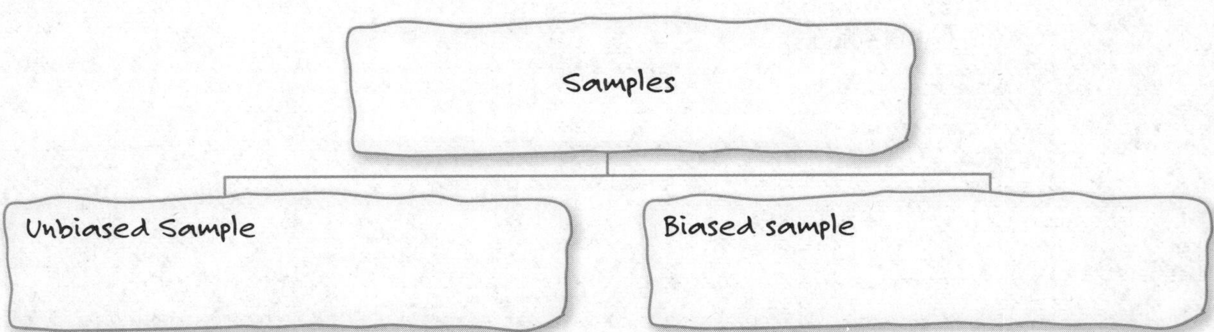

Multi-Step Problem Solving

3. An online gaming site conducted a survey to determine the types of games people play online. The results are shown in the circle graph. If 1,500 people participated in the study, how many more would play card games than arcade games? N MD MP

Ⓐ 135 people

Ⓑ 165 people

Ⓒ 315 people

Ⓓ 450 people

Games People Play Online

N = Number and Operations MD = Measurement and Data MP = Mathematical Processes

Lesson 5

Misleading Graphs and Statistics

Launch the Lesson: Real World

The Stanley Cup is awarded annually to the champion team in the National Hockey League. The graph shows the total number of points scored in Stanley Cup playoff games by three players during their careers. Is the graph representative of the actual players' points?

Texas Essential Knowledge and Skills

Targeted TEKS

7.6(G) Solve problems using data represented in bar graphs, dot plots, and circle graphs, including part-to-whole and part-to-part comparisons and equivalents.

Mathematical Processes

7.1(A), 7.1(B), 7.1(C)

Essential Question

HOW do you know which type of graph to use when displaying data?

1. According to the size of the players, how many times more points does Messier appear to have than Kurri? ______

2. Do you think this is representative of the players' number of points? Explain. ______

3. What reason could someone have for intentionally creating a misleading Stanley Cup graph? ______

Which MP Mathematical Processes did you use? Shade the circle(s) that applies.

Ⓐ Apply Math to the Real World.
Ⓑ Use a Problem-Solving Model.
Ⓒ Select Tools and Techniques.
Ⓓ Use Multiple Representations.
Ⓔ Organize Ideas.
Ⓕ Analyze Relationships.
Ⓖ Justify Arguments.

Work Zone

Identify a Misleading Graph

Graphs let readers analyze data easily, but are sometimes made to influence conclusions by misrepresenting the data.

Example

Changing Scales
To emphasize a change over time, reduce the scale interval on the vertical axis.

1. Explain how the graphs differ.

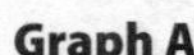

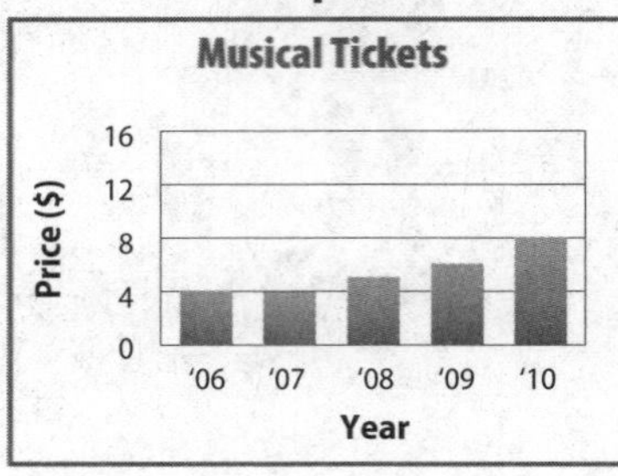

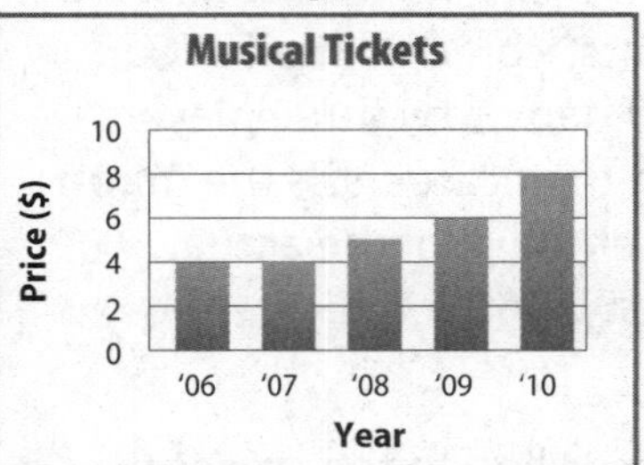

The graphs show the same data. However, the graphs differ in that Graph A uses an interval of 4, and Graph B uses an interval of 2.

Which graph appears to show a sharper increase in price?
Graph B makes it appear that the prices increased more rapidly even though the price increase is the same.

Which graph might the Music Club use to show that while ticket prices have risen, the increase is not significant? Why?
They might use Graph A. The scale used on the vertical axis of this graph makes the increase appear less significant.

Got It? Do this problem to find out.

Show your work.

a. The line graphs show monthly profits of a company from October to March. Which graph suggests that the business is extremely profitable? Is this a valid conclusion? Explain.

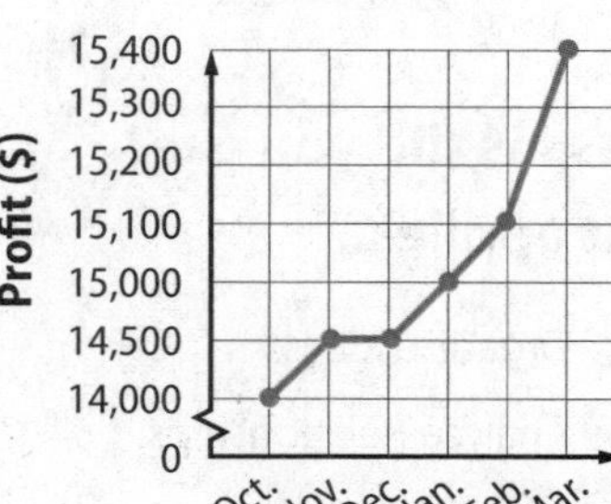

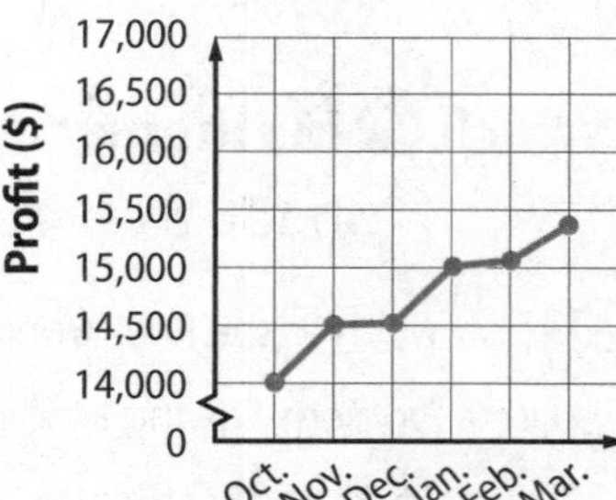

a. ________

Misleading Statistics

Statistics can also be used to influence inferences or conclusions.

Example

Tutor

2. An amusement park boasts that the average height of their roller coasters is 170 feet. Explain how this might be misleading.

Park Roller Coaster Heights	
Coaster	**Height (ft)**
Viper	109
Monster	135
Red Zip	115
Tornado	365
Riptide	126

Mean $\frac{109 + 135 + 115 + 365 + 126}{5} = \frac{850}{5}$

$= 170$

Median 109, 115, 126, 135, 365

Mode none

The average height used by the park was the mean. This measure is much greater than most of the heights listed because of the coaster that is 365 feet. So, it is misleading to use this measure to attract visitors.

A more appropriate measure to describe the data is the median, 126 feet, which is closer to the height of most of the coasters.

Mode
The mode is the number or numbers that appear most often in a set of data.

Got It? Do this problem to find out.

b. Determine the mean, median, and mode of the sofa prices shown in the table. Which measurement might be misleading in describing the average cost of a sofa? Explain.

Sofa Prices	
Sofa Style	**Cost**
leather	$1,700
reclining	$1,400
DIY assembly	$350
sectional	$1,600
micro-fiber	$1,400

b. __________

Guided Practice

1. The graph suggests that Cy Young had three times as many wins as Jim Galvin. Is this a valid conclusion? Explain. (Example 1)

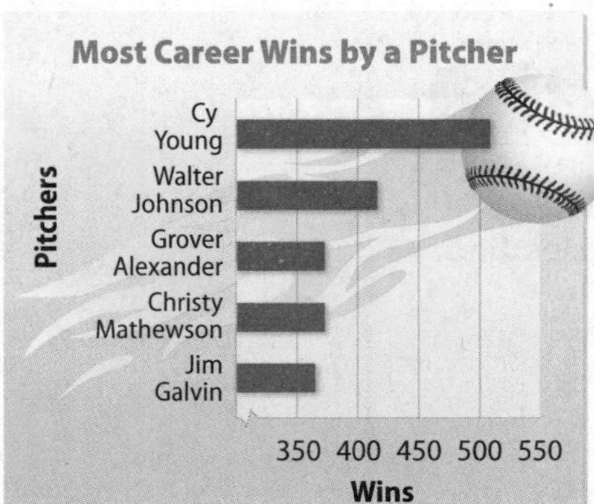

2. The graph at the right shows the results of a survey to determine students' favorite pets. Why is the graph misleading? (Example 1)

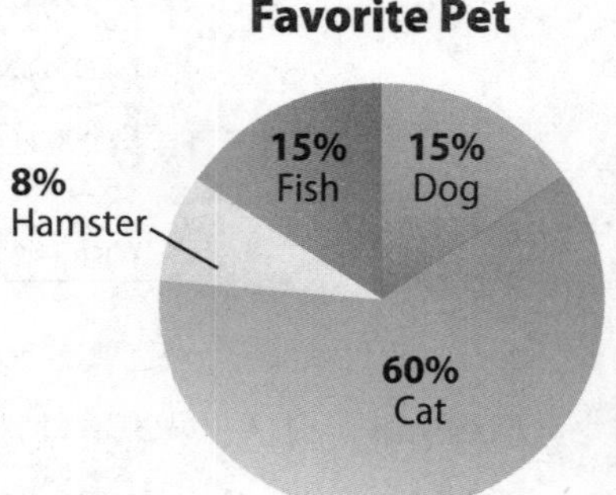

3. The table lists five counties with the largest area in Texas. Write a convincing argument for which measure of center you would use to emphasize the average area of the counties. (Example 2)

County	Area (mi^2)
Brewster	6,193
Pecos	4,764
Hudspeth	4,571
Presidio	3,856
Culberson	3,813

4. **Building on the Essential Question** Describe at least two ways in which the display of data can influence the conclusions reached.

Rate Yourself!

How well do you understand misleading graphs and statistics? Circle the image that applies.

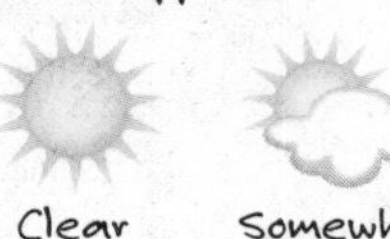

Clear Somewhat Clear Not So Clear

Find out online. Use the Self-Check Quiz.

Check

Name ________________ My Homework ________________

Independent Practice

7.6(G), 7.1(A) TEKS

1. Which graph could be used to indicate a greater increase in monthly gas prices? Explain. (Example 1)

Graph A

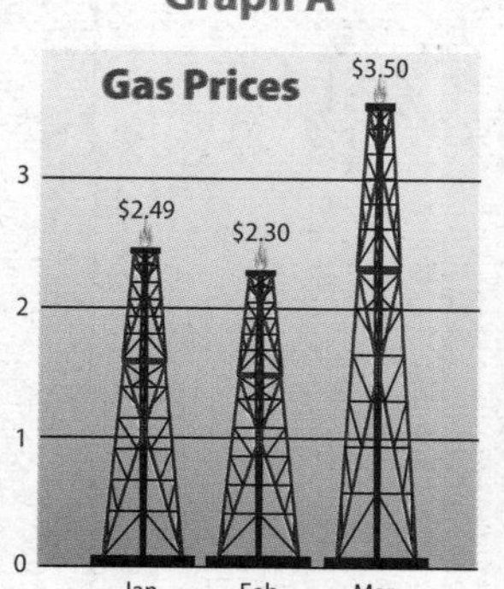

Graph B

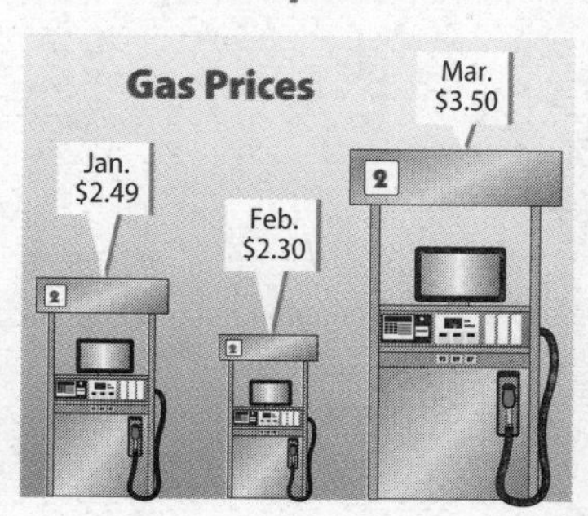

For Exercises 2 and 3, use the table. (Example 2)

2. Determine the mean, median, and mode of the data. Which measure might be misleading in describing the average annual number of visitors who visit these sights? Explain.

Annual Sight-Seeing Visitors	
Sight	**Visitors**
Cape Cod	4,600,000
Grand Canyon	4,500,000
Lincoln Memorial	4,000,000
Castle Clinton	4,600,000
Smoky Mountains	10,200,000

3. Which measure would be best if you wanted a value close to the most number of visitors? Explain.

4. MP **Apply Math to the Real World** Refer to the graphic novel frame below.

Which measure of center should the students use? ________________

For Exercises 5 and 6, create a display that would support each argument. The monthly costs to rent an apartment for the last five years are $500, $525, $560, $585, and $605.

5. Rent has remained fairly stable.

Show your work.

6. Rent has increased dramatically.

H.O.T. Problems Higher-Order Thinking

7. Analyze How could the graph you created in Exercise 5 help influence someone's decision to rent the apartment?

8. Evaluate Does adding values that are much greater or much less than the other values in a set of data affect the median of the set? Give an example to support your answer.

9. Create Give a real-world example of a set of data of which the mean is not representative.

10. Analyze The circle graph shows the results of a survey. In what way is this graph misleading? Explain.

Favorite Time of Year

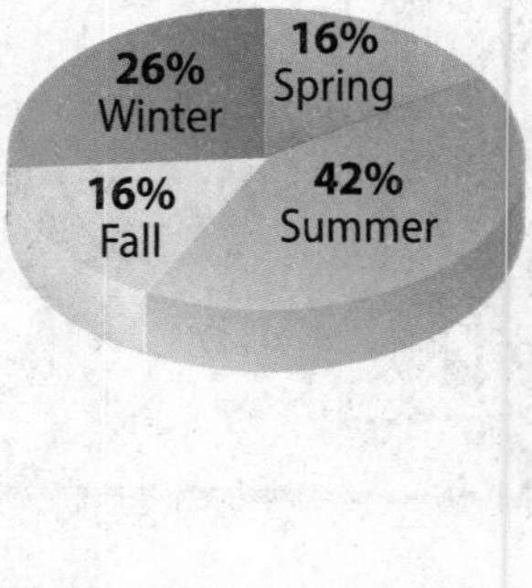

Name ______________________________

Multi-Step Problem Solving

11. Four models of televisions are on sale this week at the local electronic store. In their advertisement, the store claims that their average price for a television is $2,106.25. The sale prices of the televisions are shown in the graph. By how much should they increase this amount to give a more accurate representation of the average price, in dollars, of the televisions on sale? (P) (MD) (N) (MP)

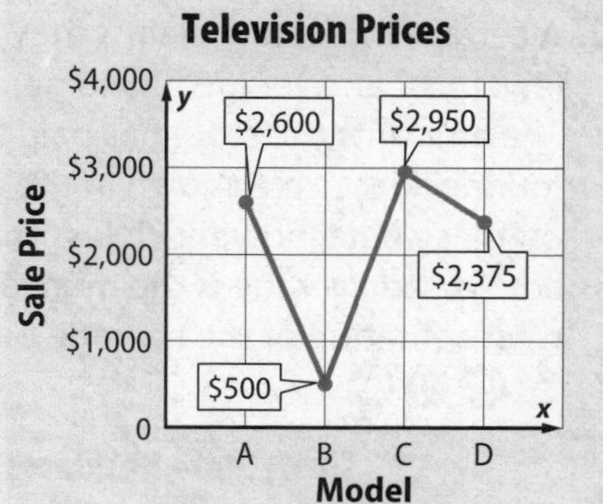

Ⓐ $381.25
Ⓑ $450.50
Ⓒ $535.42
Ⓓ $575.00

Use a problem-solving model to solve this problem.

1 Analyze

Read the problem. Circle the information you know.
Underline what the problem is asking you to find.

2 Plan

What will you need to do to solve the problem? Write your plan in steps.

Step 1 Determine the more appropriate ________ to describe to data.

Step 2 Determine the ________ between the mean and median.

3 Solve

Use your plan to solve the problem. Show your steps.

The median is the more appropriate measure. Determine the median.

$2,375 + $2,600 = ________ ________ ÷ 2 = ________

________ − $2,106.25 = ________ Subtract.

The more accurate price would be the median that is ________ greater than the mean.

So, the correct answer is ______. Fill in that answer choice.

Read to Succeed!
There is no mode for the data. You should only compare the mean and median to determine which is more appropriate for the data.

4 Justify and Evaluate

How do you know your solution is accurate?

____

____

____

(P) = Proportionality (MD) = Measurement and Data (N) = Number and Operations (MP) = Mathematical Processes

More Multi-Step Problem Solving

Use a problem-solving model to solve each problem.

12. A certain thrift store claims they will buy used jewelry at an average of $48 per necklace. The amounts the store has paid for the last four necklaces are shown in the graph. Based on these data, how much less than the store's advertised average is the more appropriate representation of the average payment? P MD N MP

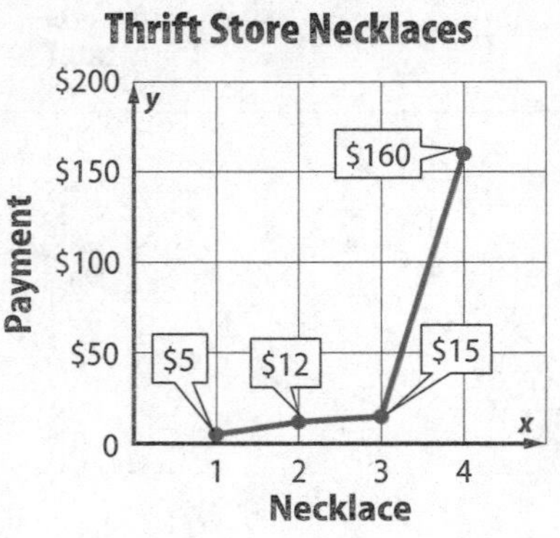

Ⓐ $13.50
Ⓑ $25.75
Ⓒ $34.50
Ⓓ $61.50

13. The table shows the times, in minutes, of the jogs that Fernando and Nakita ran last week. What is the difference, in minutes, between the measures that best describe Fernando's running times and Nakita's running times? P N MP

Running Times (in min)	
Fernando	**Nakita**
16	5
20	20
12	23

14. A ski resort claims they have an average of 190,000 visitors per year. The circle graph shows the number of visitors to the resort during each of the four seasons. Explain why 190,000 is a misleading descriptor of the average number of visitors. What would be a better way to convey the appropriate information? P MP

Ski Resort Visitors by Season

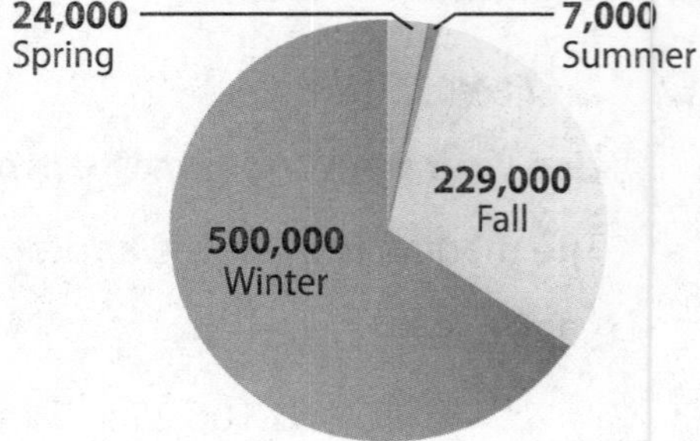

Hands-On Lab 6-a

Collect Data

INQUIRY **HOW can I select tools and techniques to use the measures of center and the range to compare two populations?**

Studies show that teens need around 9 hours of sleep each night to stay healthy.

Texas Essential Knowledge and Skills TEKS

Targeted TEKS
7.12(A) Compare two groups of numeric data using comparative dot plots or box plots by comparing their shapes, centers, and spreads. *Also addresses 7.12(C).*

Mathematical Processes
7.1(C), 7.1(D), 7.1(E), 7.1(F)

Hands-On Activity

Step 1 The results of a survey that asked 24 teens how many hours they slept last night are shown below. The teens were split into two populations, male and female.

Males	7	7	6	8	6	8	7	6	7	6	8	6
Females	8	8	7	6	8	7	6	6	7	8	9	7

Step 2 Graph the data for each population on a single dot plot.

Number of Hours of Sleep

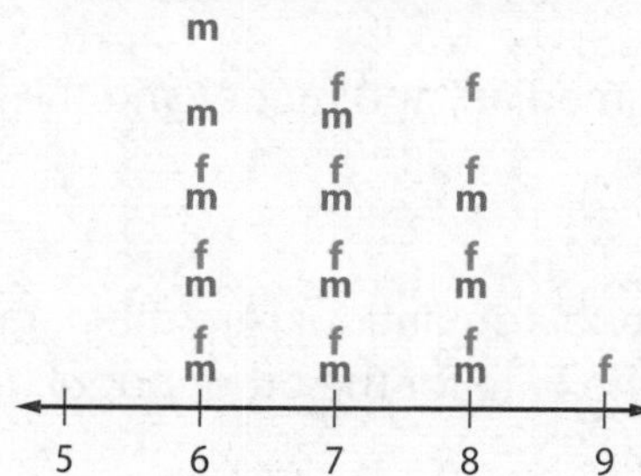

m male
f female

Step 3 Determine the measures of center and range for each population.

	Mean	Median	Mode	Range
Males	$6.8\overline{3}$			
Females				

Are the data for males more or less varied than females? ______

1. Which measure most accurately represents the data of the whole class?

Explain. ______

______

Investigate and Create

Work with a partner to design your own survey that meets the following guidelines.

- Create a survey question that involves two populations. For example, you might want to know about how many hours of sleep per night male students get in your school versus female students. Write your survey question below.

  ____

- Survey a random sample that is representative of your school's population. Survey at least 25 people.

  Collect the data and record your results in a table on a separate piece of paper. ____

- Create a display of your data, such as a dot plot. Be sure that the display shows the two populations. For example, you might use the line plot below.

  ____

Analyze and Reflect

Work with a partner to complete the exercises below based on the data you collected above.

2. Determine the measures of center (mean, median, and mode) and the range for each population's set of data. ____

3. **Analyze Relationships** Compare the two populations. Are the data for one population more or less varied than the data for the other population? Justify your response. ____

4. Describe any other comparative *inferences*, or conclusions, you can make about differences in the two populations. ____

Create

5. **INQUIRY** HOW can I select tools and techniques to use the measures of center and the range to compare two populations?

   ____

   ____

   ____

Lesson 6

Compare Populations

Launch the Lesson: Real World

Mr. Singh surveyed the students in his first period gym class to find out how many times they exercised this month. The box plot below shows the results. What inferences can you make from this data?

How Many Times Have You Exercised This Month?

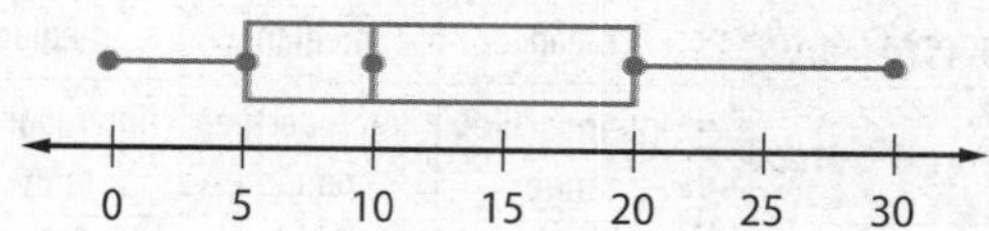

1. Determine the following values.

Minimum: ☐ First Quartile: ☐

Maximum: ☐ Third Quartile: ☐

Range: ☐ Interquartile Range: ☐

2. What is the median? What does the median represent?

3. Write an inference that you can make from the box plot.

Which MP Mathematical Processes did you use? Shade the circle(s) that applies.

Ⓐ Apply Math to the Real World.
Ⓑ Use a Problem-Solving Model.
Ⓒ Select Tools and Techniques.
Ⓓ Use Multiple Representations.
Ⓔ Organize Ideas.
Ⓕ Analyze Relationships.
Ⓖ Justify Arguments.

Texas Essential Knowledge and Skills

Targeted TEKS
7.12(A) Compare two groups of numeric data using comparative dot plots or box plots by comparing their shapes, centers, and spreads. *Also addresses 7.12(C).*

Mathematical Processes
7.1(A), 7.1(B), 7.1(E)

Vocabulary
double box plot
double dot plot

Essential Question
HOW do you know which type of graph to use when displaying data?

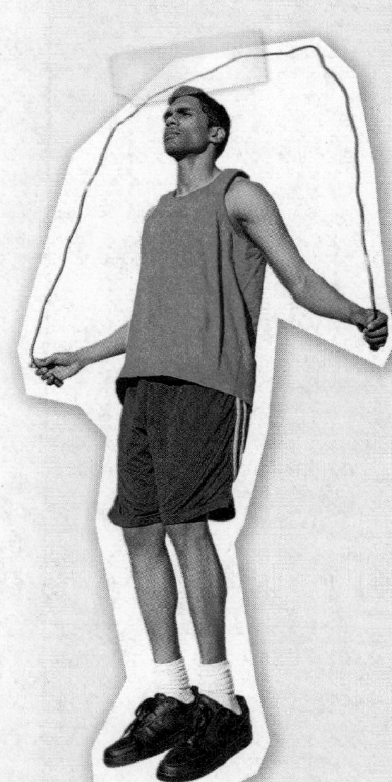

Work Zone

Compare Two Populations

A **double box plot** consists of two box plots graphed on the same number line. A **double dot plot** consists of two dot plots that are drawn on the same number line. You can make inferences about two populations in a double box plot or double dot plot by comparing their shapes, centers, and spreads. The centers and spreads to use are shown.

Shapes of Box-plots

A box plot is symmetric if the data are balanced at the center.

Symmetric

Not Symmetric

Most Appropriate Measures			
	Both sets of data are symmetric.	Neither set of data is symmetric.	Only one set of data is symmetric.
Measure of Center	mean	median	median
Measure of Spread	interquartile range	interquartile range	interquartile range

Real World

Example

Tutor

1. **Kacey randomly surveyed a different group of students in her science and math classes. The double box plot shows the results for both classes. Compare their shapes, centers, and spreads. Write an inference you can make about the two populations.**

How Many Times Have You Sent a Text This Month?

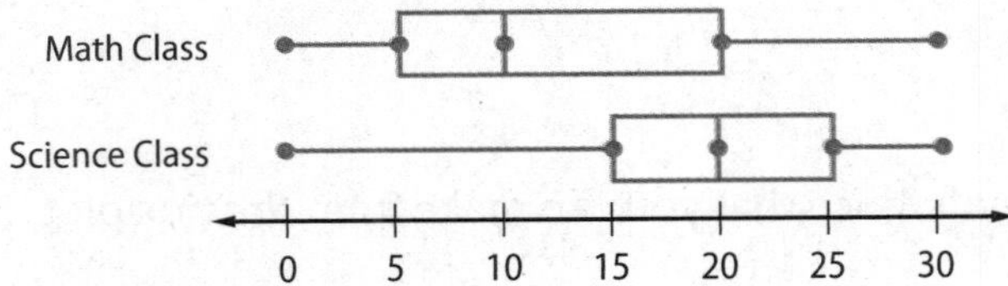

Neither box plot is symmetric in shape. Seventy five percent of the math class data is greater than 5 texts, while 75% of the science class data is greater than 15 texts.

Use the median to compare the centers and the interquartile range to compare the spreads.

	Math Class	Science Class
Median	10	20
Interquartile Range	20 − 5, or 15	25 − 15, or 10

Overall, the science students sent more texts than the math students. The median for the science class is twice the median for the math class. There is a greater spread of data around the median for the math class than the science class.

Got It? **Do this problem to find out.**

Show your work.

a. The double box plot shows the costs of MP3 players at two different stores. Compare the shapes, centers, and spreads of the two populations. Write an inference you can make about the two populations.

a. ____________

Cost of MP3 Players ($)

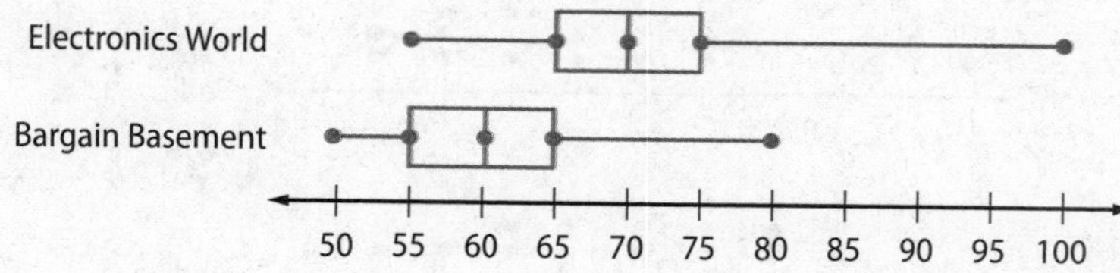

Real World

Example

Tutor

2. **The double dot plot below shows the daily high temperatures for two cities for thirteen days. Compare the shapes, centers, and spreads of the two populations. Write an inference you can make about the two populations.**

Daily High Temperatures (°F)

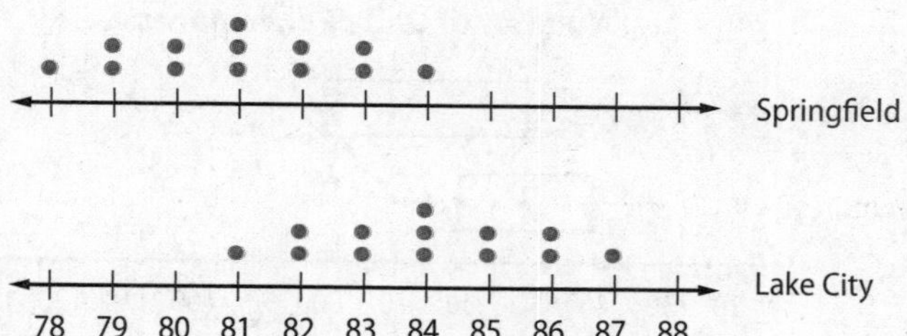

Both dot plots are symmetric in shape. The peak for Springfield, 81, is less than the peak for Lake City, 84.

Use the mean to compare the centers and use the interquartile range to compare the variations.

	Springfield	Lake City
Mean	81	84
Interquartile Range	82.5 − 79.5, or 3	85.5 − 82.5, or 3

While both cities have the same variation, or spread of data about each of their means, Lake City has a greater mean temperature than Springfield.

Interquartile Range

To determine the interquartile range, first determine the median, first quartile, and third quartile. Then subtract the first quartile from the third quartile of the set of data.

Show your work.

b. ____________

Got It? Do this problem to find out.

b. The double dot plot shows the number of new E-mails in each of Pedro's and Annika's inboxes for sixteen days. Compare the shapes, centers, and spreads of the two populations. Write an inference you can make about the two populations.

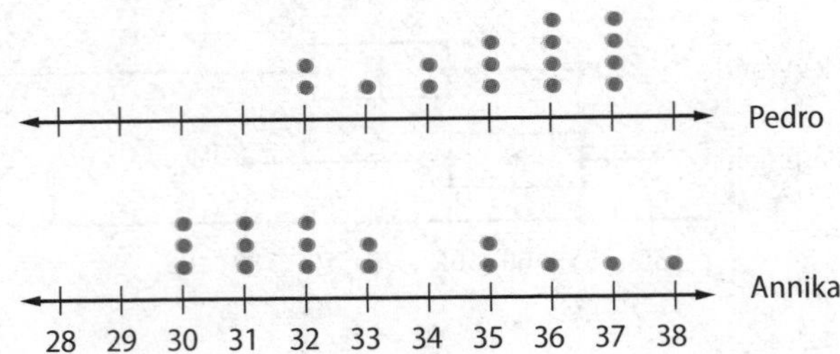

Real World

Examples

3. The double box plot shows the daily participants for two zip line companies for one month. Compare the shapes, centers, and spreads of the two populations. Which company has the greater number of daily participants?

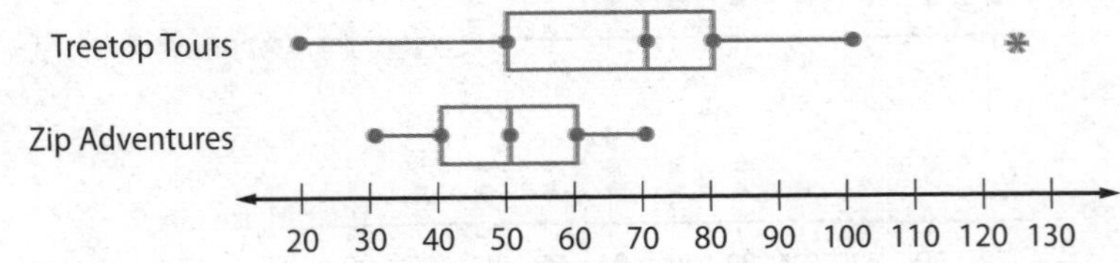

What can you tell about the shape of the set of data for Zip Adventures by looking at its box plot? Write your answer in the space below.

The distribution for Zip Adventures is symmetric, while the distribution for Treetop Tours is not symmetric.

Use the median and the interquartile range to compare the populations.

	Treetop Tours	Zip Adventures
Median	70	50
Interquartile Range	30	20

Overall, Treetop Tours has a greater number of daily participants. However, Treetop Tours also has a greater spread, or variation, so it is more difficult to predict how many participants they may have each day. Zip Adventures has a greater consistency in their distribution.

4. The double dot plot shows Jada's and Angel's number of hours worked in 2 weeks at their part-time jobs. Compare the shapes, centers, and spreads of the two populations. Who typically works the greater number of hours in a week?

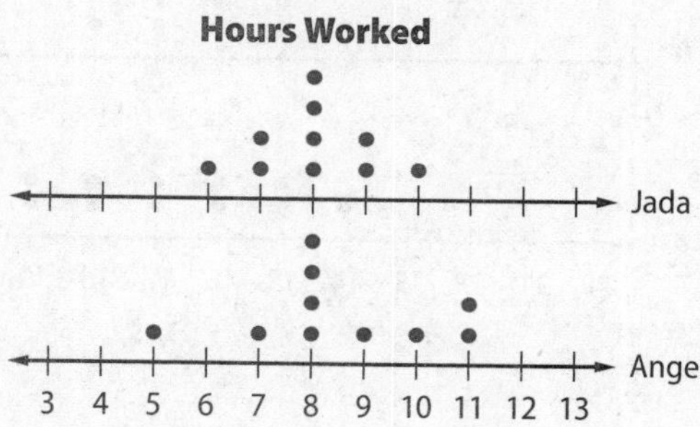

The distribution for Jada's number of hours is symmetric, while the distribution for Angel's number of hours is not symmetric. Use the median and interquartile range to compare the populations.

	Jada	Angel
Median	8	8
Interquartile Range	2	2

The median and interquartile range for both sets of data are the same. However, the interquartile range for Angel's number of hours worked is the difference of 10 and 8, while the interquartile range for Jada's number of hours is the difference of 9 and 7. So, Angel typically works more per week.

Got It? Do this problem to find out.

c. The double dot plot shows Kareem's and Martin's race times for a three-mile race. Compare the shapes, centers, and spreads of the two populations. Which runner is more likely to run a faster race?

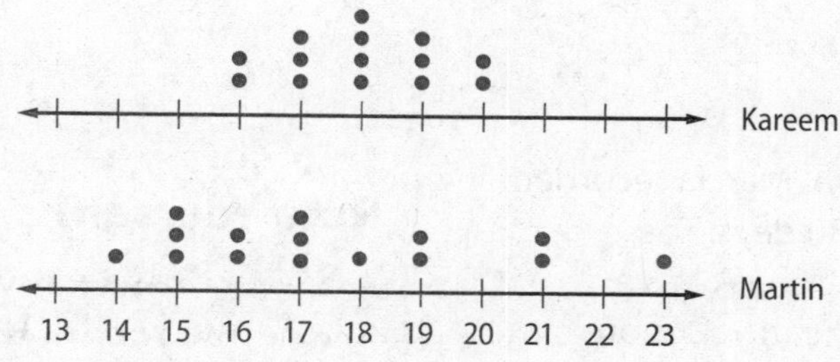

c. ______________

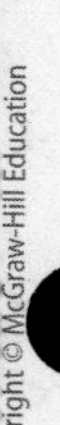

Guided Practice

1. The double dot plot below shows the quiz scores out of 20 points for two different class periods. Compare the shapes, centers, and spreads of the two populations. Round to the nearest tenth. Write an inference you can make about the two populations. (Examples 1 and 2)

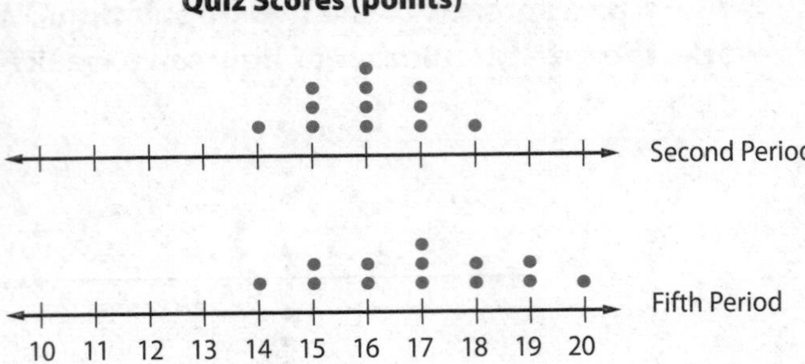

2. The double box plot shows the speeds of cars recorded on two different roads in Hamilton County. Compare the shapes, centers, and spreads of the two populations. On which road are the speeds greater? (Examples 3 and 4)

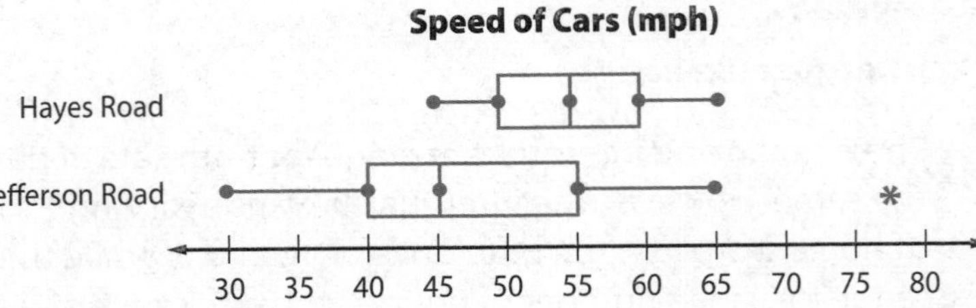

3. **Building on the Essential Question** Marcia recorded the daily temperatures for two cities for 30 days. The two populations have similar centers, but City A has a greater spread than City B. For which city can you more accurately predict the daily temperature? Explain.

Rate Yourself!

Are you ready to move on? Shade the section that applies.

YES ? NO

Find out online. Use the Self-Check Quiz.

Name ______________________ My Homework ______________

Independent Practice

7.12(A), 7.12(C), 7.1(A), 7.1(E) TEKS

1. Jordan randomly asked customers at two different restaurants how long they waited for a table before they were seated. The double box plot shows the results. Compare their shapes, centers, and spreads. Write an inference you can make about the two populations. (Examples 1 and 2)

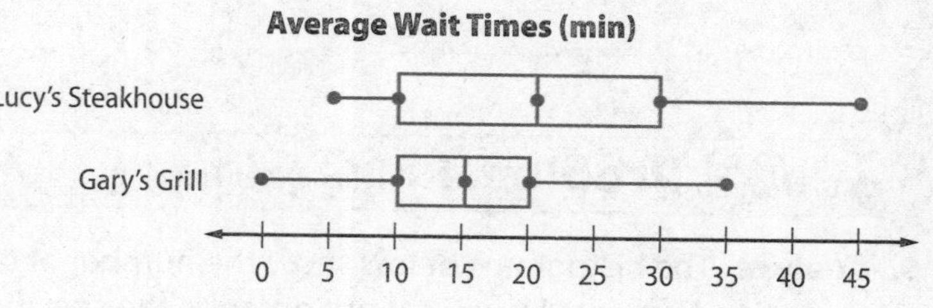

Show your work.

2. The double dot plot shows the times, in hours, for flights of two different airlines flying out of the same airport. Compare the shapes, centers, and spreads of the two populations. Which airline's flights had shorter flight times? (Examples 3 and 4)

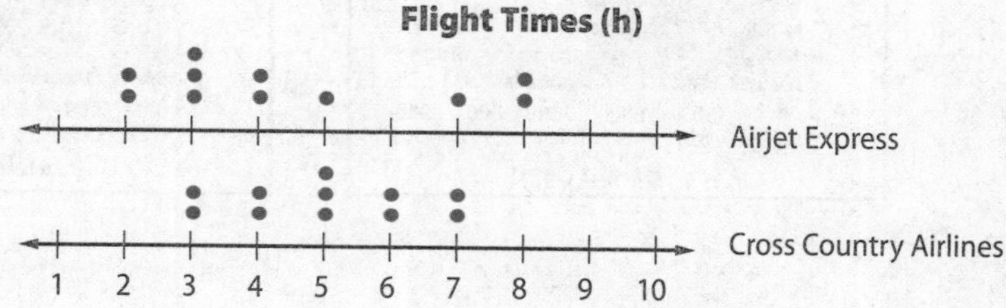

Copy and Solve **Write your answers for Exercise 3 on a separate piece of paper.**

3. MP **Use Multiple Representations** For a science project, Mackenzie is measuring the growth of two plants.

Weekly Plant Growth (cm)								
	Week 1	Week 2	Week 3	Week 4	Week 5	Week 6	Week 7	Week 8
Plant A	2	3	2	2.5	3.4	3	2.5	3
Plant B	3	2.5	3	3.4	3.2	3.8	3.5	2.5

a. **Numbers** Determine the median and interquartile range for both plants.

b. **Graphs** Graph the data using a double box plot.

c. **Words** Write an inference you can make about the two populations.

4. The median and interquartile range of a set of data is shown. Write a set of data consisting of seven values for the pair of measures.

Median: 6 Interquartile Range: 5

H.O.T. Problems Higher-Order Thinking

5. **Analyze** The histograms below show the number of tall buildings for two cities. Explain why you cannot describe the specific location of the centers and spreads of the histograms.

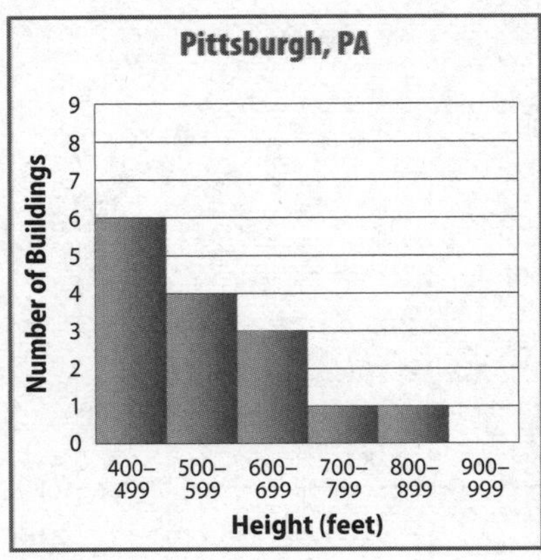

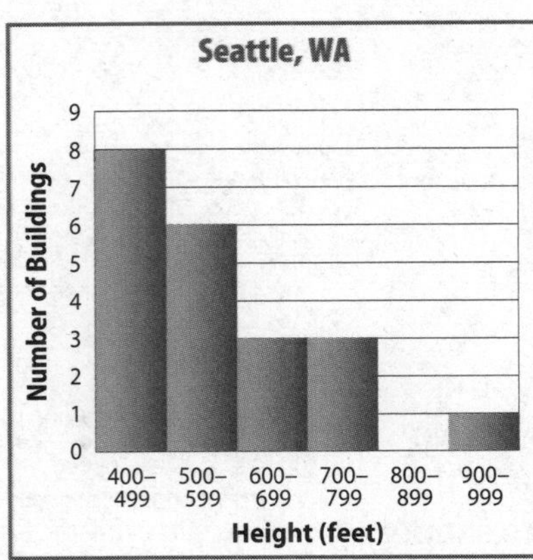

6. **Analyze** Refer to Exercise 1. What is a specific question you could ask about the two populations?

7. **Create** Design a random sample survey for two populations. Display the data in a double box plot or double dot plot. Then describe any comparative inferences about differences between the two populations.

8. **Analyze** Two hockey teams, the Warriors and the Bulldogs, played 15 games each during a month. Both scored a minimum of 0 goals and a maximum of 8 goals. The Bulldogs generally scored fewer goals than the Warriors. Draw a possible double box plot for the situation.

Name ____________________

Multi-Step Problem Solving

9. The double box plot shows the test scores for two different math classes. Use the information to determine which of the following inferences is *not* true. MD N MP

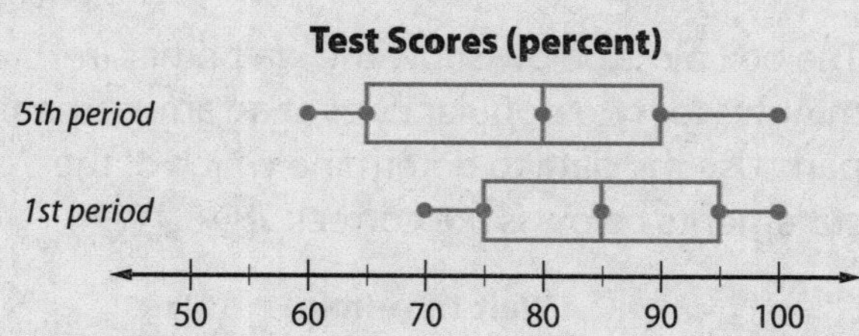

Ⓐ Only one of the data sets is symmetric.

Ⓑ The median test score in 1st period is greater than 5th period.

Ⓒ The highest test score is the same in both periods.

Ⓓ The interquartile range of 1st period is larger than 5th period.

Use a problem-solving model to solve this problem.

1 Analyze

Read the problem. Circle the information you know.
Underline what the problem is asking you to find.

2 Plan

What will you need to do to solve the problem? Write your plan in steps.

Step 1 Determine the ____________________ of the two scores.

Step 2 Determine which inference is ________.

3 Solve

Use your plan to solve the problem. Show your steps.

The 1st period is ____________, but the 5th period is ____________.

The median for 1st period is _____. The median for 5th period is _____.

Both periods have a high test score of _____.

The interquartile range for 1st period is _____, and it is _____ for 5th period.

So, the correct answer is _____. Fill in that answer choice.

4 Justify and Evaluate

How do you know your solution is accurate?

____

____

____

MD = Measurement and Data N = Number and Operations MP = Mathematical Processes

More Multi-Step Problem Solving

Use a problem-solving model to solve each problem.

10. The box plots below show the wait times in minutes for two popular rides at an amusement park. Use the data to determine which of the statements below is *not* correct. MD N MP

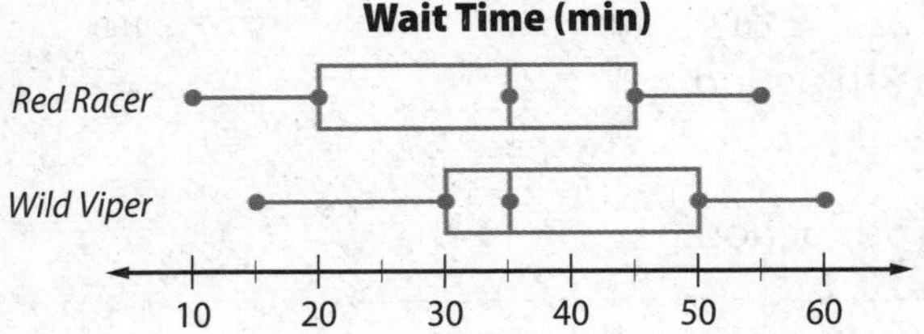

Ⓐ The median wait time for both rides is 35 minutes.

Ⓑ The Red Racer has a shorter maximum wait time than the Wild Viper.

Ⓒ The Wild Viper has a larger range of wait times than the Red Racer.

Ⓓ The Red Racer has a larger interquartile range than the Time Warp.

11. The double dot plot below shows the number of hours Kayla and Carmen studied during a two week period in college. Determine the most appropriate measure of variation for each data set. What is the difference between the centers? MD N MP

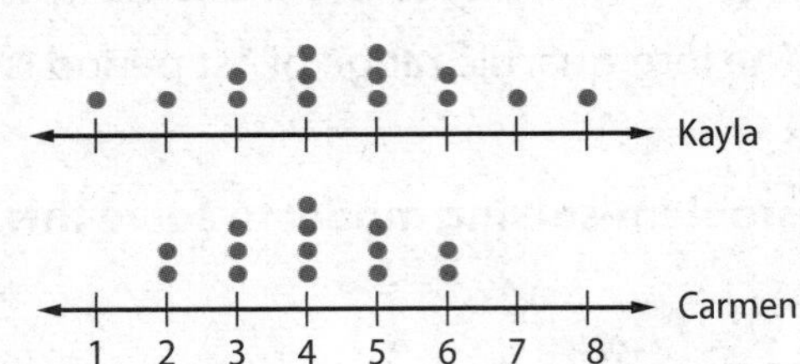

12. Juan works for an agricultural company and is studying the growth of two different types of corn. The table below shows the growth of each type of corn in inches for each month. Compare the shapes, centers, and spreads for both types of corn. Make an inference based on your findings. MD N MP

	Corn A	Corn B
1st month	20	28
2nd month	20	19
3rd month	26	15
4th month	18	7
5th month	13	26

MD = Measurement and Data N = Number and Operations MP = Mathematical Processes

Visual Overlap of Data Distributions

INQUIRY HOW can I analyze relationships to compare the visual overlap between two data distributions?

Texas Essential Knowledge and Skills

Targeted TEKS

7.12(C) Compare two populations based on data in random samples from these populations, including informal comparative inferences about differences between the two populations. *Also addresses 7.12(A).*

Mathematical Processes

7.1(A), 7.1(B), 7.1(E)

A survey was done. The tables below show the number of text messages sent and received daily for two different age groups.

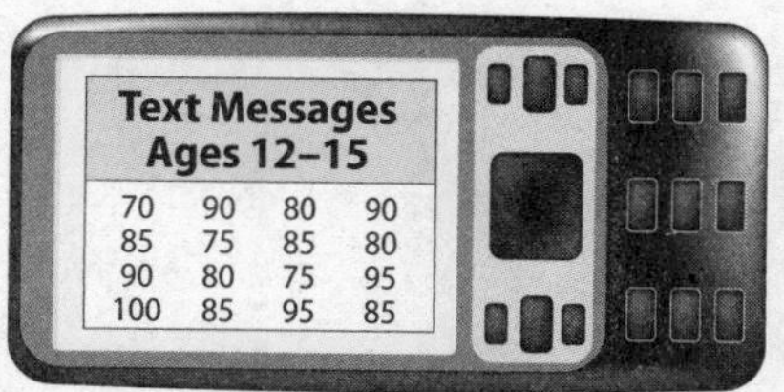

Text Messages Ages 12–15			
70	90	80	90
85	75	85	80
90	80	75	95
100	85	95	85

Text Messages Ages 16–19			
85	75	80	70
75	80	65	75
85	70	90	80
70	75	60	65

Hands-On Activity

You can compare two numerical data sets by comparing the shape of their distributions. The **visual overlap** of two distributions with similar variation is a visual demonstration that compares their centers to their variation, or spread.

Step 1 Use a double dot plot to display the data in each table.

Text Messages Sent and Received

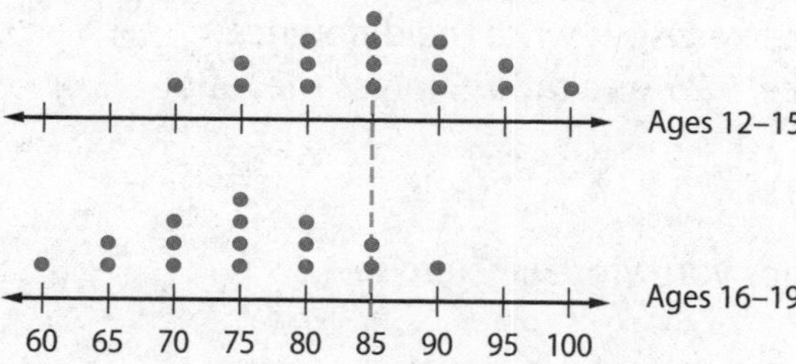

Step 2 Determine the mean number of text messages for each age group.

Ages 12–15 mean = ☐ **Ages 16–19 mean =** ☐

Step 3 A red dotted line has been drawn through both dot plots that corresponds to the mean for the age group, 12–15 years. Draw a vertical dotted line through both dot plots that corresponds to the mean for the age group, 16–19 years. The dotted lines show the visual overlap between the centers.

Investigate

Collaborate

Work with a partner. The double dot plot compares the number of text messages sent and received by a third age group to the age group, 12–15 years.

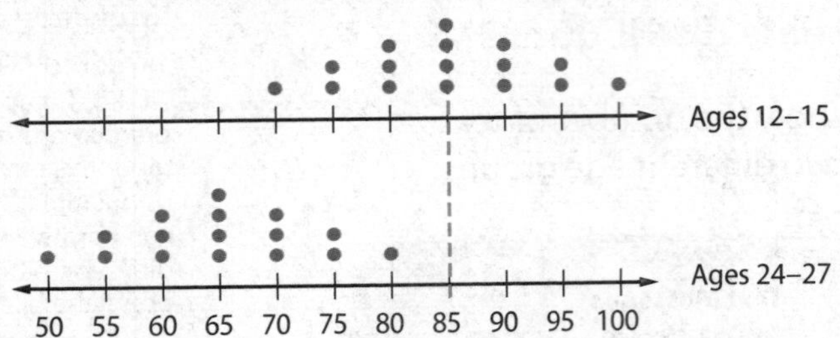

1. What is the mean number of texts for the age group, 24–27 years? ________

2. In the graph above, draw a vertical dotted line through both dot plots that corresponds to the mean for the age group, 24–27 years.

Analyze and Reflect

Collaborate

Work with a partner.

3. What is the difference between the means of the distributions for the Investigation? for Exercise 1? ________

4. The average distance between each data value and the mean of each distribution is 6.25 texts. For the Activity and Exercise 1, write the difference between the means and the average distance, 6.25, as a ratio. Express the ratio as a decimal. ________

5. **MP Analyze Relationships** Compare the ratios you wrote in Exercise 4.

____

____

Create

On Your Own

6. **INQUIRY** HOW can I analyze relationships to compare the visual overlap between two data distributions? ________

____

____

____

Lesson 7

Select an Appropriate Display

Launch the Lesson: Real World

There are many different types of graphs that are used to display all kinds of statistical data. List all of the types of graphs you can think of below.

____

____

Texas Essential Knowledge and Skills

Targeted TEKS

7.6(G) Solve problems using data represented in bar graphs, dot plots, and circle graphs, including part-to-whole and part-to-part comparisons and equivalents.

Mathematical Processes

7.1(A), 7.1(B), 7.1(C), 7.1(D)

Essential Question

HOW do you know which type of graph to use when displaying data?

The graphs below display the total number of pounds of plastic recycled each week during a ten-week period in different ways.

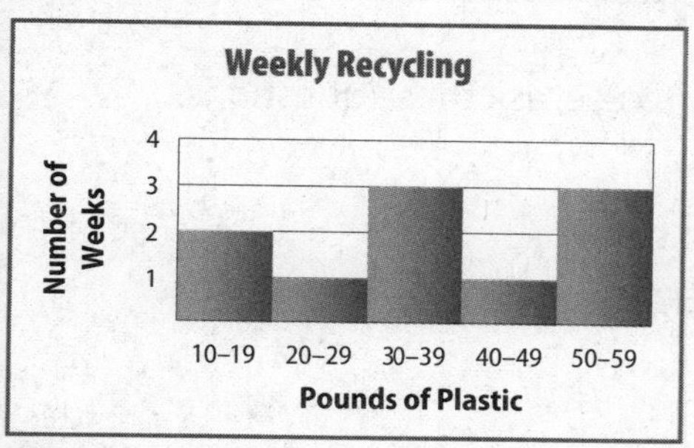

____

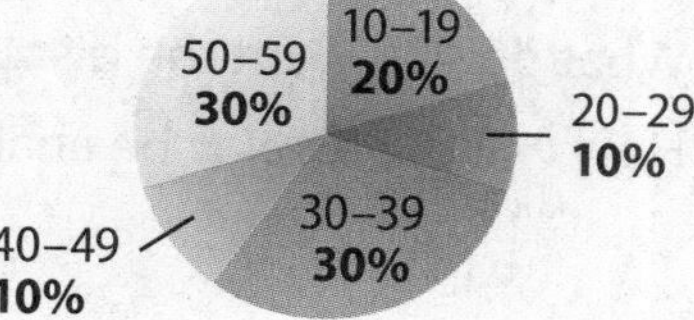

____

1. On the line below each graph, write the type of graph used.

2. Which display more easily shows the number of weeks the class collected between 30 and 39 pounds of plastic? _______________

3. Which display more easily shows the percent of time that 40 to 49 pounds of plastic was recycled? _______________

Which MP Mathematical Processes did you use? Shade the circle(s) that applies.

Ⓐ Apply Math to the Real World.
Ⓑ Use a Problem-Solving Model.
Ⓒ Select Tools and Techniques.
Ⓓ Use Multiple Representations.
Ⓔ Organize Ideas.
Ⓕ Analyze Relationships.
Ⓖ Justify Arguments.

Key Concept

Select an Appropriate Display

Type of Display	Best Used to...
Bar Graph	show the number of items in specific categories
Box Plot	show measures of variation for a set of data; also useful for very large sets of data
Circle Graph	compare parts of the data to the whole
Double Bar Graph	compare two sets of categorical data
Histogram	show frequency of data divided into equal intervals
Line Graph	show change over a period of time
Dot Plot	show frequency of data with a number line

Work Zone

Data Displays
Many situations have more than one appropriate display.

When deciding what type of display to use, ask these questions.

- What type of information is given?
- What do you want the display to show?
- How will the display be analyzed?

Example

1. Select an appropriate display to show the number of boys of different age ranges that participate in athletics.

Since the display will show an interval, a histogram like the one below would be an appropriate display to represent this data.

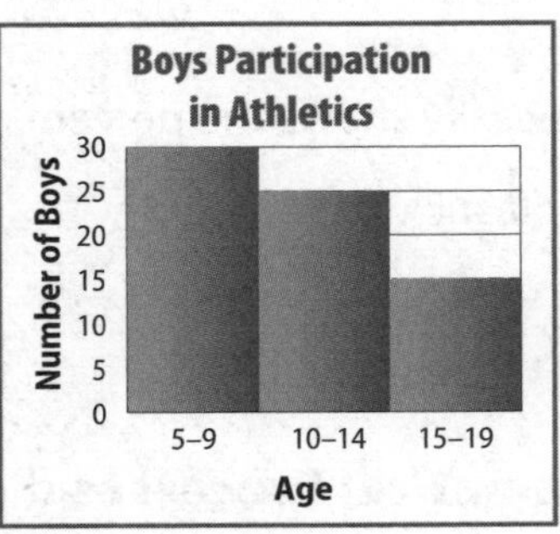

Got It? Do this problem to find out.

a. Select an appropriate display for the percent of students in each grade at a middle school.

a. ____________

Example

2. Select an appropriate type of display to compare the percent of ethanol production by state. Justify your reasoning. Then construct the display. If there were 13,608 million gallons of ethanol produced, how much more did Iowa produce than Nebraska?

Ethanol Production by State Per Year						
State	Iowa	Nebraska	Illinois	Minnesota	Indiana	Other
Percent of Total	26	12	8	8	8	38

You are asked to make a part-to-part comparison. A circle graph would be an appropriate display.

Ethanol Production by State

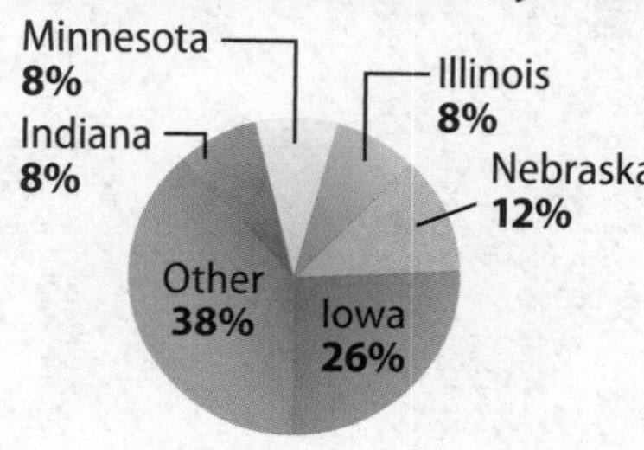

Iowa produces about $0.26 \times 13{,}608$ or 3,538 million gallons of ethanol.

Nebraska produces about $0.12 \times 13{,}608$ or 1,633 million gallons of ethanol.

So, Iowa produces about $3{,}538 - 1{,}633$ or 1,905 million gallons of ethanol more than Nebraska.

Got It? Do this problem to find out.

b. The table lists the ticket prices for school musicals during recent years. Select an appropriate display to predict the price of a ticket in 2013. Justify your reasoning. Then construct the display. What can you conclude from your display?

Ticket Prices	
Year	Price ($)
2009	5.00
2010	5.50
2011	6.50
2012	7.00

b. ______________

Guided Practice

Select an appropriate display for each situation. Justify your reasoning.
(Example 1)

1. the number of people who have different kinds of pets

2. the percent of different ways electricity is generated

3. The prices of sandwiches at a restaurant are \$4.50, \$5.59, \$3.99, \$2.50, \$4.99, \$3.75, \$2.99, \$3.29, and \$4.19. Select an appropriate display to determine how many sandwiches range from \$3.00 to \$3.99. Justify your reasoning. Then construct the display. Write a ratio that compares the number of sandwiches that are priced \$3.00 to \$3.99 to the number of sandwiches that are priced \$4.00 to \$4.99. Express this ratio as a fraction, decimal, and a percent. Then interpret the ratio's meaning. (Example 2)

Show your work.

4. A survey asked teens which subject they felt was most difficult. Of those who responded, 25 said English, 39 said social studies, 17 said science, and 19 said other subject. Construct an appropriate display of the data. Justify your reasoning. How many more total students were surveyed than prefer social studies? (Example 2)

5. **Building on the Essential Question** What are some of the factors to consider when selecting an appropriate display for a set of data?

Rate Yourself!

How confident are you about selecting an appropriate display? Shade the ring on the target.

I'm on target.

I need help.

Check

Find out online. Use the Self-Check Quiz.

Name ______________________ My Homework ______________________

Independent Practice

Select an appropriate display for each situation. Justify your reasoning. (Example 1)

1. the median age of members in a community band

Show your work.

2. the number of students that favor chocolate or vanilla as a frosting

3. Select an appropriate display for the data. Justify your reasoning. Then construct the display. What percent of the total number of push-ups are greater than 38? (Example 2)

Show your work.

Number of Push-ups			
45	35	42	37
44	40	36	42
45	40	42	39
44	43	36	39

4. MP **Apply Math to the Real World** Refer to the graphic novel frame below. What is the best type of display to use for this data? Explain.

5. Refer to the situations described below.

Situation A	Situation B
the number of customers ages 12–19 compared to all age groups	the number of customers ages 12, 13, 14, 15, and 16 who made a purchase

a. Which situation involves data that is best displayed in a bar graph?

Explain your reasoning. ______

b. Refer to the situation you selected in part **a**. Could you display the data using another type of display? If so, which display? Explain.

H.O.T. Problems Higher Order Thinking

6. **Create** Give an example of a data set that would be best represented in a circle graph. Graph the data, then make a part-to-part comparison.

7. **Analyze** Determine if the following statement is *always, sometimes,* or *never* true. Justify your response.

A circle graph can be used to display data from a bar graph.

8. **Analyze** Determine if the following statement is *true* or *false*. Explain your reasoning.

A dot plot can be used to display data from a histogram.

Name ________________________________

Multi-Step Problem Solving

9. The double bar graph shows the average January temperatures for 10 major U.S. cities. What percent of the cities have an average high temperature above 50°F?
P N MD MP

Ⓐ 20%

Ⓑ 35%

Ⓒ 60%

Ⓓ 66.7%

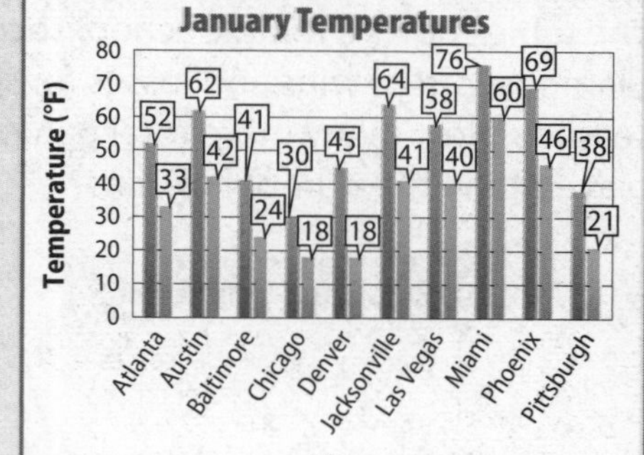

Use a problem-solving model to solve this problem.

1 Analyze

Read the problem. Circle the information you know.
Underline what the problem is asking you to find.

2 Plan

What will you need to do to solve the problem? Write your plan in steps.

Step 1 Determine the ________ of cities with an average high above 50°F.

Step 2 ________ the number of cities by the total number of cities.

3 Solve

Use your plan to solve the problem. Show your steps.

There are a total of _____ cities with an average high above 50°F.

Write the number of cities as a fraction over the total number of cities. Then express the fraction as a decimal and percent.

_____ or _____ = _____ or _____

So, _____ of the cities have an average high temperature above 50°F.

The correct answer is ___. Fill in that answer choice.

Read to Succeed!
Carefully check the data in the bar graph. The blue bar represents the average high and is greater than the average low represented in red.

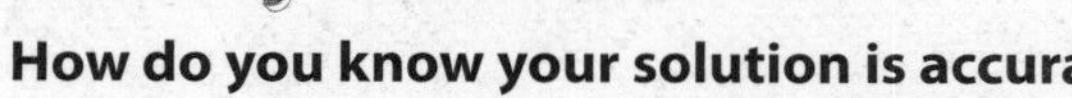

4 Justify and Evaluate

How do you know your solution is accurate?

____

____

____

P = Proportionality  N = Number and Operations  MD = Measurement and Data  MP = Mathematical Processes

More Multi-Step Problem Solving

Use a problem-solving model to solve each problem.

10. The table shows a middle school soccer team's record of wins and losses for seven seasons. How many more total games were played than the number of wins? P N MP

Boy's Soccer Team Record		
Year	**Wins**	**Losses**
1	8	5
2	9	7
3	11	2
4	10	4
5	10	3
6	8	6
7	13	1

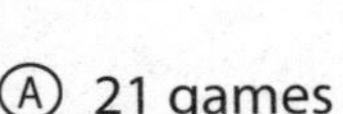

Ⓐ 21 games
Ⓑ 28 games
Ⓒ 33 games
Ⓓ 41 games

11. The circle graph shows the results of 1,132 participants in a local race. About how many more participants finished in 20–24 minutes compared to those who finished in 30 minutes or greater? P N MP

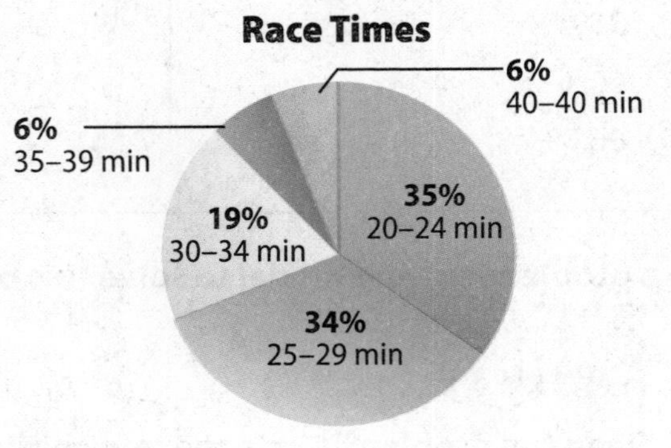

12. The data shows the test scores for two different math classes. The teacher of these classes would like to compare the two sets of scores to determine which class, overall, performed better on the exam. What type of display should the teacher use? Justify your reasoning. P MP

Class A

87	92	81	79
95	83	75	92
88	77	66	80

Class B

91	85	70	73
97	81	62	69
98	79	82	99

P = Proportionality N = Number and Operations MP = Mathematical Processes

21ST CENTURY CAREER

Market Research Analyst

Do you think that gathering and analyzing information about people's opinions, tastes, likes, and dislikes sounds interesting? If so, then you should consider a career in market research. Market research analysts help companies understand what types of products and services consumers want. They design Internet, telephone, or mail response surveys and then analyze the data, identify trends, and present their conclusions and recommendations. Market research analysts must be analytical, creative problem-solvers, have strong backgrounds in mathematics, and have good written and verbal communication skills.

Mathematical Process
7.1(A) Apply mathematics to problems arising in everyday life, society, and the workplace.

Targeted TEKS 7.6(F)

Is This the Career for You?

Are you interested in a career as a market research analyst? Take some of the following courses in high school.

- Algebra
- Calculus
- Computer Science
- English
- Statistics

Explore college and careers at ccr.mcgraw-hill.com

Keeping Your Eye on the Target Market!

Use the results of the survey in the table below to solve each problem.

1. At Hastings Middle School, 560 of the students use social networking sites. Predict how many of them use the sites to make plans with friends. ________

2. Suppose 17.9 million teens use online social networks. Predict how many will be using the sites to make new friends.

____

3. According to the survey, what percent of a teen's networking site friends are people they regularly see? ________

4. Landon randomly selects a friend from his social networking site. What is the probability that it is someone he never sees in person?

   Express as a percent. ________

5. Paris wants to compare the types of friends on social networking sites. Select an appropriate display for the situation. Justify your reasoning.

____

Survey Results: Teens and Social Networking	
Reason to Use Social Networks	**Percent of Respondents**
Stay in touch with friends	91%
Make plans with friends	72%
Make new friends	49%
Friends on Social Networking Sites	**Average Number**
People who are regularly seen	43
People who are occasionally seen	23
People who are never seen in person	33
Total	99

Career Project

It's time to update your career portfolio! Use the Internet or another source to research a career as a market research analyst. Write and prepare a brief oral presentation to your classmates that summarizes your findings. At the end, ask any clarifying questions.

What skills would you need to improve to succeed in this career?

-
-
-
-
-

Chapter Review

Vocabulary Check

Work with a partner to complete the crossword puzzle using the vocabulary list at the beginning of the chapter. Take turns reading each sentence aloud while the other student listens carefully.

Across

2. sample involving only those who want to participate (two words)
5. the group being studied
8. sample in which members of a population are easily accessed
9. part of a group
10. sample in which one or more parts of the population are favored over other parts

Down

1. random sample in which items are selected according to a specific time or interval
3. random sample in which each item is as likely to be chosen as any other item
4. a method of collecting information
6. two box plots on the same number line
7. sample that represents the entire population

Key Concept Check

Use Your FOLDABLES

Use your Foldable to help review the chapter, while the other partner listens carefully. Ask for and give help of any concept if needed. TEKS 7.1(E)

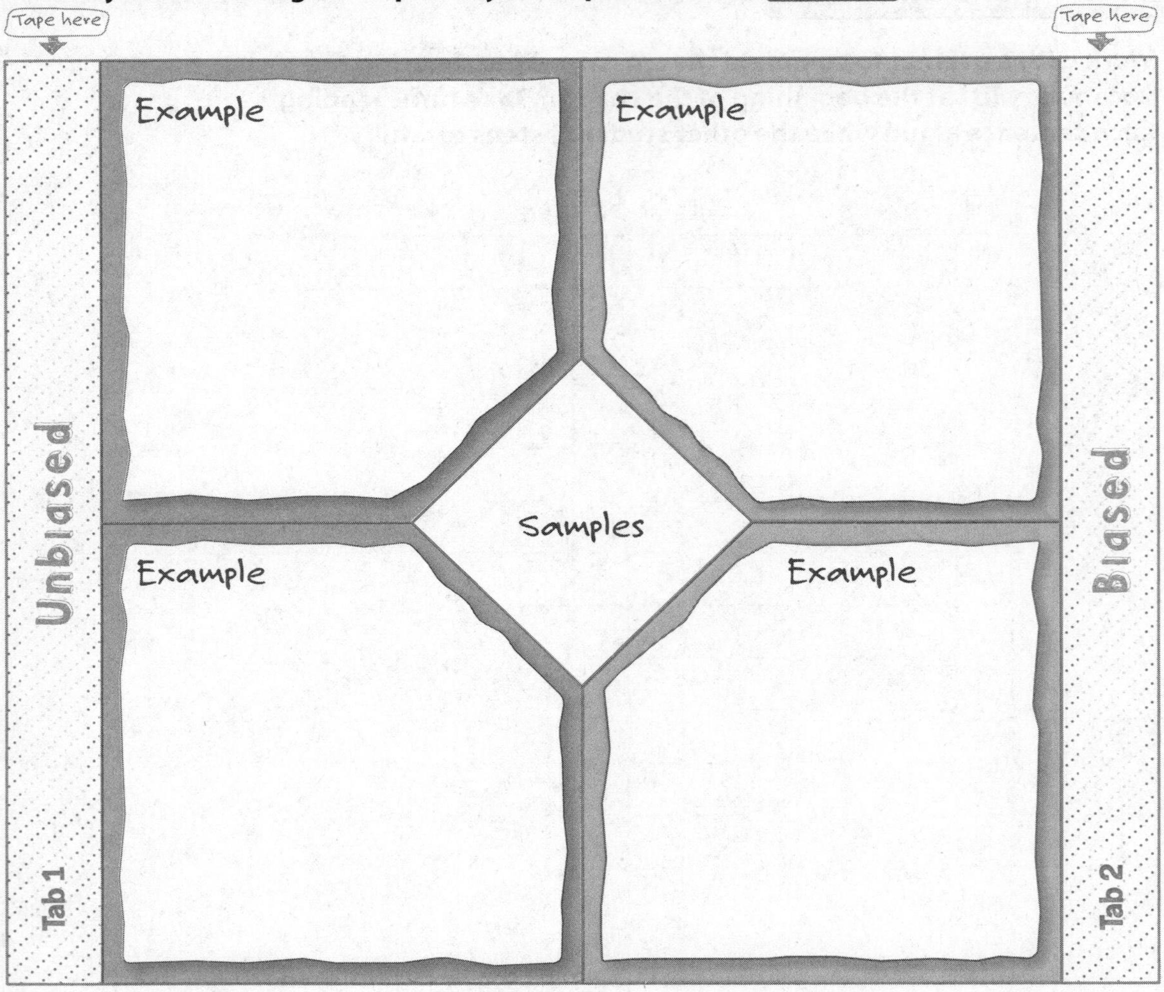

Tape here

Tape here

Unbiased

Example

Example

Samples

Example

Example

Biased

Tab 1

Tab 2

Got it?

Match each phrase with the correct term. 

1. a method of collecting information
2. the group being studied
3. when one or more parts of the population is favored
4. a sample that involves only those who want to participate

a. voluntary response sample
b. biased sample
c. survey
d. population
e. convenience sample

Multi-Step Problem Solving

5. The circle graph shows the results of a survey about the theme for the school dance. If 500 additional students were surveyed, how many students would you expect to *not* vote for Under the Sea and Travel the World? Justify your solution. P MD MP

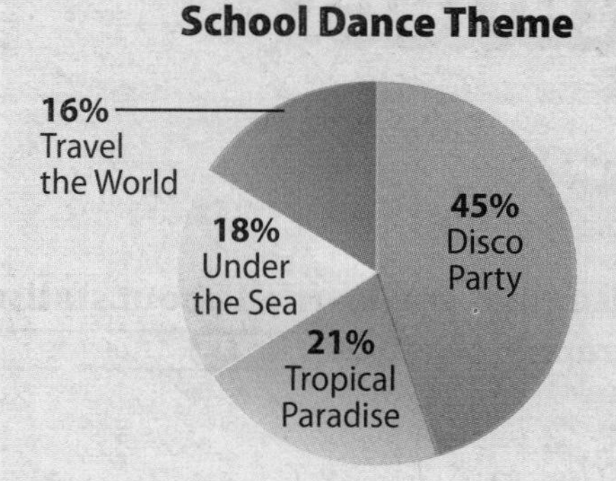

1 Analyze

2 Plan

3 Solve

4 Justify and Evaluate

Got it?

6. The double dot plot shows the number of points two teams have scored for the first five games of a basketball season. What number of points does each team need to score in game 6 in order to have an average of scoring 60 points per game? Justify your solution. P MD MP

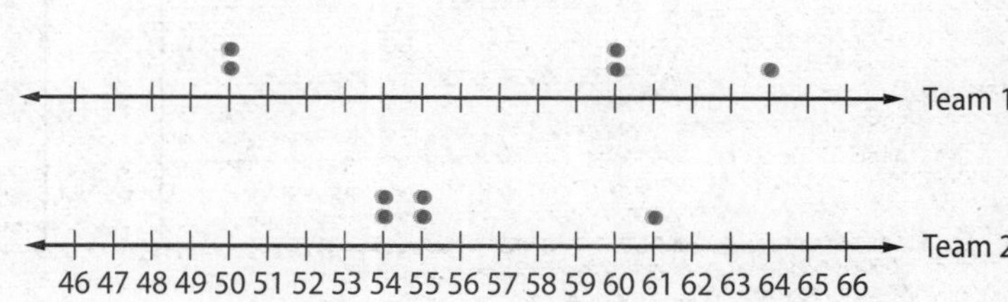

P = Proportionality MD = Measurement and Data MP = Mathematical Processes

Reflect

Answering the Essential Question

Use what you learned about statistics to complete the graphic organizer. TEKS 7.1(D), 7.1(F), 7.1(G)

Bar Graph

Line Graph

Essential Question

How do you know which type of graph to use when displaying data?

Double Dot Plot

Double Box Plot

Answer the Essential Question. HOW do you know which type of graph to use when displaying data? Verbally share your response with a partner, asking for and giving help if needed.

Chapter 10
Personal Financial Literacy

Texas Essential Knowledge and Skills

Targeted TEKS

7.13 The student applies mathematical process standards to develop an economic way of thinking and problem solving useful in one's life as a knowledgeable consumer and investor.

Mathematical Processes

7.1, 7.1(A), 7.1(B), 7.1(C), 7.1(D), 7.1(E), 7.1(F), 7.1(G)

Essential Question

HOW can I become a knowledgeable consumer and investor?

Math in the Real World

Careers Look up the salary of a career you might like to pursue. Suppose you save 10% of this salary each year, beginning at age 25. Complete the table to show the amount saved each year until you are 65 years old. How much will you have saved altogether? Assume no additional deposits or withdrawals and assume your salary remained constant.

Age (years)	Amount Saved ($)
25	
30	
35	
40	
45	
50	
55	
60	
65	

Go Online!
www.connectED.mcgraw-hill.com

Watch  Worksheets  Vocab  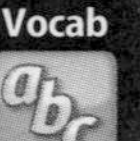 Tutor  Tools  Check 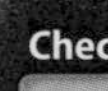

What Tools Do You Need?

Vocab abc

Vocabulary

assets
budget
compound interest
coupon
expenses
family budget
fixed expenses
income
income tax
liabilities
monetary incentives
net worth
personal budget
rebate
sales tax
simple interest
variable expenses
wages

Review Vocabulary

Interest *Interest* is a fee paid by the borrower to the owner, or lender, as a form of compensation for the use of what is being borrowed. Interest rates are usually written as a percent. As a consumer, you can *earn* interest and you can also *pay* interest. Complete the graphic organizer below by listing some examples of situations in which you would earn and/or pay interest.

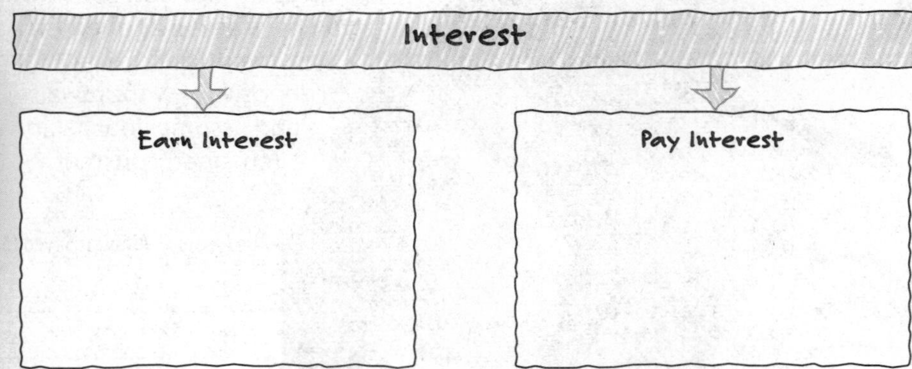

When Will You Use This?

Dario and Caitlyn in

Shoe Dilemma

I need a new pair of sneakers--which costs $44.

I want to buy a new pair of boots for $35.

LOOK! They're having a sale!

40%
OFF SINGLE-ITEM PURCHASE
MUST BUY EACH ITEM SEPARATELY.
CANNOT BE COMBINED WITH ANY OTHER COUPON.

I also have a "Buy One, Get One $\frac{1}{2}$ Off" coupon.

COUPON BUY ONE GET ONE 1/2 OFF!

But the coupon says that we'll have to pay full price on the most expensive item!

If we use the coupon, we can split the cost 50/50!

Should we use the coupon or the sale price?

40%
OFF SINGLE-ITEM PURCHASE
MUST BUY EACH ITEM SEPARATELY.
CANNOT BE COMBINED WITH ANY OTHER COUPON.

Your Turn! **You will solve this problem in the chapter.**

Are You Ready?

Quick Review

Example 1

Express 4% as an equivalent decimal.

$4\% = \frac{4}{100}$ Definition of percent

$= 0.04$ Divide 4 by 100.

So, $4\% = 0.04$.

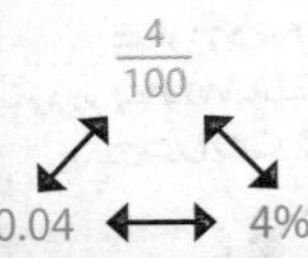

Example 2

Express each fraction as an equivalent percent.

$\frac{2{,}016}{33{,}600} = 0.06$ Divide 2,016 by 33,600.

$= 6\%$ Definition of percent

So, $\frac{2{,}016}{33{,}600} = 6\%$.

Quick Check

Express each percent as an equivalent decimal.

1. $22\% =$ ________

2. $5\% =$ ________

3. $79\% =$ ________

4. $3\% =$ ________

Express each fraction as an equivalent percent.

5. $\frac{3{,}858}{12{,}860} =$ ________

6. $\frac{50}{1{,}250} =$ ________

7. $\frac{4{,}032}{44{,}800} =$ ________

8. $\frac{1{,}496}{6{,}800} =$ ________

How Did You Do?

Which problems did you answer correctly in the Quick Check? Shade those exercise numbers below.

① ② ③ ④ ⑤ ⑥ ⑦ ⑧

Lesson 1
Sales and Income Tax

Launch the Lesson: Real World

Sales tax is a tax calculated as a percentage of the cost of a good or service. Sales tax in Texas is currently 6.25%. The table shows several items that Yolanda spent for her dog.

Item	Cost ($)
leash	15.00
treats	6.50
brush	8.50

1. Is $10 a reasonable estimate for the amount of sales tax? Explain.

2. Is $5 a reasonable estimate for the amount of sales tax? Explain.

3. Is $2 a reasonable estimate for the amount of sales tax? Explain.

4. How could you calculate the exact amount of sales tax?

Which MP **Mathematical Processes** did you use?
Shade the circle(s) that applies.

Ⓐ Apply Math to the Real World.
Ⓑ Use a Problem-Solving Model.
Ⓒ Select Tools and Techniques.
Ⓓ Use Multiple Representations.
Ⓔ Organize Ideas.
Ⓕ Analyze Relationships.
Ⓖ Justify Arguments.

Texas Essential Knowledge and Skills

Targeted TEKS
7.13(A) Calculate the sales tax for a given purchase and calculate income tax for earned wages.

Mathematical Processes
7.1(A), 7.1(B), 7.1(E), 7.1(F)

Vocab

Vocabulary
sales tax
income
income tax
wages

Essential Question
HOW can I become a knowledgeable consumer and investor?

Work Zone

Calculate Sales and Income Tax

To calculate the sales tax of a given purchase, express the sales tax rate as a decimal, then multiply by the amount of the purchase.

Income is a financial gain from capital or labor. Payments for labor or services are called **wages**. **Income tax** is a tax on the net income of an individual or a business. Federal withholding tax is one type of income tax. To calculate the income tax for earned wages, express the income tax rate as a decimal, then multiply by the amount of the earned wages.

Calculating the Total Purchase Amount

To calculate the total purchase, you could also add the sales tax to 100% and multiply $120 by 106.25%. This eliminates the added step of calculating the amount of sales tax first. Read each problem carefully. If you are not asked for the amount of the sales tax, you could omit that step.

Tutor

Multi-Step Example

1. **Calculate the sales tax and the total cost, including 6.25% sales tax, of a $120.00 costume.**

Step 1 Calculate the amount of the sales tax.

6.25% of $120.00 = 0.0625 × $120.00 — Express 6.25% as 0.0625.

= $7.50 — Multiply.

Step 2 Add the sales tax to the cost of the purchase.

$120.00 + $7.50 = $127.50

So, including sales tax of $7.50, the costume costs $127.50.

Example

2. **Calculate the income tax for Morgan's pay stub shown. Round to the nearest cent.**

Morgan Davis 82 E. Beaumont Road Startown, Texas 77777	
Gross Pay (wages)	$2,135.28
Medicare	$21.05
Social Security	$60.98
Federal Withholding Income Tax (15%)	$______

15% of $2,135.28 = 0.15 × $2,135.28

= $320.29

So, the income tax is $320.29.

Show your work.

Got It? Do these problems to find out.

Calculate the sales tax and the total cost, including sales tax, of each given purchase.

a. 6.5% sales tax on a $20 ticket **b.** 7% sales tax on a $160 bike

c. Calculate a 15% income tax on wages of $1,410. Round to the nearest cent.

a. ________

b. ________

c. ________

Name ______________________ My Homework ______________________

Independent Practice

7.13(A), 7.4(D), 7.1(A) TEKS

Calculate the sales tax for each given purchase. Then calculate the total cost. Round to the nearest cent, if necessary. (Example 1)

1. 7% sales tax on a $156.00 camera

sales tax:

total cost:

2. 6.25% sales tax on a $875.00 television

sales tax:

total cost:

3. 6% sales tax on a $129.99 coat

sales tax:

total cost:

4. 5.75% sales tax on a $12.95 book

sales tax:

total cost:

5. 5.25% sales tax on a $38.20 theater tickets

sales tax:

total cost:

6. 7.5% sales tax on a $42.65 jacket

sales tax:

total cost:

For Exercises 7 and 8, calculate each income tax for Cedric's pay stub shown. Round to the nearest cent. (Example 2)

CEDRIC JOHNSON 4368 RIDGEPATH DRIVE STARTOWN, TEXAS 77777	
Gross Pay (wages)	$2,195.00
Medicare	$31.82
Social Security	$______
Federal Withholding Income Tax (15%)	$______

7. 4.2% Social Security tax ______

8. 15% Federal Withholding income tax ______

9. Cedric's *net pay* is his take-home pay after medicare, social security tax, and federal income taxes are paid. Calculate Cedric's net pay. ______

10. What percent of Cedric's gross pay is his net pay? Round to the nearest tenth of a percent. ______

11. Cedric received a 10% pay raise, but still paid the same amount for Medicare. Calculate the amount of Social Security tax and Federal Withholding income tax, using the percents from Exercises 7 and 8. Round to the nearest cent.

______

Multi-Step Problem Solving

Use a problem-solving model to solve each problem.

12. James is visiting a state where the sales tax rate is 5%. He bought a travel guide that cost $22. What is the total cost of the travel guide? FL P MP

Ⓐ $1.10

Ⓑ $33.00

Ⓒ $22.00

Ⓓ $23.10

13. Felisa worked at the library for three months. She earned $4,500.00 and must pay a total of 15% in taxes, which includes federal withholding, Medicare, and Social Security taxes. What is her net pay? FL P MP

Ⓐ $3,825.00

Ⓑ $3,875.00

Ⓒ $4,825.00

Ⓓ $5,175.00

FL = Personal Financial Literacy 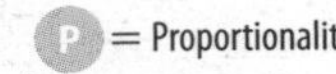

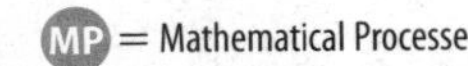

FL Personal Financial Literacy Project

Sales Tax Imagine that the citizens of your city are voting to decide whether to raise the city sales tax by 1% to fund the library system. Determine how much this will affect you. Make a list of all of the items you buy in a week, and calculate the sales tax you would contribute based on this change. Determine how many students are in your school. If everyone would pay the same additional tax as you, how much more would the library receive from the students receive from your school alone?

TEKS 7.13(A), 7.1(B)

Lesson 2

Personal and Family Budgets

Launch the Lesson: Real World

The Lorenzo family is building their **budget**, which is a plan for spending. The circle graph shows their total income after taxes are deducted, and their monthly spending, or **expenses**. Knowing both income and expenses is necessary to build their family plan for spending, or **family budget**.

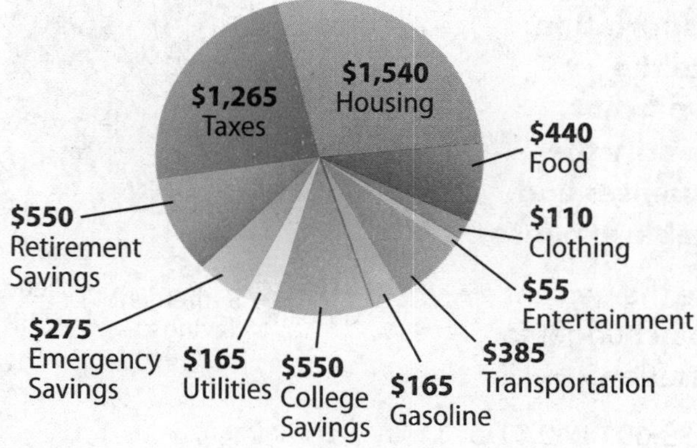

1. Determine the total of all budgeted expenses. ____________

2. What percent, of the total budget, is for college savings? for food?

____

3. If each parent worked 160 hours during the month, and earned a total of $35 per hour, would their income be less than, equal to, or greater than their budgeted expenses? Explain.

____

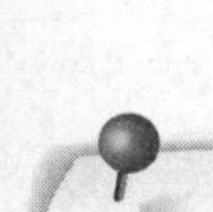

Which MP Mathematical Processes did you use? Shade the circle(s) that applies.

Ⓐ Apply Math to the Real World.
Ⓑ Use a Problem-Solving Model.
Ⓒ Select Tools and Techniques.
Ⓓ Use Multiple Representations.
Ⓔ Organize Ideas.
Ⓕ Analyze Relationships.
Ⓖ Justify Arguments.

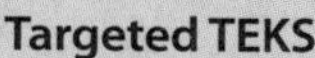

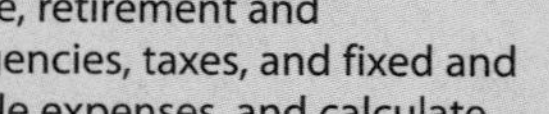

Texas Essential Knowledge and Skills

Targeted TEKS

7.13(B) Identify the components of a personal budget, including income, planned savings for college, retirement and emergencies, taxes, and fixed and variable expenses, and calculate what the percentage of each category comprises of the total budget. *Also addresses 7.13(D).*

Mathematical Processes

7.1(A), 7.1(B), 7.1(F), 7.1(G)

Vocab

Vocabulary

budget
personal budget
family budget
expenses
fixed expenses
variable expenses

Essential Question

HOW can I become a knowledgeable consumer and investor?

Work Zone

Build Personal and Family Budgets

Your **personal budget** is a plan for your own spending. **Fixed expenses** are costs that do not change based on the amount you use, while **variable expenses** do change based on the amount you use.

Tutor

Example

1. The components of Zac's personal monthly budget are shown. Calculate the percent of the total budget for transportation. Round to the nearest percent. Then identify the fixed expenses and the variable expenses.

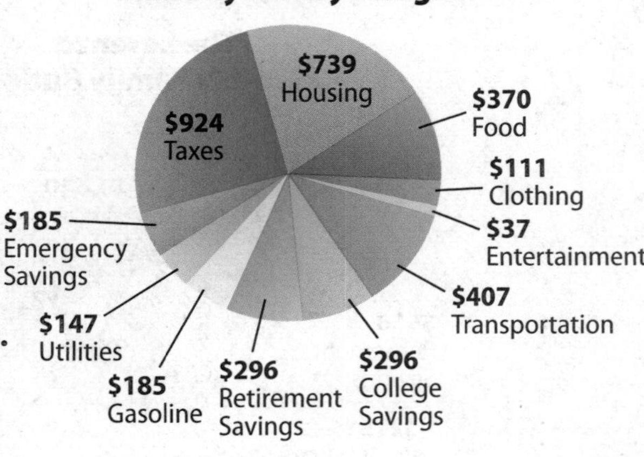

Calculate the percent of the total budget for transportation.

$\$407 \div \$3,697 \approx 0.11$ or 11%   Divide $407 by the total expenses, $3,697.

The fixed expenses are housing, transportation, college savings, utilities, emergency savings, retirement savings, and taxes. The variable expenses are food, clothing, gasoline, and entertainment.

Tutor

Example

2. The Lorenzo family budget is shown on page 791. Use a family budget estimator to determine the minimum household budget and average hourly wage for one working parent to meet the budget. Assume the parent works 160 hours in one month.

The minimum household budget is the sum of the expenses, $5,500.

Determine the average hourly wage rounded to the nearest cent.

$\$5,500 \div 160 = \$34.375$ Divide the expenses by the number of hours worked.

The minimum household wage for one working parent is $34.38.

Percent

After you round expense percents to the nearest 1%, your total budget percentage might fall above or below 100%.

Got It? Do this problem to find out.

a. Refer to Example 1. Calculate the percent of Zac's total budget for college savings. Round to the nearest percent.

a. ____________

Name ______________________ My Homework ______________________

Independent Practice

For Exercises 1–7, refer to Anna's personal monthly budget. (Example 1)

1. Identify the components of her budget. ______________________

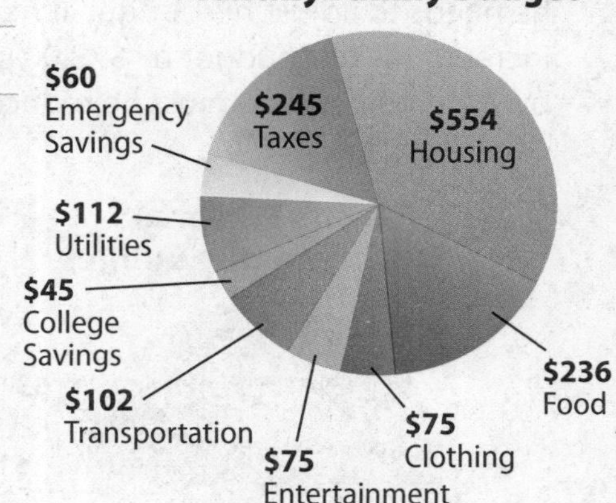

2. Calculate the percent of her budget for housing. Round to the nearest percent. __________
3. Calculate the percent of her budget for taxes. Round to the nearest percent. __________
4. Which two categories are the same percent of her overall budget? ______________________
5. Identify the fixed expenses and the variable expenses. ______________________
6. What percent of Anna's budget is for variable expenses? ______________________
7. If Anna needed to reduce her monthly budget, which expenses would most likely be easier to adjust? ______________________

For Exercises 8–11, refer to the Martin family monthly budget. (Example 2)

8. Determine the minimum household budget. __________

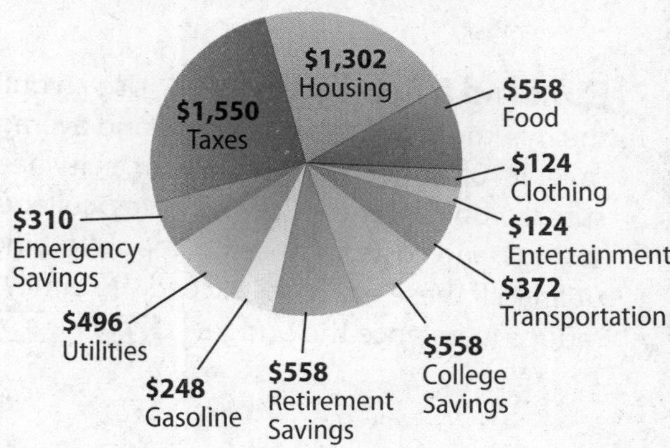

9. Determine the average hourly wage for one working parent to meet the budget. Assume the parent works 160 hours in one month. __________
10. Determine the average hourly wage for one working parent to meet the budget. Assume the parent works 170 hours in one month. Round to the nearest cent. __________
11. Determine the average hourly wage for each of two working parents to meet the budget. Assume each parent works 160 hours in one month and is paid at the same hourly rate. __________

Multi-Step Problem Solving

Use a problem-solving model to solve each problem.

12. Zac will spend $185.00, or 5%, of his budget on gasoline. Gas prices have increased, and he needs to adjust his budget. If he needs to increase his gas budget by $78.00 per month, by what percentage must he reduce his other expenses? FL P MP

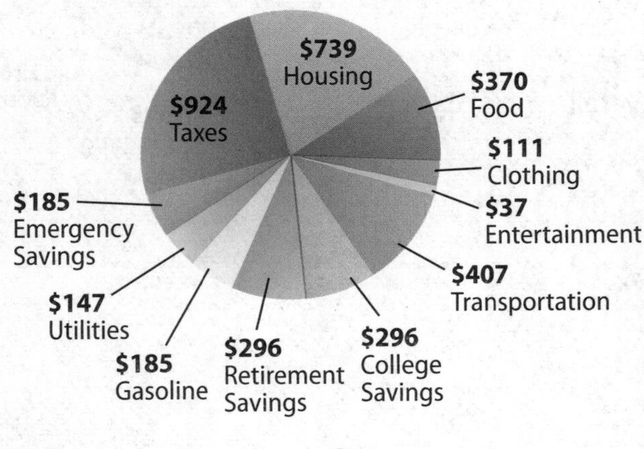

Ⓐ 7%
Ⓑ 2%
Ⓒ 5%
Ⓓ 12%

13. Mr. Martin will spend 9% of his budget, or $558.00, on college savings. His son received a scholarship, so Mr. Martin decided to put one-third of the college savings budget towards his emergency fund. What is his new monthly emergency fund expense? FL P MP

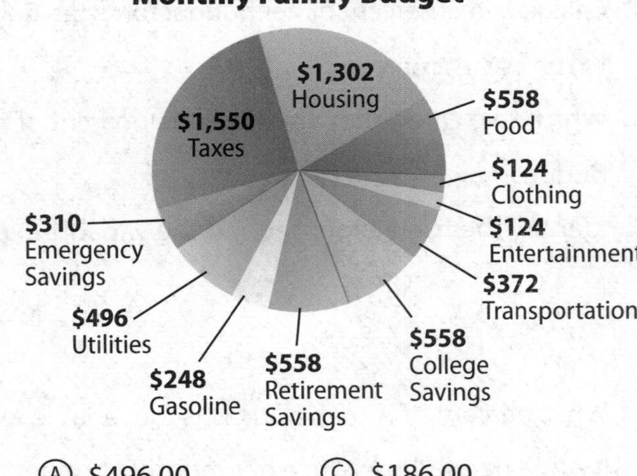

Ⓐ $496.00
Ⓑ $682.00
Ⓒ $186.00
Ⓓ $372.00

FL = Personal Financial Literacy P = Proportionality MP = Mathematical Processes

FL Personal Financial Literacy Project

Building a Family Budget Use an online family budget estimator to determine the minimum household budget and average hourly wage needed for a family to meet its basic needs in your city or a city near your home. To build a family budget, be sure to consider the following: taxes, college savings, retirement savings, emergency savings, and costs for housing, food, clothing, transportation, entertainment, and utilities. If these expenses exceed the family's income, which expenses could you reduce to balance the budget? TEKS 7.13(B), 7.13(D), 7.1(B)

Lesson 3

Assets and Liabilities

Launch the Lesson: Vocabulary

Assets are the things you own. **Liabilities** are the debts you owe. Your **net worth** is the value of assets minus liabilities.

Use the terms *net worth*, assets, and *liabilities* to label the graphic organizer.

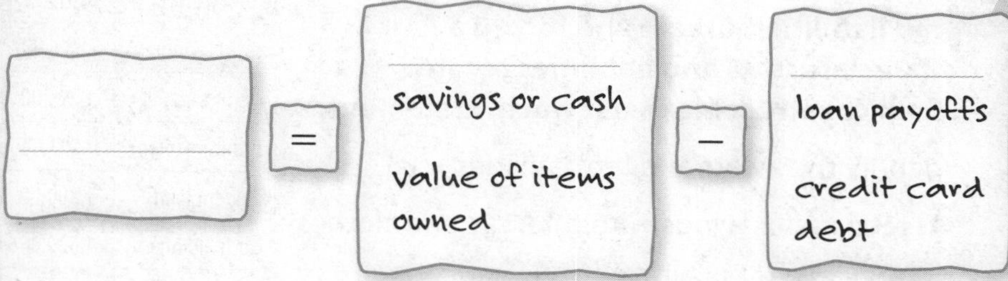

1. The value of items that you own are considered assets. List some of these assets. ______________________

2. Debts and loans are considered liabilities. List some examples of debts or loans. ______________________

Real-World Link

David has assets totaling $2,998.87 and liabilities of $898.37. Write a subtraction sentence to determine his net worth.

____

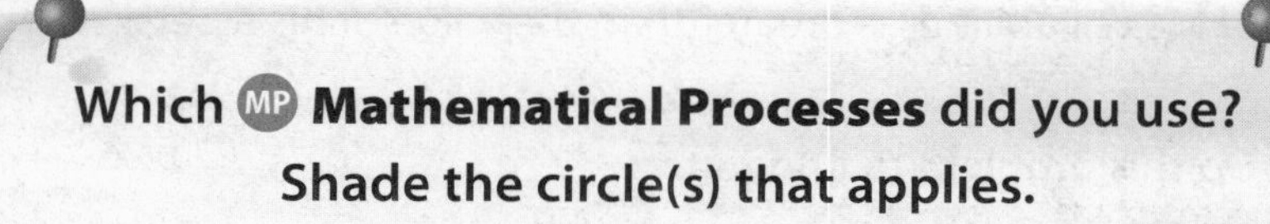

Which MP Mathematical Processes did you use? Shade the circle(s) that applies.

Ⓐ Apply Math to the Real World.
Ⓑ Use a Problem-Solving Model.
Ⓒ Select Tools and Techniques.
Ⓓ Use Multiple Representations.
Ⓔ Organize Ideas.
Ⓕ Analyze Relationships.
Ⓖ Justify Arguments.

Texas Essential Knowledge and Skills

Targeted TEKS
7.13(C) Create and organize a financial assets and liabilities record and construct a net worth statement.

Mathematical Processes
7.1(A), 7.1(B), 7.1(F)

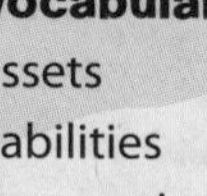

Vocabulary
assets
liabilities
net worth

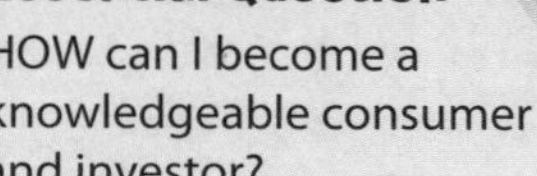

Essential Question
HOW can I become a knowledgeable consumer and investor?

Work Zone

Determine Assets, Liabilities, and Net Worth

You can create and organize a financial assets and liabilities record to construct a net worth statement. Net worth is equal to the value of the assets minus the value of the liabilities.

net worth = assets − liabilities

Example

Net Worth

A positive net worth indicates that the value of your assets is greater than the value of your liabilities. A negative net worth indicates that the value of your liabilities is greater than the value of your assets.

1. The table shows some of Max's assets and liabilities. Create and record a financial assets and liabilities record. Then construct Max's net worth statement.

Item	Value ($)
cash/savings	376.00
credit card debt	1,295.00
furniture (own)	207.00
student loan	1,800.00
car (paid off)	1,500.00
clothes	875.00

Identify the assets and the liabilities.

Assets: cash/savings, furniture, car, and clothes

Liabilities: credit card debt, student loan

Create and organize a financial assets and liabilities record. Organize the assets in one column and the liabilities in another column.

Assets	Value ($)	Liabilities	Value ($)
cash/savings	376.00	credit card debt	1,295.00
furniture (owned)	207.00	student loan	1,800.00
car (paid off)	1,500.00		
clothes	875.00		

Determine the total value of the assets and liabilities.

Assets: $376.00 + $207.00 + $1,500.00 + $875.00 = $2,958

Liabilities: $1,295.00 + $1,800.00 = $3,095

Construct the net worth statement.

$2,958 (assets) − $3,095 (liabilities) = −$137 (net worth)
Max's net worth is −$137. A negative net worth means that the value of Max's liabilities is greater than the value of his assets.

Got It? Do this problem to find out.

a. The table shows several of Jacinta's assets and liabilities. Construct Jacinta's net worth statement.

Item	cash	car (paid off)	credit card debt	motorcycle payoff	savings
Value ($)	395.52	2,500.00	672.98	1,125.00	3,120.00

a. ______

Name ______________________ My Homework ______________________

Independent Practice

7.13(C), 7.1(A) TEKS

For Exercises 1–3, refer to the table that shows several of Jordan's assets and liabilities.

Item	Value ($)
house (owned)	42,365.00
car payoff	980.00
boat payoff	2,200.00
credit card debt	3,298.00
savings	1,255.00
cash	355.00
student loan	1,500.00

1. Complete the table to record a financial assets and liabilities record. (Example 1)

Assets	Value ($)	Liabilities	Value ($)

2. Construct Jordan's net worth statement. (Example 1)

____

3. Interpret Jordan's net worth statement.

____

____

For Exercises 4–7, refer to the table that shows several of Mei-Ling's assets and liabilities.

Item	Value ($)
house payoff	32,695.00
car (paid off)	7,000.00
cash	728.65
savings	3,415.00
borrowed from parents	2,680.00
credit card debt	1,207.80
jewelry (owned)	900.00

4. Complete the table to record a financial assets and liabilities record. (Example 1)

Assets	Value ($)	Liabilities	Value ($)

5. Construct Mei-Ling's net worth statement. (Example 1)

____

6. Interpret Mei-Ling's net worth statement.

____

____

7. If Mei-Ling paid off her credit card debt and the money she owed her parents, what would be her new net worth?

____

Multi-Step Problem Solving

Use a problem-solving model to solve each problem.

8. Lizzie's net worth is $3,285.22. Her assets are $6,255.85. What will the dollar amount of her liabilities be if she increases them by 10%? Round to the nearest cent. FL P MP

Ⓐ $2,970.63

Ⓑ $3,267.69

Ⓒ $3,613.74

Ⓓ $5,630.27

9. Mario's net worth is $8,250.63. His liabilities are $3,222.35. If he doubles his net worth but keeps his liabilities the same, what will be the new value of his assets? FL P MP

Ⓐ $6,444.70

Ⓑ $5,028.28

Ⓒ $10,056.56

Ⓓ $13,278.91

FL = Personal Financial Literacy 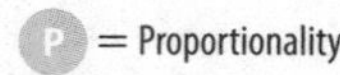 P = Proportionality 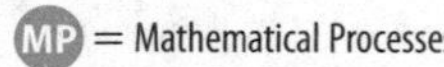 MP = Mathematical Processes

FL Personal Financial Literacy Project

Net Worth Create a financial assets and liabilities record to determine a friend or family member's net worth. Show total assets, total liabilities, and calculate the individual's net worth. Have the friend or family member think of one item they would like to purchase. Using the financial assets and liabilities record, add the amount of the liability to show how purchasing the item would affect the individual's net worth. TEKS 7.13(C), 7.1(B)

Lesson 4

Simple and Compound Interest

Launch the Lesson: Real World

Simple interest earnings are paid on a fixed amount of money, or *principal*. The table shows the simple interest on an investment of $2,000 with an interest rate of 3% for four years.

Principal	Interest Rate	Time	Interest Earned
$2,000.00	3%	4 years	$2,000.00 • 0.03 • 4

1. Determine the total interest earned in four years.

Compound interest earnings are calculated on the original amount plus accumulated interest. The principal increases each year based on the interest earned. The table shows how compound interest on an investment of $2,000 with an interest rate of 3% grows each year for four years.

Principal	Interest Rate	Time	Interest Earned
$2,000.00	3%	1 year	$2,000.00 • 0.03 • 1
$2,060.00	3%	1 year	$2,060.00 • 0.03 • 1
$2,121.80	3%	1 year	$2,121.80 • 0.03 • 1
$2,185.45	3%	1 year	$2,185.45 • 0.03 • 1

2. Determine the total interest earned in four years.

3. In these two scenarios, which interest plan earns the most interest?

Which MP Mathematical Processes did you use? Shade the circle(s) that applies.

Ⓐ Apply Math to the Real World.
Ⓑ Use a Problem-Solving Model.
Ⓒ Select Tools and Techniques.
Ⓓ Use Multiple Representations.
Ⓔ Organize Ideas.
Ⓕ Analyze Relationships.
Ⓖ Justify Arguments.

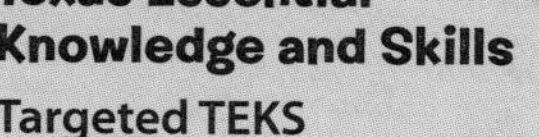
Texas Essential Knowledge and Skills

Targeted TEKS
7.13(E) Calculate and compare simple interest and compound interest earnings.

Mathematical Processes
7.1(A), 7.1(B), 7.1(E), 7.1(F)

Vocabulary
simple interest
compound interest

Essential Question
HOW can I become a knowledgeable consumer and investor?

Work Zone

Simple and Compound Interest

To calculate simple interest, use the formula $I = prt$, where I is the interest earned, p is the principal, or amount invested, r is the interest rate, expressed as a decimal, and t is the time invested, in years.

To calculate compound interest that is *compounded*, or added, annually, use the simple interest formula for each single year, but add the interest to obtain the new starting balance each year.

Tutor

Examples

1. Kedron deposits $1,000 into an account that earns 4% simple interest each year. Calculate the interest he earns after 3 years.

$I = prt$ — Use the simple interest formula.

$I = 1{,}000 \cdot 0.04 \cdot 3$ — $p = 1{,}000, r = 0.04, t = 3$

$I = 120$ — Multiply. Kedron will earn $120 in simple interest.

2. Marcie deposited $1,000 into a savings account that earns 4% compounded interest, compounded annually, each year. Calculate the interest Marcie will earn after three years. Round to the nearest cent.

Use a table. Add the interest earned to obtain the starting balance for each year. After three years, the total interest will be $124.86.

Year	Starting Balance ($)	prt	I (Interest Earned, $)
1	1,000	1,000 • 0.04 • 1	40
2	1,040	1,040 • 0.04 • 1	41.60
3	1,081.60	1,081.60 • 0.04 • 1	43.26

Compound Interest
Compound interest can be compounded annually, semi-annually, quarterly, monthly, daily, or continuously. By increasing the frequency that interest is compounded, the interest that is earned also increases.

3. Compare the simple interest and compound interest earned in Examples 1 and 2.

With simple interest, the average earned each year is $120 ÷ 3, or $40. With compound interest, the interest is added to obtain the starting balance for each year. Compound interest earns more interest when the principal, interest rate, and time invested are the same.

Got It? Do this problem to find out.

a. Calculate the interest earned and the total balance if $1,470 is deposited into a savings account that earns 6% compound interest, compounded annually, for 4 years. Round to the nearest cent.

a. ____________

Name ______________ My Homework ______________

Independent Practice

Calculate the simple interest earned and the total balance. Round to the nearest cent, if necessary. (Example 1)

1. $485 is deposited into a savings account that earns 3.75% simple interest for 3 years. ______________

2. $2,275 is deposited into a savings account that earns 4.4% simple interest for 5 years. ______________

3. $5,600 is deposited into a savings account that earns 5.5% simple interest for 12 years. ______________

Complete the table to calculate the compound interest earned and the total balance. (Example 2)

4. $1,800 is deposited into a savings account that earns 5% compound interest, compounded annually, for 3 years. Round to the nearest cent.

Year	Starting Balance ($)	*prt*	*I* (Interest Earned, $)

The total balance after three years is ______________.

5. $2,275 is deposited into a savings account that earns 4.4% compound interest, compounded annually, for 5 years. Round to the nearest cent.

Year	Starting Balance ($)	*prt*	*I* (Interest Earned, $)

The total balance after five years is ______________.

6. Compare the interest earned and total balance in Exercises 2 and 5. ______________

Multi-Step Problem Solving

Use a problem-solving model to solve each problem.

7. Estella will deposit $2,000 into an account that pays 4% annual simple interest. Veronica will deposit the same amount into a savings account that pays 4% compound interest, compounded annually. After 10 years, with no additional deposits or withdrawals, how much more will Veronica have earned in interest than Estella? Round to the nearest cent. FL P MP

Ⓐ $60.49

Ⓑ $160.49

Ⓒ $800.00

Ⓓ $960.49

8. Mike will deposit $12,000 in an account that pays 3% simple interest yearly. How many years will it take for his account to more than double? FL P MP

Ⓐ 31 years

Ⓑ 32 years

Ⓒ 33 years

Ⓓ 34 years

FL = Personal Financial Literacy 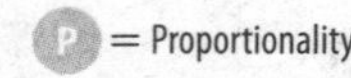

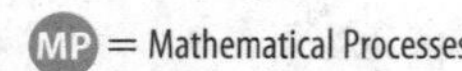

FL Personal Financial Literacy Project

College Savings Determine the cost of tuition, for the first year, for the college of your choice. Assume you receive a scholarship for half of this tuition cost. Research the rates of bank savings accounts in your area. Choose the interest plan that will earn the most money. Assuming you have a principal amount of $1,000, how much would you need to deposit each year until your senior year in high school to have enough money available for the other half of your college tuition? TEKS 7.13(E), 7.1(B)

Lesson 5

Shopping: Monetary Incentives

Launch the Lesson: Real World

Emma is shopping for two 15-pound bags of dog food. The pet store will offer her a **monetary incentive**, or a financial reason to buy. One type of monetary incentives is a sale, like the ones below.

1. If Emma buys two bags of Wagon Train, how much will she pay altogether? ______
2. What is the average cost per bag of Wagon Train? Round to the nearest cent. ______
3. If Emma buys two bags of Tall Tail Dog Food, how much will she pay altogether? ______
4. What is the cost per bag of Tall Tail Dog Food? ______
5. **Evaluate** If the nutritional value of each dog food is the same, which dog food is the best bargain?

______

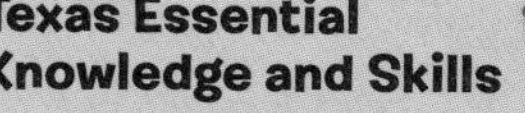

Texas Essential Knowledge and Skills

Targeted TEKS
7.13(F) Analyze and compare monetary incentives, including sales, rebates, and coupons.

Mathematical Processes
7.1(A), 7.1(B), 7.1(D), 7.1(F), 7.1(G)

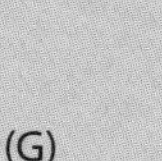

Vocabulary
monetary incentive
rebate
coupon

Essential Question
HOW can I become a knowledgeable consumer and investor?

Which MP Mathematical Processes did you use? Shade the circle(s) that applies.

Ⓐ Apply Math to the Real World.
Ⓑ Use a Problem-Solving Model.
Ⓒ Select Tools and Techniques.
Ⓓ Use Multiple Representations.
Ⓔ Organize Ideas.
Ⓕ Analyze Relationships.
Ⓖ Justify Arguments.

Work Zone

Analyze and Compare Monetary Incentives

One type of monetary incentive is a **rebate**, which is a partial return or refund on an amount paid. Another type of monetary incentive you is a **coupon**, a voucher entitling its user to a cash refund.

Tutor

Multi-Step Examples

1. Determine the cost after the rebate is applied.

CUT IT OUT
Electric Weed Puller
15% Rebate
Original Price $120.00

Step 1 Determine the amount of the rebate.

15% of $120.00 = $18 Multiply 0.15 by $120.00.

Step 2 $120.00 − $18.00 = $102.00 Subtract.

So, after the rebate, the cost of the electric weed puller is $102.00.

Determine the Final Cost

In Example 1, you could also subtract the percent from 100% and multiply $120.00 by 85% to determine the final cost.

2. Compare the incentives to determine the better bargain.

Step 1 Determine the final price after each coupon is applied.

Clean Carpets: $4.99 − $1.50 = $3.49

Magic Carpet: 25% of $4.99 = 0.25 × $4.99

= $1.25

Subtract. $4.99 − $1.25 = $3.74

Step 2 Compare the incentives. Since $3.49 < $3.74, the coupon for Clean Carpets is the better bargain.

Got It? Do these problems to find out.

Determine the final price of each item.

a. 15% rebate on a $75 printer

b. $12 coupon on a $75 printer

c. Which is the best incentive to buy the printer, the 15% rebate or the $12.00 coupon?

a. ______

b. ______

c. ______

Name ______________________ My Homework ______________________

Independent Practice

For Exercises 1–3, use the following monetary incentives. (Examples 1 and 2)

1. Determine the savings after the 15% rebate. ____________

2. Determine the savings after the sale. ____________

3. Which is the best incentive to buy the pillow, the 15% rebate or the sale price? ____________

For Exercises 4–6, use the following monetary incentives. (Examples 1 and 2)

4. Deirdre wants to buy two large one-topping pizzas. How much would she pay altogether if she used the Pizza Time sale price? ____________

5. How much would Deirdre pay if she used the Pizza Parlor coupon? ____________

6. Which is the best incentive to buy the pizza, the sale price or the coupon? ____________

7. MP **Apply Math to the Real World** Refer to the graphic novel frame below and from the beginning of the chapter. Is it better to use the Buy One Get One $\frac{1}{2}$ Off coupon or take the 40% discount? Justify your response.

____

____

____

Multi-Step Problem Solving

Use a problem-solving model to solve each problem.

8. By the Wayside hotel offers 10% off their nightly rate of $89.99 if a customer stays for three or more nights. They also accept a $5 coupon, each night, for reserving the room online. If the 10% discount is applied first, what is the discounted room rate per night after using both monetary incentives? Round to the nearest cent. FL P MP

Ⓐ $74.99
Ⓑ $75.99
Ⓒ $80.99
Ⓓ $84.99

9. A grocery store is offering 10% of all purchases if you bring your own bag to carry groceries. If the total bill, after applying the monetary incentive, is $136.80, what was the amount of the bill before the incentive? FL P MP

Ⓐ $123.12
Ⓑ $146.80
Ⓒ $150.48
Ⓓ $152.00

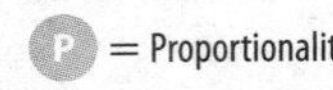

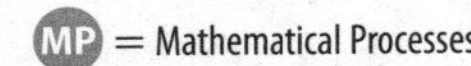

FL Personal Financial Literacy Project

Extreme Incentives Identify a product that you and three of your classmates would like to purchase. Challenge each classmate to find the best deal possible on the item. Analyze each incentive you find, including sales, rebates, and coupons. Then use what you've learned to locate and describe a product you can get for free after using monetary incentives. TEKS 7.13(F), 7.1(B)

Chapter Review

TEKS

Vocabulary Check

Work with a partner to complete the crossword puzzle using the vocabulary list at the beginning of the chapter. Take turns reading each sentence aloud while the other student listens carefully.

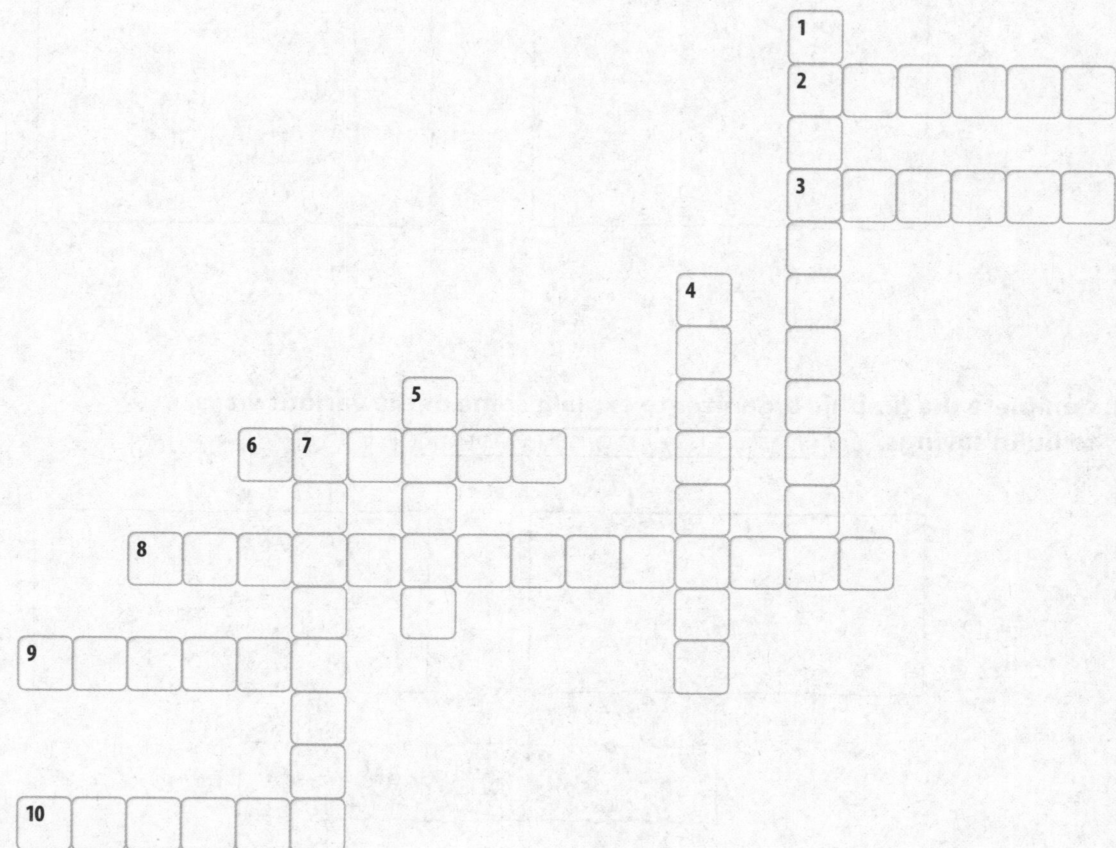

Down

1. debts you owe
4. value of assets minus liabilities
5. payments for labor or services
7. spending

Across

2. financial gain from capital or labor
3. plan for spending
6. return or refund of an amount paid
8. earnings paid on a fixed amount of money
9. voucher entitling its user to a cash refund
10. things you own

Key Concept Check

1. Complete the graphic organizer to compare and contrast simple interest and compound interest. TEKS 7.13(E), 7.1(E)

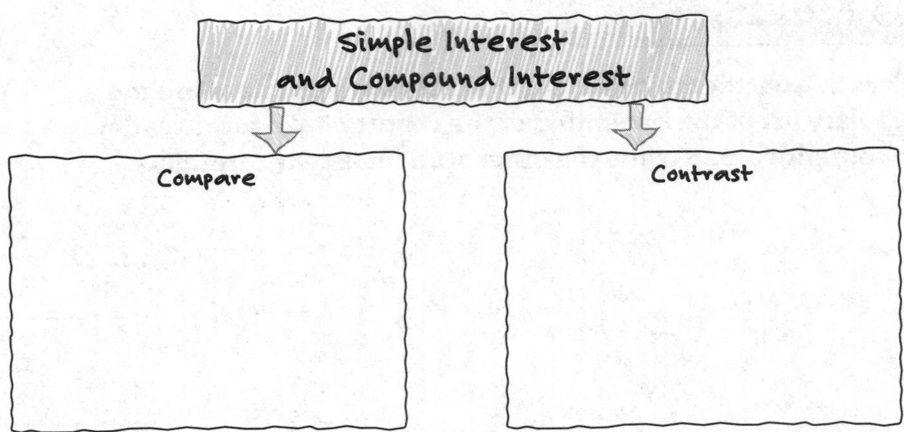

2. Complete the graphic organizer to explain some of the various ways to build savings. TEKS 7.13(A), 7.13(B), 7.13(C), 7.13(E), 7.13(F), 7.1(E)

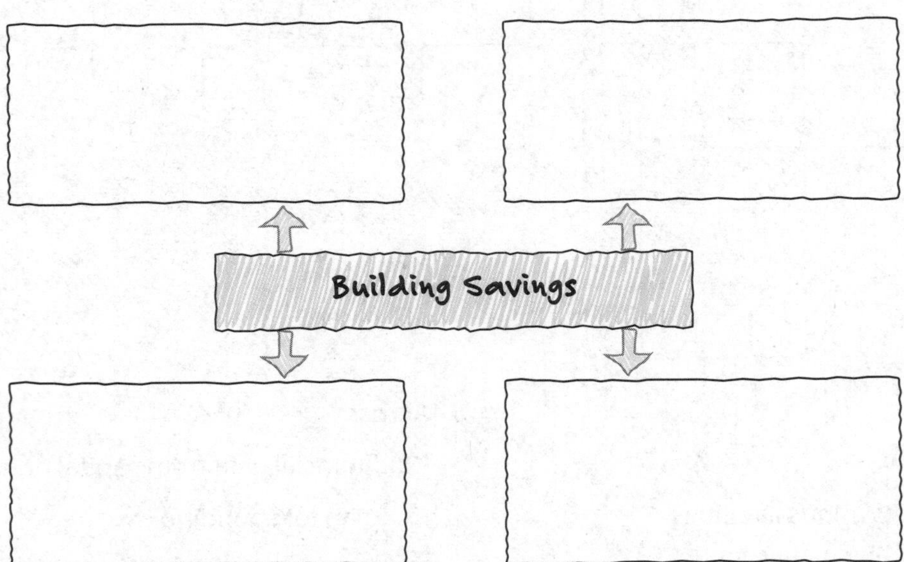

Multi-Step Problem Solving

3. The table shows the percentage of the Davisson family budget used for housing, food, and transportation. Originally, they had a $8,200 monthly income, but it was reduced by 20%. What is their new monthly income? If they leave the percent of budget for transportation the same, what is the dollar amount they now have available to spend on transportation? FL P MP

Expense	Percent of Budget
Housing	36%
Food	12%
Transportation	8%

1 Analyze

2 Plan

3 Solve

4 Justify and Evaluate

Got it?

4. The table shows the percentage of the Wheeler family budget assigned to retirement savings, gasoline, and taxes. Originally, they had a $10,200 monthly income, but Mrs. Wheeler got a 10% raise. If they leave the percent of budget for retirement savings the same, what is the new dollar amount they now have to save for retirement? FL P MP

Expense	Percent of Budget
Retirement Savings	10%
Gasoline	8%
Taxes	25%

FL = Personal Financial Literacy P = Proportionality MP = Mathematical Processes

Reflect

Answering the Essential Question

Use what you learned about financial literacy to complete the graphic organizer. TEKS 7.13(A), 7.13(B), 7.13(C), 7.13(E), 7.13(F), 7.1(E)

Taxes

Budget and Net Worth

Essential Question

HOW can I become a knowledgeable consumer and investor?

Interest

Monetary Incentives

Answer the Essential Question. HOW can I become a knowledgeable consumer and investor? Verbally share your response with a partner, asking for and giving help if needed.

Real World

Problem-Solving Projects

In the Problem-Solving Projects, you will apply the math you have learned so far to everyday life, society, and the workplace. Try them!

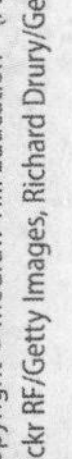

How will I get started?

Collaborate

Go Online You will work with a partner, or in a small group, to explore, research, and investigate a particular aspect of how mathematics is used in the real world. Each project will provide you with suggested activities in which to start your investigation.

You can go online to watch a video about the description of your project.

Use the guiding questions in the Analyze section to help narrow your focus in your project and to help you think critically about how specific math topics you have learned are applied in the real world.

What will I do once the project is completed?

Your group will prepare a presentation to share your results with your classmates.

Some ways in which you can demonstrate what you learned are to...

- create a powerpoint presentation.
- create a presentation, using an online presentation tool.
- create a video.
- create a music video.
- create a Web page or blog.
- create an advertisement.
- create a poster.
- create a brochure.
- write a letter.

PROJECT 1

Targeted TEKS
7.1(A), 7.1(B), 7.4(B), 7.4(D)

Watch

Become a Travel Expert Without proper planning, a family vacation could end up costing a fortune! In this project you will:

- **Collaborate** with your classmates as you research the cost of a family vacation.
- **Share** the results of your research in a creative way.
- **Reflect** on how you use mathematics to describe change and model real-world situations.

By the end of this project, you will be ready to plan a family vacation without breaking the bank.

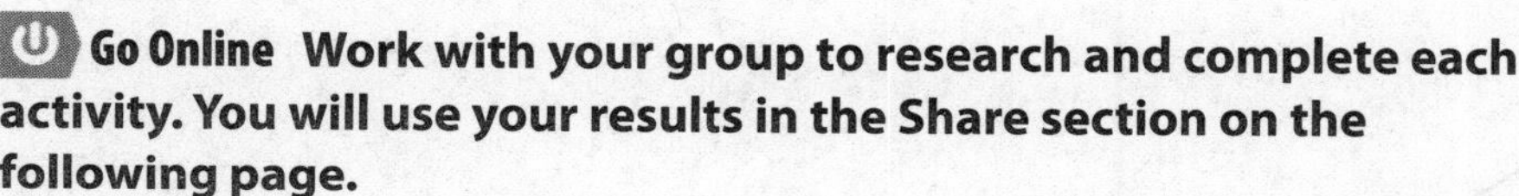

Go Online Work with your group to research and complete each activity. You will use your results in the Share section on the following page.

1. Research the cost for a family of four to fly round trip to a destination of your choosing. Record the cost of a flight that is nonstop and one that has at least one extra stop. Make sure to include the cost of the tax.

2. Research two different rental cars that would be available at a local company. Compare the miles per gallon (mi/gal) that each car averages on the highway. How much gas would you use for each car if you were going to be traveling 450 miles on your trip?

3. If you are traveling out of the country you will need to know the current exchange rates. Record the exchange rate for three different countries. How much is \$100 worth in those countries?

4. Choose a vacation spot that is a city in the United States. Find a popular restaurant for tourists in your city and look up their menu online. Calculate the cost for a dinner that feeds four people. Don't forget the tip.

5. Different states have different sales tax rates. Choose three different states. Research the sales tax rate for each of those states. Then, determine the total cost of buying jeans that cost \$50 plus the sales tax.

With your group, decide on a way to share what you have learned about the cost of a family vacation. Some suggestions are listed below, but you can also think of other creative ways to present your information. Remember to show how you used mathematics in your project!

- Use your creative writing skills to write journal entries or blogs. Your writing should describe how you were able to save money while traveling on your vacations.
- Act as a travel agent to put together one domestic and one international travel package for a family of four. Create a digital brochure to explain each package.

Check out the note on the right to connect this project with other subjects.

Financial Literacy Imagine that you are the director of tourism for Texas. Write a script for a commercial that is trying to encourage tourists to visit. Your script should include:

- unique activities found in Texas
- ways of traveling in Texas

6. **Answer the Essential Question** How can you use mathematics to describe change and model real-world situations?

   a. How did you use what you learned about ratios and proportional reasoning to describe change and model the real-world situations in this project?

   b. How did you use what you learned about percents to describe change and model the real-world situations in this project?

PROJECT 2

Targeted TEKS
7.1(A), 7.1(B), 7.2, 7.3(A), 7.3(B)

Watch

Explore the Ocean Depths For this project, imagine that your dream job is to become an oceanographer. In this project you will:

- **Collaborate** with your classmates as you research information about the ocean.
- **Share** the results of your research in a creative way.
- **Reflect** on how mathematical ideas can be represented.

Collaborate

Go Online Work with your group to research and complete each activity. You will use your results in the Share section on the following page.

1. About $\frac{2}{3}$ of Earth is covered by ocean. Research the five oceans of the world and create a table that shows about what fraction each ocean is of that $\frac{2}{3}$.

2. What is the greatest ocean depth? Find out and then display it on a vertical number line along with other facts about what you can find at different ocean depths.

3. Coral reefs are the home of many ocean creatures. Look up some facts about the state of coral reefs in the world today and display them in a creative way.

4. Choose three different types of whales that live in the ocean. Compare things like their size, the amount of food they eat, or the climate in which they live. Organize the information in a table or graph.

5. Research one of the larger icebergs in the Arctic Ocean. Sketch an image of the iceberg next to a vertical number line that shows the approximate top and bottom of the iceberg. Remember, about $\frac{7}{8}$ of an iceberg is under water.

With your group, decide on a way to share what you have learned about ocean depths. Some suggestions are listed below, but you could also think of other creative ways to present your information. Remember to show how you used mathematics in your project!

- Use presentation software to organize what you have learned in this project. Share your presentation with the class.
- Imagine you need to apply for funds to go on a deep sea exploration. Write a persuasive letter or speech that highlights the importance of studying ocean depths.

Check out the note on the right to connect this project with other subjects.

with Science

Environmental Literacy Research an animal that lives in the ocean that is on the endangered species list. Give a presentation to your class that answers the following questions:

- What are some of the causes for the animals being on the endangered species list?
- What efforts are currently being made to protect the animal you chose?

6. **Answer the Essential Question** How can mathematical ideas be represented?

   a. How were mathematical ideas involving integers represented in the information you discovered about oceans?

   b. How were mathematical ideas involving rational numbers represented in the information you discovered about oceans?

PROJECT 3

Targeted TEKS
7.1(A), 7.1(B), 7.10(A), 7.10(B), 7.10(C), 7.11(A)

Watch **Stand Up and Be Counted** The U.S. Census is used to determine the number of U.S. House of Representative members that each state is assigned. In this project you will:

- **Collaborate** with your classmates as you research Census data and the U.S. House of Representatives.
- **Share** the results of your research in a creative way.
- **Reflect** on how you can communicate mathematical ideas effectively.

Go Online Work with your group to research and complete each activity. You will use your results in the Share section on the following page.

1. Explore the official U.S. Census Web site to determine the 2010 state populations. There will be interactive maps that display this information. Write down a few facts you find interesting.

2. Create a table that displays the population and the number of U.S. Representatives for Texas and three other states. Then create a line plot for the number of U.S. Representatives.

3. Write an equation that uses any state's population x and its number of U.S. Representative members y to describe the number of people per U.S. Representative z.

4. Use your equation from Exercise 3 to determine the approximate number of people per U.S. Representative for the four states you chose. Interpret the results.

5. Look at the 2000 and 2010 census. How did the population of Texas and states in your region change? Did the population change affect the number of U.S. Representatives assigned?

6. States can be categorized by population size and density. Write at least two inequalities that compare the states using these categories.

With your group, decide on a way to share what you have learned about the U.S. House of Representatives and state populations. Some suggestions are listed below, but you can also think of other creative ways to present your information. Remember to show how you used mathematics to complete each of the activities in this project!

- Act as a Census representative and create a presentation to encourage people to participate in the census and explain why it is important.
- Write a letter or E-mail to your Representative about what you learned in this project and how it can be used to improve your community.

Check out the note on the right to connect this project with other subjects.

Civic Literacy Research the Electoral College. Some questions to consider are:

- Why was it established?
- What is the relationship between the United States House of Representatives and the Electoral College?

6. **Answer the Essential Question** How can you communicate mathematical ideas effectively?

   a. How did you use what you learned about equations to help you communicate mathematical ideas effectively in this project?

   b. How did you use what you learned about inequalities to help you communicate mathematical ideas effectively in this project?

PROJECT 4

Targeted TEKS
7.1(A), 7.1(B), 7.9(A), 7.9(D)

Watch

Turn Over a New Leaf The flatness of leaves serves an important purpose. In this project you will:

- **Collaborate** with your classmates as you research the primary function of leaves.
- **Share** the results of your research in a creative way.
- **Reflect** on how you use different measurements to solve real-life problems.

Collaborate

Go Online Work with your group to research and complete each activity. You will use your results in the Share section on the following page.

1. Suppose you have a cube that is 10 centimeters on each side. Determine the volume, surface area, and surface area to volume ratio.

2. Disassemble the cube from Exercise 1 into centimeter cubes. Arrange the cubes in a 50-by-20-by-1 prism. Determine the volume, surface area, and surface area to volume ratio.

3. Compare and contrast the volume, surface area, and surface area to volume ratio from Exercises 1 and 2.

4. Trace the outline of a leaf onto centimeter grid paper. Estimate the volume of the leaf. (Assume the height of your leaf is 0.1 centimeter.) Estimate the surface area. (You can ignore the edge of the leaf.) Determine the surface area to volume ratio.

5. Do research to find the primary function of a leaf. Explain how the surface area to volume ratio of a leaf aids in its function.

6. Find examples from nature or man-made objects that have a small surface area to volume ratio. Explain the benefits.

With your group, decide on a way to share what you have learned about the surface area to volume ratio of leaves. Some suggestions are listed below, but you could also think of other creative ways to present your information. Remember to show how you used mathematics to complete each of the activities in this project!

- Create a digital presentation that compares two types of leaves. Use what you learned about surface area to volume ratios in your presentation.
- Imagine you discovered a new type of leaf. Create an annotated diagram of your leaf. The annotations should include the type of information you learned in this project.

Check out the note on the right to connect this project with other subjects.

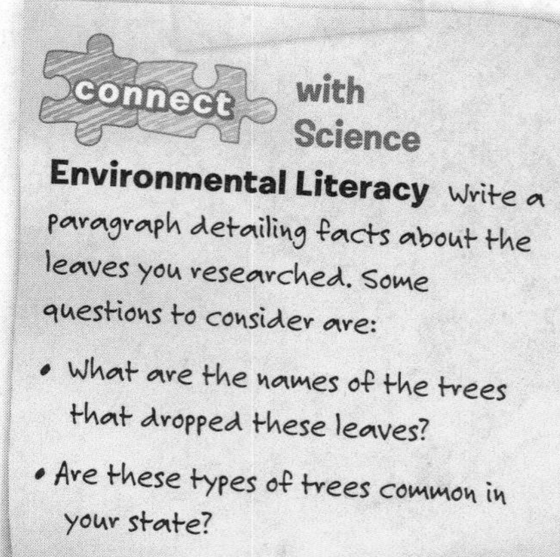

6. **Answer the Essential Question** How can you use different measurements to solve real-life problems?

   a. How did what you learned about geometric figures help you use different measurements to solve real-life problems in this project?

   b. How did what you learned about measuring figures to help you use different measurements to solve real-life problems in this project?

PROJECT 5

Targeted TEKS
7.1(A), 7.1(B), 7.6(E), 7.6(F), 7.6(G), 7.6(I)

Watch

Math Genes A Punnett Square is a graphical way to predict the genetic traits of offspring. In this project you will:

- **Collaborate** with your classmates as you research genetics and the Punnet Square.
- **Share** the results of your research in a creative way.
- **Reflect** on why learning mathematics is important.

Complete the activities below and discover the fun you can have with genetics.

Collaborate

Go Online Work with your group to research and complete each activity. You will use your results in the Share section on the following page.

1. Use the Internet to research Punnett Squares and their role in genetics. Write a paragraph describing your findings.

2. Create sample genes for pet traits. Then create a Punnett Square using those traits. Describe what each outcome represents. Include a graph with your explanation.

3. Refer to Exercise 2. How many different genetic outcomes are possible according to your Punnett Square? What is the probability of each outcome occurring?

4. Create three word problems that involve using probability and the Punnett Squares to help answer the questions.

5. Collect two or more genetic-related information samples about students in your class. For example, you can collect data on attached/unattached earlobes. Analyze the data and make a prediction about the genetics of the entire school. Draw an appropriate graph of your results.

Share

With your group, decide on a way to share what you have learned about genetics and Punnett Squares. Some suggestions are listed below, but you can also think of other creative ways to your present your information. Remember to show how you used mathematics to complete each of the activities in this project.

- Create a digital presentation of the facts you learned about genetics.
- Act as a genetic scientist. Write a journal entry that explains your current research on predicting traits passed down from generations.

Check out the note on the right to connect this project with other subjects.

with Health

Health Literacy Select a health condition or disease and research how genetics may play a part in the disease. Write 1–2 paragraphs explaining how genetics may influence someone's risk of getting the disease and steps that can be taken to reduce the risk factors.

Reflect

6. **Answer the Essential Question** Why is learning mathematics important?

 a. How did what you learned about probability help you to understand why learning mathematics is important?

 b. How did what you learned about statistics help you to understand why learning mathematics is important?

Glossary/Glosario

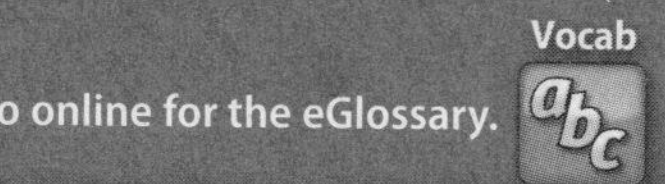

The eGlossary contains words and definitions in the following 13 languages:

Arabic	Cantonese	Hmong	Spanish	Urdu
Bengali	English	Korean	Tagalog	Vietnamese
Brazilian Portuguese	Haitian Creole	Russian		

English / Español

Aa

absolute value The distance the number is from zero on a number line.

valor absoluto Distancia a la que se encuentra un número de cero en la recta numérica.

acute angle An angle with a measure greater than 0° and less than 90°.

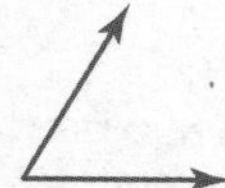

ángulo agudo Ángulo que mide más de 0° y menos de 90°.

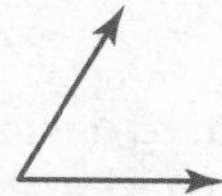

acute triangle A triangle having three acute angles.

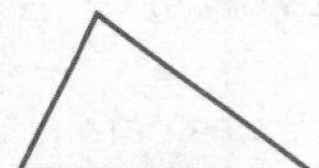

triángulo acutángulo Triángulo con tres ángulos agudos.

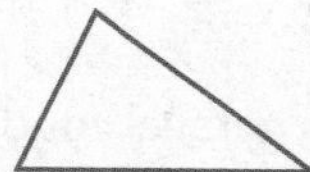

Addition Property of Equality If you add the same number to each side of an equation, the two sides remain equal.

propiedad de adición de la igualdad Si sumas el mismo número a ambos lados de una ecuación, los dos lados permanecen iguales.

Addition Property of Inequality If you add the same number to each side of an inequality, the inequality remains true.

propiedad de desigualdad en la suma Si se suma el mismo número a cada lado de una desigualdad, la desigualdad sigue siendo verdadera.

Additive Identity Property The sum of any number and zero is the number.

propiedad de identidad de la suma La suma de cualquier número y cero es el mismo número.

additive inverse Two integers that are opposites. The sum of an integer and its additive inverse is zero.

inverso aditivo Dos enteros opuestos.

adjacent angles Angles that have the same vertex, share a common side, and do not overlap.

ángulos adyacentes Ángulos que comparten el mismo vértice y un común lado, pero no se sobreponen.

algebra A branch of mathematics that involves expressions with variables.

álgebra Rama de las matemáticas que trata de las expresiones con variables.

algebraic expression A combination of variables, numbers, and at least one operation.

expresión algebraica Combinación de variables, números y por lo menos una operación.

angle Two rays with a common endpoint form an angle. The rays and vertex are used to name the angle.

ángulo Dos rayos con un extremo común forman un ángulo. Los rayos y el vértice se usan para nombrar el ángulo.

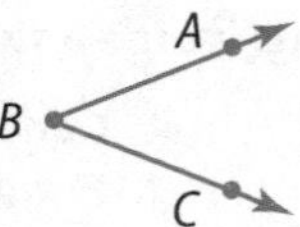

arithmetic sequence A sequence in which the difference between any two consecutive terms is the same.

sucesión aritmética Sucesión en la cual la diferencia entre dos términos consecutivos es constante.

assets Items that are owned by an individual.

activo Bienes que posee una persona.

Associative Property The way in which numbers are grouped does not change their sum or product.

propiedad asociativa La forma en que se agrupan números al sumarlos o multiplicarlos no altera su suma o producto.

attribute A characteristic of a figure.

atributo Una característica de una figura.

Bb

bar notation In repeating decimals, the line or bar placed over the digits that repeat. For example, $2.\overline{63}$ indicates that the digits 63 repeat.

notación de barra Línea o barra que se coloca sobre los dígitos que se repiten en decimales periódicos. Por ejemplo, $2.\overline{63}$ indica que los dígitos 63 se repiten.

base In a power, the number used as a factor. In 10^3, the base is 10. That is, $10^3 = 10 \times 10 \times 10$.

base En una potencia, el número usado como factor. En 10^3, la base es 10. Es decir, $10^3 = 10 \times 10 \times 10$.

base One of the two parallel congruent faces of a prism.

base Una de las dos caras paralelas congruentes de un prisma.

biased sample A sample drawn in such a way that one or more parts of the population are favored over others.

muestra sesgada Muestra en que se favorece una o más partes de una población.

box plot A method of visually displaying a distribution of data values by using the median, quartiles, and extremes of the data set. A box shows the middle 50% of the data.

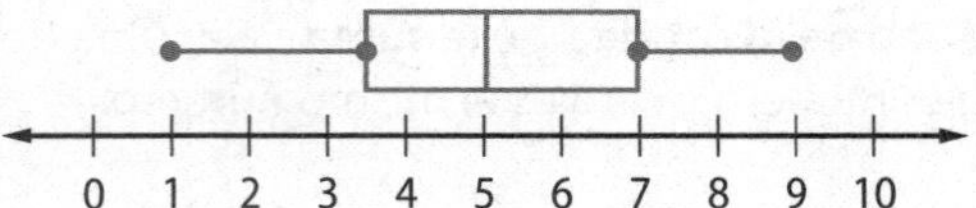

diagrama de caja Un método de mostrar visualmente una distribución de valores usando la mediana, cuartiles y extremos del conjunto de datos. Una caja muestra el 50% del medio de los datos.

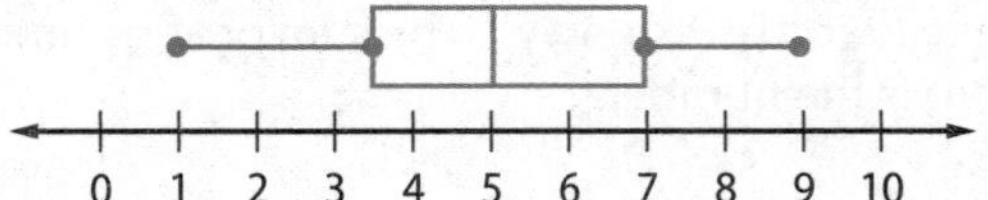

budget A plan for spending.

presupuesto Plan de gastos.

Cc

center The point from which all points on circle are the same distance.

centro El punto desde el cual todos los puntos en una circunferencia están a la misma distancia.

circle The set of all points in a plane that are the same distance from a given point called the center.

círculo Conjunto de todos los puntos de un plano que están a la misma distancia de un punto dado denominado "centro".

circle graph A graph that shows data as parts of a whole. In a circle graph, the percents add up to 100.

gráfica circular Gráfica que muestra los datos como partes de un todo. En una gráfica circular los porcentajes suman 100.

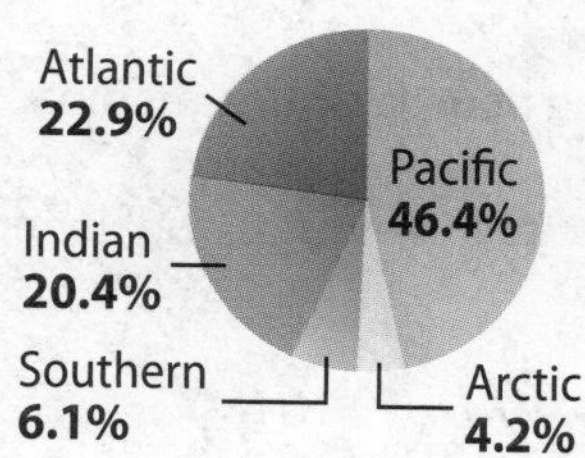

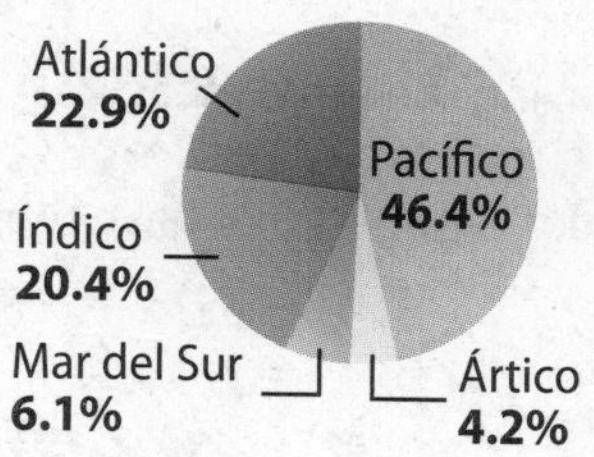

circumference The distance around a circle.

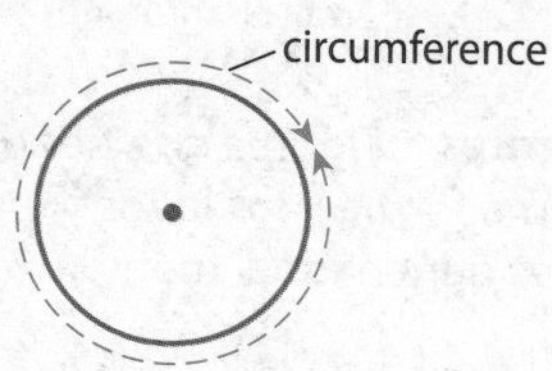

circunferencia Distancia en torno a un círculo.

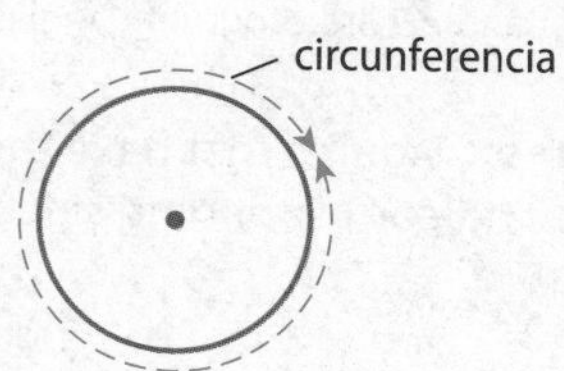

coefficient The numerical factor of a term that contains a variable.

coeficiente El factor numérico de un término que contiene una variable.

common denominator A common multiple of the denominators of two or more fractions. 24 is a common denominator for $\frac{1}{3}$, $\frac{5}{8}$, and $\frac{3}{4}$ because 24 is the LCM of 3, 8, and 4.

común denominador El múltiplo común de los denominadores de dos o más fracciones. 24 es un denominador común para $\frac{1}{3}$, $\frac{5}{8}$ y $\frac{3}{4}$ porque 24 es el mcm de 3, 8 y 4.

Commutative Property The order in which two numbers are added or multiplied does not change their sum or product.

propiedad conmutativa El orden en que se suman o multiplican dos números no altera el resultado.

complementary angles Two angles are complementary if the sum of their measures is 90°.

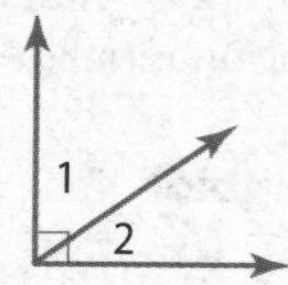

$\angle 1$ and $\angle 2$ are complementary angles.

ángulos complementarios Dos ángulos son complementarios si la suma de sus medidas es 90°.

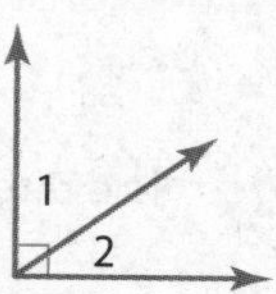

$\angle 1$ y $\angle 2$ son complementarios.

complementary events The events of one outcome happening and that outcome not happening. The sum of the probabilities of an event and its complement is 1 or 100%. In symbols, $P(\text{A}) + P(not\ \text{A}) = 1$.

eventos complementarios Los eventos de un resultado que ocurre y ese resultado que no ocurre. La suma de las probabilidades de un evento y su complemento es 1 ó 100. En símbolos $P(\text{A}) + P(no\ \text{A}) = 1$.

complex fraction A fraction $\frac{A}{B}$ where A or B are fractions and B does not equal zero.

fracción compleja Una fracción $\frac{A}{B}$ en la cual A o B son fracciones y B no es igual a cero.

composite figure A figure that is made up of two or more three-dimensional figures.

figura compuesta Figura formada por dos o más figuras tridimensionales.

compound event An event consisting of two or more simple events.

compound interest Interest paid on the initial principal and on interest earned in the past.

congruent Having the same measure.

congruent angles Angles that have the same measure.

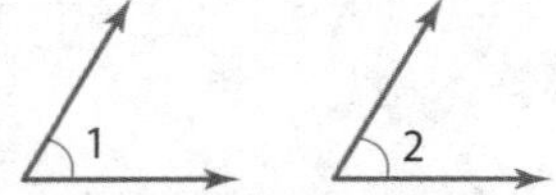

∠1 and ∠2 are congruent angles.

congruent figures Figures that have the same size and same shape and corresponding sides and angles with equal measure.

congruent segments Sides with the same length.

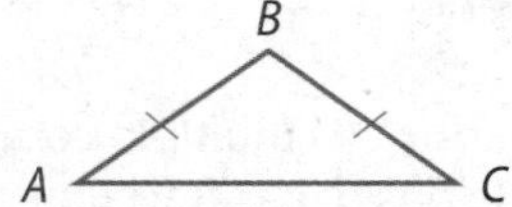

Side $\overline{AB}$ is congruent to side $\overline{BC}$.

constant A term that does not contain a variable.

constant of proportionality A constant ratio or unit rate of two variable quantities. It is also called the constant of variation.

constant of variation The constant ratio in a direct variation. It is also called the constant of proportionality.

constant rate of change The rate of change in a linear relationship.

convenience sample A sample which consists of members of a population that are easily accessed.

coordinate plane A plane in which a horizontal number line and a vertical number line intersect at their zero points. Also called a coordinate grid.

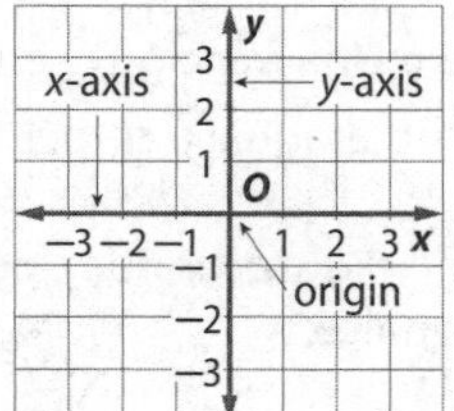

evento compuesto Un evento que consiste en dos o más eventos simples.

interés compuesto Interés que se paga sobre el capital inicial y los intereses ganados en el pasado.

congruente Que tiene la misma medida.

ángulos congruentes Ángulos que tienen la misma medida.

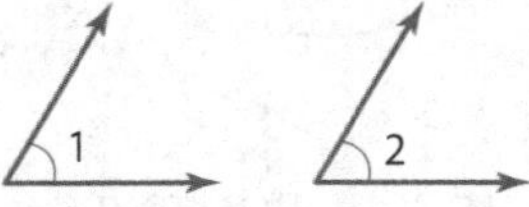

∠1 y ∠2 son congruentes.

figuras congruentes Figuras que tienen el mismo tamaño y la misma forma y los lados y los ángulos correspondientes tienen igual medida.

segmentos congruentes Lados con la misma longitud.

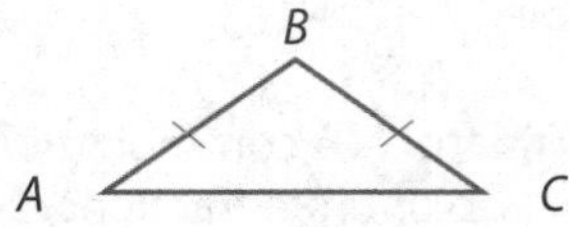

$\overline{AB}$ es congruente a $\overline{BC}$.

constante Término que no contiene ninguna variable.

constante de proporcionalidad Una razón constante o tasa por unidad de dos cantidades variables. También se llama constante de variación.

constante de variación Una razón constante o tasa por unidad de dos cantidades variables. También se llama constante de proporcionalidad.

razón constante de cambio Tasa de cambio en una relación lineal.

muestra de conveniencia Muestra que incluye miembros de una población fácilmente accesibles.

plano de coordenadas Plano en el cual se han trazado dos rectas numéricas, una horizontal y una vertical, que se intersecan en sus puntos cero. También conocido como sistema de coordenadas.

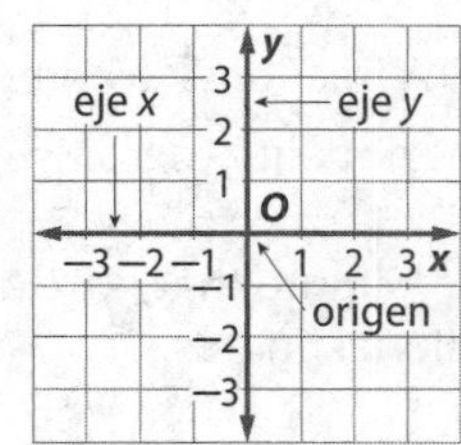

corresponding angles Angles in the same position on parallel lines in relation to a transversal.

corresponding sides The sides of similar figures that are in the same relative position.

counterexample A specific case which proves a statement false.

coupon A voucher entitling its user to a cash refund.

cross product The product of the numerator of one ratio and the denominator of the other ratio. The cross products of any proportion are equal.

cube root One of three equal factors of a number. If $a^3 = b$, then a is the cube root of b. The cube root of 125 is 5 since $5^3 = 125$.

cubed The product in which a number is a factor three times. Two cubed is 8 because $2 \times 2 \times 2 = 8$.

ángulos correspondientes Ángulos que están en la misma posición sobre rectas paralelas en relación con la transversal.

lados correspondientes Lados de figuras semejantes que estan en la misma posición.

contraejemplo Caso específico que demuestra la falsedad de un enunciado.

cupón Vale que da derecho al usuario a obtener un reembolso en efectivo.

producto cruzado Producto del numerador de una razón por el denominador de la otra razón. Los productos cruzados de cualquier proporción son iguales.

raíz cúbica Uno de tres factores iguales de un número. Si $a^3 = b$, entonces a es la raíz cúbica de b. La raíz cúbica de 125 es 5, dado que $5^3 = 125$.

al cubo El producto de un número por sí mismo, tres veces. Dos al cubo es 8 porque $2 \times 2 \times 2 = 8$.

Dd

decagon A polygon having ten sides.

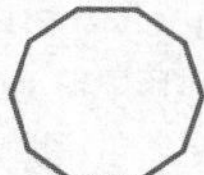

defining a variable Choosing a variable and a quantity for the variable to represent in an expression or equation.

degrees The most common unit of measure for angles. If a circle were divided into 360 equal-sized parts, each part would have an angle measure of 1 degree.

dependent events Two or more events in which the outcome of one event affects the outcome of the other event(s).

dependent variable The variable in a relation with a value that depends on the value of the independent variable.

derived unit A unit that is derived from a measurement system base unit, such as length, mass, or time.

diagonal A line segment that connects two nonconsecutive vertices.

decágono Un polígono con diez lados.

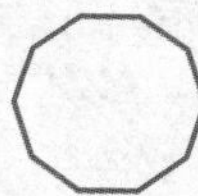

definir una variable El eligir una variable y una cantidad que esté representada por la variable en una expresión o en una ecuacion.

grados La unidad más común para medir ángulos. Si un círculo se divide en 360 partes iguales, cada parte tiene una medida angular de 1 grado.

eventos dependientes Dos o más eventos en que el resultado de un evento afecta el resultado de otro u otros eventos.

variable dependiente La variable en una relación cuyo valor depende del valor de la variable independiente.

unidad derivada Unidad que se deriva de una unidad básica de un sistema de medidas, como la longitud, la masa o el tiempo.

diagonal Segmento de recta que une dos vértices no consecutivos de un polígono.

diameter The distance across a circle through its center.

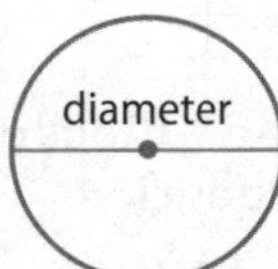

diámetro Segmento que pasa por el centro de un círculo y lo divide en dos partes iguales.

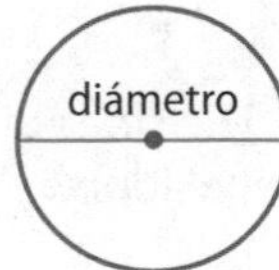

dimensional analysis The process of including units of measurement when you compute.

análisis dimensional Proceso que incluye las unidades de medida al hacer cálculos.

direct variation The relationship between two variable quantities that have a constant ratio.

variación directa Relación entre las cantidades de dos variables que tienen una tasa constante.

discount The amount by which the regular price of an item is reduced.

descuento Cantidad que se le rebaja al precio regular de un artículo.

disjoint events Events that cannot happen at the same time.

eventos disjuntos Eventos que no pueden ocurrir al mismo tiempo.

Distributive Property To multiply a sum by a number, multiply each addend of the sum by the number outside the parentheses. For any numbers a, b, and c, $a(b + c) = ab + ac$ and $a(b - c) = ab - ac$.

Example: $2(5 + 3) = (2 \times 5) + (2 \times 3)$ and $2(5 - 3) = (2 \times 5) - (2 \times 3)$

propiedad distributiva Para multiplicar una suma por un número, multiplíquese cada sumando de la suma por el número que está fuera del paréntesis. Sean cuales fuere los números a, b, y c, $a(b + c) = ab + ac$ y $a(b - c) = ab - ac$.

Ejemplo: $2(5 + 3) = (2 \cdot 5) + (2 \cdot 3)$ y $2(5 - 3) = (2 \cdot 5) - (2 \cdot 3)$

Division Property of Equality If you divide each side of an equation by the same nonzero number, the two sides remain equal.

propiedad de igualdad de la división Si divides ambos lados de una ecuación entre el mismo número no nulo, los lados permanecen iguales.

Division Property of Inequality When you divide each side of an inequality by a negative number, the inequality symbol must be reversed for the inequality to remain true.

propiedad de desigualdad en la división Cuando se divide cada lado de una desigualdad entre un número negativo, el símbolo de desigualdad debe invertirse para que la desigualdad siga siendo verdadera.

double box plot Two box plots graphed on the same number line.

doble diagrama de caja Dos diagramas de caja sobre la misma recta numérica.

double dot plot A method of visually displaying a distribution of two sets of data values where each value is shown as a dot above a number line.

doble diagrama de puntos Un método de mostrar visualmente una distribución de dos conjuntos de valores donde cada valor se muestra como un punto arriba de una recta numérica.

edge The line segment where two faces of a polyhedron intersect.

borde El segmento de línea donde se cruzan dos caras de un poliedro.

enlargement An image larger than the original.

ampliación Imagen más grande que la original.

equation A mathematical sentence that contains an equals sign, =, stating that two quantities are equal.

ecuación Enunciado matemático que contiene el signo de igualdad = indicando que dos cantidades son iguales.

equiangular In a polygon, all of the angles are congruent.

equiangular En un polígono, todos los ángulos son congruentes.

equilateral In a polygon, all of the sides are congruent.

equilátero En un polígono, todos los lados son congruentes.

equilateral triangle A triangle having three congruent sides.

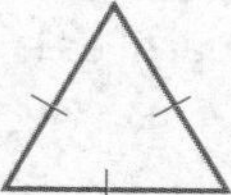

triángulo equilátero Triángulo con tres lados congruentes.

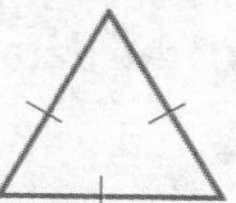

equivalent equations Two or more equations with the same solution.

ecuaciones equivalentes Dos o más ecuaciones con la misma solución.

equivalent expressions Expressions that have the same value.

expresiones equivalentes Expresiones que tienen el mismo valor.

equivalent ratios Two ratios that have the same value.

razones equivalentes Dos razones que tienen el mismo valor.

evaluate To find the value of an expression.

evaluar Calcular el valor de una expresión.

expenses The cost required to buy an item or service.

gastos Costos necesario para comprar un artículo o un servicio.

experimental probability An estimated probability based on the relative frequency of positive outcomes occurring during an experiment. It is based on what *actually* occurred during such an experiment.

probabilidad experimental Probabilidad estimada que se basa en la frecuencia relativa de los resultados positivos que ocurren durante un experimento. Se basa en lo que *en realidad* ocurre durante dicho experimento.

exponent In a power, the number that tells how many times the base is used as a factor. In 5^3, the exponent is 3. That is, $5^3 = 5 \times 5 \times 5$.

exponente En una potencia, el número que indica las veces que la base se usa como factor. En 5^3, el exponente es 3. Es decir, $5^3 = 5 \times 5 \times 5$.

exponential form Numbers written with exponents.

forma exponencial Números escritos usando exponentes.

face A flat surface of a polyhedron.

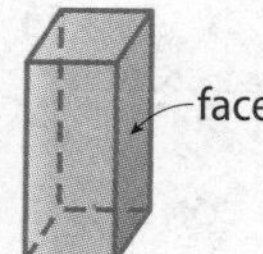

cara Una superficie plana de un poliedro.

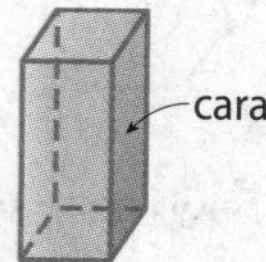

factor To write a number as a product of its factors.

factorizar Escribir un número como el producto de sus factores.

factored form An expression expressed as the product of its factors.

forma factorizada Una expresión expresada como el producto de sus factores.

factors Two or more numbers that are multiplied together to form a product.

factores Dos o más números que se multiplican entre sí para formar un producto.

fair game A game where each player has an equally likely chance of winning.

juego justo Juego donde cada jugador tiene igual posibilidad de ganar.

family budget A family plan for spending.

presupuesto familiar Plan de gastos de una familia.

first quartile For a data set with median M, the first quartile is the median of the data values less than M.

primer cuartil Para un conjunto de datos con la mediana M, el primer cuartil es la mediana de los valores menores que M.

fixed expenses Costs that do not change based on the amount that is used.

gastos fijos Costos que no cambian con la cantidad usada.

formula An equation that shows the relationship among certain quantities.

fórmula Ecuación que muestra la relación entre ciertas cantidades.

Fundamental Counting Principle Uses multiplication of the number of ways each event in an experiment can occur to find the number of possible outcomes in a sample space.

Principio Fundamental de Contar Este principio usa la multiplicación del número de veces que puede ocurrir cada evento en un experimento para calcular el número de posibles resultados en un espacio muestral.

Gg

gram A unit of mass in the metric system equivalent to 0.001 kilogram.

gramo Unidad de masa en el sistema métrico que equivale a 0.001 de kilogramo.

graph The process of placing a point on a number line or on a coordinate plane at its proper location.

graficar Proceso de dibujar o trazar un punto en una recta numérica o en un plano de coordenadas en su ubicación correcta.

gratuity Also known as a tip. It is a small amount of money in return for a service.

gratificación También conocida como propina. Es una cantidad pequeña de dinero en retribución por un servicio.

Hh

heptagon A polygon having seven sides.

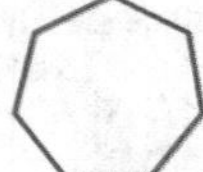

heptágono Polígono con siete lados.

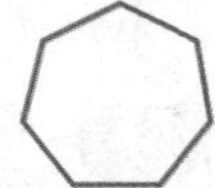

hexagon A polygon having six sides.

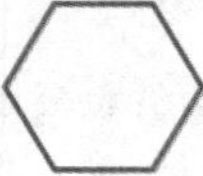

hexágono Polígono con seis lados.

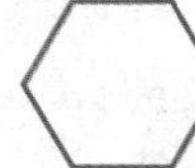

histogram A type of bar graph used to display numerical data that have been organized into equal intervals.

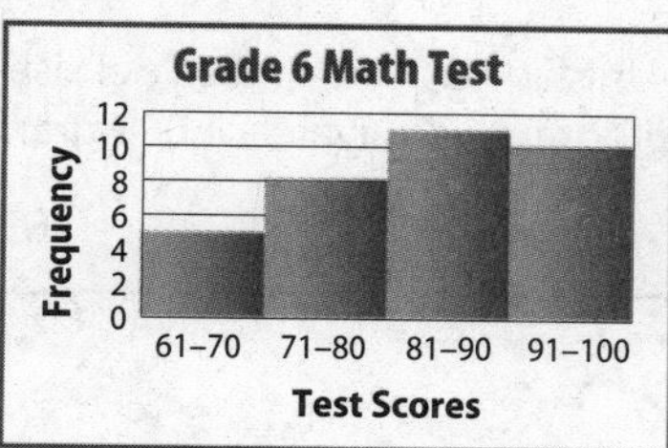

histograma Tipo de gráfica de barras que se usa para exhibir datos que se han organizado en intervalos iguales.

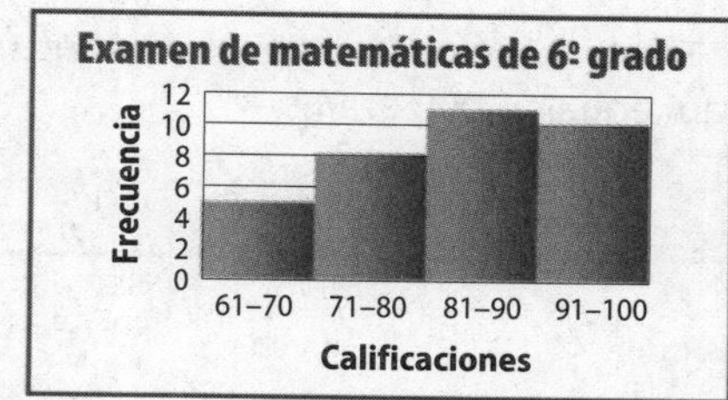

Identity Property of Zero The sum of an addend and zero is the addend. Example: $5 + 0 = 5$

propiedad de identidad del cero La suma de un sumando y cero es igual al sumando. Ejemplo: $5 + 0 = 5$

income A financial gain from capital or labor.

ingreso Ganacia financiera por el capital o el trabajo.

income tax A tax on the net income of an individual or business.

impuesto a los ingresos Impuesto sobre el ingreso neto de una persona o un negocio.

independent events Two or more events in which the outcome of one event does not affect the outcome of the other event(s).

eventos independientes Dos o más eventos en los cuales el resultado de uno de ellos no afecta el resultado de los otros eventos.

independent variable The variable in a function with a value that is subject to choice.

variable independiente Variable en una función cuyo valor está sujeto a elección.

inequality An open sentence that uses $<, >, \neq, \leq$, or $\geq$ to compare two quantities.

desigualdad Enunciado abierto que usa $<, >, \neq$, $\leq$ o $\geq$ para comparar dos cantidades.

integer Any number from the set $\{\ldots, -4, -3, -2, -1, 0, 1, 2, 3, 4, \ldots\}$, where … means continues without end.

entero Cualquier número del conjunto $\{\ldots, -4, -3, -2, -1, 0, 1, 2, 3, 4, \ldots\}$, donde … significa que continúa sin fin.

interquartile range A measure of variation in a set of numerical data. It is the distance between first and third quartiles of the data set.

rango intercuartil Una medida de la variación en un conjunto de datos numéricos. Es la distancia entre el primer y el tercer cuartiles del conjunto de datos.

inverse variation A relationship where the product of x and y is a constant k. As x increases in value, y decreases in value, or as y decreases in value, x increases in value.

variación inversa Relación en la cual el producto de x y y es una constante k. A medida que aumenta el valor de x, disminuye el valor de y o a medida que disminuye el valor de y, aumenta el valor de x.

irrational number A number that cannot be expressed as the ratio of two integers.

número irracional Número que no se puede expresar como el razón de dos enteros.

isosceles triangle A triangle having at least two congruent sides.

triángulo isósceles Triángulo que tiene por lo menos dos lados congruentes.

Kk

kilogram The base unit of mass in the metric system. One kilogram equals 1,000 grams.

kilogramo Unidad básica de masa del sistema métrico. Un kilogramo equivale a 1,000 gramos.

Ll

lateral face In a polyhedron, a face that is not a base.

cara lateral En un poliedro, las caras que no forman las bases.

lateral surface area The sum of the areas of all of the lateral faces of a solid.

área de superficie lateral Suma de las áreas de todas las caras de un sólido.

least common denominator (LCD) The least common multiple of the denominators of two or more fractions. You can use the LCD to compare fractions.

mínimo común denominador (mcd) El menor de los múltiplos de los denominadores de dos o más fracciones. Puedes usar el mínimo común denominador para comparar fracciones.

liabilities Debts that are owed by an individual.

pasivo Deudas que tiene una persona.

like fractions Fractions that have the same denominators.

fracciones semejantes Fracciones que tienen los mismos denominadores.

like terms Terms that contain the same variables raised to the same power. Example: $5x$ and $6x$ are like terms.

términos semejante Términos que contienen las mismas variables elevadas a la misma potencia. Ejemplo: $5x$ y $6x$ son *términos semejante*.

line graph A type of statistical graph using lines to show how values change over a period of time.

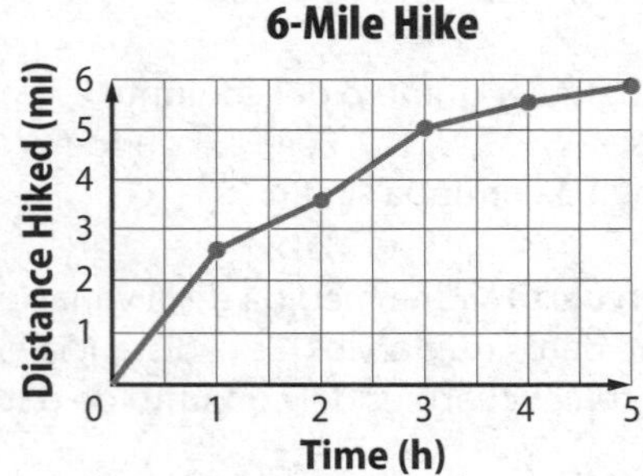

gráfica lineal Tipo de gráfica estadística que usa segmentos de recta para mostrar cómo cambian los valores durante un período de tiempo.

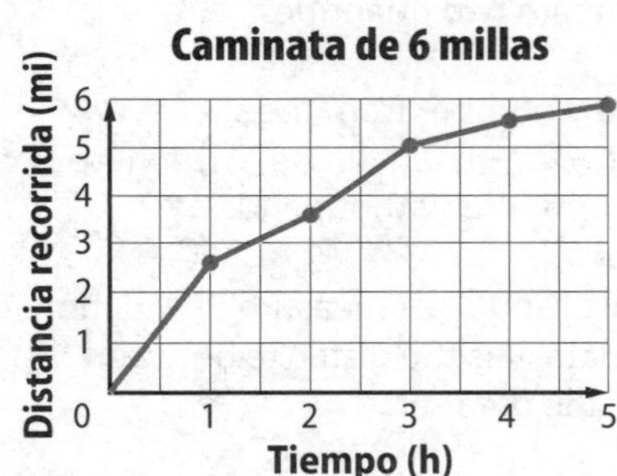

linear equation An equation with a graph that is a straight line.

ecuación lineal Ecuación cuya gráfca es una recta.

linear expression An algebraic expression in which the variable is raised to the first power.

expresión lineal Expresión algebraica en la cual la variable se eleva a la primera potencia.

linear relationship A relationship for which the graph is a straight line.

relación lineal Una relación para la cual la gráfica es una línea recta.

liter The base unit of capacity in the metric system. The amount of dry or liquid material an object can hold.

litro Unidad básica de capacidad del sistema métrico. La cantidad de materia líquida o sólida que puede contener un objeto.

Mm

markdown An amount by which the regular price of an item is reduced.

rebaja Una cantidad por la cual el precio regular de un artículo se reduce.

markup The amount the price of an item is increased above the price the store paid for the item.

margen de utilidad Cantidad de aumento en el precio de un artículo por encima del precio que paga la tienda por dicho artículo.

mean The sum of the data divided by the number of items in the data set.

media La suma de los datos dividida entre el número total de artículos en el conjunto de datos.

mean absolute deviation A measure of variation in a set of numerical data, computed by adding the distances between each data value and the mean, then dividing by the number of data values.

desviación media absoluta Una medida de variación en un conjunto de datos numéricos que se calcula sumando las distancias entre el valor de cada dato y la media, y luego dividiendo entre el número de valores.

measures of center Numbers that are used to describe the center of a set of data. These measures include the mean, median, and mode.

medidas del centro Números que se usan para describir el centro de un conjunto de datos. Estas medidas incluyen la media, la mediana y la moda.

measures of variation A measure used to describe the distribution of data.

medidas de variación Medida usada para describir la distribución de los datos.

median A measure of center in a set of numerical data. The median of a list of values is the value appearing at the center of a sorted version of the list—or the mean of the two central values, if the list contains an even number of values.

mediana Una medida del centro en un conjunto de dados númericos. La mediana de una lista de valores es el valor que aparace en el centro de una versíon ordenada de la lista, o la media de dos valores centrales si la lista contiene un número par de valores.

meter The base unit of length in the metric system.

metro Unidad fundamental de longitud del sistema métrico.

metric system A decimal system of measures. The prefixes commonly used in this system are kilo-, centi-, and milli-.

sistema métrico Sistema decimal de medidas. Los prefijos más comunes son kilo-, centi- y mili-.

mode The number or numbers that appear most often in a set of data. If there are two or more numbers that occur most often, all of them are modes.

moda El número o números que aparece con más frecuencia en un conjunto de datos. Si hay dos o más números que ocurren con más frecuencia, todosellos son modas.

monetary incentives Financial reasons, such as sales, rebates, and coupons, to buy a particular item.

incentivos monetarios Razones financieras, como ventas, reembolsos y cupones, para comprar un artículo en particular.

Multiplication Property of Equality If you multiply each side of an equation by the same nonzero number, the two sides remain equal.

propiedad de multiplicación de la igualdad Si multiplicas ambos lados de una ecuación por el mismo número no nulo, lo lados permanecen iguales.

Multiplication Property of Inequality When you multiply each side of an inequality by a negative number, the inequality symbol must be reversed for the inequality to remain true.

propiedad de desigualdad en la multiplicación Cuando se multiplica cada lado de una desigualdad por un número negativo, el símbolo de desigualdad debe invertirse para que la desigualdad siga siendo verdadera.

Multiplicative Identity Property The product of any number and one is the number.

propiedad de identidad de la multiplicación El producto de cualquier número y uno es el mismo número.

Multiplicative Property of Zero The product of any number and zero is zero.

propiedad del cero en la multiplicación El producto de cualquier número y cero es cero.

multiplicative inverse Two numbers with a product of 1. For example, the multiplicative inverse of $\frac{2}{3}$ is $\frac{3}{2}$.

inverso multiplicativo Dos números cuyo producto es 1. Por ejemplo, el inverso multiplicativo de $\frac{2}{3}$ es $\frac{3}{2}$.

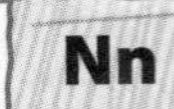

Nn

negative exponent Any nonzero number to the negative *n* power. It is the multiplicative inverse of its *n*th power.

exponente negativo Cualquier número que no sea cero a la potencia negative de *n*. Es el inverso multiplicativo de su *enésimo* potencia.

negative integer An integer that is less than zero. Negative integers are written with a − sign.

entero negativo Número menor que cero. Se escriben con el signo −.

net A two-dimensional figure that can be used to build a three-dimensional figure.

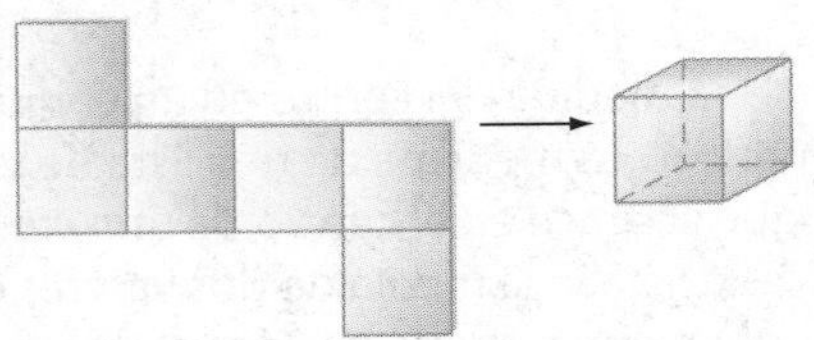

red Figura bidimensional que sirve para hacer una figura tridimensional.

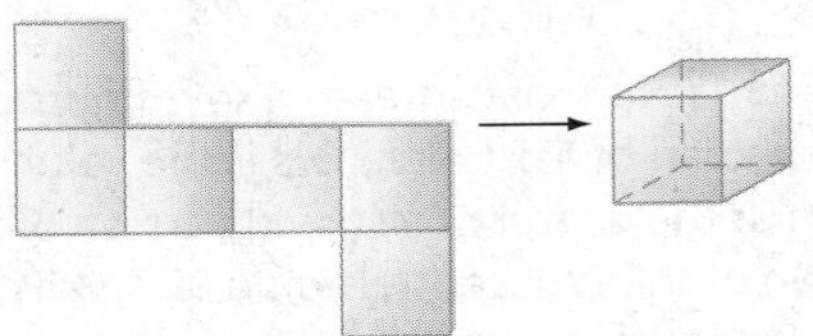

net worth The value of one's assets minus one's liabilities.

patrimonio neto Valor del activo menos el pasivo de una persona.

nonagon A polygon having nine sides.

enágono Polígono que tiene nueve lados.

nonproportional The relationship between two ratios with a rate or ratio that is not constant.

no proporcional Relación entre dos razones cuya tasa o razón no es constante.

numerical expression A combination of numbers and operations.

expresión numérica Combinación de números y operaciones.

Oo

obtuse angle Any angle that measures greater than 90° but less than 180°.

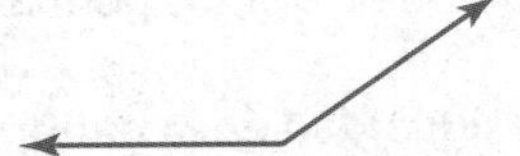

ángulo obtuso Cualquier ángulo que mide más de 90° pero menos de 180°.

obtuse triangle A triangle having one obtuse angle.

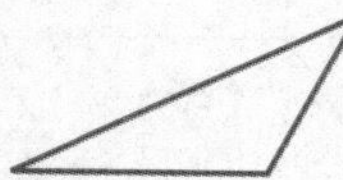

triángulo obtusángulo Triángulo que tiene un ángulo obtuso.

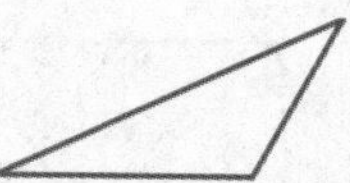

octagon A polygon having eight sides.

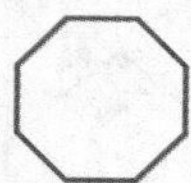

octágono Polígono que tiene ocho lados.

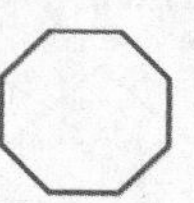

opposites Two integers are opposites if they are represented on the number line by points that are the same distance from zero, but on opposite sides of zero. The sum of two opposites is zero.

opuestos Dos enteros son opuestos si, en la recta numérica, están representados por puntos que equidistan de cero, pero en direcciones opuestas. La suma de dos opuestos es cero.

order of operations The rules to follow when more than one operation is used in a numerical expression.

1. Evaluate the expressions inside grouping symbols.
2. Evaluate all powers.
3. Multiply and divide in order from left to right.
4. Add and subtract in order from left to right.

orden de las operaciones Reglas a seguir cuando se usa más de una operación en una expresión numérica.

1. Primero, evalúa las expresiones dentro de los símbolos de agrupación.
2. Evalúa todas las potencias.
3. Multiplica y divide en orden de izquierda a derecha.
4. Suma y resta en orden de izquierda a derecha.

ordered pair A pair of numbers used to locate a point in the coordinate plane. An ordered pair is written in the form (x-coordinate, y-coordinate).

par ordenado Par de números que se utiliza para ubicar un punto en un plano de coordenadas. Se escribe de la siguiente forma: (coordenada x, coordenada y).

origin The point at which the x-axis and the y-axis intersect in a coordinate plane. The origin is at (0, 0).

origen Punto en que el eje x y el eje y se intersecan en un plano de coordenadas. El origen está ubicado en (0, 0).

outcome Any one of the possible results of an action. For example, 4 is an outcome when a number cube is rolled.

resultado Cualquiera de los resultados posibles de una acción. Por ejemplo, 4 puede ser un resultado al lanzar un cubo numerado.

outlier A data value that is either much *greater* or much *less* than the median.

valor atípico Valor de los datos que es mucho *mayor* o mucho *menor* que la mediana.

parallel lines Lines in a plane that never intersect.

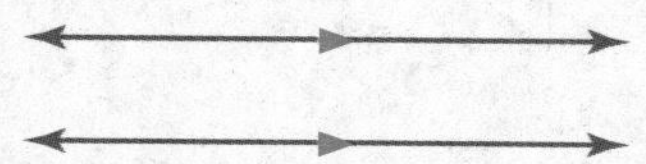

rectas paralelas Rectas en un plano que nunca se intersecan.

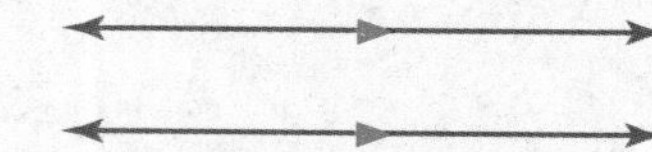

parallelogram A quadrilateral with opposite sides parallel and opposite sides congruent.

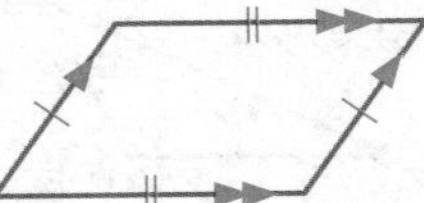

pentagon A polygon having five sides.

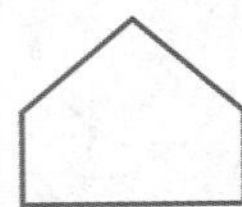

percent equation An equation that describes the relationship between the part, whole, and percent.

part = percent • whole

percent error A ratio that compares the inaccuracy of an estimate (amount of error) to the actual amount.

percent of change A ratio that compares the change in a quantity to the original amount.

$$\text{percent of change} = \frac{\text{amount of change}}{\text{original amount}}$$

percent of decrease A negative percent of change.

percent of increase A positive percent of change.

percent proportion One ratio or fraction that compares part of a quantity to the whole quantity. The other ratio is the equivalent percent written as a fraction with a denominator of 100.

$$\frac{\text{part}}{\text{whole}} = \frac{\text{percent}}{100}$$

perfect squares Numbers with square roots that are whole numbers. 25 is a perfect square because the square root of 25 is 5.

perpendicular lines Lines that meet or cross each other to form right angles.

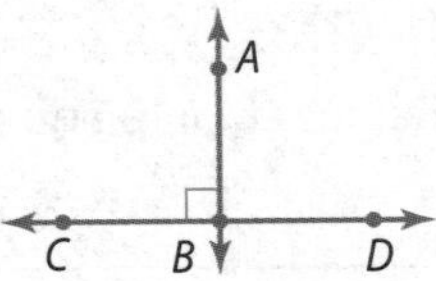

personal budget An individual plan for spending.

pi The ratio of the circumference of a circle to its diameter. The Greek letter π represents this number. The value of pi is 3.1415926. . . . Approximations for pi are 3.14 and $\frac{22}{7}$.

paralelogramo Cuadrilátero cuyos lados opuestos son paralelos y congruentes.

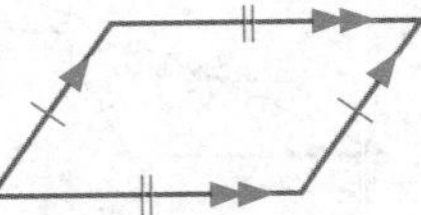

pentágono Polígono que tiene cinco lados.

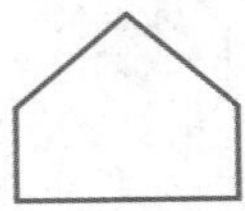

ecuación porcentual Ecuación que describe la relación entre la parte, el todo y el por ciento.

parte = por ciento • todo

porcentaje de error Una razón que compara la inexactitud de una estimación (cantidad del error) con la cantidad real.

porcentaje de cambio Razón que compara el cambio en una cantidad a la cantidad original.

$$\text{porcentaje de cambio} = \frac{\text{cantidad del cambio}}{\text{cantidad original}}$$

porcentaje de disminución Porcentaje de cambio negativo.

porcentaje de aumento Porcentaje de cambio positivo.

proporción porcentual Razón o fracción que compara parte de una cantidad a toda la cantidad. La otra razón es el porcentaje equivalente escrito como fracción con 100 de denominador.

$$\frac{\text{parte}}{\text{todo}} = \frac{\text{porcentaje}}{100}$$

cuadrados perfectos Números cuya raíz cuadrada es un número entero. 25 es un cuadrado perfecto porque la raíz cuadrada de 25 es 5.

rectas perpendiculares Rectas que al encontrarse o cruzarse forman ángulos rectos.

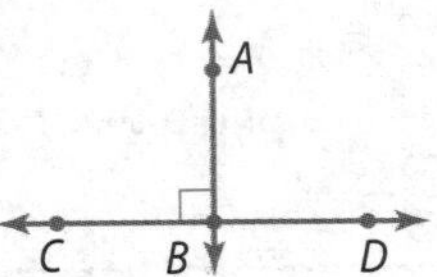

presupuesto personal Plan de gastos de una persona.

pi Relación entre la circunferencia de un círculo y su diámetro. La letra griega π representa este número. El valor de pi es 3.1415926. . . . Las aproximaciones de pi son 3.14 y $\frac{22}{7}$.

plane A two-dimensional flat surface that extends in all directions.

plano Superficie bidimensional que se extiende en todas direcciones.

polygon A simple closed figure formed by three or more straight line segments.

polígono Figura cerrada simple formada por tres o más segmentos de recta.

polyhedron A three-dimensional figure with faces that are polygons.

poliedro Una figura tridimensional con caras que son polígonos.

population The entire group of items or individuals from which the samples under consideration are taken.

población El grupo total de individuos o de artículos del cual se toman las muestras bajo estudio.

positive integer An integer that is greater than zero. They are written with or without a + sign.

entero positivo Entero que es mayor que cero; se escribe con o sin el signo +.

powers Numbers expressed using exponents. The power 3^2 is read three to the *second power*, or *three squared*.

potencias Números que se expresan usando exponentes. La potencia 3^2 se lee *tres a la segunda potencia* o *tres al cuadrado*.

precision The ability of a measurement to be consistently reproduced.

precisión Capacidad que tiene una medición de poder reproducirse consistentemente.

principal The amount of money deposited or borrowed.

capital Cantidad de dinero que se deposita o se toma prestada.

prism A polyhedron with two parallel congruent faces called bases.

prisma Un poliedro con dos caras congruentes paralelas llamadas bases.

probability The chance that some event will happen. It is the ratio of the number of favorable outcomes to the number of possible outcomes.

probabilidad La posibilidad de que suceda un evento. Es la razón del número de resultados favorables al número de resultados posibles.

probability model A model used to assign probabilities to outcomes of a chance process by examining the nature of the process.

modelo de probabilidad Un modelo usado para asignar probabilidades a resultados de un proceso aleatorio examinando la naturaleza del proceso.

properties Statements that are true for any number or variable.

propiedades Enunciados que son verdaderos para cualquier número o variable.

proportion An equation stating that two ratios or rates are equivalent.

proporción Ecuación que indica que dos razones o tasas son equivalentes.

proportional The relationship between two ratios with a constant rate or ratio.

proporcional Relación entre dos razones con una tasa o razón constante.

pyramid A polyhedron with one base that is a polygon and three or more triangular faces that meet at a common vertex.

pirámide Un poliedro con una base que es un polígono y tres o más caras triangulares que se encuentran en un vértice común.

Qq

quadrant One of the four regions into which the two perpendicular number lines of the coordinate plane separate the plane.

cuadrante Una de las cuatro regiones en que dos rectas numéricas perpendiculares dividen el plano de coordenadas.

quadrilateral A closed figure having four sides and four angles.

cuadrilátero Figura cerrada que tiene cuatro lados y cuatro ángulos.

qualitative predictions Predictions that deal with numerical data or measurable data.

predicciones cualitatives Las predicciones de que tratan los datos numéricos o datos cuantificables.

quantitative predictions Predictions that deal with descriptions, observable data, or non-numerical data.

predicciones cuantitatives Las predicciones que tienen que ver con las descripciones, datos observables, o los datos no numéricos.

quarter circle One-fourth of a circle. The formula for the area of a quarter circle is $A = \frac{1}{4}\pi r^2$.

cuarto círculo Un cuarto do un círculo. La fórmula de la superficie de un cuarto círculo es $A = \frac{1}{4}\pi r^2$.

quartile A value that divides the data set into four equal parts.

cuartil Valor que divide el conjunto de datos en cuatro partes iguales.

Rr

radical sign The symbol used to indicate a nonnegative square root, $\sqrt{}$.

signo radical Símbolo que se usa para indicar una raíz cuadrada no negativa, $\sqrt{}$.

radius The distance from the center of a circle to any point on the circle.

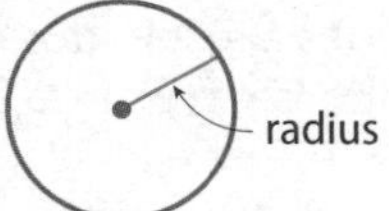

radio Distancia desde el centro de un círculo hasta cualquiera de sus puntos.

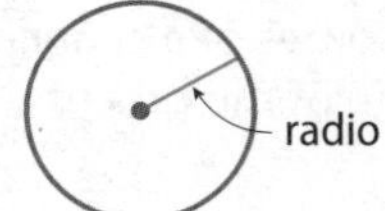

random Outcomes occur at random if each outcome occurs by chance. For example, rolling a number on a number cube occurs at random.

azar Los resultados ocurren aleatoriamente si cada resultado ocurre por casualidad. Por ejemplo, sacar un número en un cubo numerado ocurre al azar.

range The set of output values for a function.

rango Conjunto de valores de salida para una función.

range The difference between the greatest and least data value.

rango La diferencia entre el número mayor y el menor en un conjunto de datos.

rate A ratio that compares two quantities with different kinds of units.

tasa Razón que compara dos cantidades que tienen distintas unidades de medida.

rate of change A rate that describes how one quantity changes in relation to another. A rate of change is usually expressed as a unit rate.

tasa de cambio Tasa que describe cómo cambia una cantidad con respecto a otra. Por lo general, se expresa como tasa unitaria.

rational numbers The set of numbers that can be written in the form $\frac{a}{b}$, where a and b are integers and $b \neq 0$.

Examples: $1 = \frac{1}{1}, \frac{2}{9}, -2.3 = -2\frac{3}{10}$

real numbers A set made up of rational and irrational numbers.

rebate A partial return or refund on an amount paid.

reciprocal The multiplicative inverse of a number.

rectangle A parallelogram having four right angles.

rectangular prism A prism that has two parallel congruent bases that are rectangles.

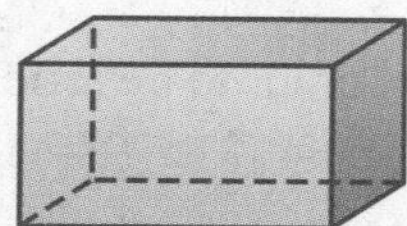

reduction An image smaller than the original.

regular polygon A polygon that has all sides congruent and all angles congruent.

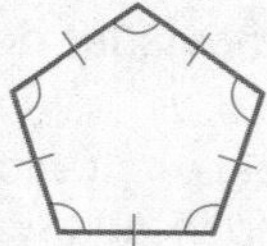

regular pyramid A pyramid whose base is a regular polygon and in which the segment from the vertex to the center of the base is the altitude.

relative frequency A ratio that compares the frequency of each category to the total.

repeating decimal A decimal whose digits repeat in groups of one or more.

rhombus A parallelogram having four congruent sides.

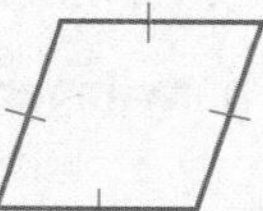

right angle An angle that measures exactly 90°.

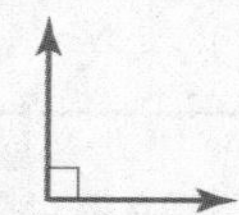

números racionales Conjunto de números que puede escribirse en la forma $\frac{a}{b}$ donde a y b son números enteros y $b \neq 0$.

Ejemplos: $1 = \frac{1}{1}, \frac{2}{9}, -2.3 = -2\frac{3}{10}$

números reales Conjunto de números racionales e irracionales.

reembolso Reintegro o devolución parcial de una cantidad pagada.

recíproco El inverso multiplicativo de un número.

rectángulo Paralelogramo con cuatro ángulos rectos.

prisma rectangular Un prisma con dos bases paralelas congruentes que son rectángulos.

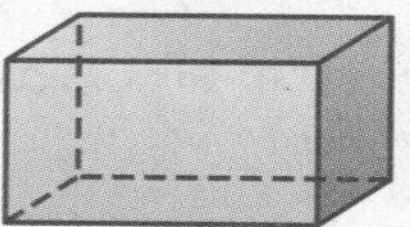

reducción Imagen más pequeña que la original.

polígono regular Polígono con todos los lados y todos los ángulos congruentes.

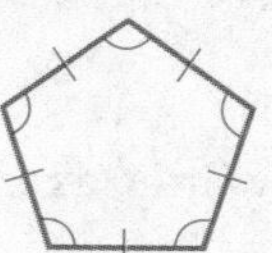

pirámide regular Pirámide cuya base es un polígono regular y en la cual el segmento desde el vértice hasta el centro de la base es la altura.

frecuencia relativa Razón que compara la frecuencia de cada categoría al total.

decimal periódico Una decimal cuyos dígitos se repiten en grupos de uno o más.

rombo Paralelogramo que tiene cuatro lados congruentes.

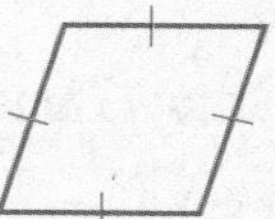

ángulo recto Ángulo que mide exactamente 90°.

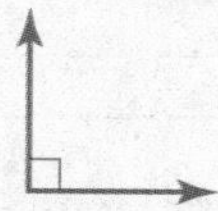

right triangle A triangle having one right angle.

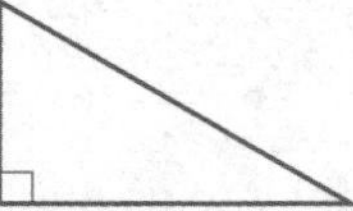

triángulo rectángulo Triángulo que tiene un ángulo recto.

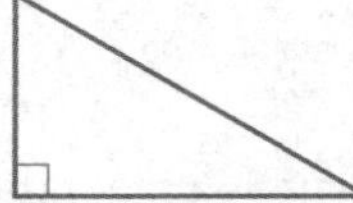

sales tax An additional amount of money charged on items that people buy.

impuesto sobre las ventas Cantidad adicional de dinero que se cobra sobre los artículos que compra la gente.

sample A randomly selected group chosen for the purpose of collecting data.

muestra Grupo escogido al azar o aleatoriamente que se usa con el propósito de recoger datos.

sample space The set of all possible outcomes of a probability experiment.

espacio muestral Conjunto de todos los resultados posibles de un experimento probabilístico.

scale The scale that gives the ratio that compares the measurements of a drawing or model to the measurements of the real object.

escala Razón que compara las medidas de un dibujo o modelo a las medidas del objeto real.

scale drawing A drawing that is used to represent objects that are too large or too small to be drawn at actual size.

dibujo a escala Dibujo que se usa para representar objetos que son demasiado grandes o demasiado pequeños como para dibujarlos de tamaño natural.

scale factor A scale written as a ratio without units in simplest form.

factor de escala Escala escrita como una razón sin unidades en forma simplificada.

scale model A model used to represent objects that are too large or too small to be built at actual size.

modelo a escala Réplica de un objeto real, el cual es demasiado grande o demasiado pequeño como para construirlo de tamaño natural.

scalene triangle A triangle having no congruent sides.

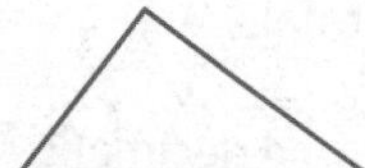

triángulo escaleno Triángulo sin lados congruentes.

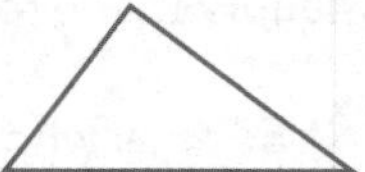

scatter plot In a scatter plot, two sets of related data are plotted as ordered pairs on the same graph.

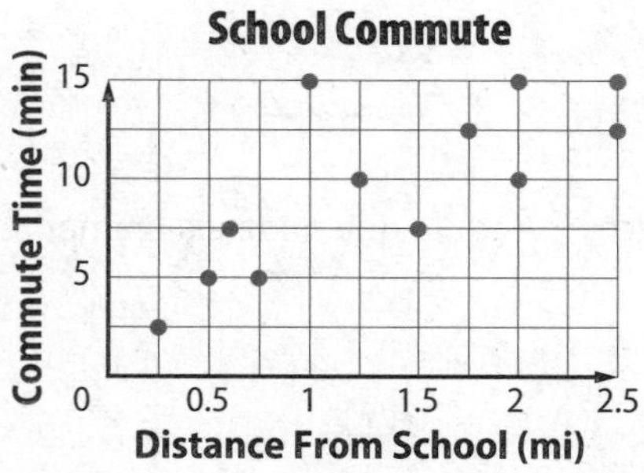

diagrama de dispersión Diagrama en que dos conjuntos de datos relacionados aparecen graficados como pares ordenados en la misma gráfica.

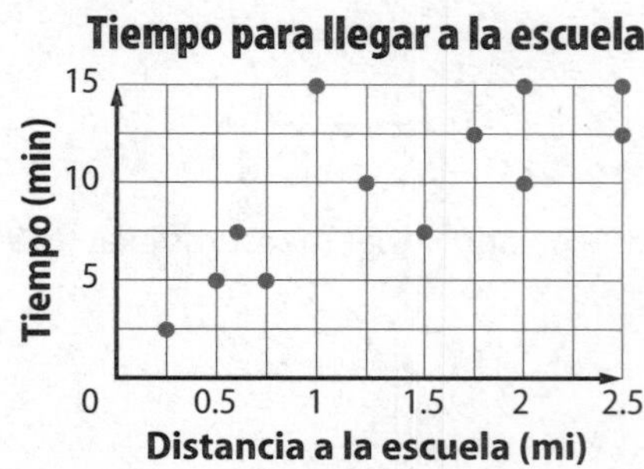

selling price The amount the customer pays for an item.

precio de venta Cantidad de dinero que paga un consumidor por un artículo.

semicircle Half of a circle. The formula for the area of a semicircle is $A = \frac{1}{2}\pi r^2$.

semicírculo Medio círculo La fórmula para el área de un semicírculo es $A = \frac{1}{2}\pi r^2$.

sequence An ordered list of numbers, such as 0, 1, 2, 3 or 2, 4, 6, 8.

sucesión Lista ordenada de números, como 0, 1, 2, 3 ó 2, 4, 6, 8.

similar figures Figures that have the same shape but not necessarily the same size.

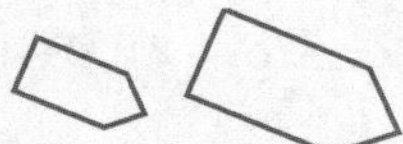

figuras semejantes Figuras que tienen la misma forma, pero no necesariamente el mismo tamaño.

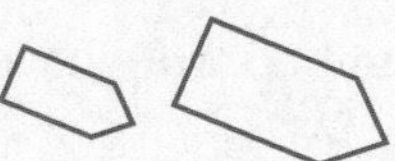

similar solids Solids with the same shape. Their corresponding linear measures are proportional.

sólidos semejantes Sólidos con la misma forma. Sus medidas lineales correspondientes son proporcionales.

simple event One outcome or a collection of outcomes.

eventos simples Un resultado o una colección de resultados.

simple interest The amount paid or earned for the use of money. The formula for simple interest is $I = prt$.

interés simple Cantidad que se paga o que se gana por el uso del dinero. La fórmula para calcular el interés simple es $I = prt$.

simple random sample An unbiased sample where each item or person in the population is as likely to be chosen as any other.

muestra aleatoria simple Muestra de una población que tiene la misma probabilidad de escogerse que cualquier otra.

simplest form An expression is in simplest form when it is replaced by an equivalent expression having no like terms or parentheses.

expresión mínima Expresión en su forma más simple cuando es reemplazada por una expresión equivalente que no tiene términos similares ni paréntesis.

simplify Write an expression in simplest form.

simplificar Escribir una expresión en su forma más simple.

simulation An experiment that is designed to model the action in a given situation.

simulación Un experimento diseñado para modelar la acción en una situación dada.

slant height The height of each lateral face.

altura oblicua Altura de cada cara lateral.

slope The rate of change between any two points on a line. It is the ratio of vertical change to horizontal change. The slope tells how steep the line is.

pendiente Razón de cambio entre cualquier par de puntos en una recta. Es la razón del cambio vertical al cambio horizontal. La pendiente indica el grado de inclinación de la recta.

slope-intercept form An equation written in the form $y = mx + b$, where m is the slope and b is the y-intercept.

forma pendiente intersección Ecuación de la forma $y = mx + b$, donde m es la pendiente y b es la intersección y.

solution A replacement value for the variable in an open sentence. A value for the variable that makes an equation true. Example: The *solution* of $12 = x + 7$ is 5.

solución Valor de reemplazo de la variable en un enunciado abierto. Valor de la variable que hace que una ecuación sea verdadera. Ejemplo: La *solución* de $12 = x + 7$ es 5.

square The product of a number and itself. 36 is the square of 6.

square A parallelogram having four right angles and four congruent sides.

square root The factors multiplied to form perfect squares.

squared The product of a number and itself. 36 is the square of 6.

standard form Numbers written without exponents.

statistics The study of collecting, organizing, and interpreting data.

straight angle An angle that measures exactly 180°.

Subtraction Property of Equality If you subtract the same number from each side of an equation, the two sides remain equal.

Subtraction Property of Inequality If you subtract the same number from each side of an inequality, the inequality remains true.

supplementary angles Two angles are supplementary if the sum of their measures is 180°.

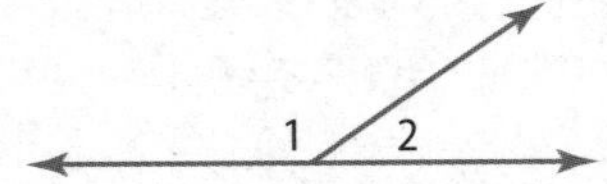

$\angle 1$ and $\angle 2$ are supplementary angles.

surface area The sum of the areas of all the surfaces (faces) of a three-dimensional figure.

survey A question or set of questions designed to collect data about a specific group of people, or population.

systematic random sample A sample where the items or people are selected according to a specific time or item interval.

cuadrado Producto de un número por sí mismo. 36 es el cuadrado de 6.

cuadrado Paralelogramo con cuatro ángulos rectos y cuatro lados congruentes.

al cuadrado Factores multiplicados para formar cuadrados perfectos.

raíz cuadrada El producto de un número por sí mismo. 36 es el cuadrado de 6.

forma estándar Números escritos sin exponentes.

estadística Estudio que consiste en recopilar, organizar e interpretar datos.

ángulo llano Ángulo que mide exactamente 180°.

propiedad de sustracción de la igualdad Si restas el mismo número de ambos lados de una ecuación, los dos lados permanecen iguales.

propiedad de desigualdad en la resta Si se resta el mismo número a cada lado de una desigualdad, la desigualdad sigue siendo verdadera.

ángulos suplementarios Dos ángulos son suplementarios si la suma de sus medidas es 180°.

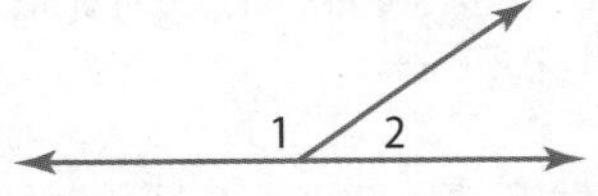

$\angle 1$ y $\angle 2$ son suplementarios.

área de superficie La suma de las áreas de todas las superficies (caras) de una figura tridimensional.

encuesta Pregunta o conjunto de preguntas diseñadas para recoger datos sobre un grupo específico de personas o población.

muestra aleatoria sistemática Muestra en que los elementos o personas se eligen según un intervalo de tiempo o elemento específico.

Tt

term Each number in a sequence.

term A number, a variable, or a product or quotient of numbers and variables.

término Cada número en una sucesión.

término Número, variable, producto o cociente de números y de variables.

terminating decimal A repeating decimal which has a repeating digit of 0.

decimal finito Un decimal periódico que tiene un dígito que se repite que es 0.

theoretical probability The ratio of the number of ways an event can occur to the number of possible outcomes. It is based on what *should* happen when conducting a probability experiment.

probabilidad teórica Razón del número de maneras en que puede ocurrir un evento al número de resultados posibles. Se basa en lo que *debería* pasar cuando se conduce un experimento probabilístico.

three-dimensional figure A figure with length, width, and height.

figura tridimensional Figura que tiene largo, ancho y alto.

third quartile For a data set with median *M*, the third quartile is the median of the data values greater than *M*.

tercer cuartil Para un conjunto de datos con la mediana *M*, el tercer cuartil es la mediana de los valores mayores que *M*.

tip Also known as a gratuity, it is a small amount of money in return for a service.

propina También conocida como gratificación; es una cantidad pequeña de dinero en recompensa por un servicio.

transversal The third line formed when two parallel lines are intersected.

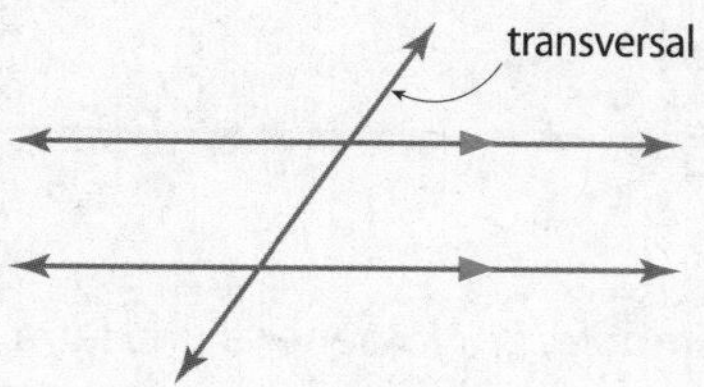

transversal Tercera recta que se forma cuando se intersecan dos rectas paralelas.

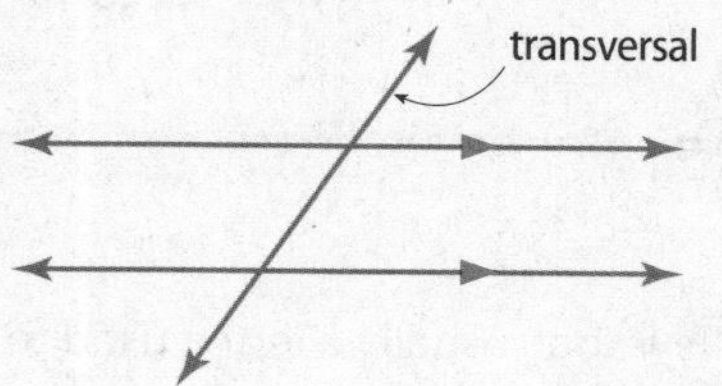

trapezoid A quadrilateral with one pair of parallel sides.

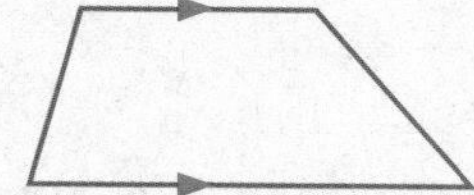

trapecio Cuadrilátero con un único par de lados paralelos.

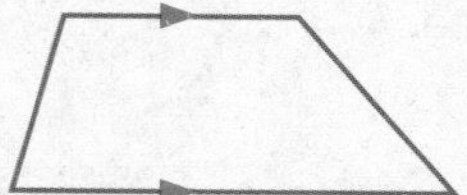

tree diagram A diagram used to show the sample space.

diagrama de árbol Diagrama que se usa para mostrar el espacio muestral.

triangle A figure with three sides and three angles.

triángulo Figura con tres lados y tres ángulos.

triangular prism A prism that has two parallel congruent bases that are triangles.

prisma triangular Un prisma que tiene dos bases congruentes paralelas que triángulos.

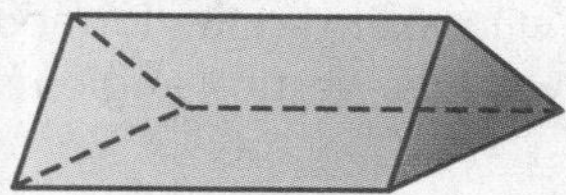

two-step equation An equation having two different operations.

ecuación de dos pasos Ecuación que contiene dos operaciones distintas.

two-step inequality An inequality than contains two operations.

desigualdad de dos pasos Desigualdad que contiene dos operaciones.

unbiased sample A sample representative of the entire population.

unfair game A game where there is not a chance of each player being equally likely to win.

uniform probability model A probability model which assigns equal probability to all outcomes.

unit rate A rate that is simplified so that it has a denominator of 1 unit.

unit ratio A unit rate where the denominator is one unit.

unlike fractions Fractions with different denominators.

muestra no sesgada Muestra que se selecciona de modo que se representativa de la población entera.

juego injusto Juego donde cada jugador no tiene la misma posibilidad de ganar.

modelo de probabilidad uniforme Un modelo de probabilidad que asigna igual probabilidad a todos los resultados.

tasa unitaria Tasa simplificada para que tenga un denominador igual a 1.

razón unitaria Tasa unitaria en que el denominador es la unidad.

fracciones con distinto denominador Fracciones cuyos denominadores son diferentes.

variable A symbol, usually a letter, used to represent a number in mathematical expressions or sentences.

variable expenses Costs that do change based on the amount that is used.

vertex A vertex of an angle is the common endpoint of the rays forming the angle.

vertex

vertex The point where three or more faces of a polyhedron intersect.

vertical angles Opposite angles formed by the intersection of two lines. Vertical angles are congruent.

1 2

$\angle 1$ and $\angle 2$ are vertical angles.

volume The number of cubic units needed to fill the space occupied by a solid.

variable Símbolo, por lo general una letra, que se usa para representar un número en expresiones o enunciados matemáticos.

gastos variables Costos que cambian con la cantidad usada.

vértice El vértice de un ángulo es el extremo común de los rayos que lo forman.

vértice

vértice El punto donde tres o más caras de un poliedro se cruzan.

ángulos opuestos por el vértice Ángulos opuestos formados por la intersección de dos rectas. Los ángulos opuestos por el vértice son congruentes.

1 2

$\angle 1$ y $\angle 2$ son ángulos opuestos por el vértice.

volumen Número de unidades cúbicas que se requieren para llenar el espacio que ocupa un sólido.

voluntary response sample A sample which involves only those who want to participate in the sampling.

muestra de respuesta voluntaria Muestra que involucra sólo aquellos que quieren participar en el muestreo.

Ww

wages Payments for labor or services.

remuneración Pago por trabajo o servicios.

Xx

***x*-axis** The horizontal number line in a coordinate plane.

eje *x* La recta numérica horizontal en el plano de coordenadas.

***x*-coordinate** The first number of an ordered pair. It corresponds to a number on the *x*-axis.

coordenada *x* El primer número de un par ordenado. Corresponde a un número en el eje *x*.

Yy

***y*-axis** The vertical number line in a coordinate plane.

eje *y* La recta numérica vertical en el plano de coordenadas.

***y*-coordinate** The second number of an ordered pair. It corresponds to a number on the *y*-axis.

coordenada *y* El segundo número de un par ordenado. Corresponde a un número en el eje *y*.

***y*-intercept** The *y*-coordinate of the point where the line crosses the *y*-axis.

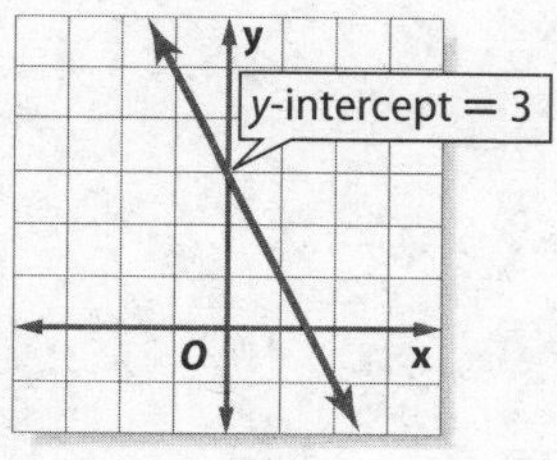

intersección *y* La coordenada *y* del punto donde cruza la gráfica el eje *y*.

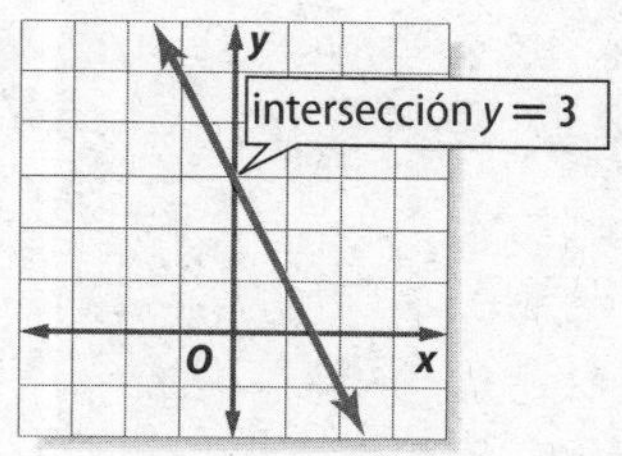

Zz

zero pair The result when one positive counter is paired with one negative counter. The value of a zero pair is 0.

par nulo Resultado de hacer coordinar una ficha positiva con una negativa. El valor de un par nulo es 0.

Selected Answers

eHelp
Go online for Step-by-Step Solutions.

Chapter 6 Multiple Representations of Linear Relationships

Page 436 Chapter 6 Are You Ready?

1. (−3, 4) **3.** (2, 2) **5.** (4, 3) **7.** 121 **9.** 2.5 **11.** $\frac{s}{2} = 35$; 70 mph

Pages 445–446 Lesson 6-1 Independent Practice

1. Linear; the rate of change is constant; as x increases by 2, y increases by 1. **3** Linear; the rate of change is constant; as x increases by 5, y increases by 15. **5** Yes; the rate of change is constant; as the time increases by 1 hour, the distance increases by 65 miles. **7.** Linear; Not linear; Not linear; Not linear **9.** Sample answer: The number of stories a building has to its height.

Stories	35	40	45	50
Height (ft)	510	515	545	582

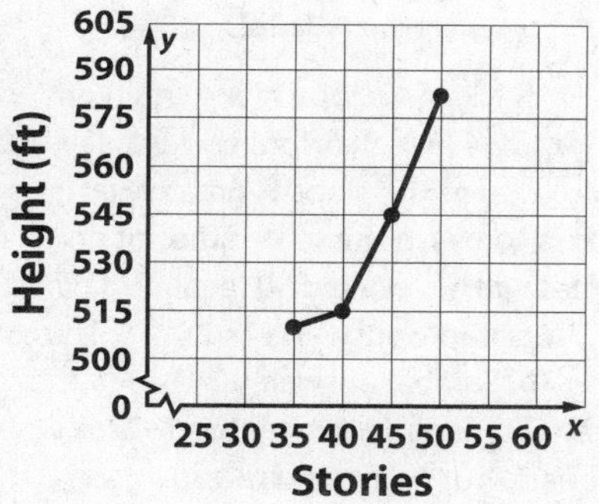

Pages 447–448 Lesson 6-1 Multi-Step Problem Solving

11. C **13.** 8 **15.** yes; Sample answer: Since 25% is being donated to charity, that means that for every dollar raised, 25 cents will be donated. The rate is constant.

Pages 453–454 Lesson 6-2 Independent Practice

1

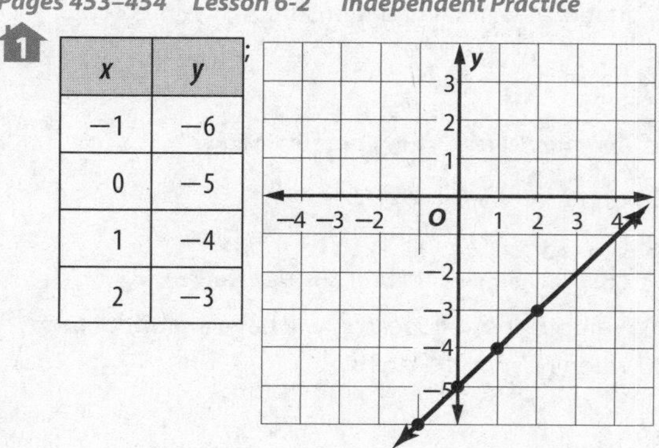

x	y
−1	−6
0	−5
1	−4
2	−3

3 a.

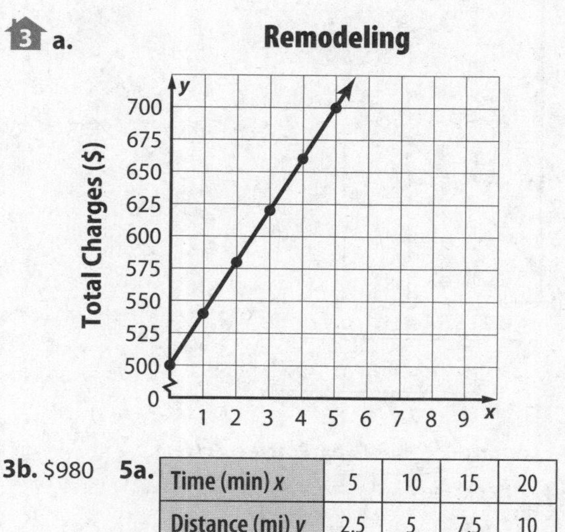

3b. $980 **5a.**

Time (min) x	5	10	15	20
Distance (mi) y	2.5	5	7.5	10

5b. Sample answer: The rate of change is 0.5 mile per minute. The rate of change is constant.

5c.

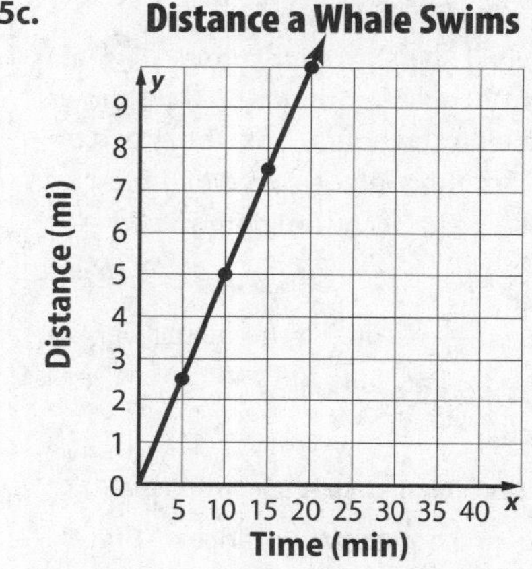

7. Sample answer: The graph is still a straight line. The line is steeper.

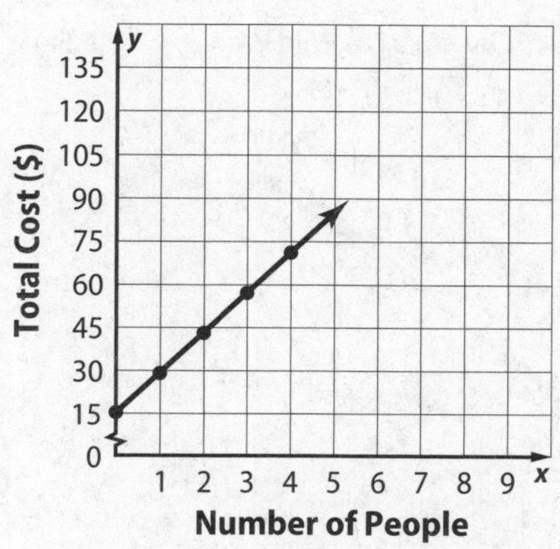

9. Sample answer: Mindy walks 3 miles each day. She has already walked 3 miles, How many total miles will Mindy walk in 7 days?; 24 miles

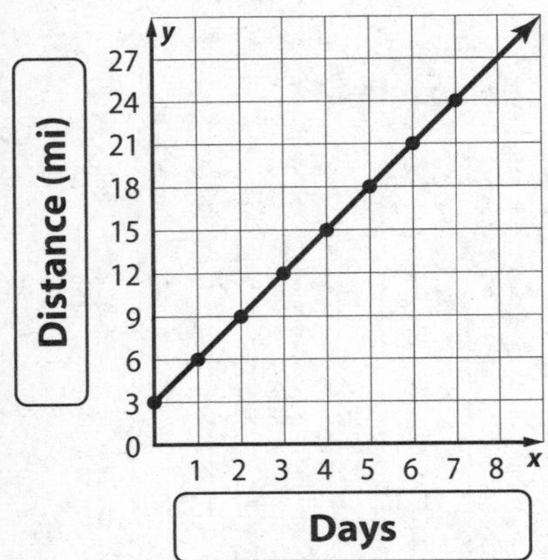

Page 456 Lesson 6-2 Multi-Step Problem Solving

11. C **13.** 2 necklaces

Page 459 Focus on Mathematical Processes

1. 26 containers **3.** $2n + 2$; 18 toothpicks

Pages 465–466 Lesson 6-3 Independent Practice

1 $\frac{50}{1}$ or 50; Adriano read 50 pages every hour. **3 a.** It shows that car A travels 120 miles in 2 hours. **3b.** It shows that car B travels 67.5 miles in 1.5 hours. **3c.** the speed of each car at that point **3d.** the average speed of the car **3e.** Car A; the slope is steeper **5.** Marisol determined $\frac{\text{run}}{\text{rise}}$. Her answer should be $\frac{3}{2}$ or $1\frac{1}{2}$. **7.** No; the slope of $\overline{AB}$ is $\frac{0-1}{1-5}$ or $\frac{1}{4}$ and the slope of $\overline{BC}$ is $\frac{-3-0}{-3-1}$ or $\frac{3}{4}$. If the points were on the same line, the slopes would be equal.

Pages 467–468 Lesson 6-3 Multi-Step Problem Solving

9. C **11.** 0.2 foot rise over a horizontal distance of 1 foot; $\frac{2}{5} - \frac{1}{5} = \frac{1}{5}$ or $\frac{0.2 \text{ ft}}{1 \text{ ft}}$ **13.** -3

Pages 477–478 Lesson 6-4 Independent Practice

1 $-\frac{5}{2}$; -2 **3.** $\frac{3}{8}$; 7 **5.** 8; -5 **7a.** Wild Waves: $y = 16.5x + 200$; Coaster Haven: $y = 14.5x + 250$

7b.

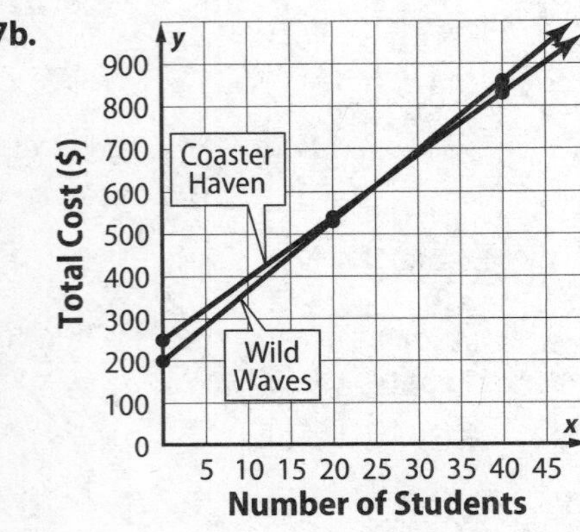

25 students; The point at which both lines intersect is where the cost is the same. **7c.** Wild Waves; Coaster Haven; Sample answer: The line for Coaster Haven is below the line for Wild Waves at 20 and above it at 28. **9** Sample answer: Theresa incorrectly determined the y-intercept. The y-intercept is -4. **11.** Sample drawing shown;

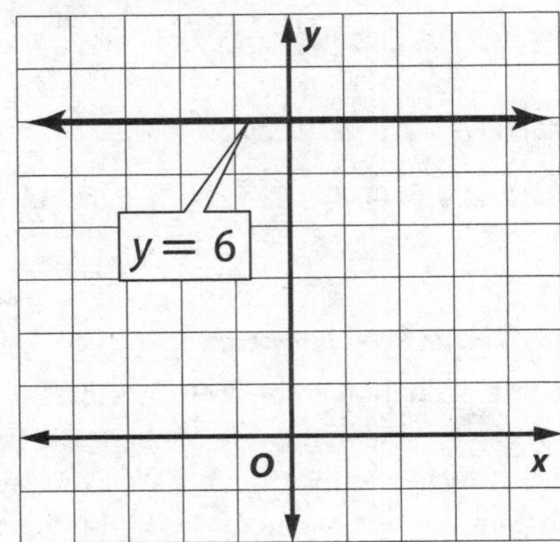

horizontal line; slope = 0

Pages 479–480 Lesson 6-4 Multi-Step Problem Solving

13. 2 **15.** 2 miles per hour **17.** $y = -\frac{3}{5}x + 12$; y-intercept: 12; slope: $-\frac{3}{5}$; x-intercept: 20

Pages 485–486 Lesson 6-5 Independent Practice

1 $y = 2x$ **3** $y = -\frac{5}{3}x + 12$ **5a.** slope = 3; y-intercept = 35 **5b.** $y = 3x + 35$ **5c.** 32,435 feet; 6.1 miles **5d.** Javier hikes at a faster pace, which means the slope is greater. Javier hikes a further distance than Tomás in the same amount of time. After 5 seconds, Tomás will have hiked 50 feet and Javier will have hiked 55 feet. **7a.** Sample answer: $y = 2x + 5$; The line moves up the y-axis. **7b.** Sample answer: $y = 3x + 3$; The line becomes steeper. **7c.** Sample answer: $y = -2x + 3$; The line is the same steepness, but slants downward.

Page 488 Lesson 6-5 Multi-Step Problem Solving

9. B **11.** $40

Page 493 Chapter Review Vocabulary Check

1. linear equation **3.** linear relationship **5.** y-intercept **7.** slope

Page 494 Chapter Review Key Concept Check

1. $y = 2x - 3$ **3.** $y = x$ **5.** $y = -3x + 4$

Page 495 Chapter Review Multi-Step Problem Solving

7. 6 lawns: Sample answer: Jackson will have a profit of more than $100 when he mows 6 lawns.

Chapter 7 Equations and Inequalities

Page 500 Chapter 7 Are You Ready?

1. $p + 3$ **3.** $g + 10$ **5.** 17 **7.** 1 **9.** 35

Pages 507–508 Lesson 7-1 Independent Practice

1. −2 **3** 35 **5.** −13 **7.** 3.5 and 4.5 **9** 3 games **11.** 5 books **13.** −3 **15.** False; this is an equation, so both sides of the equation must equal the same value. Therefore, $3m + 13$ must equal 7 and m can only have one solution, −2. **17.** Sample answer: $3x - 5 < 2$

Pages 509–510 Lesson 7-1 Multi-Step Problem Solving

19. C **21.** 7 pencils **23.** Sample answer: He spent \$46 or less on clothing because $50 + 1.07(46) = 99.22$ which is less than 100 and $50 + 1.07(47) = 100.29$ and is greater than 100.

Pages 515–516 Lesson 7-2 Independent Practice

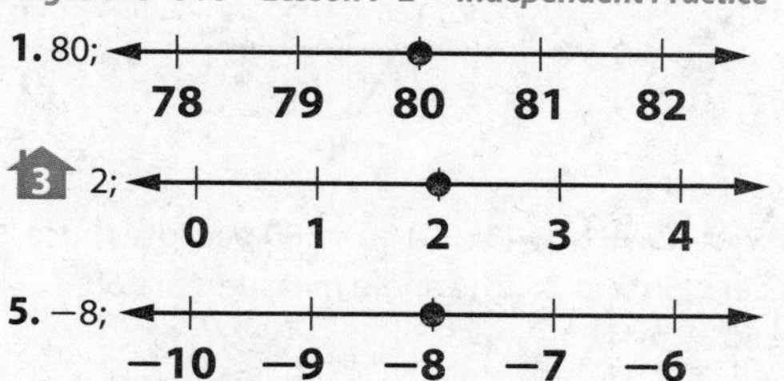

7 $3r = 615$; $r = 205$; $2.5r = 575$; $r = 230$; The jet travels 230 miles per hour. **9.** She should have subtracted 5 from each side; $b = -13$ **11.** Sample answer: $20 + x = 30$; $30 - x = 20$ **13.** Sample answer: A football player can run 10 yards in 1 second. Write an equation to find d, the distance, in yards, the football player can run in 4.5 seconds?; $\frac{d}{4.5} = 10$; 45 yd **15.** The absolute value of a positive or negative number is always positive. So, $x = 4$ or $x = -4$.

Page 518 Lesson 7-2 Multi-Step Problem Solving

17. C **19.** 121 sq ft

Pages 525–526 Lesson 7-3 Independent Practice

1. 5 **3** 3 **5.** $\frac{20}{3}$ or $6\frac{2}{3}$ **7** $\frac{3}{4}p = 46.50$; \$62 **9.** Emily's homeroom class; Sample answer: Write and solve the equations $0.75e = 15$ and $\frac{2}{3}s = 12$; $e = 20$ and $s = 18$; Since $20 > 18$, Emily's homeroom class has more students. **11.** 20; Sample answer: Solve $8 = \frac{m}{4}$ to determine that $m = 32$. So, replace m with 32 to determine $32 - 12 = 20$. **13.** Sample answer: Multiply each side by 2. Then divide each side by $(b_1 + b_2)$. So, $\frac{2A}{b_1 + b_2} = h$.

Pages 527–528 Lesson 7-3 Multi-Step Problem Solving

15. 4 **17.** 0.5 **19.** \$85.50; Sample answer: Add each amount. The sum is $(-30 + 10.20 + 45.50 - 60) = -34.30$. Since the overall effect of the transactions is a withdrawal of \$34.30, I used the equation $s - \$34.30 = \$51.20$ to solve for s. The starting balance was \$51.20 + \$34.30 or \$85.50.

Pages 537–538 Lesson 7-4 Independent Practice

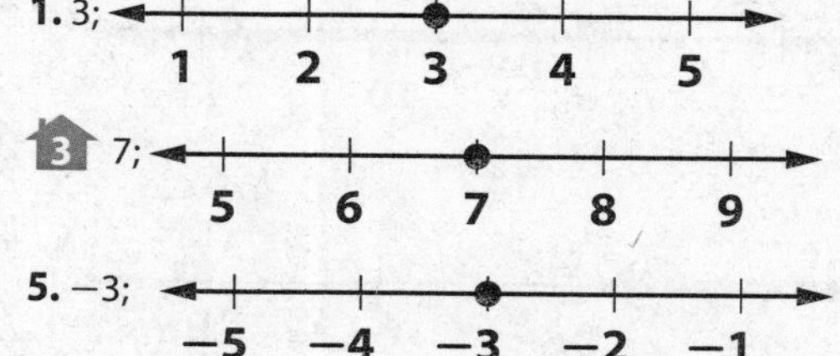

7. Sample answer: Makayla has a collection of 20 rare coins. This is 6 more than one half as many coins as Axel. How many rare coins x does Axel have?; Axel has 28 rare coins.

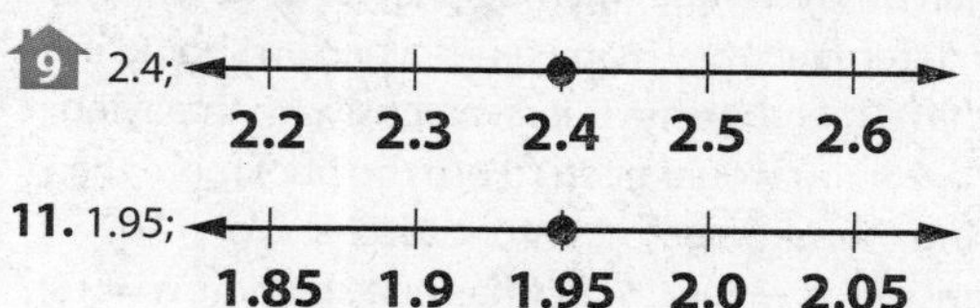

13. $19x + 39 = 100$; $x = 3.21$; Since it is not possible to purchase part of a movie, they can purchase 3 movies. **15.** $\frac{1}{2}(20x) - 18 = 200$; 22 subscriptions

Pages 539–540 Lesson 7-4 Multi-Step Problem Solving

17. C **19.** $\$88.40 = \$9.80h + \$7.00 + \$3.00$; $h = 8$; 8 hours **21.** Sample answer: The equation that describes the rule is $y = 3x - 7$. If a student guesses the number 10, the teacher response should be 23, not 3.

Page 543 Focus on Mathematical Processes

1. 1,250 ft **3.** 6:25 A.M.

Pages 553–554 Lesson 7-5 Independent Practice

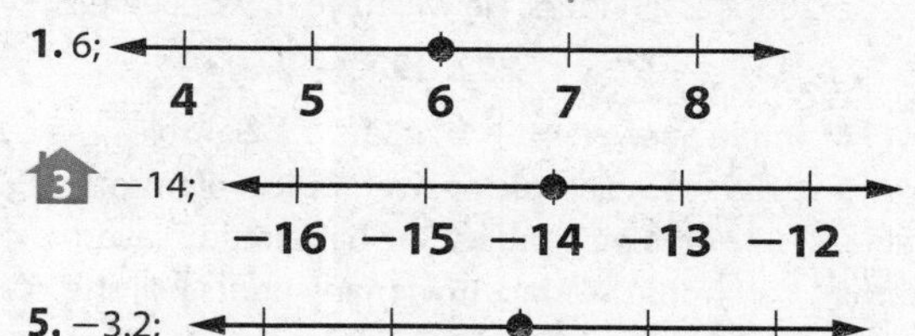

7 $3(\ell + 5) = 60$; 15 in. **9a.** $12(m - 2.57) = 0.36$ **9b.** Sample answer: I first divided each side by 12 and then added 2.57 to each side; \$2.60. **11.** $x = \frac{r}{p} - q$ **13.** $k = 7$; The value of the expression in parentheses must be 0, so $x - k = 0$ and $x = k$.

Page 556 Lesson 7-5 Multi-Step Problem Solving

15. A **17.** 4

Pages 561–562 Lesson 7-6 Independent Practice

1. $m \geq -6$;

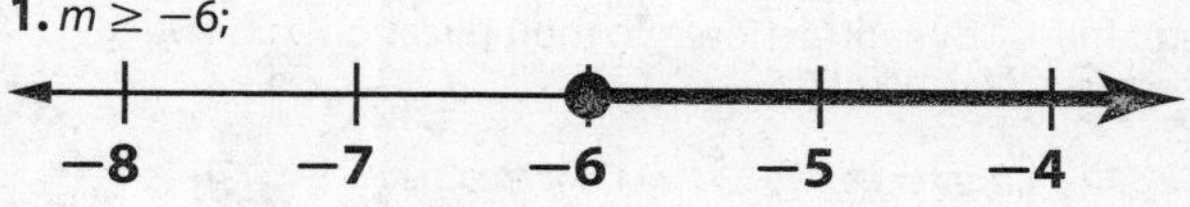

3. $x \geq 9$;

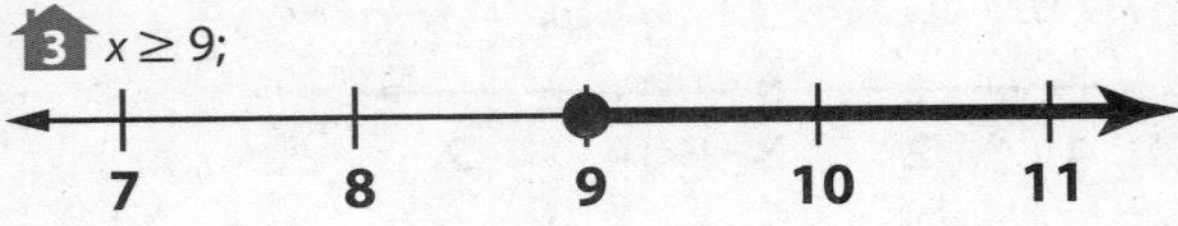

5. $s < 96$;

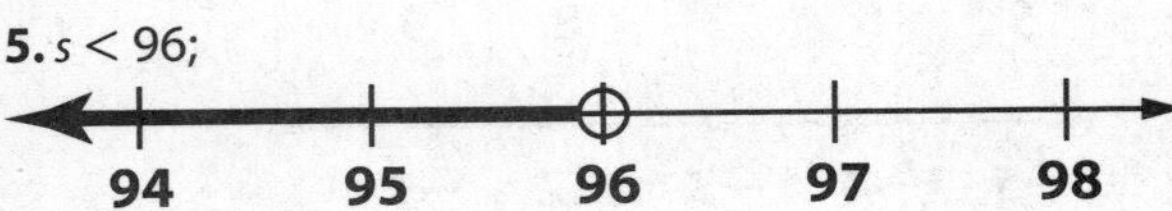

7. $p + 17 \leq 26$; $p \leq 9$; Nine additional players or fewer can make the team. **9.** Sample answer: A pool charges $4 each visit, or you can buy a summer membership for $100. Write an inequality to determine how many times a person should use the pool so that a membership is less expensive than paying each time; $x > 25$; You would need to use the pool more than 25 times during the summer. **11.** $16 < 8n$; $2 < n$ or $n > 2$ **13.** Sample answer: $a - 3 = 15$ only has one solution, $a = 18$; $a - 3 \geq 15$ has an infinite number of solutions. **15.** $x > c - b$ **17.** Sample answer: $12x > 8$

Page 564 Lesson 7-6 Multi-Step Problem Solving

19. A **21.** 7.2 feet

Pages 573–574 Lesson 7-7 Independent Practice

1. $x \geq 1$;

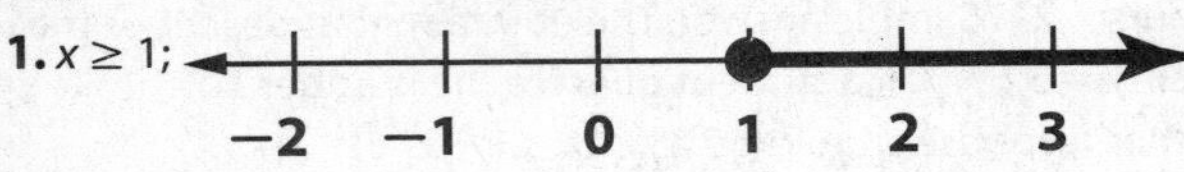

3. $x > 12$;

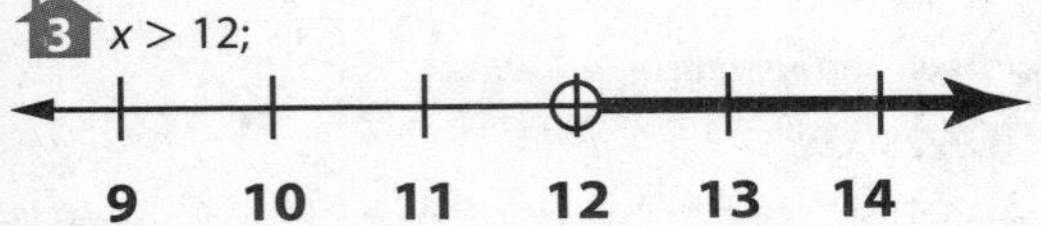

5. $30 + 7x \geq 205$; $x \geq 25$ hours; He will have to work at least 25 hours. **7.** $3x + 4 < -62$; $x < -22$ **9.** $\frac{x}{3} - 2 \geq -12$; $x \geq -30$ **11.** Sample answer: $4x + 1 > 53$ **13.** Sample answer: $2x - 6 \leq 186$ **15.** Sample answer: Felicia plans on spending at least $32 on a new purse. She has already saved $8. If she earns $4 an hour tutoring, how many hours will she need to tutor to save at least $32?; $x \geq 6$ **17.** $x > -10$;

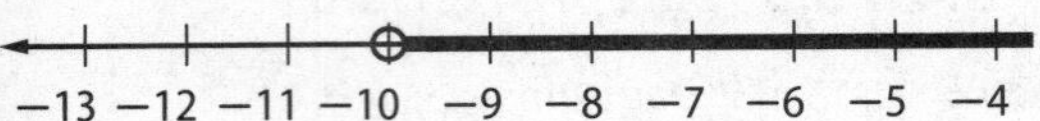

Pages 575–576 Lesson 7-7 Multi-Step Problem Solving

19. A **21.** 3
23. −2, −1, 0, 1, 2, 3, 4, 5, 6;

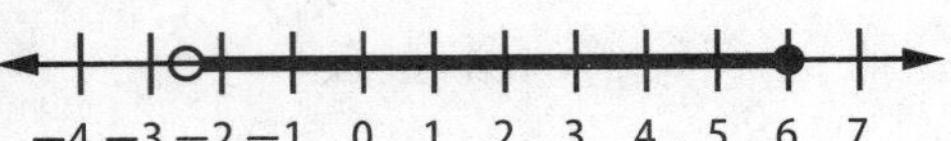

Page 579 Chapter Review Vocabulary Check

1. equation **3.** subtraction **5.** multiplication **7.** two-step

Page 580 Chapter Review Key Concept Check

1. solution **3.** equivalent equations

Page 581 Chapter Review Multi-Step Problem Solving

5. 4 years and 8 months

Chapter 8 Develop Geometry with Algebra

Page 586 Chapter 8 Are You Ready?

1. 42 sq m **3.** 76.5 sq mm

Pages 593–594 Lesson 8-1 Independent Practice

1. $\angle ABC$, $\angle CBA$, $\angle B$, $\angle 4$; acute **3.** $\angle MNP$, $\angle PNM$, $\angle N$, $\angle 1$; obtuse **5.** neither **7.** adjacent **9.** vertical
11. $15x + 15 = 180$; 11

15. True; Sample answer:

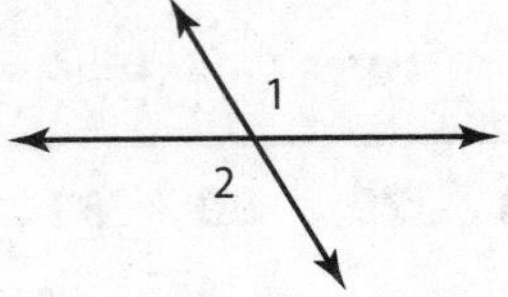

17. Sample answer: $(2x + 8) + (5x - 10) = 180$ because those angles are adjacent. So, $x = 26$. The angle measures are 60°, 120°, 120°, and 60°.

Page 596 Lesson 8-1 Multi-Step Problem Solving

19. A **21.** 1 student

Pages 601–602 Lesson 8-2 Independent Practice

1. neither **3.** supplementary **5.** $6x + 60 = 180$; 20
7. $6x + 42 = 180$; 23 **9.** Sample answer: $\angle CGK$, $\angle KGJ$
11a. adjacent; adjacent; vertical **11b.** $m\angle 1 + m\angle 2 = 180°$; $m\angle 2 + m\angle 3 = 180°$ **11c.** $m\angle 1 = 180° - m\angle 2$; $m\angle 3 = 180° - m\angle 2$; Sample answer: $m\angle 1$ and $m\angle 3$ are equal.
11d. Sample answer: Vertical angles are congruent.
13. $m\angle E = 39°$, $m\angle F = 51°$ **15.** $m\angle B = 60°$, $m\angle C = 120°$

Pages 603–604 Lesson 8-2 Multi-Step Problem Solving

17. A **19.** 20 seconds or 30 seconds **21.** Each of the four angles has a measure of 90°.

Pages 613–614 Lesson 8-3 Independent Practice

1. acute equilateral; Sample answer:

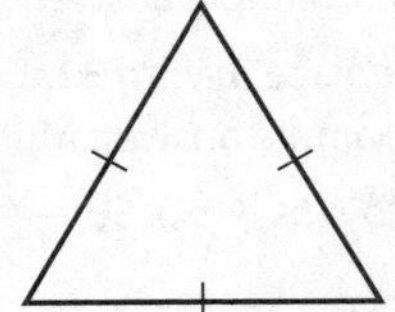

3. acute equilateral **5.** obtuse isosceles **7.** $2x + 29 + 33 = 180$; 59 **9.** $x + x + 2x = 180$; 45°, 45°, 90° **11.** $3x + 4x + 13x = 180$; 27°, 36°, 117° **13.** $2x + 47 + 61 = 180$; so $x = 36$ or $x + 11 = 47$, so $x = 36$ $m\angle A + 72 + 47 = 180$; so $m\angle A = 61$
15. equilateral **17.** $125 + a = 180$, so $a = 55$; $a + b + 60 = 180$, so $b = 65$; $60 + d = 90$, so $d = 30$; $c + d + 90 = 180$, so $c = 60$

19a. never; Sample answer: The sum of the interior angles of a triangle is 180°. Two right angles have a sum of 180°. This means the third angle would equal 0°, which is not possible.
19b. never; Sample answer: The sum of the interior angles of a triangle is 180°. The measure of an obtuse angle is greater than 90°. So, triangle cannot have more than one obtuse angle.
19c. always; Sample answer: There can be at most one right or one obtuse angle. So, the sum of the two remaining angles must be greater than or equal to 90°.

Page 616 Lesson 8-3 Multi-Step Problem Solving

21. D **23.** 25°

Pages 623–624 Lesson 8-4 Independent Practice

1. $3.14 \times 6 \times 6 = 113.0$ cm^2 **3** $3.14 \times 5.5 \times 5.5 = 95.0$ ft^2 **5.** $3.14 \times 6.3 \times 6.3 = 124.6$ mm^2 **7.** 4.9 ft^2 **9** 226.1 in^2 **11.** 163.3 yd^2 **13.** large; Sample answer: The medium pizza's area is 78.5 square inches and costs \$0.102 per square inch. The large pizza's area is 153.86 square inches and costs \$0.097 per square inch. **15.** Sample answer: When the radius of a circle is doubled, the circumference doubles and the area is 4 times as large. In the formula for area of a circle, the radius is squared, so when the radius of a circle is doubled, the area is 2^2 or 4 times as large. **17.** 5.9 in^2

19. Sample answer: 113.0 m^2;

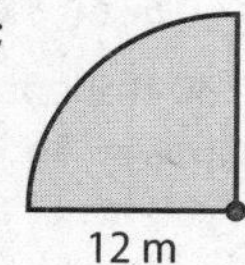

Page 626 Lesson 8-4 Multi-Step Problem Solving

21. 235.5 **23.** 132 square feet

Pages 631–632 Lesson 8-5 Independent Practice

1. 64 cm^2 **3.** 220.5 cm^2 **5** 38.6 ft^2 **7** 48 yd^2 **9.** 218 ft^2; 66 ft **11.** 44.6 ft^2; 30.3 ft **13.** 110.8 ft^2

Pages 633–634 Lesson 8-5 Multi-Step Problem Solving

15. A **17.** 359.25 square inches **19.** 232 ft^2; $12(9) = 108$; $4(3) = 12$; $10(14) = 140$; $108 + 12 + 140 = 260$. $\frac{1}{2}(2 \times 2) = 2$; $3(2) = 6$; $10(2) = 20$; $2 + 6 + 20 = 28$. $260 - 28 =$ 232 square feet

Page 637 Focus on Mathematical Processes

1. 80 chairs **3.** Sample answer: The area of Asia is about 17,251,712.4 square miles and the area of North America is about 9,488,441.8 square miles. So, 17,251,712.4 − 9,488,441.8 or about 7,763,270.6 square miles larger.

Pages 643–644 Lesson 8-6 Independent Practice

1 192 m^3 **3** 108 m^3 **5a.** 96 ft^3; 128 ft^3; 168 ft^3; 160 ft^3; 120 ft^3 **5b.** The height must allow the water to be deep enough for someone to get wet and the length and width must allow a person to fit. So the first and last sets of dimensions would not work. **7a.** Sample answer: There is a direct relationship between the volume and the length. Since the length is doubled, the volume is also doubled. **7b.** The volume is eight times greater. **7c.** Neither; Sample answer: doubling the height will result in a volume of $4 \cdot 4 \cdot 10$ or 160 in^3; doubling the width will result in a volume of $4 \cdot 8 \cdot 5$ or 160 in^3.

Pages 645–646 Lesson 8-6 Multi-Step Problem Solving

11. B **13.** 22 bags **15.** Sample answer: The volumes are equal. The height of each triangle is equal. The base of the first prism is twice the length of the second prism and the height of the first prism is half the height of the second prism.

Pages 655–656 Lesson 8-7 Independent Practice

1 80 ft^3 **3.** 42 ft^3 **5.** 14 in. **7a.**

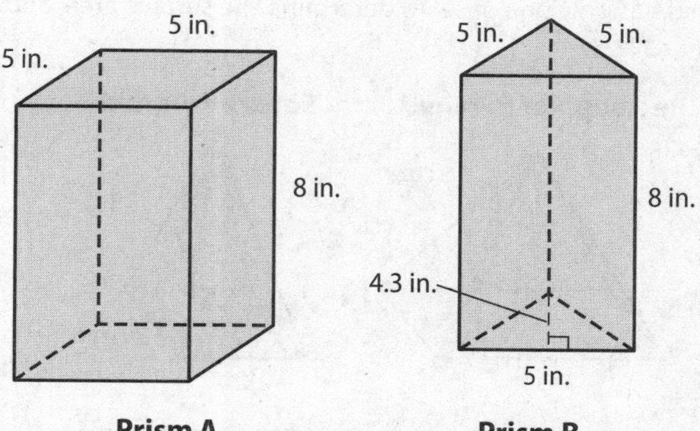

7b. Pyramid A: 66.7 in^3; Prism A: 200 in^3; Pyramid B: 28.7 in^3; Prism B: 86 in^3 **7c.** Sample answer: The volume of a pyramid is one third the volume of a prism with congruent base areas and heights. **7d.** Volume of Prism: $V = Bh$; Volume of Pyramid, with congruent bases and heights: $V = \frac{1}{3}Bh$ **9** 38,520,000 ft^3 **11.** $4\frac{4}{5}$ meters **13.** The height of the pyramid is 3 times the height of the cube. **15.** True; Sample answer: Both volumes are $\frac{1}{3}Bh$.

Page 658 Lesson 8-7 Multi-Step Problem Solving

17. D **19.** 280 in^3

Pages 667–668 Lesson 8-8 Independent Practice

1. 1,372 yd^2; 2,352 yd^2 **3** 1,848.24 m^2; 3,668.94 m^2 **5.** 1,162 cm^2 **7** Package A: 492 in^2; Package B: 404 in^2; Package A has a greater surface area. No, the volume of Package B is greater. **9.** 48 in^2; 144 in^2 **11.** Sample answer: Prism A with dimensions 3 by 3 by 3 and Prism B with dimensions 10 by 2 by 1. Prism A has the greater volume while Prism B has the greater surface area.

Pages 669–670 Lesson 8-8 Multi-Step Problem Solving

13. B **15.** 5 units **17.** Sample answer: The left container has a volume to surface area ratio of about 1.946. The right container has a volume to surface area ratio of 2. They should use the right container.

Pages 677–678 Lesson 8-9 Independent Practice

1. 540 yd^2; 1,152 yd^2 **3.** 11.2 m^2; 13.6 m^2 **5.** about 21.4 yd^2 **7.** 259.2 in^2 **9.** 7.5 in. **11.** Sample answer: Prism A with bases that are right triangles measures 3 by 4 by 5 and a height of 1. Prism B with bases that are right triangles measures 1 by 1 by 1.4 and a height of 10. Prism A has a greater volume while Prism B has a greater surface area.

Pages 679–680 Lesson 8-9 Multi-Step Problem Solving

13. A **15.** 4 times **17.** No; Sample answer: The surface area of the triangular prism is 1,320 square feet, and the surface area of the rectangular prism is 1,620 square feet.

Pages 689–690 Lesson 8-10 Independent Practice

1. 20 m^2; 24 m^2 **3.** 105 cm^2; 126.35 cm^2 **5.** 108 mm^2; 143.1 mm^2 **7.** 132 in^2 **9.** 110 ft^2; Sample answer: A pyramid has only one base. To determine the surface area, add $25 + (4 \cdot 21.25)$.

11. **Rectangular Pyramid** **Square Pyramid**

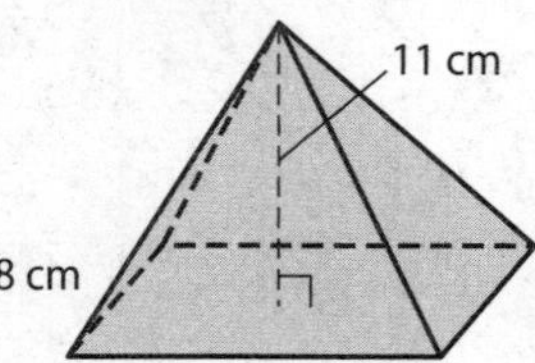

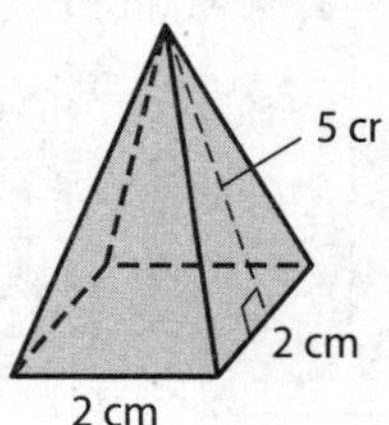

Sample answer: Both a square pyramid and a rectangular pyramid have isosceles triangles as their lateral faces. All the lateral faces are congruent on a square pyramid but, on a rectangular pyramid, the opposite pairs of lateral faces are congruent.

Pages 691–692 Lesson 8-10 Multi-Step Problem Solving

13. D **15.** 58.2 cm^2 **17.** 780 in^2; Sample answer: The two pyramids share a base and therefore only the lateral surface area is needed. $\frac{1}{2}(10)(19.5) = 97.5$ and $97.5(8) =$ 780 square inches

Page 695 Chapter Review Vocabulary Check

1. congruent **3.** complementary **5.** prism **7.** vertical

Page 696 Chapter Review Key Concept Check

1. twice **3.** height

Page 697 Chapter Review Multi-Step Problem Solving

5. 7.065 m^2

Chapter 9 Statistics and Sampling

Page 702 Chapter 9 Are You Ready?

1. Rihanna **3.** 75

Pages 709–710 Lesson 9-1 Independent Practice

1 a. There were 1.8 times as many students that went to the movie theater four or more times than less than three times. **1b.** $\frac{2}{9}$ of the students went to the movie theater to watch 4 movies **1c.** There were 3.6 times as many students that were surveyed than those who went to watch 2 or less movies at the theater.

3 a.

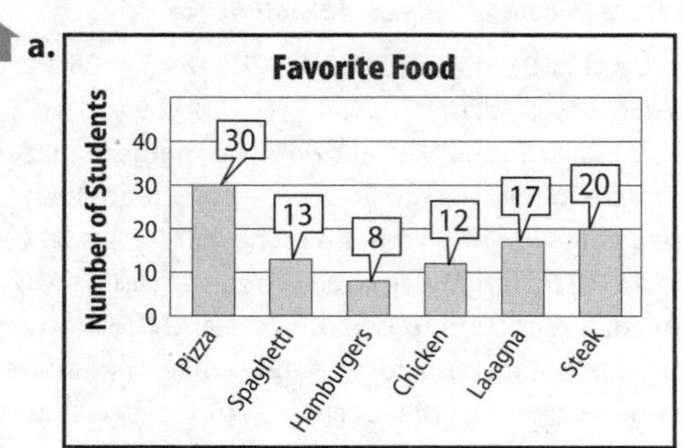

3b. $\frac{3}{10}$ **3c.** 20 : 30; $\frac{2}{3}$; $0.\overline{6}$; $66.\overline{6}\%$; For every 20 students that prefer steak, there are 30 students who prefer spaghetti and lasagna. **5.** Sample answer: Both allow me to make comparisons and equivalents of the parts to the whole. It is easier to determine the total on a bar graph than a dot plot.

Page 712 Lesson 9-1 Multi-Step Problem Solving

7. 69 minutes **9.** 20 : 25; $\frac{4}{5}$; 0.8; 80%; For every four million people that make up the 2000 population in Texas, there are five million people that make up the 2010 population in Texas.

Pages 719–720 Lesson 9-2 Independent Practice

1 a. 8% : 12%; $\frac{2}{3}$; $0.\overline{6}$; $66.\overline{6}\%$; For every 8% of people that favor birds, 12% of the people favor hamsters. **1b.** 576 people **1c.** 240 people **3 a.** 39%; $\frac{39}{100}$ **3b.** 246 students

5a. Sample answer: **Favorite Lunch**

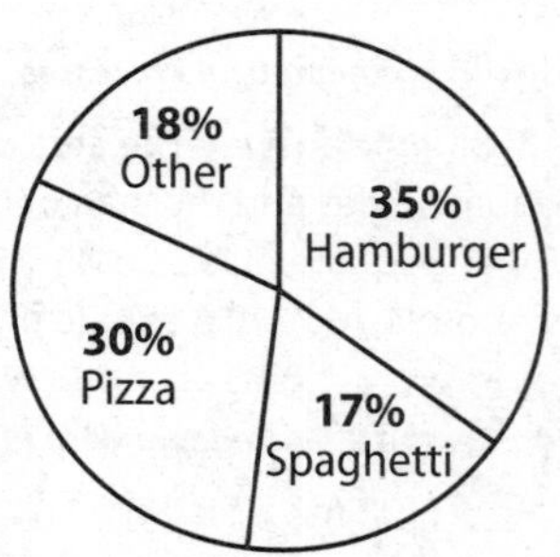

5b. Sample answers: There were 100 students surveyed. How many more total students were surveyed than favor pizza? 70 students; How many more students preferred hamburgers than spaghetti? 18 students

Pages 721–722 Lesson 9-2 Multi-Step Problem Solving

7. 9 **9.** 35% **11.** Sample answer: A 25%, B 20%, C 40%, D 10%, E 5%

Pages 727–728 Lesson 9-3 Independent Practice

1. $\frac{3}{10}$, 0.3, or 30% **3** $\frac{2}{25}$, 0.08, or 8% **5** 9 students
7. About 143 students prefer humor books, and the number of students that prefer nonfiction is 88. So, there are about 55 more students who prefer humor books to nonfiction books.
9. about 100 times

Pages 729–730 Lesson 9-3 Multi-Step Problem Solving

13. B **15.** 1 student **17.** 516 families

Pages 735–736 Lesson 9-4 Independent Practice

1 The conclusion is valid. This is an unbiased systematic random sample. **3** This is a simple random sample. So, the sample is valid; about 205 people. **5.** Sample answer: The sample will be biased because it is a convenience sample. Marisol will be asking only basketball fans. **7.** Never; Sample answer: A biased sample favors one or more parts of the population over others. **9.** Never; Sample answer: A voluntary response sample involves only those who want to participate in the sampling.

Pages 737–738 Lesson 9-4 Multi-Step Problem Solving

11. B **13.** 30 shoes **15.** Sample answer: Each sample is not a random sample. Customers who have already made a purchase may not provide useful information as they may not buy another chain. Also, the sample size for customers who did not make a purchase is very small. A better method would be to survey every 5th person who comes into the store about their chain preference.

Page 745 Focus on Mathematical Processes

1. Sample answer: 2017 **3.** $38.20

Pages 751–752 Lesson 9-5 Independent Practice

1 Graph B; Sample answer: The ratio of the area of the gas pumps in the graph on the right are not proportional to the cost of gas. **3** The median or the mode because they are much closer in value to most of the data.

5.

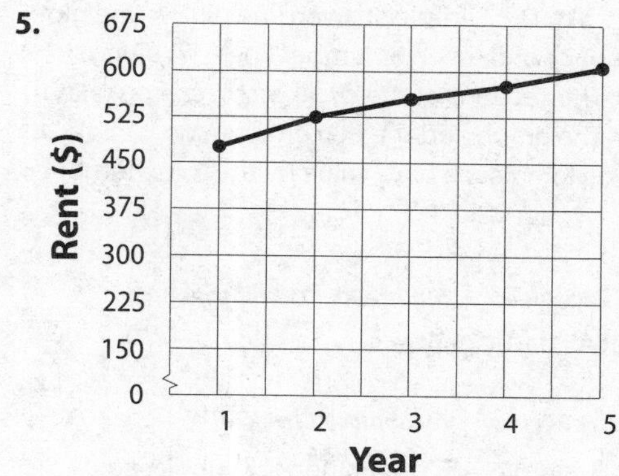

7. Sample answer: Since the graph makes it seem as if rent has been stable, a person may choose to become a tenant.
9. Sample answer: Gia went fishing and caught five fish. The weights of the fish were 2, 1, 4, 2, and 21 pounds.

Pages 753–754 Lesson 9-5 Multi-Step Problem Solving

11. A **13.** 4 minutes

Pages 763–764 Lesson 9-6 Independent Practice

1 Sample answer: Neither plot is symmetric in shape. The times at Lucy's Steakhouse have a median of 20 minutes with an interquartile range of 20 minutes. The times at Gary's Grill have a median of 15 minutes with an interquartile range of 10 minutes. In general, a customer will wait longer at Lucy's Steakhouse. **3** **a.** Plant A: 2.75, 0.75; Plant B: 3.1; 0.7

3b.

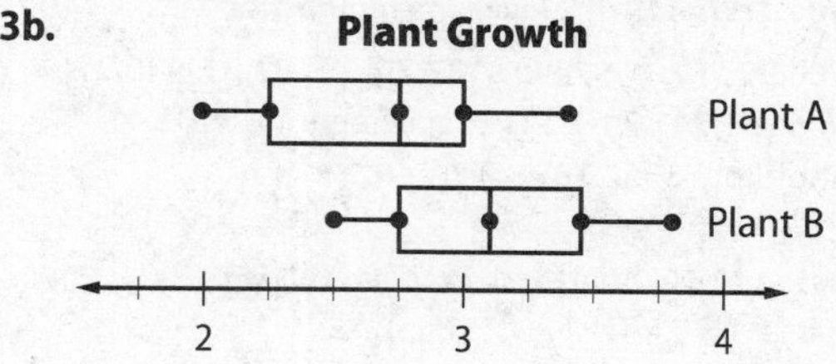

3c. Sample answer: Both populations have similar interquartile ranges. The median for Plant B is higher. So, Plant B generally showed more growth. **5.** The data shown in the histograms are only shown in intervals. Specific values are not shown.

Pages 765–766 Lesson 9-6 Multi-Step Problem Solving

9. D **11.** 0.5 hour

Pages 773–774 Lesson 9-7 Independent Practice

1 box plot; shows the median

3

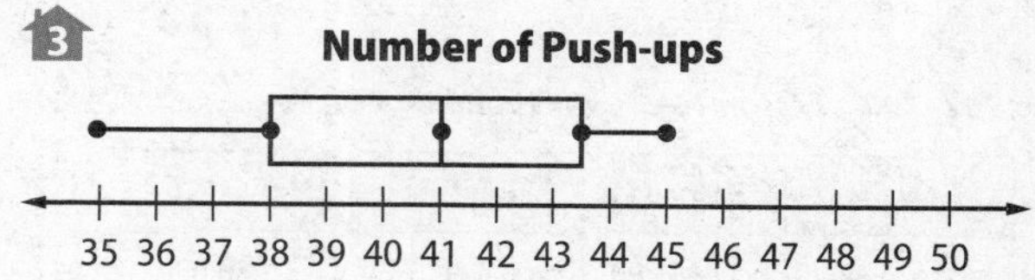

A box plot is an appropriate graph because there is a large set of data and it will show the measures of variation of the data set. The graph shows that 75% of the push-ups are greater than 38. **5a.** Situation B; Sample answer: A bar graph can show the number of customers who made a purchase by each individual age. **5b.** Yes; Sample answer: line plot; A line plot shows the frequency of data on a number line. **7.** always; Sample answer: The sections of the circle graph can be taken from the bars of the graph and the percents can be determined by dividing each bar's value by the total number of data values.

Pages 775–776 Lesson 9-7 Multi-Step Problem Solving

9. C **11.** about 45 participants

Page 779 Chapter Review Vocabulary Check

1. systematic **3.** simple **5.** population **7.** unbiased **9.** sample

Page 780 Chapter Review Key Concept Check

1. survey **3.** biased sample

Page 781 Chapter Review Multi-Step Problem Solving

5. 330 students

Chapter 10 Personal Financial Literacy

Page 786 Chapter 10 Are You Ready?

1. 0.22 **3.** 0.79 **5.** 30% **7.** 9%

Pages 789–790 Lesson 10-1 Independent Practice

1. $10.92; $166.92 **3** $7.80; $137.79 **5.** $2.01; $40.21 **7** $92.19 **9.** $1,741.74 **11.** Social Security: $101.41; Federal Withholding: $362.18

Page 790 Lesson 10-1 Multi-Step Problem Solving

13. A

Pages 793–794 Lesson 10-2 Independent Practice

1. housing, food, clothing, entertainment, transportation, college savings, utilities, emergency savings, taxes **3** 16% **5.** fixed: housing, transportation, college savings, utilities, emergency savings, taxes; variable: food, clothing, entertainment **7.** variable expenses: food, clothing, entertainment **9** $38.75 per hour **11.** $19.38 per hour

Page 794 Lesson 10-2 Multi-Step Problem Solving

13. A

Pages 797–798 Lesson 10-3 Independent Practice

1

Assets	Value ($)	Liabilities	Value ($)
house (owned)	42,365.00	car payoff	980.00
savings	1,255.00	boat payoff	2,200.00
cash	355.00	credit card debt	3,298.00
		student loan	1,500.00

3. Sample answer: Since Jordan's net worth is positive, he owns more than he owes. **5.** $12,043.65 − $36,582.80 = −$24,539.15 **7** −$20,651.35

Page 798 Lesson 10-3 Multi-Step Problem Solving

9. D

Pages 801–802 Lesson 10-4 Independent Practice

1. $54.56; $539.56 **3** $3,696; $9,296

5

Year	Starting Balance ($)	*prt*	*I* (Interest Earned, $)
1	2,275	2,275 • 0.044 • 1	100.10
2	2,375.10	2,375.10 • 0.044 • 1	104.50
3	2,479.60	2,479.60 • 0.044 • 1	109.10
4	2,588.70	2,588.70 • 0.044 • 1	113.90
5	2,702.60	2,702.60 • 0.044 • 1	118.91

; $2,821.51

Page 802 Lesson 10-4 Multi-Step Problem Solving

7. B

Pages 805–806 Lesson 10-5 Independent Practice

1 $4.20 **3.** 15% rebate **5** $16.99 **7.** Sample answer: If they each take the 40% discount, Dario will pay $26.40 and Caitlyn will pay $21. If they use the coupon, Dario will pay $44 and Caitlyn will pay $11.50, $44 + $11.50 = $55.50. So, each will pay $27.75. It is better for them to each take the 40% discount.

Page 806 Lesson 10-5 Multi-Step Problem Solving

9. D

Page 807 Chapter Review Vocabulary Check

1. liabilities **3.** budget **5.** wages **7.** expenses **9.** coupon

Page 808 Chapter Review Key Concept Check

1.

Simple Interest and Compound Interest

Compare	Contrast
Sample answer: Both simple interest and compound interest represent earnings on an investment.	Sample answer: Simple interest is calculated on the principal only, while compound interest is calculated on both principal and interest.

Page 809 Chapter Review Multi-Step Problem Solving

3. $524.80

Index

Dd

Ee

Tt

Uu

Vv

Ww

Xx

Yy

Name ____________________

Name ______________________________

Modeling the Math

Name ____________________

Fold the circle in half four times to divide it into 16 equal sections.

Cut out each section and reassemble the sections to form a parallelogram-shaped figure.

Determine the area of the circle.

Name ______________________________

Modeling the Math

Cut out the net to form each rectangular prism. Use the net to determine the surface area of the prism.

Name ______________________________

Cut out the net to form each rectangular pyramid. Use the net to determine the surface area of the pyramid.

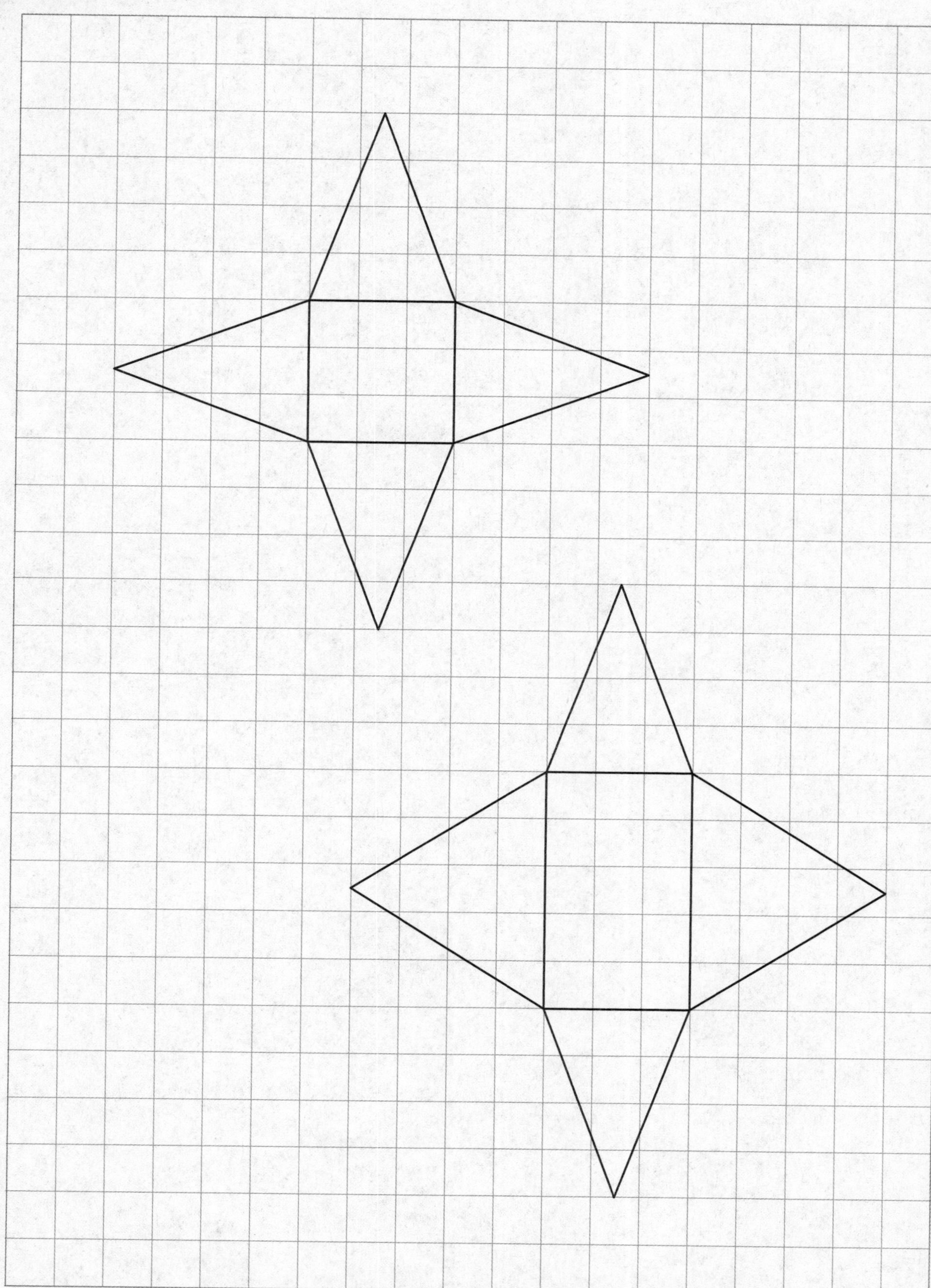

Name ______________________________

Cut out the net to form the triangular prism. Use the net to determine the surface area of the prism.

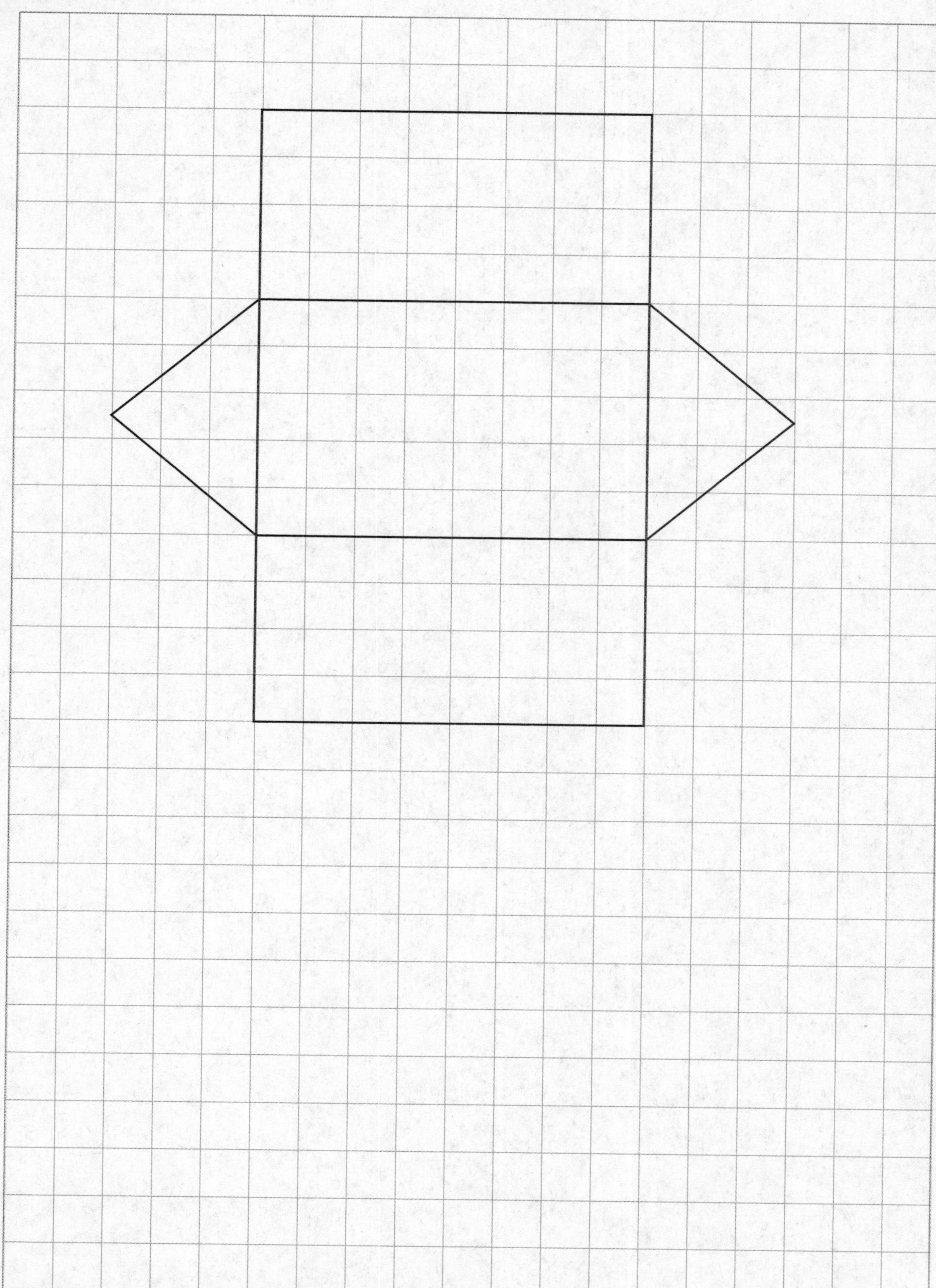

Modeling the Math

Name ____________________

Cut out the net to form the triangular pyramid. Use the net to determine the surface area of the pyramid.

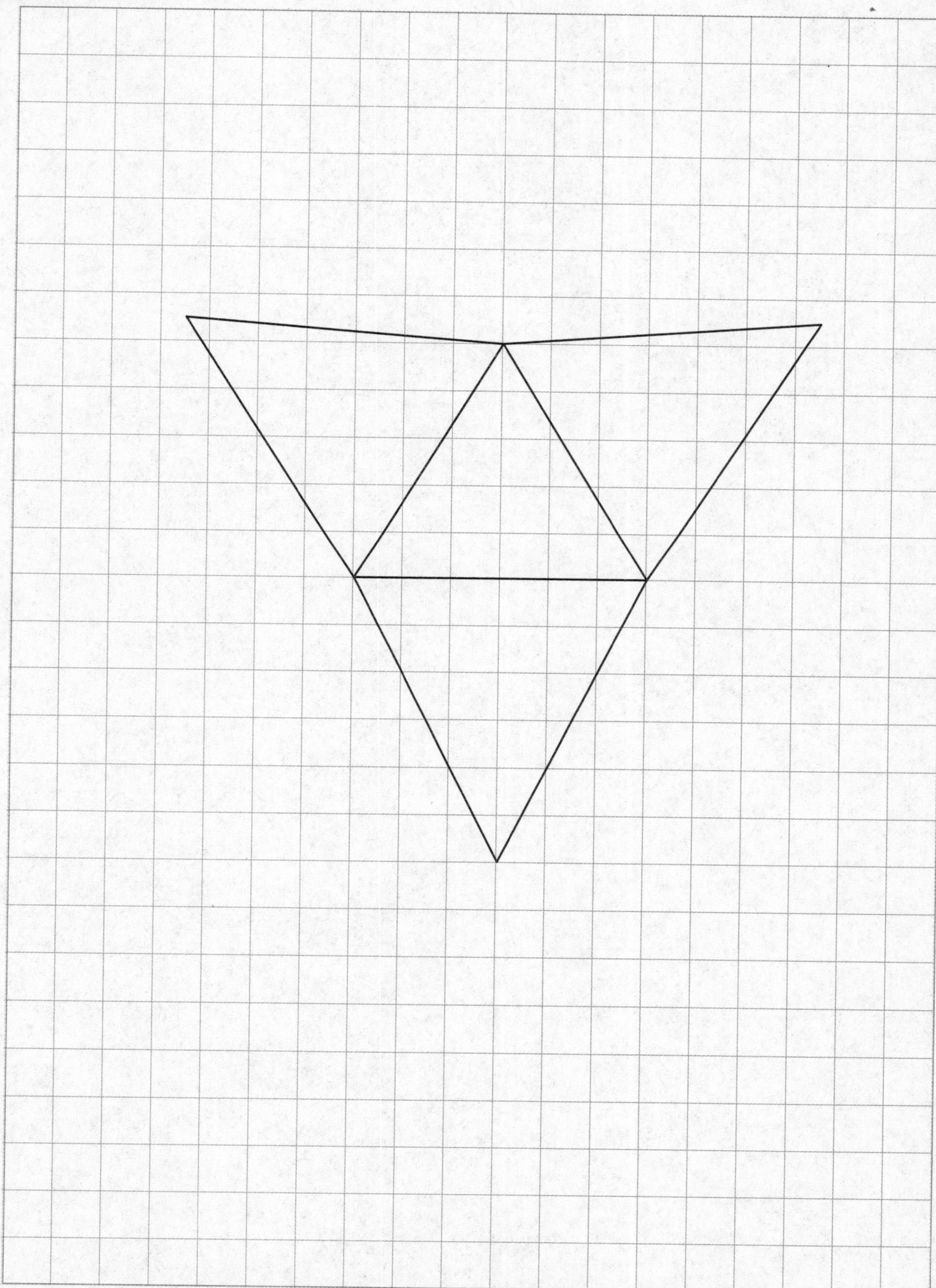

What are VKVs® and How Do I Create Them?

Visual Kinethestic Vocabulary Cards® are flashcards that animate words by focusing on their structure, use, and meaning. The VKVs in this book are used to show cognates, or words that are similar in Spanish and English.

Step 1

Go to the back of your book to find the VKVs for the chapter vocabulary you are currently studying. Follow the cutting and folding instructions at the top of the page. The vocabulary word on the BLUE background is written in English. The Spanish word is on the ORANGE background.

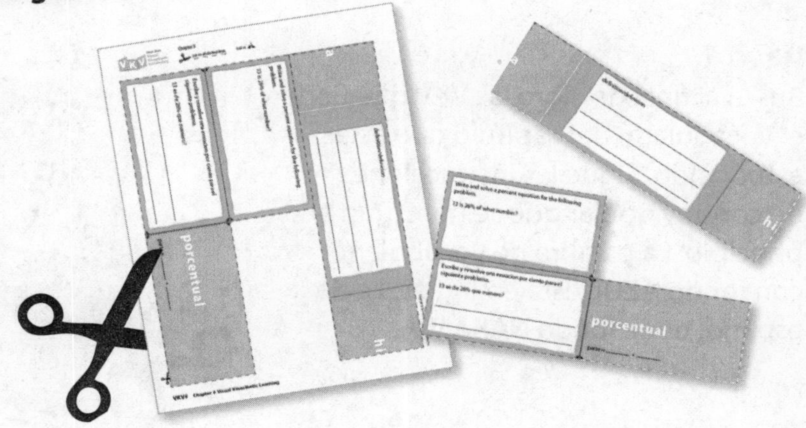

Step 2

There are exercises for you to complete on the VKVs. When you understand the concept, you can complete each exercise. All exercises are written in English and Spanish. You only need to give the answer once.

Step 3

Individualize your VKV by writing notes, sketching diagrams, recording examples, and forming plurals (radius: radii or radiuses).

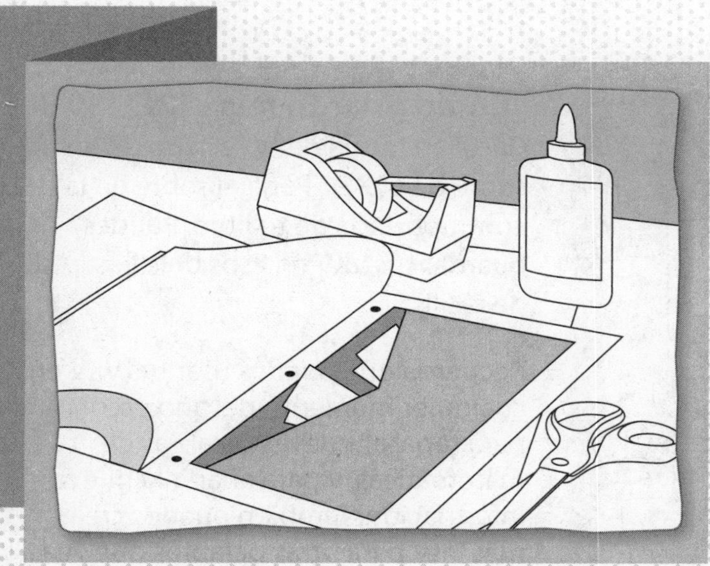

How Do I Store My VKVs?

Take a 6" x 9" envelope and cut away a V on one side only. Glue the envelope into the back cover of your book. Your VKVs can be stored in this pocket!

Remember you can use your VKVs ANY time in the school year to review new words in math, and add new information you learn. Why not create your own VKVs for other words you see and share them with others!

¿Qué son las VKV y cómo se crean?

Las tarjetas de vocabulario visual y cinético (VKV) contienen palabras con animación que está basada en la estructura, uso y significado de las palabras. Las tarjetas de este libro sirven para mostrar cognados, que son palabras similares en español y en inglés.

Paso 1

Busca al final del libro las VKV que tienen el vocabulario del capítulo que estás estudiando. Sigue las instrucciones de cortar y doblar que se muestran al principio. La palabra de vocabulario con fondo AZUL está en inglés. La de español tiene fondo NARANJA.

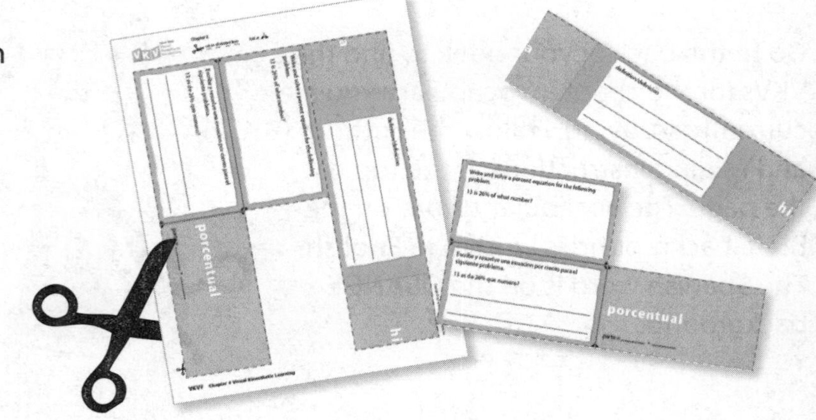

Paso 2

Hay ejercicios para que completes con las VKV. Cuando entiendas el concepto, puedes completar cada ejercicio. Todos los ejercicios están escritos en inglés y español. Solo tienes que dar la respuesta una vez.

Paso 3

Da tu toque personal a las VKV escribiendo notas, haciendo diagramas, grabando ejemplos y formando plurales (radio: radios).

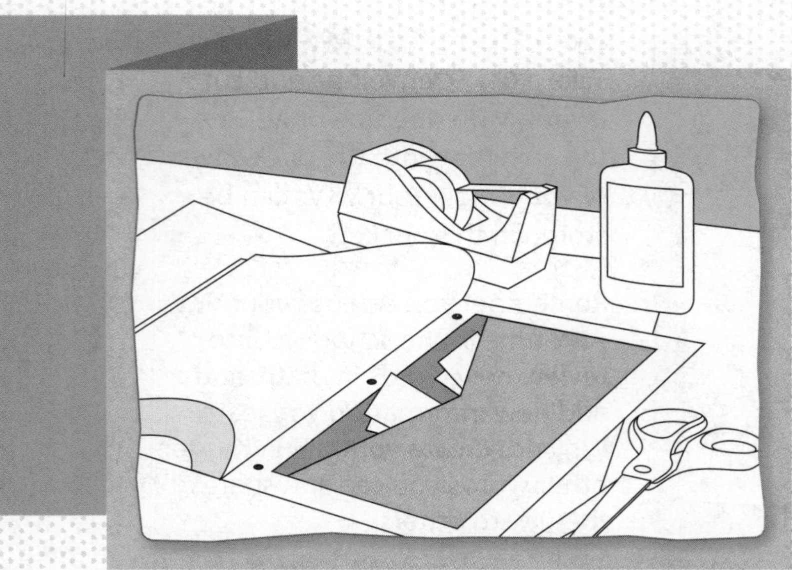

¿Cómo guardo mis VKV?

Corta en forma de "V" el lado de un sobre de 6" X 9". Pega el sobre en la contraportada de tu libro. Puedes guardar tus VKV en esos bolsillos. ¡Así de fácil!

Recuerda que puedes usar tus VKV en cualquier momento del año escolar para repasar nuevas palabras de matemáticas, y para añadir la nueva información. También puedes crear más VKV para otras palabras que veas, y poder compartirlas con los demás.

cut on all dashed lines

fold on all solid lines

Define linear relationship.
(Define relación lineal.)

linear relationship

What does a linear relationship look like when it is graphed? (¿Cómo se ve la gráfica de una relación lineal?)

Dinah Zike's
Visual
Kinesthetic
Vocabulary®

Chapter 6

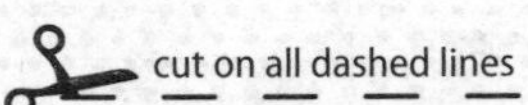

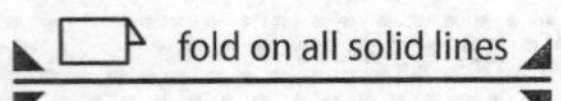

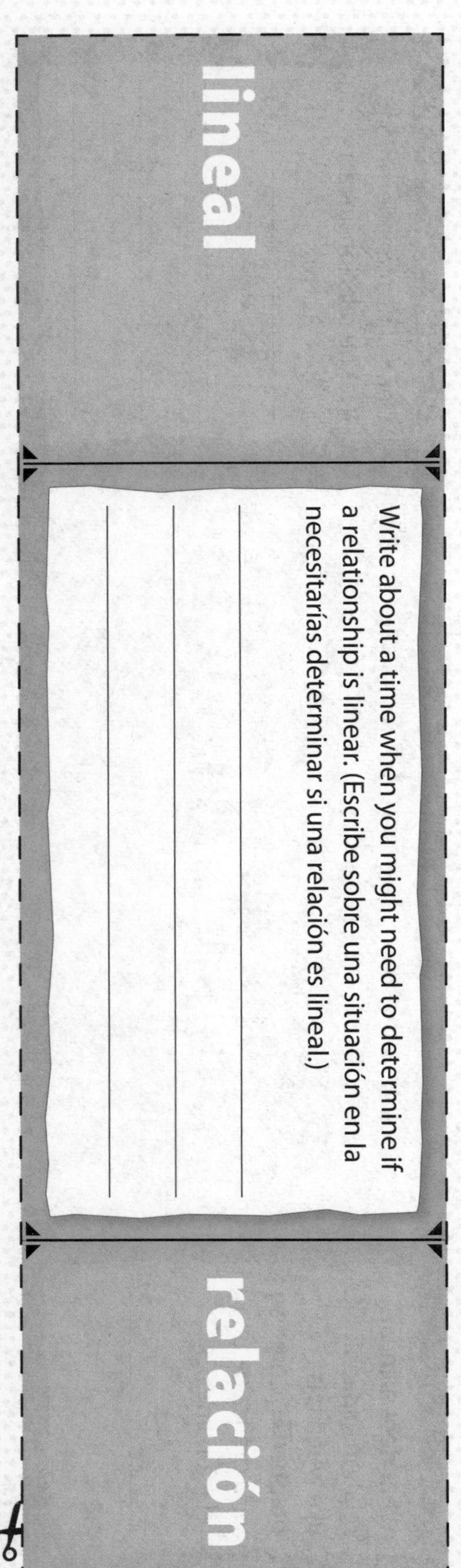

cut on all dashed lines

fold on all solid lines

solution

What value of x makes the equation true? (¿Qué valor de x hace la ecuación verdadera?)

$x + 8 = 13$ ______

Circle the equations that are equivalent to $x = 9$. (Encierra en un círculo las ecuaciones equivalentes a $x = 9$.)

$x + 12 = 20$ $x - 5 = 4$ $3 + x = 12$

equivalent equation

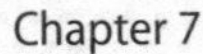

Chapter 7

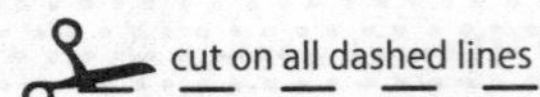

cut on all dashed lines

fold on all solid lines

ecuación equivalente

ción

Determine the solution of each equation. (Halla la solución de cada ecuación.)

$x - 12 = 8$ ________

$9 + y = 17$ ________

Are the equations $x + 11 = 14$ and $x = 3$ equivalent? Explain. (¿Son las ecuaciones $x + 11 = 14$ and $x = 3$ equivalentes? Explica.)

____

____

____

Dinah Zike's Visual Kinesthetic Vocabulary®

Chapter 8

cut on all dashed lines

fold on all solid lines

The formula for the area of a circle is $A = \pi r^2$. Write the formula for the area of a semicircle. (La fórmula para calcular el área de un círculo es $A = \pi r^2$. Escribe la fórmula para calcular el área de un semicírculo.)

$A =$ __________

semicircle

lateral surface area

Define lateral surface area. (Define área de superficie lateral.)

____

____

____

cut on all dashed lines

fold on all solid lines

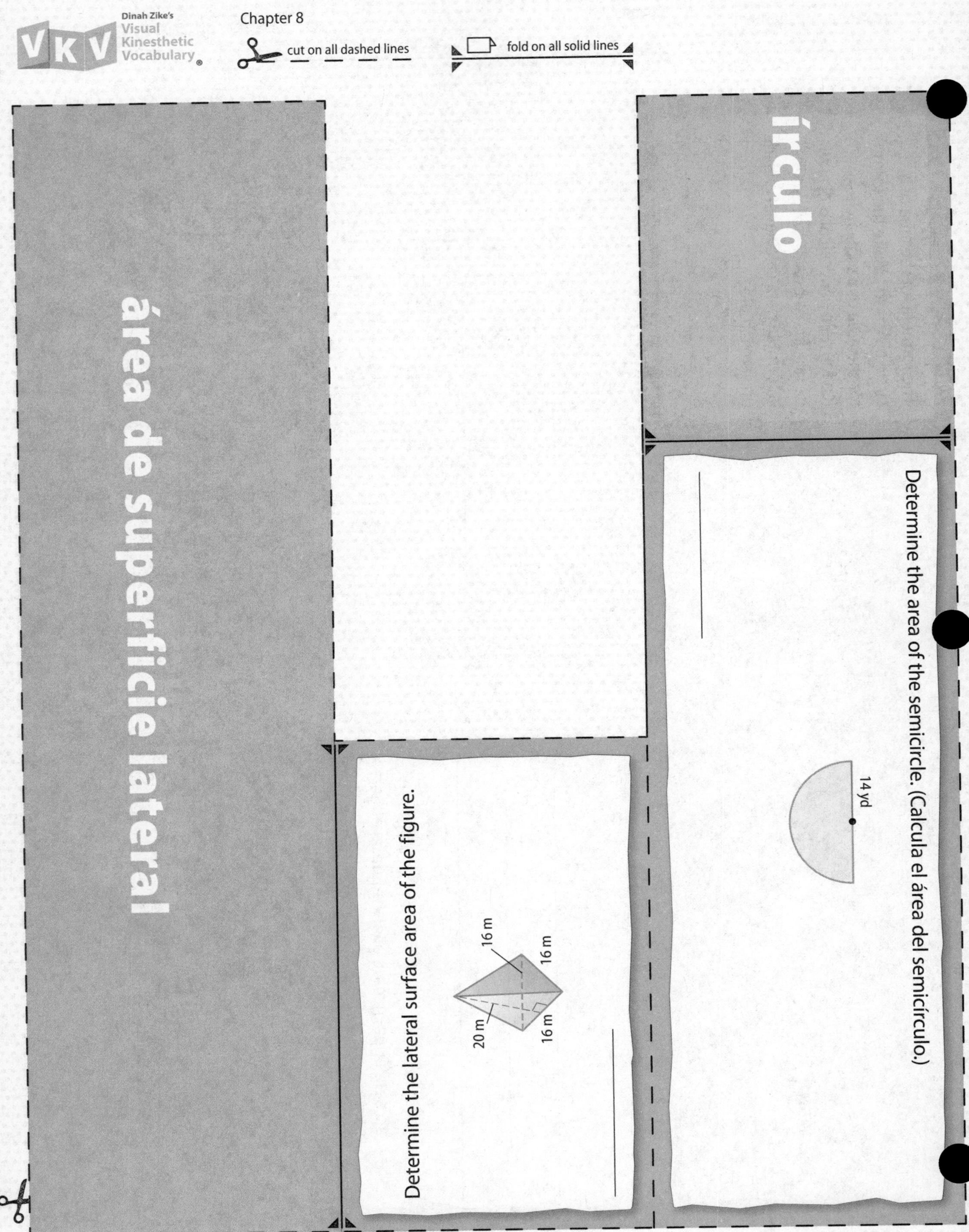

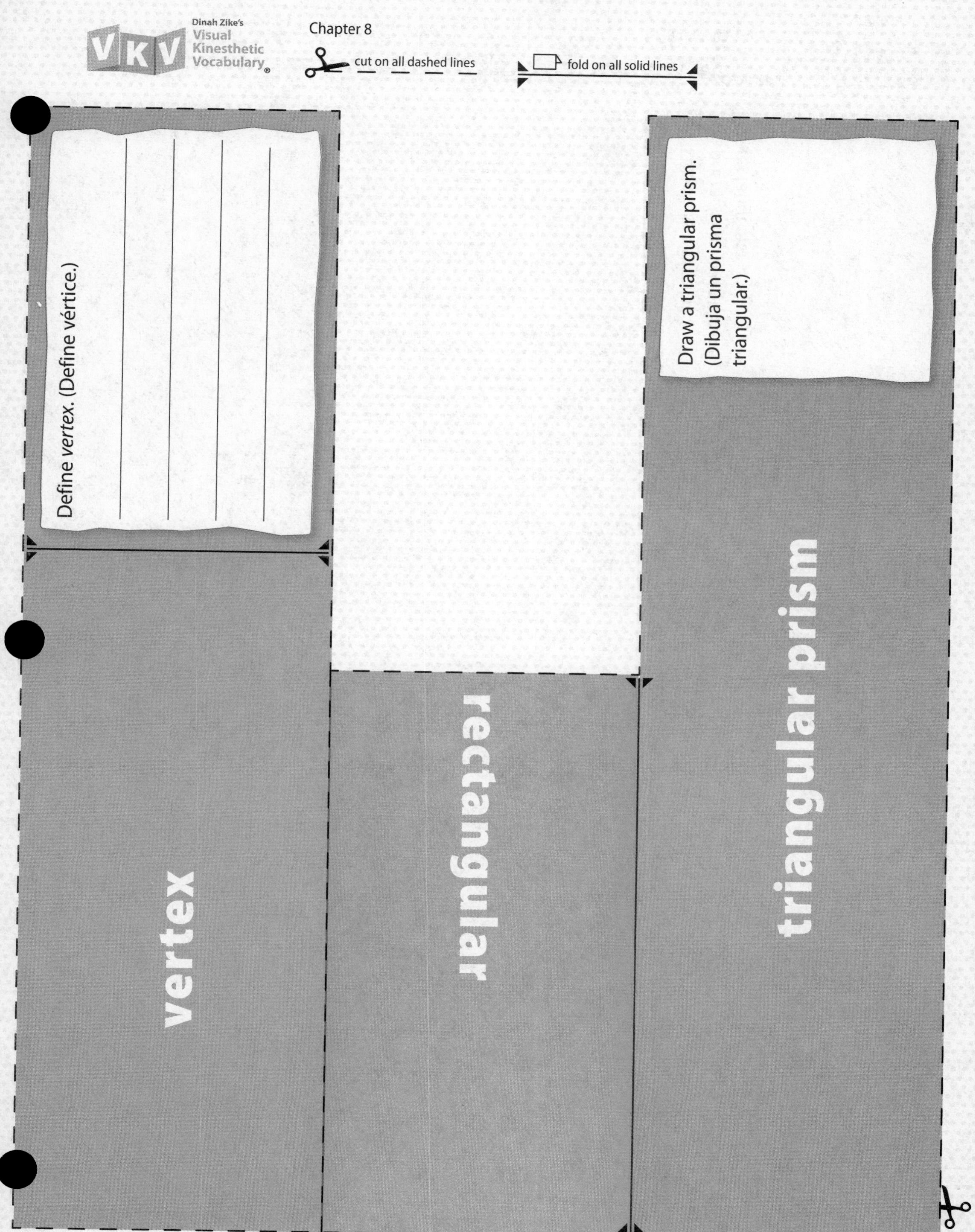

Dinah Zike's
VKV
Visual
Kinesthetic
Vocabulary®
Chapter 8
cut on all dashed lines
fold on all solid lines
Define *vertex*. (Define vértice.)
Draw a triangular prism. (Dibuja un prisma triangular.)
vertex
rectangular
triangular prism

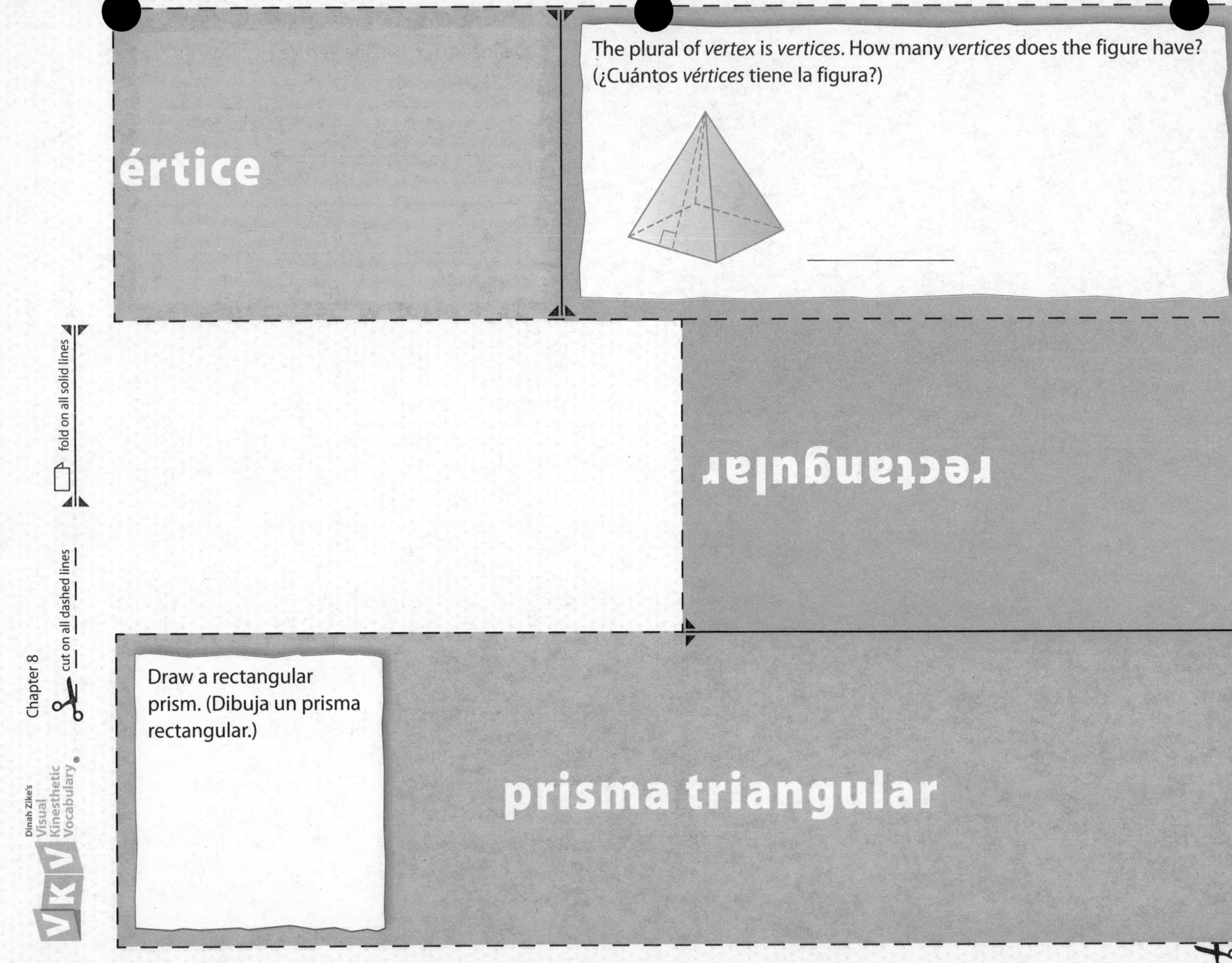
értice
The plural of vertex is vertices. How many vertices does the figure have? (¿Cuántos vértices tiene la figura?)
rectangular
Draw a rectangular prism. (Dibuja un prisma rectangular.)
prisma triangular
Dinah Zike's Visual Kinesthetic Vocabulary®
Chapter 8
cut on all dashed lines
fold on all solid lines

cut on all dashed lines

fold on all solid lines

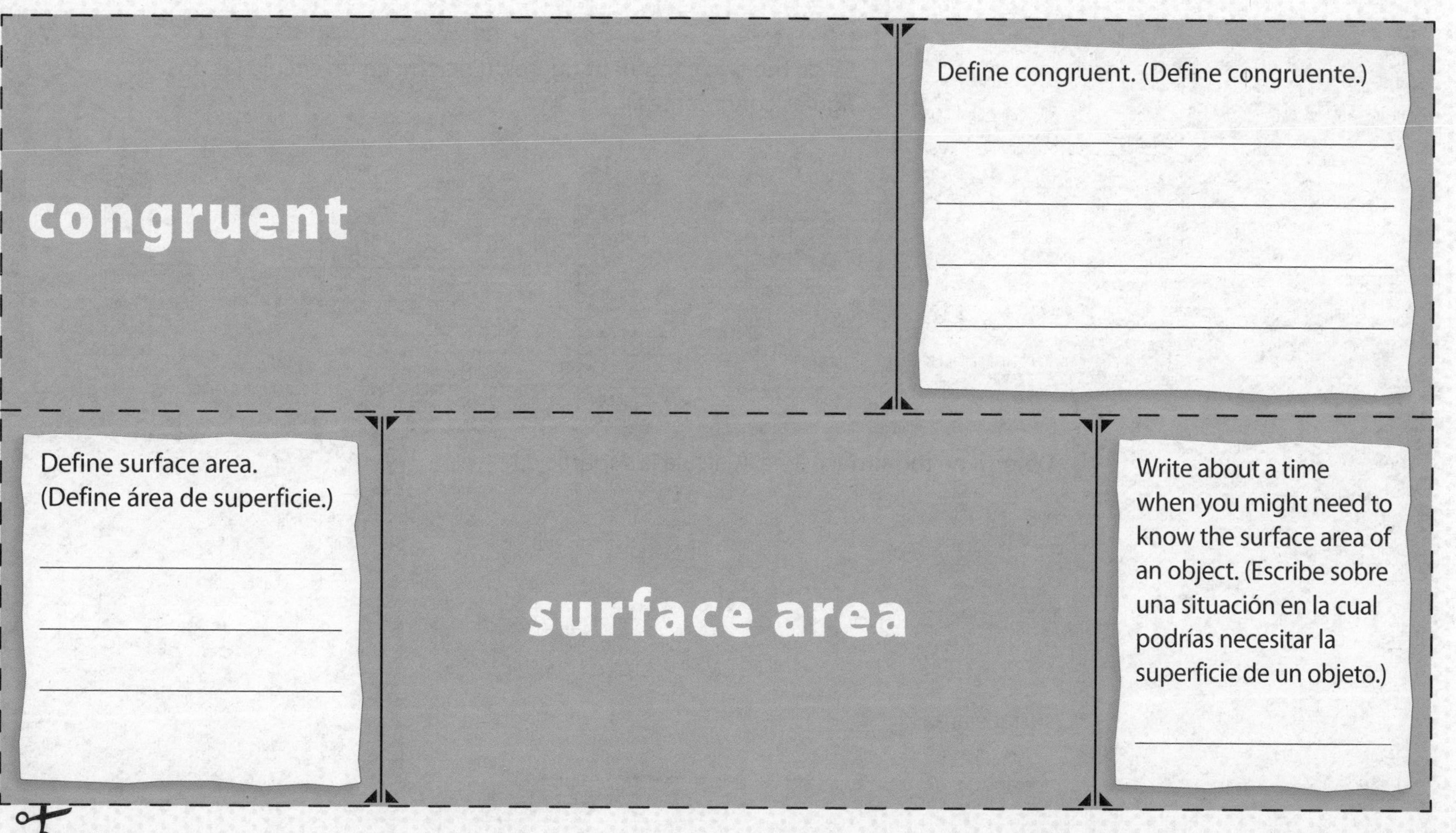

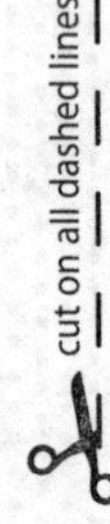

fold on all solid lines

e

Circle the two congruent figures. (Encierra en un círculo las dos figuras congruentes.)

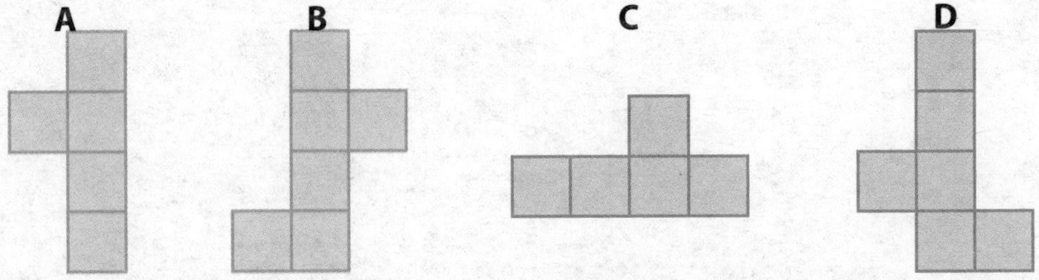

A

B

C

D

superficie

Determine the surface area. (Calcula la superficie.)

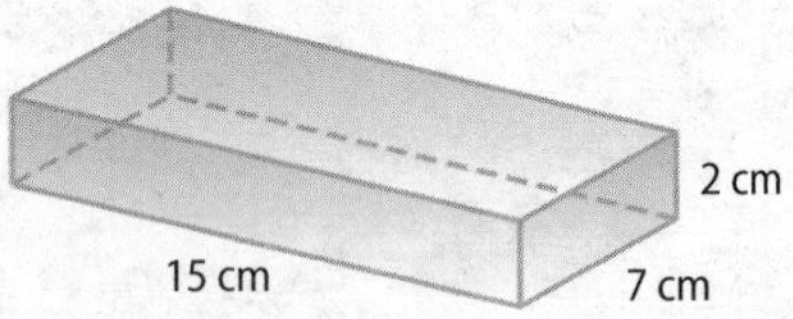

15 cm

7 cm

2 cm

surface area = ________

área de

cut on all dashed lines

fold on all solid lines

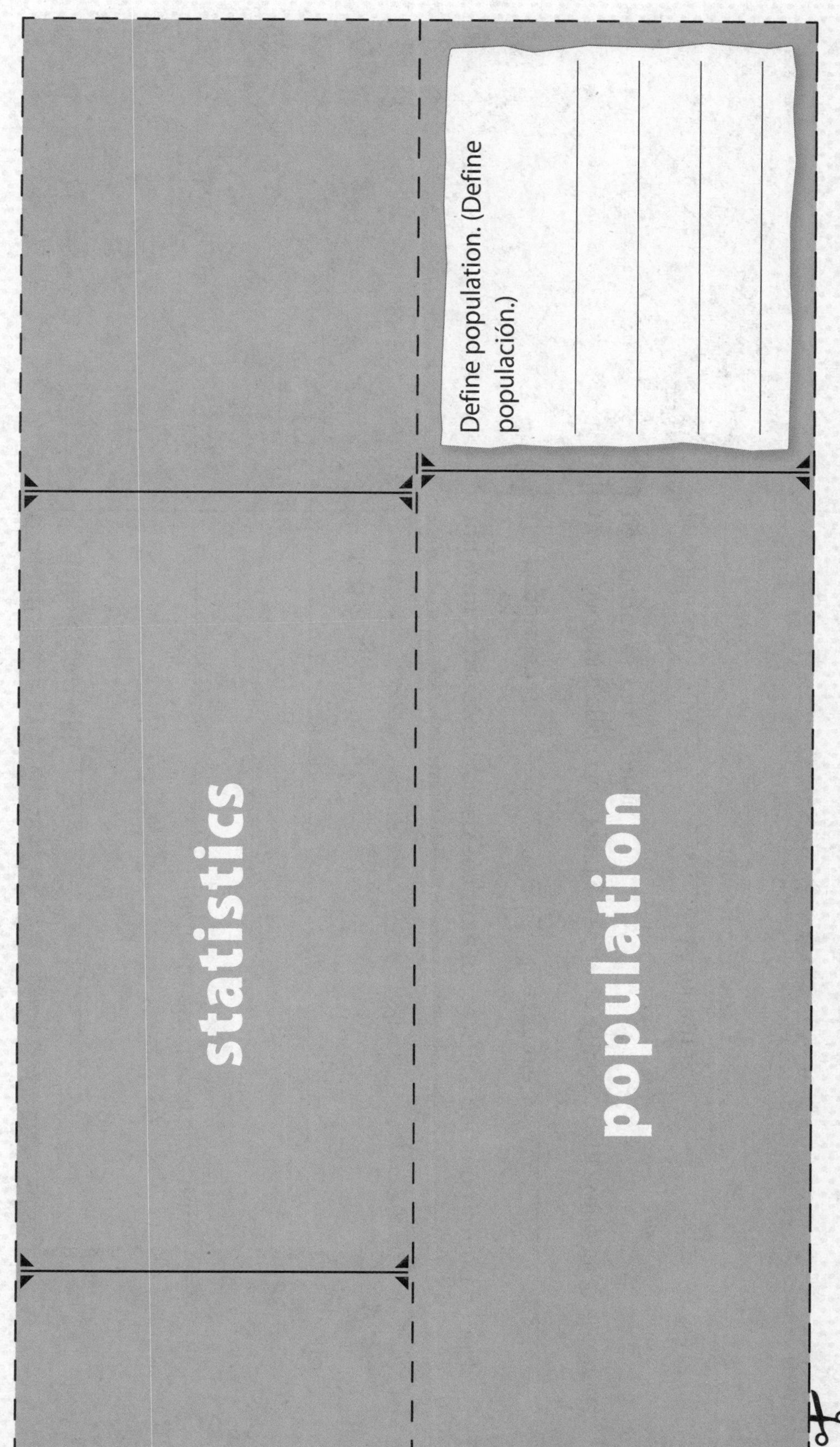

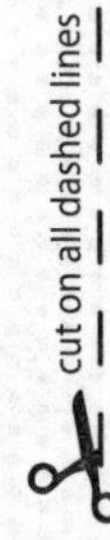

fold on all solid lines

dística

Statistics deal with ____________________,

____________________, and

____________________ data. (La estadística tiene que

ver con ____________________,

____________________ y ____________________

de datos.)

e

ción

You want to survey customers at a store to see which dog food is most popular.

The population is ______________. The sample is ______________.

(Vas a hacer una encuesta a los clientes de un almacén para averiguar cuál comida para perros es más popular.

La población es ______________. La muestra es ______________.)

Grade 7 Mathematics Reference Materials

LENGTH					
Customary			**Metric**		
1 mile (mi)	=	1,760 yards (yd)	1 kilometer (km)	=	1,000 meters (m)
1 yard (yd)	=	3 feet (ft)	1 meter (m)	=	100 centimeters (cm)
1 foot (ft)	=	12 inches (in.)	1 centimeter (cm)	=	10 millimeters (mm)

VOLUME AND CAPACITY					
Customary			**Metric**		
1 gallon (gal)	=	4 quarts (qt)	1 liter (L)	=	1,000 milliliters (mL)
1 quart (qt)	=	2 pints (pt)			
1 pint (pt)	=	2 cups (c)			
1 cup (c)	=	8 fluid ounces (fl oz)			

WEIGHT AND MASS					
Customary			**Metric**		
1 ton (T)	=	2,000 pounds (lb)	1 kilogram (kg)	=	1,000 grams (g)
1 pound (lb)	=	16 ounces (oz)	1 gram (g)	=	1,000 milligrams (mg)

Inches 0 1 2 3 4 5 6

LINEAR EQUATIONS

Slope-intercept Form	$y = mx + b$
Constant of Proportionality	$k = \frac{y}{x}$

CIRCUMFERENCE

Circle	$C = 2\pi r$	or	$C = \pi d$

AREA

Triangle	$A = \frac{1}{2}bh$
Rectangle or Parallelogram	$A = bh$
Trapezoid	$A = \frac{1}{2}(b_1 + b_2)h$
Circle	$A = \pi r^2$

VOLUME

Prism	$V = Bh$
Pyramid	$V = \frac{1}{3}Bh$

ADDITIONAL INFORMATION

Pi	$\pi \approx 3.14$	or	$\pi \approx \frac{22}{7}$
Distance			$d = rt$
Simple Interest			$I = Prt$
Compound Interest			$A = P(1 + r)^t$

Centimeters 0 1 2 3 4 5 6 7 8 9 10 11 12 13 14 15 16 17 18 19 20